Handbook of Peace and Conflict Studies

The fields of peace and conflict studies have grown exponentially since their initiation in Scandinavia about a half century ago by Johan Galtung. They have forged a transdisciplinary and professional identity distinct from security studies, political science and International Relations.

The Routledge Handbook of Peace and Conflict Studies offers a cutting-edge and transdisciplinary overview of the main issues, debates, state-of-the-art methods and key concepts in peace and conflict studies today. The volume is divided into four sections, commencing with 'Understanding and Transforming Conflict', moving sequentially through 'Creating Peace' and 'Supporting Peace', and culminating with 'Peace Across the Disciplines'. Each section features new essays by distinguished international scholars and/or professionals working in peace studies and conflict resolution and transformation. Drawing from a wide range of theoretical, methodological and political positions, the editors and contributors offer topical and enduring approaches to peace and conflict studies.

This book will be essential reading for students of peace studies, conflict studies and conflict resolution. It will also be of interest and use to practitioners in conflict resolution and NGOs, as well as policymakers and diplomats.

Charles Webel is currently Fulbright Senior Specialist in Peace and Conflict Studies. During 2005, he was Director of the Centre of Peace Studies and a professor of social science at the University of Tromsø, Norway. He is the author of *Terror, Terrorism, and the Human Condition* (2005) and co-author with David P. Barash of *Peace and Conflict Studies* (2002).

Johan Galtung is widely acknowledged as the founder of peace studies and peace research. He has published extensively in these fields. He is currently co-director of TRANSCEND, a global network of peace scholars and conflict transformers.

Handbook of Peace and Conflict Studies

Edited by
Charles Webel and Johan Galtung

LONDON AND NEW YORK

First published 2007
by Routledge
2 Park Square, Milton Park, Abingdon, Oxon, OX14 4RN

Simultaneously published in the USA and Canada
by Routedge
270 Madison Avenue, New York NY 10016

Routledge is an imprint of the Taylor and Francis Group, an informa business

Typeset in Bembo by RefineCatch Ltd, Bungay, Suffolk
Printed and bound in Great Britain by
The Cromwell Press, Trowbridge, Wiltshire

British Library Cataloguing in Publication Data
A catalogue record for this book is available from the British Library

Library of Congress Cataloging in Publication Data
Handbook of peace and conflict studies / edited by Charles Webel and Johan Galtung.
p. cm.
Includes bibliographical references and index.
1. Peace-building. 2. Conflict management. I. Webel, Charles. II. Galtung, Johan.
JZ5538.H36 2007
303.6′6—dc22

2006027025

ISBN10: 0–415–39665–4 (hbk)
ISBN10: 0–203–08916–2 (ebk)

ISBN13: 978–0–415–39665–3 (hbk)
ISBN13: 978–0–203–08916–3 (ebk)

Contents

List of Illustrations

Tables

Figures

Notes on Contributors

Pamela R. Aall is Vice President for Education at the US Institute of Peace. She is also President of Women in International Security, an organization dedicated to promoting the visibility and influence of women in foreign affairs. With Chester A. Crocker and Fen Osler Hampson, she is co-editor of several books, including *Turbulent Peace: The Challenges of Managing International Conflict* (2001) and *Grasping the Nettle: Analyzing Cases of Intractable Conflict* (2005). She also is co-author of *Taming Intractable Conflicts: Mediation in the Hardest Cases* (2004) and the *Guide to IGOs, NGOs and the Military in Peace and Relief Operations* (2000). Her research interests include mediation in inter- and intra-state conflicts, non-official organizations in conflict management and resolution, and the role of education in exacerbating conflict and promoting reconciliation.

Chadwick F. Alger is Mershon Professor of Political Science and Public Policy Emeritus, the Ohio State University. His research and teaching has focused on three linked themes. First is the development of long-term strategies for peace-building. He was Secretary General of the International Peace Research Association from 1984 to 1987. Second is the expanding peace-building roles of some 30 organizations in the UN system, with special interest in the roles of NGOs/civil society. For a number of years he conducted extensive field research at the UN Headquarters in New York City and at the headquarters of the UN and UN Specialized Agencies in Geneva, Switzerland. Third is the world relations of people and organizations in local communities. He is author of *The United Nations System: A Reference Manual* (2006) and editor of *The Future of the UN System: Potential for the Twenty First Century* (1998). He was President of the International Studies Association, 1978–79.

Neil Arya is a family doctor involved with projects on violence reduction in El Salvador (post-conflict) and mental health in Palestine (active conflict). He has been a lecturer on Peace through Health both at McMaster and the University of Waterloo, and holds academic positions in Environment and Resource Studies at the University of Waterloo, and Family Medicine both at McMaster University and the University of Western Ontario. He has served as President of Physicians for Global Survival and Vice President of International Physicians for the Prevention of Nuclear War. Dr Arya has published on health effects of small arms and nuclear weapons, peace through health, a health-based model of security, as well as various health and environmental issues. He is co-editor of a book with Joanna Santa Barbara on *Peace through Health* (forthcoming).

Anat Biletzki is Professor of Philosophy, Tel Aviv University and was a former chairperson of B'Tselem – the Israeli Information Centre for Human Rights in the Occupied Territories. Professor Biletzki's research interests range from Wittgenstein and Hobbes to analytic philosophy, political thought and human rights. Her professional and philosophical activities converge in the area of human rights and she is often invited abroad – for public lecturing, for seminars at human rights conferences, for interviews, and for meetings with human rights counterparts all over the world. Publications include *Paradoxes* (1996), *Talking Wolves: Thomas Hobbes on the Language of Politics and the Politics of Language* (1997), *What Is Logic?* (2002) and *(Over)Interpreting Wittgenstein* (2003).

Alicia Cabezudo, from Argentina, specializes in Education for Democracy, Cultures of Peace, and Human Rights, as rooted in recent Latin American history. She is Professor at the School of Education, University of Rosario, Argentina, and Education Coordinator at the UNESCO Chair on Culture of Peace and Human Rights, University of Buenos Aires. Her recent publications include *Educacion en Derechos Humanos. Un ejercicio para la Construccion de la Ciudadania* (2006); *Educacion para la Paz y los Derechos Humanos: un desafio actuala* (2006); *Learning to Abolish War: Teaching toward a Culture of Peace,* with Betty Reardon (2002); and 'Tasks and directions for the global campaign for peace education', also with Betty Reardon, in *Disarmament Forum Newsletter*, Volume 3, United Nations Institute for Disarmament Research, Geneva (2001).

Chester A. Crocker is James R. Schlesinger professor of strategic studies at the Walsh School of Foreign Service, Georgetown University. He served as chairman of the board of the United States Institute of Peace (1992–2004), and continues as a member of its board. From 1981 to 1989, he was US Assistant Secretary of State for African affairs. He is the author of *High Noon in Southern Africa: Making Peace in a Rough Neighborhood* (1992), co-author (with Fen Osler Hampson and Pamela Aall) of *Taming Intractable Conflicts: Mediation in the Hardest Cases* (2004) and co-editor of *Grasping the Nettle: Analyzing Cases of Intractable Conflict* (2005), *Turbulent Peace: The Challenges of Managing International Conflict* (2001) and *Herding Cats: Multiparty Mediation in a Complex World* (1999).

Richard Falk is Albert G. Milbank Professor of International Law Emeritus, Princeton University and since 2002 Distinguished Visiting Professor, Global Studies, University of California at Santa Barbara. He is also Chair of the Board, Nuclear Age Peace Foundation and on the editorial board of *The Nation* and *The Progressive*. His recent books include a co-edited volume, *Crimes of War: Iraq* (2006). *The Decline of World Order: America's Neoimperial Foreign Policy* (2004) and *The Great Terror War* (2003).

Dietrich Fischer is Academic Director of the European University Centre for Peace Studies, Burg Schlaining, Austria. He is a former MacArthur Fellow in International Peace and Security Studies at Princeton University and Co-Director of TRANSCEND. He is the author of *Preventing War in the Nuclear Age* (1984) and *Non-Military Aspects of Security: A Systems Approach* (1993) and co-author of *Warfare and Welfare: Integrating Security Policy into Socio-Economic Policy* (with Nobel Laureate Jan Tinbergen, 1987), *Winning Peace: Strategies and Ethics for a Nuclear-Free World* (with Wilhelm Nolte and Jan Oberg, 1989), and *Conditions of Peace: An Inquiry* (with

Grace Boggs et al., 1991). He has been a consultant to various United Nations agencies on issues of disarmament and development.

Johan Galtung is a Professor of Peace Studies and the founder and Co-director of TRANSCEND: A Peace and Development Network. Born in Oslo, Norway, he has doctorates in mathematics and sociology. He is the founder of the International Peace Research Institute, Oslo, and of the *Journal of Peace Research*. His recent book publications include: *Human Rights in Another Key* (1994); *Peace By Peaceful Means* (1996); *Conflict Transformation by Peaceful Means* (1998, 2000); *Searching for Peace* (with Carl G. Jacobsen and Kai Frithjof Brand-Jacobsen) (2000); *Rethinking Conflict: The Cultural Approach* (2002); 'Democracy works: people, experts and the future' (with Håkan Wiberg, eds), *FUTURES*, Special Issue, March 2003; *USA Glasnost* (with Rick Vincent) (2003); *Transcend & Transform* (2004); and *Pax Pacifica: The Pacific Hemisphere and Peace Studies* (2005).

Wilfried Graf holds a PhD in Sociology. He is Senior Researcher at the Institute for Sociology of Law and Criminology and Co-Director of the Institute for Integrative Conflict Transformation and Peacebuilding in Vienna, Austria. Between 1983 and 2005, he was Senior Researcher at the Austrian Study Centre for Peace and Conflict Resolution. Currently he is conducting dialogue workshops in order to support the peace process in Sri Lanka, and is also engaged in similar projects in Central Asia, the South Caucasus and West Balkans. Dr Graf is a lecturer and trainer at numerous universities and academies. His main research interests are the study of culture and the collective unconscious in processes of violence, war, peace and conflict transformation.

Magnus Haavelsrud is a Professor of Education at the Norwegian University of Science and Technology in Trondheim, Norway. His work deals with the critique of the reproductive role of education and the possibilities for transcendence of this reproduction in light of the traditions of educational sociology and peace research. His publications include *Education in Developments* (1996); *Perspectives in the Sociology of Education* (1997, 2nd edition); *Education Within the Archipelago of Peace Research 1945–1964*, co-authored with Mario Borrelli (1993); *Disarming: Discourse on Violence and Peace*, editor (1993); and *Approaching Disarmament Education*, editor (1981).

Fen Osler Hampson is the Director of the Norman Paterson School of International Affairs, Carleton University, Ottawa, Canada. His books include *Taming Intractable Conflicts: Mediation in the Hardest Cases* (2005), *Grasping the Nettle: Analyzing Cases of Intractability* (2005), *Madness in the Multitude: Human Security and World Disorder* (2002). *Turbulent Peace: The Challenges of Managing International Conflict* (2001). *Herding Cats: Multiparty Mediation in a Complex World* (1999). *Nurturing Peace: Why Peace Settlements Succeed or Fail* (1996). *Multilateral Negotiations: Lessons From Arms Control, Trade and the Environment* (1995 and 1999) and *Unguided Missiles: How America Buys Its Weapons* (1986).

Sara Horowitz is a Professor of Negotiation in the School of Agriculture of the University of Buenos Aires. She is a TRANSCEND member and Co-Director of the TRANSCEND Peace University, mediator and peace worker. She is Secretary of the Latin American branch of IPRA, the International Peace Research Association. She is the author of six books in Spanish, dealing with adoption; mediation in general; mediation at school; community; and peace in school.

Jim Ife has been Professor and Head of Department of Social Work and Social Policy at both the University of Western Australia and Curtin University. He was the inaugural Head of the Centre for Human Rights Education, and Haruhisa Handa Professor of Human Rights Education, at Curtin University, until his retirement in 2006. He has published in the fields of community development and human rights, and his books include *Community Development* (3rd ed. 2006) and *Human Rights and Social Work* (2001). He is a former Chair of Amnesty International Australia.

Tony Jenkins is the Co-Director of the Peace Education Center at Teachers College, Columbia University and the Global Coordinator of the International Institutes on Peace Education (IIPE). He has extensive consultative experience, including work with universities, NGOs and several UN agencies. His current work focuses on pedagogical research and educational design and development, with special interest in alternative security systems, disarmament and gender. Among his recent publications are 'Disarming the system, disarming the mind', in *Peace Review* (2006) and 'A peace education response to modernism: reclaiming the social and pedagogical purposes of academia', in Jing Lin and Christa Bruhn (eds) *Educators as Peacemakers: Transforming Education for Global Peace* (in press).

Jørgen Johansen is a freelance peaceworker, lecturer and researcher. He is affiliated with the Transcend Peace University, and the Centre for Peace and Reconciliation Studies, Coventry University. He is author of *Bombemålet Norge, Atomstrategi, Ytringsfrihet og Razzia* [Norway the Bombtarget, Nuclear Strategy, Freedom of Speech and Police Raid] (1984); *Aldri Mer 9. April* [Never More April 9] (1987); *Socialt Försvar – en ickevåldsrevolution* [Social Defence – A nonviolent Revolution] (1990); *Den Nødvendige Ulydigheten* [The Necessary Disobedience] (with Åsne Berre Persen, 1998); and *Sosialt Forsvar, ikkevoldskamp mot vår tids trusler* [Social Defence, Nonviolent Struggle Against the Threats of Our Time] (2000).

Gudrun Kramer is Co-Director of the Institute for Integrative Conflict Transformation and Peacebuilding in Vienna, Austria and Co-Director of TRANSCEND International. Between 1999 and 2005, she was Programme Director for projects related to conflict regions at the Austrian Study Centre for Peace and Conflict Resolution. Ms Kramer was also responsible for the training courses that are designed to prepare civilians for peace-building activities in crisis areas. Currently she is conducting dialogue workshops in order to support the peace process in Sri Lanka, and is also engaged in similar projects in Central Asia, the South Caucasus and West Balkans. She is a lecturer and trainer at numerous universities and academies.

David Krieger is a founder of the Nuclear Age Peace Foundation, and has served as President of the Foundation since 1982. Under his leadership the Foundation has initiated many innovative and important projects for building peace, strengthening international law and abolishing nuclear weapons. He is the author of many studies of peace in the nuclear age, including the book *Nuclear Weapons and the World Court* (1998).

Jake Lynch is Director of the Centre for Peace and Conflict Studies at Sydney University. With Annabel McGoldrick, he is the joint author of *Peace Journalism* (2005) and many book chapters and articles about conflict, peace and the ethics of reporting. He is a member of the Toda Institute working group on Peace Journalism and a founder member of the Peace Journalism commission of the International Peace Research Association. He was previously a senior international journalist, having worked as a Political Correspondent for Sky News, Sydney Correspondent for the Independent newspaper and a news anchor for BBC World.

Graeme MacQueen taught Buddhist text and narrative in the Religious Studies Department of McMaster University for 30 years. In 1989, he became founding Director of the Centre for Peace Studies at McMaster, after which he helped develop an undergraduate programme in Peace Studies and co-directed a peace-building programme with projects in Sri Lanka, Gaza, Serbia and Afghanistan. He has published numerous peer-reviewed articles and book chapters, as well as three books, including a novel.

Patrick McCarthy is a painter and sculptor, living in Los Angeles. Besides his daily painting, he is also at work on a philosophical manuscript entitled 'Supreme Happiness', as well as a fictional narrative about an artist going about his life in Los Angeles. His website is: patrickmccarthygallery.com.

Annabel McGoldrick is an experienced international reporter in television and radio news. She has covered conflicts in the Philippines, Indonesia and Israel–Palestine. She produced the BBC documentary, 'Against the War', with Harold Pinter, during the NATO bombing of Yugoslavia in 1999. With Jake Lynch, she is the joint author of *Peace Journalism* (2005) and many book chapters and articles about conflict, peace and the ethics of reporting. She has taught in the universities of Sydney, and Queensland, Australia. Annabel is a qualified psychotherapist with a special interest in journalism and trauma.

Kinhide Mushakoji, Director of the Peace Research Institute at Meiji Gakuin University in Tokyo, was Vice Rector for Regional and Global Studies at the United Nations University in Tokyo from 1976 to 1989. He is a Japanese authority on international affairs and particularly interested in peace research. He is the former Director of the Institute for International Relations at Sophia University in Tokyo, which he founded in 1969, a year after joining the Sophia faculty. He has been a Visiting Professor at Princeton and Northwestern Universities in the USA and subsequently a Senior Scholar at the East West Center in Hawaii and Consultant to the Commission on Society, Development and Peace in Geneva. He was Vice President of the International Political Science Association. Among his publications are 'Introduction to Peace Research', 'Japanese Foreign Policy in a Multi-Polar World', and 'Behavioral Science and International Politics'.

Augustin Nicolescou is Project Coordinator and Researcher at the Institute for Integrative Conflict Transformation and Peace-building in Vienna, Austria. He is the coordinator of the IICP dialogue workshops for the support of the peace process in Sri Lanka. Mr Nicolescou received his BA in Political Science from McGill University in Montreal, Canada and his MA in Peace and Conflict Studies from the European University Centre for Peace Studies in Stadtschlaining, Austria. His current research focus is on the role of networks, norms and trust in conflict transformation processes.

Jan Oberg is co-founder and Director of the Transnational Foundation for Peace and Future Research, TFF, in Lund, Sweden (www.transnational.org). His main books are *Myth About Our Security, To Develop Security and Secure Development, Winning Peace* (co-author) and *Predictable Fiasco: The Conflict with Iraq and Denmark as an Occupying Power* (2004).

Marc Pilisuk is Professor Emeritus, the University of California, and a Professor at the Saybrook Graduate School and Research Center. He is the author of *International Conflict and Social Policy* (1972); *The Healing Web: Social Networks and Human Survival* (1986); *The Triple Revolution: Social Problems in Depth* (1968); *Triple Revolution Emerging* (1971); *Poor Americans: How the White Poor Live* (1971); and *How We Lost the War on Poverty* (2005).

Betty A. Reardon is a peace educator with a half century of experience in the field. She is the founding Director of the Peace Education Center at Teachers College Columbia University and of the International Institute on Peace Education, an international experience in peace education offered annually, each year in a different world region. She has taught at all levels of formal education. Her work has been in the development of pedagogies relevant to the substance and purposes of peace knowledge, with emphasis on gender issues, human rights and human security. Among her many publications are *Sexism and the War System* (1985) and *Education for a Culture of Peace in a Gender Perspective* (2001).

Jack Santa-Barbara is currently Director of the Sustainable Scale Project, an NGO focusing on the relationship between economic theory and practice and the biophysical limits of global ecosystems. He is also an Associate of the Centre for Peace Studies at McMaster University in Hamilton, Ontario, and a Member of Transcend: A Peace and Development organization. He is co-author, with Johan Galtung, of *Peace Business: The Role of Business in Reducing Violence, Inequity and Ecological Degradation*, (in press).

Joanna Santa-Barbara is affiliated with the Department of Psychiatry and Centre for Peace Studies, McMaster University, Hamilton, Ontario, Canada, as well as with Physicians for Global Survival Canada, Science for Peace and TRANSCEND. Her research interests include conflict transformation, Peace through Health and the impact of war on children. Publications include *Peace through Health* (forthcoming).

Antonella Sapio is a medical doctor, child neuropsychiatrist and social psychologist. Currently, she is Professor of Peace Psychology at the University of Florence in Italy. She is the author of many scientific publications, including the important volume *Per una Psicologia della Pace* (2004, ed. F. Angeli). She has founded, together with other collegues, the Società Italiana di Scienze Psicosociali per la Pace [Italian Society of Psychosocial Sciences for Peace] (SISPa) and is involved in many activities for peace, emphasizing the promotion of a culture of nonviolence in institutional peacebuilding.

Charles Webel is currently a Fulbright Senior Specialist in Peace and Conflict Resolution. Previously, he was Director of the Centre for Peace Studies at the University of Tromsø, Norway, and was a Guest Professor at the UNESCO Chair for the Philosophy of Peace at the University of Castellon, Spain. He studied and taught at Harvard University and at the University of California at Berkeley, and is a research graduate of the Psychoanalytic Institute of Northern California. He is author of *Terror, Terrorism, and the Human Condition* (2004), co-author (with David Barash) of *Peace and Conflict Studies* (2002), and has published widely in philosophy, psychology, and social science journals. He has also been active in many peace organizations, having also served as West Coast Secretary of Concerned Philosophers of Peace.

Adriano Zamperini is Professor of Social Psychology at the University of Padua, Italy. The promoter of many scientific and cultural initiatives on peace, together with other colleagues he has founded the Società Italiana di Scienze Psicosociali per la Pace [Italian Society of Psychosocial Sciences for Peace] (SISPa), of which he is the President. His books include *Psicologia sociale della responsabilità: Giustizia, politica, etica e altri scenari* [Social Psychology of Responsibility: Justice, Politics, and Other Scenarios] (1998); *Psicologia dell'inerzia e della solidarietà: Lo spettatore di fronte alle atrocità collettive* [Psychology of Inertia and Solidarity: The Bystander Before Collective Atrocities] (2001); and *Prigioni della mente. Relazioni di oppressione e resistenza* [Mind Prisons: Oppression and Resistance Reports] (2004).

Introduction

1

Introduction

Toward a philosophy and metapsychology of peace

Charles Webel

The importance of securing international peace was recognized by the really great men of former generations. But the technical advances of our times have turned this ethical postulate into a matter of life and death for civilized mankind today, and made the taking of an active part in the solution to the problem of peace a moral duty which no conscientious man can shirk.

(Albert Einstein 1984: 43)

Although attempting to bring about world peace through the internal transformation of individuals is difficult, it is the only way. . . . Peace must first be developed within an individual. And I believe that love, compassion, and altruism are the fundamental basis for peace. Once these qualities are developed within an individual, he or she is then able to create an atmosphere of peace and harmony. This atmosphere can be expanded and extended from the individual to his family, from the family to the community and eventually to the whole world.

(Dalai Lama, in Thich Nhat Hanh 1991: vii)

If we begin with the need to survive, we immediately see that peace is a primary requirement of the human condition itself.

(Johan Galtung, in Galtung and Ikeda 1995: 110)

Love, work, and knowledge are the well-springs of our life. They should also govern it.

(Wilhelm Reich 1971: Epigraph)

Nonviolence is a weapon of the strong. . . . The law of love will work, just as the law of gravitation will work, whether we accept it or not. . . . The more I work at this law the more I feel the delight in life, the delight in the scheme of the universe. It gives me a peace and a meaning of the mysteries of nature that I have no power to describe.

(M. K. Gandhi 1930/2002: 46)

The history of human civilization shows beyond any doubt that there is an intimate connection between cruelty and the sexual instinct; but nothing has been done towards explaining the connection, apart from laying emphasis on the aggressive factor in the libido.

(Sigmund Freud 1905/1989: 252)

> And how long shall we have to wait before the rest of mankind becomes pacifists too? There is no telling. . . . But one thing we can say: whatever fosters the growth of culture works at the same time against war.
>
> (Sigmund Freud 1932/1959: 287)

> . . . peace (the sum total of the love objects to be preserved) is the new mother symbol threatened by the dragon-war; not to fight for the mother-peace against the dragon-war is to desert what we love because the need to prove that we know how to fight . . . is narcissistically more important than the preservation of what we love.
>
> (Fornari 1974: 231)

> Justice and power must be brought together, so that whatever is just may be powerful, and whatever is powerful may be just.
>
> (Pascal, in Ackerman and DuVall 2000: 1)

Preface

For millennia, philosophers, religious thinkers and political activists have written about and demonstrated for 'peace' and decried war. Yet a 'philosophy' of peace is still in its infancy. And while theorists, strategists, tacticians and planners of war and 'security studies' dominate both the academy and the halls of power, philosophers who profess and march for peace do so outside the mainstream philosophical curriculum, far removed from those with the power to make and enforce important political decisions, and often to the dismay and castigation of their more '*echt* philosophical' colleagues.

For over a century, psychologists and psychoanalysts have attempted to illuminate the often elusive and murky depths of the human psyche. But a 'depth psychology' of peace is also merely inchoate. Psychologists who research and teach peace, like their philosophical comrades, do so on the margins of their discipline, and usually as a supplement to more 'rigorous, scientific' investigations.

Philosophers and psychologists are all 'for' peace. But those who attempt to bring peace studies and peace research into their 'professional' work, at least in much of the Anglophonic world, risk marginalization and even exclusion from their disciplinary practices, powers and perks. As a result, scholars who wish to study, research, teach and practise peace have begun in the past half century to create their own counter-institutions, where they may do so without the risk of continued academic and professional isolation.

And psychoanalysts, perhaps modernity's most acute probers of conflicts unconscious and interpersonal, are shunned almost entirely by the halls of academic learning and medical research and shun, almost entirely, a depth analysis of the emotional and cognitive hallmarks of inner peace (or harmony) and outer discord (or conflict). Unlike Freud, who engaged in an epistolary discussion with Albert Einstein about the depth-psychological origins of war and mass violence, most analysts in the mainstream 'object relations' and 'drive-theoretical' traditions are reluctant to stray from the inner sanctum of the clinical case conference and take a public stand on the unconscious sources of bellicose and peaceful behaviour. In contrast, an earlier generation of analysts, including Wilhelm Reich and Erich Fromm, actively sought to understand and transform the characterological and cultural sources of authoritarianism and militarism. But in our time, analytic 'silence' tends to extend far beyond the analytic hour with the analysand.

There are some hopeful contraindications, however. In the US and UK, progressive and peace-oriented philosophers have banded together in such organizations as 'Concerned Philosophers for Peace', 'Radical Philosophy' and 'International Philosophers for the Prevention of Nuclear War' (created by John Somerville as a sister group of 'International Physicians for the Prevention of Nuclear War'). Several journals and many conferences have been held by these organizations. And psychologists have their own division of 'Peace Psychology' in the American Psychological Association and have recently published two books about peace psychology (Christie et al. 2001; Macnair 2003).

Psychoanalysts, while speaking as individuals in favour of peaceful means of conflict resolution and in opposition to war in general and to recent wars in particular, still tend, at least in the English-speaking world, to shy away from 'politicization' of their 'science'. Many Latin American and European analysts are less reluctant to publicize their privately held pacifist sentiments. On the whole, however, most contemporary philosophers, psychologists and psychoanalysts remain publicly mute about war and peace.

Consequently, in large part because of the modernist and postmodernist shifting of peace analysis and research to the fringes of 'elite' professional discourse and outside the institutional reward structure of mainstream academia and politics, a philosophical theory of 'outer' peace and a depth psychological comprehension of 'inner' peacefulness seem as desirable today as they did thousands of years ago. And just as evasive and elusive.

Hence we are confronted with a seeming paradox – peace is something we all desire, and yet, except for relatively brief intervals between wars, seem unable to attain (except on paper). And peace studies, peace research, peacekeeping and peacemaking are almost universally acclaimed to be laudable activities, but not for 'serious' scholars and clinicians doing their 'day' jobs.

Is an ontology, a metaphysics of peace possible, or even desirable? If so, what might it look like?

Can a deep psychological account of emotional well-being, and its opposite(s), be offered, possibly on scientific principles rooted in contemporary psychoanalysis and neuroscience? If so, what might this contribute to contemporary theories and practices of nonviolence and peacemaking?

In this chapter, I will not attempt to give a comprehensive, much less a definitive response to these questions. There is neither sufficient knowledge nor adequate space to do so. Instead, what is possible in this brief introduction is to raise, and perhaps to reframe, these questions, to look at peace and its philosophical and metapsychological prerequisites in a provocative, possibly novel, way.

What is, and might be, peace?

Perhaps 'peace' is like 'happiness', 'justice', 'health' and other human ideals, something every person and culture claims to desire and venerate, but which few if any achieve, at least on an enduring basis. Why are peace, justice and happiness so desirable, but also so intangible and elusive? But perhaps peace is different from happiness, since it seems to require social harmony and political enfranchisement, whereas happiness appears, at least in Western culture, to be largely an individual matter.

Alternatively, perhaps peace does indeed resemble individual happiness – always there, implicit in our psychological make-up and intermittently explicit in our social behaviour and cultural norms. Peace is a pre-condition for our emotional well-being, but a peaceful state of mind is subject to cognitive disruptions and aggressive eruptions.

Peace is a linchpin of social harmony, economic equity and political justice, but peace is also constantly ruptured by wars and other forms of violent conflict. Like happiness, peace remains so near . . . and yet, like enduring love, so far . . ..

Spiritual and religious leaders from the Buddha and Jesus to Gandhi and the Dalai Lama have been inclined to equate peace and love, both in their inner dimensions and in the manner in which people who are spiritually developed interact with others, most acutely with those who may hate and envy them. In the twentieth century, Freud and other depth psychologists explored the vicissitudes of our loving and hating feelings, both toward our 'selves', and to others both near and dear (especially our mothers), and to those distant and often dangerous (the 'enemy' within and without).

Eros and aggression, love and hate, are intermingled from birth to burial. Understanding and pacifying our conflicted inner worlds – our need for and flight from love of ourselves and others – is an intellectual and political project of the highest and most urgent order. This undertaking must run in tandem with the necessity of comprehending and transforming the conflicts rampant in our interpersonal and political realms of interaction and division.

If peace, like happiness, is both a normative ideal in the Kantian sense – a regulative principle and ethical virtue indicating how we *should* think and act, even if we often fail to do so – as well as a psychological need – something of which we are normally unaware but sporadically conscious – then why are violence and war (the apparent contraries of social, or outer, peace), as well as unhappiness and misery (the expressions of a lack of inner peace), so prevalent, not just in our time but for virtually all of recorded human history? Given the facts of history and the ever-progressing understanding of our genetic and hormonal nature, is peace even conceivable, much less possible?

These are issues that have been addressed from time immemorial, in oral form since the dawn of civilization and in written form since at least the periods of the great Greek and Indian epochs. But they seem no closer, and perhaps even farther, from resolution than they were at the times of the *Iliad* and the *Mahabharata*.

'Peace', like many theoretical terms, is difficult to define. But also like 'happiness', 'harmony', 'love', 'justice' and 'freedom', *we often recognize it by its absence*. Consequently, Johan Galtung and others have proposed the important distinction between 'positive' and 'negative' peace. 'Positive' peace denotes the simultaneous presence of many desirable states of mind and society, such as harmony, justice, equity, etc. 'Negative' peace has historically denoted the 'absence of war' and other forms of widescale violent human conflict.

Many philosophical, religious and cultural traditions have referred to peace in its 'positive' sense. In Chinese, for example, the word '*heping*' denotes world peace, peace among nations. While the words '*an*' and '*mingsi*' denote an 'inner peace', a tranquil and harmonious state of mind and being, akin to a meditative mental state. Other languages also frame peace in its 'inner' and 'outer' dimensions.

The English lexicon is quite rich in its supply of terms that refer to and denote peace. In *Webster's Third New International Dictionary*, for example, the meanings of peace are clearly defined.

Initially, in *Webster's*, peace is defined negatively, as 'freedom from civil clamor and confusion', and positively as 'a state of public quiet' (*Webster's* 1993: 1660). This denotes –peace and +peace in their political or 'outer' sense. *Webster's* proceeds further to define (political or outer) peace positively as 'a state of security or order within a community provided for by law, custom, or public opinion' (ibid.).

Webster's second distinct definition of peace is a 'mental or spiritual condition marked by freedom from disquieting or oppressive thoughts or emotions' (–peace in its personal or 'inner' sense) as well as 'calmness of mind and heart: serenity of spirit' (+inner peace) (ibid.). Third, peace is defined as 'a tranquil state of freedom from outside disturbances and harassment (+inner peace resulting from –peace) (ibid.). Fourth, peace denotes 'harmony in human or personal relations: mutual concord and esteem' (this is what I will call *interpersonal or intersubjective peace*) (ibid.).

Next, peace is defined by *Webster's* as (1) 'a state of mutual concord between governments: absence of hostilities or war' (+outer peace caused by –outer peace) and (2) 'the period of such freedom from war' (–outer peace) (ibid.). The sixth definition of peace is the 'absence of activity and noise: deep stillness: quietness' (+inner peace caused by –inner peace) (ibid.). And the final lexicographical meaning of peace in the English language (American version) personifies peace as 'one that makes, gives or maintains tranquility' (as God being the ultimate cause of peace on earth and as identified with peace, or Peace, itself) – 'divine peace' (or Peace?). (ibid.).

Dictionary definitions of abstract terms can only go so far. But in the case of the English lexicon, the semantics of peace gets us remarkably far. For in this important dictionary, the meanings of peace are clearly classified into both + and –, as well as 'inner and outer' components. Two additional denotations are what I am calling 'interpersonal or intersubjective' (ITP) peace, and 'divine peace' or the divine peacemaker (God, or in polytheistic and mythological cosmologies, the gods). I will not go into various spiritual, theological and/or religious views of peace and Peace, but I will explore some aspects of intersubjective peace, especially in what I shall call its 'dialectical' determination. For it is in this intersubjective zone that some important contemporary and cutting-edge philosophical, psychological and psychoanalytic theories and research strategies converge.

A dialectical determination of peace

Peace is often defined or determined negatively. Peace is 'the absence of war'. Peace is '*non*-violence'. Etc. We know peace by its absence.

We would agree that the Second World War was certainly not a time of peace, at least for much of the Northern Hemisphere. But what about much of the Southern Hemisphere from 1919 to 1945? Were sub-Saharan Africa, most of Latin America, and the homelands of the Anzus countries 'at peace' because they were *not* battlegrounds? And what about the period of the 'Cold War'? Was that a 'Cold Peace' as well?

These historical considerations lead us back to first, perhaps to 'ultimate', principles, regarding not just the meaning(s) of peace, but its 'essence', its ontology. Is peace like other theoretical terms–justice, freedom, virtue and equality, to name a few? Something intangible but which virtually all rational people prize? Or is it even less tangible, less perceptible, an ideal without an essence, an 'ideal type' (in Max Weber's formulation) but still bearing a 'family resemblance' to other, more tangible human desiderata? *Perhaps peace is both an historical ideal and a term whose meaning is in flux*, sometimes seemingly constant (as in 'inner peace of mind') but also noteworthy for its relative absence on the field of history (as in 'world peace').

Peace is dialectical. In this world, peace is neither a timeless essence – an unchanging ideal substance – nor a mere name without a reference, a form without content. Peace should neither be reified by essentialist metaphysics nor rendered otiose by postmodernist and sceptical deconstruction.

Peace is also not the mere absence of war in a Hobbesian world of unending violent conflict. *Peace is both a means of personal and collective ethical transformation and an aspiration to cleanse the planet of human-inflicted destruction*. The means and the goal are in continual, dialectical evolution, sometimes regressing during periods of acute violent conflict and sometimes progressing non-violently and less violently to actualize political justice and social equity. Like history and life, peace is a terrestrial creation struggling for survival in a constantly changing, and sometimes threatening environment.

Thinking peace

In thinking about and thinking peace, it is helpful to make clear distinctions between what peace is and might be, and what peace is not and should not be. Thinking 'negatively' (critically or dialectically), it is important to note that peace is not mere pacification: it is not active or subtle domination and manipulation of less by more powerful actors (or –pacification). Peace is also not quiescence and acquiescence by a 'pacified' population (+ pacification) fed 'bread and circuses' by a 'benevolent' empire or autocrat.

On the contrary, *peace in its progressive or dialectical mode denotes active individual and collective self-determination and emancipatory empowerment.* Peace entails continuous peacekeeping and peace-making. And peacemaking requires active and continual personal and collective transformation, pacifistic rather than pacifying in its means of psychological and political development.

Similarly, the belief system of those who both think and practise peace and who actively seek to attain it by peaceful (nonviolent) means – true pacifism – is not passivism. *Genuine pacifism is transformative and activist, employing nonviolent means of social and personal change to resist oppression, war, and injustice and to promote personal and social moral integrity and radical, peaceful means of transforming conflicts and actors.*

Given the history of the recent past and the current parlous state of our world, one might understandably be tempted to be sceptical about the prospects for enduring peace on earth in an era (error?) of potential instantaneous global war with weapons of mass and vast destruction. But it is worth recalling that other political ideals once thought unachievable also came to pass.

It took centuries, even millennia, to outlaw slavery and legitimize human rights. It might take at least as long to delegitimize political violence, both from above (by the state) and from below (by non-state actors).

And 'peace on earth' might in fact be unachievable, at least for a sustained period of time. That does not invalidate the struggle to achieve a world with greater justice and equity and without violence, or at least with significantly less violence, injustice and inequity. On the contrary, the nonviolent struggle to liberate humanity from its means of self-destruction and self-enslavement is its own end. The absence of a guarantee of 'success' in the effort to bring peace to humanity, and the real possibility of the failure of the human experiment, do not undermine the effort to pacify existence but instead bestow on it a kind of existential nobility and political virtue.

Peace and its antitheses: terror and terrorism

The antithesis of peace is not conflict. Conflicts appear historically inevitable and may be socially desirable if they result in personal and/or political progress. Conflicts may, perhaps paradoxically, promote and increase peace and diminish violence if the conflicting parties negotiate in good faith to reach solutions to problems that are achievable and tolerable, if not ideal.

And sometimes the antithesis of peace is not violence, even political violence, since violent means (such as the Second World War and wars of independence/national liberation) have sometimes historically helped to bring about periods of less violence and fragile peace. During the long Cold War from 1945 to 1991, for example, when the major powers – the US and its NATO allies on the one hand, and the former Soviet Union and its Warsaw Pact allies on the other hand – did not attack each other directly. Simultaneously, the defeated Second World War axis powers – Germany, Italy, and Japan – experienced unprecedented political and economic development with vastly less militarism than before 1939.

War-prone nations can become peace-prone (Switzerland, the Scandinavian countries, and Costa Rica come to mind) if their real and perceived security and resource needs are met and their standing armies are dramatically reduced or are retired. Even the most striking personal example of the unification of peace thinking and peacemaking – M. K. Gandhi – believed that under certain circumstances it is preferable to act violently on behalf of a just cause than not to act at all. Gandhi said, 'It is better for a man to be violent, if there is violence in our breasts, than to put on the cloak of nonviolence to cover impotence. Violence is any day preferable to impotence. There is hope for a violent man to become nonviolent. There is no such hope for the impotent' (Gandhi, in Webel 2004: 141).

Rather the polar opposite of peace is violence, or the threat of violence, employed either for its own sake – that is, on behalf of political and/or criminal terrorism – or for the primary purpose of achieving, maintaining and/or expanding personal and/or political power for the sake of conquest and domination. Peace and reflexive acts of interpersonal violence, perpetrated on the spur of the moment against real and/or perceived threats to one's or one's loved ones' existence, are not always mutually exclusive. Similarly, certain acts of political violence may at times advance peaceful ends, as during revolutionary struggles employing controlled and generally non-lethal violence against clear state representatives of tyranny and oppression. The less violence the better. But in a world of murder and murderers, it is often not possible, no matter how ethically desirable, simultaneously to have justice and 'clean hands'.

On the other hand, there is a kind of political and psychological violence that seems always to be reprehensible and avoidable. For this kind of violence – *terrifying, terroristic violence* – almost always increases human pain and suffering and usually diminishes personal safety and peace of mind, without accomplishing 'higher order' political goals, such as national liberation and political or socioeconomic emancipation.

Some kinds of violence may, especially if non-lethal and not directed intentionally or foreseeably at civilians and other non-combatants, at least in the short run, seem to augment national security or to promote 'just causes'. But in the long run, the chronic use of violence for political and/or criminal means turns back on those who deploy it (as the recent film *Munich* concretely illustrates at the international level and *A History of Violence* shows at the interpersonal level) and ultimately decreases both the psychological and political security of those who use violence ostensibly to protect themselves from real and/or perceived antagonists or as a means of retaliation to avenge attacks on them, their families and/or their property.

Peace and conflict are not antagonists, especially if the conflicting parties use nonviolent, less violent and non-lethal means of conflict resolution and transformation. Even peace and war are not always antitheses if parties who find themselves reluctantly pulled into war make every effort to reduce the incidence and lethality of violent conflicts and operations during a war and in good faith resolve to end the violence as expeditiously as possible and not to inflict violence on civilian and military non-combatants (*jus in bello*).

Terror and terrorism, however, are incompatible with peace, peacemaking and the struggle to pacify existence. As I have argued elsewhere, terrorism is a dual phenomenon, a tactic used by states (terrorism from above) and by non-state actors (terrorism from below) to induce fear in terrorized people for the purpose of influencing another, less vulnerable, population, such as government officials (Webel 2004; Barash and Webel 2002: 80–3). To be at peace in our inner worlds means, inter alia, to be free from the anxiety and terror that are induced or threatened both from above and from below.

Being at peace: toward a metapsychology of peace

'Metapsychology' is a term used by Freud to denote a number of essays he wrote just after the start of the First World War, commencing with two papers written in 1915, 'Instincts and their Vicissitudes' and 'The Unconscious', and continuing two years later with 'Mourning and Melancholia'. In his 'Autobiographical Study', Freud said that what is meant by 'metapsychology' is 'a method of approach according to which every mental process is considered in relation to three coordinates, which I described as dynamic, topographical, and economic, respectively; and this seemed to me to represent the furthest goal that psychology could achieve' (Freud 1925/1995: 37).

Freud's 'metapsychology' was his theoretical effort to provide a three-dimensional portrait of the dynamics of emotional life, as 'determined' by mostly unconscious mental processes. In this essay, I am appropriating and revising the Freudian notion of 'metapsychology' and am using it to denote a three-dimensional portrayal of the political psychology of peace and conflict formation.

As I have previously claimed, there are three dialectical, dynamic 'spheres' or 'spectra' of greater or lesser peace. The first is the realm of 'inner', or psychobiological peace (IP). I will use IP to correspond to the 'topographical' (or 'inner spatial') representation of Freud's metapsychological theory. Unconscious, pre-conscious and conscious thoughts, impulses, needs, desires and perceptions constitute the mental and emotional lives of sentient beings.

The second part of this spectrum is the 'outer' sphere of sociopolitical, domestic and international peace (OP). This is the 'economic' arena, both in the psychodynamic sense of 'economy' (drives, instincts and their vicissitudes operating, roughly, according to and beyond the pleasure principle), and in the literal sense of the term. Macroeconomic and political forces constitute the commonly understood field of global and local market and power-driven agents and agencies.

And the third, and least discussed sphere in peace studies and conflict research, is intersubjective or interpersonal peace (ITP). This corresponds to the 'dynamic' element of Freudian metapsychological theory. It is the behavioural field of human interaction in daily life and work.

Like Freud's tripartite 'structural theory', in which the ego, the superego and the unconscious are in continuous interaction, IP, OP and ITP are similarly dynamic processes. States of inner peace, or psychological harmony and well-being, are characterized by low degrees of 'inner conflict' and malignant aggression (directed either against oneself, as in masochism, or against others, as in sadism), and by high ego functioning, successful sublimation and non-pathological object relations with significant (and even insignificant) others.

But even the most psychologically healthy persons have difficulty maintaining their equilibrium in pathogenic environments. Their tranquility may be undermined and even uprooted by pathology-inducing familial, organizational, social and political systems, ranging from conflict-laden interactions with kith and kin, bosses and subordinates, to such stress- and potentially violence-inducing structural factors as under- and unemployment, racism, sexism, injustice, need-deprivation, famine, natural catastrophes, poverty, exploitation, inequity and militarism. The intersubjective zone, which mediates and straddles the topographies of inner and outer peace, is accordingly the catalyst for environmental and interpersonal agents, energies and institutions that reinforce or subvert psychological equilibrium, or inner peace.

Being-at-peace is possible but improbable in an environment that is impoverished. Being peaceful is an enormous challenge when others with whom one interacts are hostile, aggressive, very competitive, and violent. And living in peace is almost inconceivable in desperately poor and war-ridden cultures.

Accordingly, the three zones of inner, outer and intersubjective peace are never static and always in interaction. A metapsychology of peace would lay out the structural dynamics of these interactions (the descriptive component), assess the strengths and weaknesses of their current historical alignment (the analytic component), and propose a practicable strategy for remediating the inequities and infelicities in the respective spheres of IP, OP, ITP and their interactions (the prescriptive or therapeutic component). This is a considerable challenge for peace researchers and peacemakers alike.

A spectral theory of peace

Peace is like light, intangible but discernible either by its absence or by its sporadic and often startling appearances (like a flash of lightning against a black sky). Peace is a background condition for the perception of everything else, a physical phenomenon affecting all sentient beings, something whose presence or absence is best measured on a continuum or spectrum.

Peace ranges from what I shall call 'Strong, or Durable, Peace' (roughly equivalent to Johan Galtung's term 'Positive Peace' – a condition in which there is relatively robust justice, equity, and liberty, and relatively little violence and misery at the social level) to weak or fragile peace. Strong peaceful cultures and societies reflexively promote personal harmony and satisfaction.

On the other end of the spectrum is what I will call 'Weak, or Fragile, Peace' ('Negative Peace' in Galtung's formulation), where there may be an overt absence of war and other widespread violence in a particular culture, society or nation-state, but in which there is also pervasive injustice, inequity and personal discord and dissatisfaction. Very few human cultures and societies historically have qualified for the designation of 'Strong Peace', while very many tend toward 'Weak Peace'. The spectrum that measures the relative presence or absence of the necessary and sufficient conditions for sociocultural and national Strong or Weak Peace illuminates what I shall call '*External Internal Peace* (EIP)'.

At times of weak peace, peace is a background condition for social existence in general and of personal happiness in particular, something taken for granted – until it is no longer present. During times of war, people yearn for peace in ways they could not have imagined during less violent times. They imagine and desire an often idealized and all-too-evanescent 'peaceable kingdom', a blissful condition, a *status quo ante bellum*, to which they long to return and for which they would pay literally any price.

Personal survival is the absolutely necessary condition, the sine qua non, for peace at the personal level. And 'national security', or the collective survival of a culture, people or nation-state, has in modern times become the macroscopic extension of individual 'defensive' struggles, sometimes ruthless, unscrupulous and murderous during times of perceived and real threats to individual and familial existence.

This spectrum is also descriptive of the mental/emotional lives of individuals, which range from extremely conflicted, or Weak Harmony (similar but not identical to psychotic) to conflict free, or Strong Harmony (what ego psychologists once referred to as 'the conflict-free zone' of ego-syntonicity). This is a measure of an individual person's '*Internal Internal Peace*' (IIP).

Similarly, cultures and societies also range on a spectrum from 'very violent and warlike' to 'very nonviolent and warfree' in terms of their inter-cultural and international behaviour. The United States, especially since 1941, has vacillated between periods of 'Weak Peace' and 'very violent and warlike' behaviour, both internally (domestically) and internationally. The spectrum that places nation-states and cultures on a continuum ranging from continual and high casualty warfare to no warfare and no casualties is a measure of *External External Peace* (EEP).

Finally, individual persons, when interacting with others, exhibit a range of behaviours ranging from 'very conflicted' to 'very unconflicted'. There are a variety of reasons and motivations, from the intrapsychic and hormonal to the sociocultural, why certain individuals behave in antagonistic and hyper-competitive ways on the one hand, to peaceable and cooperative on the other hand. And the continuum of personal feelings, needs, inclinations and desires manifested in behaviours ranging from Very Conflicted to Very Unconflicted is a measure of *Internal External Peace* (IEP). This is the zone of *intersubjective peace*, a dialectical stage comprising the public and familial spheres, in which people's most aggressive and compassionate qualities are elicited, reinforced or rejected by their peers and bosses. Inner peace can often be made or unmade by interpersonal and socioeconomic (or class) conflict.

But peace is also spectral in another way. Peace seems very illusory, almost ghost-like. It is sometimes fleeting and barely visible, like an apparition, especially during times of continual warfare and collective violence. Peace is a future end-point and 'goal' of war in virtually all cultures and societies. War has been allegedly conducted 'for the sake of peace' from Homeric to present times. As such, peace is a vision, often otherworldly, of a human and individual condition that is violence and terror free.

Absolute peace, like absolute pacifism, may also be ghost-like in that it may not exist at all. It may be an illusion or delusion, something for which we are inclined by our natures and cultures to yearn for and idealize, but also something deeply resisted by those same natures and cultures.

Instead of desiring and idealizing what may be unachievable – 'Perfect Peace' (PP), or, in Kant's formulation, 'Unending Peace' – might it be more prudent and realistic to think of PP as what Kant sometimes called a 'regulative ideal', a norm (like the Platonic form of perfect virtue or complete happiness) that ought to guide and regulate our behaviour but which is also unlikely to be universally observed? So instead of vainly trying to achieve the impossible – a world completely without war and violence – should we be willing instead to strive for '*Imperfect Peace*' (IP)?

What I mean by IP is not Negative Peace (–P) or Positive Peace (+P), but their unification in what I will call *Strong Peace (SP), at both the internal and external levels.* SP is not perpetual peace, although peacemakers and peacekeepers, like those who sincerely strive for justice and happiness, have PP as their 'regulative ideal'. Rather, Strong, or Imperfect Peace, denotes those points on the EEP, EIP, IIP and IEP continua that veer toward the nonviolent and harmonious ends of the spectra.

Conclusion: imperfect but durable peace?

Peace is not and probably cannot be either perfect or unending – at least not on this island Earth as we now know it. But that does not imply that peace is also chimerical and 'not in our genes.' Rather peace, like justice and happiness, is an historically shifting condition of our individual and collective natures, of our psyches and polities, that at some times is less intangible and at other historical moments shines in the most distant horizons of our imaginations and desires.

Peace is, like all desired and desirable human ideals and needs, always potentially within us, even if difficult to discern and seemingly impossible to accomplish. The quest for peace may seem quixotic, but that is part of it allure.

Peacemaking is and ought to be heroic. Peace is and must be the heroic quest of this new millennium – if we are to survive.

Bibliography

Ackerman, P. and DuVall, J. (2000) *A Force More Powerful: A Century of Nonviolent Conduct*, New York: Palgrave.

Barash, D. and Webel, C. (2002) *Peace and Conflict Studies*, Thousand Oaks, CA: Sage.

Christie, D., Wagner, R. and Winter, D. (2001) *Peace, Conflict, and Violence: Peace Psychology in the 21st Century*, Upper Saddle River, NJ: Prentice Hall.

Einstein, A. (1984) *The World as I See It*, Secausus, NJ: Citadel Press.

Fornari, F. (1974) *The Psychoanalysis of War*, Garden City, KS: Doubleday Anchor Books.

Frank, J.D. (1968) *Sanity and Survival: Psychological Aspects of War and Peace*, New York: Random House Vintage Books.

Freud, S. (1959) *Collected Papers, Volumes 4 and 5*, New York: Basic Books.

Galtung, J. and Ikeda, D. (1995) *Choose Peace: A Dialogue between Johan Galtung and Daisaku Ikeda* (translated and edited by R. L. Gage.) London: Pluto Press.

Galtung, J., Jacobsen, C.G. and Brand-Jacobsen, K.F. (2002) *Searching for Peace: The Road to TRANSCEND*, London: Pluto Press.

Gay, P. (ed.) (1989) *The Freud Reader*, New York: W. W. Norton.

Kant, I. (1983) *Perpetual Peace and Other Essays on Politics, History, Morals*, Indianapolis, IN: Hackett Publishing Company.

Kernberg, O.F. (1992) *Aggression in Personality Disorders and Perversions*, New Haven, CT: Yale University Press.

Macnair, R.M. (2003) *The Psychology of Peace: An Introduction*, Westport, CT: Praeger.

Merton, T. (ed.) (1965) *Gandhi on Non-Violence*, New York: New Directions Press.

Reich, W. (1971) *The Mass Psychology of Fascism*, New York: Farrar, Straus and Giroux.

Rose, J. (1993) *Why War? Psychoanalysis, Politics, and the Return to Melanie Klein*, Oxford: Blackwell.

Somerville, J. (1954) *The Philosophy of Peace*, New York: Liberty Press.

Thich Nhat Hanh in Kotler, A. (1991) *Peace is Every Step, the Path of Mindfulness in Everyday Life*, New York: Bantam Books.

Webel, C. (2004) *Terror, Terrorism, and the Human Condition*, New York: Palgrave Macmillan.

Webster's Third New International Dictionary of the English Language Unabridged (1993) Springfield, IL: Merriam-Webster, Inc.

2

Introduction

Peace by peaceful conflict transformation – the TRANSCEND approach

Johan Galtung

Towards a model relating conflict, violence and peace

What is new in this approach is already in the title. First, the focus is on peace, a relation between parties, not on security. Compatible goals lead to ever higher levels of peace, conviviality, and incompatible goals, conflict, are handled peacefully. The security approach, still dominant, including in the UN *Security* Council (not Peace, or Peace and Security, Council) sees some party as a threat to be deterred or eliminated. There is no focus on improving relations. But there may be room for both approaches.

Second, peace depends on transformation of another relation between parties, conflict. And, the opposite of peace, violence, is seen as the outcome of untransformed conflict. But the conflict transformation has itself to be peaceful in order not to make the situation worse by sowing new seeds for future violence.

Third, for conflict transformation we need transcendence, going beyond the goals of the parties, creating a new reality like the European Community so that the parties can live and develop together. A child may struggle with 5–7, but a new mathematics with negative numbers accommodates the problem. Much politics is done by people with 5–7 problems and no idea of negative numbers.

Fourth, whereas classical mediation brings parties together for negotiation and compromise, the TRANSCEND approach starts with one party at a time, in deep dialogue, and in a joint creative search for a new reality. After that comes the classical approach, bringing them together for negotiation, with a facilitator.

Fifth, there is more to this than mediation. The approach is holistic, with a dynamic process model relating conflict and peace.

What should we demand of a model for violence-peace? The same as of a medical model for individual or collective disease-health. We would demand *diagnosis*, analysis of the type of disease and its conditions/causes ('pathogens'), *prognosis* to explore what we might call the natural history or process of a disease, given the conditions/causes, and a *therapy* that would list the *interventions* ('sanogens') necessary and sufficient to prevent unacceptable consequences/effects such as death, by the patient or by Others. We want a cure so as to restore health, ease, wellness; if possible by the patient himself and his immune system.

So we need insight in the *past* for diagnosis, and in the *future* for prognosis and therapy. We need *description* for diagnosis and prognosis, and *prescription* for therapy. And we need a counterfactual therapy of the past: 'What could have been done in the past to stop or soften the process?' We need a broad spectrum of thought, speech and action, knowledge and skills; focusing both on universalizable, general aspects cases of the same type have in common; and on the specific, particular aspects of any patient, including the context.

Academic research and universities, tied to the empirical, to facts, meaning past and present, and to the descriptive, meaning the verifiable, tend to be limited to diagnosis, to the 'is', not the 'ought'. No value-judgements. But medical schools break through both walls and are found in any good university. The physician is devoted to betterment through therapy, not only to patients as sources of data. Schools of engineering and architecture are also devoted to creating new realities, such as bridges and houses. But peace and conflict studies have to struggle to get a foothold, possibly because they may be as disturbing to established dogma (security?) as were medical studies to the church some time ago.

We should demand exactly the same of violence–peace models. We are dealing with actors who are human beings, individual and collective. Violence/war, or the threat thereof, corresponds to disease, ill-ness. Something has gone wrong. But exactly what? In what kind of process are we? Which are the 'bellogens' that lead to violence/war, and the 'paxogens' that might not only stay that course, but produce a sustainable peace? What are the key context conditions? Including in the actors themselves?

We have been riding on a fruitful medical analogy. Something has gone wrong in some system. Positive feedback makes bad things worse. Some negative feedback is badly needed. Time has come to identify the violence-peace system components in a violence prevention process, and then proceed to a violence cure process.

But could not some violence, like some disease, and some crime (Durkheim's thesis) be useful, strengthening the mechanisms to prevent them and undo the damage? Like an induced TBC once a week producing anti-bodies that may also prevent cancer of the prostate? Maybe. But by and large we feel safer with peace by peaceful means.

For better understanding we ask the same question as for disease: *what happened before violence*, the intended hurt and harm to human beings? Before *aggression*, including the inner aspect, the hatred – eating at one's heart – of some Other, even of oneself?

Answer: *polarization*, with dehumanization of Other removing the aversion humans have against intra-species killing and maiming. And before polarization? Some kind of *frustration*. And where did that frustration come from? From a blocked goal.

More specific answer: from a *blocked goal because Self and/or Other pursue incompatible goals*. And that means *conflict*; between goals, and between the carriers of those goals, Self and Other.

More precisely: from *untransformed conflict*, a problematic *relation* rather than a problematic actor; person, nation, state.

An untransformed conflict is a major bellogen. It becomes like a festering wound, whether visible to the untrained eye or located deeper down in the body, personality, structure and/or culture, like a genetically pre-programmed tumour. Medical studies identify immune systems as a sanogen to prevent disease. And peace studies identify the capability and intent to solve the conflict, to transform it, blunting the contradiction, as a major paxogen. The division of prevention into *primary prophylaxis* by removing the patho-/bellogens, and *secondary prophylaxis* by strengthening the sano-/paxogens, the self-healing capacity, expands this vision.

But it does not put an end to our questioning. If conflict = incompatible/contradictory goals, where do the goals come from?

We can identify three broad categories of answer: from Nature, Culture and Structure. Nature is in us, and around us; Culture is in us as internalized values and norms; and Structure is around us as institutionalized, positive and negative, sanctions.

Marx focused on Nature as basic needs, on Structure as class relations, and was Culture-blind; Freud focused on Nature as Id, drives, on Culture as Super-Ego, and was Structure-blind; Darwin focused on Nature as struggle between species for survival and 'the preservation of the favoured races', and was Culture- and Structure-blind. The combination of three single-minded foci is not sufficient. But they are necessary; we cannot do without them.

We can use Marx's answer that goals are structure-induced *interests*, Freud's answer that goals are Other-transmitted *values*, and Darwin's focus on self- and species-*preservation*, the first and foremost need for survival. And then add the actors' private goals.

Let us now repeat this exercise, this time from top to bottom:

- individual actors are conditioned, not determined, by Nature and Culture inside us, and Nature and Structure outside us, giving us humans a window of freedom for our spiritual capacity to transcend;
- there are collective actors such as genders and generations, races and classes, countries and nations, regions and civilizations;
- actors have goals, among them are basic needs derived from Nature, values from Culture and interests from Structure;
- goals are positively coupled (harmonious, compatible), negatively coupled (disharmonious, incompatible), or decoupled, if pursuit of one is productive, counterproductive or indifferent to pursuit of others;
- harmonious-indifferent goals offer potentials for positive peace, disharmonious-incompatible-contradictory goals define conflict;
- where there is conflict there may be frustration because the pursuit of one goal is blocked by the pursuit of other goal(s);
- where there is frustration there may be polarization, organizing inner and outer worlds as a dualist *gestalt* of 'Self vs Other';
- where there is polarization there may be dehumanization of Other;
- where there is dehumanization the frustration may translate into aggression, with hatred growing in the inner world of attitudes and violence growing in the outer world of behaviour, all of them reinforcing each other in processes of escalation;
- where there is hatred and violence there will be traumatization; of victims harmed by the violence, and of the perpetrators harmed by their own hatred *and* by having traumatized the victims;
- where there is trauma victims may dream of *revenge* and *revanche*, and perpetrators of more *glory*, deposited in Culture and Structure as values and interests and in History as vicious feedback cycles.

In Table 2.1 this is put together as a model in a 9-step flow chart. Reading Table 2.1 downwards makes us ask whether one step really is necessary or sufficient for the next. We start with 'necessary'.

Is there always an unresolved conflict underlying violence? Thus, the imperial powers were extremely violent in their overseas conquest, but they had no prior conflict with those peoples. They did not even know them, they 'discovered' them, and most were friendly. The conflict was not over invasion but over unlimited submission, politically as subjects, economically as forced labour, culturally as converts (in the 4 May 1493 papal bull *Inter Caetera*). If they

Table 2.1. Peace by peaceful conflict transformation: a TRANSCEND model

	Diagnosis and prognosis of conflict without intervention	I. Inner narrative: Diagnosis–prognosis	II. Outer narrative: Diagnosis–prognosis	III. Between narrative: Diagnosis–prognosis	IV. Interventions: To prevent negative prognoses	
DIAGNOSIS	1) Context	**Culture**	**Nature**	**Structure**	**Research**	THERAPY
	2) Deep ABC triangle	Deep Attitudes = deep culture = collective subconscius – cultural violence A	Deep Behaviour = deep nature = basic needs – nature violence B	Deep Contra-dictions = deep structure = infra structure - structural violence C	**Needs** **Rights** **Dignity** **Satisfaction** **Peace culture** **Peace structure**	
	3) Goal production	Values (actors): Actor conflict	Goals - compatible - indifferent - incompatible	Interests (parties): Structural conflict	**Goal restraint** **Consequence analysis**	
	4) Conflict Surface ABC triangle	A Attitude (meta-conflict) Empathy ACCEPTABILITY	B Behaviour (meta-conflict) Nonviolence + NO VIOLENCE	C Contradiction (root-conflict) Creativity + SUSTAINABILITY	**Mediation** **Dialogue:** **- Mapping** **- Legitimizing** **- Bridging** = SOLUTION	
PROGNOSIS	5) First order consequences	Frustration Negative - cognitions - emotions	Frustration Negative - speech - behaviour	Apathy Low participation	**Anger transformation** **Anger control**	
	6) Second order consequences	Polarization Dehumanization Attitudinal polarization	Polarization Dehumanization Behavioural polarization	Polarized structure: Two blocs, Cold war	**Peacebuilding** **Depolarization** **Humanization**	
	7) Third order consequences	Aggression Escalation of hatred: Self-destructive	Aggression Escalation of violence: Other-destructive	Self-sustained vivious cycles of violence: Hot war	**Non-violence** **Soft peace-keeping**	
	8) Basic consequences	Trauma to self Healing and closure	Trauma to other Healing and closure	Destructuration Vertical Empty	**Conciliation** **- Past cleared** **- Future together**	
	9) Producing vicious cycles	War culture: Winner goal: More glory Loser goal: Revenge, revanche	War behaviour: - Aggressive speech - Body language - Behaviour	War structure: - Vertical - Filled with obedience	**Creating self-sustaining virtuous cycles of peace**	

submitted, they could be admitted as slaves; if they resisted, military power, violence/war, was used to force them or kill them. In addition, imperial powers had conflicts with each other.

If violence is the smoke, then conflict is the fire. Search and you will find. But some conflict may be festering, like a smoke-less glow.

Is polarization always underlying violence? Polarization means social distance; horizontally, like countries separated by borders, or vertically, like classes separated by unequal power, or both. Social distance means human distance. Even the most violent bully person, or bully country, has somebody he would not harm/hurt, some untouchable buddy, even if his own family might not be exempt from his violence.

Gandhi's identity was with all humanity; buddhism with all sentient life experiencing a *dukkha-sukha*, suffering-well-being, gradient. Romans spoke of *homo res sacra hominibus*. Identity impedes polarization and violence. However, the less polarized can employ the more polarized, dehumanizing riff-raff for the dirty job of violence, and train them to kill. Scratch the surface and you will find elements of polarization.

We do not rule out that aggression, due to frustration, may be for lack of adequate means, not because of blocking by another goal. Violence may also come out of sheer greed. One therapy might be *goal-restraint*; a promising new field of peace studies. Another: creativity.

The 'sufficiency' part is more problematic.

Will frustration always lead to aggression, violence? In a *deep conflict*, with basic needs as irrepressible goals, aggression is likely. But even so there may also be *suffering in silence*, seeing a predicament as an unavoidable part of the human condition, dwelling in human nature. Or in God's wisdom, even in his love (like his 'love' for Job).

This holds particularly for structural conflicts, built into the social structure, between those high up who want status quo and those lower down who do or do not reconcile themselves to their fate: the dangerous classes. They are 'dangerous' because one day they may wake up and see the injustice. In actor conflicts, with a very concrete actor on the other side – real conflicts are mixes of the two – the subject standing in the way is easily identified. 'What can we do about Him' then quickly becomes a 'What can we do about It', Buber's I–It relation.

Will polarization always lead to direct violence? No, it can go on for ages as between countries with no contact. The polarization between classes is structural violence if those lower down are really hurt or harmed, meaning that their basic needs are molested/left unsatisfied by a structure of exclusion. Will direct violence be added? Yes, if basic needs are deeply insulted. But states and nations have kept apart for ages with no violence and so have classes, within and between countries. And direct contact with everybody is impossible.

What would make unresolved conflict with polarization violent? An answer in addition to Nature, basic needs conflict, would be a deep *culture of violence*, making violence look natural/normal, thereby lowering the threshold. There is frustration. The blood is boiling. The culture demands Go Ahead! instead of anger transformation. Do not accept any insult! Be a man! The result is violence, with male deep culture as a key factor behind the close to male monopoly on physical violence. Another answer is a deep structure of exploitation.

The TRANSCEND model read vertically and horizontally

Table 2.1 can be read both ways. The conditions–consequences flow constitutes a model, something that can be falsified, not only a typology. Let us read vertically, with horizontal deepening.

Row 1–4 is Diagnosis, and includes unresolved incompatibilities, the contradictions, the root conflicts. They may be over more or less deeply held goals. If the goals are basic needs – survival–wellness–freedom–identity – by definition non-negotiable – the conflict is deep. If left unresolved, it becomes a festering wound, deeper down the deeper the conflict, and starts activating rows 5–9. And that is the Prognosis.

If the unresolved root conflict is the bellogenic insult to the system of actors (conscious) or parties (less conscious), then, where is the self-healing resistance capacity to withstand that insult?

Answer: in Column IV, Therapy, to the extent the parties, as actors, are conscious about what is going on and themselves able to apply them. Like a good couple they may have been able to satisfy each other's needs, rights and dignity, and build a micro peace culture and peace structure in and around themselves. Very importantly, they may have exercised some restraint in their own goal-production, like learning not to demand too much of themselves and others. And they may have developed mediation capacity inside themselves and between the two of them. Thus equipped they should be in a position to weather many a storm. A focus on the marital relation as such and not only on each other already helps a lot.

But more is needed if frustration produces escalating aggression, inflicting traumas in increasingly vicious cycles. Anger control, peacebuilding in the midst of struggle, abstention from violence, physical and verbal, and efforts to conciliate and find a new joint life project are called for. If the immune system of Self-therapy cannot cope, then some Other-therapy, some intervention, help, may be indispensable.

Column I – favoured by religionists and psychologists – and Column II – favoured by sociologists, anthropologists, political scientists and economists – are the inner and outer versions of this general narrative. Column III is the relational, between, version.

They start with Culture and Structure. Basic are the ideas of the true, the good, the right, the beautiful and the sacred that have been *internalized* in people. And basic are not all kinds of patterned interaction, meaning structure, but behaviour *institutionalized* in the system. Running against Culture or Structure may become very painful; running with them may be very pleasant. Negative sanctions are the bad conscience for insulting Culture and the punishment for insulting Structure, and the positive sanctions are the good conscience and positive rewards when acting downstream, aligned with Culture and Structure. Happy the actor who wants culturally to do what he has to do structurally anyhow – and even happier the ruler presiding over a contradiction-free system peopled by such contradiction-free actors.

But such totalitarian alignment obtains only in small, controlled systems like guerrilla cells and bomber crews, and for a short time. The human actor is always squeezed between the pressures from Culture and Structure and the urges of Nature, but we can use our spirit to carve out more space. We are capable of self-reflection, including on how we are programmed, and transcendence to create new realities. In our era we recognize easily the spirit of the scientific creator, and reward him/her with prizes. The economic creator, called 'entrepreneur', is rewarded with profit. We are more ambiguous toward an ethical genius like Gandhi, and the religious genius we marginalize as a 'mystic'.

Contradictions, conflicts, should be welcomed, not avoided. They are challenges to expand our spaces, and to furnish them creatively with new, feasible, realities. *Conflict* = crisis + opportunity. Freedom is both a consequence of conflict, and a condition for its transformation.

Sticking to the Nature-Structure-Culture context, we then go deeper down, to the deep triangle. What constitutes a *deep culture*, of emotions and cognitions, is always a matter of dispute. Here it is identified with the 'collective subconscious', and Freud and Jung are still our best guides to the individual and collective subconscious. But that does not mean any blind acceptance beyond such simple axioms as these:

1 There is something deep down, conditioning thought-speech-behaviour.
2 To master yourself(ves) be conscious of that subconscious.
3 Internalize a better consciousness for a better subconscious.

What is floating 'down there' may be elements, 'atoms', archetypes of cognitive emotions and emotive cognitions, such as Chosenness as person or group, by god, history or anything Above, the Glory of the past or the future, and the Trauma of having been hurt or harmed by the non-chosen, filled with envy. Such mutually-reinforcing elements may come together in syndromes like a CGT 'molecule'. Trauma is then taken as proof of chosenness (the martyr), and the dream of the glory calls for much perseverance, under guidance from Above. An individual with this syndrome built into the personality may be psychiatrized as suffering from megalomania-narcissism (the CG part) and paranoia (the T part). In a nation the same syndrome may be culturally legitimized as patriotism. In both cases, the syndrome may be pathological in its consequences.

Another syndrome is DMA, Dualism-Manicheism-Armageddon, dividing the world into two parts, Good and Evil, in a battle with no compromise, no transcendence, only the victory of one over the other. An actor with this baggage is prepolarized, in need of no frustration from unresolved contradictions, nor of mental and behavioural preparation for aggression through dehumanization of Other, including of his/her own Alter Ego.

And there are counteracting archetypes: unity, equality and peace. They need reinforcement.

All of this can then unfold from the neutral 4 to the apocalyptic 9, at all levels, with inner and outer factors reinforcing each other.

The *deep structure* can be identified with the 'infrastructure' – hidden to the unguided eye – whose presence or absence is conditioning much of what happens. Marxists and liberals alike focus on economic infrastructure; liberals on the presence or absence of a free market for capital, goods and services, marxists on ownership or not of means of production. Smith and Marx are less useful as guides than Freud and Jung, who furnished the subconscious with what they deemed important and left space for others to do the same. Smith and Marx were convinced that the key dimensions are economic, and knew which ones. But, how about Table 2.2.

All 20 are patterned interactions, structures, but far beyond what Smith and Marx identified as infra-structure. Three rules apply:

1 There are structures deep down conditioning surface structures.
2 To master structures be conscious of that infrastructure.
3 Institutionalize better structures for a better infrastructure.

If peace is about equity the task is to build 20 equitable structures. More equity to draw upon, more acceptable and sustainable outcomes.

Now, back to *deep culture*, also with many dimensions to explore:

- time cosmology: crisis, with heaven *or* hell; or more oscillating?
- space cosmology I: dualistic, Self wins, *or* Other; or transcending?
- space cosmology II: Is Other Evil, Barbarian or Periphery; or human?
- archetypes I: History God/good vs Satan/evil; or transcending?
- archetypes II: History as war-hero vs peace-saint; or ordinary people?
- episteme I: atomistic/deductive vs holistic/dialectic; or all four?
- episteme II: contradiction philosophy: *tertium non datur*, or else?

Table 2.2. Ten faultline dimensions and two levels of organization

	Dimension	*Individual level*	*State level*
1	Nature	Humans vs environment	States vs environment
2	Gender	Men vs women	Penetrator vs penetrated
3	Generation	Old vs middle-aged vs young	Old vs middle-aged vs young
4	Race	White vs yellow/brown vs black/red	White vs yellow/brown vs black/red
5	Class political	Repressors vs repressed	Repressors vs repressed
6	Class economic	Exploiters vs exploited	Exploiters vs exploited
7	Class military	Killers vs killed	Killers vs killed
8	Class cultural	Conditioners vs conditioned	Conditioners vs conditioned
9	Nation	Dominant culture vs dominated	Dominant civilization vs other civilizations
10	State	State vs other states	Region vs other regions

The most unfortunate deep culture combination, if the goal is peaceful conflict transformation, would be (reading upwards):

- a view of contradictions as absolute, this goal *or* that goal;
- a focus on few actors and goals, and a deductive approach;
- projecting Self on God and Other on Satan, with strong gradients;
- war-hero and peace-saint with strong Egos, no ordinary people;
- seeing Other as Evil, Barbarian or Periphery, as pre-dehumanized;
- seeing world space dualistically as Self vs (all) Others;
- seeing time as moving toward crisis = catharsis or apocalypsis.

This most unfortunate combination is a good guide to *Occident (I), hard*, with expressions like (Hitlerite) nazism, (Stalinist) bolshevism, fundamentalist US/Israeli exceptionalism and fundamentalist Islam. Or, seeing the winner in Spain as Madrid *or* ETA, not as transcending Spain as a community of nations.

The most fortunate deep culture combination for peace would be:

- a view of contradictions as mutable, e.g. as *yin/yang*;
- a holistic and dialectic view of the conflict formation;
- a civilization with no Satan/Principle of Evil, but of Unity;
- a civilization with conflict transformation by common people;
- a civilization identifying all humans (all life?) as part of Self;
- a civilization without Self–Other dualism;
- a civilization with an oscillating time cosmology.

This most fortunate combination is a good guide to *Occident (II), soft*, with expressions in soft Christianity-Judaism-Islam, some women's approaches; soft Hinduism and non-ritualized Buddhism; and 'indigenous' civilizations (like in Polynesian *ho'o pono pono*, Somalian *shir*, etc.).

The Sinic and Nipponic civilizations can be seen as occupying an in-between position, with unfortunate and fortunate characteristics. Particularly unfortunate is Sinic dehumanization of Other as barbarian; and the Nipponic view of Self as God-chosen and Other as Periphery. Fortunate are the flexible epistemes.

In general: there are cultural impediments and resources everywhere. A typical example is dualism, the tendency to see only two parties in a conflict. Hidden in the deep culture the tendency may be hidden to the parties themselves.

Conflict conceptualization and the mainstream security model

The model has three columns for three conflict aspects A, B and C. 'Conflict' comes from *confligere*, 'shocking together'; compatible with the usual Anglo-American *Behavioural interpretation* as parties 'shocking together', in *violence*. But it also opens for a subjective *Attitudinal interpretation* in the inner worlds of the actors, the *Lebenswelten*, as an inner shock that may cause a *hatred* that may be expressed as violence. Then the trans-subjective, relational *Contradiction interpretation*. What is 'shocking together' are goals held by the parties when the realization of one excludes the realization of other(s). There is *incompatibility*, or *contradiction* of goals, like between 'independence' for a province, and 'unitary state' for the country. No inter-actor violence is assumed, nor that the 'shocking' is known to the actors, the goal-holders. 'Incompatible goals' does not imply 'incompatible actors'.

That leads to A-, B- and C-oriented conflict interpretations, focused on attitude, behaviour, contradiction. In the sequence C- > A- > B, a conflict starts objectively, takes on inner, attitudinal life, and finds an outer, behavioural expression, verbally and/or physically, violent, or not. But any other ABC sequence is possible empirically.

Since all three interpretations are valid we pick up all three: *Conflict = Attitude + Behaviour + Contradiction*. But our definition tilts in favour of the C-orientation. We define the C aspect as the *root* conflict, and A and B as *meta*-conflicts, after C.

This broad definition enables us to talk about A, B and C *orientations* in conflict theory and practice; about A, B and C *phases* in conflict dynamics as was also done above; and about A, B and C *approaches* where solutions are concerned, as will be done below. Any one-sided A, B *or* C orientation will seriously distort conflict research, theory and practice. Hence A, B *and* C.

In the behaviourist B-orientation of mainstream Anglo-American approaches, 'conflict' and 'violence' often stand for the same, for 'violent behaviour'. With no conflict concept independent of violence, 'Violent conflict' becomes an oxymoron. If conflict equals violence, however, then 'conflict' is bracketed between outbreak of violence and ceasefire. And if in addition 'peace' equals absence of violence, then the implication is that there was peace before and there will be peace after violence. That makes *work for peace* = work for violence control, a behaviourist reductionism easily turned into a political disaster. *Realist* may be, militarist, and behaviorist. But highly *unrealistic*.

Behaviourism focuses on the human outside, constructing people like hordes of animals, fish shoals, cars in traffic studies; 'shocking' in violence, power struggle.[1] Researchers identify causes and conditions, effects and consequences, like season, climate, any external correlate of violent behaviour, *but not human inner reality*. Like the ahistorical construction of a terrorist as fueled by blind hatred only, no cause.

'Greed' fits easily into an A-orientation, 'grievance' not, being more C-oriented, more relational. Goals are psychologized and may invite psyche control in addition to violence control. If psyche and violence control are unsuccessful, a country may be attacked. The psyche of Self is left unexamined. A and B problems are in Other, as *actors*, not in Self. The focus is autistic, not reciprocal (Piaget). There is no C focus on the Self–Other *relation*.

But all reductionisms are problematic. A-orientations disregard contradictions not reflected in the party's life world, at a high level of consciousness. There is no space for Freud, Jung and

Marx. And pure C-orientations dehumanize conflict to abstract contradictions, with no concern for attitude and behaviour. So we add classical *liberal*, and *marxist*, reductionisms and errors to the *realist* reductionism above.

How it became like that is easily seen. If Self wants to control the world, some may not submit. There will be 'security problems' when Self's good intent clashes with Other's evil capability. An A focus for Other might give Other a voice better left unheard. B focus for Self and C focus for the relation might both shed serious doubts on Self. Hence: A-orientation for Self, B-orientation for Other, and C for neither. The result of this autism is security studies, and current media practice. Peace and conflict studies have to focus on A, B and C symmetrically.

A behaviourism that leaves out Other's subjective inner reality and the objective contradiction between them, has two clear consequences. First, the behaviourist approach is so incompatible with subjective and lived experience of what the conflict is about that Other feels dehumanized and humiliated. The approach reduces subjects to objects, depriving Other of personal identity. One more major conflict is added. Second, in doing so a basic approach to violence control and peace is lost: empathic, creative dialogue before and after violence, with a view to transforming the relation to solution or at least to settlement.

If violence must be controlled to restore law and order and reduce real and potential suffering, humanitarian intervention is one method. This may lead to a court case against Other, and it is worth noting how behaviourism focuses on intersubjectively observable and confirmable eyewitness reports that fit into due process of law. Motives are left out, and so is the context (the C aspect). It becomes like empiricist, natural science approaches for earthquakes, tsunamis, landslides, opening for natural and social engineering with upside-down control.

Other has been made nameless, faceless, deindividualized. Only what is seen is believed, like gender, age, colour and physiognomy, in other words race, perhaps elements of class; like in 'male, youth, black, poor'. Not strange if a dehumanized Other does not cooperate.

Two discourses for coping with violence: security and peace

The preceding paragraph can be used to analyze the kind of security and peace flowing from how conflict is conceptualized. The mainstream security discourse applies A and B to Other, at the expense of C. The peace discourse focuses on C, sometimes at the expense of A and B.

The *security approach* is based on four components:

1 *An evil party*, with strong capability and evil intention;
2 *A clear and present danger of violence*, real or potential;
3 *Strength*, to deter or defeat the evil party, in turn producing
4 *Security*, which is the best approach to 'peace'.

The approach works when evil/strong/active parties are weakened through deterrence or defeat, and/or converted to become good/passive.

The *peace approach* is also based on four components:

1 *A conflict*, which has not been resolved/transformed;
2 *A danger of violence* to 'settle the conflict once and for all';
3 *Conflict transformation*, empathic-creative-nonviolent, producing
4 *Peace*, which is the best approach to 'security'.

The approach works through acceptable and sustainable outcomes.

The security approach presupposes superior strength (of whatever kind, Sun Tzu or Clausewitz), implying inequality, superiority. The peace approach presupposes a conflict outcome acceptable to all parties and sustainable, implying equality, parity, also in the process.

What would favour a preference for the security approach?

1 *A deep culture of Dualism/Manicheism/Armageddon*, a hard reading of the abrahamitic religions. The security approach is a secular version of Good/God/Christ vs Evil/Satan/ Anti-Christ, with war as final arbiter.
2 *Construction of the Other as evil, with no legitimate goal*, driven by greed or envy, somebody with no grievances to negotiate or conflicts to solve; inviting extermination/crushing, containment or conversion.
3 *The absence of 'diversity with equality' as category*, the Columbus fallacy (Todorov). There is an underlying social code of verticality to be implemented, based on ascribed categories like gender, generation, race, class/caste, nation, state. Different means inferior or superior.
4 *A preference for a structure of inequality*; a Hobbesian reading of 'social order'. The expression 'dangerous classes' or 'dangerous genders/generations/races/nations/states' updates evil/ Satan and witch-burning, close to massive category killing, genocide, of races and nations in modernity, making superiority the best self-defence.
5 *Monopoly on the 'ultima ratio regis/regnum'*, concentrating the means of coercion in the state, or in a community of states like NATO and the EU, defined through their monopoly (Weber) to uphold 'law and order' by force, and legitimized by long lists of threats.
6 *'To He Who Has a Hammer the World Looks Like a Nail'*, making the security machinery self-reinforcing with secret police to assess how strong is Other's capability and how evil his motivation, with police to spy on and arrest suspects, covert and overt operations to preempt, extra-judicial execution, and overwhelming force to defeat and deter.

And what would favour a preference for the peace approach?

1 *A culture of unity of human beings*, soft readings of abrahamitic religions, and of others like the African *ubuntu*, mainstream readings of hinduism/buddhism and daoism, with women focusing on compassion, and ideologies like *liberté, egalité, fraternité*. There is no Armageddon as final arbiter, but the ever-lasting effort of human beings to transcend.
2 *'There is that of God in everybody'*, meaning a legitimate goal in every party, however violent and repulsive. The way of identifying legitimate goals is mutual inquiry; in other words by dialogue.
3 *Diversity as a source of mutual enrichment*, presupposing curiosity, respect, dialogue, for mutual exploration and learning. Reciprocity and symmetry have to be extended to any other party with legitimate goals as defined by legality, human rights and basic human needs. Diversity with inequality is mutual impoverishment, and so is equality with uniformity. Diversity with equality spells peace.
4 *A preference for a structure of equality*. Thus, 'security' is located to the right politically, and 'peace' to the left. Peace is an equality-oriented, some say revolutionary, proposition. Democracy and human rights are already great equalizers. Reciprocity is the norm. If you want peace, then give to others what you want; if they also want it.
5 *A culture and practice of nonviolent countervailing power*, based on a strong identity, high level of self-reliance and much courage and fearlessness, to counter brainwashing, bribery and threats.

6 *A culture and practice of conflict transformation*, not only for specialists, more like hygiene and healthy life styles for everybody to practise by identifying legitimate goals in all parties and bridging creatively the contradictions between such goals, building peace. Also for the parties themselves to do, not by calling in outside specialists.

The peace argument against the security approach is strong: it works like a bandage over a festering wound. The conflict formation of parties with goals with too many incompatibilities has to be transformed into a peace formation by bridging the legitimate goals nonviolently, empathically, creatively. An untransformed conflict will reproduce violence sooner or later. Not going to the roots, transcending the contradictions, leads to a spiral of violence and counter-violence.

But the security argument against the peace approach is also strong. Not all parties are driven by legitimate grievances, some are driven by illegitimate greed. The latter have to be stopped before they destroy us all. After a 'peaceful conflict transformation' the greedy may get at everybody's throat, producing neither security, nor peace.

That conflict between two approaches can itself be transcended by *soft peacekeeping*, combining soft strength with mediation:

- peacekeeping by very large numbers, with defensive weapons, but
- with at least 50 per cent women, and the adequate cultural underpinning, and
- equally trained in police methods, nonviolence and mediation.

In the preceding section, the tendency by some actors in the state system to use an incomplete, even distorted conflict analysis was explored. If we now combine that with a tendency to prefer the security discourse, how would state action relate to the TRANSCEND approach?

Of course, states are no strangers to conflict, usually referred to as 'disputes', even 'situations'. Such words may soften encounters, but also open for distorted conflict analysis. Nor are they strangers to mediation by bringing the parties together at the Table, negotiating, searching for compromises. The TRANSCEND approach is based on mediators meeting the parties one-to-one, dialoguing, searching for new realities that would accommodate conflict transformation. Then comes the Table.

States, however, tend to be triggered into serious action not by conflicts but by acts of violence, by the first stone thrown or the first shot fired in anger. That anger may have been observed for a long time, and they know fully well that this Step 7 may 'get out of hand' and lead to Steps 8 and 9. Standard remedy is military intervention as the second party, or as an outside 'third' party, to stop the violence. If successful, the next step is depolarization at the top, bringing the parties together with no display of anger, around a negotiation table, for a settlement which, given military victory, may be a dictate rather than a compromise. With that, the conflict is presumably closed.

In this model of a classic state system 'peace process', only four of the nine steps are used, and in the opposite order: 7–6–5–4. First comes military intervention with ceasefire and peacekeeping, then diplomacy depolarizing at the top, attention to anger control, and then settlement for the conflict. There will be monitoring and review conferences. What is left out is the (Step 8) towering significance of trauma with the need for conciliation, and (Step 9) creation of virtuous peace cycles; assuming deep attention to the missing Steps 1, 2 and 3.

To summarize: omissions when using the security discourse only:

1 *They leave out the unresolved conflict and focus only on violence*, which then looks unmotivated, irrational, autistic, fundamentalist.
Example: 'Terrorism', as explored in Chalmers Johnson's *Blowback* (2000).

2 *They confuse conflict arena – where violence/action is found – with conflict formation*, all the parties with a stake in the outcome.
Example: focus in Ulster only on violent parties, not on 85 per cent moderates.

3 *DUALISM, the focus on violence reduces the number of conflict parties to two, and the number of issues to one, as dominant discourse*; disregarding hidden parties posing as mediators, and underlying issues.
Example: missing Germany as major conflict party in Yugoslavia, with her own goals; missing class and gender as major issues in Yugoslavia.

4 *MANICHEISM, the focus on violence casts one party as evil and the other as good*, (re)enforcing polarization, denying the 'evil' a voice.
Example: standard image of Serbia, Indonesia, Iraq, Iran, North Korea, and theirs of US/UK taking sides, with governments or anti-governments.

5 *ARMAGEDDON, presenting Other's violence as autistic and own military intervention as the only solution*, omitting alternatives.
Example: the NATO war against Yugoslavia (Serbia), omitting the many alternative causes of action, even denying their existence.

6 *Disregarding structural and cultural conflict and violence*, like refugee camps or the role of *shoa*, reporting only the direct violence.
Example: 100,000 plus dying daily from hunger and curable diseases.

7 *Omitting the bereaved* (except 'our own'), easily ten per victim, and their sentiments of revenge and revanche, fueling spirals of violence.
Example: with 100,000 killed in Iraq, a pool of one million revengers.

8 *Failing to explore causes of protraction and escalation*, and particularly the role of media war journalism in keeping violence going.
Example: arms supply to the parties continuing, e.g. in Sri Lanka.

9 *Failing to explore the goals of intervening parties*, how big powers tend to move in when a system is shaken loose by conflict and violence, picking up morsels, getting footholds like bases and contracts.
Example: the 'international community' in Yugoslavia, missing the Camp Bondsteel story and German protectorate policy.

10 *Failing to explore peace proposals and nonviolent action.*
Example: missing the Pérez de Cuéllar proposal December 1991 for the Yugoslavia conflict; downplaying citizens' action like in DDR 1989.

11 *Confusing ceasefire and meeting at the table with peace*, with exaggerated expectations when warring parties meet, following standard government agendas with victory or ceasefire- > talks- > negotiation- > peace.
Example: Afghanistan, with no regard for the peace ideas of others.

12 *Leaving out reconciliation*, as opposed to efforts at pacification.
Example: almost any conflict, with the seeds of renewed violence intact. A highly unintelligent approach, guaranteeing perpetual violence.

Interventions for peaceful conflict transformation: an overview

After the readings of the model demonstrated in Table 2.1, we have tried to clarify two important problems, the conceptualization of conflict (A-, B- *or* C-oriented versus A-, B- *and* C-oriented) and the discourses (mainstream security discourse versus the peace discourse). Now comes the therapy, Column IV, and an exploration of what this counter-trend model offers.

The first major point is the variety of the nine approaches, both for the preventive and the more curative stages of the 'natural history' of violence. With a good job done in all stages the horrible aftermath, feeding the vicious cycle of violence with trauma sedimented in deep cultures and structures, as values and interests, should be avoidable.

The repertory is diverse. The knowledge and skills are available in the world today, some at governmental levels. The nine approaches could be sections in Ministries of Peace. But most governments focus on the security discourse because of the factors favouring that approach. That leading discourse is also the discourse of the leading states, two of the most belligerent states in the world: the USA and the UK.

However, a *caveat*: the nine tasks are not easy, as will be made clear below. Like for health, the preparation is a complete university study, not a 'programme', a summer school or a workshop. There will be professionalization, with the danger of excessive institutionalization, of 'school peace', like 'school medicine', against people's peace.

Today the security approach is 'school peace', pitted against the approaches like the nine steps model. Like 'school medicine' much money is involved. Security business is good business. The TRANSCEND approach is inexpensive. We have highlighted seven of the nine steps: peace culture/structure, mediation, peacebuilding, nonviolence, conciliation, virtuous cycles. All with the 'mantra', often mentioned, of *empathy*, *non-violence*, *creativity*. Or *peace by peaceful means*, a check-list.

Peace culture

The underlying *problem* is the numerous *collective subconscious elements legitimizing direct or structural violence*, in syndromes like CGT (Chosenness, Glory, Trauma) and DMA (Dualism, Manicheism, Armageddon), combining into the security discourse. And others.

There is a *goal*: (1) reject those elements that impede peace by peaceful means; and (2) bring subconscious peace cultures to the forefront, trying to build a peace culture at both conscious and subconscious levels. An example would be *yin/yang* thinking to blunt the absolutism of true/false, good/bad, right/wrong; *horizontality*, equality as preferred mode of interaction; and *pragmatism* as to the effects, checking empirically, udogmatically, whether things work. As opposed to mainstream dualism, verticality and dogmatism.

There are *practices*, such as increased consciousness about bellogens and sanogens, about that which impedes and promotes peace, through massive peace education. Example: awareness of such carriers as street names for their impact on the collective mind (like the strong males in Paris street names), and as tools of change.

This is deep culture work, calling on cultural anthropology, philosophy, history of ideas, etc. The major instrument is peace education. But people associate that with schooling and think they have graduated from schools. So we need peace journalism, observing and reporting events within a solution-oriented peace discourse, not only within the victory-oriented security discourse.

Then there is the entire cultural environment, particularly in public space, the street names mentioned, monuments, museums, the very structure of public space – is it made for military parades or for relaxed conviviality in a park? The messages of the major means of communication, language, let alone art, are certainly also in it.

Peace structure

The underlying *problem* is the role of the infrastructure of *interacting faultlines* – gender, generation, race, class (political-economic-military-cultural), normal/deviant, nation, territory – at the individual as well as state/nation levels, and the *high or low entropy distribution of actors*, disequilibrated and equilibrated. There is a *goal*: an infra-structure with equality, equity and reciprocity across faultlines to facilitate conflict transformation, to prevent genocide, and legitimized by a deep culture of peace.

And there is a *practice*: nonviolent struggle for equality and equity across faultlines. Have another look at Table 2.2: that type of work is today going on, skillfully or not, successfully or not, for all twenty; even for equality in killing by People's War balancing superpower killing capability. Nuclear proliferation is the old-fashioned method. Terrorism with suicide bomb belts against state terrorism from 40,000 feet and against state torturism, is another. The peaceful approach wold be to establish equality by widespread use of the nonviolent, assertive approaches included in this model.

Obviously this is political work, mobilizing the knowledge and possible skills of jurisprudence, political and military science, international studies and economics. Law and politology have done more for egalitarian political power structures than economics for egalitarian economic relations. In that backward discipline, from a peace angle, equity still has to be defined.

Above all, this is the work of myriads of people suppressed in inegalitarian structures now arguing that the time for parity has come. NGO representatives from world civil society can increasingly negotiate in an egalitarian setting, as opposed to the dress-and-manners equality of diplomats from an inegalitarian state system.

Mediation

The underlying *problem* is a *contradiction* among goals (and means), with attitudes inclining toward hatred and behaviour toward violence in the whole underlying *A, B, C-triangle*.

Mediation has its own *goal*: a *new, acceptable and sustainable, reality* where the parties feel at home with each other because any contradiction is less sharp, blunted, and attitudes and behaviour have also been softened. We are not talking in absolutist terms about solution, resolution or dissolution. We talk about conflict transformation, meaning blunting and softening to a level the parties can live with and handle themselves, with empathy with each other, creativity in searching for something new, and by nonviolent behaviour, speech, and – if possible – even thoughts. 'Love thy enemy' may be demanding too much; but 'hate him less' may already help.

There is a *practice* linking the problem and the goal: *dialogue* with all actors, (1) to map the conflict formation (parties, goals and contradictions), (2) to assess legitimacy, or not, of all goals, and (3) to bridge legitimate goals by a creative jump, imagining a new reality, with contradictions transcended, and conflicts transformed. Much empathy is needed.

In deep conflicts the mediator meets with one party at a time. They dialogue by questioning each other, aiming at a new reality, like the European Community, not at a tepid compromise.

There is a time order. Generally, softening of A and B will be easier when progress is made on C rather than vice versa. To soften A and B with no progress on C is pacification, not peacemaking. Work on A, B and C should be parallel activities, with a heavy focus on C. Solve C, and the sunshine at the end of the tunnel will melt icy A and B. Needed is the creativity of artists, wedded to the knowledge and skills of architects and engineers. With no violence.

Peacebuilding

The underlying *problem* is mental and behavioural dualism, frozen into gestalts and structures. The inner world sees only Good and Evil and only the good in Self and the negative in Other. The outer world is divided in two blocs with all positive interaction within, and all negative interaction, or no interaction at all, between. The mental polarization legitimizes the behavioural polarization, which in turn reinforces the former. After some time, Other is no longer seen as human but as an evil object ready to be killed, legitimized by slogans like 'there is no good German but a dead German'.

There is a *goal*: depolarization, humanization (not *re* as there may have been no positive image or any image at all, earlier). That means a more normal view of both Self and Other, with shades of grey and mixes of black and white all over. Human, not all too human.

There are many *practices* to draw upon, and to be developed, in peacebuilding. An elementary practice is the civil disobedience of establishing contact with the appointed enemy, engaging in positive, helping, cooperative relations instead. The mental task would be cognitive/emotional disobedience, refusing to structure the inner world in that polarized way, also identifying the negative in Self and the positive in Other. Avoiding the trap of Self-hatred combined with Other-love; that is only polarization in reverse, not reversed.

Thus, peacebuilding moves people not only into new action, but also new speech and new thoughts. A primary condition is an open, not closed, mind with expanding inner space, and then the will and ability to take the risk of thinking, speaking and acting upon it. Like talking with terrorists, state terrorists and state torturists.

What do we call a person capable of this? A *peace builder*; peace worker being the generic term for all nine steps.

Nonviolence

The underlying *problem* is that *violence breeds violence*, as defence against attack, and as revenge for the traumas inflicted. There is a *goal*: reducing *dukkha*, increasing *sukha*; getting nonviolent results by using nonviolent means. 'Peace is the road.'

There is a *practice*: Nonviolence breaking that vicious cycle, by some called 'the security dilemma', refusing to use violence, engaging in constructive action across conflict borders instead.

Nonviolence actually has two meanings. One is broader, more or less co-extensive with what here is called 'peace by peaceful means', including most steps and most therapies in the model. And one is more narrow, seeing nonviolence as a better way of doing legitimate jobs violence is supposed to do, such as defence against direct violence attacks, and offense against structural violence.

Within the narrow interpretation there are first-, second- and third-party nonviolence, all taking the risk of police surveillance, imprisonment, maiming, killing. Without risk-taking, no nonviolence. But writing and speaking, meetings, resolutions, demonstrations, the classical peace movement repertory, are also very valuable. The underlying philosophy is readiness to receive violence without returning it, breaking the cycle of violence for the benefit of all, 'stirring sluggish consciences' (Gandhi). First-party nonviolence could be designed to break the power of structural violence, like through massive economic boycott. Second-party nonviolence could be designed as defence against occupation, like through massive civil disobedience. And third-party nonviolence could be designed for in-between roles, as witness for peace, accompanying victims and others, for conflict facilitation bringing the parties together.

Conciliation

The underlying *problem* is *trauma*, wounds to the body, mind and spirit, of both victims (V) and perpetrators (P), including the wounds to the community, the togetherness whose wholeness has been wounded by the P–V rift and has itself become a victim.

There is a *goal*: *healing and closure*; that the traumas no longer hurt, and that there is a shared feeling that the traumas, although not forgotten, can be put behind us. Certain violent events in the past can be removed from the political agenda, liberating that agenda for cooperative, constructive acts. The parties are ready to close a chapter or book, and open a new one.

There are *practices* linking the underlying problem and this goal, like presenting the approaches to conciliation in a seminar with the parties, encouraging discussion of which approaches to use. One empirical experience is that such dialogues, opening for more spiritual, transcending processes, are in themselves conciliating.

At a deeper level, there are two gaps to bridge. First, between the conscious and the subconscious, in both V and P, making deep trauma memories and effects conscious, to the conciliator and to each other. Second, the gap between V and P, if possible as a *joint life-long project*, as sometimes happens when marriages are renewed, or, as happened inside EC/EU, with Germany as P and the rest as V. Could that happen to Israel–Palestine in a Middle East Community?

The task of the conciliator is different from the mediator. The mediator is more cognitive, bringing in vast knowledge of successful conflict transformation, stimulating cognitive openings of new spaces. The conciliator is more emotional, encouraging P and V to let go the traumas that make them prisoners of the past. Time order enters: conciliation without mediation can become pacification.

Creating virtuous cycles

If we do all this there would be *absence of direct violence* engaged in by military and others. And the work on structure and culture leads to *absence of structural violence*, the non-intended slow, but massive suffering by economic, political and cultural structures; *and* to the *absence of cultural violence* that legitimizes direct and/or structural violence. All these absences add up to *negative peace*. A much simpler approach would be mutual isolation, with no joint structure and culture. But *positive peace* would be missing – see Table 2.3.

These are six peace tasks, three 'absences' and three 'presences'.

First, by eliminating direct violence causing suffering, the structures causing suffering through economic inequity or political walls placing Jews or Palestinians in ghettos, and cultural themes justifying one or the other.

Second, by building direct, structural and cultural peace. The parties exchange goods and services, not 'bads' and 'disservices', like violence. Cooperation is built into the structure as something automatic, and sustainable under the heading of equity for the economy[2] and equality for the polity:[3] reciprocity, equal rights, benefits and dignity, 'what you want for yourself also be willing to give to Other'. And then a culture of peace confirming and stimulating all these 'presences' in self-reinforcing peace cycles. Peace is very holistic. Thus, the task

Table 2.3. Peace: negative and positive, direct, structural, cultural

	Direct peace (harming, hurting)	*Structural peace (harming, hurting)*	*Cultural peace (justifying harm/hurt)*
Negative peace	[1] absence of = ceasefire; or a desert, cemetery	[2] absence of = no exploitation; or no structure = *atomie*	[3] absence of = no justification; or no culture = *anomie*
Positive peace	[4] presence of = cooperation	[5] presence of = equity, equality	[6] presence of = culture of peace, and dialogue
Peace	negative + positive	negative + positive	negative + positive

known as ceasefire is only one-sixth of a complete peace process, yet often mistaken for the real thing.

Research, needs–rights–dignity, goal restraint and anger transformation

Let us then conclude with some words about the therapies or peace tasks not highlighted: research, needs-rights-dignity satisfaction, goal restraint and anger transformation. Incidentally, we get a total of 7 + 4 = 11 therapies, not nine, because there are three for Step 2.

The most important point about *peace research* is to open new spaces for peace action, often done through reconceptualization. An example is the triple diagnosis-prognosis-therapy taken from health studies. Obviously diagnosis and prognosis are more descriptive, of past and future, since diagnosis is based on data, and only the past can produce data, whereas in prognosis there is projection into a data-free future. On the other hand, therapy is prescriptive. A searching mind will identify the missing fourth category: the prescription, or therapy of the past, making 'at that time, what could/should have been done' a major question in a mediation dialogue.

Another important point is, of course, research to evaluate processes engendered by the mainstream security discourse and the counter-trend conflict/peace discourse. Does it really work the way they both claim?

The most important point about *needs–rights–dignity* is their status as rock bottom, necessary conditions for peace. The arduous work to satisfy them can also be identified with *development*, or at least with a major part of that exercise. That makes development a condition for peace: without development no peace. But peace is also a condition for development because violence insults all needs. It insults survival through killing and wellness through maiming in a war, and then freedom through repression and identity through alienation in a subsequent occupation. That brings the two concepts of peace and development very close to each other.

A point to be highlighted: a person deprived of basic needs may become an angry, violent person. But he may also become manipulable, humiliated, begging for mercy. The opposite is dignity, a major peace component.

The most important point about *goal restraint* is the effort to forestall conflict by putting some limits to goals. The Limits to Growth debate may serve as a good example, using Gandhi's formula 'there is enough for everybody's need, but not for everybody's greed'. Limits to egoism is among the conditions for harmonious marriages, and what does that mean? Not a farewell to pursuing own goals but a welcome to the question, what does this imply for my spouse? The basic point lies in the distinction above between harmonious, disharmonious and indifferent goals. Ideally the satisfaction curves for spouses and family members in general should harmonize, what is good/bad for one is good/bad for the other(s). But, even so, a harmonious family at the top of society may be a disaster to the society, depriving it of means of satisfaction, and correspondingly for a harmonious country at the top of the world community. Much holism and foresight are needed for consequence analysis, missing in some cultures more than others.

The most important point about *anger control* is the effort to cut the frustration–aggression link or at least to insert a delay-loop. 'Breathe deeply' is one approach, 'sleep on it' another. Not very convincing in a country like Afghanistan where the failure to respond with the aggression of hatred and violence to the frustration of an 'insult' is met with the accusation *you are not a man*. Anger control might include training in verbal responses, like 'this is your problem, not mine', or 'so what?'. Or to transform, channel, the anger energy for more constructive purposes.

There are tall bills in this text, with costs in mental rather than money terms. Like the mega conflict Anglo-American Christianity vs the Arab-dominated Islam world, a mix of current conflicts relating to integration of immigrants and to Afghanistan, Iraq and Israel/Palestine, and past conflicts over colonization and trauma. The therapy is mediation for present and conciliation for past conflicts. The basic cost is for all parties to adopt reciprocity, equality. And as to the gains: *the sky is the limit*.

For more about these topics by the present author, see Galtung (1996, 2004).

Notes

1 Thus, the carriers of violent behaviour, violent people, are looked upon like the carriers of such pathogens as viruses and micro-organisms. The slogan used during the 'war against Viêt Nam' was 'seek and destroy', and for the present 'war against terrorism' it is 'identify and crush' (the terrorists).

2 Very weak, a very undeveloped field, both in economic theory and practice, with the social, economic and cultural rights of 1966 being an effort, but not yet ratified by the leading state in the state system, the United States.

3 And that is where democracy (one person one vote) and human rights (every one is entitled) enter, but not only within countries, also among them.

References

Galtung, J. (1996) *Peace by Peaceful Means*, London: Sage.
Galtung, J. (2004) *Transcend and Transform*, London: Pluto; Boulder, CO: Paradigm.
Johnson, C. (2000) *Blowback: The Costs and Consequences of American Empire*, New York: Henry Holt.

Part 1

Understanding and transforming conflict

3

Negotiation and international conflict

Fen Osler Hampson, Chester A. Crocker and Pamela R. Aall

Prior to the Second World War, interstate conflict was the predominant form of organized violence in international relations. During the Cold War and the period that has followed it, intrastate violence and intercommunal conflict have replaced interstate violence as the principal form of conflict in international relations. However, what is striking about the international conflict trends is that over the past two decades the number of civil wars, measured by their frequency and aggregate levels of violence, has been on the decline. This trend is now well-documented in a large number of studies, including, most recently, the *Human Security Report* (Mack 2005) of the Liu Institute of International Studies at the University of British Columbia. What is also borne out in these studies is that *many* of these conflicts – Bosnia, Northern Ireland, South Africa, Mozambique, the conflict between North and South Sudan, El Salvador, Guatemala, the border dispute between Peru and Ecuador, and now perhaps the conflict in Aceh – have been settled or 'resolved' through a process of negotiation, upsetting a longstanding, post-Westphalian trend where wars traditionally ended when one party defeated the other on the battlefield. And even in those cases of those perennial conflicts – Israel–Palestine, Sri Lanka, Kashmir, Mindanao, and Korea – that are still on-going, negotiations between the warring parties have rarely been off the table.

In terms of war termination, there are two trends to explore. The first is the apparent decline in the outbreak of wars. There is obviously a need to explore the factors or forces that are shaping and influencing these international conflict trends in order to understand better why some conflicts are diminishing and whether or not this *tendency* will continue (Marshall and Gurr 2005).[1] The second trend is the growing interest in negotiated settlements, which is the area that this paper will explore. The objectives of this paper are as follows: (1) to discuss why warring parties in recent years have increasingly turned to the 'negotiation option' – usually with the assistance of third parties, including third-party mediators – in order to settle their differences; and (2) to explore some of the different approaches to the study and practice of negotiation in the burgeoning conflict management literature.

The negotiation option

First, it must be said that the preference for the negotiation option in the settlement of violent international disputes is one that has taken place against a backdrop marked by a growing preference for international negotiation as the principal means for dealing with international disputes on a wide range of issues. This is partly due to a stronger understanding of the processes of interest-based negotiations, a method of structuring negotiations toward a 'win-win' solution in which both parties reach a satisfactory agreement on issues critical to each (Fisher et al. 1991). At the same time, globalization processes have brought states and the societies that inhabit them into increasingly close proximity – a proximity characterized by a growing density of interactions that cross the economic, commercial, social, cultural and political spheres of life. As the frequency and depth of these interactions has grown, so too has the potential for conflicts of interest, beliefs and values. Generally speaking, in matters of 'low politics' – that is to say the politics of trade, investment, natural resources, the environment, economic policy and so forth – these conflicts have been resolved through processes of informal dialogue and negotiation directed at identifying new norms, rules and procedures that will govern future interactions while lowering transaction costs (Keohane 1984; Keohane and Nye 2000).

The rapid growth in the number of international institutions in the twentieth century, which accelerated after the Second World War with the founding of the United Nations and a host of regional and sub-regional institutions and arrangements, has also given further impetus to international negotiation processes, especially multi-party and multi-issue negotiations which have taken place within the formal multilateral and rule-bound settings of these institutions (Hampson 1989; Kremenyuk 1991; Umbricht 1989). The obvious importance states attach to these somewhat ritualized bargaining processes is also reflected in the sizeable cadre of professional international negotiators who are to be found not just in foreign ministries, but also in the many different functional departments and agencies of national governments that now deal with cross-border issues.

Although adjudication, arbitration and various judicial means are frequently used to deal with interstate disputes (Bilder 1997), as well as disputes between private actors that cross international borders, the continued importance that states attach to their sovereignty in international affairs has meant that the opportunities for judicial recourse generally tend to be limited. Bargaining and negotiation are thus the default option when disputes arise. This is because states are often reluctant to let themselves be governed by extra-national legal institutions even if they have formally agreed to submit themselves to the legal rules and norms of those institutions. For instance, shunning Law of the Sea provisions, East Timor and Australia have negotiated a temporary arrangement dividing the income from off-shore petroleum resources, but have put off the settlement of the borders in question for 50 years as part of the deal. This reluctance to be governed by international law is especially true for those great powers that see themselves as completely independent actors in the international system, as the US's refusal to ratify the International Criminal Court illustrates (Hampson and Reid 2003: 22–33).

When it comes to the great issues of war and peace, international negotiation and diplomacy have generally been the preferred means for dispute settlement at the global level since the Second World War. There are a number of reasons for this, not least of which is the advent of nuclear weapons technology. As many scholars and commentators have pointed out, the advent of nuclear weapons had a progressively sobering effect on the way the two superpowers managed their strategic and ideological rivalries during the Cold War (George et al. 1988). Nuclear brinksmanship, which reached its highest and most dangerous point during the Cuban missile crisis, eventually yielded to a more business-like relationship characterized by regular summits between the leaders of the United States and the Soviet Union and negotiations on arms control, troop deployments and other kinds of confidence-measures directed at reducing tensions and the risks of escalation in crisis situations. The leaders of the West, but especially the United States, also invested their diplomatic political capital and energy in negotiating a relatively smooth and trouble-free transition when the Soviet Union collapsed and the Berlin Wall came tumbling down.

But it is not just technology and the costs of war that have influenced strategic calculations and the pursuit of the negotiation option, *realist* theories of international relations also stress that the prospects for diplomacy and negotiation in international relations have historically been influenced by the balance of power, the presence or absence of military stalemate and domestic political pressures (Organski 1968; Stein 1990). All of these variables have salience in recent international relations, including the management of superpower relations during the Cold War.

Liberal theories of international relations point to another set of factors that help to explain why negotiation is the preferred option for resolving international disputes, especially in recent years. An important body of scholarship argues that there is a strong relationship between democracy and peace, which, following the writings of Immanuel Kant, suggests that democratic states have an overwhelming tendency to resolve their differences via peaceful, i.e. diplomatic, as opposed to violent means (Russett 1993). However, there are some important exceptions to this rule. Weak democracies have a tendency to exhibit both illiberal and belligerent tendencies, which suggests that the 'democratic peace' thesis should not be interpreted and applied simplistically (Mansfield and Snyder 1995). Even so, the spread of pluralist values throughout the world with the rise in the number of democratic states – what Samuel Huntington (1993) refers to as the 'third wave of democracy' – has buttressed a preference for diplomacy and negotiation in international relations, a trend that is likely to continue if democracy is consolidated in those states where liberal norms are shaky or weak. This is because political solutions and the peaceful settlement of disputes are highly valued in democratic polities and because there are a variety of constitutional checks on executive power in democratic states, which further encourage negotiation processes between the different branches of government.

Finally, the continued importance that states attach to sovereignty (Chayes and Handler Chayes 1995; Krasner 1999) itself has generally tended to act as a brake on temptations to challenge the status quo or to try to redraw state boundaries through the use of force, especially in former colonial territories like the African subcontinent. The normative appeal of Westphalian principles remains strong in international affairs, although, in some respects, the 'pillars' of this system are crumbling with the emergence of new normative principles that are centred on the concept of human security. Sovereignty has come under challenge when there are violations of human rights and governments fail to protect or respect the basic rights and freedoms of their citizens. International interventions in the Balkans, Kosovo, East Timor and elsewhere were carried out in the name of higher humanitarian principles (Blechman 1996). But even the strongest champions of humanitarian intervention when there are gross violations of human rights believe that the international community should only use force as a last resort, and only after all other peaceful means, including the negotiation option, have been exhausted (ICISS 2001).

The puzzle of civil war termination

In the case of intrastate conflicts, the embrace of the negotiation option by the parties to these conflicts nonetheless remains something of a puzzle. As Mack (2005) and others have documented, there was a steady rise in the frequency and magnitude of civil wars during the Cold War up until the late 1980s–early 1990s, when the trend reversed itself and intrastate conflicts experienced a steady decline. However, unlike civil wars in the past the majority over this decade ended in a negotiated settlement, usually with the assistance of a third party – and typically more than one – in helping secure a negotiated outcome.

One possible explanation why many of these conflicts ended in a negotiated settlement is because many of them fall into the category of what Roy Licklider refers to as 'long civil wars'. As Licklider observes, 'We have some evidence that long civil wars are disproportionately likely to be ended with negotiated settlements rather than military victory. This is plausible since a long civil war means that neither side has been able to achieve a military victory' (Licklider 2005: 39). The logic of this process is spelled out by Robert Harrison Wagner. He notes, 'that a military stalemate merely transforms a counterforce duel into a contest in punishment, in which war becomes indistinguishable from bargaining. Thus in deciding whether to accept some proposed settlement, there are two ways in which a party to a stalemate might expect to do better if it continued fighting instead: it might be able to overcome the stalemate and achieve a military advantage, or its opponents might, after further suffering, decide to settle for less. A negotiated settlement therefore requires that all parties to the conflict prefer the terms of the settlement to the expected outcome both of further fighting and of further bargaining' (Wagner 1993: 260).

The parallel ending of many of these civil conflicts with the end of Cold War also suggests that broader, systemic forces may have been at play. Many conflicts in the Third World during the Cold War were aided and propelled by the two superpowers who were busy arming insurgents (or governments) in order to strengthen and expand their respective spheres of influence. The desire to end these so-called 'proxy wars' as the Cold War wound down encouraged the two superpowers to pursue negotiated solutions so that they could gracefully exit from their regional commitments, which had also become very costly (Weiss 1995). Nowhere was this desire for a negotiated 'exit' to their difficulties more evident than in the case of Cambodia (Solomon 2000). Negotiation efforts there, which were led by the five Permanent Members of the Security Council, were tied to a wider exit strategy so that China, Russia, Vietnam and the United States could disengage from their military commitments in the region and move towards the normalization of relations. Similarly, in Southern Africa, US efforts to negotiate a peaceful termination to the conflict in Namibia were tied more broadly to a negotiated withdrawal of Cuban troops from Angola, which became the cornerstone of the US policy of 'constructive engagement' in the region (Crocker 1992).

Although the end of the Cold War had its positive effects in some regions, it is important not to stack the historical deck. It is also the case that the bipolar system checked and prevented many conflicts from breaking out, and the Soviet collapse followed by US disengagement coincided with a number of 1990s conflicts that might never have occurred in Cold War times, including wars in Somalia, Sudan, the Democratic Republic of the Congo, Liberia (and its neighbours), Afghanistan (between the Mujahadeen and Taliban), Aceh/Moluccas/Timor, Tajikistan, Nagorno-Karabakh, Georgia, Moldova, and the Balkans.

The transformation of the international system from the Cold War period to the post-Cold War period also had other important consequences. At least initially, the United Nations suddenly assumed greater relevance as the great powers looked to international institutions to play a greater role in conflict management processes, including the mediation and negotiation of international disputes (Skjelsbaek 1991; Skjelsbaek and Fermann 1996; Vayrynen 1985). The same was true of regional and sub-regional organizations, which also began to expand their roles in conflict management in their own neighbourhoods, sometimes with the support and backing of the international community (Smock and Crocker 1995; Thornton 1991; Wedgwood 1996).

The changing US global position has also expanded the range of potential US responses to individual conflict scenarios. On the one hand, the unipolar environment enables Washington to enjoy a freer hand as a potential intervener in both the political and military sense. On the other hand, the absence of an adversary pole may reduce the perceived necessity for action or leadership in the broad global service of order and stability. At the end of the day, it has depended and may continue to depend on the circumstances of individual cases. The US capacity to conduct an essentially discretionary foreign policy looks likely to continue.

What is also quite striking is that a wide variety of small-state and non-state actors also began to offer their services in conflict management and resolution processes. For example, small and medium-sized powers, like Australia, New Zealand, Norway and Switzerland, who had long been active in international peacekeeping operations, began to actively market their negotiation and intermediary services to warring parties (see Princen 1991, 1992a, 1992b). From the Middle East to Central America to Africa and the Asia-Pacific region, these countries have played key roles in instigating negotiations between warring sides, backstopping negotiations once they got underway, and ensuring that the parties remained committed to the peace process once a negotiated settlement was concluded. Prominent international nongovernmental organizations, like the Community of Sant'Egidio – a Catholic lay organization that has been active as a mediator in Mozambique, Algeria and Kosovo (Bartoli 1999) – have also played key roles in bringing parties to the negotiating table and creating much-needed forums for dialogue, discussion and negotiation, especially at the intercommunal and societal levels – although such roles are by no means new (Yarrow 1978).

From the point of view of the conflicting parties, negotiation becomes a more desirable option when hope of winning the war on the battlefield fades. The condition of ripeness – the point at which a conflict is ripe for resolution – has been associated with mutually hurting stalemates, or situations in which the parties to the conflict are unable to muster or deploy their armies or militias in order to change the facts on the ground. The parties cannot win militarily by themselves, they cannot persuade outsiders to provide extra firepower, and they cannot lessen the capacity of their enemies to continue the fight. This was the situation in Mozambique when the Community of Sant'Egidio became involved in the mediation there. In addition to depleting the fighting capacities of the combatants, a long civil war leads to exhaustion in the wider community by destroying economies and taking a psychological toll on civilians affected by the conflict. Popular backing for the fight diminishes, and the drop in popular support makes it difficult for the parties to recruit and retain their militaries. The general revulsion after the market bombing at Omagh killed nine children diminished support markedly for the Irish Republican Army among Northern Irish Catholics. This change – brought on by exhaustion – helped create support for the Good Friday Agreement that had been negotiated just weeks before. (Without this exhaustion or mutually hurting stalemate, civil conflicts are difficult to bring to negotiation: for many years, the Angolan government and the rebel force UNITA were at a stalemate – neither could win, but neither were 'hurting' as each had access to a resource (oil and diamonds) that allowed the fight to go on for decades.) *At the point at which the conflict seems unwinnable and popular support evaporates, the negotiation alternative becomes more attractive to the parties themselves* (Haass 1988; Zartman 1985, 1989).

In sum, superpower disengagement from regional conflicts and the collapse of the bipolar system may have triggered a number of conflicts during the first post-Cold War decade, and there was a transition in conflict management approaches in the early–mid-1990s toward greater engagement by the UN, individual states and NGOs. At the same time, this period witnessed a 'learning curve' as conflict parties benefited from the 'demonstration effect' of parallel efforts to wind down wars and negotiate peace agreements.

The study of negotiation

The obvious importance of negotiation to the settlement and resolution of international conflicts of both the interstate and intrastate/civil conflict varieties has prompted renewed interest by scholars in different disciplines about the conditions that underpin bargaining and negotiation processes. Although it is impossible in a brief review of this kind to give proper justice to this literature, there are a number of important aspects to this debate about the conditions that are conducive to the 'negotiation option', especially in civil conflict situations, which have been the principal form of organized violence in the modern age.

Oversimplified, the debate about international negotiation processes in conflict settings can be classified into major approaches – those that stress the importance of communications and dialogue as trust-building activities that help change the perceptions of warring parties by promoting cooperative solutions and those that view the negotiation process as a risk management process directed at changing the utility preferences of the parties and their strategic ability to commitment themselves to a negotiation process – what we refer to here as 'realist' approaches to negotiation, which are grounded in rational-actor assumptions about negotiation processes. These two approaches involve alternative assessments about appropriate bargaining strategies, risk, comparative advantage, and the sources of leverage in bargaining relationships. Each approach also points to a different set of conclusions about the possibilities for third-party intervention in conflict processes and the kinds of bargaining strategies that are likely to be most effective in these situations.

Communication-based approaches

Communication-based approaches typically stress the importance of negotiation as a vehicle or means for changing the parties' perceptions in a conflict so that they learn to trust each other to the point where they are prepared to engage in a reciprocal exchange of concessions. Trust is developed by bringing the parties into direct contact with each other in forums that encourage dialogue, discussion and ultimately negotiation. The negotiation process therefore should be viewed as a trust-building activity that taps into the deeply rooted needs of the parties and elicits empathic responses in the way they view the needs of their negotiating partners. In the communications' frame of reference, negotiation is also a learning process where the parties progressively redefine their own perceptions about their own needs that can be met by eschewing violence as the 'preferred' option. The establishment of a dialogue, of a pattern of informal as well as formal exchanges and contacts between and among official parties or other influential representatives, helps set the stage for cooperation and the search for more lasting negotiated political solutions to their differences. A key to this process is often the involvement in the dialogue not just of the principal political authorities but of a wider group of civil and opinion leaders whose support is essential for the long-term sustainability of the peace process.

In communications-based approaches, an important assumption is that although parties identify specific issues as the causes of conflict, conflict also reflects subjective, phenomenological and social fractures and, consequently, analyzing 'interests' can be less important than identifying the underlying needs that govern each party's perception of the conflict (Doob 1993; Lederach 1995). Because much of human conflict is anchored in conflicting perceptions and in misperception, negotiation processes must be directed at changing the perceptions, attitudes, values and behaviours of the parties to their conflict (Kriesberg 1992, 1997). Accordingly, the negotiation process should begin with an informal dialogue – sometimes referred to as a prenegotiation – that allows conflict parties to develop personal relationships before they actually begin to discuss the different dimensions of their conflict. These relationships are viewed as critical to building a basis for trust that will, in the long run, help to sustain the negotiation process. Attitudinal change can be fostered through a variety of instruments, including, for example, consultative meetings, problem-solving workshops, training in conflict resolution at the communal level, and/or third-party assistance in developing and designing other kinds of dispute resolution systems which are compatible with local culture and norms and are directed at elites as different levels within society (Bloomfield 1997).

The problem-solving workshop is directed at communication and creating more open channels of communication which allow the participants to see their respective intentions more clearly and to be more fully aware of their own reactions to the conflict (Kelman 1996, 1997). Workshops are aimed at cultivating respect and objectivity so that the parties develop a mutual commitment to cooperative exchanges in their relationship. Based on findings which show that individuals are more disposed to cooperative behaviour in small, informal, intergroup activities, the problem-solving workshop establishes relations among significant players who may be in a position to influence the parties to the conflict and, in so doing, to contribute to the de-escalation of conflict. The approach seems to work best if individuals are middle-range elites such as academics, advisers, ex-officials or retired politicians who continue to have access to those in power. By helping to establish communications between parties at the sub-elite level, these workshops help to undermine 'we–they' images of conflict, establish linkages among influentials, begin a discussion of framework solutions, identify steps that will break the impasse, and in general create an understanding of these steps and processes that the participants can feed back into the track one effort where actual decisions get made.

A somewhat different kind of prenegotiation activity is third-party assisted dialogue, undertaken by both official and nongovernmental structures. This activity is directed at ethnic, racial or religious groups who are in a hostile or adversarial relationship (Wehr and Lederach 1991, 1996). Like 'circum-negotiation', this dialogue occurs at a quasi-official level around or prior to the formal peace process (Saunders 1996). Dialogue is directed at both officials and civic leaders, including heads of local nongovernmental organizations, community developers, health officials, refugee camp leaders, ethnic/religious leaders, intellectuals and academics. This dialogue process can be assisted by specialized training programmes that are directed at exploring ways of establishing and building relationships, furthering proficiency in facilitation, mediation, brokering, data collection, fact-finding, and other kinds of cooperative decision making. As Kriesberg notes, much of this activity is directed at developing 'constituency support for peace efforts' (Chigas 2005; Kriesberg 1996a: 228; Rouhana 2000; Saunders 2000).

The practice of dialogue and communication is not confined to the nongovernmental sector, but in fact underlies the approach of regional organizations in promoting dialogue and confidence-building prenegotiations. Lacking in some instances the resources of individual states or the UN and in other instances reluctant to use the resources they have, regional organizations have used consultation, problem-solving, dialogue, and a kind of moral example to shift perceptions and change attitudes among conflict parties. A prime example of the use of this approach is found in the conflict prevention work of the OSCE's High Commission on National Minorities (Chigas et al. 1996).

Communications-based approaches typically stress the importance of third-party interveners in establishing communication channels between different groups in society, initiating discussions of framework solutions to problems of mutual concern, identifying steps for breaking impasses, developing new norms and creating an understanding of the kinds of decision-making processes that can lead parties out of conflict. In these kinds of activities, third parties are supposed to play a neutral and essentially facilitating role, enabling and encouraging a mutual learning process rather than guiding or still less influencing and directing the parties to mutually acceptable approaches to problem-solving. Their involvement is based on their expert and/or reputational authority or on their ability to represent a normative or real community to which the combatants aspire. However, if such third parties are successful at promoting dialogue, their importance as conveners will diminish over time as the parties to the dispute take ownership of their dialogue and learn to manage the negotiation process by themselves.

Realist approaches

Realists typically view the negotiation process in utility maximizing terms where the parties' expected utility calculations exercise a decisive influence over negotiating incentives, behaviours and outcomes. There are several different points of emphasis in this literature. Some scholars stress the 'costing' aspects of negotiation, where the costs of negotiation and bargaining outcomes must be compared to costs of the conflict itself, including its sunk and future anticipated costs. Using the insights of game theory, other scholars argue that concession and commitment problems are acute in these kinds of conflict situations because the parties do not trust each other and that it is difficult to elicit trust simply through a process of dialogue and communication. Instead, bargaining processes and interactions have to be designed to manage risk while strengthening the parties' commitment to negotiation. This includes the use of enforcement mechanisms and security guarantees (typically provided by a third party) that lower negotiation costs while raising the costs of noncompliance.

Expected utility calculations figure prominently in the work of I. William Zartman and Richard Haass, who have written extensively about negotiation and conflict management processes in civil conflict situations. These authors argue that the parties to a conflict are unlikely to entertain the possibility of negotiation as long as they continue to believe that 'conflict pays'. That is to say, they believe that they have a good prospect of defeating their adversary through violent means and at a lower cost to themselves (and their supporters) than if they were to opt for a negotiated agreement that would require them to make concessions. The negotiation option only becomes attractive if this expectation changes. And, according to Zartman and Haass, this change is more likely to occur if the parties are deadlocked militarily, the conflict is prolonged and shows no signs of abating, and the parties are denied the opportunity to seize the military initiative and escalate the conflict to a higher level. At this moment, the conflict becomes 'ripe for resolution' because the parties are willing – perhaps for the first time – to entertain their negotiated options and a political 'solution' that ultimately promises lower costs than a continuation of the conflict. This is sometimes referred to as the moment of 'ripeness'. As Zartman suggests, the prime 'condition' for negotiations is if the parties perceive the costs and prospects of continuing war to be more burdensome than the costs and prospects of settlement (Zartman 1985, 1987).[2] The prospects for a negotiated settlement to a dispute are thus greater when war weariness has set in among the parties and a conflict has reached a plateau or 'hurting stalemate' in which unilateral solutions are no longer believed to be credible or achievable.

Under this approach, timing is critical. For those third parties who wish to assist with the negotiation process through the provision of various kinds of intermediary services they must recognize that their interventions are going to be more successful if the parties are sufficiently 'exhausted' on the battlefield to look for a negotiated political settlement (Rubin 1991). In stressing the importance of timing, the theory of ripeness has its greatest utility in setting up benchmarks and signposts that help third parties calibrate their strategies to help ripen the conflict. Commitment tactics also have an important role to play in changing the parties' expected utility calculations about the costs of an agreement. By denying military assistance, or taking measures that alter the balance of power between warring sides, external actors can strengthen the incentives for negotiation. At the same time, the offer of side-payments and other kinds of inducements can make a negotiated agreement appear more attractive all other things being equal (Crocker 1992: 469–72). However, the kinds of penalties and inducements have to be introduced with great care. For example, if offers of military assistance are presented in such a way that the parties feel that it will allow them to defeat their enemies, they may accept them but not live up to their commitment to pursue a negotiated solution. And the ill-timed withdrawal of such benefits can also produce similar unintended consequences.

Triadic bargaining situations, where third parties offer side-payments and/or penalties and sanctions to get the parties to the dispute to change their cost/benefit calculations about the utility of a negotiated settlement, though conceivably desirable are also quite unstable for the reasons just mentioned (Touval 1996a, 1996b). Thus what may be required in some situations is what Saadia Touval calls 'mediators with muscle' (Touval 1982a). According to this formulation, impartiality and objectivity are less important to achieving influence than 'power potential considerations' (Touval and Zartman 1985: 256). The ability to exercise leverage may also be positively influenced by close ties between a third party and one or more parties to the dispute, thus allowing the mediator to elicit cooperative behaviour and concessions (Princen 1991). The less 'muscle' a third party has, and the more removed or distant it is from the conflict, the weaker will be its intervention potential (Zartman 1989; Zartman and Touval 1985). And if third-party pressure is the only factor that keeps the parties at the negotiating table, negotiations will fall off the rails as soon as that pressure is relaxed or withdrawn (Azar and Burton 1986; Burton 1987).

Some scholars go one step further and argue that it is not just the costs of negotiation and settlement that matter to the parties as they consider their negotiation options but also the 'risks' of negotiation, i.e. the probabilities that are associated with negative outcomes. Because the parties in civil conflict situations are distrustful of each other and will refuse to cooperate even if there are indeed powerful incentives to consider negotiations as a way out of their current impasse, ways have to be found to reduce the risks of defection so that the parties can entertain the possibility of a negotiated, reciprocal exchange of concessions. The theoretical basis for this position is spelled out in (1) 'prisoner's dilemma' and (2) 'games of chicken', where defection is the dominant bargaining strategy and cooperative solutions are confounded in the first instance by information problems (because of the absence of proper and reliable channels of communication between the parties), and, in the second, the problems of credible commitment.

In inter-ethnic bargaining situations, or civil conflict situations where the parties have deeply antagonistic relations towards each other, efforts to reach some sort of political accommodation via negotiations may be thwarted by the 'domestic' equivalent of the security dilemma because the parties distrust each other so acutely that even defensive measures are viewed as offensive and threatening by the other side (Posen 1993). As Touval (1982a) argues, in these kinds of situation the persistence of high levels of mutual distrust need not pose an insurmountable obstacle to negotiations if ways can be found to effectively reduce risks and 'insure' the parties against the costs of negotiation failure.[3] There are a number of risk management options available to the parties. These include measures to transfer or shift risk, such as (1) bringing a third party into the negotiations who can quietly probe and assess the intentions of the other side; (2) developing deliberately ambiguous commitments during the course of negotiations that can be reinterpreted, manipulated or even withdrawn as circumstances change (also known as hedging); sharing risks so that potential losses if a negotiation fails are more or less equally distributed among the parties; and (3) segregating assets to limit liability, by, for example, separating issues and taking a step-by-step or incremental approach to negotiations.

However, these kinds of bargaining tactics may be insufficient to control strategic behaviour and prevent defection. In those situations where the problems of the security dilemma are compounded by the problem of *moral hazard* – the risk that a party has not entered into negotiations in good faith, different remedies may be called for. Stedman, for example, argues that the moral hazard problem is especially acute in civil conflict situations because of the prevalence of 'spoilers' or extremist elements or groups in a conflict who are generally not interested in compromise and will do their best to create the conditions that will destroy or upset compromise. Because spoilers are predisposed to reckless or uncooperative behaviour, effective strategies of spoiler management may be required to prevent peace negotiations from being blown off course. Spoilers come in different shapes and sizes. The only way to deal with 'total spoilers' – who 'see the world in all-or-nothing terms' and seek a 'violent transformation of society' – may be coercion. On the other hand, the best defence against spoilers who have more limited political goals and can be 'bought off' is to bring them into the negotiation process but to lay clear ground rules for their participation that include penalties for intransigent behaviour and rewards for cooperation.

Barbara Walter and Andrew Kydd (Kydd and Walter 2002; Walter 2002) argue that policymakers and negotiators must also concern themselves with the impact of extremist violence on domestic political support for the peace process. An effective strategy of spoiler management is one inter alia that is directed at neutralizing the impact of extremist violence through exchanges of information and other kinds of trust-building activities that shore up public support for the peace process.

A growing body of scholarship which looks at the requirements for the successful negotiated settlement of civil wars also suggests that it is not sufficient for the parties to a conflict to hammer out an agreement but the negotiated terms of an agreement must necessarily be complemented by ironclad security guarantees – usually provided by external actors – that enforce the terms of the settlement (Walter 2002). The actual terms or content of an agreement also affect its long-term prospects for success. Strong agreements are ones that contain mechanisms that include demilitarized zones, demobilization of troops, dispute resolution commissions, peacekeeping, as well as political provisions for effective power-sharing among previously warring parties (Page Fortna 2004; Sisk 1996).

Negotiation and the conflict cycle

Both of the above perspectives hinge on different assessments about the role of trust and political risk in bargaining relationships among combatants in civil conflict situations.

Communication-based approaches argue that the foundations for trust and reciprocal bargaining can be laid through a sustained process of dialogue and communication, especially if there are forums for dialogue and negotiation that allow the parties to treat each other as individuals, break down stereotypes, and identify common interests and needs. Realists argue that the parties will not be interested in negotiations as long as they continue to believe that they can pursue their goals through violent means. And once they do sit down at the negotiating table, communication and dialogue, though viewed as desirable, are often not enough to overcome the high levels of mistrust that infect intercommunal relationships in war-torn settings. Accordingly, the parties must structure their interactions in ways that reduce the upfront costs/risks of defection from negotiated solutions. In addition, confidence-building measures, third-party security guarantees and strategies of spoiler management may also be required to change their strategic calculus and move negotiations forward.

As we have argued elsewhere in greater depth, these two approaches are not necessarily incompatible if we consider that most conflicts pass through different stages or phases, which are marked by different levels of violence (Bercovitch and Langley 1993; Crocker et al. 1999; Lund 1996; Mitchell 1994). These include a period of rising tensions between or among parties during its early stage or phase, followed by confrontation, the outbreak of violence, and the escalation of military hostilities. In the post-agreement or post-settlement phase, a conflict may go through several de-escalatory phases as well, such as a ceasefire, followed by a formal settlement, rapprochement and eventual reconciliation. And in unfortunate cases, as the situation in Angola in the late 1980s and early 1990s reminds us, some conflicts reverse themselves, doubling back into violence even in the implementation stage (Hampson 1996).

During these various phases or stages of conflict, the intensity of the security dilemma among rival communal groupings will vary. Parties will tend to feel more secure in their relations with other groupings when the level of violence is low, formal ties exist between different groups, and institutionalized channels of communication, though perhaps frayed, are still available. At this stage of the conflict style, there may well be more chances for direct, face-to-face negotiations because attitudes and perceptions have not hardened and parties are still willing to talk to each other (Adelman and Suhrke 1996; Carnegie Commission 1998; Jones 1995; Lund 1996). As Princen notes, negotiation at this stage is a relatively low risk strategy for the disputants 'because it is not equated as conceding' (Princen 1992a: 54). The downside is that negotiated solutions will seem less attractive because the parties, having not yet experienced the full cost and limits of what can typically be achieved through other means, may consider violence in support of unilateral goals to be a viable alternative to compromise and politically-based solutions.

As violence increases, different groups start to arm themselves, and factions become increasingly aware of the real power asymmetries that exist between themselves and other groups, the security dilemma will become more acute and the desire for peaceful and cooperative strategies of conflict management will weaken (Lake and Rothchild 1996). This will tend to thwart the prospects for successful negotiations unless instruments of outright strategic leverage and coercive diplomacy can be found (Corbin 1994; Crocker 1992; Hampson 1996). Once violence has reached a threshold where no further escalation is possible without major costs, the disputants may be willing to consider other alternatives than the use of force *and turn to* negotiation.

There are a whole set of conflicts, however, for which this change in calculation never seems to occur. These conflicts, characterized as intractable or protracted, endure for decades at the middle range of the escalation curve, i.e. violence is ongoing and episodic but not sufficient to make the idea of a political solution an attractive alternative to the status quo. Intractable conflicts are marked by self-sustaining patterns of hostility and violence and have multiple sources or causes – including greed, self-interest, security dilemmas, and bad neighbours or neighbourhoods (Albin 1997; Azar 1990). As the conflict wears on, the intensity and duration of the adversarial relationship make the idea of entering into talks or reaching an agreement unacceptable to the conflict parties' leadership. At the same time, the conflict permeates every aspect of life in the societies in question from the economy to the education system. These conflicts – the Middle East, Kashmir, Korea, Sudan – seem to lack any apparent deadline, impending disaster or sense of time shifting to the other side's advantage. And yet even some of the hardest cases yield to negotiation, for a variety of reasons. Openings may come to intractable conflicts because of systemic changes – the prospect of European Union membership, for instance, provided a brief opening for the end of the Cyprus conflict. There may be changes in leadership, as happened in Angola with the death of the rebel leader Savimbi. And there may be changes in situation on the ground, as happened in Bosnia just before the signing of the Dayton Accords. A critical element, however, in the resolution of most intractable conflicts is long-term, committed involvement of third-party peacemakers that intervene and encourage the parties to change their strategic calculus and consider their negotiation options (Crocker et al. 2004, 2005).

Conclusion

As this chapter has shown, there is much fertile ground in the study of international negotiation processes, not least because the main protagonists in today's conflict situations have demonstrated a greater propensity to come to the negotiating table to address their differences. This propensity has been affected by many factors on both the demand and supply side of the equation. On the demand side, the negotiation option is affected by stalemate on the battlefield and the prospect of a war (or violence) of indefinite duration, which encourages combatants to look to their negotiated options – perhaps for the first time – as a way out of their current impasse. On the supply side, the abundance of third parties of the intergovernmental, state and nonstate variety who are willing to offer their negotiation and intermediary services has meant that warring parties do not have to struggle to reach a negotiated compromise on their own. And because the strategic incentives to look for negotiated solutions are adversely affected by the acute security dilemma communities and their leaders experience in civil conflict situations, pressuring tactics, security guarantees and other kinds of positive and negative inducement are often necessary to instigate, manage and sustain the negotiation process. At the same time, once intercommunal tensions ease, dialogue and negotiation processes that voluntarily engage a wide range of different groups in society, not just elites, are critical elements to building trust and laying the foundations for the kinds of social and political relationship that will sustain civil society. These factors underscore the reality that conflict parties increasingly turn to third parties for help when they decide to explore the negotiation option and find a way out of their dilemma. But, the reality is that there is no one-size-fits-all approach to negotiation and conflict management processes in today's world.

Notes

1 The Marshall and Gurr (2005: 25) data include these findings related to armed conflicts for self-determination, which account for a high percentage of all conflicts: 'The number of armed conflicts over self-determination spiked sharply upward at the end of the Cold War (17 new such conflicts in the

1991–5 period), but they had been building in number since the late 1950s, doubling between 1970 and the early 1980s. From five ongoing wars in the 1950s, numbers swelled to a high of 49 by the end of 1991. The numbers have declined steadily since then to 25 at the end of 2004, a level that has not been reached since 1976.'

2 For critical discussions of the concept of ripeness, see Kleibor (1994) and Kleibor and Hart (1995).

3 Thomas Schelling (1960: 135) makes the same point in his classic study, *The Strategy of Conflict*. He states that, 'Agreements are unenforcible if no outside authority exists to enforce them or if noncompliance would be inherently undetectable. The problem arises, then, of finding forms of agreements, or terms to agree on, that provide no incentives to cheat or that make noncompliance automatically visible or that incur the penalties on which the possibility of enforcement rests. While the possibility of "trust" between two partners need not be ruled out, it should also not be taken for granted; and even trust itself can usefully be studied in game-theoretic terms. Trust is often achieved simply by the continuity of the relation between the parties and the recognition by each that what he might gain by cheating in a given instance is outweighed by the value of the tradition of trust that makes possible a long sequence of future agreement. By the same token, "trust" may be achieved for a single discontinuous instance, if it can be divided into a succession of increments.'

References

Adelman, H. and Suhrke, A. (1996) 'Early warning and response: why the international community failed to prevent the genocide', *Journal of Disaster Studies and Management*, 20, 4: 295–304.

Albin, C. (1997) 'Negotiating intractable conflicts: on the future of Jerusalem', *Cooperation and Conflict*, 32, 1: 29–77.

Azar, E.E. (1990) *The Management of Protracted Social Conflict: Theory and Cases*, Dartmouth, MA: Aldershot.

Azar, E.E. and Burton, J.W. (eds) (1986) *International Conflict Resolution: Theory and Practice*, Sussex: Wheatsheaf Books.

Bartoli, A. (1999) 'Mediating peace in Mozambique: the role of the Community of Sant'Egidio', in C. A. Crocker, F. O. Hampson and P. Aall (eds) *Herding Cats: Multiparty Mediation in a Complex World*, Washington, DC: United States Institute of Peace Press, 245–74.

Bercovitch, J. (1986) 'International mediation: a study of the incidence, strategies and conditions of successful outcomes', *Cooperation and Conflict*, 21, 3: 155–68.

Bercovitch, J. (ed.) (1997) *Resolving International Conflicts: The Theory and Practice of Mediation*, Boulder, CO: Lynne Rienner.

Bercovitch, J. and Langley, J. (1993) 'The nature of the dispute and the effectiveness of international mediation', *Journal of Conflict Resolution*, 37, 4: 670–91.

Bilder, R.B. (1997) 'Adjudication: international tribunals and courts', in J. Bercovitch (ed.) *Resolving International Conflicts: The Theory and Practice of Mediation*, Boulder, CO: Lynne Rienner, 155–90.

Blechman, B.M. (1996) 'Emerging from the intervention dilemma', in C. A. Crocker and F. O. Hampson, with P. Aall (eds) *Managing Global Chaos: Sources of and Responses to International Conflict*, Washington, DC: United States Institute of Peace Press, 287–96.

Bloomfield, L.P. (1997) 'Why wars end: a research note', *Millennium: Journal of International Studies*, 26, 3: 709–26.

Burton, J.W. (1987) *Resolving Deep-rooted Conflict: A Handbook*, Lanham, MD: University Press of America.

Carnegie Commission on Preventing Deadly Conflict (1998) *Preventing Deadly Conflict: Final Report*, New York: Carnegie Corporation of New York.

Chayes, A. and Handler Chayes, A. (1995) *The New Sovereignty: Compliance with International Regulatory Agreements*, Cambridge, MA: Harvard University Press.

Chigas, D. (2005) 'Negotiating intractable conflicts: the contribution of unofficial intermediaries', in C. A. Crocker, F. O. Hampson and P. Aall (eds) *Grasping the Nettle: Analyzing Cases of Intractability*, Washington, DC: United States Institute of Peace Press, 123–60.

Chigas, D., with McClintock, E. and Kamp, C. (1996) 'Preventive diplomacy and the organization for security and cooperation in Europe: Creating incentives for dialogue and cooperation' in A. Chayes and A. Handler Chayes (eds) *Preventing Conflict in the Post-Communist World*, Washington, DC: Brookings Institution, 25–98.

Corbin, J. (1994) *The Norway Channel: The Secret Talks That Led to the Middle East Peace Accord*, New York: Atlantic Monthly Press.
Crocker, C.A. (1992) *High Noon in Southern Africa: Making Peace in a Rough Neighborhood*, New York: W. W. Norton.
Crocker, C.A., Hampson, F.O. and Aall, P. (eds) (1999) *Herding Cats: Multiparty Mediation in a Complex World*, Washington, DC: United States Institute of Peace Press.
Doob, L.W. (1993) *Intervention: Guides and Perils*, New Haven, CT: Yale University Press.
Fisher, R., Ury, W. and Patton, B. (1991) *Getting to Yes: Negotiating Agreements Without Giving In*, 2nd edn, New York: Penguin.
George, A.L., Farley, P.J. and Dallin, A. (eds) (1988) *US–Soviet Security Cooperation: Achievement, Lessons, Failures*, New York: Oxford University Press.
Haass, R.N. (1988) *Conflicts Unending: The United States and Regional Disputes*, New Haven, CT: Yale University Press.
Hampson, F.O. (1989) *Multilateral Negotiations: Lessons From Arms Control, Trade, and the Environment*, Baltimore, MD: Johns Hopkins University Press.
Hampson, F.O. (1996) *Nurturing Peace: Why Peace Settlements Succeed or Fail*, Washington, DC: United States Institute of Peace.
Hampson, F.O. and Reid, H. (2003) 'Coalition diversity and normative legitimacy in human security negotiations', *International Negotiation*, 8, 1: 7–42.
Huntington, S.P. (1993) *The Third Wave: Democratization in the late Twentieth Century*, Tulsa: University of Oklahoma Press.
International Commission on Intervention and State Sovereignty (ICISS) (2001) *The Responsibility to Protect*, Ottawa: International Development Research Centre.
Jones, B.D. (1995) 'Intervention without borders: humanitarian intervention in Rwanda, 1990–94', *Millennium: Journal of International Studies*, 24, 2: 225–49.
Kelman, H.C. (1996) 'The interactive problem-solving approach', in C. A. Crocker and F. O. Hampson, with P. Aall (eds) *Managing Global Chaos: Sources of and Responses to International Conflict*, Washington, DC: United States Institute of Peace Press, 501–20.
Kelman, H.C. (1997) 'Social-psychological dimensions of international conflict', in I. W. Zartman and J. L. Rasmussen (eds) *Peacemaking in International Conflict: Methods and Techniques*, Washington, DC: United States Institute of Peace Press, 191–238.
Keohane, R.O. (1984) *After Hegemony: Cooperation and Discord in the World Political Economy*, Princeton, NJ: Princeton University Press.
Keohane, R.O. and Nye, J.S. Jr. (2000) *Power and Interdependence*, 3rd edn, New York: Longman.
Kleibor, M. (1994) 'Ripeness of conflict: a fruitful notion?', *Journal of Peace Research*, 31, 1: 109–16.
Kleibor, M. and Hart, P. (1995) 'Time to talk? Multiple perspectives on timing of international mediation', *Cooperation and Conflict*, 30, 4: 307–48.
Krasner, S. (1999) *Sovereignty: Organized Hypocrisy*, Princeton, NJ: Princeton University Press.
Kremenyuk, V.A. (ed.) (1991) *International Negotiation: Analysis, Approaches, Issues*, San Francisco, CA: Jossey-Bass.
Kriesberg, L. (1992) *International Conflict Resolution: The US–USSR and Middle East Cases*, New Haven, CT: Yale University Press.
Kriesberg, L. (1996a) 'Coordinating intermediary peace efforts', *Negotiation Journal*, 12, 4: 341–52.
Kriesberg, L. (1996b) 'Varieties of mediating activities and mediators in international relations', in J. Bercovitch (ed) *Resolving International Conflicts: The Theory and Practice of Mediation*, Boulder, CO: Lynne Rienner, 219–34.
Kriesberg, L. (1997) 'Preventing and resolving destructive communal conflicts', in D. Carment and P. James (eds) *The International Politics of Ethnic Conflict: Theory and Evidence*, Pittsburgh, PA: University of Pittsburgh Press, 232–51.
Kydd, A. and Walter, B.F. (2002) 'Sabotaging the Peace: The Politics of Extremist Violence', *International Organization*, 56, 2: 263–96.
Lake, D.A. and Rothchild, D. (1996) 'Containing fear: the origins and management of ethnic conflict', *International Security*, 21, 2: 41–75.
Lederach, J. Paul (1995) *Building Peace: Sustainable Reconciliation in Divided Societies*, Washington, DC: United States Institute of Peace Press.
Licklider, R. (2005) 'Comparative studies of long wars', in C. A. Crocker, F. O. Hampson and P. Aall (eds)

Grasping the Nettle: Analyzing Cases of Intractability, Washington, DC: United States Institute of Peace Press.

Lund, M.S. (1996) 'Early warning and preventive diplomacy', in C. A. Crocker and F. O. Hampson, with P. Aall (eds) *Managing Global Chaos: Sources of and Responses to International Conflict*, Washington, DC: United States Institute of Peace Press, 379–402.

Mack, A. (2005) *Human Security Report: War and Peace in the 21st Century*, New York: Oxford University Press.

Mansfield, E. and Snyder, J. (1995) 'Democratization and the danger of war', *International Security*, 20, 1: 5–38.

Marshall, M.G. and Gurr, T.R. (2005) *Peace and Conflict*, College Park, MD: Center for International Development and Conflict Management, University of Maryland.

Mitchell, C. (1994) 'The process and stages of mediation', in D. R. Smock (ed.) *Making War and Waging Peace: Foreign Intervention in Africa*, Washington, DC: United States Institute of Peace Press, 139–59.

Organski, A.K.F. (1968) *World Politics*, 2nd edn, New York: Random House.

Page Fortna, V. (2004) *Peace Time: Cease-Fire Agreements and the Durability of Peace*, Princeton, NJ: Princeton University Press.

Posen, B. R. (1993) 'The security dilemma and ethnic conflict', in M. E. Brown (ed.) *Ethnic Conflict and International Security*. Princeton, NJ: Princeton University Press.

Princen, T. (1991) 'Camp David: problem solving or power politics as usual?', *Journal of Peace Research*, 28, 1: 57–69.

Princen, T. (1992a) 'Mediation by a transnational organization: the case of the Vatican', in J. Bercovitch and J. Rubin (eds) *Mediation in International Relations: Multiple Approaches to Conflict Management*, New York: St Martin's Press.

Princen, T. (1992b) *Intermediaries in International Conflict*, Princeton, NJ: Princeton University Press.

Rouhana, N.N. (2000) 'Interactive conflict resolution: issues in theory, methodology and evaluation', in P. C. Stern and D. Druckman (eds) *International Conflict Resolution after the Cold War*, Washington, DC: National Academy of Sciences.

Robin, J.Z. (ed.) (1981) *Dynamics of Third Party Intervention: Kissinger in the Middle East*, New York: Praeger.

Russett, B. (1993) *Grasping the Democratic Peace: Principles for a Post-Cold War World*, Princeton, NJ: Princeton University Press.

Saunders, H.H. (1996) 'Prenegotiation and circum-negotiation: arenas of the peace process', in C. A. Crocker and F. O. Hampson, with P. Aall (eds) *Managing Global Chaos: Sources of and Responses to International Conflict*, Washington, DC: United States Institute of Peace Press, 419–32.

Saunders, H.H. (2000) 'Interactive conflict resolution: a view for policy makers on making and building peace', in P. C. Stern and D. Druckman (eds) *International Conflict Resolution after the Cold War*, Washington, DC: National Academy of Sciences.

Schelling, T. (1960) *The Strategy of Conflict*, Cambridge, MA: Harvard University Press.

Sisk, T. (1996) *Power Sharing and International Mediation in Ethnic Conflict*, Washington, DC: United States Institute of Peace.

Skjelsbaek, K. (1991) 'The UN Secretary-General and the mediation of international disputes', *Journal of Peace Research*, 28, 1: 99–115.

Skjelsbaek, K. and Fermann, G. (1996) 'The UN Secretary-General and the mediation of international disputes', in J. Bercovitch (ed.) *Resolving International Conflict: The Theory and Practice of Negotiation*, Boulder, CO: Lynne Rienner, 75–104.

Smock, D.R. and Crocker, C.A. (eds) (1995) *African Conflict Resolution: The US Role in Peacemaking*, Washington, DC: United States Institute of Peace.

Solomon, R.H. (2000) *Exiting Indochina: US Leadership of the Cambodia Settlement and Normalization with Vietnam*, Washington, DC: United States Institute of Peace Press.

Stedman, S. John (1997) 'Spoiler problems in the peace process', *International Security*, 22, 2: 5–53.

Stein, A. (1990) *Why Nations Cooperate: Circumstances and Choice in International Relations*, Ithaca, NY: Cornell University Press.

Thornton, T.P. (1991) 'Regional organizations in conflict management', *Annals of the American Academy of Political and Social Science*, 518: 132–42.

Touval, S. (1982a) *The Peace Brokers: Mediators in the Arab–Israeli Conflict 1948–1979*, Princeton, NJ: Princeton University Press.

Touval, S. (1982b) 'Managing the risks of accommodation', in N. Oren (ed.) *Termination of Civil Wars: Processes, Procedures, and Aftermaths*, Jerusalem: Magnes Press, Hebrew University.

Touval, S. (1996a) 'Coercive mediation on the road to Dayton', *International Negotiation*, 1, 1: 547–70.

Touval, S. (1996b) 'Lessons of preventive diplomacy in Yugoslavia', in C. A. Crocker and F. O. Hampson, with P. Aall (eds) *Managing Global Chaos: Sources of and Responses to International Conflict*, Washington, DC: United States Institute of Peace Press, 403–18.

Touval, S. and Zartman, I.W. (eds) (1985) *International Mediation in Theory and Practice*, Boulder CO: Westview Press.

Umbricht, V.H. (1989) *Multilateral Mediation: Practical Experiences and Lessons*, The Hague: Martinus Nijhoff Publishers.

Vayrynen, R. (1985) 'The United Nations and the resolution of international conflicts', *Cooperation and Conflict*, 20, 3: 141–71.

Wagner, R.H. (1993) 'The causes of peace', in R. Licklider (ed.) *Stopping the Killing: How Civil Wars End*, New York: New York University Press, 235–68.

Walter, B.F. (2002) *Committing to Peace: The Successful Settlement of Civil Wars*, Princeton, NJ: Princeton University Press.

Wedgwood, R. (1996) 'Regional and subregional organizations in international conflict management', in C. A. Crocker and F. O. Hampson, with P. Aall (eds) *Managing Global Chaos: Sources of and Responses to International Conflict*, Washington, DC: United States Institute of Peace Press, 275–86.

Wehr, P. and Lederach, J.P. (1991) 'Mediating conflict in Central America', *Journal of Peace Research*, 28, 1: 85–98.

Wehr, P. and Lederach, J.P. (1996) 'Mediating in Central America', in J. Bercovitch (ed.) *Resolving International Conflicts: The Theory and Practice of Mediation*, Boulder, CO: Lynne Rienner, 55–74.

Weiss, T.G. (1995) *The United Nations and Civil Wars*, Boulder, CO: Lynne Reinner.

Yarrow, C.H.M. (1978) *Quaker Experiences in International Conciliation*, New Haven, CT: Yale University Press.

Zartman, I.W. (1989) *Ripe For* Resolution: *Conflict and Intervention in Africa*, New York: Oxford University Press.

Zartman, I.W. (ed.) (1985) *Elusive Peace: Negotiating an End to Civil Wars*, Washington, DC: Brookings Institution.

4

Mediation

Sara Horowitz

Introduction

Definitions

> The word ***mediate*** comes from *mediato*, which in turn comes from the Latin noun *medius* (means) and verb *mediare* (separate into halves). Yale (1992) compares it with *immediate* (direct, without intermediaries), and with the Indo-European word *medhyo*, from which the Germanic compound word *midja-gardaz* derives – *gardaz* (middle garden or garden in the middle) is the name of Earth, the zone between Heaven and Hell.

Given this framework, we define mediation in a dispute or negotiation as the 'intervention of a third party unfamiliar to the conflict, trustable, unbiased and intending to be neutral'. According to Moore (1986), being a mediator involves artful skills to assist the parties in reaching a mutually acceptable agreement on the issues in dispute. The task of a mediator is creating the conditions for an open dialogue and assuring the parties involved in the conflict freedom of speech and, above all, autonomy in decision making.

The mediator is 'a facilitator, educator or communicator who helps to clarify issues, identify and manage emotions, and create options, thus making it possible to reach an agreement avoiding an adversarial battle in court'.

Historical background

Contrary to what happens with most other conflict resolution processes, there is evidence of mediation far back in time. In the Bible, Moses is referred to as the mediator between God and men; since the origin of catholic religions, members of the congregations have turned to priests or preachers for intercession as mediators; and even today, in primitive hunter-gatherer societies in Asia, America and Oceania, the shaman or witch doctor, who is supposed to have supernatural powers to heal the sick, foretell, and communicate with spirits, is trusted to act as mediator for his wisdom.

In many cultures, the most respected elderly people were used to mediate in family conflicts.

Landau et al. (1987) report that in China, Japan and Africa people also resorted to mediation to solve conflicts other than domestic, especially disputes between neighbours.

After the development of states, diplomats were the ones to intervene in social conflicts, modifying conflicting interests and sharing valuable information for the parties involved in the dispute.

Moving forward in history, other processes similar to modern western mediation can be found: the 'Water Court' (*Tribunal de las Aguas*) in Spain, certain towns in Latin America, such as the Mexican village of Ralua, where a judge helps the parties make a decision based on consensus, and the people in Melanesia (Oceania), where a counsellor and a committee meet regularly and analyze disputes in the community.

It is in the 1960s that this alternative practice shows a substantive growth in the US, UK and Canada. At a local level, community justice centres which offer mediation services either for free or minimum fees spread. Mediation is also applied in schools and higher education institutions, and criminal justice uses it to solve disputes at prisons, especially in cases of riots with hostages (Spain, US).

In American colonies and the US, mediation has its own history. Puritans, Quakers and other religious communities or sects settled there, usually resorted to these procedures, but the first field where mediation was formally applied in that country was the labour field during the Great Depression. And it is particularly in the US where mediation expands greatly in the resolution of family conflicts. The legal system and individual practitioners offer mediation services for cases of child custody, divorce, parent–child conflicts, adoption and parental rights, domestic violence, etc. The resulting agreements are more appropriate for these cases; the parties are more satisfied with them rather than with imposed or contentious agreements, and experience shows that these agreements are honoured longer than court ordered ones.

In the last years, mediation also spread to other fields such as in- or intra-company disputes involving environmental or public policy issues, owner–tenant conflicts and provider–client disputes.

The global evolution observed in the mediation system implementation was triggered by both the oversaturation of the traditional ways – courts – and a sociocultural change, which dictated that individuals in litigation claim greater protagonism in the process.

In the twentieth century, mediation played an important role in international conflicts. (The role of mediators or intervenors will be discussed later in this chapter.)

Key elements of the process: trust and persuasiveness

Trust

As mentioned before, the 'natural' mediators were priests, shamans or elderly members of the community, because people *trusted* them. Why is it so important that mediation be based in the trust of people? Because the mediator intervenes in situations of disagreement, struggle, misunderstanding, and conflict, and in these situations, the antagonists' distrust predominates. The parties in crisis are in a negative rather than positive position; they know what they do not want but are not very clear regarding their expectations, wishes, or a positive way out of the conflict. If parties trusted each other, they could use their creativity to transform the conflict and find a solution. However, distrusting and perceiving the other party as an enemy or opponent drive them to use hard tactics, making the conflict more complex and distant from a possible solution.

The core issue is that in a conflict situation, parties consider that outcomes are excluding:

only one can win, as in a zero-sum situation. Consequently, seeking integrative solutions is not feasible. Therefore, it is crucial for a mediator to be trusted by the parties to a conflict, and in order to achieve that, he must be an upright and honourable person, who shows will and determination to help the parties, and has no hidden agendas. He should also be a good communicator, able to listen and give good feedback, capable of following the parties' thoughts and, especially important, patient. Another essential condition is that he should be unfamiliar with the conflict and the sociocultural environment where the conflict takes place.

At the beginning of the process, the mediator should create an atmosphere of trust based on his integrity and ethics, which would allow the process to flow in moments of negative emotional commitment (anger, hate, reference to former negative events, betrayal, etc.).

Persuasiveness

Another key to success in mediation is persuasion. The mediator, as the politician, publicist or salesperson, can influence unintendedly but persuade intendedly without pushing or manipulating. It should be made clear that negative manipulation is used by a mediator who wishes to profit from the conflict, whereas positive manipulation is used for the benefit of the parties in order to find a solution to the conflict. This kind of manipulation is generally needed to prevent conflict escalation or avoid stalemate, and Tidwell considers this skill as part of the mediator's role.

Persuasion is a constant in human matters. The difference between persuasion and influence is that *persuasion is a conscious activity* (and many times intentional), whereas *influence* is the result of communication, and usually does not carry an open intention. The difference between persuasion and effective communication lies in the following: a person can be more persuasive for having greater information and/or understanding than the other, or for speaking in more precise terms, while being an effective communicator does not assure achieving persuasion. Persuasion is an interactive process. When the process is successful, the persuaded person becomes more cooperative.

Description of the traditional role of the mediator

In plain terms, a mediator is a person who puts his knowledge and skills at the service of the parties in a voluntary and confidential process whose result is expected to be *impartial* for it does not benefit or have to do with the mediator. The mediator has *authority*; although the parties acknowledge his mediation skills, the mediator does not hold or abuse power.

A mediator's power is different from a judge's. A judge decides on the result and his decision is bonding, contrary to the mediator, who does not make a decision. This is an important attribute of mediation, but also its most vulnerable aspect. Among the risks it entails, there is the possibility of one party pushing the other, or using false information to drive the deceived party into an unfair settlement. Williams (1993) calls this possibility 'strategic interaction', and compares it to deceit in games such as poker. In order to face this risk, it is essential for the mediator to be 'on the alert', checking the truthfulness of the given information to avoid preventable deceits.

Positive neutrality, the essence of mediation

The fact that the mediator's role does not imply imposing his values and principles on the parties but following the parties, does not mean that it is a passive role. Gary Friedman (1993) states that the mediator should have an active participation, although respectful and without impositions, while helping the parties assume their responsibility in the process and in decision making. Friedman defines *positive neutrality* as the mediator's constant effort to fully understand each party. He considers that, in order to be completely objective and fully understand the parties, the mediator should have been deeply subjective before and, if possible, put himself in the position of each party to the dispute. Active empathy is the characteristic of positive neutrality, and it is the contrary to keeping emotional distance.

Goals of traditional mediation

The goal of mediation is assisting the parties in conflict so that they can solve their differences. Fisher and Ury (1981), and other Harvard scholars, speak of *joint problem solving* to reach a win-win settlement or *integrative solution*. Unfortunately, that is not always possible. Dates, deadlines, scarce resources, different needs, and especially emotional issues that raise feelings such as hate and resentment, prevent reaching an agreement.

Although Landau et al. (1987) listed the following 'goals of a mediator' as typical of family mediation, they can be perfectly applied to mediation in other fields. To emphasize their comprehensive nature, the comments about aspects specific to family conflict have been omitted.

- *To develop trust and cooperation between the parties*, so they can share relevant tasks and information.
- *To improve communication between the parties*, or, in other words, to understand the feelings of their counterpart, and share the decision making.
- *To assure all the relevant parties their perspectives will be heard*, and therefore, make them feel they are fairly treated.
- *To reduce tension and conflict*, so those who have a close relationship with both parties are not involved in a conflict of loyalties.
- *To help the parties appreciate relevant information*, in order to make decisions based on proper data, after having considered alternative proposals to solve the same issues.
- *To favour confidentiality*, while developing a voluntary resolution to the conflict.
- *To reach a reasonable and fair agreement*, unlike what usually happens in court.

The mediator's role is crucial, but *his skill must focus on granting the continuity and successful conclusion of the process rather than substituting the parties at the moment of proposing or deciding on a solution*. The importance of the mediator's role becomes greater when negotiations come to a standstill and are at risk of breaking off or reaching a stalemate.

The mediator should guarantee a favourable environment for negotiation, allowing parties to *listen and understand themselves and each other; acknowledge and appreciate their own interests and needs, and arrange them in order of importance; and build – together with the mediator – options that would let them reach a fair, feasible and long-lasting agreement, flexible enough to consider the possibility of future adjustments to its clauses*.

When the mediator meets the parties at the beginning of the process, he finds them entrenched in their own personal views regarding their perspectives and demands, which they consider to be the best and fairest. Both parties are fixed in those *positions*, since they are unwilling to resign their values and views. The mediator must build an atmosphere of trust in himself and the process, which will allow working towards the conflict resolution, each party leaving aside their fantasy of recreating life according to their own wishes.

Bush and Folger's (1994) 'transformative orientation to conflict' in mediation creates the scenario for the mediator to accompany the parties in the design of a new reality, consistent with their values and including both perspectives. In the transformative approach, the ideal response is not the 'solution to the problem'; it is helping transform the parties involved so that they:

(a) Use their potential, resources and opportunities.
(b) Belong and relate to their society (the others) . . .
by means of two kinds of approaches: (1) *empowerment* and (2) *recognition*.

Empowerment allows parties to turn from being disorganized and unable to be in control into being calm, clear, safe, organized and able to make decisions. This approach enhances the parties' capacities and resources to meet their goals; when parties acknowledge their power and capacity for self-determination, empowerment is achieved. On the contrary, if the mediator decides for the parties, there is no transformative process. Therefore, it is the concrete steps to transformation rather than the nature of the outcome or solution that constitutes *empowerment*.

Recognition in mediation means that the parties voluntarily treat each other fairly, decide to be more open, polite and empathic, and respond to their own and other's needs. That is to say, they expand their perspective to include the situation of the others, and are willing to recognize it in concrete actions, thoughts and words. Recognition favours empathy when trying to understand things from the other's point of view. Recognition depends on the parties.

It is worth mentioning the ethical and humanistic level of transformative mediation. The mediator assists the parties, empowering them so they can decide for themselves, use their potential and recognize the other as a human being – a brother or sister. 'The experience of interdependence, in fact, is a key part of problem-solving mediation' (Bush and Folger 1994).

Following the mediators' standard of ethics, the first thing a mediator should point out at the beginning of the process, is that he is not a representative of one party or the other but a neutral third party. Acting on a neutral and impartial basis does not mean that he cannot have an opinion on the issues at stake, but implies that the dispute resolution process is not guided by these opinions. His perspective or vision should accompany those of the parties in dispute, for his role is expanding the parties' understanding and satisfying their needs.

Traditional approaches to conflict

Regarding roles, the mediator plays a certain number of different roles in the mediation process:

- *Facilitator:* He ensures the continuity of the mediation process, focusing on negotiation rather than on hardening positions.
- *Opener of negotiation channels:* When, for any reason, the dialogue between parties is interrupted, the mediator intervenes to re-establish communication.
- *Translator of information or communicator:* If parties speak but do not understand each other, or are not aware of certain facts, or both have different perceptions, the mediator acts as a communicator or translator of information.
- *Reformulator:* In some cases, the mediator should reframe or reformulate the conflict within the codes acceptable for all the parties, even running the risk of considering only the general aspects of the conflict and missing the particular aspects.
- *Differentiator of positions and interests:* The mediator knows that the positional bargaining can be an expression of grief, anger or desire for revenge, while representing a realistic

hope for concessions. In general, the parties *do not come to an agreement without changing the presentation or the content of their original demands.*

- *Creator of options:* The mediator's role is not always passive. In order for the sessions to advance, he should sometimes suggest options to the parties. This creative aspect of mediation should not be discarded, but the mediator should remember that his role will never be that of 'selling' a solution but suggesting ideas to the parties.
- *Agent of reality:* This is a critical role of the mediator. As parties come to an agreement, one of the mediator's functions is raising awareness regarding the needs of each party, and building a realistic framework to assess the costs and benefits of solving the conflict in that way.

Responses to conflict

According to Moore (1986), when a conflict arises, and there are different perceptions regarding how to solve it or by what means, the first response to conflict is denying or avoiding it. But this response – denial or avoidance – does not solve the conflict, since it continues to exist. The second step could be trying an informal negotiation and, in case it is not successful, the following steps to take consist of the two approaches discussed in this section: negotiation and mediation.

Negotiation

Two parties or more open a dialogue and use offers and counter-offers in an effort to build a mutually acceptable agreement (decide on company policies, regional treaties like the EU, etc.). Negotiations can be either distributive or integrative. In distributive negotiations, there is only one variable at stake, and the outcome implies that if one party gets more, there will be less for the other (zero-sum). In integrative negotiations, there is an exchange of items and issues in dispute, allowing a more complex and beneficial solution.

Third parties: mediators, facilitators and intervenors

If the negotiation turns out to be unsuccessful, a third party unfamiliar to the conflict or dispute may be included to help parties identify issues and reach an agreement. For example, a neighbour could mediate in a conflict between two other neighbours, or as it happened in Chile, where a conflict arose between companies with a mining lease for 3,200 hectares around Lleu Lleu Lake, an ancient mapuche territory, part of the mapuche nation. In this case, the law protects the rights of the mining companies but, on the other hand, there are the native communities and small owners who feel they are not protected by the law. The mapuche communities are agricultural and have lived in that territory for a long time. There are sacred places where they conduct their religious ceremonies and which are therefore spiritually significant to these people. Including a third party to act as an intervenor or facilitator is especially relevant to solve conflicts of this kind, since this practice is both related to their ancient tradition and accepted as a means of conflict resolution by the modern culture.

Watkins and Winters (1997) use another term to refer to a third party who assists the others, and who has influencing power or power to put either economic or military pressure on the parties: the *intervenor.* Intervenors are third parties who, whether invited by the parties in conflict or by unilateral action, seek affecting the outcome of the conflicts. Because of their power, sometimes they do not build the agreement but 'buy' it (as happened when the US acted as intervenor in the conflict between Israel and Egypt).

If the person who enters the process to assist parties in search of a solution is unfamiliar with the system or conflicting situation, he is called a *mediator*. On the other hand, if the person is part of the system where the conflict arose, he is called a facilitator. 'The traditional view which featured mediators as unbiased third parties has been for a long time inadequate to describe situations in which third parties have interests and the power to influence in the results, as it happens in international (Pruitt 1981; Touval and Zartman 1991) and in-company conflicts (Kolb 1985). However, we still lack a good conceptual scheme to understand the range of roles played by third parties with interests and power in the resolution of conflicts. We do not know either enough regarding the impact of interests and power on the third parties' role in the conflicts, or the difficult choices that arise during intervention. . . . As a starting point in our attempt to understand the role of third parties, we do not focus on the mediators but on a broader group. In these terms, the traditional mediators are a kind of intervenor. Other kinds are the negotiators who seek promoting their own interests in the conflict through negotiation, and the arbitrators, whose coercive power allows them to impose the terms of an agreement to the litigants' (Watkins and Winters 1997).

The intervenors in international conflicts play a wide variety of roles. While sometimes they try to act as conventional unbiased mediators, they seldom behave in that way. Although all mentioned forms can be present in interpersonal, intergroup and interorganizational conflicts, some of the approaches are more accessible than others, depending on who the protagonists of the dispute are. For example, it is easier to move away from conflicts between people rather than conflicts between countries, or resort to negotiation when one belongs to the structure that provides for and regulates it.

Kolb (1985) recommends differentiating interpersonal conflicts from disputes between groups or organizations, and those between strangers from those affecting pre-existing relationships. According to this author (Horowitz), the relationship between the mediator and the parties is different in each case. On the other hand, Robert Benjamin (1995) considers that there is not such a marked difference between international, business, financial and family conflicts. He states that in every conflict, the following three areas can be found:

- Economic aspects.
- Legal or regulatory aspects.
- Feelings – emotions.

Benjamin suggests that the professional mediator should be trained to deal with the three areas. He believes that the mediator's role is helping the parties get a clearer vision in order to make informed decisions.

Trends in mediation

Within the scope of traditional mediation, there are different trends. Some focus on (a) the process, others on (b) the outcome, or *resolution of problems*, and still others on (c) the transformative approach, each trend using different strategies.

In the first approach, the scholars focus on the process, assigning the power of mediation to the parties, and the mediator assumes the role of 'traffic lights', facilitating the dialogue between the parties in conflict.

In the second approach, focusing on the outcome, or *resolution of problems*, the mediator focuses his capacity on finding solutions and generating mutually acceptable agreements. The mediator uses a greater number of moves which influence and put pressure on the parties in order to come to an agreement on general and even specific issues. In this process, the potential to solve problems is stressed, and so this kind of directive mediation, oriented towards the settlement, has become today the dominant practice.

The third approach, or *transformative approach* (Bush and Folger 1994), emphasizes the capacity of mediation to promote empowerment and recognition. Mediators oriented towards transformation focus their efforts in an attempt to enable the parties to define issues and decide the settlement terms by themselves, as well as to help the parties to better understand each other's perspectives. The effect of this approach is avoiding the directive orientation of the mediation focused on the resolution of problems.

An equally important fact is that transformative mediation helps parties recognize and benefit from the opportunities of moral growth inherent to the conflict. I consider this approach a bridge between traditional mediation and Johan Galtung's transcendent transformative mediation.

Summing up traditional mediation

As previously stated, if a third party is included in a negotiation to assist the parties in conflict, then we have a mediation (that is why it is called a 'three-way negotiation'). In mediation, parties have self-determination, for they are the only ones who make decisions regarding their differences. Thus, they can decide upon what is convenient or appropriate to agree or, on the contrary, when it is not the right moment to reach an agreement.

It is necessary for the parties to understand to what they are committing, i.e. if reaching an agreement is convenient or not for them. This is called *informed consent*. Informed consent is one of the positive pillars of mediation: it is useful to clarify and understand whether it is preferable to come to an agreement at present or in the future, or if it is better never to reach a settlement.

To sum up, there are two trends in mediation: a less directive one, in which the mediator facilitates the flow of dialogue as the traffic lights facilitate the flow of cars, and a more directive one, in which the mediator focuses on the outcome of the mediation, thus he gives personal opinions and even gives advice on the content of the agreement. It is noteworthy that in financial and family mediations, the parties consider that a directive mediator is more effective than a mediator who only assists them and favours the flow of dialogue.

Mediation, based on Johan Galtung's theory

Johan Galtung, the 'father' of Peace Studies as a science, developed the *Transcendent Transformative Theory of Conflict*. Instead of the term *mediator*, he prefers to use 'peace worker' or 'conflict worker', for *mediator* is someone who is in the middle. However, in this section, the peace worker will be referred to as 'the mediator'.

Galtung offers a different and interesting view of traditional mediation when he points out that it is better for the mediator to enter the process being ignorant of the culture and customs of the place where he will mediate, so he will have to ask and receive 'inside information' from the parties in conflict. The tool of every mediator is the word; the goal is opening a sincere and committed dialogue. Of course, the mediator needs to achieve a deep understanding of the culture in which the conflict is immersed and nurtured. Then, the mediator is like a diplomat who travels to different countries, learning the local culture by speaking and asking questions of local residents. When the mediator cannot learn more, it is time to be recycled, change community and start learning a new culture.

Along the same lines, another author, Alan Campbell (1996), states that the mediator plays two roles. First is the *inquisitive tourist*, curious, eager to learn the society – the culture – he is visiting, and for whom everything is pleasant and fine. (As happens with tourists, he is not expected to condemn or be bothered by different local customs; on the contrary, he is curious and wants to learn about the new culture. In a conflict situation, the mediator wants to learn about both parties, considering them as different cultures.) Second is the *tourist guide*, presenting to each party the subculture of the other. It does not matter whether the parties share background and culture; at the moment of conflict, both act as if they belonged to different subcultures.

An interesting proposal of Galtung is that in a mediation process, there should be the same number of mediators and parties; in this scheme, the mediator's role is that of an 'auxiliary I',[1] assisting and helping the parties in conflict, taking into account their feelings, thoughts and goals. He considers that having a greater number of parties and issues in conflict is enriching and positive, since it allows for a greater number of integrative solutions.

The mediator enters the conflict as a third party, whether invited or not, and he must know that his duty is to assist the parties, respecting their goals and needs, and seeking to generate a dialogue based on the idea that:

- We are all part of the humankind, in which we are united in suffering. From this perspective, there is the responsibility[2] to reduce violence and destruction.
- The mediator is independent,[3] does not conceal information or have a hidden agenda. He does not make use of threats, punishments, rewards or promises to get the parties to yield. Only fair play is accepted.
- The mediator brings to the conflict general knowledge, skills, empathy, nonviolence, creativity, compassion and persistence.
- It is essential for the mediator to be willing to learn about the parties and speak with them, exchanging general and local knowledge. He needs to know, grasp, understand and explore the conflict, in order to assist the parties in the resolution of it.

The mediator's profile should be low, even as regards his fees; they should be accessible to all parties, not very high in case one of the parties cannot afford them. The world needs a huge number of humble and competent conflict workers (mediators), good at transforming conflicts, able to transcend them with creativity and respect for human rights, working on a legitimacy criteria.

This third party should not limit his work to the analysis of the situation, predictions and/or to speak and write. The mediator's task is based on self-reflection. In order to explore oneself, Galtung suggests the following ten-item list, which includes possible questions, and has been respectfully reproduced:

1 *Motivation:* Why do I do this job? For them? For me? To get a promotion? Fame? Reputation? Experience? Out of scientific curiosity?
2 *General knowledge:* Do I know the conflict and the local culture in depth? Do I have and make use of common sense?
3 *Specific local knowledge:* Do I have information enough to make good, pertinent and helpful questions, or do I wish to understand only certain aspects? We are trying to understand if the worker is unbiased, and is really eager to learn.
4 *Skills:* Do I have skills enough to make myself clear? To understand others? To listen

(including silence)? Do I tend to impose my thoughts? Do I have sense of humour? Am I optimistic?

5 *Empathy:* Am I mature and sensitive enough to understand the others in a peaceful and unbiased way?
6 *Non-violence:* Am I a nonviolent person in action, word and thought? Do I easily lose my mind? Am I verbally violent? In my manners? Do I think it is alright to disagree?
7 *Creativity:* Can I get detached from the problem and project a positive future? Do I find it appealing to challenge logics? Can I understand the positive and healing aspects of the conflict? Do I like and enjoy finding original and different solutions?
8 *Compassion:* Am I sensitive to the suffering of others or are they mere objects to me? Do I consider that it is fine to take care of others? Am I governed by individualistic behaviours, letting each person take care of their own issues?
9 *Persistence:* Do I have the capacity to go on despite difficulties or negative conditions? Do I get impatient when the others do not follow my advice?
10 *Process:* Do I understand that life is a continuous process? Do I understand that it is not linear? Do I seek to expand my knowledge and feelings? Do I consider myself smart?

The psychoanalyst Donald Winnicott (1994) refers to the good mother as a 'sufficiently good mother', who understands her child, accompanies his growth without pushing, creating a space that allows him to be different, and assists him in case of need. I consider that, on the same lines, a good mediator could be defined as the 'sufficiently good mediator', who provides a service to the parties in dispute without putting pressure on it with his own desires.

The mediator's task is very complex and stressing; that is why it is advisable to include relaxation habits, meditation or some kind of self-reflection to allow him to focus and 'cool down'. If a mediator wants to help others, before each session he should work on his own prejudices, the negative influence from other environments, and his strengths or weaknesses, as well. Self-knowledge is a basic requirement to work as a mediator or peace worker.

Regarding the knowledge of the social and cultural context of the parties in conflict, it is interesting to note that the nongovernmental organizations which offer help worldwide and assist in cases of war, often send mediators who belong to an academic elite – high-class white scholars from the West, mainly men. The war in Bosnia-Herzegovina and natural catastrophes like the tsunami give an account of the phenomenon. However, in his *requirements for the mediator's profile*, Galtung considers that it would be more positive for the mediator to be a woman, since women get less involved in situations of physical violence and are more sensitive and empathic concerning somebody else's grief. As regards age, it would be better to look for young, idealistic people, or older experienced mediators. Race is indifferent to him, although racists would not accept mediators of other race than theirs. He prefers middle-class mediators to high-class or elite mediators, since the latter better understand the government and their leaders rather than the people. Regarding nationality and religion, he is keener on the 'soft' rather than the 'hard' ones (among the Christians, the Quakers; among the Muslims, the Sufis; and in Judaism, the humanists who follow Martin Buber's line of work). Galtung also suggests that a mediator who comes from smaller towns is likely to be humbler, and will also tend to solve problems without using weapons.

How to relate to the parties in conflict

The basic attitude is *respect*, even if the mediator might have difficulties in feeling empathy or friendliness for any of the parties. In every conflict there is a part of legitimate claim. The parties to the dispute are in crisis, and many times they show their darker or harder side. When the mediator comes to intervene, the conflict has already escalated, and many times there is nothing but hate and a desire for revenge between the parties. Actually, they are trapped and tend to blame the others for the difficult situations through which they are going.

The positive aspect of being a third party unfamiliar to the conflict is that, if not emotionally involved, the mediator will be able to help the parties speak and find their own solution to the conflict. Which are the risks of getting emotionally involved? The mediator may be tempted to:

- *Psychiatrize* the parties, labelling them as mentally ill.
- *Criminalize* the parties, seeing them as morally wrong and deserving punishment.
- *Idiotize* the parties, considering them simple and dumb, needing to be educated.

Human beings identify[4] themselves with some people (positive feelings) and reject others. In the context of transcendent transformative mediation, openness to dialogue is the goal, and the dialogue itself is the tool.

Empathy to soften attitudes

Empathy is the capacity to deeply understand the other at a cognitive and emotional level and it is the mediator's basic skill. Galtung is very strict regarding empathy. He states that, 'being in somebody else's shoes' is not enough. It does not matter how the conflict worker reacts; the core is how 'they' – the parties in conflict – react and how the peace worker understands the parties. Should the mediator be guided by these feelings, he would react as the parties themselves and that is not the task of a mediator. Hence, the importance of the conflict worker being somebody from the outside.

Empathy allows mediators not to get trapped in the negative feelings that are part of the mediation process but identify themselves as human beings, seeking legitimate goals based on respect for human rights, especially those related to the fulfilment of basic needs. Every party to a conflict, over and above violent means or expressions, has valid and legitimate goals and demands on which nonviolent and creative solutions can be built.

Dehumanizing a party (the opposite to empathy) prevents the mediator from identifying the legitimate claims present in every dispute. The mediator needs to stimulate the search for a settlement which would not make parties feel rejected. We must remember that sometimes to understand is to forgive, and that the role of the mediator is assisting the parties to end a situation by nonviolent means, opening a dialogue between them.

Generating empathy has to do with establishing a respectful and deep relationship with the different people. It may also be necessary, in order to build mutual trust and generate empathy, to allow parties to share their feelings, establish an open dialogue with each party and, after achieving a deep understanding of each one, foster communication between them.

Attitudes should be softened, trying to reach the goals without violence, without the intention of hurting the other, and working with nonviolence at four levels:

1. In *thought*, meditating and promoting an inner, self-reflective dialogue.
2. In *speech*, avoiding labelling, blaming, demonizing the other while searching for common roots and sharing the future responsibilities, calming anxieties and fears, helping the parties to visualize a future in which they could live.
3. In *action*, making use of different resources, meeting to negotiate, avoiding repressive answers and the use of weapons.

4 In *creativity to overcome contradictions*. Creativity implies that the solution transcends the conflict; it goes beyond saving the 'honour' or 'face' of the parties or the actual situation. This is an interesting way of implementing creativity to prevent the parties from building defences and opposing new ideas; it is considering the new situations as possibilities rather than statements, since the original ideas suggested by others tend to be rejected by those who have not considered or proposed them.

In order to get people to transcend contradiction and become creative, it is necessary to enter a new perspective, a new dimension. Galtung goes deeper in this issue and differentiates *individual* creativity from *collective* creativity. Individual creativity can be worked on by analogy, by comparing similar situations, by placing situations at the same level, and by establishing the complete difference. Collective creativity can be worked on doing brainstorming, pasting sheets of paper on the wall and giving pencils to people, debating, discussing, imagining, writing on cards and organizing them according to CCC (Condition, Consequence, Context). Creativity is a turn, a spin of basic dimensions such as space and time. We need to add who? and how? to this. For Galtung, the best solution is that which can be reverted.

Conclusions

The *basics* of the mediator's task are to be a trustworthy and honourable person, unfamiliar to the conflict or problem, who has the skills and the will to help in an empathic way, understand and assist in an unbiased way the parties to the dispute. In mediation, there are three central issues that all mediators should learn and consider:

1 The *communication*, including the divergence of perceptions present in every conflict.
2 The *conflict process*, since it has a predictable path, the mediator should recognize and predict escalation, stalemate and other variables that may arise during the conflict.
3 His or her own *negotiating style* when facing a disagreement situation, as well as identifying the different negotiating styles of others.

It is also important that the mediator should know how to ask, listen and recognize differences in a sensible way; consider each party as a human being; and be able to follow each party's speech without getting involved or imposing his personal values. The mediator should be a person who asks a lot and generates empathy in the response; who is external to the society or group he will try to assist. Mediation is a confidential process, embedded in the parties' values and wishes rather than the mediator's.

In order to help solve a conflict, the mediator seeks to create an appropriate atmosphere; share the existing information on the parties' interests; and help them suggest and reduce options, until they can make a rational decision, located in some point between the prospective agreement and what they claimed.

To conclude dealing with traditional mediation, we must insist that the mediator's role is crucial, but *his skill must focus on granting the continuity and successful conclusion of the process rather than substituting the parties at the moment of proposing or deciding on a solution.*

In the transcendent transformative mediation, when a mediator knows enough of the local culture, he should be recycled, go to another place and start the task once again, as diplomats do. Finally, a transcendent solution is oriented towards a legitimate, positive and constructive future. Sometimes this solution does not agree with the law or with the structural violence that may exist in a society in which there is enough food but the population is starving because they do not have the money to buy the food. Therefore, it can be legal – according to local laws – but not legitimate. *Human rights* and *basic needs* are non-negotiable, and so should be for the whole of humankind.

If mediation implies opening the dialogue between two parties which see themselves as antagonist, maybe the education of future generations should be focused on the development of the virtues which, according to Comte-Sponville (2004), are *applied values*, instead of on teaching theoretical values which have fallen in disuse.

Slavery seemed a natural event, impossible to be eradicated at that time; the use of violence and war also seems natural and difficult to eradicate. We must imagine and design a peaceful world so maybe, in the future, dialogue outweighs weapons and the use of power. We need a positive, legitimate and fair world, not only a legal one.

Notes

1 Term coined by Sara Horowitz.
2 For Galtung, the responsibility may be 'by commission', regarding a violent or improper event, or 'by omission', for not having intervened in an unfair, and therefore, illegitimate situation.
3 This is similar to the concept of impartiality in the traditional theory, in which impartiality means not getting benefits from the process or the outcome.
4 *Identification* is a way of projecting in others the positive aspects we believe to have in common. This leads to the loss of neutrality.

References

Benjamin, R. (1995) *The Mediation of Business, Family and Divorce Conflicts: Practice Forms and Handbook* Buenos Aires: University of Buenos Aires Press.

Bush, R.A. Baruch and Folger, J.P. (1994) *The Promise of Mediation*, San Francisco, CA: Jossey-Bass.

Campbell, A. (1996) 'Mediation of children's issues when one parent is gay: a cultural perspective', *Mediation Quarterly*, 14, 1: 79.

Comte-Sponville, A. (2002) *A Small Treatise on the Great Virtues*, New York: Owl Books.

Fisher, R. and Ury, W. (1981) *Getting to Yes*, New York: Houghton Mifflin.

Friedman, G. (1993) *A Guide to Divorce Mediation: How to Reach a Fair, Legal Settlement at a Fraction of the Cost*, New York: Workman Publishing.

Kolb, D. (1983) *The Mediators*, Cambridge, MA: MIT Press.

Kolb, D.M. (1985) 'To be a mediator: expressive tactics in mediation', *Journal of Social Issues*, 41, 2: 11–26.

Landau, B., Bartoletti, M. and Mesur, R. (1987) *Family Mediation Handbook*, London: Butterworth.

Moore, C. (1986) *The Mediation Process: Practical Strategies for Resolving Conflict*, San Francisco, CA: Jossey-Bass.

Pruitt, D.G. (1981) *Negotiation Behavior*, New York: Academic Press.

Tidwell, A. (1994) 'Not effective communication, but effective persuasion', *Mediation Quarterly*, 12, 1.

Touval, S. and Zartman, I.W. (1991) 'Mediation', in S. Brown and K. Schraub (eds) *Resolving Third World Conflict*, Washington, DC: United States Institute of Peace Press.

Watkins, M. and Winters, K. (1997) 'Intervenors with interests and power', Harvard University, Kennedy School of Government.

Williams, G. (1993) 'Style and effectiveness in negotiation', in L. Hau (ed.) *Negotiation: Strategies for Mutual Gains*.

Winnicott, D. (1994) *El Ambiente Familiar y el Proceso Facilitador* [The Family and Individual Development] Buenos Aires: Editorial Paidos.

Yale, D. (1992) 'Metaphors in mediating', *Mediation Quaterly*, 22: 15–25.

5

Former Yugoslavia and Iraq: a comparative analysis of international conflict mismanagement

Jan Oberg[1]

Among dozens of serious, protracted conflicts in the post-Cold War global system, former Yugoslavia and Iraq have attracted major attention in politics as well as media. While severe in human terms, other conflicts and wars have harvested many more deaths and wounded people, these two stand out because of their significant impact on the global society.

Major powers such the US and members of the European Union, international organizations such as the United Nations, NATO, OSCE as well as numerous humanitarian and other civil society organizations engaged in these two conflicts in a unique multitude of ways. Undoubtedly, these actors themselves have changed through their engagement and so have the norms and operational modes of the wider global society.

One purpose of this chapter is to highlight some of the major similarities and differences between the two cases from the perspective of international conflict management.[2] This means that, although both former Yugoslavia and Iraq display very complex internal conflict dynamics, the analysis gives priority to the question: What did the international community[3] do in the two cases and to what extent were the implemented conflict-management policies similar or at least indicative of a similarly underlying philosophy?

Traditionally, comparative studies in this field are based on a security-strategic perspective and focus on who lost and who gained. The road taken here is built on decades of peace studies and what this field can offer with two different angles: (1) was peace attained and how; and, if not, why? – and (2) what can be learnt about the case of Iraq by studying the case of the Balkans, and vice versa, and what general patterns repeat themselves although the countries, their problems and cultures are quite different?

Another purpose, hinted at in the title of this chapter, is to show how both cases display characteristics more indicative of conflict mismanagement than management. This means that important cases of lost opportunities for true peacemaking are highlighted. Admittedly this approach can be perceived as somewhat counterfactual – thinking about a possible violence-reducing past that did not happen – and thus the argument will contain a heuristic-hypothetical dimension. But to criticize a policy, it is important: (a) to point out that alternatives could be thought out or were actually available to the decision-makers; and (b) to argue (with some realism) that today's situation would have been better in some defined ways, had such options been tried at the time.

Naturally, therefore, the chapter ends with a few suggested lessons that should be learnt and applied to future cases of international conflict management. This is the chapter's constructive perspective, following naturally the theoretical-empirical analysis and the critical-normative phases of the argument. In this sense, the chapter adheres to the tradition of modern Nordic-rooted peace and conflict studies.[4]

Some similarities between former Yugoslavia and Iraq

Here follows a non-prioritized list of some of the similarities between former Yugoslavia and Iraq *as conflict formations and as objects of international conflict management.*

Leadership roles that challenged Western hegemony

Both countries aspired to leadership roles in organizations that were sceptical to Western hegemony: Yugoslavia in the Non-Aligned movement, Iraq in the pan-Arabic, nationalist movement, e.g. the Arab League. In a contemporary historical perspective, both were countries that had tried hard to carve out a niche for themselves as 'different', neither fully with the US/NATO bloc nor with the Soviet Union/Warsaw Pact bloc. Yugoslavia's manifest position as neutral and non-aligned became problematic to some extent when the bloc system dissolved. Both relied on a strong military defence, both had contemplated acquiring nuclear weapons.

The global time and space

Although the underlying conflicts are much older, violence broke out and came to the attention of the international community at about the same time: Iraq invaded Kuwait in autumn 1990 and violence broke out in Slovenia and Croatia in spring 1991. It was right after the old bipolar Cold War-related world order had broken down with the dissolution of the Soviet Union. Western dualist triumphalism was rapidly on the rise; since the Soviet Union was finished it must have been weak/evil and the US, now the logical only superpower, by definition strong/good. A more risk-free global interventionist policy became possible coupled with a much more blurred and unpredictable global conflict formation than the old one hinged upon the two-bloc pact system, quite clear traffic rules between them and two counterpoised ideologies that structured a considerable part of the rest of the world community.

Societal complexities ignored or misunderstood by the international community

Yugoslavia's ethnic and other complexities may have been appreciated by some international decision-makers and media. By and large, however, the conflict formation was cast by them in the shape of two conflicting parties only: the majority 'bad' Orthodox Serbs/Greater Serbia versus all the rest. This would resemble a known – but now irrelevant – prism of the past: the generalized Western image of the expansionist Orthodox Russians (read Serbs) planning to conquer Western democratic Europe: in the Yugoslav space, read Slovenia, Croatia and Bosnia-Herzegovina.

Thus, the ethnic interpretation which promoted the historically untenable view that these groups cultivated an age-old, permanent hatred against each other (in addition to being perceived as non-modern, quite primitive and lacking a civil society altogether) conveniently left other highly relevant, deeper contributing conflict causes aside such as, e.g. Yugoslavia's historical role as 'exchange coins' in transactions among bigger European powers and Yugoslavia's deep economic crisis in the wake of being victimized in the 1970s and 1980s by Western multinationals outsourcing their production in Yugoslavia to low-wage countries in Southeast Asia. It left aside also such factors as the complex centrifugal constitutional dynamics, the multiple buried fears and traumas dormant from earlier conflicts and the physical leopard skin-like ethnic map of the country which, if it had been known to European politicians, ought to have made them think twice about choosing to split up the country along its purely administrative republic borders as the foremost method of conflict management and solution.

The Dayton Agreement for Bosnia-Herzegovina and other constructions were based on simplifying interpretations of the remarkable complexities; for instance, it stipulated that this republic consisted of three pure nations only, the Muslims/Bosniaks, the Croats and the Serbs. That the picture on the ground was and remains vastly more mixed and displayed all kinds of mixtures and people who would be neither willing nor able to categorize themselves as belonging to any of these three identities played virtually no role.

The dominant image of Iraq still being used in the West is that it consists of three significantly different groups: the majority Shiites in the southern parts, the minority Sunnis in the middle 'triangle' and the Kurds in the north. Two simple observations would debunk this type of gross simplification that shaped parts of the basis of the Western US-led warfare and occupation.

Of Baghdad's roughly five million inhabitants, one million or 20 per cent are Kurds; that makes Baghdad the largest Kurdish city in Iraq. Secondly, during his visit this author repeatedly asked people he interviewed to tell him which group they belonged to. One late evening in the Ministry of Foreign Affairs, for instance, the question caused five–six high-level people in a meeting to burst into laughter. It turned out that (a) the majority of them had a mixed background and (b) that none of them, having worked together for years, knew what any of the others were. This pattern repeated itself elsewhere, and nowhere did he get the impression that the categories were of any relevance whatsoever to the people of Iraq. This was confirmed by internationals in various UN missions and humanitarian organizations who had been living and working in Iraq for months or years. The Iraqis feel Iraqi more than anything else and have never fought a civil war among themselves.

This resembles the pattern of Yugoslavia to quite some extent. The author has met many people in all republics – with the exception of the Kosovo province – who as adults did not even know what ethnic identity they had; they knew they were of mixed origin and felt 'Bosnian' for instance or 'Yugoslav'. In passing it should be noted that no one can uphold such identities in any of today's newly formed republics; they have mono-ethnic constitutions with the exception of that of Serbia-Montenegro, which stipulates that the State consists of anyone living there irrespective of national identity.

However, in contrast to Iraq the higher-level Yugoslav identity was declared by a small minority only and it was much weaker even in the days of Tito's leadership than the Iraqi-cum-Arab identity in Iraq. And while these deeply felt overarching identities were present among many with quite some intensity, it should also not be forgotten that they were, to some extent, driven or at least underpinned by the 'party line' that was espoused by the central leaderships as an ideological self-identification with an emphasis on standing out as 'different'.

Finally, while national-ethnic belonging is a dominant dimension in former Yugoslavia, the extended family and clan is much more basic for an understanding of Iraqi society.

Strongmen perceived to hold their countries together who had once been loyal to the US/UK and other Western countries, had deviated and thus deserved to be demonized by the international community

Tito had enjoyed tremendous respect in Western circles due to his partisan role in the Second World War. He had sent Milovan Djilas (who later broke with Tito and became the first and probably greatest East European 'dissident') to negotiate a break with Stalin as early as 1948 and oriented about 60 per cent of Yugoslavia's foreign trade toward the West. In spite of this, he has repeatedly been called a 'dictator' in the 1990s by Western politicians and commentators. And while virtually all nations in Yugoslavia did perceive him as a great leader and visionary who led the country to play a role in world politics (albeit also as a person obsessed with personality cult and displaying some quite authoritarian traits), they all re-interpreted him during the dissolution process as 'bad', particularly from their own more or less nationalistic vantage points.

Serb leader Slobodan Milosevic served as both the main leader for Western actors to do political business with up to as late as autumn 1998 and as the villain par excellence, the mastermind of all the wars allegedly to create a fascist 'Greater Serbia'. Remarkably exaggerated, propagandistic comparisons of him with Hitler, Stalin and Pol Pot[5] to the extent that similar policies pursued at the time by other leaders and suspect war criminals (such as Franjo Tudjman in Croatia, Alija Izetbegovic in Bosnia-Herzegovina and Agim Ceku first in Croatia and then in Kosovo) have been deleted from the contemporary historical records.

Saddam Hussein, the strongman of Iraq, was undoubtedly more ruthless than Tito and Milosevic and more obsessed with a personality cult. He too had been the darling of the West only to become demonized beyond recognition by Western media, opinion leaders and politicians. As a young man in exile in Egypt, he allegedly worked for the CIA;[6] as leader of Iraq he obtained the vast majority of his weapons and technologies from NATO countries. Politically, his socialist Baath Party distanced itself early from both the Soviet Union and China and he vehemently protested the Soviet invasion of Afghanistan. What made the West turn against Saddam was his invasion of Kuwait which, in passing, was a more complicated event than is usually recognized in the media.[7]

Notably, most of those who demonized Saddam Hussein had never visited Iraq. If they had, they would have seen that Iraq was a secular society with a huge Western-educated and -fascinated middle class that exhibited an infrastructure, a health system and an educational standard as well as a status for the women that was indisputably second to none in the region. Whatever the dictator's motives behind these welfare-oriented policies, his personal cruelty, his invasion of Kuwait, and his programmes for acquiring weapons of mass destruction, there was this famous other side of the coin that was never explored by the allegedly pluralist Western media. This was a main reason for some of the bizarre assumptions on which the 2003 invasion was based, for instance that the Iraqi people would line the road with flowers when their liberators rolled in.

Common for all three were their personal roles as allies or favoured 'son-of-bitch' of the West for as long as the West needed them to play a role compatible with their own interests. Common was also that they trespassed their masters, so to speak, and were abandoned and then demonized beyond recognition. Common for Tito and Saddam, while not for Milosevic, is a still not sufficient explored ability to instil, through a mixture of charisma and authoritarian rule, a sense of popular vision and higher common identity, cultural pride and a unique regional or world role for their respective countries. For good or for bad, you may add, none of those succeeding them in various capacities have so far shown even a remotely similar capacity.

Countries situated at cultural faultlines with a macro-history with foreign intervention and humiliation as well as a desire to appear strong

Both Yugoslavia and Iraq have been visited by war and destruction, foreign troops and big powers trying to occupy, divide and rule them. While there have been periods of stability, various types of political violence and murders, coup d'états and elite intriguing have been a conspicuous part of their history. Both are – and have been for centuries – situated at the faultlines of a combination of civilizations, strategic interests of major powers and ideological struggles.

While it is plausible that the existence of natural resources provides some of the explanation as to why strong countries intervene abroad, it is certainly not the only causal factor, not even in the case of Iraq. On the other hand, in the Yugoslav case there has been a considerable public ignorance about that region's relationship to strategic raw materials, i.e. the Middle East and Central Asia.

It can be argued that both have, more or less continuously, served as stepping stones, real or desired for extended strategic resource policies. Iraq served as such for the British on their way to India and do so now for US base-building with a view to secure its oil, fence in Iran and be closely positioned the day Saudi Arabia may fall apart. Yugoslavia served as a stepping stone for both NATO and Warsaw Pact war scenarios during the Cold War[8] and today Macedonia and Kosovo (together with Bulgaria, Romania and Albania) function as support points for Central Asian gas and oil pipelines and as transport corridors.[9]

It is in this historical perspective one must see the fascination in both countries with military power. Iraq aspired to become second to none in the region and possess nuclear weapons until virtually disarmed by the UN inspection teams around 1995–6. Yugoslavia was close to acquiring nuclear weapons and developed a special military force structure consisting of the JNA, the Yugoslav Peoples' Army, for the federation as an entity combined with the decentralized territorial defence forces in each republic. The citizens in both countries had lots of weapons and ammunition stored in their homes; should national defence fail, they could switch to a guerrilla-like insurgency-cum-liberation struggle that hardly any occupier would be able to control. In their defence doctrines, Yugoslavia made the best use of its mountains, Iraq of its cityscape and political underground. No one, they decided, should be able to pacify or rule them after what they had been through in their respective history. NATO, the strongest alliance in human history and nuclear-based, consequently decided to only bomb (not very successfully from a military point of view) in 1999 but not send in ground troops to occupy and control Serbia with Kosovo. The US and other occupying powers in post-2003 Iraq are likely to discover what others found out before them, that the Iraqis are simply not possible to control militarily.

Offending the US and Europe by accepting neither their political dictates nor neo-liberal globalization

Tito's Yugoslavia did not conform to the West; it was a founding member of the Non-Aligned movement and it stood outside the Warsaw Pact–NATO conflict formation. Slobodan Milosevic had been trained in banking in the United States, but he never bought globalization. His Socialist Party programme propagated a Sweden-inspired (at the time) mixed economy consisting of a strong state with a free market.

No other Yugoslav leader embraced wholeheartedly the neo-liberal globalization agenda; it was rather forced upon the country by the IMF and the World Bank in the 1980s and created devastating impoverishment of the people as well as a breakdown of the ethnic-republican balance in Yugoslavia's financial and constitutional spheres.[10] Indeed, the ensuing economic misery became a fertile ground for the emerging conflicts and violence that were *played out through* ethnicity but were not ethnic conflicts at the root.

Saddam Hussein too was an independent-minded leader who did not take orders. The Baath Party, knowing full well the unique oil wealth of Iraq, had no inclinations toward globalization; it would rather fuel it than be an object of it. Prime Minister Tariq Aziz told the author in 2002 that Iraq would sell any amount of oil to the United States and everybody else under two conditions: that the buyer paid the market price at any given time and – with special emphasis – that the buyer would treat the Iraqi people and government decently and with respect.

Saddam became known as the leader who did not bow down to pressure, including the devastating economic sanctions, the man who defied UN Security Council resolutions, and who 'expelled' the inspectors (that some of them actually conducted intelligence work for Israel and the United States was usually omitted in Western media).[11] In November 2002 Saddam demanded payment for Iraq's oil in Euros, not in dollars; that was probably the last straw that broke the camel's back in the eyes of the Bush administration. If such a demand would snowball among OPEC members and other oil-exporting countries, it would have disastrous consequences for the US empire, for the strength of the dollar and for the domestic American economy.

In summary, for the international community what mattered the least were the noble goals stated for public consumption about creating peace, bringing democracy, welfare, human rights and freedom to former Yugoslavia and Iraq. The raw political driving force and what really mattered to the United States and Europe in Real Psyko-Politik terms was that somebody had disobeyed them and remained stubborn adherents – as they saw it – of some kind of socialism. In addition, they refused to submit to or become pawns in the game of a neo-liberal agenda for globalization and the unipolar world order under US leadership. And as the respective crises built up, both Milosevic and Saddam defied a series of concrete Western/US demands-cum-threats.

Western powers repeatedly used the threat of military action: 'Do as we say or face our consequences.' Having done so for a sufficiently long time, they finally felt cornered by their own rhetoric. If they turned out to have issued threats that they were never willing to carry out on the ground, they would have lost credibility and thus – as the twisted logic has it – humiliated themselves or 'lost' by giving in to dictators and terrorists.[12]

Applying economic sanctions with increasingly devastating human and societal consequences

Iraq suffered history's most comprehensive and tight economic sanctions from August 1990 to May 2003.[13] Reliable United Nations data collections and analyses[14] offer overwhelming evidence on their inhuman results; thus, today's Iraqi population is between 500,000 and one million fewer than it is estimated that it would have been without these sanctions (i.e. excluding the accumulated deaths caused by the invasion and occupation in March 2003). Women and children in particular died because of malnutrition and lack of medicine, as well as the overall societal consequences of the sanctions on Iraq's health sector, research, education and infrastructure.

Independent analyses offer evidence that the negative effects on Iraqi civil society was caused far more by the sanctions regime itself than by the two factors mentioned repeatedly by Western powers, namely (a) that oil income and the supplies under the Oil for Food Programme was systematically appropriated by Saddam's regime and (b) that it spent the revenues on ever more weapons, palaces and mosques. While there may be some truth to that, at least from the point of view of opportunity costs, it never explained the tremendous suffering of the Iraqi people and the destruction of civil society. Britain's DFID states that, 'The country's position on the Human Development index dropped from 76 in 1990 to 126 in 2000. In many respects Iraq's social and economic indicators now resemble those of a low-income country rather than a major oil producer.'[15] As a matter of fact the UNDP Human Development Index shows that Iraq fell from a position around #90 among the world's countries to about #130, probably the fastest fall of any country in the post-1945 world.[16] Before the invasion in 2003, Iraq's standard of living was estimated to be about the same as Lesotho's.[17]

The UN Security Council decided on an arms embargo pertaining to all parts of former Yugoslavia in 1991.[18] On 15 December 1991, the Council established an economic sanctions committee; that was the same day as the EU decided prematurely to recognize Slovenia and Croatia as independent states without having any kind of plan for the rest of the country's future shape. This decision increased tremendously the risk of war breaking out in Bosnia-Herzegovina which the EU, spearheaded by Germany, granted independence on 6 April 1992 – incidentally on the fifty-first anniversary of Hitler's bombardment of Belgrade. With the exception of a few thousand, the Bosnian Serbs (33 per cent of the people in that republic) had boycotted the referendum that lead to the independent Bosnia-Herzegovina. The Security Council imposed economic sanctions selectively on Serbia and Montenegro in May 1992 and on the Bosnian Serbs in 1994. Both were lifted again in late 1996.

These sanctions of course hit Serbia itself, but also its smaller trading partners such as Macedonia. While the human suffering was far smaller than in Iraq, it can safely be argued that by 2006 Serbia has not yet recovered from the combined effects of the sanctions and the bombing in 1999. A serious side effect of these sanctions was to boost and to a certain extent create a mafia elite. Smuggling weapons, oil, prostitutes, cigarettes, etc. in and out of Serbia and the region (in criss-crossing cooperation with the Montenegrin, the Kosovo-Albanian, the Macedonian and the Albanian-Macedonian mafias) has not exactly promoted transparency and lawful government. It has also not helped the economies of the region to recover. Various types of funds going into the region for post-war reconstruction have ended up in the wrong pockets in all republics. And we have seen mafia-related killings in Serbia (Prime Minister Zoran Djindjic in Belgrade) and mafia-related politics in Kosovo.

Finally, the psycho-political effects of sanctions have shown similar characteristics. By and large, they proved the Western assumptions behind them to be grossly mistaken. The basic assumption seems to have been that when life becomes miserable due to the sanctions, the people will blame their authoritarian leaders and rise against them. The counter-hypothesis is that sanctions undermine the resource base, energy and health of the citizens who, under normal circumstances, *might* have been able to mobilize an opposition to the regime. Secondly, if applied together with other threats, such as that of bombings or invasion, and are perceived therefore as part of a serious threat to the very existence of their country, citizens gather around the leaders and postpone whatever plans they may have had to change the leadership. Thus, there is hardly any doubt that the economic sanctions in and of themselves hit civil society the hardest and functioned as a de facto support to both Saddam and Milosevic, including offering opportunities for certain elites to enrich themselves by smuggling and by other types of circumvention of the sanctions.

Simplified dualistic conflict analysis

Whether based on a collective, subconscious dichotomization of everything (black/white, left/right, male/female, either/or, etc.) or something else, there is a pervasive tendency throughout

Western culture to perceive conflicts as made up of two parties, despite the de facto complexities. One side is appointed good and only good characteristics, the other evil and only evil – no grey nuances – and, thus, conflict management is about neutralizing/punishing/destroying the evil party and rewarding the victimized good side.

In the case of Iraq two such dichotomies were made: (a) evil Saddam versus the Iraqi people and (b) Saddam versus neighbours in the region (Kuwait and Israel)/threat to the whole world. In the case of Yugoslavia, it was basically the evil Serbs against everybody else good, innocent and victimised, i.e. the Croats, the Bosniaks and the Albanians in Kosovo.

With this as their basic intellectual tool, most conflict managers are bound to make things worse on the ground.

Differential and discriminatory treatment of minorities

As a subset of the mentioned simplifying and empirically faulty interpretation of what are actually hugely complex conflict *formations*, we find the treatment of minorities. Some are evil/guilty minorities not worthy of our compassion or human rights protection; those were the Serbs in Croatia, Bosnia and Kosovo who were driven out from their homes and today make up the largest refugee problem in Europe: almost half a million living in Serbia with little prospect of returning to their respective republics.

The minorities in Iraq who are largely ignored in the general Western understanding are those who are neither Shiites, Sunni or Kurds such as Assyrians, Jews, Christians, Mandeans, Turkomans and Romas. Kurds can be divided into several subcategories, one of them being Yezidis[19] who are ethnically Kurdish, but many of those in Iraq do not see themselves as Kurdish in terms of ethnicity, culture and religion. This has led to Kurdish authorities forcing Yezidis to register as Kurdish during the 2005 elections. As has been pointed out earlier in this chapter, Iraq is more mixed than generally assumed in the West. However, the West has concentrated wholly on supporting one minority, the Kurds in the North. During the 1990s they were given such preferential treatment, including 13 per cent of all of Iraq's total oil revenues, that they have reasons to believe that the West will, sooner or later, grant them an independent state in the North. This will of course become more likely should an all-encompassing civil war break out in Iraq. The similarities with the way the West has favoured the Kosovo-Albanians because they were 'enemies of our enemy' are obvious.

The main unworthy minorities in former Yugoslavia were, of course, the Serbs.[20] The West, for all practical purposes, sided with the authoritarian-nationalist Croatian government under Dr Franjo Tudjman, not with the 12 per cent Serb citizens of that republic for whom terrible Second World War memories were coming up to the surface when they listened to his speeches and observed his policies. Moderate Serb pleas for cultural autonomy, then political autonomy and finally their self-declared 'Krajina' Republic in Croatia literally never met with any attention, let alone sympathies, in Western decision-making circles. Neither did the 33 per cent Serbs in Bosnia who did not want to become a minority in an independent state under Muslim leader Ilija Izetbegovic – Tito had imprisoned him for fundamentalist leanings in his books – in Sarajevo whose manoeuvring had so threatened Serb leaders there that they left and set up the headquarters in Pale.[21]

Likewise, the Serb fears that they would become a repressed minority under a 90 per cent majority of Albanians should Kosovo become an independent state also fell on deaf ears in Western circles. In these three cases Serb minorities fought against becoming minorities in republics, the majority of whose leaders had served as extended hands of Hitler and Mussolini during the Second World War. These Serbs were all guilty by association in that the Serb leader was the designate evil Enemy # 1 of the West, the Butcher of the Balkans, Milosevic. Secondly, the West seems to have believed that the Croat, Bosniak and Kosovo-Albanian leaders were modern, Western-oriented and – if not quite so – could be coached into behaving as if they were.

Only a few thousands of the ethnically cleansed but legitimate Serb citizens from the mentioned three places have been able to return. No international organization has made the point that their host countries *must* let them back, somewhat like the Palestinians; contrast the Western concern for Muslims in Bosnia and the Kosovo-Albanians. The EU could have put pressure on Croatia as part of its membership negotiations with Croatia. Kosovo is, at the time of writing, stipulated to become an independent state. These are facts that support the hypothesis that the Serbs – too – may have had a point when they felt let down and discriminated by the international community.

Among other Yugoslav minorities hardly mentioned by the West are the Gorani, Egyptians and the Romas in particular in Kosovo, as well as those who perceived themselves as Yugoslavs and as Bosnians and whoever else feels that he or she is of mixed origin and does not want an ethnic identity at all. These minorities would make up a fairly high percentage of all peoples in former Yugoslavia, but for them the Western conflict managers and peacemakers have provided little political, psychological and constitutional space.

The divided European Union

The proposed Constitution for the European Union,[22] as well as numerous policy statements coming out of EU bodies, make it abundantly clear that the Union shall have a common foreign and security policy and that that includes an ever closer integration of the armed forces and the members' arms industry as well as the establishment of a European Defence Agency. However, anyone who followed EU member actions in former Yugoslavia through the 1990s would look in vain for signs of a common analysis, understanding and policy for this region, sometimes called the 'backyard' of Europe. The most important wartime decision the EU took as a Union was the one in the night between December 15 and 16 1991, by which they selectively and prematurely recognized Croatia and Slovenia as independent states out of the Federal Republic of Yugoslavia. The decision was driven through by Germany's then foreign minister, Hans-Dietrich Genscher, as part of a multi-item member horse-trading deal, including the 'social dimension'.

Genscher had repeatedly been warned by his ambassador in Belgrade, by mediator Lord Carrington and by then UN Secretary-General Perez de Cuellar, that such a decision would cause war to break out in Bosnia-Herzegovina. And so it did a few months later.[23]

Concerning the Iraq conflict, it is well known that Germany and France opposed the war but also that they had no alternative plans and took no political initiatives to actively prevent the US-led war. Italy, Holland, Denmark, Spain and other EU members sent troops in support of the invasion and occupation. And a number of EU members, including Sweden, gave their unreserved political support without committing troops on the ground.

Simply put, the conflicts in Yugoslavia and Iraq make it abundantly clear that the European Union has not yet been able to shape a coherent common policy that could serve, in the eyes of others, as some kind of alternative to US hegemony. It has also proven unable to capitalize on the widespread and intensely negative attitudes citizens have to US foreign policy in NATO allied countries, in the Middle East and elsewhere.[24] Hence the ongoing discussion as to whether the EU, an economic superpower, shall seek to become 'different' from and a 'softer' alternative to the United States or basically imitate the policies of its Western ally and compete with it as a world player.

The principle of peace by peaceful means largely ignored

By and large, the international community's handling of former Yugoslavia and Iraq was founded on the principle of punishing the bad guys rather than rewarding the good guys, and on applying violence before all peaceful means had been tried and found in vain. Western media covered the conflicts in ways that corroborated this bias – often expressed in the sentence that, 'we have to speak with capital letters to make them understand.' This philosophy seldom yields anything but escalation and worst-case scenarios, however.

It is true that, in contrast to the Iraq case, a lot of conferences, meetings, consultations and processes took place in the case of former Yugoslavia. Foreign diplomats and mediators used to queue up in the offices of Presidents Tudjman, Izetbegovic and Milosevic. There was a diplomatic presence in Belgrade, albeit at a lower level, whereas many Western countries had virtually no representatives in Baghdad for the good part of the 1990s. There have been agreements made, associated with names such as Dayton, Erdut, Ohrid, etc., that resulted from negotiations. But Kosovo remains different, much closer to the Iraq war process.

From the very early 1990s, organizations such as Amnesty International, TRANSCEND and the Transnational Foundation for Peace and Future Research warned that Kosovo would blow up in violence if no mediation initiatives were taken.[25] Regrettably, the international community felt it had its hands full with the wars already raging in Slovenia, Croatia and Bosnia. Even though the United Nations and other governmental organizations heard the early warnings, they were without the resources to prevent the violence that was looming due both to Milosevic's police state-like exertion of power in that province and, from 1993, the development of the Kosovo Liberation Army, KLA/UCK, behind the back of pacifist Kosovo-Albanian leader, Dr Ibrahim Rugova. When the war broke out in Kosovo, the international community was largely unprepared, although a few diplomats had visited from time to time during the 1990s and various ambassadors in Skopje, Macedonia, for instance had been engaged in trying to solve the conflict. None of it had been well planned or coherent and the minimum human and other resources had never been made available by the international community.

Contrary to media reports, the Rambouillet process outside Paris was not an attempt to find a negotiated solution; the Serb and the Kosovo-Albanian delegations never met face to face. It is also commonplace among connoisseurs that it was little but a fait accompli deliberately aimed at making the Serb side say no – which it did. The reason was simple and any leader of a sovereign European state would have acted likewise. At the second round of talks, Secretary of State Madeleine Albright presented the famous Military Appendix that outlined a future presence for NATO not only in Kosovo but all over Serbia. The troops would operate freely, pay nothing for the use of facilities including harbours and airports, and they could not be arrested or sued in case they broke the laws of the host country, damaged property or committed other offensive acts. Milosevic said no and the assistant Secretary of State who served as an official mediator, James Rubin, made the famous statement to his wife on CNN, senior correspondent Christiane Amanpour, that now the Kosovo-Albanians had chosen peace and the Serbs war. NATO's 78 days of day-and-night bombing began shortly after.[26]

Like Milosevic had been threatened repeatedly with military action, so was Saddam Hussein. Both were what Western media normally term 'defiant'. The author cannot remember a single case in which such a response to a fait accompli was presented as a normal protection of a country's sovereignty and integrity in the face of an existential threat.

Commensurate with this, Western conflict management consistently ignored the local forces for peace as well as proposals built on the UN Charter norm of 'peace by peaceful means'. Under the visionary, pacifist[27] leadership of Dr Rugova, the Kosovo-Albanians had developed an impressive parallel society based on nonviolence. This development earned no support anywhere in the West despite its uniqueness in all of former Yugoslavia. When after the war on Serbia the UN, NATO, OSCE and the EU came in to run Kosovo the qualities of this parallel society were completely ignored.

There were what could appropriately be called *peace pockets* and *peace lords* at many places. First and foremost, probably 95–98 per cent of the ordinary citizens were against war; they were increasingly the victims of military and political and mafia elites, their own as well as those of the other conflicting parties. Had alternatives to war been consistently presented by foreigners and supported with 'carrots' – such as a thick carpet of peacekeepers, humanitarian aid, development projects, jumpstarting of destroyed production facilities, grants, loans, scholarships for the young, rebuilding of infrastructure coupled to peace and reconciliation training, media democratization and a solid support to women and children in particular – it is quite likely that the war lords could have been undermined earlier from below. Instead, the international community systematically broke the UN arms embargo against all sides in former Yugoslavia, flew in tons of weapons and ammunition, and built and equipped the Kosovo-Albanian Liberation Army to a modern force of 20,000, etc.[28]

Secondly, moderate non-nationalist leaders who also detested violence at various levels seldom received any attention from foreign media, diplomacy or international organizations; neither were they listened to. There were moderate Serbs in Croatia who fought against Milosevic and his war lords in Krajina; there were non-nationalist Croats who saw how detrimental Tudjman's nationalism was to a future democratic Croatia. There were Bosniaks who refused to follow the hard-line ethnicity-based policies of Alija Izetbegovic, such as Tuzla's mayor, Beslagic. There was a vibrant civil society in Serbia all through the war whose leaders had to fight for years to meet with the foreigners who almost always came to see only Milosevic and his like. Macedonia's remarkably soft-spoken and peace-oriented president, Kiro Gligorov, witnessed how his country's sovereignty was ignored by Western powers and how their policies systematically undermined the economy.[29]

Finally, the word *peace pockets*, the opposite of war zones. These were towns, local areas, neighbourhoods or work places that were known, for instance by UN peacekeepers and UN Civil Affairs staff, for trying hard to remain tolerant and multi-ethnic when coming under severe pressure from their own authorities. The citizens there upheld decent relations, helped each other with everyday matters like they had always done and largely ignored ethnic and other more or less constructed divisions. Particularly during the early years of the war, the author experienced such peace pockets in both Croatia, in Sarajevo, in Serbia and in Macedonia. It was often the women and youth who upheld such humane networks while the men engaged in various types of politics or had left for the killing fields. Invariably, the only internationals who cared for them were the three legs of the UN missions, the Blue Helmets, the Police and Civil Affairs.

The international community chose to make peace from the top down, through more or less intensive horse-trading with presidents and military leaders and it chose violence-based solutions, most often in consequence of not having reacted to early warnings or committed to violence prevention. One wonders how much faster the war could have been stopped and a more genuine locally-rooted peace could have been made had the international community chosen to identify and cooperate with the local peace potentials, reward the peace lords and the peace pockets and stood by the few top leaders who advocated nonviolence. The potential of also involving peace from the ground up[30] never entered the mind set of the international community in the case of former Yugoslavia. And, one must add, even less so in the case of Iraq.

Nonviolent action has proven quite effective over recent years.[31] But it is still not recognized by mainstream media and politics as such, as a new ethos, philosophy and political tool. It wasn't diplomatic isolation, sanctions and the war on Serbia that caused Slobodan Milosevic's fall in Serbia. It was nonviolent mobilization and concerted, planned action virtually without the use of violence.[32] Other authoritarian leaders of our time have fallen and systems changed also due mainly to the force of nonviolent mobilization; cases are Iran (the shah), the Philippines (the Marcos family), Poland (Solidarnosc) and Georgia (Shevardnadze). Indeed, the most heavily armed confrontation and conflict formation in human history, the Cold War bloc system, dissolved and the Soviet Union fell apart because of millions marching in the streets, because of the enlightened policies of Mikhail S. Gorbachev and dissidents inside the Eastern bloc.

In April 2006 the Thai prime minister, Thaksin Shinawatra, was forced to resign because of nonviolent mass demonstrations (albeit with some violence and violent attitudes) and the French government had to give in after weeks of student and labour union demonstrations (with some little violence). Simultaneously, millions of Americans protested immigration reform plans with Luther King Jr.-inspired banners such as 'We have a dream too'. However, again virtually no media cover this as nonviolent politics with any of the intense interest and expertise they devote to violent politics.

Together with former UN Assistant Secretary General and United Nations Humanitarian Coordinator for Iraq, Hans von Sponeck, the author was engaged in an effort to present alternatives to war on Iraq. The *International Herald Tribune* considered the proposals we made 'unrealistic' and changed from accepting the article to declining it.[33] Unfortunately, it will never be known whether Kosovo could have achieved peace or Saddam Hussein been overthrown through nonviolent politics. But given the situation in today's former Yugoslavia and in Iraq, it is a plausible hypothesis that the international community might have succeeded in creating a little more genuine peace and a little less violence by making much better use of the peacemaking potentials in civil society.[34]

The UN became a casualty of international conflict management[35]

It merits saying it at the outset: the United Nations will never become more or better than its member states, the permanent Security Council members in particular, are willing and able to make it. The UN has been one of the real victims of the Yugoslav drama. In spite of all its deficiencies as a world organization, the image allotted the UN in most media, parliaments and the public discourse has been anything but fair. In contrast to this we here promote the hypothesis that if the basic principles of the UN Charter had actually been applied to the Balkans and to Iraq, things are likely to have turned out better.

In Iraq, the United Nations was forced to play a dual, contradictory role. It was the UN Security Council, the now outdated elite body of the United Nations, that decided about the sanctions that – as has been shown above – led to unspeakable material misery and humiliation for the Iraqi people. It was also the United Nations that, through its various bodies and its humanitarian mission in Iraq, assisted the people in ways that could not but touch the heart of a visitor.[36] The highly biased media focus on the Oil for Food Programme only does not do justice to the whole spectrum of UN activities in the country. It seems that the Iraqi people knew the difference between the 'evil' Security Council sanctions and the 'good' UN; no UN staff member was ever wounded or killed – compare the situation for foreigners ever since the occupation of the country.

Although the UN Security Council did not endorse the war and the occupation, the role of the United Nations on the ground ended with the tragic attack on the UN Headquarters in Baghdad in August 2003.

The UN presence in the various parts of former Yugoslavia was not only humanitarian, it consisted of three integrated types, namely the military peacekeepers, police and civil affairs, of which only the first-mentioned attract media attention. Over the years, there were UN missions in Croatia (in Krajina, Eastern and Western Slavonia), in Bosnia, Belgrade, Kosovo and Macedonia. Common for them was, to varying extents, an unclear mandate, a mandate too large for the resources made available by the member states (Bosnia in particular), a premature withdrawal of missions (Eastern Slavonia, Macedonia); further, that other Western policies at the same time directly worked against the missions and, in the case of Croatia in 1995, the UN was overrun and expelled by the host country's military forces (Operations Storm and Flash, assisted by the United States) and never invited back. Finally, in the case of post-war Kosovo, the UN mission there (UNMIK) was tasked by SC Resolution 1244 to both respect the sovereignty of Serbia and take over its Kosovo province after having sent away every part of Belgrade's administration and ignored the right of states to defend their borders. As a high-level UN staff member told the author shortly after UNMIK had moved into buildings legally belonging to the state, 'we are coming here on the basis of rather controversial policies in the past and on an equally disputed mandate.'

To put it somewhat bluntly, the UN missions in former Yugoslavia did an impressive job given the extremely complex and difficult circumstances on the ground and the lack of genuine commitment and support by a number of the most influential UN member states. Unfortunately, they simultaneously pursued their national interests, including selling arms, and let the UN down by not sending a minimum of personnel or funds to enable the world organization to succeed with the mandate they themselves had given the world organization.

And if the United Nations could say no – and in principle the Secretary-General can do so according to Chapter 99 and 100 – the mission in Kosovo is one of those that he should have said no to. A UN mission set up in the wake of a decade of conflict negligence, in which one side is armed to the teeth by the international community in support of violent secession after which the other side becomes the target of NATO's severest punishment, is a mission that is bound to fail, at least in terms of peace and justice,[37] no matter that it may well be the UN mission that has cost most per square kilometres anywhere.

A couple of factors aggravated the situation in the region from the point of view of the UN. First, there was mission 'creep' combined with minimum or no long-range planning. Mandates were renewed with short intervals and staff rotated with little institutional learning possible. Hardly observed by the media, there was a constant lack of funds. While accused by the editorials and columnists, Western politicians and various groups in the region of not saving the victims in Srebrenica, few paid attention to the fact that the UN was literally financially broke and that its mission in Bosnia had received only 1200 soldiers of the more than 30,000 required by its mission leaders to make the officially designated safe zones safe.[38]

In addition, the UN *Agenda for Peace*, published by Butros-Ghali's office in 1992, introduced the possibility of (violent) peace enforcement on top of peacekeeping, peacemaking and peace-building, thereby – for sure unintentionally – making everyone on the ground confused. Peacekeeping requires impartiality, peace enforcement means military action against one side. Thus when NATO threatened to bomb Serb positions in Bosnia, it automatically threatened the safety of its own Blue Helmets on the ground. When it decided to bomb Serbia, it had to secure the advance withdrawal of the UNPREDEP mission on the Macedonian side of the border with Serbia; it was co-located with American soldiers there and would risk being hit if Serbia tried to retaliate against them, as they were the nearest in the region.

Secondly, the problems were severely compounded by the very opposite of what was often stated at the time, namely that the international community did too little too late in the former Yugoslavia. Various countries and organizations of the international community tried at one and the same time to play multiple roles and ended up in a series of rather unsolvable dilemmas. For example, they played the roles of both neutral mediators and peace enforcers; humanitarian aid workers and bomber pilots; peacemakers and arms dealers; champions of democracy and human rights while being authoritarian and ignoring 'unworthy' minorities; using the UN while for all practical purposes undermining its authority; helping countries to develop by adopting market economies while making them victims of sanctions without any compensation; denouncing nationalism and pursuing their own national(ist) interests and supporting those nationalisms (Croatian, Bosnian-Muslim and Albanian) they saw fitting. The list could be extended.

In sum, the UN – until something else emerges, undoubtedly the most important world institution with a Charter containing essential norms – has suffered very severely blows to its strength. This has been caused much less by the UN itself being incompetent or inefficient and much more by member states' neglect, lack of appropriate support and, not least, overt attempts to sideline and undermine it.

Failed conflict management and peacemaking due to deficient competence

We ask lawyers to draft constitutions. We hope that the medical doctor who performs surgery on us has been educated in some relevant branch of medicine. We take for granted that the pilots in the cockpit have been trained professionally and are well-rested. Surprisingly, few ask what minimum kinds of competence should be required of official conflict managers.

None of those appointed to mediate on the ground in former Yugoslavia had any professional training in, say, conflict analysis, mediation and negotiation skills, nonviolence, reconciliation or forgiveness. They were career diplomats, former high-level officials, militaries, many trained as lawyers. It is true that, as one can become a good artist without having been educated at an arts academy, there are certainly those whose personality, life experience and values integrate to produce extraordinary peacemakers. The author would mention former Secretary of State Cyrus Vance, whom he had the privilege to meet in person in Belgrade. On the – famous – other hand, however, it would hardly hurt if conflict managers had taken at least a basic, one-week, academic training course as a minimum before being sent out to help solve complex protracted conflicts and negotiate peace plans that lay the foundation for the lives of millions of people and future generations.

The author's survey of one of the first batch of Americans arriving after the occupation to run Iraq shows that not one had a professional background in, say, post-war reconstruction, peace-building, reconciliation, negotiation, conflict analysis and resolution and similar subjects that one would consider relevant for the task of building a new democratic, peaceful, just and well-governed Iraq.[39]

And there were, as mentioned, several other similarities at various levels that space does not permit an elaboration of here.[40]

Some differences between the two cases

For sure, there are differences between the two countries and regions and between the conflict management applied to them by the international community. Here we shall mention the most important.

Different country structures, conflict formation and wars

Yugoslavia was a federation the constituent parts of which had certainly added fuel to the flames by creating the preconditions for the civil war since the 1970s. Iraq was neither a confederation nor a federation and had never seen civil war. But then there is the similarity in the difference: Iraq had invaded Kuwait and should be punished for that, somewhat similar to the interpretation that the Serbs had started the entire Yugoslav drama by invading the other republics with the goal of creating a 'Greater Serbia'.

In the case of Iraq, the overall conflict formation was different. Because of its oil, Iraq was more important for the long-term future of both the United States and Europe than the former Yugoslavia was – and would ever be. Iraq was part and parcel of the wider Middle East conflict formation with all the prestige invested there by the West. And then there was Israel, the regional nuclear power considered Number One enemy by the Iraqis – more so than the US and Europe – and also a close ally of the West with a comparatively strong influence on Washington. There was nothing comparable in the Yugoslav conflict formation.

Different economic structures

Iraq is heavily dependent on selling one product, its oil. Yugoslavia had a more diversified economy, albeit it shared having a strong state sector combined with some private market functions. Iraq's economy and infrastructure was deliberately destroyed by the economic sanctions before the war, while those on Yugoslavia (Serbia and Montenegro to be precise) were less cruel and successively wore down the country simultaneously with the wars.

Different cultures and levels of contact and understanding

From a Western Catholic and Protestant perspective, the cultural distance to Iraq is much larger than that to Yugoslavia. Many Europeans had visited Yugoslavia as tourists at some point and governments kept their embassies operative in Belgrade and successively set up representations when new republics emerged. In contrast, comparatively few Westerners had any personal knowledge from visiting Iraq and important countries withdrew completely from there. The same pattern describes the coverage of leading media.

It deserves mention that, while the West made the Muslims in Bosnia and Kosovo their closest allies (together with the Croats), its sanctions killed hundreds of thousands of Iraqi Muslims.

Total US occupation versus partial UN–NATO–OSCE–EU occupation

Conspicuously, Iraq is an example of invasion and occupation under the de facto control of the United States. Contrary to the Yugoslav space, the UN has had no peacekeeping or peacemaking role in wartime. The occupation of Iraq is unilateral, all-territory and complete; the only thing somewhat similar is Kosovo, a tiny but important part of former Yugoslavia run multilaterally by the four mentioned organizations under UN leadership. (And by spring 2006 it became clear that the purpose is to carve out Kosovo from Serbia for good and establish some kind of independence irrespective of what UNSC Resolution 1244 states about respecting the sovereignty and territorial integrity of Serbia.) In passing, one may air the hypothesis that the same could one day happen to Iraqi Kurdistan; it will undoubtedly meet fierce resistance in Baghdad.

A cold war and an anti-terrorism war

Yugoslavia was in a sense the last conflict and war acted out within the Cold War paradigm. The 1991 war against Iraq's Kuwait invasion could be seen as different in that it ushered in the emerging, but still far from clarified, new unipolar world order and Western triumphalism.

The invasion and occupation of Iraq in 2003 adds the important dimension of changed US perceptions in the wake of 11 September 2001, i.e. the so-called war on terrorism. In 1991 no coherent enemy image existed in the minds of Western decision-makers; rather, all through the 1990s there existed periodically shifting enemy images and engagements but the definition of who is the enemy of the West coalesced and solidified between 11 September and 7 October when the war was unleashed on Afghanistan. The unified enemy – so most Westerners believed – was terrorism in general and Muslim terrorism and nuclear proliferation with its potential for nuclear terrorism in particular. A new enemy had been born – or at least the image of him/it – that was eminently able to take the place of the enemy that had been lost with the demise of the Soviet Union and the Warsaw Pact about a dozen years before. In passing, it did not seem to matter much to Washington's decision-makers that Iraq had already been economically destroyed, had been militarily disarmed and had no relations with Osama bin Laden or possible nuclear terrorism. It was, in a sense, enough that Iraq had been pointed out by President Bush – together with Iran and North Korea – as the 'Axis of Evil'.

In the case of Yugoslavia, none of these arguments were brought forward. It was enough to point out that the people in Yugoslavia had age-old hatred, that they were primitive since they took to weapons against each other, that they were non-modern and backward compared with the rest of Europe and, specifically, that a new Hitler in Europe had emerged with 'Lebensraum-like' dreams embedded in the idea of a Greater Serbia and 'concentration camps' in Bosnia. That both the Iraqis and their leader and Serbs and their leader were backwards and brutal compared with 'us' was enough to culturally underpin the psychological warfare fought against the Western public to make it accept the actual warfare when it happened.

Differences in likely world order consequences

The Yugoslav dissolution drama undoubtedly exerted a remarkable influence on European politics. It challenged European identity and EU cohesion. It widened the gap, at least for a period, between the Europeans and the Americans. One element was a sense of humiliation; the US had intervened in the European 'backyard' that Europe itself had been so manifestly unable to handle in time and with appropriate means. For instance, it is conspicuous how, after the US-led bombing of Serbia/Kosovo in 1999, the European Union intensified its work towards a common defence policy, outlined elements of a strategy for out-of-NATO-area operations (up to 6,000 kilometres from Brussels), for military–industrial integration and for common interoperable military units. Javier Solana, who had been NATO Secretary-General during the alliance's bombing of Yugoslavia, became Secretary General of the Council of the European Union/High Representative for the Common Foreign and Security Policy (CFSP) and, just a month later, Secretary General of Western European Union (WEU).

It is a reasonable hypothesis that, despite the heavy impact of Yugoslavia *on European politics*, it will have less far-reaching consequences for *the global order* than Iraq. Interestingly, the concept of humanitarian intervention that was massively promoted in the case of Yugoslavia was hardly mentioned in the cases of the wars on Afghanistan and Iraq; with the rampant suffering of the Iraqi people repeatedly being explained with reference to Saddam's weapons purchases and palace building, what would have been more fitting than to argue for humanitarian intervention in that case? But nobody did and the concept seems now dead and gone.

So, because of the Iraq case's (more or less real) connection with the nuclear (WMD) issue, with terrorism, the wider Middle East conflict formation, with strategic raw materials, with US base proliferation and with whatever may happen in the future in the two neighbouring oil states, Iran and Saudi-Arabia, it is reasonable to conclude that the Iraq case carries more far-reaching implications than Yugoslavia for the future world (dis)order.

It cannot be safely concluded that we have seen the end of violence in former Yugoslavia. As of spring 2006, there are very complex and unpredictable situations concerning Montenegro's possible independence, Kosovo's possible independence, possible turmoil inside them both, a possible nationalistic backlash in Serbia, and – in the wake of all this – instability in Dayton Bosnia and throughout Macedonia. However, one can also not preclude that a series of negotiated solutions will make it possible to muddle through without open violence, albeit with a considerable potential for future violence.

Regrettably, in the case of Iraq such hopes fail to appreciate the darkness of its predicament. Rather, a Second World War-Yugoslavia-like combination of struggle against the foreign occupiers combined with civil war spun out of (a) a fundamental disagreement among groups on how to deal with the occupiers, (b) internal divisions crisscrossing ethnic, religious, clan, geographical borderlines, etc., and (c) struggles for de facto independence for at least parts of the North (Kurdistan) and possibly Shiite secessionist forces in the South supported by Iran is a more probable scenario.

Stated in somewhat different terms, while the US – together with Slovenia, Croatia, Bosnia-Herzegovina and Kosovo – could claim victory in the Balkans, the US is likely to be the loser in Iraq. This will have severe, negative consequences domestically and, thereby, for the future world order. To the extent Iran is drawn into the conflict formation and into an Iraq-like pattern of sanctions, isolation and military punishment by the West, the global long-range impact will increase.

A few selected lessons to learn from the two cases

Space does not permit too elaborate arguments here, towards the end of this chapter. Here simply follow some of the lessons the author would state on the basis of his multi-year experience with diagnosis, prognosis and treatment in former Yugoslavia and Iraq as well as the argument presented over the preceding pages.

Successful conflict mitigation or management requires comprehensive, unbiased diagnosis of the wider conflict formation, not just of two main actors on a medialized stage

It would greatly facilitate honest brokering if, from the outset, the international community recognized its own historical roles in the conflicting parties' history.

Underestimating or ignoring the human social-psychological dimensions of conflict prevents genuine conflict resolution, peace and stability

None of the peace agreements done in former Yugoslavia addresses these dimensions and thus hate, mistrust, non-reconciliation, non-forgiveness, trauma and a sense of humiliation characterize the republics in which the international community pride itself on having made peace. Sadly, there is less multi-ethnicity and less co-existence and cooperation across various dividing lines in each of the former Yugoslav republics than under Tito. To prevent future violence from breaking out, these deeply human issues should be addressed as energetically at least as is peace-building, human rights, good governance and whatever else the conflict-managing international community attempts to promote.

Successful conflict management requires early warning with diagnosis, early listening with prognosis and early action with treatment

Two mistakes are usually done. First, those who profess to manage conflicts and make peace have, at an earlier stage in the conflict, directly contributed to increasing the likelihood of violence; for instance, Saddam was little but the product of Western arms and high-technology trade and profit interests. The West helped him win against Iran according to the principle that 'the enemy of my enemy is my friend'. Secondly, they act far too late, either because of being overloaded with already manifest conflicts or simply they are ignorant of the danger potential in the situation and their own decisions when implemented on the ground. Kosovo is a very good example of about ten years of international warnings with no single actor in the international community taking steps to mitigate it when it would have been possible. After the 1999 bombing blunder, no just and sustainable peace is possible there.

Genuine conflict management is incompatible with the simultaneous promotion of one's own interests and playing multiple other roles. Ideally, conflict management can be done only by 'disinterested' actors who have no interest in a particular outcome of a conflict

If this is not the case, one should be suspicious that conflict management and peacemaking signifies nothing but the continuation of power politics with other means. Yugoslavia represents a particularly good example of actors trying to play far too many and contradictory roles at one and the same time, largely driven by the media-promoted pressure that they must 'do something'.

Sanctions are counterproductive from a conflict-management viewpoint

Sanctions usually hit the innocent and end up displaying a lack of humanity that is incompatible with other stated aims such as promoting human rights, market economic reforms and democracy. In addition their politico-psychological effect is to strengthen the authoritarian leader in his crisis operations and weaken the very civil society that could, in the best of cases, depose him.

Conflict management that gives priority to military threats and means and ignores 'peace by peaceful means' as well as the peace potential of civil societies in the conflict zone is bound to fail

This is not to say that military means are always counterproductive. Rather, it means that there must be a clear understanding of what military means can and can *not* achieve and how they interact with civil measures before, during and after force has been employed. For instance, peacekeeping and peace enforcement can *not* be used in the same 'theatre'; and lacking a post-occupation plan for reconstruction and peace-building as in both Kosovo and Iraq has destructive consequences for all sides. Finally, the employment of military means without first having employed the wide spectrum of civilian means and found them in vain is counterproductive and, for all practical purposes, a violation of the United Nations Charter. We need more comparative studies of predominantly nonviolent and violent conflict resolution methods and how they correlate with types of conflict formation and their cultures.

The systematic assault on the UN and the concomitant erosion of its Charter's normative functions and provisions must be halted

Until something better is created and fully in place, we shall be wise to preserve and strengthen the UN as humanity's most significant common peace and justice organization. Furthermore, the media and others should pay attention to both of the two rather different United Nations: the power house in New York, on the one hand, and the UN on the ground around the world with its specialized agencies and peace missions encompassing peacekeepers, police and civil affairs, on the other. Without that UN – which hardly ever hits the front pages – millions of ordinary citizens in conflict regions would have been much worse off today.

Politics and media should integrate knowledge from peace and conflict studies

To manage and help solve conflicts requires multiple competences. In the two cases we have discussed here, military as well as a long series of civilian professions and trainings have certainly been needed – political science, history, international affairs, diplomacy, international law, human rights, etc. Conspicuously absent, however, are people trained in peace and conflict studies in a broad sense. No conflict can be managed professionally or solved successfully to the optimum satisfaction of all sides unless that expertise is also drawn in – not as the only one, but at least as one among several.

We need much more scrutiny and self-critical assessment of Western conflict management, both governmental and non-governmental/civil society organizations

Much post-Cold War conflict management has failed to bring and root genuine peace in the conflict regions and war zones. Lids have been put on open war-fighting and social violence and the value of this reduction in direct violence should not be underestimated. However, students and practitioners of peace should require better situations than those we find, grosso modo, in today's Croatia, Bosnia-Herzegovina, Serbia, Kosovo, Macedonia and in Iraq. There are new borders, institutions and laws, there are new people at the helm – but there is, to put it in popular terms, very little peace at heart or belief in the future. There is scant economic recovery, rampant corruption and, in too many places, a dangerously close integration between politics and criminality. Everywhere ordinary citizens still suffer more than anyone believes to be reasonable and fair.

In the face of this, we need much more balanced accounts in the Western world. It is significant that one never hears Western conflict managers say that they are aware that they made mistakes in former Yugoslavia and Iraq, at least not before they have resigned or retired. If leaders are not open to self-criticism but insist again and again that whatever conflict management they undertook it was right and good – and if not, it was and remains the fault of the local conflicting parties – their institutions and successors will never get a chance to do it better, to do it right.[41]

In the eyes of the author, the international community has operated in former Yugoslavia and Iraq in ways that ought to produce much more critical awareness and public debate. In both cases, the general conflict-management approach was restricted by numerous limitations, misunderstandings were rampant and – worse – there were cases of deliberate misuse of *conflict management and peacemaking as nothing but power politics and interventionism with other means.*

Independent intellectuals and scholarship have a considerable task ahead to map out the extent and consequences on the ground of this conflict mismanagement.

Notes

1 The author's background for writing about former Yugoslavia and Iraq is 30 years in academic peace and conflict research and exactly as many years of on-and-off studies of and some 80 visits (and 3,000 interviews at all social levels) to former Yugoslavia, about which he has produced several hundred pages of articles and book chapters. He visited Iraq – Baghdad, Babylon and Basra – twice in 2002 and 2003, altogether for one month, and conducted some 160 interviews with people from the top leadership to people in the bazaars and countryside. Most of his English-language writings on Iraq can be found at http://www.transnational.org/forum/meet/TFF_Forum_Iraq.html. He has also written a book *Predictable Fiasco: On the Conflict with Iraq and Denmark as an Occupying Power* (in Danish), (2004) Copenhagen: Tiderne Skifter. Thus, this chapter is based on academic studies integrated with personal impressions and experiences.

2 The term conflict management is to some extent deceptive; it conveys the impression that some 'third party' can enter somebody else's conflict, manage it and lead it to resolution or transformation. A further underlying hypothesis is that that 'third party' – 'third' is also misleading as there are usually more than two parties to a complex conflict – has not been and is not a party to the conflict and therefore can act impartially, i.e. without having or promoting its own goals and interests and also being fair in its 'management' of the local parties. These features very seldom, if ever, characterize international conflict management, and certainly not in the two cases we deal with here.

3 The 'international community' is used here only because it is common parlance. It should be emphasized that it is a highly politicized term normally used by mainstream Western media and a small group of Western leaders as if they had been given a mandate to speak on behalf of all the world's governments or citizens. Secondly, it is highly debatable whether the world can meaningfully be defined as a community; hundreds of millions seem to be rather convinced that – for a variety of reasons – they are not included in any community but significantly excluded.

4 Galtung, J. (1977) *Methodology and Ideology: Theory and Methods of Social Research*, Vol. I, Copenhagen: Christian Ejlers, p. 60.

5 For instance, at Milosevic's death in March 2006, the self-styled peacemaker Richard Holbrooke managed in a 3–4 minute CNN interview to compare him with all three and say that it did not matter whether he had died in his cell in the Hague; he had been judged by world public opinion, as he stated it, and that was what mattered.

6 See Aburish, S.K. (2000) *Saddam Hussein: The Politics of Revenge*, London: Bloomsbury.

7 There is both the recorded story about his meeting prior to the invasion with US ambassador April Glaspie and the various theories and interpretations of why he invaded Kuwait. See for instance: http://wais.stanford.edu/Iraq/iraq_andambassaprilglaspie22303.html and Hassan, H.A. (1999) *The Iraqi Invasion of Kuwait: Religion, Identity and Otherness in the Analysis of War and Conflict*, London: Pluto Press.

8 Hackett, J. (1979) *The Third World War: August 1985*, Buckingham: Sphere Books; a war scenario that centres – quite realistically for its time – on Yugoslavia.

9 A largely overlooked angle on US policies in the former Yugoslavia is President Clinton's programme for placing US military experts in a series of ministries of defence and building bases around the former Soviet Union which commenced in 1992. The Bondsteel base in Kosovo – the largest US base outside the United States built since the Vietnam war and still there – together with similar bases in Romania and Bulgaria serve as examples here.

10 See, for instance, Woodward, S. (1995) *Balkan Tragedy*, Washington, DC: Brookings Institution, and Chossudovsky, M. (1997) *The Globalization of Poverty: Impacts of IMF and World Bank Reforms*, London: Zed Press.

11 This is very clearly pointed out by chief inspector Scott Ritter in his book *Endgame: Solving the Iraqi Crisis* (1999), New York: Simon & Schuster.

12 This reasoning builds on the kindest interpretation, namely that the bombings of Yugoslavia and the invasion of Iraq had not been planned long ago for entirely different reasons and just required the building of enough traps for Milosevic and Saddam to fall into in order to make the intervention legitimate in the eyes of the very same international community itself.

13 See the details of all the UN Security Council resolutions at: http://www.un.org/News/ossg/iraq.htm. On the sanctions and their effects, see CASI, the Campaign Against Sanctions on Iraq at: http://www.casi.org.uk/guide/, IraqAnalysis.Org at: http://www.iraqanalysis.org and former UN Assistant Secretary-General, United Nations Humanitarian Coordinator for Iraq and TFF Associate Hans von Sponeck's book and articles listed at: http://www.transnational.org/tff/people/hc_vonsponeck.html.

14 The author collected these materials in Baghdad, for instance at the UN Office of the Iraq Programme and UNICEF, both of whom produced several well-documented reports backed up by statistics.

15 See DFID at: http://www.dfid.gov.uk/countries/asia/iraq.asp.

16 More data available in various annual *UNDP Human Development Reports*.

17 The author investigated the effects of sanctions in child hospitals, with Care International and UNICEF and other sources in Iraq during his visits and finds the arguments produced by the UN and Iraq itself much more credible than any of the arguments produced by the, say, Washington and London, or Copenhagen and Stockholm for that matter.

18 See http://www.un.org/News/ossg/fy.htm.

19 See, for instance, http://en.wikipedia.org/wiki/Iraq#Minority_situation about the Kurds and their sub-groups.

20 The author remembers how in the early 1990s, he was told by the second-highest ranking official at the US Embassy in Zagreb, Croatia, that the United States would never treat the nations/minorities in former Yugoslavia according to the same principles.

21 For one highly interesting witness account of the early conflict years, see Vukovic, Z. (1993) *Mordet på Sarajevo: En krigsdagbog (The Murder of Sarajevo: A War Diary)*, Copenhagen: Brøndum (L'assassinat de Sarajevo, Sulma 1998).

22 See the EU Constitution text at: http://europa.eu.int/eur-lex/lex/JOHtml.do?uri=OJ:C:2004:310:SOM:EN:HTML and the author's (2004) *Fremmer EU Freden? Analyse, kritik og alternativer* (*EU As a Promoter of Peace? Analysis, Criticism and Alternatives*), Copenhagen: Agenda 2004.

23 Much more is given about the central importance and details of this decision in Galtung, Oberg and Wiberg, *Yugoslavia: What Could Have Been Done?* (forthcoming).

24 See Pew Research Centre for the People and the Press, for instance the survey, *A Year After Iraq War: Mistrust of America in Europe Ever Higher, Muslim Anger Persists* at: http://people-press.org/reports/display.php3?ReportID=206, and *Anti-Americanism: Causes and Characteristics* at: http://people-press.org/commentary/display.php3?AnalysisID=77.

25 See, for instance, TFF's report *Preventing war in Kosovo* from 1992 and TFF's mediation proposals in *UNTANS – Conflict-Mitigation for Kosovo: A UN Temporary Authority for a Negotiated Settlement* from 1996, available at: www.transnational.org.

26 The long list of TFF analyses of Kosovo are listed at: http://www.transnational.org/features/2005/Coll_Kosovo3–2005.html – including TFF PressInfo 58, 1999 *Read the Military Kosovo Agreement!*, TFF PressInfo 57, 1999 *Read the Civilian Kosovo Agreement!*, TFF PressInfo 56, 1999 *Rambouillet – A Process Analysis*, TFF PressInfo 55, 1999 *Rambouillet – Imperialism in Disguise*, and TFF PressInfo 54, 1999 *Why these 'peace' efforts can't bring peace to Kosovo*.

27 Ibrahim Rugova, who passed away in early 2006, did abhor war and would not advocate that his people use violence to become an independent state. It was in consultation with TFF that he and his associates developed the idea of a Kosovo without an army or membership in any military alliance, a Kosovo with open borders and a pledge to not join Albania. He was, however, not against NATO coming in to liberate the province from Belgrade's rule. Directly asked, Rugova admitted to the author that he had never read Gandhi or other leaders of principled nonviolence, but he had felt it so painful to watch the human suffering on all sides in Croatia and Bosnia that he wanted nothing of it in Kosovo.

28 The rampant violations of the UN arms embargo and the secret arming of the Muslims by the US is another aspect conveniently left unmentioned in the media coverage of Srebrenica. The Dutch government report on Srebrenica in the section on US arms deliveries is listed as one of the links in Jan

Oberg, *Srebrenica Muslims Remembered, The Rest Silenced*, in PressInfo # 222, 11 July 2005: http://www.transnational.org/pressinf/2005/pi222_Srebrenica.html.

29 The author has had the privilege to meet him three times for long discussions about the history of the dissolution process and how Macedonia's economy and sovereignty was undermined by the sanctions against Serbia, its largest trading partner (compensation was never paid); how NATO's Supreme Commander Wesley Clark failed to ask him in time whether bombings could be simulated in Macedonian airspace as a warning sign to the Serbs; how the UNPREDEP mission (see next section) was withdrawn much too early because it would be at risk when NATO started bombing Serbia and how the bombing of Serbia and Kosovo sent hundreds of thousands running to Macedonia.

30 As an example, see Schultz, K. (1994) *Build Peace from the Ground Up: About People and the UN in a War Zone in Croatia*, Lund: TFF.

31 See, for instance, Schell, J. (2003) *The Unconquerable World: Power, Nonviolence and the Will of the People*, London: Penguin.

32 It should be noticed in passing that Serbia is the only republic in which the citizens made up the account with their own wartime leader.

33 See Hans von Sponeck and Jan Oberg, *A Road to Peace with Iraq – Europe's Choice* at: http://www.transnational.org/pressinf/2003/pf170_IraqEuropeChoice.html.

34 The author gave a guest lecture at the Beit al-Hakme (Friendship House) Institute in Baghdad only a few weeks before the war on nonviolent resistance, popular mobilization, peacemaking and that sort of thing. While the distinguished audience from research, politics, defence and culture listened with keen interest, the overwhelming message was to the effect that, 'while you are surely correct in pointing out the power of nonviolence in many other places and moments of history, it won't work in Iraq. We will fight any occupier with weapons to the last Iraqi.'

35 For a much more detailed account of the strong and weak aspects of the United Nations in former Yugoslavia, please see Johan Galtung, Jan Oberg and Håkan Wiberg, *Yugoslavia – What Could Have Been Done?* (forthcoming).

36 The author met with UN heads of all missions there in 2002 and 2003 and those of UNICEF, UNDP, UNECO and WFP made a lasting impression on him.

37 And UNMIK, together with the other organizations working with it, are unlikely to find a sustainable, fair, stable, democratic, human rights-respecting and peaceful solution for Kosovo. It simply will not happen. See the ten-article *Kosovo Solution Series* (Lund: TFF, 2005) and a collection of links at: http://www.transnational.org/forum/meet/2005/Forum_Coll_Kosovo.html – for a comprehensive argument in support of that conclusion.

38 See Jan Oberg, *Srebrenica Muslims Remembered, the Rest Silenced*, TFF PressInfo 222 of 11 July 2005 at: http://www.transnational.org/pressinf/2005/pi222_Srebrenica.html.

39 See Jan Oberg, *Do You Want to Know Who the Americans Running Iraq Really Are?*, TFF PressInfo 183 Part 1–3, May 2003 at: http://www.transnational.org/pressinf/2003/pf183_AmericansInIraq Part1.html.

Instead they were diplomats and business people surrounding Pentagon, came from the military-industrial complex, former US officers from missions in Bosnia and elsewhere, members of the Israeli lobby in Washington, etc. Very few, if any, spoke Arabic or had visited Iraq, and none of them were area experts – all according to the CVs and other information that could, at the time, be found about these roughly 30 individuals by thousands of searches on the Internet.

40 It is possible to see some parallels between Serb historical claims to Kosovo and Iraqi claims to Kuwait. There are ways the media have covered massacres that seem to have served to legitimate bombings and invasions such as Merkhale and the bread queue killings in Bosnia, the Racak massacre in Kosovo, Saddam's treatment of the Kurds and the use of chemical warfare means on Halabja. And it is easy to also see a parallel in the never-documented Belgrade plan to exterminate all Albanians or cleanse them out of Kosovo (Operation Horseshoe) and the media-manufactured 'news' that Saddam was amassing weapons and troops along the Iraqi–Saudi Arabian border.

41 A foremost example is writings and speeches by the EU Foreign Policy chief, Javier Solana, and even formulations in the proposal for an EU Treaty. Another is the entirely self-congratulatory description we find in Western circles even today about the situation in, say, Bosnia or Croatia.

6

Peace studies and peace politics

Multicultural common security in North–South conflict situations

Kinhide Mushakoji

Common security building in North–South situations

This chapter will deal with the specific type of situation that we call 'North–South situations'. It is based on the author's experience in trying to transcend conflicts between the citizens of the North and the migrant workers from the South in Japan. The citizens, including NGO activists in Japan, share a common prejudice about the migrants from the South. This prejudice is especially intense in the case of 'illegal' migrants and trafficked sex workers.

Under the media campaign which treats all foreigners as potential terrorists, Japanese citizens, even feminists concerned by gender inequality, believe that the foreign migrants are a potential danger to their security. They cannot imagine the seriousness of the sense of insecurity of the migrants who experience daily the suspicion of the police as well as of the neighbours, at home, at their workplace and at school. The belief prevailing in civil society that the migrant workers are a threat to the security of that society increases the state of insecurity of the migrants, and a 'security dilemma' follows. The more the citizens become suspicious, the more the migrants feel insecure and, the less they open their heart to the suspecting citizens.

This chapter deals with the need to build an awareness among the 'good' citizens of the reality of the present globalizing world, where a new kind of North–South relation becomes part of the daily reality of the civil societies. It is necessary to understand the asymmetrical situation which exists between the citizens protected by the State and its legal system and the migrant workers, especially the undocumented ones who are in the eyes of the State and civil society part of the criminal underworld.

It is crucial to build an awareness about the different aspects of this new North–South situation among the citizens so that they can understand the structural constraints causing the anxiety and insecurity of the migrants from the South in the North, and empathize with them. This approach has been developed in Japan and needs adaptation to the different concrete situations. We believe that the concepts used in this chapter can be applied *mutatis mutandis* in other industrialized societies as well as in the developing societies among the citizens of the 'North' sectors of the South, where the middle class lives in a relatively secure society more and more detached from the increasingly insecure situation of the South in the South.

The neo-liberal capitalism and the neo-conservative war

We live in a time when humankind faces a major crisis, the crisis of Western modernity. It is a global crisis in the sense that it engulfs the globe, also in that it covers all aspects of human life and of human civilization, political, military, economic, financial, cultural and social. It is a global crisis in that it is a crisis of globalization, of the globalization of Western modernity. We will attempt in this chapter an identification of the major characteristics of this crisis, in an historical context, which enables us to choose our paths in this global crisis, full of danger, yet full of opportunities.

The contemporary global crisis cannot be grasped unless the true nature of 'global finance' and 'global hegemony' are understood. First, 'global finance'. The contemporary neo-liberal version of capitalism subordinates production to financial speculation of a global free market, and turns the states into 'welcome states' loosing interest in the 'welfare state' model. (Mushakoji 2004: 23–5) Second, 'global hegemony'. The United States has built its neo-conservative hegemony, by using its absolute military-economic supremacy to unite the states into a global coalition to protect the security of the capital and of the global financial casino economy (Mushakoji 2004: 31–7).

The above considerations on 'global finance' and 'global hegemony' do not automatically lead us to understand the insecurity of the migrant workers and trafficked people from the South. The speculative nature of the global finance is believed to be natural by the media, and by many citizens, under the influence of the neo-liberal economic analysis as enacted by the IMF. The War on Terror initiated under 'global hegemony' can be supported and justified from the point of view of national or international security.

We have to raise the ideological and civilizational questions of the present globalization under the guidance of neo-liberalism and neo-conservatism, because the two ideological positions are systematically opposed to the fundamental values which underlie the human security benefited by the civil societies of the North. It is insufficient to 'democratize' the South if the North is unable to overcome its discriminatory culture against the migrants from the South.

The citizens of the North must realize that 'democratization' or 'modernization' is not an answer to all forms of insecurity, in spite of the claim by the media that democracy brings peace. We must build awareness of the fact that modernity at this phase cannot conceal the contradictions between the universalistic values it proclaims with the ideas of the greedy *homo economicus* and power thirsty *homo politicus* at the base of its national economy and its state order (Mushakoji 2004: 213–20).

Our guiding principle in this exercise will be a deliberate choice to look at the world, not from the point of view of the market and the state, but rather from the vantage point of the peoples, whose rights, security and development are put at risk by the actions, institutions and structures of the present global neo-liberal/neo-conservative order. Human rights, human security and human development, applied to the most vulnerable individuals, will provide us with a way to look at the global realities, different from the conventional views based on the states as the unit of analysis, and the universal values defined by Western civilization as the basis of our evaluation of a world order based on the two ideal types of human persons already mentioned.[1]

It is important to build awareness among the civil society agents of the fact that the choice to look at global realities from this point of view is based not only on moral principles. It is grounded on a belief that any efforts to transcend a conflict between the beneficiaries of this system and anybody who is excluded from it will have to be based on the Gandhian principle of 'antiodia'. That is, that unless the well-being of the smallest is taken into consideration, the whole society will not survive. The citizens of the North must be able to understand that if they want their rights, security and development to be sustainable, they have to take care of the rights, security and development of the most vulnerable peoples, e.g. the migrants from the South. The citizens must become capable to undertake, on their own, a critical analysis of the present globalization from the vantage point of those excluded from its security and from its benefits.

We need therefore to build, in any North–South situation, an epistemic community among the citizens, which sees that their community cannot have a sustainable future unless it cares for its most insecure members within the present neo-liberal and neo-conservative globalization. The citizens of the North must realize that they have to build 'common sustainability' between them and the insecure members of the society who migrated from the South if they want to build a sustainable world where they can live in peace.

The migrants from the South and global colonialism

Let us, therefore, look at the present state of globalization, not from the point of view of global finance or national security, but from the point of view of human (in)security, i.e. the freedom, or the lack of freedom, from fear and wants of peoples in most insecure situations. As we have seen, these situations can be defined in terms of two of the major causes of their fear, i.e. the neo-conservative War on/of Terror, and the reason of their want, the global neo-liberal economy.

Superficially, it seems that these two causes of their insecurity are unrelated, one military-political and the other economic. We must put the War on Terror and the global neo-liberal economy in a deeper historical context, from where they both emerge, in order to find that they are closely interlinked. This historical context is nothing but 'colonialism'.

The history of colonization of the non-Western world by the Western powers (and by Japan, which was an exceptional case of a non-Western colonial power) is characterized by an economic exploitation of the colonized societies by the colonial powers' rule backed by their military supremacy. This geo-historical age of colonial rule ended in the 1950s and 1960s, and the post-colonial age which followed was characterized by a new structure of exploitation, where the exploiters were the industrialized countries of the North, and the exploited were the developing countries of the South. This neo-colonialism was also combining an economic exploitation with a political/military subjugation. The combination of a global neo-liberal structure of exploitation with the military-political hegemony can be interpreted within the historical trajectory of colonialism and its most advanced phase, which we propose to call 'global colonialism' (Mushakoji 2004: 216–27).

Seen as a single phenomenon with two sides, an economic aspect characterized by neo-liberalism, and a military-political side characterized by the War on Terror, the present process of globalization can be seen as a final phase of the colonialism which began in the sixteenth century. Traditional colonialism and neo-colonialism exploited and extracted surplus, created by value-added industrial production and services, first from the colonies and later from the developing countries. Now that there is no more frontier left to colonize, global colonialism extracts surplus from the 'multitudes', the peoples who are not protected by the states like the citizens. Such people exist in the South of both the South and the North.

The clear divide between the South (provider of primary products) and the North (specialized in value-added industrial production) which existed during the neo-colonial period does not exist any more in the age of global colonialism. There is now an outpost of the North in the

South, where the cheap labour of the South is exploited by the North in its high-tech industrial production, including information technology (IT) and bio-technology. 'Ciberabad' in India and 'Ciberjaya' in Malaysia are typical examples of this emerging North in the South.

This outpost creates a new middle class, and a small ultra-rich minority, while leaving in abject poverty and insecurity the rural communities and the urban informal sectors in the 'deep South' where the large majority of the people live. In many urban centres of the North, there are expanding informal sectors where the diaspora communities of migrant workers from the South live in a chronic state of insecurity, as a result of the massive exploitative migration from the South, often undocumented and 'illegal' (Mushakoji 2004: 146–57).

This situation where a great number of people live unprotected by the state and overexploited by the transnational corporate agents, both in the South and in the North, is a typical manifestation of global colonialism. Traditional colonialism has been a system where states and civil societies of the Western colonial powers had established a contractual relationship, with the former monopolizing all means of violence in exchange for their commitment to protect the security and welfare of the latter. This contract between the states and the civil societies did not cover the multitude living in the colonies. The people living in the Deep South and in the informal diaspora communities in the North are in the same insecure situation of exploitation as the colonial multitude, in terms of the lack of state protection of their security and welfare. Global colonialism is nothing but this new form of exploitation of the global South by the global North.

It was extremely difficult for the expatriate colonial ruling class in the traditional colonial situations to understand the feeling of frustration and insecurity of the subjugated colonized peoples. In the same way, the citizens of the North constitute a majority insensitive to the human insecurity of the minorities. It is crucial for them to realize the high degree of insecurity of the diaspora communities, and become aware of the colonial relations which exist between the civil society and the diaspora communities.

The economic exploitation, the political subjugation and the psychological exclusion which turn the dwellers of these often impoverished sectors of big cities into an insecure community. They reproduce a frustrated identity feeling, which is often strengthened by the majority citizens joining in the colonialism of the global governance often taken for granted as sustainable. Yet it creates an environment making unsustainable the communities where different cultures are forced to live together, reproducing their exploitative relationships.

The War on/of Terror and the military/police security system

The 9/11 incident has become a pretext for George W. Bush to legitimize his neo-conservative hegemonic agenda. The neo-liberal global economy is promoting the worldwide application of free market economy, attributing a minimal role to governments. This minimal role, however, concerns the security of the state, the society and especially the market.

The role of the state in traditional liberalism has often been characterized by the concept of the 'night watchman' state. The agenda of the Bush administration, as expressed in the report on 'The National Security Strategy of the United States of America', limits the role of the American state to this security function. The United States promises to play the role of an invincible night watchman, with a worldwide deployment of military bases backed by weapons of mass destruction, for the global market, promoting free market principles, as well as freedom and democracy, against possible attacks from the 'terrorists' and the 'rogue states'.

This 'War on Terror' has transformed fundamentally the Westphalian world order, which has characterized Western modernity. This world order was based on the 'balance of power' between sovereign states, which were recognized as having an absolute right to guarantee the security of their citizens, domestically through their police force, and internationally through their military. The principle of non-interference in the domestic affairs of other states was combined with the principle of clear separation between domestic security controlled by the police, and international security maintained by the military, both under civilian control, and which was supposed to provide the institutional conditions indispensable for domestic and international democracy.

Now, the aforementioned report by the government of the US officially declares its non-compliance with these principles as it engages in the War on Terror. The right of this global hegemon to wage preemptive attacks on the rogue states, and the policy to merge military and police activities indicate the hegemonic decision to ignore the above basic rules of the game adopted by all the law-abiding members of the Westphalian inter-state order.

The new military strategy of the War on Terror has put an end to the modern separation between the military and the police, an arrangement which so far had helped avert a threat to democracy, a likely scenario when the military is permitted to intervene in civilian affairs. The military-police security is based on a systematic anti-human rights surveillance, control and punishment system where 'uncivilized' others, such as the prisoners in Guantanamo, are treated as objects of fear rather than of humane compassion. They are treated as evil people who do not deserve any elementary sense of justice.

The War on Terror is, in a sense, on the antipode of a state where human security prevails. The United Nations Human Security Commission Report points out this fact by criticizing this war in the following way:

> What is now being described as the 'war on terrorism' dominates national and international security debates. In addition to military actions, it has increased attention to other tools to fight terrorism, such as tracking (and blocking) flows of funds, information and people. It has given rise to new areas of international cooperation, such as sharing intelligence. Yet these actions focus on coercive, short-term strategies aimed at stopping attack by cutting off financial, political or military support and apprehending possible perpetrators.
>
> Equally, state-sponsored terrorism is not being addressed, while legitimate groups are being labeled as terrorist organizations to quash opposition to authoritarian government policies. And fighting terrorism is taking precedence over protecting human rights and promoting the rule of law and democratic governance. . . . [T]he 'war on terrorism' has stalled that progress (i.e. multilateral strategies that focus on the shared responsibility to protect people: insert mine) by focusing on short-term coercive responses rather than also addressing the underlying causes related to inequality, exclusion and marginalization, and oppression by states as well as people.

The War on Terror is, as the report on 'Human Security Now' denounces, not only refusing to address the root causes of the insecurity it is supposed to face, but is becoming in itself a major source of human insecurity. This is not because of any miscalculation by the hegemon. It is necessary to realize that it is because of the very historical nature of this 'war'. As the aforementioned report on the national security strategy of the hegemon so clearly states, the War on Terror is providing the ground for a special reading of history particular to the neo-conservative hegemon. The present situations, opened by the War on Terror, are defined as an unprecedented age of peace among nations, which have renounced waging wars between them for the first time in history. The War on Terror creates a situation where no more wars can be envisaged by any states of the world. They all joined in with the hegemon in combating terrorism.

The War on Terror is, in this sense, a Trotskyite revolution in reverse, a permanent counter-revolution uniting the states, the transnational corporations and the technocratic elites in their common fear of the multitudes. The war is not supposed to end in a victory, but rather to continue indefinitely, justifying the monopoly of economic and military power by the global hegemon.

The permanent counter-revolution is targeted especially against the dwellers of the informal sectors of the North. The 'illegal' migrants living in the impoverished sectors of the civil societies of the North are an object of constant fear. The security of the rich requires the surveillance of the poor, the security of the national majority requires the control of the foreign minorities. This is so, in different ways and different degrees, in the trilateral regions of the North, North America, Western Europe and Japan. The 'terrorists' provide an ideal scapegoat for the surveillance, control and punishment campaign against the 'others'. The global media produces and reproduces an image of the 'threats' of the migrants, especially harsh in the case of the migrant communities where Muslim peoples live.

It is crucial, if a multicultural community is to be built in a sustainable manner, to develop among the citizens and the administrators (national and local) an awareness of the insecurity experienced by the dwellers of the migrant communities, constantly under surveillance by the police. The 'good conscience' of the citizens, believing that they have the right to be protected by the police from the potential threats from the 'illegal' migrants, should be shaken down by an education for sustainable multicultural development disclosing the unsustainability of the permanent war on terror. The citizens must learn to understand that the insecurity of the migrants is increased by their search for security under the 'War on Terror' regime, and that they must build a relationship of 'common security' between 'us' the citizens and 'them' the foreign migrants.

Global fascism calling for a new contract of citizens and multitudes

We have seen already that the present combination of two sources of human insecurity, neo-liberal global economy and neo-conservative War on Terror, is a new form of colonialism. We will also argue that it is a global form of fascism, and that it should be combated by a new anti-fascist common front.

Just as traditional fascism of the 1920s and 1930s had established itself using the fear of a proletarian revolution and of Zionist hegemony among the middle classes, the new fascism exploits the fear of the multitude and Islamophobia propagated by the global media. We must eliminate the fear and the sense of insecurity of the citizens vis-à-vis the multitudes.

It is sad to realize that the two fascisms are closely linked by the conflict between Israel and Palestine. The fear of being accused of anti-semitism is forcing an important sector of world public opinion to accept Islamophobia. The recollection of the Holocaust by the fascist states does not permit public opinion to criticize state terrorism, as so well pointed out in the report on 'Human Security Now'.

The fear of a proletarian revolution has disappeared in most parts of the world, with the exception of the Philippines with its NPA, and Nepal with its militant Maoist movement. There is, however, a new target for the fear of the middle class in both the North and the South. It is the 'multitude', identified by Negri and Heart as an emerging sector of the empire, which can play a key role in destabilizing its global rule (Virno 2002).

The multitude is seen as represented by the terrorists, thanks to their indiscriminate violence that is manipulated by the War on Terror coalition of states and media. More generally, the 'illegal' migrant workers, and the transnational criminal organizations, which exploit them, are also sources of public fear. They bring into the global North different sources of human insecurity. They bring in drugs, trafficked sex workers supposed to bring in HIV-AIDS, and disturb the public order with their crimes.

Seen as a human security problem, the insecurity of the middle class is just a mirror image of the insecurity of the multitude, i.e. all the peoples, in North and South, unprotected by the states engaged in the War on Terror. To overcome the mutual insecurity, and the 'security dilemma' which causes a vicious circle between the mutual threat perception of civil societies and the multitudes, it is indispensable to build a 'common security' between both groups.

Global fascism not only denies the rights and security of the multitude, but also the rights and security of the citizens. It also denies recognition of the multilateral system guaranteeing the rights and security of the states. A new contract must be signed between the multitude and the citizens, and should be extended to the states. They do not want to stay mere 'welcome states' in the global colonial scene.

As proposed by Antonio Gramsci in the era of national fascism, we must develop an anti-fascist common front suited to the conditions of global fascism, as the Porto Alegre World Social Forum proclaims that 'another world is possible', in opposition to the hegemonic alliance represented by the Davos World Economic Forum, which excludes any alternative to neo-liberal global governance.

This common-front argument suits better the social activists and NGOs who specialize in advocacy about specific issues, such as ecology or landmines. The citizens engaged in these social movements in specific local communities must be convinced that their objectives cannot be reached unless they cooperate with the excluded minorities in building a sustainable multi-cultural community. They must realize that global fascism divides the citizens and the foreigners, as well as other minorities, in order to rule on both the majority and the minority communities.

To break this hegemonic cooption of the majority citizens, it is necessary to overcome the majority and minority divide which originates in the contract between the state and the civil society = the majority, excluding the multitude = the minorities. A new contract should be signed between the civil society = the majority and the multitude = the minorities. The common security between the civil society and the migrant communities can be contextualized within this new contract metaphor.

Global fascism invites the civil society to sign this new contract. As was, if well understood, the case in the past, the abuse of the fundamental rights of the foreigners and the minorities is just the beginning of a process where the rights of the majority will sooner or later become the target of restriction and violation. The lessons from past fascist regimes must be learned by the citizens as a preparation for a sustainable multicultural community. The citizens who are not participating in any social activities should be made to realize that even the 'illegal' migrants should be considered as part of 'us' when it comes to face a greater danger of losing freedom in an Orwellian world.

An epistemic community for sustainable multicultural development

If we want to transcend the North–South conflicts which begin to proliferate in the neo-liberal global world of today, it is necessary to build a new awareness among the civil societies of the North about the need to cut with the past and build a new rapport with the global South represented by the migrant workers, especially the 'illegal' migrants and the victims of human trafficking. Awareness of the need to build a common security with them needs to be supported by a good knowledge and understanding of global North–South relations. The nature and structure of globalized colonialism, of the military-police complex, and of global fascism must be well grasped, not only by the social movements but also by the civil society at large, otherwise it is difficult to overcome the prejudices produced in the educational system and reproduced by the press, and to make it possible for the 'good' citizens to empathize with the minorities, especially with the 'illegal' migrants.

It is difficult to imagine, in the face of the present reality where xenophobic reactions prevail in many parts of the civil societies in the North, that such a new awareness will emerge in the North. This is where we have to refer ourselves to the concept of 'epistemic community' coined in connection with the rapid spread of an ecological awareness reaching the governments, the corporate sectors and the international organizations. The concept of the epistemic community was proposed in the literature of international relations where the existing paradigms were unable to explain the international agreements by states, accepted by MNCs, about regulating state and corporate activities breaking the sustainability of development. The *homo politicus* and *homo economicus* models do not explain altruistic decisions implied in all the environmental legislation. National interests and the interests of the firm seem opposed to the demanded sacrifices. This is where the theory of epistemic community provides a plausible explanation.

The awareness-building activities of the ecologists, which continue since the 1970s, succeeded in forming a number of ecologically concerned citizens who entered into the different decision-making institutions, be it governments, business firms or international organizations. Their insistence on the necessity to build ecological sustainability influenced the different institutions they infiltrated, and this made it possible for the states, the firms and the international organizations to agree, in spite of their interests, to different measures to build a sustainable world. They created an epistemic community of citizens convinced of the crucial role of ecology, and this community is now represented in the different decision-making agents of the global community.

If the ecological sustainability of the world has become today a matter of global consensus thanks to the ecological epistemic community, it is possible also to form an epistemic community aware of the necessity of developing social sustainability by building a common security awareness between the citizens and the multitude, the majority and the minorities, and especially between the citizens of the North and the migrants from the South. This chapter is meant to begin a process of epistemic community building as a small but crucial beginning indispensable for a sustainable multicultural development of the citizens' communities in the North. This includes not only the North in the North but also the North in the South, where the rapid growth of a new middle class often makes invisible the insecurity of the peoples living in the South of the South.

Note

1 On 'human security', cf. Commission on Human Security (2003) *Human Security Now*, New York: United Nations.

References

Mushakoji, K. (2004) *Ningen-Anzennhoshou-Ron Josetsu: Global Faschism ni Koushite (Introduction to Human Security: In Face of Global Fascism)*, Tokyo: Kokusai Shoin, pp. 23–5.

Virno, P. (2002) *Grammaire de la multitude pour une analyse des formesde vie contemporaine* Paris: Editions de l'éclat.

7

Disarmament and survival

Marc Pilisuk

The importance of the quest for disarmament seems obvious. War is hell. While it is glorified in history, revered in memory as a moment of absolute life and death involvement and of camaraderie, and used as a rallying point by political leaders in calls for unity and sacrifice, the actual human consequences of armed conflict, and its aftermath, are devastating and growing worse. War has apparently caused more than three times the number of casualties in the last 90 years than in the previous 500. Upwards of 250 major wars have occurred in the post-Second World War era, taking over 50 million lives and leaving tens of millions homeless (Peace Pledge Union 2005). Rarely considered in the costs are the displaced refugees, mostly children and women, and the soldiers who return with enduring disability and traumatic disorders that diminish their lives and those of their families.

War is also expensive (Sivard 1996). The ability to make war and the extent of destruction in warfare depend upon the availability of weapons. Production levels of military weapons have reached record levels in the past five years, with worldwide sales and transfer agreements totaling 37 billion dollars in 2004. Though patterns in arms transfers have shifted since the Cold War era, weapon sales and distribution remain concentrated on developing nations (Shanker 2005). This extensive world market in weapons trade provides the means by which ethno-political wars are being fought (Greider 1998; Renner 1998). The best of resources that might otherwise improve life are consumed in war (Piven 2004). It is most frequently in the aftermath of such costly bloodletting that people, and their governing officials, take time to evaluate whether the weapons used have produced suffering that might well have been avoided and whether the actual presence of such weapons presents a threat of their being used again. Such time for reflection leads to several responses.

The hawkish response has been to suggest that an overwhelming superiority of weapons will deter all potential enemies, a suggestion clearly not borne out historically. There are also numerous examples in which disarmament referred to the maintaining of weapons by the winning side and the forced elimination of weapons in the conquered countries. Such imposed restrictions on the armed forces of defeated countries have a long history. In classical antiquity, the Romans tried to disarm Carthage, their long-standing rival. After military victories, Napoleon also dictated limits on the size of the Prussian and Austrian military. In the twentieth century, the peace settlement that ended the Second World War placed limits set by the victorious nations on the German army and navy. The intent was to prevent Germany's military from posing a serious offensive threat to its neighbours. At the end of the Second World War, both Germany and Japan were disarmed. Although more than 50 years have elapsed since the end of the Second World War, both countries still observe important limitations on their armed forces. Neither country has tried to reassert its independent status as a great power by developing nuclear weapons. The converse of enforced disarmament by countries with large and victorious military establishments can also be seen. Tsar Nicholas II of Russia, for example, called for the convening of the Hague Conference, in 1899, to prevent wealthier great powers from modernizing their armed forces (Maurer 2005; Towle 1997).

Controlling and limiting weapons

The more dovish alternatives that have been considered in the wake of violent conflicts include arms control and disarmament. The terms reflect a spectrum of alternatives from partial to complete elimination of weapons, from phased reductions to immediately enforced elimination of certain weapon categories, from unilateral to multilateral efforts, the latter often requiring tools for inspection and enforcement, and including the concept of global disarmament. The word *disarmament* is sometimes used interchangeably with *arms control*. Actually the two terms represent somewhat different concepts. Agreements among nation states to limit or even to reduce particular weapons occur in a pragmatic context. This context does not address directly the somewhat anarchic international environment in which autonomous nation states are assumed to compete for interests as defined by their governments. Military might is seen in this context as a tool to expand such interests and as a way of protecting against the aggression by other states. With the advent of highly destructive biochemical and nuclear weapons, the costs of waging war can grow to be incommensurate with any possible gains. Arms control does not aim to eliminate the competitive assumptions that drive nation states, or even to eliminate violent conflict. The objectives of arms control are better viewed as efforts to promote international stability and to reduce the likelihood of war. Other objectives are to reduce the costs of weaponry and the damage that follows once violent conflict occurs. Major states give consideration to arms control as part of their security policy. The US Congress, for example, established the Arms Control and Disarmament Agency (ACDA) in 1961 to provide a bureaucratic institution for dealing with arms control issues (Institute for Defense and Disarmament Studies 2005).

Examples of arms control date back to twelfth-century Europe. The church at that time strived to ban crossbows in warfare among Christians. This attempt at arms control was not successful and crossbows remained in widespread use throughout Europe. During the past century, arms control negotiations played a major role in international relations. After the First World War, the major naval powers of the world made a serious effort to negotiate the relative force levels among them. The Washington Conference (1921–2) and the London Conference (1930) succeeded for a time in limiting naval armaments. Efforts by the League of Nations to advance international disarmament culminated in the Geneva Conference (1932–4). There an attempt was made to distinguish between 'defensive' and 'offensive' weapons and then to eliminate the offensive ones. That is often a difficult distinction since perceptions of intention can play a major role in what psychologists have called the *attribution error*. Armaments of an opponent are typically viewed as an indication of aggressive intent, while one's own arms are seen as a defensive response to a situation presented by the behaviour of others. With the rise of German, Italian and Japanese imperialism during the 1930s, the Western liberal democracies felt threatened and this important effort at arms control came to an end (Maurer 2005).

There are more successful stories of the disarming of borders between neighbouring states. The Rush-Bagot Agreement (1817) led to the successful demilitarization of the border between Canada and the United States. This has served as an illustration of the way disarmament between modern democracies can be achieved. The European Union has taken important steps in this direction. Such agreements do not actually call for the participating nations to reduce their weapons or the size of their military. But they affirm a non-military and collaborative relationship among the parties (Institute for Defense and Disarmament Studies 2005).

The pursuit of disarmament

The goal of general disarmament is more far reaching and speaks to the need for a world in which competing states no longer have the responsibility to promote their own security in an international environment in which might makes right. The dream of disarmament envisions a world in which conflicts still occur but the rules for their resolution preclude the possible use of lethal weapons. It prescribes a world in which enforceable restrictions on the massing of armaments, and armed forces, are in place with a universal transparency and openness for early detection of violations. Disarmament calls for the support of institutions like the International Court of Justice that might be called upon to make binding judgements in disputes and for police functions available to monitor outbreaks of violence. In the present climate, most countries are unlikely to disarm voluntarily. In fact their leaders would consider such actions as suicidal as long as other nations did not also renounce war and armaments. Moreover, disarmament has a psychological or perhaps cultural component. It requires not only laws and institutions to make it happen but also a willingness of people to respect those laws and institutions as just and to consider the goal of pursuing peace by peaceful means to be a universal value on which the survival of life depends. Hence, disarmament is often considered a long-range goal that is associated with a fundamental reordering of the international political environment. That change aims inevitably at ending the law of the jungle among nations by establishing some form of world government or an effective system of collective security (Institute for Defense and Disarmament Studies 2005; Myrdal 1982).

The ideal of a world in which access to weapons of great destructive capability is banned, is often countered by the argument that weapons are needed to prevent a potential Adolph Hitler or otherwise obsessed national leader from dominating the world, that there will always be such deviant enemies, and that to disarm is to give an upper hand to those with evil intent. The responses to this are complex. The risks of disarmament may be greatly limited by strong and enforceable universal agreements. The willingness to undertake such risks makes sense only in comparison to the risks incurred by allowing the current and costly patchwork of efforts at security to grow worse as the number of parties with access to weapons of mass destruction increases. Moreover, the core reasons for violent conflict remain with the use of weapons to deter adversaries. To address these reasons, the world will need to deal with gross inequality and exploitation of people and of habitats. We will need to address the paucity of education into effective forms of nonviolent resolution of conflict, including tools to convert rather than to confront potential enemies, and the insufficient resources now left for those committed to building cultures of peace. When resources are instead devoted to preparing for war, we continue a caste of military and corporate professionals whose life work is to find enemies and to fight them.

One early example of disarmament occurred in Japan long before the twentieth century. For almost 200 years, beginning in the mid-1600s, the Japanese renounced and avoided the use of firearms for combat. During this entire period of self-imposed restriction, the sword remained the dominant weapon. The ban changed only in the middle of the nineteenth century after powerful outside powers threatened intervention in Japanese affairs. The end of Japan's isolation within the international political system also brought this experiment in disarmament to an end (Maurer 2005).

In the Western world, the origins of the idea of disarmament arose with the nineteenth-century development of liberal doctrines about international politics. Advocates of disarmament believed that wars occurred because of the competition among major powers in armaments. The outbreak of the First World War was precipitated by an assassination of one leader and was rapidly escalated by the involvement of heavily armed states. This appeared to confirm the explanation that major increases in armaments were fundamental factors in the conflict. In a frequently quoted statement, Sir Edward Grey, Great Britain's Foreign Secretary (1906–16), observed, 'The enormous growth of armaments in Europe, the sense of insecurity and fear caused by them – it was these that made war inevitable.' This theory of why violent conflicts occur had an implication for subsequent policy. Disarmament could provide a way to reduce international tension and to prevent war. In an attempt to promote a humane international order, US President Woodrow Wilson called for disarmament as part of his peace programme known as the Fourteen Points. The disarmament called for did not actually happen and the failure of other powers to disarm after the First World War was used as an excuse by the Hitler regime for rearmament of Germany in the 1930s (Hyde 1988; Institute for Defense and Disarmament Studies 2005).

Bans upon particular weapons

Efforts to ban particular types of weapons have had some measure of success. The horrible consequences of poison gas used in the First World War led to the acceptance of the Geneva Protocol in June 1925. Eventually 132 nations signed the Protocol. The Protocol bans the use of chemical and bacteriological weapons (UNIDC 2005). In January 1989, a conference was held in Paris to strengthen the Protocol. The United Nations had created a forum for discussion of disarmament-related issues. One product of its deliberations has been the Chemical Weapon Convention: 130 countries signed the original agreement in 1993 (OPCW 2005).

In August 1992, the International Conference on Disarmament's Ad Hoc Committee on Chemical Weapons completed an effort begun in March 1980 to draft a ban on chemical weapons (CW). It was submitted to the UN General Assembly and recommended the text of the Chemical Weapon Convention (CWC); 130 states signed the convention at a ceremony in January 1993. The time spent on this indicated the concern of the member states. The committee had worked on the draft since 1980 and the CWC finally went into force in April 1997. The Organization for the Prohibition of Chemical Weapons (OPCW), the treaty's implementing organization, came into operation one month later.

Under the treaty, each signatory nation agrees never 'to develop, produce, otherwise acquire, stockpile or retain chemical weapons'. It agrees, as well, not to use or prepare to use CW and not to assist others in acting against any of the prohibitions of the convention. The convention also requires states to destroy any CW in their possession, to destroy any of their own CW abandoned on the territory of another state, and to dismantle their CW production facilities (UNIDC 2005). One problem in restricting the use of chemical weapons is that the range of products produced is quite wide and most of the research and production activity is done secretly (Barnaby 1999).

Antipersonnel landmines are a particularly insidious source of death and disability that continue long after actual combat has ended. Soldiers are typically demobilized and will usually turn in their guns when peace returns. Landmines do not recognize a ceasefire. They cannot be aimed but lie dormant until a person or animal triggers the detonating mechanism. Then, landmines kill or injure civilians, soldiers, peacekeepers and aid workers alike. Children are particularly susceptible. Mine deaths and injuries over the past decades now total in the hundreds of thousands. Estimates of 15,000 and 20,000 new casualties are caused by landmines and unexploded ordnance each year, some 1,500 new casualties each month, more than 40 new casualties a day. The numbers are an underestimate since some countries with a mine problem such as Myanmar (Burma), India and Pakistan fail to provide public information about the extent of the problem (International Campaign to Ban Landmines 2005a).

As of September 2005, 154 countries have signed on to the 1997 Convention on the Prohibition of the Use, Stockpiling, Production and Transfer of Anti-Personnel Mines and on Their Destruction. Forty countries including Russia, China and the United States have not signed up. Some antipersonnel landmines are from earlier conflicts. They claim victims in many parts of the world. The situation, though improved in recent years, nevertheless constitutes a global crisis. Antipersonnel landmines are still being planted today and minefields dating back decades continue to claim innocent victims. Vast stockpiles of landmines remain in warehouses around the world and a handful of countries still produce the weapon (Human Rights Watch 2003; International Campaign to Ban Landmines 2005b).

The impact of nuclear weapons

The advent of atomic weapons during the Second World War gave further impetus to advocates of disarmament. Many prominent writers, intellectuals and policy activists supported efforts to 'ban the bomb', even if this entailed unilateral disarmament. Nuclear disarmament became for many a moral imperative for the stakes at risk seemed nothing less than the extinction of the human species. Films and television popularized an apocalyptic vision, helping to garner significant support for the disarmament movement.

The leaders of the superpowers gave considerable attention to arms control during the period of the Cold War. A relaxation of tensions in superpower relations, or détente, was widely viewed to coincide with arms control agreements, such as the conclusion of the first round of SALT (Strategic Arms Limitation Talks) in 1972, the INF (intermediate nuclear forces) agreement in 1987 and START (Strategic Arms Reduction Talks) in 1991. To many analysts of international relations, the superpower experience showed that arms control could play a useful (if modest) role in helping rival states to manage the uncertainty of their armaments competitions. Some advocates of disarmament, however, came to view arms control as a subterfuge employed by the leaders of the great powers to frustrate genuine disarmament. The Soviet Union sometimes abetted disarmament as a way of causing domestic political embarrassment for the governments of its principal adversaries, the United States and other countries in NATO. However, both superpowers could well be accused of having used the nuclear threat as a way to make the world safe for wars of domination that used only threats, economic pressures, political assassinations and conventional weapons in efforts to create allies in a polarized world (Institute for Defense and Disarmament Studies 2005; UNIDC 2005).

Nuclear weapons add a new dimension to discussions of disarmament. Their level of potential destructiveness far outweighs any gain from their use. A major exchange of nuclear weapons would so totally destroy places and people and so contaminate the earth's capacity to provide uncontaminated food and water as to leave the planet unsuited to support life. The weapons have been typically considered a requirement for deterring an attack from other countries. The argument has critical flaws. If the deterrent failed to deter, would a sane government choose to retaliate. To do so would likely create even greater destruction to one's own country. Would an aggressive enemy not be tempted then to consider the threat to retaliate to be merely a bluff? The country with the deterrent would need to convince its adversaries that the nuclear counter-attack would come. This can be done by preparing retaliatory capacities that will be immediate, automatic and incapable of retraction. The retaliatory promise is also augmented by a bellicose posture and a depiction of the enemy as hostile, evil and committed to one's own destruction. When such hostile images are communicated they affect not only an adversar's belief that an attack would be foolhardy, but also the belief that the deterring nation is indeed sufficiently hostile to start a war. If only an irrational and deeply disturbed individual would launch an annihilating attack, how would threats of retaliation act as a deterrent? Angry and deranged individuals are far more likely to strike out, without fear of consequences, if they feel threatened. The dynamic is what game theorists have likened to the game of *chicken*, in which the drivers of opposing vehicles speed toward each other threatening not to be the first to veer off the white line (Rapoport 1960, 1965). It is not played by sane people who honour life. The degree to which actual policies mimic this game can only reflect a deep pathology of a system preparing for war but not for peace.

After the Cold War

The end of the Cold War has not dampened interest in disarmament and arms control. In the liberal democracies, organizations promoting disarmament retain some clout in the domestic political arena. A current view holds that modern liberal democracies can achieve effective disarmament among themselves because they seem less prone to make war on one another. The spread of democracy then conceivably advances the cause of disarmament (Maurer 2005). The US government has been the primary advocate of the theory that democracies are, at least, not sources of aggression. However, its own record has been one of military support for either democracies or dictatorial police states depending only upon the favourability of their policies to corporate economic interests in the US (Chomsky 2004; Pilisuk and Zassi 2006).

In the aftermath of the Cold War, attempts to limit the geographical spread of nuclear weapons and ballistic missiles, and to eliminate the use of chemical and biological agents as weapons of mass destruction, have also emerged as important policy concerns. Paradoxically, disarmament has even been used as a justification for resorting to war. The coalition that fought Iraq in 1991, for instance, aimed not only at restoring Kuwait as an independent sovereign state, but also at eliminating Iraq's ability to manufacture and use nuclear, chemical and biological weapons. The prospect for a major war in northeast Asia, brought about by North Korea's desire to build a nuclear arsenal, and the determination of the US and South Korea to prevent this development, is also part of an attempt to further international disarmament on a selective basis. The establishment of a neo-liberal world order could therefore entail the paradox of fighting wars for the sake of disarmament. Hence the plea of disarmament advocates – namely, that weapons themselves cause war – might come to have a new, more ominous meaning. Arms and their use might be justified as instruments for disarming other countries by attacking them (Maurer 2005).

The world owes much to the United Nations for whatever progress toward disarmament has occurred. UN responsibility falls upon the First Committee of the UN General Assembly (a committee of the whole), which is responsible for disarmament and security matters. All 191 Member states are included and literally hundreds of matters are discussed. The UN Disarmament Commission meets in New York once or twice a year to help refine the agenda proposed by the First Committee for the talks in the Conference on Disarmament. Resolutions are passed by a majority vote or by a two-thirds majority if deemed important issues (United Nations Department for Affairs Disarmament 1988).

The more specialized UN Conference on Disarmament (CD), currently with 66 members, meets in Geneva to produce multilateral agreements. It is the only group given authority to negotiate actual treaties. This group sets its own agenda, taking into account recommendations from the UN General Assembly (UNGA), and it submits reports at least annually to the General Assembly. Its work has been slow, reflecting wide differences among members on what should be discussed. The dividing issue frequently is linkage. Some nations will refuse to participate in discussions limiting one type of weapon or the weapons in one particular area unless weapons threats from other sources are also up for consideration. For example, the US might wish to mobilize international support for disarming what it considers 'rogue states' while others will only agree to such discussion if they include attention to the weapons within the US that threaten other nations. The US opposed any negotiating mandate on general nuclear disarmament while China, at the same time, opposed negotiating a fissile material cut-off treaty in the absence of negotiations on general nuclear disarmament. Egypt has urged Arab states not to sign the Chemical Weapons Treaty until Israel signs the Nuclear Proliferation treaty (INIDC 2005; United Nations 1996; Department for United Nations Disarmament Affairs 1988).

The UN disarmament agenda in 2005 had the following priorities: cessation of the nuclear arms race and nuclear disarmament, prevention of nuclear war (including all related matters), prevention of an arms race in outer space, effective international arrangements to assure non-nuclear weapon states that they would be protected against the use or threat of use of nuclear weapons (negative security assurances), new types of weapons of mass destruction and new systems of such weapons, radiological weapons, comprehensive programme of disarmament, transparency in armaments, and landmines (UNIDC 2005). While talks provide more basis for hope than belligerent unilateral proclamations, little significant progress was achieved on any of the items. To understand why, it is important to place the issue of disarmament in a larger economic, political and psychosocial context.

Profits from weapons

Arms make money. Small weapon transfers, for example, are a business in which independent entrepreneurs are often involved. Arms brokers have engaged in disturbing weapons transfers to highly abusive armed groups and to countries that are under UN arms embargoes. One well-known arms broker, Victor Bout, has been implicated in violating or contributing to violating UN arms embargoes in Sierra Leone, Angola, Liberia and the Democratic Republic of Congo. The armed groups wreak havoc on innocent civilians. Yet, many arms brokers, including Bout, remain free and continue to traffic arms to human rights abusers outside of the purview of international regulations. In one example, arms brokers were reported to have shipped 3,117 surplus assault rifles from Nicaragua to Panama. The weapons were diverted to Colombia's paramilitary Autodefensas Unidas de Colombia (AUC). At the time, the AUC was accused of killing thousands of civilians and was on the US Department of State list of terrorist organizations (Institute for Defense and Disarmament Studies 2005).

There have been US and international efforts to stem such arms transfers. The US government adopted a law on arms brokering in 1996. The law covers a wide range of activities, including transporting and financing. It requires arms brokers both to register and to apply for a license for each activity. The US used this law to prosecute a British citizen for attempting to sell shoulder-fired missiles in the United States to a group intending to use the missiles to shoot down a commercial airliner. Many governments, however, have no law, or only very weak law, on arms brokering. For example, Irish law does not restrict brokers who arrange weapons supplies from foreign countries. Hence Ireland was unable to prosecute an arms broker that was reportedly involved in 2004 in efforts to supply 50 T72 tanks from Ukraine to the Sudanese military. In January 2004, the EU strengthened its arms embargo on Sudan out of concern for its ongoing civil war. The US law cannot be fully effective until similar laws are adopted and enforced by other governments. Since the adoption of the law, the US has only prosecuted five individuals. Because small arms transfers are quite important in abuses of human rights, Amnesty International has called for an international agreement to prevent arms brokering activity, such as transfers to governments and groups with consistent records of gross human rights violations (Institute for Defense and Disarmament Studies 2005; Multilateral Arms Regulation and Disarmament Agreements 2005).

Weapons of mass destruction

Most of what is happening in the development of weapons of mass destruction has been occurring with little public awareness. With the Cold War long past, one might have expected that the US would be a leader in the effort to fulfill its 30-year-old promise, embodied in Article VI of The Nuclear Non-proliferation Treaty, 'to pursue negotiations in good faith on effective measures relating to cessation of the nuclear arms race at an early date and to nuclear disarmament'. There has been a dramatic change in the last decade regarding the words used to describe US nuclear and missile development programmes. But the content of these programmes speaks to escalation in the efforts to produce new, high-technology weapons (see Kreiger, this volume).

The Department of Energy's nuclear weapons research facilities at Livermore, Los Alamos and Sandia (now partnered with the Bechtel Corporation) have long been the advocates and the producers of new nuclear weapons. They each play a major role in the research needed to enter this new era of military expansion. Among such projects, the National Ignition Facility, which will house a laser 40 times more powerful than any yet in existence, will have many nuclear weapon applications. Space-based laser weapons are viewed as a means to destroy chemical or biological weapons that might be lodged against the US.

Whether such threats are real, whether they might be better prevented by establishing peaceful economic and social relations with other countries, whether the costs are worth the dubious feasibility of the efforts are matters that should concern us. Surely they will lead to greater proliferation of nuclear weapons and surely they will interfere with international hopes for the US to ratify the Comprehensive Test Ban Treaty. What is clear is that the US is not living up to its promise to reduce nuclear weapons capabilities. The ballistic defence system will make progress toward the elimination of nuclear arsenals impossible and is part of a plan that provides for indefinite continuation of nuclear weapons testing and development.

The costs of such activity in the past have been great. The activity has produced severe consequences to human health and to the environment (Bertell 2004; Boly 1989, 1990). Weapons produced have created incentives for other countries to develop their arsenals.

Espionage activities have been aimed at the US. Secrecy has led to the cover-up of dangerous activities. And the diversion of public funds from needed programmes in health, education, housing and renewable energy development has been a part of our history. Even funds for peacekeeping activities that might provide greater security have suffered. Now, in the period after the end of the Cold War, when the US has no credible military adversaries, the tragedy is that the opportunity to end preparedness for nuclear war will be lost. To understand how such policy comes into being it is important to note that the weapons laboratories operate in relative secrecy. They employ bright scientists and provide them with unparalleled support and facilities. They provide lucrative contracts to defence industries, which in turn provide extensive consultation to government. Behind closed doors, weapons are conceived, justified, funded and developed (Pilisuk 1999).

The US and disarmament

Nation states in general are poorly designed for the responsibilities of disarmament. They sometimes operate in the old model as vehicles for the expansion of the interests of rulers. More recently, many exist as the vassals for large corporate interests (Johnson 2004; Korten 1998; Pilisuk 2001), but even those professing to do what is best for their own citizens find the lure of weapons to be great and are cautious about agreements that might weaken military forces or weapons. True progress toward disarmament will likely require the development of some form of world government with the policing authority to limit weapons and the moral authority to require mediated or judicial resolution of disputes. The role of the US as the remaining superpower is particularly important to progress in moving toward disarmament and the record is not promising.

After two world wars, the nations of Europe were ready to forgo the weapons and policies that had created such devastation. The animosity of governments in capitalist economies to the communist experiment in the Soviet Union remained, but primarily as a battle to prevent the colonized world from developing socialist governments and controlling their own resources. The US, as the first atomic power, assumed this role of containment primarily through military superiority. Efforts by Stalin, and later by Khrushchev, to offer the unification of Germany in exchange for substantial mutual reductions and controls in armaments were dismissed (Potyarkin and Kortunov 1986) and the US has won the competition to become the most heavily armed state. It is the US, then, that will have to modify its policies if movement toward disarmament is to occur (Chomsky 2004).

Between the Second World War and the end of the last century, the US led 73 military interventions throughout the world, almost double the total from the preceding 55-year period (Grossman 1999). If we include all covert operations in which casualties occurred, the figure rises to 196 (Ferraro 2005). The Pentagon has an ever-expanding empire of over 6,000 domestic bases, and 725 overseas. The US $455 billion military expenditure in 2004 was larger than the combined amount the 32 next-most-powerful nations spent on their militaries (Anderson 2005).

United States policy has often been guided by an assumption that interests defined by the US take precedence over international agreements. This has occurred first in matters that might constrain US military activities. In August 2001, the US withdrew from a major arms control accord, the 1972 Antiballistic Missile Treaty. In July 2001, the US walked out of a conference to discuss adding on-site inspectors to strengthen the 1972 Biological and Toxic Weapons Convention, which was ratified by 144 nations, including the US (DuBoff 2001). Meanwhile,

US preparations to use chemical and biological weapons at Fort Dietrich and other sites have been extensive (Barnaby 1999). The US was the only nation to oppose the UN Agreement to Curb the International Flow of Illicit Small Arms. The Land Mine Treaty (banning mines) was signed in 1997 by 122 nations but the US refused to sign, along with Russia, China, India, Pakistan, Iran, Iraq, Vietnam, Egypt and Turkey. Clinton's promise that the US would 'eventually' comply in 2006 was disavowed by President George W. Bush. In February 2001, the US refused to join 123 nations pledged to ban the use and production of antipersonnel bombs (DuBoff 2001).

Preparedness for war has been costly

The US spent $10.5 trillion on the military during the Cold War (Markusen and Yukden 1992). The nuclear powers of that time spent an estimated $8 trillion on their nuclear weapons (Sivard 1996). If current annual US expenditures for such weapons were instead invested in global life-saving measures, the result could have covered *all* of the following – the elimination of starvation and malnutrition, basic shelter for every family, universal health care, the control of AIDS, relief for displaced refugees and the removal of landmines (Gobel 1997). The US is pouring more than a billion dollars a week into the Iraq war that could otherwise be spent on health care, schools and infrastructure at home. One might think this would raise the demand for a conversion from weapons spending in the direction of disarmament. However, the dollars are not evaporated. They go largely to contractors, specialized in the production not only of weapons but in the marketing of strategies in which such weapons appear to be needed and the support of officials sharing their views.

US plans for the future are no more promising than the record of the past. These involve nuclear weapons and their use in outer space (see Kreiger, this volume). The National Missile Defense proposal (previously referred to as 'Star Wars') poses the greatest threat to the erosion of existing arms control agreements. In preparation for the transition to the use of space for warfare, the Air Force science and technology community has doubled its commitments in 'space only' technologies from 13 per cent in FY 1999 to 32 per cent in FY 2005. This activity jeopardizes the modest stability afforded by the ABM Treaty. Yet major lobbies for the defence industries, like the Missile Defense Advocacy Alliance, provide constant pressure for continued development of space weapons. According to a scientific panel assembled by the National Resources Defense Council, the Bush team assumes that nuclear weapons will be part of US military forces at least for the next 50 years; it plans an extensive and expensive series of programmes to modernize the existing force, including a new ICBM to be operational in 2020 and a new heavy bomber in 2040. In addition, the US administration has ordered the Pentagon to draft contingency plans for the use of nuclear weapons against at least seven countries, naming not only the 'axis of evil' (Iraq, Iran and North Korea) but also Russia, China, Libya and Syria. The Pentagon in addition has launched programmes for research and testing of a missile defence system. While technically dubious, the large programme has been viewed by other nations with alarm as a signal that the US is working toward being able to attack other nations with the security that it could intercept missiles sent in retaliation. Such planning has the obvious consequence of provoking other nations to develop their own arsenals, a process already taking place. Russia and China have responded with plans for new or updated development for nuclear weapons. Without enforceable controls nuclear weapons technology is spreading (Roche 2002).

Disarmament is more than a set of formal agreements. It is also a commitment to a worldview that differs from the dominant view in developed countries. If one envisions the world as a place in which mutual cooperation can provide more of what is important to all parties than violent conflict, then the possibilities for disarmament become more promising. The reliance upon weapons to provide security has been outmoded by technology. It is clear to psychologists that the threatened use of force more typically begets retaliatory force. Retribution continues a cycle of animosity and violence. Conversely, a proposal for graduated reciprocation in tension reduction (GRIT) suggests that a series of small unilateral moves toward conciliation, announced in advance, are likely to be gradually reciprocated and move the adversaries to more trustful and less threatening relations (Osgood 1962). A period of thaw in the Cold War included a speech in 1961 by President Kennedy calling for a reappraisal of the Cold War, for new modes of cooperation and suspending nuclear weapons tests in the atmosphere. The USSR broadcast the Kennedy speech intact and premier Khrushchev responded with a conciliatory speech. The USSR stopped production of strategic bombers and removed objections to the presence of UN observers in Yemen. The US then removed objections to restoration of the full recognition of the Hungarian delegation to the United Nations. A limited nuclear weapons test ban was signed. The Soviet Foreign Minister, Gromyko, called for a non-aggression treaty between NATO and the Warsaw Pact. Kennedy called for joint efforts to 'explore the stars together'. Direct flights were scheduled between Moscow and New York. The US agreed to the sale of wheat to the USSR. Gromyko called for a pact outlawing nuclear weapons in outer space. Kennedy responded favourably and an agreement was reached on the exchange of captured spies (Etzioni 1967). Studies in the laboratory provide confirming evidence that humans in conflict situations can use the GRIT strategy to reduce the distrust that keeps them armed and start a process toward mutually beneficial disarmament (Pilisuk 1984; Pilisuk and Skolnick 1968). To appreciate why such a conciliatory strategy is not more actively pursued, it is important to examine the stakes of powerful decision-makers. The perceived short-term benefits to certain beneficiaries of war often dominate the policy process. The small group of persons obsessed with weapons development and with military support for corporate expansion is unduly influencing a dangerous direction for American policy (Pilisuk 1999; Pilisuk and Zazzi 2006). It is a policy that blurs the lines of reality between video game dueling and the actual domination of space by lethal weapons. The public has not been told this story and has surely not been asked if this should be the national direction. The survival of the planet will require progress toward disarmament. Public demand for, and involvement in, a culture of peace appears necessary if leaders are to respond to the challenge.

References

Anderson, G. (2005) 'US defense budget will equal rest of world's combined within 12 months', *Janei Defense Industry*, 4 May.

Barnaby, W. (1999) *The Plague Makers: The Secret World of Biological Warfare*, London: Vision.

Bertell, R. (2004) 'Health and environmental costs of militarism', presented in Barcelona, 24 June.

Boly, W. (1989) 'Behind the nuclear curtain', *Public Citizen*, 9, 1: 12–16.

Boly, W. (1990) 'Downwind', *In Health*, July/August: 58–69.

Chomsky, N. (2004) *Hegemony or Survival: America's Quest for Global Dominance*, New York: Holt and Co.

Etzioni, A. (1967) 'The Kennedy experiment', *Western Political Quarterly*, 20: 361–80.

Ferraro, K. J. (2005) 'The culture of social problems: observations of the Third Reich, the Cold War, and Vietnam', *Social Problems*, 52, 1: 1–14.

Gabel, M. (1997) *What the World Wants and How to Pay for it*, Philadelphia, PA: World Game Institute.

Greider, W. (1998) *Fortress America: The American Military and the Consequences of Peace*, New York: Public Affairs.

Grossman, Z. (1999) 'Over a century of US military intervention', at: http://www.redrat.net/thoughts/criminal-behavior/interventions.
Human Rights Watch (2003) *Landmine Monitor Report: August 2003*, at: http://www.icbl.org/lm/2003/.
Hyde, H.A. (1988) *Scraps of Paper: The Disarmament Treaties between the World Wars*, 1st ed, Lincoln, NE: Media Publishers.
Institute for Defense and Disarmament Studies (2005) at: html http://www.idds.org/.
International Campaign to Ban Landmines (2005a) http://www.icbl.org/treaty.
International Campaign to Ban Landmines (2005b) http://www.icbl.org/problem/what.
Johnson, C. (2004) *The Sorrows of Empire: Militarism, Secrecy, and the End of the Republic*, New York: Metropolitan Books.
Korten, D.C. (1998) *Globalizing Civil Society*, New York: Seven Stories Press.
Landmine Monitor Report (2003) *Toward a Mine-free World*, International Committee to Ban Landmines, at: http://www.icbl.org/lm/2003/findings.html.
Markusen, A. and Yukden, J. (1992) *Dismantling the War Economy*, New York: Basic Books.
Marrow, A.J. (1977) *The Practical Theorist: The Life and Work of Kurt Lewin*, New York: Teachers College Press.
Multilateral Arms Regulation and Disarmament Agreements (2005) http://disarmament.un.org/TreatyStatus.nsf.
Myrdal, A.R. (1982) *The Game of Disarmament: How the United States and Russia Run the Arms Race*, New York: Pantheon Books.
OPCW (2005) 'Chemical weapons', at: http://www.opcw.org/.
Osgood, C. (1962) *An Alternative to War or Surrender*. Urbana: University of Illinois Press.
Peace Pledge Union (2005) *War and Peace: What's it all About?*, at: http://www.ppu.org.uk/war/war_peace-modernwar.html retrieved 11/20/05
Pilisuk, M. (1984) 'Experimenting with the arms race', *Journal of Conflict Resolution*, 28, 2: 296–315.
Pilisuk, M. (1999) 'Addictive rewards in nuclear weapons development', *Peace Review*, 11, 4: 597–602.
Pilisuk, M. (2001) 'Globalism and structural violence', in D. Christie, R. Wagner and D. Winter (eds) *Peace, Conflict, and Violence: Peace Psychology for the 21st Century*. Englewood, NJ: Prentice Hall, 149–160.
Pilisuk, M. and Skolnick, P. (1968) 'Inducing trust: a test of the Osgood proposal', *Journal of Personality and Social Psychology*, 8, 2: 121–133.
Pilisuk, M. and Joanne Zazzi, J. (2006) 'Toward a psychosocial theory of military and economic violence in the era of globalization', *Journal of Social Issues*, 62, 1: 41–62.
Piven, F.F. (2004) *The War at Home: The Domestic Costs of Bush's Militarism*, New York: New Press.
Potyarkin, Y.E. and Kortunov, S. (1986) *The USSR Proposes Disarmament, 1920s–1980s* (translated from the Russian), Moscow: Progress Publishers.
Rapoport, A. (1960) *Fights, Games and Debates*, Ann Arbor: University of Michigan Press.
Rapoport, A. (1965) 'Chicken a la Kahn', *Virginia Quarterly Review*, 41: 370–89.
Renner, M. (1998). 'Curbing the proliferation of small arms', in L. R. Brown, C. Flavin and H. French (eds) *State of the World 1998*, New York: Norton, 131–48.
Roche, D. (2002) 'Rethink the unthinkable', *Globe and Mail*, 12 March, p. A19.
Shanker, T. (2005) 'Weapons sales worldwide rise to highest level since 2000', *New York Times*, at: http://www.nytimes.com/2005/08/30/politics/30weapons.html.
Sivard, L. (1996) *World Military and Social Expenditures*, Washington, DC: World Priorities.
Towle, P. (1997) *Enforced Disarmament: From the Napoleonic Campaigns to the Gulf War*, Oxford: Clarendon Press; New York: Oxford University Press.
United Nations (1996) *The United Nations and Disarmament since 1945*, New York: Pantheon Books.
United Nations Department for Disarmament Affairs (1988) *The United Nations and Disarmament: A Short History*, New York : United Nations Department for Disarmament Affairs.
UNIDC (2005) United Nations Institute for Disarmament Research, Geneva, Switzerland, at: http://disarmament.un.org/TreatyStatus.nsf.

8

Nuclear disarmament

David Krieger

The effort to achieve nuclear disarmament cannot be understood without providing an historical perspective going back to the pre-nuclear Age, at least to the formative years of the late 1930s. The US initiative to develop nuclear weapons emerged from the tensions in Europe that would lead to the Second World War, mainly from concerns about the potential of the Nazi-controlled German government to harness the power of the atom for destructive purposes.

The origins of the US nuclear weapons programme centre on two scientific giants, both émigrés to the US from Nazi-threatened Europe: Leo Szilard, a brilliant Hungarian physicist and his famous friend, Albert Einstein. Fearing that the Germans were capable of developing an atomic bomb – and hoping that Einstein's advice would be heeded – Szilard urged Einstein to warn the US president of this potential danger. Einstein's subsequent letter to President Roosevelt expressing this fear, dated 2 August 1939, led to the establishment of the Advisory Committee on Uranium, which first met on 31 October 1939 (Atomic Archive 2006a). This committee was eventually replaced in December 1941 by the Manhattan Engineering Project, a US programme to develop an atomic bomb. While the Germans did not succeed in developing atomic weapons, the US programme led the world into the Nuclear Age, with its dire threats to all humanity (Bird and Sherwin 2005).

By July 1945, two months after the defeat of the Nazis in Europe, the US had succeeded in creating the world's first nuclear device, which it tested at Alamogordo, New Mexico. Just three weeks later, the US dropped an atomic bomb on the Japanese city of Hiroshima, destroying it; and then three days later, a second atomic weapon was dropped, destroying the city of Nagasaki.

In a world in which the US was the only nuclear power, the US did not hesitate to attack population centres of an enemy that was already largely defeated and seeking to surrender. This use of nuclear weapons was a major turning away from the aspirations of the scientists who created the world's first nuclear weapons, who had been motivated by a determination to deter a potential German atomic weapon. To forestall the possibility that innocent civilians would be victims of this terrible destructive device, some of the scientists, led by Leo Szilard, tried futilely to convince US political leaders to demonstrate the power of the weapon by dropping an atomic bomb on uninhabited territory rather than use the bombs on cities (Lanouette and Silard 1994).

But once the US weapons were built and ready to use, the decisions about their use were out of the hands of the scientists. It was the politicians who had the ultimate power of decision, and they chose to use the new weapons on Japanese cities. While the scientists had succeeded technologically in creating atomic weapons, they failed in the political realm because they were unable to persuade top political and military leaders to desist from using their weapons. Once the nuclear genie was unloosed, the battle for nuclear disarmament would be one that would have to be fought in the corridors of power. It is a battle that is still being fought, and its outcome may determine the future of humankind and other forms of life on earth.

The Nuclear Age

The radical change that came with the initiation of the Nuclear Age was that humankind had created the means of its own destruction. Human societies had always made war against other societies, but the Nuclear Age opened the door to the destruction of the entire human species by tools of its own invention. The explosion of the first atomic device in the desert of New Mexico on 16 July 1945 brought us into a new era, and the dropping of these frightful weapons on the cities of Hiroshima and Nagasaki alerted the world to a sobering existential crisis. Some six months later, on 24 January 1946, the first resolution of the newly formed United Nations created an Atomic Energy Commission and called for the 'elimination from national armaments of atomic weapons and all other major weapons adaptable to mass destruction' (United Nations General Assembly 1946). But its original intent would over time unravel, as the world's superpowers and other players in the world community sought to advance their own perceived national interests. This struggle became one of the major themes of the second half of the twentieth century, and continues unabated in the twenty-first century.

When the US succeeded in developing nuclear weapons, its political leaders believed incorrectly that the country would be able to indefinitely hold this power unchallenged. In June 1946, the US government put forward what became known as the Baruch Plan to place nuclear weapons under international control. But it would do so only after the Soviet Union, its wartime ally, submitted to inspections to assure that it was not pursuing the development of nuclear weapons (Atomic Archive 2006b).[1] The US was willing to disarm its nascent nuclear arsenal after the Soviet Union demonstrated its willingness to give up its nuclear weapons potential. The Soviet Union countered by offering to submit to inspections after the US disarmed its nuclear arsenal. Neither side trusted the other enough to make the first move. As a result, and as some of the original nuclear scientists in the US nuclear weapons programme, including J. Robert Oppenheimer and Leo Szilard, had predicted, the Soviet Union was able to become a nuclear weapons state in a relatively short period. In just four years, the Soviet Union tested its first nuclear weapon and became the world's second nuclear power.[2]

Over the next four decades the US and USSR communicated to each other by means of nuclear tests, always on the lands of indigenous peoples. These tests, in effect, said to each other and to the world, 'See how powerful I am and what havoc and destruction I can rain down upon you.' The era of Cold War nuclear posturing and threats from 1946 to 1991 was one in which both the US and USSR developed ever more powerful nuclear weapons, including weapons that were thousands of times more powerful than the weapons that destroyed Hiroshima and Nagasaki. At the same time, each side developed ever more sophisticated delivery systems for their weapons, including missile systems capable of bringing ruin to the other side from across the earth in approximately 30 minutes of the order to launch. Doctrines of first use and launch on warning continue to place civilization and humankind at the razor's edge of annihilation.

Despite the end of the Cold War, the residue of this madness remains embedded in the nuclear policies of the US and Russia as the successor state to the Soviet Union. Even today, with arsenals reduced in size from Cold War highs, the two dominant nuclear weapons states maintain nuclear arsenals approximating or exceeding 10,000 weapons each, with some 2,000 of these weapons on each side poised on hair-trigger alert. The Cold War may have ended, but nuclear dangers persist and have taken on new forms with the increasing threats and acts of terrorism aimed at both states.

The defects of deterrence

The dominant strategic thinking of the Cold War was based on the theory of deterrence, a theory in which each side threatened the other with massive retaliation should it or its allies be attacked by the other side. Deterrence theory relies heavily on the alleged rationality of the key decision-makers, since it would be irrational for any leader to attack an opponent that was capable of annihilating it in retaliation. But if we know anything about human behaviour, it is that humans do not always act rationally and the possibilities for irrational behaviour increase in times of stress and crisis. Each side must believe that the other is committed to unleashing massive retaliation in the event of an attack, a policy that itself may be viewed as irrational.

Over the years of the Cold War, there were many near failures of deterrence, the most prominent being the Cuban Missile Crisis of 13 tense days in October 1962 when the US and USSR stood on the cusp of nuclear war over the Soviet placement of nuclear weapons in Cuba (Kaku and Axelrod 1986; Kennedy 1999). When decision-makers from the US, Russia and Cuba met years later in conference to dissect the crisis, each side found that they were acting on limited, even false, information about the situation. Nuclear war was averted more by good fortune and the grace of God than by the rationality of the decision-makers (Allison and Zelikow 1999; Scott and Smith 1994).

In the early 1950s controversy broke out in the United States over whether or not to build thermonuclear weapons, capable of generating explosive power more than a thousand times greater than the bombs that destroyed Hiroshima and Nagasaki. J. Robert Oppenheimer, the scientific director of the Manhattan Project, opposed this leap to far more powerful nuclear weapons. The strongest booster of these weapons, sometimes called 'the super', was scientist Edward Teller. In the end, those who wanted these earth-shattering weapons prevailed, and the US went forward with their production, followed soon by the Soviet Union. It was a great and treacherous leap forward in the nuclear arms race.

The dangers of the Nuclear Age have always brought forth calls for moderation and control, and by the late 1950s, the effects of nuclear testing in the atmosphere were raising public concerns. There were scientific reports that radiation was finding its way into the food chain and into the milk that mothers were breastfeeding to their infants. Scientists, such as Nobel Laureate chemist Linus Pauling, entered into the public debate, pressing for an end to atmospheric testing. With the help of his wife, Pauling initiated a petition of scientists to the United Nations, resulting in some 10,000 signatures of scientists throughout the world (Pauling 1983). By 1963, in the aftermath of the Cuban Missile Crisis, the US and USSR signed and ratified a Partial Test Ban Treaty (PTBT), in which they agreed to end the testing of nuclear weapons in the atmosphere, in outer space or under water. While this treaty was important in limiting the environmental and health effects of atmospheric nuclear testing, it did not stop the arms race, as the US and USSR continued to test to improve their arsenals by moving their nuclear testing underground.

The Non-Proliferation Treaty

In the 1950s and 1960s, the UK, France and China joined the US and USSR in the 'nuclear club', and the possibility of other states joining loomed large. Some experts predicted that by the end of the twentieth century there could be 20–30 nuclear weapons states, with the dangers of nuclear war increasing exponentially. While the nuclear arms race between the US and USSR continued unabated, these states, along with the UK, worried about the consequences of potential nuclear proliferation to other states. In an effort to stem the proliferation of nuclear weapons, they joined together in putting forward the Non-Proliferation Treaty (NPT), a treaty to halt proliferation, but that for the first time included a commitment to achieve nuclear disarmament within the structure of a multinational treaty (Nuclear Files 2006a).

The NPT, which came into force in 1970, sought to prevent the proliferation of nuclear weapons, but also to promote the peaceful uses of atomic energy, referring to such uses as an 'inalienable right'. The treaty sought to both promote nuclear energy and prevent the transfer of nuclear materials into weapons programmes. The International Atomic Energy Agency (IAEA), which would in 2005 receive the Nobel Peace Prize along with its director general, Mohamed ElBaradei, was to be the international agency charged with keeping separate the peaceful and warlike uses of the atom. Its task was extremely difficult, perhaps impossible. But, although the potential to divert materials from peaceful to warlike uses of nuclear power exists, so far only one such case of diversion, North Korea, has led to a state under IAEA safeguards becoming in all probability a nuclear weapons state. In North Korea's case, it withdrew from the NPT before announcing that it would develop its nuclear arsenal, although the CIA had earlier concluded that North Korea had at least one or two nuclear weapons.

Three other states that never became parties to the NPT also joined the 'nuclear club' – Israel, India and Pakistan. Israeli leaders have always said ambiguously that Israel will 'not be the first to introduce nuclear weapons into the Middle East', but it is widely understood that Israel has developed an arsenal of 100 to 200 nuclear weapons along with sophisticated delivery systems (Federation of American Scientists 2006a). Indian leaders claimed that India would remain a non-nuclear weapons state in a world in which the existing nuclear weapons states would disarm but, dissatisfied with progress toward nuclear disarmament, India is thought to have secretly tested a nuclear device in 1974 and then publicly tested nuclear weapons in May 1998. Pakistan followed India's latter tests almost immediately with tests of its own. It was deeply disconcerting at the time to see news footage of ordinary people in both countries enthusiastically celebrating in the streets the respective testing of their nuclear arms. It was as though they had bestowed upon themselves a new prestige for having joined the initial nuclear weapons states, the permanent members of the United Nations Security Council, in demonstrating their technological capacity to threaten such massive destruction.

The central bargain of the NPT was a promise by the non-nuclear weapons states to forego the acquisition of nuclear weapons, and the promise of the nuclear weapons states to engage in good faith negotiations to achieve nuclear disarmament. This promise was contained in Article VI of the treaty, and constitutes the only multinational agreement by the nuclear weapons states parties to the treaty to disarm their nuclear arsenals. Article VI of the NPT states: 'Each of the Parties to the Treaty undertakes to pursue negotiations in good faith on effective measures relating to cessation of the nuclear arms race at an early date and to nuclear disarmament, and on a treaty on general and complete disarmament under strict and effective international control' (Nuclear Files 2006a).

Nuclear arms limitations and reductions

The nuclear weapons state parties to the NPT have moved excruciatingly slowly in demonstrating their good faith. The US and USSR sometimes talked to each other and sought ways to reduce the risk of nuclear weapons, but they made few efforts to actually end the nuclear arms race or to achieve nuclear disarmament. One of the first steps that was taken was the signing of an Anti-Ballistic Missile (ABM) Treaty in 1972 by the US and USSR. Both sides agreed to limit the emplacement of antiballistic missiles for defensive purposes on the theory that improved defences would ratchet up the nuclear arms race by leading to further improvements in offensive missiles as well as greater numbers of offensive missiles to overcome the defences. There was a realization that improved defences made the countries that employed them less secure rather than more so.

The two major nuclear weapons states, the US and the former USSR, also signed the first Strategic Arms Limitation Treaty (SALT I) in 1972, in a complex treaty that sought to freeze the number of ballistic missile launchers on each side, but did not require the downsizing or elimination of nuclear weapons (Federation of American Scientists 2006b). This treaty, along with a second SALT agreement, SALT II, signed in 1979 (Federation of American Scientists 2006c), sought to maintain strategic stability and to manage the nuclear arms race rather than end it. These treaties led to a new set of negotiations on nuclear arms reductions culminating in two Strategic Arms Reduction Treaties, START I signed in 1991 (Federation of American Scientists 2006d) and START II signed in 1993 (Federation of American Scientists 2006e). These treaties continued to try to impose strategic parity between the US and USSR. They were not treaties seeking nuclear disarmament, but rather the management of the nuclear arms race at somewhat lower levels.

When the Non-Proliferation Treaty entered into force in 1970, there were some 38,000 nuclear weapons in the world, all but 400 in the arsenals of the US and USSR (Norris and Kristensen 2002). Although the nuclear weapons states sought to prevent proliferation to other countries and promised good faith negotiations for nuclear disarmament, they continued to add to their own nuclear arsenals, engaging in 'vertical proliferation'. The size of the world's nuclear arsenals reached its highest point in 1986, shortly after Mikhail Gorbachev came to power in the Soviet Union (Norris and Kristensen 2002). From this apogee, it took until 1993 for the number of nuclear weapons in the world to again fall to the 1970 level. Twenty-three years after the coming into force of the Non-Proliferation Treaty, the overall number of nuclear weapons in the world had not diminished. In the interim, both the US and USSR had improved the quality of their nuclear arsenals. With higher accuracy and more reliable delivery systems, even rabid nuclear warriors conceded that there was no longer the need for as many nuclear weapons. In addition, Mikhail Gorbachev was a visionary who began working early in his ascendancy to power for the elimination of all nuclear weapons (Wittner 2004).

In October 1986, Gorbachev and Reagan held a summit in Reykjavic, Iceland, and came close to agreeing to eliminate all their nuclear weapons. The sticking point was that Reagan wanted to pursue his dream of an extremely costly and probably unworkable anti-ballistic missile system called the Strategic Defense Initiative (SDI). Reagan had been told by scientist Edward Teller, among others, that SDI would protect the US from a nuclear attack. Although Reagan offered to share the SDI technology with the Soviet Union, Gorbachev was uncomfortable with the offer. The world had come close in that summit to an agreement in principle to eliminate nuclear weapons, but in the end no agreement was reached. On 13 October 1986, the *Washington Post* reported, 'The summit meeting between President Reagan and Soviet leader Mikhail Gorbachev collapsed tonight after the two leaders had tentatively agreed to sweeping reductions in nuclear arsenals but deadlocked on the crucial issue of restricting the US space-based missile defense program widely known as "Star Wars" '(Cannon 1986).

The improved relationship between the two leaders, however, along with widespread public pressure in Europe, did lead to the signing by Reagan and Gorbachev of the Intermediate-Range Nuclear Forces (INF) Treaty in 1987 (Federation of American Scientists 2006f).[3] By 1991, the INF Treaty resulted in the elimination of all ground-launched ballistic and cruise missiles with a range between 300–3,400 miles. The improved relationship between the two leaders also gave impetus to the START talks and to later unilateral reductions in tactical nuclear forces by each side. In 1991, the USSR initiated a unilateral moratorium on nuclear testing, and called for an international moratorium. The next year, the US initiated its own moratorium on nuclear testing. By the end of 1991, the Soviet Union had dissolved into independent states and was replaced by Russia as the dominant successor state.

The NPT Review and Extension Conference

In 1995, the parties to the Non-Proliferation Treaty held a Review and Extension Conference, 25 years after the treaty's coming into force, as called for by the terms of the treaty. Although the number of nuclear weapons in the world had dropped appreciably from Cold War highs, there were still some 27,000 nuclear weapons, enough to destroy civilization many times over and perhaps end life on earth (Norris and Kristensen 2002). The delegates to the treaty conference had to decide whether to extend the treaty indefinitely or for a period or periods of time. Some delegates felt that the progress in fulfilling the Article VI requirements for nuclear disarmament were not sufficient, and argued for a limited extension of the treaty. But the US and other nuclear weapons states lobbied hard for an indefinite extension of the treaty. Those who opposed an indefinite extension, including many non-governmental organizations, argued that insufficient progress had been made on the Article VI commitment by the nuclear weapons states to engage in 'good faith' negotiations to achieve nuclear disarmament; that such an extension could be likened to giving a blank cheque to those who habitually overdraw their account; and that instead the extensions should be for periods of time and contingent upon progress toward eliminating nuclear arsenals. The nuclear weapons states countered by arguing that the treaty was essential for preventing nuclear proliferation and should be made permanent.

In the end, the position of the nuclear weapons states prevailed and the Non-Proliferation Treaty was extended indefinitely, but only after the nuclear weapons states agreed to '[t]he determined pursuit of systematic and progressive efforts to reduce nuclear weapons globally, with the ultimate goals of eliminating those weapons . . .' (1995 Review and Extension Conference 1995: 10). The parties also took note of the security assurances given by the nuclear weapons states in April 1995 (United Nations Security Council 1995), while calling for further steps, including an internationally binding legal instrument, 'to assure non-nuclear-weapons states party to the Treaty against the use or threat of use of nuclear weapons' (1995 Review and Extension Conference 1995: 10).

In 1996, a year after the NPT Review and Extension Conference, the International Court of Justice issued an opinion on the illegality of nuclear weapons. The Court found that the threat or use of nuclear weapons would be generally illegal under the international law of armed conflict. The Court, however, left open one circumstance in which it could not definitively conclude legality or illegality, that being 'an extreme circumstance of self-defense, in which the very survival of a state would be at stake' (United Nations General Assembly 1996: 36). As a result, the Court went further and unanimously ruled: 'There exists an obligation to pursue in good faith and bring to a conclusion negotiations leading to nuclear disarmament in all its aspects under strict and effective international control' (United Nations General Assembly 1996: 37).

Also in 1996, a long-awaited agreement on a Comprehensive Test Ban Treaty (CTBT) was opened for signatures (Federation of American Scientists 2006g). This agreement was called for in the Preamble to the 1963 Partial Test Ban Treaty, when the parties expressed their determination for 'continued negotiations' to achieve 'the discontinuance of all test explosions of nuclear weapons for all time' (Nuclear Files 2006b). The promise to achieve a CTBT was again reiterated at the 1995 NPT Review and Extension Conference, and the opening of the CTBT for signatures in 1996 was widely hailed as an important step toward putting a cap on the nuclear arms race. To enter into force, the treaty requires the ratification of all nuclear-capable states, 44 in total, a goal that has not been achieved in a decade. Although the US was the first country to sign the treaty, the US Senate turned down ratification in 1999, and the Bush administration has not resubmitted the treaty for ratification.

13 Practical Steps for Nuclear Disarmament

In 2000, the parties to the NPT held their five-year Review Conference, their first since agreeing in 1995 to an indefinite extension of the treaty. At this meeting, the delegates reviewed the progress in 'systematic and progressive' efforts to achieve nuclear disarmament and agreed to 13 Practical Steps for Nuclear Disarmament (see Appendix) (Federation of American Scientists 2006h). These steps included, *inter alia*, early entry into force of the Comprehensive Test Ban Treaty, a Fissile Material Cut-Off Treaty, early entry into force and full implementation of START II and the conclusion of START III, preserving and strengthening the Anti-Ballistic Missile Treaty, and the application of the principle of irreversibility to nuclear disarmament. The 13 Practical Steps also included, '[a]n unequivocal undertaking by the nuclear-weapon States to accomplish the total elimination of their nuclear arsenals . . .' (Federation of American Scientists 2006h).

It soon became clear that the Bush administration would not be bound by the agreed upon 13 Practical Steps. Given this stance of the Bush administration, it became apparent that the hopeful promises of the 2000 NPT Review Conference would not fare well. In December 2001, the Bush administration gave formal notice of its intention to unilaterally withdraw from the Anti-Ballistic Missile Treaty. In 2002, the US and Russia entered into a new treaty, the Strategic Offensive Reductions Treaty (SORT) (Nuclear Files 2006c) and gave up efforts to implement START II or to pursue START III. The SORT agreement called for reducing the deployed strategic nuclear warheads for each side to between 2,200 and 1,700 by 31 December 2012. There were no requirements to make these reductions irreversible, and no timetable for interim steps. Both sides were free to put the warheads taken off deployed status onto the shelf to be held in reserve, and both were free to resume deployment of any number of warheads after 31 December 2012. It was a treaty that, while reducing the number of deployed strategic weapons, allowed the principal nuclear weapons states to retain maximum flexibility with their nuclear arsenals, thus holding open the possible resumption of the nuclear arms race. For these reasons, the SORT agreement appears to be a step backward from the 'unequivocal undertaking' to eliminate nuclear weapons.

The principal nuclear weapons states, led by the US, seem intent upon retaining their nuclear arsenals, perhaps at lower levels, but with the open-ended possibility of keeping these weapons for the indefinite future. They have shown no inclination to engage in, let alone conclude, the 'good faith' negotiations toward nuclear disarmament required by the NPT. In addition to the moral and legal implications of taking this stance, there are also practical security implications raised. Those who possess nuclear weapons are also the targets of nuclear weapons. The longer the nuclear weapons states continue to rely upon these weapons for security, the more potential is created for these weapons to proliferate, thus increasing the danger to all. Previously, when nuclear weapons were used in warfare at Hiroshima and Nagasaki, they were directed at an enemy already largely defeated in military terms that was incapable of retaliating. In today's world, the use of nuclear weapons by one country against another country that also possesses nuclear weapons would be suicidal, perhaps omnicidal. In the final analysis, nuclear weapons have no legitimate purpose, including deterrence.

Weapons for the weak

Nuclear weapons may prove to be far more effective in the hands of the weak than in the hands of powerful countries. Even a few nuclear weapons in the arsenal of a country such as Iran or North Korea could be successful in deterring a far more powerful country from imposing its political or military will on that country. This is likely the reason that Iran and North Korea, both named by the US, along with pre-war Iraq, as part of an 'axis of evil', appear to be seeking to develop nuclear weapons. They recognize the asymmetric value of these weapons. Even more striking would be the value of nuclear weapons in the hands of a terrorist organization. With nuclear weapons, an extremist group such as al Qaeda might conceivably bring even the most powerful country to its knees. And it could do so without fear of retaliation, since such a group could not be located. In other words, even the most powerful state in possession of nuclear weapons would have little hope of deterring a determined terrorist group that had obtained nuclear weapons.

In light of the asymmetric value of nuclear weapons to relatively weak actors, it would be highly beneficial to the current nuclear weapons states to pursue nuclear disarmament in a serious manner. Failure to do so may turn them into helpless giants, the victims of their own weapons in the hands of those who would not hesitate to use these weapons in acts of terror. In thinking about nuclear weapons in this way, it should also become clear that those who possess and threaten the use of nuclear weapons, even powerful states, are also assuming a terrorist role in that their threat, if carried out, would result in the massive destruction of innocent women, men and children.

Cowardly and anti-democratic weapons

Nuclear weapons have two additional characteristics that should give pause to any state that relies upon them for security: they are by their very nature cowardly and anti-democratic. Military valour was once based upon bravery in battle, but nuclear weapons provide no possibility of such exercise of valour. With nuclear weapons, the military virtue of bravery in battle is replaced by the willingness to annihilate populations from a distance. For those who create, deploy and make the decision to use nuclear weapons, the targets can be little more than abstractions or coordinates on a map. For those involved with the threat or use of nuclear weapons, the enemy can have no face.

Nuclear weapons kill indiscriminately. When targeted on cities and their inhabitants, their destructive potential is overwhelming. They are also weapons that release radiation, poisoning the surroundings and adversely affecting present and future generations. As such, they cannot be conceived of as ordinary weapons of war. Their use is *per se* illegal and immoral. There can be no valour in using nuclear weapons. They are weapons of those who hide in dark bunkers, ready to unleash terrible destruction upon the innocent. Neither military nor political leaders can take pride in the threat or use of these weapons of brutal annihilation. Nor should the citizens of nuclear-armed countries forget that they are complicit in the possession and brandishing of these cowardly weapons that threaten humanity.

Nuclear weapons concentrate power in the hands of the few, in some cases in the hands of a single individual. They undermine constitutional powers of democracies to make war, for the use of these weapons could be the beginning and the end of war all at once. Jimmy Carter described a nuclear war in his 1981 Farewell Address to the nation: 'In an all-out nuclear war, more destructive power than in all of World War II would be unleashed every second during the long afternoon it would take for all the missiles and bombs to fall. A World War II every second – more people killed in the first few hours than all the wars of history put together. The survivors, if any, would live in despair amid the poisoned ruins of a civilization that had committed suicide' (Jimmy Carter Library 2006).

Do nuclear weapons keep the peace?

It is argued by proponents of deterrence theory that nuclear weapons kept the peace throughout the Cold War. The basic argument is that the existence of nuclear arsenals in the US and USSR prevented each side from attacking the other for fear of overwhelming retaliation. This perception of the power of nuclear weapons to keep the peace seems to be widespread among the public at large. But there are some important reasons to question this assumption. First, the assumption has a logical fallacy in that it seeks to prove a negative by suggesting that something didn't happen (war) because something else did happen (the threat to use nuclear weapons). In logic, a negative cannot be proven. If war didn't happen, it cannot be proven that it didn't happen because there were nuclear weapons or because the countries didn't intend to start a war against each other for different reasons. For example, the fact that the Soviet Union did not attempt to overrun and conquer Western Europe during the Cold War may have been because they had suffered enough losses in the Second World War and had no intention of initiating another war, rather than because they were threatened by nuclear retaliation for doing so. The Soviet Union had lost some 20 million people in the Second World War, and they likely had little enthusiasm for more losses in new wars.

If someone truly believed that nuclear weapons keep the peace, then logic would dictate that they should seek the spread of nuclear weapons. By this logic, the more countries that possessed nuclear weapons, the less war there would be. If these weapons were effective in preventing a war between the US and USSR for four decades in the Cold War, then shouldn't it stand to reason that the more countries with nuclear weapons the better? But, in fact, the nuclear weapons states fear such a world bristling with nuclear weapons, and prefer to limit the number of nuclear weapons states, which they have attempted to do by means of the Non-Proliferation Treaty and other approaches to preventing nuclear proliferation.

Another reason to question the assumption that nuclear weapons keep the peace is that wars did occur despite the possession of nuclear weapons. US nuclear weapons did not prevent a war with North Korea, nor with China when the US crossed its border in the Korean War. Nor did US nuclear weapons prevent a war with Vietnam. The same can be said about the war of the UK against Argentina, or the war of the Soviet Union against Afghanistan. Nuclear weapons neither kept the peace, nor gave the nuclear armed state any significant advantage in the war.

The truth is that nuclear weapons do not keep the peace, but rather inflame passions of distrust by demonstrating a willingness to utterly destroy another country and annihilate its people. One must ask: What possible moral justification could exist for threatening mass murder as a means of preserving the peace? The proponents of deterrence would argue that nuclear weapons have kept the peace, but as we discussed above this is a fallacious argument not subject to proof. Deterrence can fail for many reasons, including irrationality under stress, miscommunication and false or falsely interpreted information. The belief that nuclear deterrence keeps the peace could fail spectacularly and this has come close to happening on many occasions, including the Cuban Missile Crisis (Kaku and Axelrod 1986). The only sure way to eliminate the threat of nuclear weapons is to eliminate all nuclear weapons. Eliminating other weapons of mass destruction, such as chemical and biological weapons, and moving forward in other areas of disarmament, including missiles, landmines and small arms, are also of critical importance, but no task more urgently confronts humanity than that of eliminating nuclear weapons.

Why has nuclear disarmament been so difficult to achieve?

Despite the repeated warnings to humanity, nuclear disarmament has proven very difficult to achieve. Understanding why this is so should be a challenge to all of us, but most especially to the political and military leaders of the world. Although nuclear weapons cast a dark shadow over the human future, they are often perceived as useful to political and military leaders. There are many reasons for this. One of the most important is the politics of fear. Knowing that it is possible to create nuclear weapons, countries seek to possess this power in order to prevent others from threatening them with such power. Every country that possesses nuclear weapons has created them out of fear of being subjugated by another country in possession of these weapons. Even the first nuclear weapons state, the US, created its first weapons out of fear that Nazi Germany might succeed in creating the weapons.

In addition to the politics of fear, there is also the prestige that these weapons bestow, and the modeling of the principal states in possession of these weapons. The Allied victors in the Second World War all aspired to and attained nuclear weapons, starting with the US, and none of these states has shown an inclination to take the lead in eliminating the weapons. There is a sense among these states, and others such as India and Pakistan, that the weapons, despite the inhibitions on their use, confer both greater degrees of freedom in a dangerous world and also greater prestige. In fact, for whatever degrees of freedom these weapons provide, they place the populations of the possessing states in danger of annihilation. The weapons themselves are a bargain with the devil. Their prestige, at once a standard of scientific achievement, is also a reflection of moral compromise, on basing the security of one's country on the threat of massive destruction of the people of another country.

When India and Pakistan tested their nuclear weapons, the people celebrated the scientific achievement and the symbolic elevation to 'great power' status without seeming to recognize the moral descent of the technical triumph. In the case of India, this moral descent was from the lofty principles of nonviolence fostered by Mohandas Gandhi to the willingness to possess and threaten the ultimate violence of the use of these weapons of mass annihilation.

The five permanent members of the United Nations Security Council are the original five nuclear weapons states. Not only do they possess the special elevated status of permanent membership on the Security Council with the power of veto, but they possess the world's most powerful weapons. It is perhaps not surprising that other countries wishing to elevate their status in the international community, including India and Pakistan, have also chosen this path. It is perhaps more interesting to explore why other countries have chosen not to pursue this path. Many advanced countries, including Canada, Sweden, Germany, Japan, Brazil and Italy, have all made the choice not to develop nuclear arsenals. They have made a conscious choice that their security is better pursued without nuclear weapons than with them.

Another factor in the equation of why nuclear disarmament has been so difficult to achieve is the enormous amounts of money that have gone hand in hand with nuclear weapons programmes. The US alone is estimated to have spent some $6 trillion on its nuclear weapons programmes from the beginning of the Nuclear Age (Schwartz 1998). This enormous amount of money undoubtedly creates corporate and political constituencies that are advantaged by the continuation of nuclear weapons programmes. Among the strongest constituencies in the US lobbying for a continuation of US nuclear weapons programmes are the nuclear weapons laboratories, the Los Alamos National Laboratory and the Lawrence Livermore National Laboratory, in which thousands of scientists and technicians are well paid for developing and maintaining the US nuclear arsenal. In addition, there are major corporations, including Boeing, Honeywell International, Northrop Grumman and United Technologies, making billions of dollars annually from work on nuclear weapons and their delivery systems (BBC News 2006).[4]

Humanity has been repeatedly warned

Humanity has been repeatedly warned about the dangers of nuclear weapons and the need for nuclear disarmament. These warnings have come from presidents, prime ministers, Nobel Laureates, scientists and a host of other prominent individuals and organizations. The warnings have come from those who have suffered the effects of nuclear weapons, and from those who have been instrumental in controlling these weapons. Yet, for six decades nuclear disarmament has languished in a two-tier system of nuclear 'haves' and 'have-nots'.

It is an unjust and intolerable system that cannot hold in the long run and, in fact, is already breaking down. India and Pakistan have demonstrated that they will not allow themselves to become victims of what they believe is the injustice of nuclear apartheid. Israel, fearful for its national survival, has laid claim to the right to surreptitiously develop a nuclear arsenal. North Korea has chosen to develop a nuclear deterrent force against a more powerful perceived enemy. The future of humanity and all of life is being held hostage to those countries that refuse to relinquish their claim to these weapons of mass annihilation.

The path to a nuclear weapons-free world requires strengthened international law and cooperation, as well as dramatically increased public awareness of the ongoing dangers these weapons pose to life on earth. The way forward toward the elimination of nuclear weapons will require an ethical and moral base transformed into social and political action. Pursuing a nuclear weapons-free world has its own set of dangers, but certainly not greater dangers than continuing to live in a world of nuclear anarchy and apartheid.

Some countries with the technological capacity to develop nuclear weapons have chosen not to do so. Others have inherited nuclear weapons, as did Ukraine, Kazakhstan and Belarus when the Soviet Union broke apart, and agreed to have these weapons dismantled and to join the Non-Proliferation Treaty as non-nuclear weapons states. One country, South Africa, secretly developed nuclear weapons and then chose to dismantle these weapons. Nearly the entire Southern hemisphere has chosen to organize nuclear weapons-free zones, banning nuclear weapons in the regions of Latin America, the South Pacific, Africa and Southeast Asia (Nuclear Files 2006d). Many examples exist of states that have chosen, despite their technological capacity, to live without the burdens and dangers of nuclear weapons. Unfortunately, not all states have chosen this path, nor will they until there is a strong grassroots demand from the public and the leadership of courageous and visionary political and military officials.

The elimination of these weapons is the greatest challenge confronting humankind. It is the challenge of all individuals alive at the outset of the Nuclear Age or born into it, a challenge that cannot be avoided. It is a challenge that cannot be left to political and military leaders alone, for they have failed to demonstrate vision and courage in meeting their long-standing obligations. This failure is not for technical reasons, for technical issues can be solved, but rather it is a question of political will. Were there the political will to reach an accord to eliminate nuclear weapons, the technical solutions to nuclear disarmament could be found. It would require vision and patience, intrusive inspections and verification. But mostly, it would require real leadership from courageous leaders in the nuclear weapons states to confront the dangers not only to their own citizens, but also to the entire world – which are inherent in a continuation of a nuclear-armed status quo.

Unfortunately, one scans the horizon in vain to find such leaders in the nuclear weapons states. Rather than propose a way to rid the world of nuclear weapons, most political and military leaders today seem content to stay the dangerous course toward the nuclear abyss. They appear to be comfortable holding onto their nuclear arsenals as instruments of power and symbols of prestige.

We cannot count on the emergence of political leaders with the vision and courage of Mikhail Gorbachev. Rather than waiting for such a leader to come along and save humanity, ordinary people must become leaders and create the necessary political will so that leaders of nuclear weapons states will have no choice but to act nobly and in the interests of all humanity. Awakening the people of the world to accept this responsibility is the work of civil society.[5] The responsibility lies with each of us.

The dangers of honest efforts to achieve a world free of nuclear weapons would be far less than the dangers posed in our current nuclear-armed environment, and the rewards of achieving such a world would be immense. Humankind would have conquered an enemy of its own making and could turn its collective attention and resources to building a world at peace based upon principles of universal justice.

Appendix: 13 practical steps for nuclear disarmament

The following text is excerpted from the 2000 Non-Proliferation Treaty Review Conference Final Document.

The Conference agrees on the following practical steps for the systemic and progressive efforts to implement Article VI of the Treaty on the Non-Proliferation of Nuclear Weapons and paragraphs 3 and 4(c) of the 1995 Decision on 'Principles and Objectives for Nuclear Non-Proliferation and Disarmament':

1 The importance and urgency of signatures and ratifications, without delay and without conditions and in accordance with constitutional processes, to achieve the early entry into force of the Comprehensive Nuclear Test Ban Treaty.
2 A moratorium on nuclear-weapon-test explosions or any other nuclear explosions pending entry into force of that Treaty.
3 The necessity of negotiations in the Conference on Disarmament on a non-discriminatory, multilateral and internationally and effectively verifiable treaty banning the production of fissile material for nuclear weapons or other nuclear explosive devices in accordance with the statement of the Special Coordinator in 1995 and the mandate contained therein, taking into consideration both nuclear disarmament and nuclear non-proliferation objectives. The Conference on Disarmament is urged to agree on a programme of work which includes the immediate commencement of negotiations on such a treaty with a view to their conclusion within five years.
4 The necessity of establishing in the Conference on Disarmament an appropriate subsidiary body with a mandate to deal with nuclear disarmament. The Conference on Disarmament is urged to agree on a programme of work which includes the immediate establishment of such a body.
5 The principle of irreversibility to apply to nuclear disarmament, nuclear and other related arms control and reduction measures.
6 An unequivocal undertaking by the nuclear-weapon States to accomplish the total elimination of their nuclear arsenals leading to nuclear disarmament to which all States parties are committed under Article VI.
7 The early entry into force and full implementation of START II and the conclusion of START III as soon as possible while preserving and strengthening the ABM Treaty as a cornerstone of strategic stability and as a basis for further reductions of strategic offensive weapons, in accordance with its provisions.
8 The completion and implementation of the Trilateral Initiative between the United States of America, the Russian Federation and the International Atomic Energy Agency.
9 Steps by all the nuclear-weapon States leading to nuclear disarmament in a way that promotes international stability, and based on the principle of undiminished security for all:

   - Further efforts by the nuclear-weapon States to reduce their nuclear arsenals unilaterally.
   - Increased transparency by the nuclear-weapon States with regard to the nuclear weapons capabilities and the implementation of agreements pursuant to Article VI and as a voluntary confidence-building measure to support further progress on nuclear disarmament.
   - The further reduction of non-strategic nuclear weapons, based on unilateral initiatives and as an integral part of the nuclear arms reduction and disarmament process.
   - Concrete agreed measures to further reduce the operational status of nuclear weapons systems.
   - A diminishing role for nuclear weapons in security policies to minimize the risk that these weapons ever be used and to facilitate the process of their total elimination.

- The engagement as soon as appropriate for all the nuclear-weapon States in the process leading to the total elimination of their nuclear weapons.

10 Arrangements by all nuclear-weapon States to place, as soon as practicable, fissile material designated by each of them as no longer required for military purposes under IAEA or other relevant international verification and arrangements for the disposition of such material in peaceful purposes, to ensure that such material remains permanently outside of the military programmes.
11 Reaffirmation that the ultimate objective of the efforts of States in the disarmament process is general and complete disarmament under effective international control.
12 Regular reports, within the framework of the NPT strengthened review process, by all State parties on the implementation of Article VI and paragraph 4(c) of the 1995 Decision on 'Principles and Objectives for Nuclear Non-Proliferation and Disarmament', and recalling the Advisory Opinion of the International Court of Justice of 8 July 1996.
13 The further development of the verification capabilities that will be required to provide assurance of compliance with nuclear disarmament agreements for the achievement and maintenance of a nuclear-weapon-free world.

Notes

1 This plan was submitted to the United Nations Atomic Energy Agency by Bernard Baruch on 14 June 1946. Baruch said famously, 'We are here to make a choice between the quick and the dead. . . . Let us not deceive ourselves: We must elect World Peace or World Destruction.'
2 The Soviet Union tested its first nuclear weapon on 29 August 1949.
3 Treaty Between the United States of America and the Union of Soviet Socialist Republics on the Elimination of their Intermediate-Range and Shorter-Range Missiles. Entered into force 1 June 1988.
4 A very good example was recently shown by the government of Norway, which divested some $500 million from its state retirement account by selling shares of companies involved in making nuclear weapons.
5 Some tools for becoming involved in working to eliminate nuclear weapons can be found at the Nuclear Age Peace Foundation website: www.wagingpeace.org. You can sign up there for *The Sunflower* e-newsletter, which provides monthly updates on important nuclear disarmament, proliferation, missile and missile defence issues. Additionally, you can sign up for Turn The Tide Action Alerts to communicate with elected representatives in the US on a variety of nuclear-related issues. Another important website is www.abolition2000.org, the website of a global network of over 2000 organizations and municipalities working for a nuclear weapons-free future. Another important citizen-based campaign is the Mayors for Peace Emergency Campaign to Eliminate Nuclear weapons. Information on this campaign can be found at www.mayorsforpeace.org.

References

1995 Review and Extension Conference (1995) *1995 Review and Extension Conference of the Parties to the Treaty on the Non-Proliferation of Nuclear Weapons, Final Document, Part I*, New York: NPT/CONF.

Allison, G.T. and Zelikow, P. (1999) *Essence of Decision: Explaining the Cuban Missile Crisis*, Harlow: Longman.

Atomic Archive (2006a) *The Uranium Committee*, at: http://www.atomicarchive.com/History/mp/p2s1.shtml.

Atomic Archive (2006b) *Baruch Plan*, at: http://www.atomicarchive.com/Docs/Deterrence/BaruchPlan.shtml.

BBC News (2006) 'Norway culling nuclear shares', 5 January 2006.

Bird, K. and Sherwin, M.J. (2005) *American Prometheus: The Triumph and Tragedy of J. Robert Oppenheimer*, New York: Alfred A. Knopf.

Cannon, L. (1986) 'Reagan-Gorbachev talks collapse as deadlock on SDI wipes out other gains', *Washington Post*, 13 October 1986, p. A01.

Federation of American Scientists (2006a) *Nuclear Weapons*, at: http://www.fas.org/nuke/guide/israel/nuke/.

Federation of American Scientists (2006b) *Strategic Arms Limitations Treaty I (SALT I)*, at: http://www.fas.org/nuke/control/salt1/text/salt1.htm.

Federation of American Scientists (2006c) *Strategic Arms Limitation Treaty II (SALT II)*, at: http://www.fas.org/nuke/control/salt2/text/salt2–2.htm.

Federation of American Scientists (2006d) *Strategic Arms Reduction Treaty I (START I)*, at: http://www.fas.org/nuke/control/start1/text/index.html.

Federation of American Scientists (2006e) *Strategic Arms Reduction Treaty II (START II)*, at: http://www.fas.org/nuke/control/start2/text/treatyar.htm.

Federation of American Scientists (2006f) *Intermediate-range Nuclear Forces (INF) Treaty*, at: http://www.fas.org/nuke/control/inf/text/index.html.

Federation of American Scientists (2006g) *Comprehensive Test Ban Treaty*, at: http://www.fas. org/nuke/control/ctbt/text/ctbt1.htm.

Federation of American Scientists (2006h) *Final Document Issued by 2000 NPT Review Conference*, 20 May 2000, at: http://www.fas.org/nuke/control/npt/docs/finaldoc.htm.

Jimmy Carter Library (1981) *President Jimmy Carter's Farewell Address, 14 January 1981*, at: http://www.jimmycarterlibrary.org/documents/speeches/farewell.phtml.

Kaku, M. and Axelrod, D. (1986) *How to Win a Nuclear War: The Pentagon's Secret War Plans*, Cambridge, MA: Southend Press.

Kennedy, R. (1999) *Thirteen Days: A Memoir of the Cuban Missile Crisis*, New York: W. W. Norton & Co.

Lanouette, W. and Silard, B. (1994) *Genius in the Shadows: A Biography of Leo Szilard, the Man behind the Bomb*, Chicago: University of Chicago Press.

Norris, R.S. and Kristensen, H.M. (2002) 'Global nuclear stockpiles 1945–2002', *Bulletin of the Atomic Scientists*, 58, 6: 103–4. Also available at: http://www.thebulletin.org/article_nn. php?art_ofn=nd02norris.

Nuclear Files (2006a) *Treaty on the Non-Proliferation of Nuclear Weapons, 5 October 1970*, at: http://www.nuclearfiles.org/menu/library/treaties/non-proliferation-treaty/index.htm.

Nuclear Files (2006b) *Treaty Banning Nuclear Weapons Tests in the Atmosphere, Outer Space and Under Water*. 480 UNTS 43, at: http://www.nuclearfiles.org/menu/library/treaties/partial-test-ban/trty_partial-test-ban_1963–10–10.htm.

Nuclear Files (2006c) *Treaty Between the United States of America and the Russian Federation on Strategic Offensive Reductions*, 24 May 2002, at: http://www.nuclearfiles.org/menu/library/treaties/strategic-offensive-reduction/trty_strategic-offensive-reduction_2002–05–24.htm.

Nuclear Files (2006d) *Nuclear Weapons Free Zones*, at: http://www.nuclearfiles.org/menu/library/treaties/nuclear-free-zones/trty_nuclear-free-zone-index.htm.

Pauling, L. (1983) *No More War!* (25th anniversary ed.), New York: Dodd, Mead & Co.

Schwartz, S.I. (1998) *Atomic Audit: The Costs and Consequences of US nuclear Weapons since 1940*, Washington, DC: Brookings Institution Press.

Scott, L. and Smith, S. (1994) 'Lessons of October: historians, political scientists, policy-makers and the Cuban missile crisis', *International Affairs (Royal Institute of International Affairs 1944–)*, 70, 4: 659–84.

United Nations General Assembly (1946) *United Nations General Assembly Resolution I(1)*, 24 January.

United Nations General Assembly (1996) *Advisory Opinion of the International Court of Justice on the Legality of the Threat or Use of Nuclear Weapons*, United Nations General Assembly, A/51/218, 15 October.

United Nations Security Council (1995) *United Nations Security Council Resolution 984*, 11 April.

Wittner, L. (2004) 'Gorbachev wages the good fight against WMDs', at: http://www. wagingpeace.org/articles/2004/10/01_wittner_gorbachev-wages-good-fight.htm.

Part 2

Creating peace

9

Counselling and training for conflict transformation and peace-building

The TRANSCEND approach

Wilfried Graf, Gudrun Kramer and Augustin Nicolescou

Gate, gate, paragate, parasamgate, bodhi svaha
Go, go, go beyond, go further beyond, towards enlightenment
The Heart Sutra

The field of peace and conflict counselling and training has significantly developed in the past few decades. The first part of this chapter gives an overview of the field's development and the challenges which have been faced. The second part gives an overview of the method which we have been using in our work in Sri Lanka, Central Asia, South Caucasus, Macedonia, Kosovo/a and the Great Lakes Region in Africa. Based on the work of Johan Galtung, the TRANSCEND approach that we are using is constantly being refined and developed for use in training, research, counselling and mediation. For counselling and training purposes, we have developed a series of training workshops called 'The Art of Conflict Transformation and Peacebuilding', a six-step process, based on the TRANSCEND approach. This chapter gives an outline of what we consider the most essential elements of peace and conflict counselling and training as an overview of the TRANSCEND approach.

The failure of diplomacy and the development of conflict transformation approaches

The 1990s, far from ushering in a peaceful era after the end of the Cold War, were marked by new phenomena of postmodern wars, the majority taking the form of so-called 'ethnic conflicts' – intrastate wars based on the politicization of faultlines of nationality. The responses to these conflicts were based on a framework of 'humanitarian' intervention. Since 11 September, politicization along religious and civilizational faultlines has emerged into the foreground. These postmodern wars, in which the killing of civilians is the main strategy for all sides, surpass the classical modern war in complexity and have proven resistant to the traditional approaches of resolving armed conflicts. These new forms of direct violence are only the tip of the iceberg of the new structural and cultural conflict formations in the new era of global, multinational world capitalism called 'globalization'.

Even in cases in which traditional agreements were eventually reached, violence has on occasion broken out again. This has happened, for example, in Angola, Palestine/Israel and Rwanda. In the cases of Angola and Rwanda, there were more deaths after the agreements were signed than during the preceding civil war (O'Toole 1997). Since then, a new constitution has failed to bring peace to Afghanistan, the Iraq war is possibly turning into a civil war, and the issue of the final status of Kosovo/a is raising the prospects of renewed violence, while in Bosnia the Dayton Accord's complex political system imposed by the outside forces of the international community has not lived up to expectations.

The need for a different, more complex approach, made clear by the persistence of violent conflict over the past decades, has led to the development of new forms of conflict transformation. The traditional approach to negotiation is based on a win–lose understanding of conflict, where there is a definite and fixed amount of resources which must somehow be allotted. Parties have goals, and the parties must give in on some points in order for the goals to be compatible with each other. The language of this approach is 'win–lose', 'zero-sum', 'pure conflict', 'competitive', 'legalistic', with tactics including 'carrot and stick', 'power-coercive', 'threats, bluffs, concealment', and 'compromise towards the middle'. This approach to ending conflicts is reminiscent of Zhou Enlai's definition of diplomacy as 'a continuation of war by other means'. And the record for this type of diplomacy is not promising.

The rise of a Track II approach to conflict resolution

Some of the earliest efforts at developing workshops for dealing with conflicts can be found in the 1940s, when the Connecticut Advisory Committee on Inter-group Relations was looking for ways to deal with problems of race relations in communities, and a workshop was developed by a group of researchers (Fisher 1997). The first analytical problem-solving workshops in which high-level representatives of conflicting nations met on an unofficial basis began to take place in the 1950s (Rothman and Olsen 2001).

This approach aimed at international conflicts developed further for application in intrastate conflicts in the late 1960s, emerging from diplomatic and law-related circles, such as the efforts of Harold Saunders and Roger Fisher, as well as from the field of social psychology, with efforts by Ronald Fisher and Vamik Volkan among others. These lead to 'Track II' initiatives, problem-solving workshops and negotiation trainings (Lumsden 1996). Although there are no calls for Track II efforts to replace Track I efforts, a strong Track II initiative can make all the difference when the parties officially meet at the negotiating table (Rothman and Olson 2001). And they can even create the possibility of having negotiations in the first place.

The role for NGOs and academic groups in assisting in the resolution of intrastate conflict, where it is difficult for traditional international organizations and governments to engage, has been particularly important for these approaches. Counselling and training for conflict transformation and peace-building brings new perspectives and alternatives to current approaches which have proven to be ineffectual. It moves away from traditional prescriptive trainings, and moves towards an elicitive training model. The difference is that the conflict/peaceworker is no longer there to be the expert, to lecture *to* the participants and impart certain content, but rather to be a facilitator, in dialogue *with* the participants, who together are engaged in a process-oriented activity (Lederach 1995).

The arena is unofficial, and the activities take place outside of government offices, and through NGOs, rather than embassies. It offers a space for the participants to think creatively without being held accountable to what they discuss in these closed sessions. This is especially important when the issues are too sensitive to be discussed publicly. The interactions can furthermore help overcome some of the trust issues which are inherent between conflict parties (Chigas 1997). As such, it can have an impact on the 'ripeness' of the conflict for a negotiated solution, allowing for official negotiations much sooner than would otherwise be the case.

Gaps in conflict transformation and peace-building

Even within the new approaches to conflict transformation and peace-building which have gained prominence since the end of the Cold War, there are important deficits which must be addressed in order that this new approach to conflict transformation can lead to peace. The simple fact remains that peace processes more often fail than succeed.

John Paul Lederach identifies three gaps which he has noticed in his experience as a peaceworker. These gaps refer to an 'inability or insufficiency in our conceptual and practice frameworks that weaken our capacity to sustain a desired process' (1999: 2). He points to an interdependence gap, a justice gap and a process-structure gap. He has also since pointed out an additional authenticity gap (Lederach 2005). Addressing these gaps is a critical concern for the further development of peace-building, conflict transformation and peace and conflict counselling and training.

Usual approaches to conflict resolution have equals meet equals: generals with generals or the equivalent (para)-military position, leaders with leaders, grassroots with grassroots. Efforts have tended towards these kinds of horizontal relationship, with the idea of fostering interdependence, building relationships across the major line of social cleavage along which the conflict is formed. There have been, for example, numerous projects aimed at bringing Palestinian and Jewish Israeli youth together, while at the negotiating table, there is a meeting of the political elite.

Different practitioners work at these different levels. And the practitioners from each level have the tendency to believe that their approach, at their level of interaction, will be the basis of peace. Those who, at the grassroots, bring youths from the different conflict parties together see these youths as the leaders of tomorrow, as the ones who will foster new nonviolent movements, and having developed a level of interdependence with their counterparts, will have the resources and relationships to bring peace. Similar things can be said of bringing journalists, intellectual leaders, religious leaders community leaders and military personnel together.

However, the vertical links *within* a conflict party are overlooked. The relationship between the elite level, the midlevel leaders and the grassroots level has not been addressed, and there is a gap in the interdependence between these vertical levels, which is what Lederach is referring to.

A second gap in peace work emerges most prominently when some sort of agreement, which is supposed to bring an end to the conflict, is signed. It is clear that there is generally a significant decrease in direct violence once this happens. Yet the original structural origins of the conflict often remain unaddressed. Direct violence is often the response of one group to the structural violence which is perpetrated by another group. When a peace agreement, or even a ceasefire, is signed, there is an expectation that the decrease of direct violence will also be accompanied by a decrease in structural violence, that the population will experience the benefits of a peace dividend. However, as Lederach writes, 'the expectations for social, economic, religious, and cultural change are rarely achieved, creating a gap between the expectations for peace and what it delivered' (Lederach 1999: 5). One can say that the justice gap is the difference between the expected reduction in structural violence (the expected peace dividend) and the actual outcome.

A further gap which Lederach identifies is between process and structure and it has much to do with the confusion between whether peace is an end product or a process. This gap is most clearly visible after a negotiated peace agreement is signed. A peace process will often lead to the creation of new institutions, positions, even new constitutional structures. These are important structural changes, but with them must come attitudinal changes, new relationships need to be fostered, a culture of peace needs to be developed and the entire way in which conflicts are approached needs to change. This is a dynamic process. A peace structure is empty if it is not used as the framework for an ongoing, dynamic peace process.

To say that peace has happened when an agreement has been signed is akin to saying that the end and be all of owning a home is signing a mortgage. Much like a home, a peace agreement must be lived in, must be amended and changed to suit emerging needs, and it must be maintained. Peace also requires a new structure and new culture, a very real change in the previous, violent structure and culture, into one that is conducive to peace in much the same way that a new home gives a growing family the physical structure and culture it needs to develop.

What these peace-building gaps have in common is that they arise from an incomplete vision of what peace work entails. One can attribute this in part to the legacy of the traditional approach to conflict resolution through military, diplomatic, legal means. This legacy, hammered into the deep psyche of most societies over a period of millennia, has left us with the notion that once an agreement is settled, however it may have been settled, it is final and the problem is resolved. The result is an overemphasis on elite negotiation and interdependence between elites, while neglecting the elites' need for interdependence with the people they aim to lead and govern. It also results in an overemphasis on the structure of peace, in the form of a peace or ceasefire agreement, while the complex processes necessary for peace and the transformation of conflict are neglected. The final result of this legacy is a superficial peace without roots or chances for development.

An additional factor which is missing is something less tangible. Beyond techniques, approaches to negotiation, mediation and intervention need something more. What is missing is peace as an organic process fuelled by the creativity, dedication and vision of those who live in conflict.

Peace must be organic. This means that it must be developed from within as opposed to imported or imposed from without. There should be ownership of the peace by those who have to live with it. This corresponds to what Lederach refers to in *The Moral Imagination* as the 'authenticity gap' (2005: 49).

The basis of a good peace and conflict counselling and training approach: between technique and art

A successful peace and conflict counselling and training approach needs to take into account the lessons learned and address the challenges that have been identified. Peace and conflict counselling and training usually seeks to impart knowledge and skills, a specific method that can be used to resolve conflicts. Lederach (2005) points out that in the process of professionalizing the field of peace-building the emphasis on technique has overshadowed the fact that peace-building is also an art. Peace and conflict counselling and training approaches generally seek to 'rationalize' conflict. The shortcoming is often that these counselling and training approaches fail to impart the fact that many conflict dynamics are 'irrational' and unconscious to the conflict parties; in particular, they fall short on imparting the need for creativity, spontaneity, self-reflection and empathy. Lederach also writes that the 'moral imagination' is needed in order to transform conflicts. This is what we refer to as the potential to 'TRANSCEND' a conflict, the capacity to go beyond the existing reality and to jump into a new reality. In

Mahayana Buddhism this idea is expressed in the mantra of the heart sutra, for the calming of all suffering. '*Gate, gate, paragate, parasamgate, bodhi svaha* – Go, go, go beyond, go further beyond, towards enlightenment.'

Peace and conflict counselling and peace training must be both technical and artistic, and we use the term 'the art of conflict transformation' or 'the art of peace-building' in order to characterize our peace and conflict counselling and training approaches. In order to reach the goal of transcending conflicts, counselling and the training of a technical methodology are not sufficient. A comprehensive approach must be complex and integrative, and continuously revised according to the findings and experiences of practical work. At the same time, it cannot be a fixed recipe or a ready-made product; a comprehensive approach requires elements of artistic creativity. And it has to be personal. A good conflict trainer/worker, once engaged, is part of the process, and cannot be replaced easily. The relationships with the conflict parties are personal. Trust and confidence in the conflict trainer/worker is not transferable to another. But, of course, good relationships are not enough. There needs to be a balance between the technique and the art.

A craftsman needs both tools and artistic talent. A layperson can be given all the tools of the trade, but the result will not be the same. In the broadest definition, a layperson may create art. But peace work is not simply an aesthetic concept. The end product needs to fulfil a purpose. Take the tools away from a craftsman, and he will not be able to do the job with talent alone. Even with training in using the tools, without creativity, the result is bland, unoriginal and inadequate. Both technique and creativity are needed, or the result is insufficient for conflict transformation.

The role of the peace and conflict worker, consultant or trainer[1] is to support a process of self-reflection, to strengthen the capacity for empathy, to awaken the creative potential for imagining a new reality and to empower nonviolent strategies, through a dialogue with the participants – while constantly questioning the approach.

A complex peace and conflict counselling and training approach needs to combine a philosophy, theories and a praxeology. The philosophy defines the worldview of the conflict worker/trainer, which consists of their attitudes and assumptions. It is the carrier of the values according to which one acts. Conflict workers/trainers often do not reflect on their own values, which derive from their own culture. Confronted with conflicts embedded in other cultures, they will, often unconsciously, analyze the conflict through their culture-tinted glasses and try to lobby for possible solutions that impose their own values.

In the established understanding, conflict workers/trainers should be all-partial, which enables the development of empathy for the conflict parties. Yet at the same time, this concept of all-partiality implies that conflict workers/trainers have no biases of their own. Therefore, this concept can hinder their ability to reflect upon their own opinions and the source of those opinions. Conflict workers/trainers need to not only ask themselves the question, 'What is it that guides me really?' but the philosophy that is imparted must itself be culturally-sensitive, so that it can serve as the conflict worker/trainer's anchor, a point of reference when faced with the uncertainties of practical peace work. Philosophical values also guide the axioms chosen as the basis for a theory, which is a second component of what makes a complex peace and conflict counselling and training approach.

The 'complex' part refers to the analysis of the conflict, and the amount of complexity which can be attained, and this is dependent on the theories used to reach it. Any good theory must be robust enough to address at least the majority of the empirical cases it is applied to. However, the basic axioms should be as simple and few as possible. As Albert Einstein put it, 'The supreme goal of all theory is to make the irreducible basic elements as simple and as few as possible without having to surrender the adequate representation of a single datum of experience.' And theories are one of the most practical things. Theories build the paradigm from which we operate, and without an adequate theory, what should be clear is obscure. If one believes that peace comes from balance of power rather than through the transformation of contradictions rooted in deep culture and structure, military training assistance becomes the logical choice, and dialogue is the last thing to have in mind – at best, negotiation is conceivable. In short, better theory leads to better practice.

Praxeology refers here in particular to the conflict transformation process as a dialogue process, starting with a dialogue with each conflict party separately, in order to accompany each conflict party in a process of self-reflection and exploration of the unconscious dimensions of conflict formation. Therefore the counselling and training in this approach must counsel and train 'the art of dialogue', based on the philosophy and theories. The methods come out of the philosophy, theory and praxeology, and are guided by them. Methods are more specific tools to deal with a particular issue or challenge. A good peace and conflict counselling and training approach needs to have methods which address the existing gaps in the field.

Each of these components – a philosophy, theories and a praxeology providing concrete methods and tools – are necessary for a complex, integrative approach to conflict transformation and peace-building work, counselling and training. Inadequacies in one can affect the other components, and the whole must be continuously re-evaluated according to their effects in the field. Peace and conflict counselling and training needs to address all of the components. So equipped, the conflict worker/trainer may be able to not only grasp 'serendipitous appearances of moral imagination', described by Lederach (2005) but also to actively work towards the *kairos* points that enable creative social change with peaceful means.

A complex, integrative approach to conflict transformation and peace-building: an overview of the TRANSCEND approach

Developed over the past 50 years, beginning with the groundbreaking work of Johan Galtung, the TRANSCEND approach seeks for answers not only to how to stop direct violence, but also how to transform structural and cultural violence. Over time, it has developed through the research and practices of many peace practitioners and has incorporated the work of numerous researchers and practitioners from a wide range of backgrounds. Today it consists of a philosophy, a set of values, theories that are continuously empirically evaluated, and a praxeology with a set of various methods and techniques. In that regard, TRANSCEND today is comparable with other approaches of cultural work, social work and group work, such as Paolo Freire's emancipatory pedagogy, Jakob Levy Moreno's psycho/sociodrama or Fritz Pearl's Gestalt work. However, in contrast to these approaches, TRANSCEND deals with conflicts not only on the micro and meso levels, but also on the macro and mega levels. The following section is meant as a brief overview of the TRANSCEND approach to peace-building and conflict transformation, and is the basis for our integrative peace and conflict counselling and training approach.

From a TRANSCEND perspective, the goal of peace-building and conflict transformation is to enable people to be self-reliant in dealing with conflicts using peaceful means. Especially when working in foreign societies, the aim of a TRANSCEND conflict trainer/worker is to intervene as little as possible. Peaceworkers from outside, who move to and then live in the country of conflict, often become part of the conflict themselves. They are often no longer able to distance themselves from the conflict; they perceive the conflict as their conflict, becoming 'conflict thieves'. This provokes counter-productive dynamics. On the one hand, the conflict worker/trainers start competing with each other, on the other, confronted with deadlocks or backlashes, they themselves feel helpless and become frustrated and cynical. Therefore the TRANSCEND approach focuses primarily on strengthening local capacities through counselling and training.

When directly working with conflict parties, the TRANSCEND approach stresses the importance of working with the conflict parties separately, in order to facilitate a process of self-reflection. Self-reflection enables the conflict parties to better understand themselves, the others and the conflicts which divide them. In doing so, conflict parties are better able to formulate and/or reformulate their goals, and to come up with better, nonviolent strategies in order to achieve their goals. In the best case scenario, the conflict parties do not need third-party mediation anymore, but are able to engage in a genuine autonomous dialogue and agree on solutions to their common problems.

The TRANSCEND approach integrates behaviour-oriented, process-oriented and solution-oriented approaches. 'Integrative' in this context means the integration of different approaches to conflict resolution, conflict transformation and 'sociotherapy', rather than to the differentiation between 'integrative' and 'competitive' approaches referred to in the 'win–win' approach. Although the TRANSCEND approach is also in favour of integration, consensus, cooperation, mutual learning and creative collaboration, the aim is for equity and symmetric power structures. Therefore it is sometimes necessary to choose disintegrative, dissociative, non-cooperative strategies, but always using nonviolent methods of resistance.

TRANSCEND philosophy

The TRANSCEND philosophy is grounded in scientific epistemology, historical anthropology and a political philosophy of peace. It is marked by a complex peace philosophy of 'peace by peaceful means', inspired by Gandhi's satyagraha – meaning not only nonviolent behaviour, but also structural autonomy and cultural self-realization. Additionally, it integrates many critical social philosophies going beyond classical leftist and classical liberal approaches. Key elements of the TRANSCEND philosophy are nonviolence, creativity and empathy.

Epistemologically, TRANSCEND is based on the trilateral concept of science: empiricism, criticism and constructivism, which can correspond to realism, idealism and art.[2] Empiricism looks at what has happened – the data – and interprets it according to the theory, which itself is tested by the data. This focuses on the past or what has happened. Criticism looks at the data, and gives a positive or negative judgement based on values. It is examining what is happening in the present. Constructivism is the possibility for the future, looking at what is desired according to values, and using theory to achieve it (Galtung 2002). Empiricism helps us to distinguish between correct or incorrect. Criticism helps us distinguish between better or worse, and constructivism between adequate or inadequate. All three components of the concept are necessary to answer the basic corresponding questions: 'Why did it happen?', 'What is it about?' and 'How can it be better?'

TRANSCEND'S historical anthropology puts the human being at the centre of conflict transformation. Human beings have basic needs which are universal, regardless of one's culture or societal structures. Basic human needs are what define us as human beings. Contrary to Karl Marx's or Abraham Maslow's specific hierarchies of human needs, Galtung's basic human needs concept, like that of Max Neef's (1991), assumes that there is no hierarchy in basic human needs. Galtung distinguishes four categories of basic human needs: *survival*, as opposed to death; *well-being*, which refers to what we need to live from, such as food, clothes, shelter, access to a healthcare system, access to an educational system; *identity*, which means a sense of life, something to live for, not only to live from; and *freedom*, meaning having equal choices (Galtung 1996). Using Ken Wilber's (1995) terminology, one could also refer to them as physiological, social, spiritual and psychological needs.

Although there is no objective hierarchy, human beings and societies tend to prioritize basic human needs, and tend to base ideologies on this prioritization. Marxism puts the basic human need of well-being at the centre of its ideology, liberalism puts the need for freedom at the centre, and conservatism puts the need for identity at the centre. For Hobbes, survival is at the centre. In deep-rooted conflicts, one can often observe a pathological fixation on one of the basic needs. People are known to sacrifice their lives for their religious and cultural identity (such as the right to use their own language). Well-being and survival are often sacrificed in the struggle for freedom. TRANSCEND tries to go beyond these ideologies or pathological fixations. It assumes that all basic human needs are equally important and that, if there is to be a sustainable solution to a conflict, all of these basic human needs must be fulfilled.

TRANSCEND'S political philosophy of peace follows the core value of 'peace by peaceful means'. It recognizes that the dominant approaches of 'peace through balance of power' and 'peace through law' are insufficient in order to transform conflict in a sustainable manner. Nonviolence is essential as the cornerstone of the approach, as violence only serves to further entrench conflict parties, and closes doors to possible solutions.

The way out of violence is through creativity and empathy. Creativity, in all its forms, is what distinguishes human kind from other living beings. It is the mental capacity to see something which does not exist, and to then achieve that. Going from a structurally and culturally violent condition where the basic needs of many are unfulfilled, and imagining and fulfilling the achievement of basic needs for all, within a culturally and structurally peaceful system, requires that individuals make full use of their creative potential. The work of conflict transformation must be less technical, less legalistic and more creative in order to overcome the limitations of what has been done, to go beyond and create something new.

However, creativity can be used in less beneficial ways, such as finding creative new ways of killing, maiming and oppressing. Empathy with the other ensures that the creative power is used for peaceful purposes rather than violent ones. Like in Moreno's psycho-, socio- and axiodrama, it is putting oneself in the shoes of the other, reversing the roles to which one is accustomed (Graf 2006). This should not be confused with sympathy, which involves an affinity for the other or their actions. Through compassion and empathy one can understand the other, even if the other's ideas and actions are anathema to one's own.

In the TRANSCEND philosophy, especially in the basic human needs for all approach, there is also the basis for a new legitimacy of the intervention of the conflict trainer/worker, beyond classical neutrality, impartiality or even all-partiality. A perennial question is 'What right do you have to stick your nose into our business?' It is good to have an answer to that question, especially in the context of individuals from the Western world working in other parts of the world. In the TRANSCEND philosophy, legitimacy for any kind of intervention is based on the fulfilment of the basic human needs for all conflict parties and on the following points:

> As fellow human being you are party to human suffering anywhere [. . .] because their suffering is yours; as fellow human being your agenda is to reduce destruction and enhance the creative aspect of conflict; [. . .] you bring in general conflict knowledge and skills; [. . .] you may be short on local conflict knowledge but willing to learn from dialogues with inside participants [. . .]
>
> (Galtung 2000: 58)

The last point is perhaps the most important part of the answer to the question of legitimacy. It is the assurance that ownership remains with the conflict parties, not with some outside force. It is the assurance that whatever comes out of the process, it will be, as Lederach writes, authentic.

TRANSCEND theories: peace theory

On a theoretical level, the TRANSCEND approach is based on a complex critical-constructivist peace theory, on the basis of a tridimensional theory of violence: direct, structural and cultural violence. It encompasses what is violence, what is the conflict formation underlying the violence, what is the perspective of a peaceful solution and what is the way to conflict transformation and peace-building.

Direct, structural and cultural violence as a theoretical model for violence goes beyond the common understanding of violence. A riot, a revolt or a revolution with the accompanying violence remains puzzling without a deeper understanding of violence. Mass violence does not erupt without a reason, although the reason is not a justification. This type of direct violence is an event. To understand the event one needs to understand the process which led to it. Structural violence is the difference between the potential and the actual. Although the potential and the actual can in practice never coincide completely, it is more the enormous gulf between the two which is worrisome. A violent structure impedes the development of the group and the self through a structure which is generally invisible. Cultural violence is the hardest to change, it is the deep-rooted constant which legitimates structural and direct violence, especially when there is a reaction (violent or not) against the structural violence by those who are victims of it.

The majority of approaches to dealing with conflict are limited to the understanding of violence as direct violence. At best, the result can be a compromise that brings an end to direct violence. In general, the conflict is put on ice, until at some point it re-emerges. In the worst cases, of which there are a number, the violence is worse than before. There is, in any case, no sustainable peace to be had. The justice gap needs to be addressed; the violent structures and cultures need to be transformed.

Conflict theory

In the TRANSCEND theory, conflict is seen as having three main components: attitudes, behaviours and Contradictions (ABC). Conflict is not the same as violence. Conflict is a challenge – and when an individual has a conflict within himself, it is a dilemma. A conflict over food shortage (which is a contradiction) can lead to better agriculture because of a creative solution which transforms the conflict through an increase in crop productivity by using a creative new method. However the outcome, whether it is creative, constructive and peaceful, or whether it becomes violent and destructive, depends mainly on behaviour – whether it is peaceful or not, and influenced by attitudes towards the other. The behaviour is the visible element of the conflict, what people, when they see it, say, 'Look those two are having a fight.' Often, the contradiction, the incompatible goal, is eventually forgotten as the cycle of animosity and violence spirals. This is especially the case of protracted violent conflicts, in which violence creates a self-perpetuating dynamic, and the violence obscures the real contradiction.

When faced with a conflict, the TRANSCEND approach stresses all three points of the attitude–behaviour–contradiction triangle. In order to reverse the cycle of violence, the contradiction itself must be transformed, as do the violent behaviours and attitudes. Although a ceasefire (change in behaviour) can open a window for transforming the conflict and reversing the cycle of violence, it is insufficient.

In Cyprus there has been a change in behaviour since the arrival of UN peacekeepers, yet decades later, there is still no end to that conflict. Attitudes remain polarized, and the contradictions remain unaddressed. A change of behaviour is also not a prerequisite for the reversal of the conflict dynamic. It can start with a change of attitudes or a transformation of the contradiction. This is the case for Aceh, where there was no ceasefire prior to the signing of the Memorandum of Understanding which officially has brought an end to the violent conflict, and this itself was made possible by changes in the attitudes of the main conflict parties. The cession of hostilities was the last part of the conflict cycle to go. Therefore, it is important not to focus too heavily on a linear approach of ceasefire, then negotiation, then agreement, then reconciliation. The process should start where there is the best opening and, if possible, on multiple levels.

The process–structure gap also can occur when a peace and conflict counselling and training approach focuses too much on attitudes (the process) or too much on finding a solution (structure). One of the benefits of this understanding of conflict is that it helps ensure proper attention to both process and structure.

Civilizational theory: deep structure and deep culture

The third central component of the TRANSCEND theory is an understanding of the deeper dimension of conflict. At the deeper level, there is unconscious behaviour, which has the aim of fulfilling one's basic needs, and can have implications for the fulfilment of the basic human needs of others. There is also the deep (latent) structure and the deep (implicit) culture of the conflict formation. These are, respectively, the deeper levels of the psyche (and body), the social and the cultural.

Deep structure can be defined as the patterns of relations between the segments of society – between the old and the young, men and women, between races and ethnicities, between powerful and powerless, along every social cleavage.

Deep structure is always present, and as such is neither a good thing nor a bad one. However, a deep structure where an asymmetry of power between the different segments of society and violations of the basic needs of others occurs is structurally violent. It is then linked with discrimination and exploitation. Violent deep structures include slavery, colonialism and patriarchy. Deep structure influences every aspect of a society's organization, and the patterns of power relations are often recreated in the family, workplace and government.

Deep structure can exhibit certain pathologies, and Galtung identifies these as the PSFM Syndrome (1996). PSFM stands for Penetration, Segmentation, Fragmentation and Marginalization. Penetration is the extent to which those with power are able to condition those without to accept the structure. Segmentation is the extent to which information is controlled by the elite, and where the average individual does not have access to the whole picture. Fragmentation is the extent to which those without power are isolated along the different faultlines and therefore do not have contact with each other. Marginalization is the extent to which a segment of the population is prevented from interacting in society and in the world at large.

There is a counterpart to PSFM, which is the basis for a peaceful deep structure. It is autonomy instead of penetration, integration instead of segmentation, solidarity instead of fragmentation and participation instead of marginalization.

If attitudes are on the surface, then below them are deeper attitudes and assumptions, which form the deep culture, the sum of unconscious, usually unspoken, directives, rules, assumptions and prejudices about the self and the other. The unconscious, that which belongs to the realm of what once was conscious and has sunk into unconsciousness, informs the patterns of thinking and the conscious, surface level attitude which one sees in the attitude point of the ABC triangle. More specifically, deep culture is composed of the operating paradigms and cosmology of a society. It is 'a web of notions about what is true, good, right, beautiful, sacred' (Galtung 2000: 33).

In conflicts, and in particular in protracted conflicts, these deep attitudes and assumptions often work to impede a peaceful end to the conflict, and are the raw materials for the dynamics of escalation and polarization, which are in turn exacerbated by populist and fundamentalist policies. Throughout culture (in religion and ideology, language and art, empirical and formal science) such deep cultural meanings can be identified, and they can be used to legitimize direct or structural force, and are transferred from one generation to the next.

Deep culture has its own pathologies. There is a cognitive pathology of Dichotomy, Manichaeism and Armageddon (the DMA Syndrome) and an emotional pathology of Glory Chosenness and Trauma (the CGT syndrome). The DMA syndrome reduces each conflict constellation to only two conflict parties (dichotomy), about which there is one good side, with an apposing bad or evil other (Manichaeism), so that a final decisive encounter becomes inevitable (in the form of Armageddon). Nations with a CGT syndrome suffer from heavy traumata (multiple traumatic events), and dwell on injuries and defeats that were perpetrated by enemies. They maintain and publicize myths which tell of their past and future glory. And they live with the conception of being chosen by transcendental forces for political missions. With both syndromes, the three respective components have a tendency for mutual reinforcement.

In times of crisis, when a group is faced with a complex situation yet needs to maintain consensus in order to (re)act effectively, these deeper dimensions of conflict assert themselves on the surface level. The way in which the situation is understood, and the ensuing reaction, will be guided on the group level by the deep culture. A basic hypothesis of TRANSCEND is that a just, sustainable solution can only be achieved if the deeper dimensions are addressed and brought into the consciousness of the conflict parties. Then new, transformed attitudes and assumptions, goals and strategies, and behaviour can be achieved.

TRANSCEND praxeology

The TRANSCEND approach's praxeology is based on deep dialogue – and *polilogue*[3] as a method for delving below the superficial level, and into the 'collective unconscious'. This, however, cannot be achieved at the negotiating table. The parties must be ready to negotiate before taking their place at the round table. Therefore the TRANSCEND praxeology stipulates that each conflict party should be worked with separately in order to develop their understanding of their own goals as well as developing vertical interdependence (in order to prepare the conflict parties for creative negotiation and mediation). This means bringing a broad range of individuals together, coming from different backgrounds; government officials, NGO representatives, local leaders, military personnel, journalists, religious leaders and intellectuals, from the same conflict party, must meet.

The participants of such seminars and trainings take part in their personal capacity and the sessions are carried out under the Chatham House Rule. The unofficial, private, nature of the meeting allows for individuals to express ideas and explore possibilities which would be against the position of their respective organizations. It also helps build a collegial and trusting atmosphere necessary for an honest and deep dialogue. As well, if possible, it is best to take the participants out of the context of the conflict and into a third country which is not party to the conflict. Participants have often commented that this has allowed them to gain a different perspective on the issues.

The participants come from one conflict party, but the composition of the group is heterogeneous, allowing the process to go along vertical lines rather than horizontal ones. Each segment of the population represented brings in insights which would normally not be shared with those from such different backgrounds. In this way, vertical interdependence is fostered. Each participant on their return can act as multipliers, and their efforts within their segment of the population should be assisted by conflict trainer/workers. Such activities are especially important at the grassroots level, empowering them as well as conveying the insights developed during dialogue seminars.

The praxeology also includes a multiple-orientation approach. Attitudes, behaviours and contradictions must be worked on simultaneously. On the attitude, or process, level, the stress is on developing empathy for the other parties. On the behaviour level, the stress is on non-violence. On the level of the contradiction, the solution is elaborated based on the principle of creative conflict transformation and the attainment of basic human needs for all.

The goal of the conflict trainer/worker is the achievement of basic human needs for all. With this ethical anchor, the peace trainer can better deal with the realities on the ground. It also reassures the conflict parties that the conflict trainer/worker will not be sympathizing with one conflict party against another. When a conflict party may have committed a disproportionate amount of the violence, they know it, and become very defensive and sensitive to criticism. The use of basic human needs as the clear bias of a conflict trainer/worker allows the party to understand that criticism is not against them as individuals or from a moralizing standpoint. This happens to be the biggest difference between a conflict trainer/worker and a peace activist, the latter, by definition, takes sides.

A further characteristic of the TRANSCEND praxeology is that the conflict trainer/worker may put forth ideas and possible solutions, especially when there is an impasse on an issue. This must be done carefully, and with the clear message that this is a proposal for consideration, not an imposition. It should always remain up to the conflict party to decide whether to follow that proposal or reject it. In that regard, case studies are very useful.

The art of conflict transformation lies in asking the right question at the right time, and making the right proposal at the right time. This is not something that can be trained for or analyzed scientifically. And art has a place. During a seminar, the process is intense, and it is difficult to go through an entire re-evaluation of one's self. At times tempers may erupt. To see a group which is undergoing this process come together and share their songs and poetry is both a fantastic healing process and a development of their relationships as they share such creative moments. There is nothing which unites people so much as when they come together and create something new – whether it is singing a song or a list of recommendations to take back home with them, it is the same process.

Complex conflict analysis

Human beings, in order to fulfil their basic human needs, become part of a group, and develop specific individual as well as group goals. In the outside world these goals meet the goals of others, and when the goals are incompatible, a contradiction occurs and a conflict emerges. If the contradiction is perceived negatively and no solution can be found, it is likely that it will lead to an act of violence. This act does not resolve the contradiction. On the contrary, violence has the effect of worsening the contradiction. Violence then often leads to counter-violence, further polarizing the attitudes and assumptions about the others, setting in motion a process of de-humanization.

Experiencing violence is always a traumatic event. When a society is exposed to large-scale violence, it needs to come up with coping mechanisms. Myths are created and passed on from one generation to the next. In this way, collective traumas can endure for centuries. They are stored within the deep culture and are often reactivated in situations of crisis, once again influencing the actions and goals of the individual or group.

Similar dynamics can be analyzed with regard to the structures. The experience of trauma through violence and the inability to resolve the contradiction(s) lead to the creation of structures which only serve the purpose of achieving the fulfilment of basic needs of one's own people, excluding the needs of the others. Since the others are perceived as an obstacle to achieving their goals, this leads to discrimination, exploitation and, in the worst case, an attempt to destroy the others, even if this leads to self-destruction.

The aim of conflict transformation, peace-building, counselling and training initiatives is to empower participants to be able to escape this vicious cycle by reframing their goals. This should occur at the level of positions, at the level of interests, as well as at the level of basic human needs, in order to overcome the incompatibility of goals.

Conflict transformation dialogue: three phases, six steps

A TRANSCEND Dialogue Project is organized along three phases. The first phase is to understand the goals of the conflict parties. The second phase is the reframing of illegitimate goals into legitimate goals on the basis of the fulfilment of basic human needs of all conflict parties. The third phase consists of the elaboration of an overarching formula for a sustainable solution on the basis of the integration of these legitimate goals. In each phase, there are two steps, each addressing a particular conflict transformation concern, alternating according to a double dialectic between analysis (or observation) and therapy (or solution), and between past and future.

The six steps were elaborated for didactical purposes and it has to be noted that, in actual peace and conflict work, such a linear process cannot be followed. The six steps only serve the purpose of making trainees become acquainted with the different dimensions and dynamics of conflict formations, and providing them with a mental landscape for finding the right questions in the right time, when working with each conflict party separately.

Phase one: understanding the conflict formation

Conflict transformation work is not scientific conflict analysis. The aim in phase one therefore is not to try to come up with an 'objective' understanding of the conflict, but rather to understand how the conflict party itself perceives the conflict. The process-oriented goal in phase one is to build up trust between the conflict worker/trainer and the conflict party. The structure-oriented goal in phase one is to give each conflict party the possibility for a better understanding of the contradiction, their goals and the goals of the other conflict parties.

Step one: understanding all actors, their behaviour and their relations in the context of the contradiction (Analysis of the Present)

The underlying question of the first step is, 'What is the conflict about?' It is a question about the present; what is happening at that point. It is an analysis of the antagonism which exists between the conflict parties. The analysis takes place on the level of attitudes, behaviours and contradictions.

The conflict party should start out by identifying their goals and those of the other conflict parties. The forgotten and hidden actors should also be identified. These are generally parties to the conflict who are involved in some way, but not always visibly so. The relationships between the conflict actors should then be examined.

One tool for the whole six-step process is a diagram of five possible outcomes along the lines of a standard *x-y* graph. The points are laid out as follows: 'Either' is at the end of the *y*-axis (0, 1); 'Or' is at the end of the *x*-axis (1, 0); 'Neither/Nor' is at the point of origin (0, 0); between 'Either' and 'Or' there is 'Compromise' (0.5, 0.5) extending the line between 'Neither/Nor' and 'Compromise' leads to the 'TRANSCEND' point (1, 1).

Originating in Taoist and Buddhist logic, it offers five possible outcomes instead of the usual either/or framework of Aristotelian logic. To these two options, it adds 'neither/nor', 'compromise' and 'transcendence.' Transcendence means not only 'win-win' (or integration, consensus, collaboration), but 'both and – something more', meaning the overcoming of the incompatibility of the goals on the basis of the fulfilment of the basic human needs of all conflict parties.

A first way of making use of this diagram is to place the two main contradicting goals as perceived by the conflict party at the positions *either* and *or*. Then the conflict parties are placed along the diagram relative to the five possible outcomes. In general, most conflict parties fall somewhere on a line between the two either/or positions. This line is the one along which traditional approaches to negotiations seek to move the actors, with the goal being some form of compromise in the middle. Except for the point of compromise, when moving along this line between the goals, there is a constant power asymmetry in the possible outcomes. It is a competitive process, and the dynamics of competition lead to a bad compromise, since each side must give in on some points, yet tries to hold on to as much of their original goal as possible.

The diagonal between the neither/nor position and the transcend position, also going through the compromise point, is what we refer to as the 'peace diagonal'. Even if the outcome of the process is a compromise, a negotiation running along this line is a more peaceful one, as it does not arise out of competition, but out of a dialogue, and with symmetry. What one party has, so does the other.

By placing the conflict parties within the diagram it is possible to identify which actors are already at a point where they are not satisfied with the stated goals of either major conflict party. Such a conflict actor will often fall somewhere close to the neither/nor point of the schema. As the Transcend process is one of changing the (inadequate) pre-existing patterns, these conflict actors can play a key role as they are more amenable to finding creative solutions which would also take into account their goals and needs.

Furthermore, the application of this framework to the conflict is the first step in putting forward the idea that there are more options out there than win-lose or compromise, that there is a possibility that the needs of all can be satisfied, through a creative solution.

Step two: understanding the assumptions, attitudes and how they interact with contradictions and the goals (Therapy of the Past)

Step two is primarily one of self-reflection for the conflict party. It focuses on the past, looking to identify both what happened, as well as what failed to happen, leading to the present situation. When a conflict party does not see any hope in the present, then it is useful to look into the past, and see what could have been done then to make the situation better. The process of analyzing the past is an anamnetic one, a reflection aimed at remembering, and to a certain extent, reliving what has happened before. It is a form of therapy for the past. The guiding question of step two is, 'How did the conflict occur?'

The aim is to develop an understanding of how the assumptions and attitudes of the conflict parties affect their goals. The assumptions are used to justify the goals. However, since they are not as visible, they are often not discussed, but taken as self-evident 'truths'. In the case of Sri Lanka, the Tamil Tigers assume that the rights of Tamils in a predominantly Sinhalese state will never be guaranteed. Their goal of *Tamil Eelam* – an independent Tamil state – arises from this assumption.

During this step, the assumptions, and the resulting goals and strategies, are examined. It is important to bring up also the strategies used by the conflict parties. Since the conflict is ongoing, it is clear that the strategies have not sufficed. Usually these strategies are violent, and it is a good opportunity for the conflict party to reflect on how well violence has served their needs.

Within a dialogue, nonviolence as an alternative should be explored as a strategy. Often the response is that this was tried and failed. Yet in almost every case, the nonviolent period of the conflict is relatively short compared to the violent struggle which followed, and the nonviolent strategies from the time were not adequately developed or pursued. One example of a deeper assumption on the deep culture level is the belief that violence offers better results than non-violence, a kind of 'presumption of the supremacy of violence', sometimes also rooted in the biblical metaphor of Armageddon.

When a violent strategy fails, it is generally taken to imply that more violence is needed, or that new violent strategies and weapons need to be developed. Failures in achieving a goal through a nonviolent strategy are generally taken to imply that violence is needed. There is no thought of developing new nonviolent techniques or of perseverance. And the greatest irony is that when the conflict parties, exhausted and suffering, come to the negotiating table, it is violence that receives the credit for bringing them there. 'See, with violence, we have at least come this far.' Changing this assumption completely is a long and difficult process; however, bringing up the issue is already an important step.

To strengthen the idea that there are alternatives to violence and to the current situation, looking back to how conflicts were dealt with in the past can offer an insight into alternatives which have worked in a concrete way. This brings out the positive experiences which may help guide and bring hope to the ongoing process.

To look into what has happened, and to begin the process of re-evaluating assumptions is something very emotional for participants. It is important not to avoid these emotions, and it is important to acknowledge these feelings. The therapy of the past begins here, but the entire process is an ongoing one.

Phase two: differentiating between 'just/legitimate' and 'unjust/illegitimate' goals

The process-oriented aim of phase two is to create 'analytical empathy' within each conflict party for the other conflict parties, to create understanding that the conflict can only be transformed if basic human needs for all are fulfilled. The structure-oriented goal is to give the conflict parties the possibility to reflect upon the unconscious dimensions of the conflict and to prepare the ground for formulating new legitimate goals, assumptions and attitudes.

An indicator of whether this aim has been achieved is whether the conflict party can identify what is illegitimate within their own goals and what is legitimate within the goals of the others.

Step three: exploring unconscious assumptions and attitudes and unconscious contradictions and goals (Analysis of the Past)

The third step goes into a deeper understanding of what the conflict is 'really about', by examining the deeper contradictions, the assumptions and attitudes, and the interests of the conflict parties. The idea is to gain insight into the historical development of the conflict, the structural and cultural context, as well as the unconscious obstacles and resources to peace which exist in the collective unconscious. This is an analysis of the past, of what happened, what could have happened, and why things happened. The conflict trainer/worker accompanies the conflict parties in this exploration of the deeper dimensions of the conflict. One guiding question is, 'What are the structural and cultural obstacles and resources?'

After this process, the conflict trainer/worker should have a basic idea of the deep culture and deep structures of the conflict formation in question. For example, in the analysis of ethno-nationalistic deep cultures, it is important to look at the national anthems, street names, national myths, literature, sagas, music, statues, specific proverbs, and other similar carriers of the deep culture and to reflect with the conflict party about the meanings that are associated with these symbols. It is also important, at this stage, to reflect on collective trauma and glory and how this influences the conflict constellation on the surface. It might also be useful to start reflection on religious and cultural values and frameworks and how these influence the way we interpret reality.

The deep structure can be observed by looking at what the major societal faultlines are, and which groups are favoured over others. The conflict trainer/worker is there to help identify those aspects of the society which have sunk into the unconscious, and make the conflict parties aware of those deeper elements.

This process of deep dialogue cannot be done overnight. Identifying and recognizing the recurring themes and patterns which are deeply ingrained in the society and culture requires continuous attention and numerous discussions. This process is perhaps the most difficult one of a conflict transformation process because it requires conflict parties to dig deep into their past and collective unconscious, and to find what is constructive as well as what is destructive and therefore needs to change. Again, this is not something which can be achieved by a few people over a few discussions. For meaningful change in the deep structure and culture of a society to occur, the discussions must take place throughout the society over an extended period of time. As with the conflict transformation process in general, one cannot expect for this entire process to be completed in a short time. It is simply important for this process to start, making the conflict parties aware that there are deeper dimensions to the current situation, and to understand that they are influenced by the deeper level and therefore need to understand it better.

Having, to the extent possible, recovered the deeper underlying elements of the conflict from the level of the collective unconscious, the conflict parties can then proceed to examine how the deeper levels have influenced the progression of the conflict at the surface level, especially the attitudes, assumptions and goals.

Step four: the analysis of basic needs constellations and fixations (Analysis of the Future)

Step four moves again from an analysis of the past to one of the future, posing the questions of what the situation will be like if basic human needs will not be satisfied in the longer run (negative scenario), and what needs to be changed in order to ensure the basic needs of all conflict parties on the basis of structural symmetry and intercultural learning (positive scenario).

When the conflict parties bring up one of their positions, the conflict trainer/worker's role is to place those positions within the context of the social and cultural interests and more deeply within the individual basic human needs which are not being fulfilled. If a group is not allowed to use their language in their interaction with their government or in the educational system, then it is their need for cultural identity that is not being addressed, and the conflict trainer/worker should point this out. Awareness of how the denial of basic needs on the deeper level emerges as particular grievances on the surface level, and the connection between the two levels, needs to be raised.

Basic human needs are non-negotiable. Therefore, it is one of the tasks of the conflict worker/trainer to create an environment which allows the conflict parties to become aware of their basic human needs and the behaviours, strategies, fixations or pathologies linked to their needs. This is done through dialogue, but also through non-cognitive methods like sociodrama, systemic constellation work, and large group psychology. Differentiating between actors and their goals and strategies, The conflict trainer/worker is all-partial towards the actors, but undertakes a value-centred, dialogue-based exploration of their goals and strategies. Goals and strategies that violate basic human needs are not legitimate, and this must be clearly communicated to the conflict parties. Goals that need to be achieved in order to make the fulfilment of basic human needs possible need to be supported. The conflict trainer/worker, neither neutral nor all-partial, needs to take the side of basic needs, simultaneously challenging and supporting a conflict party depending on the compatibility of the party's strategies and goals with the respect of the basic human needs of the others.

If this principle is clearly communicated to the conflict parties and at the same time, through dialogue, the concept of basic human needs within the specific cultural and social context is constantly re-evaluated, then conflict parties are willing to accept this frame of reference. It has been our experience that conflict parties find this concept more understandable than all-partiality or impartiality, which goes counter to their very partial viewpoints. The fulfilment of basic human needs for all as the frame of reference guarantees the transparency of the conflict trainer/worker. It also minimizes the risk of unconsciously referring to one's own cultural values.

The concept of basic human needs is used to differentiate the legitimate goals from the illegitimate ones. The litmus test is whether a goal prevents the attainment of the basic needs of the individuals from another conflict party. The conflict parties need to examine which particular basic needs they are focused on, and also which basic needs they may be neglecting in order to maintain that focus. As well, the basic needs of the other conflict parties need to be explored, putting the one conflict party into the position of their antagonists which leads to an increase in the understanding of the other as well as empathy. Often, the preprogrammed responses to the perceived goals of other conflict parties make it difficult for this process to take place, and the work of the conflict trainer/worker is to develop the capacity for empathy.

One method is to ask the participating conflict party to go through a role reversal and argue the position of the other side, expressing the basic needs of the other side. A second important reason for such an activity is that the understanding at that moment which one conflict party has of the other is expressed clearly. This gives not only the conflict trainer/worker a clearer understanding of how one conflict party perceives the other, but also improves the conflict party's understanding of their own perceptions. However, care must be taken when engaging participants in such a role reversal. It is only possible under certain conditions, when the setting is safe, trust exists and care is taken to not (re)traumatize the participants.

Phase 3: integrating the legitimate goals with an overarching formula

Once the conflict party is able to empathically perceive its adversaries, it is ready to think about possible solutions. The conflict party should at this point perceive the situation no longer as a destructive conflict, but as a common, challenging problem that needs to be addressed. The process-oriented aim of phase three is to evoke spontaneity and creativity within the conflict party, so that an overarching vision, strategy and formula (which are the solution-oriented aims) can be found.

Step five: the construction of new attitudes, new assumptions and goals (Therapy of the Future)
Step five is the integration of the legitimate goals of all conflict parties into an overarching framework, through each conflict party alone, without the presence of the others, in order to prepare them for future negotiations or mediations. There is a return to the five outcomes, with the focus on finding transcending solutions to the problem, finding the structure for peace which enables the attainment of well-being, freedom, identity and survival for all. The conflict trainer/worker, together with the conflict parties, continues the process of examining the deep dimensions, but with more of an emphasis on the positive aspects which can be used in transforming the conflict. The solution must reflect the positive deep behaviours, cultures and structures of the conflict parties. Doing so ensures that the new peace culture, structure and praxis will be legitimate in the eyes of the conflict parties and will have the benefit of deep roots within the society.

Using the diagram of the five possible outcomes, the 'either' and 'or' points are relabeled with the newly elaborated legitimate goals of the conflict parties. The parties should then undergo a brainstorming process of coming out with possible solutions which address the legitimate basic needs of all parties. In this creative process, some of the best ideas are those which may sound impossible at first. This is generally a good sign, because such a reaction is typical when someone is faced with a completely new idea, different from those which have been discussed before. Time needs to be given in order to allow this new idea to be assimilated. Conflict trainers/workers are also there to help elaborate proposals and ideas without, however, trying to impose those ideas. Rather, these proposals should serve as examples of the kind of creative thinking necessary for the conflict transformation process.

New structures, culture and strategies for peace and the overarching formula should fall along the peace diagonal, with a creative integration of aspects of neither/nor, compromise and transcendence. Working along this peace diagonal ensures that the new structures fulfill the requirements of equity and reciprocity necessary for a just peace through a cooperative process. The elaboration of solutions according to these principles engages the conflict parties to develop a common vision of the future. It is a therapy of the future. And it is at this point that the conflict parties are truly ready for the round table, for honest negotiations because they are internally prepared to do so, rather than being externally coerced.

Step six: creating new behaviours, an action plan for the present (Therapy of the Present)
The process returns full circle to the issues of the present, but now focused on the therapeutic elaboration of the actions necessary in order to transform the conflict. This is done in the light of the deeper understanding of the conflict and of the alternatives developed in order to address the inequities of the past and present. The most important thing about step six is the creation of a new reality, a reality in which there is a palpable change in the relationship and a transcendence of the conflict. With a conflict party, having reached this point in the conflict transformation process, the action plan can be to bring forward this new vision to the other

conflict parties, to share with them this new vision. The sixth step is also the first step to (re)conciliation. Any agreement, no matter how just or creative, must be accompanied by a process of (re)conciliation, transforming the relationships, structures and cultures, and establishing a permanent dialogue between all communities and segments of the society in order to ensure that peace will have the deep roots it requires in order to thrive.

It is important to stress that this is not a sequential process. It is not about getting from steps one to six, and thinking that the process is complete. The complexities of reality do not allow for such a theoretically ideal situation. A conflict trainer/worker will not be able to joyfully announce that the conflict parties have now reached step four of the process. It is much more complex than that. The process goes from one phase to the others and back again. All six steps can occur within a day, yet not be achieved after a period of years. However, each step is an important element of the conflict transformation process, the analysis and therapy for the past, present and future necessary for a sustainable process of conflict transformation and peace-building. The six-step process is both therapy and analysis (or, in the terminology of systemic therapy, observation and solution-orientation). And there is a dialectic between past and future, both anchored in the present.

In most of the cases, the conflict parties should not be informed of the six steps at all. Rather, it should be considered as a mental map for the conflict trainer/worker to be use to keep track of the numerous processes which must occur, and the tools which can be used to achieve them. It is the mental map, but not the landscape of a conflict. But in our view, it is a very useful tool for conflict and peace counselling and training.

Notes

1 To avoid using the unwieldy 'peace/conflict worker, consultant or trainer', the more general term of conflict worker/trainer will be used.

2 For more on the Transcend scientific approach, see Galtung, J. (1977) 'Empiricism, criticism and constructivism: three aspects of scientific activity', in *Methodology and Ideology*, Copenhagen: Ejlers, Ch. 2.

3 This differs from Platonic dialogue, in that there is not one side with the answers, trying to elicit that answer from a pupil. Rather, the idea is one of many equal-sided and open discussions – hence going from the Greek dia – meaning two, to poli – meaning many. It is going from two parties, to many, with each party sharing with the others. This breaks free from the dichotomous thinking entrenched in formal mediation, legal and diplomatic approaches and allows for much greater creativity and complexity.

References

Chigas, D. (1997) 'Unofficial interventions with official actors: parallel negotiation training in violent intrastate conflicts', *International Negotiation*, 2, 3: 409–36.

Fisher, R. (1997) 'Training as interactive conflict resolution: characteristics and challenges', *International Negotiation*, 2, 3: 331–51.

Galtung, J. (1996) *Peace by Peaceful Means: Peace, Conflict, Development and Civilization*, London: Sage.

Galtung, J. (2000) *Conflict Transformation by Peaceful Means (the Transcend Method)*, New York: United Nations Disaster Management Program.

Galtung, J. (2002) 'The epistemology and methodology of peace studies', paper presented at the Centre for Peace Studies at the University of Tromsø, Tromsø, Norway, January, available at: http://uit.no/getfile.php?PageId=3324&FileId=37.

Graf, W. (2006) 'Soziometrie, Friedensforschung und kreative Konfliktbearbeitung. Einladung zu einer

Begegnung zwischen J. L. Moreno und Johan Galtung', *Zeitschrift für Psychodrama und Soziometrie*, 2, 5: 191–206.

Lederach, J.P. (1995) *Preparing for Peace: Conflict Transformation across Cultures*, Syracuse, NY: Syracuse University Press.

Lederach, J.P. (1999) 'Just peace: the challenges of the 21st century', in *People Building Peace: 35 Inspiring Stories from Around the World*, Utrecht: European Centre for Conflict Prevention.

Lederach, J.P. (2005) *The Moral Imagination: The Art and Soul of Building Peace*, Oxford and New York: Oxford University Press.

Lumsden, M. (1996) 'The evolution of the problem-solving workshop: introduction', *Peace and Conflict: Journal of Peace Psychology*, 2, 1: 37–67.

Neef, M. (1991) *Human Scale Development*, New York: Apex Press.

O'Toole, K. (1997) 'Why peace agreements often fail to end civil wars', *Stanford Report Online*, 19 November, at http://news-service.stanford.edu/news/1997/november19/civilwar.html.

Rothman, J. and Olson, M.L. (2001) 'From interests to identities: towards a new emphasis in interactive conflict resolution', *Journal of Peace Research*, 38, 3: 289–305 (Special Issue on Conflict Resolution in Identity-based Disputes).

Volkan, V.D. (1999) *Das Versagen der Diplomatie: Zur Psychoanalyse nationaler, ethnischer und religiöser Konflikte*, Giessen: Psychosozial-Verlag.

Wilber, K. (1995) *Sex, Ecology, Spirituality*, Boston, MA: Shambhala Publications.

10

Nonviolence

More than the absence of violence

Jørgen Johansen

Introduction

Research on nonviolence has never dominated the academic field of Peace Research. Compared to the focus on violent conflicts, peaceful ones have always been a minor sideline. The practice of nonviolence has on the other hand developed a lot over the last 100 years. In the following chapter, I will introduce the two main forms of nonviolence and then go deeper into the more nuanced views and advanced discussions in each of these fields. The most influential use of nonviolence in recent decades has been in political revolutions. This chapter will go through the waves of nonviolent revolutions that have washed over the world since the 1980s. At the end, I will try to look into the crystal ball and see what the future can bring.

The word

Nonviolence is a word we can find in very many contexts. It is often used as a specifier for other topics and hence followed by another word – nonviolent action, nonviolent philosophy, nonviolent communication, nonviolent defence and many more. In itself it is almost impossible to define. It consists of two words most people regard as negative: no and violence. In most languages it has the same construction. Among the European languages German stands out as a little different: *gewaltfrei* (free from violence). None of them have a completely positive connotation. In recent years some have done their best to introduce new concepts with a more attractive meaning. The German *Gütekraft* (good power) is one example.

Why nonviolence?

Nonviolence is not always the first choice for people in conflict. Why some use nonviolence is a relevant and important question not only for theoretical reasons. It can also give guidance for those who search for help in how to act when in the midst of a conflict.

For many pacifists life itself has an inviolable or sacred value and hence it will always be wrong to hurt other living beings. Some will restrict this to humans, for others all forms of life have an ultimate value.

For the more pragmatic minded, the situation is different. Many argue that by using violence to influence the outcome of a conflict it is often very difficult to reverse your actions in case you are wrong. It is easy to acknowledge for any honest person that we from time to time make wrong judgements. If we act violently based on wrong assumptions it is seldom possible to reverse our actions. It is obvious in extreme forms of violence: killing someone cannot be reversed, but the same goes for many forms of physical or serious psychological violence.

In the same way, many argue that violence is too wide-ranging a tool. All persons have a number of 'roles' and in most cases it is only one or a few of them we have conflicts with. Let us say you are a trade unionist, a woman, a mother, a football player, a friend, a daughter, an environmentalist, a Christian, a sociologist, a social democrat, a soldier and a Norwegian. Maybe it is only your role as a soldier I have a conflict with. If you are part of the occupation of Afghanistan by volunteering as an officer in ISAF forces in Afghanistan, I don't have problems with any role other than that you are a foreign soldier in an occupied country. If I shoot you, I will also kill all the other roles you have. Violence is not specific enough to separate the different roles. This is one of the main reasons against Weapons of Mass Destruction (WMD). The nuclear bombs the US dropped over Hiroshima and Nagasaki in 1945 killed all forms of life within several square kilometres and destroyed life for many more. Violence is blind. Most nonviolent means are much more specific. They could be directed to one precise role of a person or a group of persons. It is, for instance, possible to boycott the owner of your local shop because he sells products from child labour and still cooperate with him as your trainer in football. Or you can take part in a protest against a decision by local politicians but still be friendly neighbours.

When violence is used it will often result in counter-violence and be the first twist in a violent spiral which can escalate out of control. For many of those who opt for nonviolence, the fear of the consequences of violent means is a strong argument in favour of nonviolence. A long discussion within political movements is how the means influence the ends. Many of the most prominent figures within nonviolent movements have argued strongly that violent means result in violent ends. In recent years these discussions have been given attention in more than a few armed movements as well. Former guerrilla soldiers describe how military means grow from being a tool to totally dominating the movement. Some argue that armed means became the only focus for the movement and the political goals became less important. An intensive discussion on what are the most effective means takes place in many movements these days.

Most of the discussions on the relations between means and ends have been focused on the problematic consequences of violent means. The degree to which the traditional nonviolent means always end up with nonviolent ends has not gotten the same attention. As we will see in the next section, on waves of nonviolence, there is need for more research on the long-term results of the nonviolent revolutions in recent decades. It is not obvious that all nonviolent means will always result in nonviolent ends.

Another frequent argument in favour of nonviolence is that the activists are fighting problems rather than persons. Violence can hit humans but not ideologies, decisions and policies. The roles of individuals in political conflicts have a tendency to be exaggerated. When individuals in central positions are replaced, the systems seem to survive and continue more or less as before.

Many argue that nonviolence is more effective than violence. In most social movements there is not even a discussion about violent means; the only interesting topic is which nonviolent techniques are appropriate for the campaign in front of them.

That violence creates new problems is an experience many have discovered. New conflicts, often far away from the focus they are interested in, pop up as a result of the use of violence. These conflicts remove the centre of attention and withdraw resources they could otherwise have used on their main goals.

Two overlapping traditions

The history of nonviolence has two traditions with some connecting points: the pacifistic and the pragmatic traditions. In the pacifist tradition, we include nonviolent ideas, aspects, views and visions from religions, philosophies, ethics and lifestyles. For pacifists no goal justifies killing other human beings. Many pacifists are against all forms of harming humans and other living beings. The pragmatic school regards nonviolent actions as being important and effective as political tools, a collection of techniques, and as means for communication, for revolutions, for a social movement, and as a system of defence. Many within the pacifist school actively use the methods within the pragmatic tradition, but the majority of those using the nonviolent skills do not share the pacifist views.

In the past, the pacifist traditions were larger. Pacifism has never been a majority view, but historically pacifist practitioners of nonviolence used to outnumber pragmatists. In modern times, we have the opposite situation. Those using active nonviolence for pragmatic reasons now outnumber pacifists.

In the following section, I shall tell the history of both these traditions and distinguish the characteristics of each of them. Then I will see where there are overlaps and describe the latest developments within the research on and practice of nonviolence.

The pacifist tradition

Religious traditions tend to dominate the history of pacifist nonviolence. Inspired by holy scriptures, gurus, gods, imams, priests and other leading persons from different religions, there have probably always been groups of religious believers who were committed to nonviolence. Theistic pacifists believed that acts of violence were against the will of God and hence sinful. Some authors argue that prior to the rise of the leading religions of today, other faith systems with female goddesses rather than male gods were more peaceful than those now prevalent.

Within all religions you will find representatives who do not find any justifications for the use of violence in their respective scriptures and oral traditions. But these are usually exceptions: most religious believers justify the use of violence as a means of defence in conflict situations, be that defence of attacked individuals, groups or states. There is no one 'correct' interpretation of holy books, but nearly all of them tell stories where the god(s) goes to war for a good cause and uses extremely violent means against the enemies. Holy texts, such as The Lun Yu,[1] Wu Ching,[2] Bhagavad Gita,[3] Koran,[4] New Testament,[5] Tanakh,[6] Talmud,[7] Tao-te-ching,[8] Guru Granth Sahib[9] and Veda[10] are all interpreted in many different ways on the question of justification of violence. For many followers it is just as easy to find quotations in these texts which give good reason for the use of violence as it is for others to find guidance for a pacifistic conviction.

Within every religion we find denominations that are more consistent pacifists than the mainstream followers. Within Christianity, so-called 'peace churches' such as the Brethren, the Mennonites and the Quakers, are examples of such religious communities. Two religions, Jainism and Bahá'í, are very firm in their nonviolent views and practice. For them the philosophy of nonviolence is the core of their religions.

The central part of a nonviolent philosophy is that the use of violence is morally wrong; that the aims do not justify the means. The most widespread understanding of nonviolence is the rejection of killing human beings. But most nonviolent philosophies have a much more nuanced view than this. They regard all sorts of physical and psychological harm against human beings as violations of the nonviolent norm. And many expand the scope to include not only human beings, but all sorts of living creatures. Some will include the whole global ecosystem as well as material objects.

Mohandas Karamchand Gandhi used the concept *ahimsa* in his philosophy. *Ahimsa* occurs in Bhagavad-Gita and is normally translated as 'nonviolence' or 'non-harm'. In the Bhagavad Gita, the concept is used narrowly, with other terms describing many other forms of 'no injury' or 'no harm'. Gandhi expands the use of it to include a number of different injuries. In the Gandhian philosophy it is not only a question of physical actions but he argued that *ahimsa* should be a principle guiding humans in their thoughts, words and deeds. Well aware of human nature, he was clear about the impossibility to completely fulfil such a norm, but that does not make it impossible to make every effort to reduce injury on other living creatures to an absolute minimum.

Gandhi has wrongly been criticized for promoting passivity, whereas in reality he argued that passivity itself could be violence: 'every act of injury to a living creature and endorsement of such an act by refraining from non-violent effort, whenever possible, to prevent it, is a breach of ahimsa.'[11] This attitude so widens the concept as to make it an act of violence to abstain from efforts to prevent injurious acts, for instance suppression, manipulation, exploitation (Næss 1974: 48).

It can be useful to ask a few questions of this view. The first one is, is it universal? Shall the norm guide us in all situations and is it applicable for all human beings? Gandhi himself was not always clear on this point. There are situations in his text where he argues in favour of putting an end to life of a living being. One example is euthanasia. He describes a situation with a sick calf and the only way to end the terrible suffering is by giving the calf a deadly dose of poison. He adds: 'It was a surgical operation, and I should do exactly the same thing with my child, if he were in the same predicament' (Galtung and Næss 1955: Ch. 3) This is a side of the Gandhian view on nonviolence not widely known or accepted today.

What about other exceptional cases? What if someone falls in the river and cannot swim? When a brave swimmer tries to help, if the person in danger panics, the only way to rescue him is to knock him unconscious. Is that a violation of the *ahimsa* norm? Even if it includes physical violence, most people would easily justify such an act of unselfish and brave action. There are similarities in some of the common arguments for a national military defence and the situation with someone trying to save the life of others by inflicting some pain on them. The moral justification for military defence includes the idea that it can be right to sacrifice a few to save many. Few wars have been started without someone trying to justify them with arguments that they are carried out to defend higher values. The pacifist traditions do not accept such justifications of the use of violence in war situations. Neither do they justify slavery, colonialism, patriarchy or imperialism. These are all violent institutions justified by the majority just a few generations ago. Moral norms are seldom static. They change over time and differ from context to context.

For pacifists, it is more complicated to judge actions which include the harming of oneself. Many persons within the nonviolent traditions have of their own free will done harm to their own bodies. Fasts and hunger strikes are two well-known types of action. Prisoners all over the world have used hunger strikes as a means to get attention for their demands. Gandhi went on open-ended hunger strikes on several occasions. On 11 June 1963, the Buddhist monk, Thich

Quang Duc, burned himself to death in protest against the Vietnam War. Thich Quang Du was protesting against the way the administration of the Vietnamese prime minister, Ngo Dình Diệm, was oppressing the Buddhist religion during the war. Several monks and nuns followed him. Four US citizens also self-immolated in protest against the US attack on Vietnam. These extremely painful forms of suicide are controversial in many respects. Within most religions, actions like these have relatively few supporters even if there is a deep respect for those who do end their lives in this way. Many believe that such actions will be rewarded after they pass away.

It is important to understand the variations among different religious contexts when it comes to judging actions like these. For some, like most Christians, the death is much more definite than for others. For a Hindu, with thousands more lives on earth, the passing away is much less dramatic. For Gandhi, the hunger strike was an action to show how much he was willing to suffer for the cause he was struggling with. He was solely responsible for the action and possible death. When political prisoners in Christian cultures are close to dying in hunger strikes, the media and public opinion often blame others (for instance, political leaders) for the possible death of a prisoner. To die is a very different process in different religions.

Another factor of difference, when it comes to the use of violence, is whether or not ethical norms are seen as universal. Do they apply to all human beings? In the Western traditions there are widespread views that norms are valid for all or none. In, for instance, the Hindi tradition there are different norms depending on your karma and cast. For a Sadhu,[12] it is a norm to avoid the use of violence in every situation, while someone from the warrior caste, the Kshatriyas,[13] has a duty to use violent means to defend his people. Gier characterizes Hinduism as 'relative nonviolence' and gives several reasons for this: '(1) the prohibition against killing is relative to the person, yogis and Brahmins taking the vow most strictly; (2) it is also relative to the occasion, such as killing in war, in self-defence, and in sacrifice; and (3) it is relative to individual self-interest' (Gier 2004: 34).

Gandhi was not advocating a traditional Hindu view on these matters. He argued that the norm of *ahimsa* was universal and he opposed the common view among Hindus that a military defence is a necessity. Gandhi was often in doubt and experimented with different activities. He tested a number of diets, political actions and views on political and moral questions. Most of his writings are dated. In his original writings you can always see on which specific date he wrote each letter, article or comment. The reason is that he was always prepared to change his mind when he learned new things. He told his readers that, if in his writings they found several opinions on the same subject, they should trust the latest. This option for changing even your core values is important to remember when reading texts by or on Gandhi.

Gandhi grew up in a home with a very strong relationship with his deeply religious mother. She belonged to a sect that combined Hindu and Muslim beliefs and she welcomed Christians and Jains in their house. One of the great Jain saints of modern India, Shrimad Rajchandra, settled many of Gandhi's spiritual doubts and was a significant personal inspiration for him: local people referred to Rajchandra as 'Gandhi's Guru' (Hunter 2003).

For Gandhi, philosophy was not enough. His vision was to develop and build a whole lifestyle based on nonviolent principles. He used the terms 'Nonviolence for the Weak' about the pragmatic use of nonviolent techniques and 'Nonviolence of the Strong' for those who committed themselves to a nonviolent lifestyle. That lifestyle was a totality of self-discipline, undemanding lifestyle, an inner search for truth, the use of non-cooperation against unjust laws and decisions, constructive work,[14] and civil courage to confront the opponent.

Among the famous advocates of nonviolence based on a religious belief we find Leo Tolstoy, Martin Luther King, Jr. and Gandhi. For them, human life had an ultimate value, higher than everything else. Nothing was important enough to sacrifice human lives. This faith led them to a pacifist position and guided their activities in life. For many, nonviolence became part of their lifestyle and influenced all parts of their life. In daily life, nonviolence could decide what to eat, how to travel, what to consume, how to relate to other human beings (and nature), how to act in order to take responsibility for your local community, and what to do for leisure. People who lived with Gandhi, like 'JP'[15] (Narain 1978) and Narayan Desai[16] (Desai 1980), use the term 'Total Revolution' to describe the extensive implications of a nonviolent lifestyle. Political and social revolution are not enough; in addition there must be an inner revolution in each individual. And both JP and Narayan Desai are clear that the change within every individual is by far the most difficult one.

Within this lifestyle-orientation we find the most obvious overlap between the pacifist tradition and the pragmatic tradition. Many, although not all, of those committed to a nonviolent lifestyle also tend to be engaged in nonviolent actions of different sorts. They include in their lifestyle a societal engagement and take part in civil society activities against what they regard as unjust, immoral or simply wrong policies and decisions.

The pragmatic tradition

The pragmatic tradition of nonviolence has its roots in those parts of society that have fought with peaceful means for freedom, democracy and respect for human rights. These tools are used by stakeholders to influence a conflict situation. They have adopted different nonviolent strategies and techniques and used them in their struggle against inhuman ideologies, policies, systems, decisions and laws. Their choice of means has been based more on what is effective than on ethical guidelines and moral values. Even if we can trace their history back further, it is fair to say that they have developed and been used more in the last 100 years. Today, the majority of those who deal with nonviolence, whether they use the term or not, belong to the pragmatic tradition.

Nonviolent techniques are frequently used in most modern social and political movements. Within women's networks, trade unions, environmental groups, solidarity movements, peace organizations and other parts of civil society, nonviolent actions are used regularly to promote their ideas and struggle for their causes. Nonviolent actions are used either to create wider support for their goals, to directly reach their aims, or in order to prevent their opponents from achieving theirs.

What is meant by 'nonviolence' in the pragmatic school? It is obvious that there are diverse definitions used by different authors and activists. Many practitioners have never needed or wanted to propose a full and distinct definition, but when asked have said that they 'don't use serious physical violence against other human beings'. Others have wider definitions. Some will exclude all forms of psychological violence as well. At one extreme of a spectrum we find people who merely 'try to avoid killing humans', while at the other there are those who will avoid 'all disturbance of the harmony in life'. The latter ones you will find among those who use nonviolent actions as a part of their lifestyle. The majority of nonviolent activists belong somewhere in the middle, but closer to 'not killing' than 'perfect harmony'.

Whatever definition is used, there is one more aspect of these actions we need to clarify. Is it a nonviolent action just because it avoids the use of violence? In the early phase of his writing, Gandhi used the term 'passive resistance'. That could be interpreted as nonviolence being some form of passivity; not doing anything. This is a misunderstanding we still find used in present discussions and in media coverage of nonviolent actions and movements. Gandhi changed the term to *ahimsa* and the English interpretation: nonviolence. Later he used Satyagraha, which literally means 'to keep to the truth'.[17] The point here is that we need to make clear what we mean by nonviolence. Vinthagen (2005: 136–46) has developed and clarified the definition of the concept. He argues that in addition to 'without violence' it must also be 'against violence'. It is not enough that an activity is carried out without the use of violence. To fulfil the criteria of being labelled nonviolence it must in addition be done with the aim of reducing or eliminating violence or oppression.

Nonviolent actions can be categorized in three broad groups: protests, non-cooperation and interventions.

Nonviolent protests

Nonviolent protests are actions of peaceful opposition but not going as far as refusing to cooperate or directly intervene in the situation. The use of symbols, marches, picket-lines and protest meetings are typical examples of nonviolent protest. A wide variety of actors are using such techniques on a regular basis. For more examples, see Chapter 3 in *The Politics of Nonviolent Action* (Sharp 1973). A frequent goal for nonviolent protests is to communicate a message of opposition. It can be seen as a voice against the establishment when the formal political channels do not give them a say in decision making. The protests themselves are a visual means of communication, but often they are combined with slogans, symbols or catchphrases which explain the message. Protests are normally just one step in a chain of activities which leads to more communication between representatives from the opposition and delegates from those in positions of power. Thousands of protests take place in the local, regional and global arena every day.

Non-cooperation

Non-cooperation is well known from trade unions and their use of strikes. They put pressure on their employers by refusing to fulfil their role as producers. But these same methods are used by many other actors and in many different contexts.

To decrease or withdraw completely the normal level of cooperation changes the power relation between the actors. The main idea behind such actions is that political, social or economic power depends on some level of cooperation. These types of power can be influenced by changing the level of cooperation. The level of cooperation is based on several factors. Cooperation may exist because it benefits the involved actors or it can be based on fear of the consequences of refusing to cooperate. The fear is normally based on knowledge about possible forms of punishments. States are well known for threats of punishments like trials, fines, imprisonments, tortures and death penalties. Other actors can force people to be obedient by threats of social exclusion, withdrawal of support and – as for state actors – physical or psychological punishment. The most frequent reasons for people's cooperation, in addition to self-benefit, are ignorance and unawareness. The norm is to obey, follow orders and regulations and not behave differently from others. For non-cooperation to take place it is necessary, but not sufficient, to remove, fear, ignorance and obedience.

Nonviolent interventions

Nonviolent intervention is the last of the three categories of nonviolent actions. These are actions in which some form of direct involvement from someone who originally was not part in the conflict takes place. By directly intervening in a situation, the persons taking part in it often expose themselves to higher risks and the consequences can be both more immediate and more serious. The interventionists can, depending on their activity, be stakeholders in the conflict. Nonviolent interventions take place in many contexts. Someone intervening when a single person is attacked on the street is a small-scale example. Members of Shanti Sena[18] interpositioning themselves between fighting Muslims and Hindus in Indian cities is an example on a group level. In the last two decades we have seen people from the peace movement act not just in their home country but by going to war zones. During the Vietnam War most activists demonstrated in their own cities or gathered outside US embassies around the world. With the wars in the Balkans we saw the first massive wave of activists moving into the battle field. It had been done earlier, but only in small numbers. In the present wars in Palestine, Colombia, Sri Lanka and Iraq the nonviolent actions inside the countries at war are substantially bigger than in any previous war. Some of these actions are there to support the local civil society; others are carried out as 'third'[19] parties acting with their own agendas. Still, it is important to recognize that for most wars there are no strong movements, neither inside nor outside the combat zone. For the majority of wars, the nonviolent initiatives are still to be born.

Civil disobedience

Civil disobedience is one traditional form of nonviolent action that deserves some extra attention. It is a form of action that often triggers strong reactions and it is used in all cultures, many contexts and by all sorts of actors. The definition of civil disobedience is an action which fulfils the following four criteria:

1 A violation of a law or generally accepted norm.
2 It is done without the use of violence.
3 It is done in full openness.
4 It is done with a serious commitment.

A few words of explanation for each of these four points will make it easier to grasp this form of nonviolent intervention. The first one just says that the action is illegal or contradicts generally accepted norms in the society. This makes it controversial and provokes reactions from several actors. The second criterion is the one which specifies that civil disobedience is a nonviolent action. Exactly what is meant by nonviolence is debated. That no humans shall be physically hurt is commonly accepted, but many will accept some degree of psychological aggression and symbolic sabotage of material objects. The third criterion is the one which makes these illegal actions unique. Commiting an illegal activity and being open about it puts strong demands on the actor and creates reactions among those who are observing or are parts in the conflict. Here there is a requirement that the people using this form of action shall face the consequences of their activities. The implications of that are that the activists shall not try to avoid being arrested or stay away from coming trials. A public 'confession' of what they have done is often included in these actions. The last criterion is included in order to separate these actions from 'funny' or purely spectacular activities.

That the action by definition is illegal makes it very controversial. No establishment can ever support such actions and they frequently condemn them as 'anti-democratic' and dangerous. From history we know that such actions have been used by most movements that have worked for more and better democracy. Well known are the actions of civil disobedience used by the Abolitionist Movement in the US against slavery, the suffragists in their struggle for the universal right to vote, the Civil Rights Movement for equal rights for all citizens, the workers' movements for their right to organize themselves in unions, the anti-conscription movements for their right to conscientious objection, and the environmental movement for the right to a safe environment. Looking back, it is obvious that the uses of civil disobedience have been to the benefit of democratic development.

Nonviolence as antithesis of violence

Violence has been defined and categorized by Johan Galtung (Galtung 1969, 1990, 1996). His terminologies are direct violence, structural violence and cultural violence. In short: direct violence is harming others with intention. Structural violence is the harm done by sociopolitical structures and decisions that deprive someone of their access to basic needs necessary for fulfilling one's full potentials in life. Cultural violence is the cultural justification of direct and structural violence. Each of them has their antithesis in the context of nonviolence.

Direct nonviolence

Direct nonviolence is the use of nonviolent techniques to influence conflicts without the use of violence. The full scale of pragmatic nonviolent methods and strategies are integrated parts of direct nonviolence. Direct nonviolence is used to directly confront those decisions, laws and systems that do not treat all humans equally. The struggle for the abolition of slavery, decolonialization, removal of patriarchal structures, resistance against wars and imperialistic policies are all full of direct nonviolence. People have used direct nonviolence against illegitimate powerholders and faced armed police and military forces for hundreds of years. Many of them with successful results.

Structural nonviolence

Structural nonviolence consists of those structures in our society that promote cooperation, reconciliation, openness, equality and peaceful actions in conflict situations. Democratic institutions and systems are examples of such structures. Democracy is here meant as something much more than the parliamentarian state systems we find in many Western states today. Consensus, inclusiveness, transparency and accountability are important elements in a real democracy. And these are all elements in many traditional communities. A nonviolent societal structure will to a large degree be the result if political, economical, cultural, and social human rights are fulfilled. More specifically, structural nonviolence is those parts of a society which open up for nonviolent handling of conflicts regarding human rights. When there is unequal distribution of resources, freedoms, and rights, a nonviolent structure gives people the possibility to handle such conflicts by peaceful means. In this case, 'peaceful' involves more than the tools of direct nonviolence. It includes many sorts of mediation, conflict transformation and reconciliation as well.

Cultural nonviolence

Cultural nonviolence includes those parts of our culture that transmit traditions of nonviolent behavior and which commemorate and honour nonviolent values and qualities. We can find nonviolent traditions in most cultures, religions and philosophies. While rarely the dominant tendency, they still formed important parts of norms and systems of behaviour in relation to other human beings and/or nature. Nonviolent ways of handling conflicts can be traced far back in history. Even in times of instability and in the midst of violent conflicts we find individuals and groups who have approached the situation with the use of nonviolent techniques. We have in mind here not those who avoided conflict, but rather those who actively took part, but using peaceful means. Often they have been regarded as wise and sensible women and men. Among indigenous people many of these nonviolent values, techniques and ethics are still ruling their communities. Within movements, organizations and networks many of these qualities are integrated and important elements.

The Culture of Nonviolence has deep roots in human history. Just as in today's media, so too our written history is dominated by actions of violence. But despite violent clashes, the capabilities to cooperate have characterized human life since early days. Individual humans have sacrificed their lives for the community on many occasions in our history. Altruistic behaviour has always been regarded as a respected virtue. Human societies could not have developed without a strong force of cooperation and the capacity to solve conflicts without the use of violence.

A problem for those who search for the peaceful roots in our civilizations is that the nonviolent behaviours have not been recognized as important enough to be documented. Probably nonviolent ways of handling conflicts have been so widespread that they have never been paid any specific attention. We still see that tendency today. Almost all research on conflicts focuses on the most violent ones. Societal conflicts seem only to be interesting when the groups involved are using belligerent means, and domestic conflicts are only studied when individuals are beating and/or killing each other. This focus has been so strong that some have redefined conflict and only count those cases which include violence. Other conflicts are hardly regarded as conflicts at all. But it is among the peaceful conflicts that we can find the most interesting cases of how to handle conflicts nonviolently. One of the aims for research on conflicts should be to learn about how to handle future conflicts as peacefully as possible. In order to be skilled at peaceful conflict handling we should carefully study the most peaceful cases in our history. When military officers of today have almost every military battle since the Napoleonic wars in their curriculum, peaceworkers should have a similar history of nonviolent conflicts in theirs. The need to document nonviolent cases cannot be underestimated.

Waves of nonviolence

The concept of Nonviolent Revolution has in the past two decades gone through a renovation and transformation. From the early 1980s and up till today the number of movements that successfully have confronted governments and parliaments and demanded change in their leadership has increased enormously. The pragmatic use of nonviolent strategies in struggles for revolutionary goals is the dominant tendency. In the same period only a handful of armed movements have achieved successes in their fight against states. This change in means for victorious revolutionary movements will have an impact on the concepts, theories, research on and use of nonviolence for decades to come.

The focus in the following is those movements that have used mainly nonviolent means in their struggle and which have been successful in toppling the leadership of a state. Only cases from countries with a relatively strong and organized civil society are included. The numerous examples of movements that have not (or not yet) achieved their goals are not forgotten, but are not included in this chapter. Neither are the many social movements which effectively have used nonviolent means in their struggle for other goals than a regime change. The large majority of social movements from all parts of civil society use nonviolence on an almost daily basis in their struggles. For those focusing on questions of gender equality, environmental problems, human rights, solidarity with the oppressed, freedom of speech and other important issues, almost all apply only nonviolent techniques in their repertoire of means.

There is also a chronological limitation in the cases taken up in this chapter, namely the period from the early 1980s to the present time. Preliminary research indicates that an important change in the use of means by those movements who worked for a change took place around that time. The trend for such movements had since 1945 been that successful movements who aimed for a change in the present regime based their strategies mainly on the use of armed struggle. Since Solidarity in Poland, an important strategy for successful movements has been holding massive demonstrations in central places of the capitals.

This is not the place to describe in detail each of these cases, but a few from the first wave will be used as illustrative cases. The key lesson here is that the nonviolent strategies and techniques *characterize* the successful nonviolent revolutions in recent decades. Most of the cases can be categorized into four more or less separate waves. The cases in each wave are linked together in different ways. Cooperation and inspiration are the main common factors.

Wave one: Poland, Bolivia, Uruguay and the Philippines

Poland, 1980

The first case in this wave is Solidarity in Poland. After two centuries of armed uprising, the Polish workers in 1980 tried to fight the regime with non-armed means and they formed the independent trade movement, Solidarity. The Catholic Church and the Polish pope played a crucial role in inspiring and giving courage to individuals in the years ahead. The visit to Poland by the Pope in June 1979 mobilized some of the largest gatherings in Poland ever. No one was in doubt about the Pope's view on communism.

Solidarity is noted for its use of symbols in its struggle. Not only its flag and the Catholic cross, but a number of monuments, historic dates and well-known persons were used to express solidarity's views in times of censorship. Kubik, in his book *The Power of Symbols against the Symbols of Power* (1994), gives the reader an excellent and sophisticated cultural understanding of these nonviolent means.

On 1 July 1980, localized strikes broke out all over the country as the result of a government decree that raised meat prices by almost 100 per cent.[20] In August 1980, the Gdansk Strike Committee (MKS) was formed and 21 demands were presented. By early September, agreements were signed in three cities giving the workers the right to form trade unions and to strike.

On 21 September, the Sunday Mass was heard on national radio for the first time since the Second World War. During the whole autumn, strikes and court cases were intermingled with talks between Solidarity and the government. The Supreme Court officially registered Solidarity on 10 November. On 5 December, Warsaw Pact countries met for a summit in Moscow and four days later the Soviet Union initiated military exercises all around Poland; fears grew of an invasion like in Hungary 1956 or Prague 1968. By early February next year General Jarulzelski was named prime minister, asking for a three-month 'truce'. Industrial and general strikes occurred in several parts of the country. Starting in the shipyards in Gdansk, the strikes spread to many sectors and cities in the country. The scope of the protests and the lack of violence created a situation where the government was forced to start negotiations with Solidarity. By the end of autumn close to 10 million people in a total population of 35 million joined the protests. The unions created a multitude of diverse forums for free expression of opinions. An Independent Student Union won recognition, farmers began to organize the independent Rural Solidarity. The whole of 1981 continued with strikes and recognition of more organizations. The peak was reached on 13 December, when Jaruzelski declared 'martial law' and a number of Solidarity leaders and activist were arrested.

The coming spring, Solidarity started to organize underground and formed a Temporary Co-ordinating Commission (TKK). During the following 12 months, a number of demonstrations took place but not with large numbers of participants. In October, a new law dissolved independent self-governing trade unions, and by New Year martial law is suspended. The following year the visit by the Pope in June resulted in the lifting of martial law and in October Lech Walesa was awarded the Nobel Peace Prize. The struggle continued and Solidarity asked people to boycott the local government elections 1984. The following year a major shift starts in the Soviet Union with the election of Gorbachev as the General Secretary of the Communist Party. In 1989, Solidarity got 35 per cent of the seats in Sejm[21] and 99 out of 100 seats in the new upper house, the Senate. It is a without doubt a good result after almost a decade of nonviolent actions. That Lech Walesa was elected president on 9 December 1989 can be seen as the end of the revolution.

Poland became some sort of model and source of inspiration for many other movements worldwide. Even if the contexts were very different and the means also differed, the Polish example encouraged other oppositional movements to organize large-scale nonviolent resistance and confront those in power.

Bolivia, 1982

Bolivia became the next scene for a nonviolent revolution. The nonviolent mobilization started in 1977 when three women from the mining districts started a hunger strike in the capital, La Paz. The well-known woman Domitila Barrios de Chungra joined them and soon many activities around the country followed. Bolivia is a country from a different political and cultural context, but with some similarities to Poland. A strong trade union is one important common factor. General Luis Garcia Meza led a bloody coup in 1980. The committee for Defence of Democracy (CONADE) was established in spring 1980 and mobilized the political opposition. The Bolivian trade union, Central Obrera Boliviana (COB), joined them and started to organize for strikes in the mines and, later, general strikes. Since the majority of the population are farmers, the opposition gathered new strength when the farmers union joined them. After five general strikes with increasing participation and a growing number of farmers in demonstrations, the generals had to step down in 1982 and give governmental power to those who won the elections in 1980. Bolivia is not well known for nonviolent resistance, but there are many interesting parallels to Poland. When Lech Walesa got the Nobel Peace Prize he invited representatives from the trade union, COB. There were obviously good links between Solidarity and COB. In both cases, the workers' organizations cooperated with the farmers' unions and generated a strong coalition which decided to use nonviolent means. The armed tradition from Che Guevara turned out to be less effective and popular than the strikes, demonstrations and boycotts.

Uruguay, 1985

After the coups d'etat in June 1973, nobody challenged the military junta in Uruguay. It was regarded as one of the most totalitarian and brutal regimes in Latin America. All forms of opposition were met with cruel reactions. People got tortured, killed or disappeared. In an effort to legitimate its power, the dictatorship organized a referendum over a new constitution in 1980. The proposed constitution would institutionalize the military rule over the country, but was rejected by 57 per cent of the population.

In the end of August 1983, a small demonstration was organized in front of the small office of Servicio Paz y Justicia (Serpaj) in Montevideo. Inside, three people had been fasting for 15 days and more and more people gathered outside in solidarity. The authorities had cut off light, water and the telephone to the office. One night a new form of protest was born: *caceroleada*. It means banging on pots, pans and other kitchen equipment to make sounds in protest. The sound was soon heard everywhere in the city. Police and military could not do much as long as people were inside their houses. With open windows the sounds got around.

Serpaj was declared illegal by the government soon after the first large *caceroleada* but grew quickly to a major national human rights movement through these actions. Labour and student organizations demonstrated separately in the capital Montevideo on several occasions that autumn. The common and main demand was new elections. In early 1984, labour and civil strikes pressed the military into negotiations with the major opposition parties. A result of these discussions was the military's agreement to hold national elections in November, in which the opposition Colorado Party's Julio Maria Sanguinetti emerged victorious. He took office in March 1985.

The Philippines, 1986

Asia was the next continent to experience a successful nonviolent revolution. Corazon Cojuangco Aquino went into exile with her husband, opposition leader Beningno Aquino. On his return to the Philippines, he was shot dead on the airport runway on the orders of Marcos. When Corazon returned home for his wake and funeral, she was persuaded to become leader of the opposition. In the years following her husband's death, she led numerous demonstrations and stood against Marcos in the election of 1986. In February that year, popular uprisings took place at military camps in Quezon City, outside Manilla. President Ferdinand Marcos met serious opposition after 13 years of martial law. Marcos felt confident that he would win and announced presidential elections. So blatant was Marcos' use of fraud in the elections that several electoral returning officers walked out in protest. The Catholic Bishops Conference of the Philippines issued a document that was read from pulpits throughout the nation. They declared that the people had a duty to resist, nonviolently. One million people took part in demonstrations at Lueta Park on 4 February. Two weeks later, more than two million turned up in the park. Thousands of civilians surrounded the military tanks Marcos ordered out on the streets to stop the demonstrations. Active 'fraternization' by the demonstrators turned many soldiers into supporters of the opposition. Later, parts of the armed forces declared that Mrs Aquino was the true winner of the elections. Massive demonstrations of people in yellow t-shirts took place in the capital to support Mrs Aquino. The yellow colour was used by Aquino as the symbol of her movement. Whenever she was seen in public she dressed in clear yellow clothes. That was why she got the nickname the 'Canary bird'. By the end of February, Marcos fled the country and Corazon Aquino took her place as the Philippines' legally elected president.

Wave two: Eastern Europe and the former Soviet Union

The year of change in Eastern Europe was 1989. With the collapse of communism in Poland, the legitimacy for one-party systems in the rest of the Soviet bloc disappeared. In country after country people took to the streets and demanded change in the regimes. The most spectacular event was of course the fall of the Berlin Wall, but quite a few other episodes worth mentioning took place in several countries east of the 'Iron Curtain'.

By the year 1989, the communist regimes in six Eastern and Central European countries met nonviolent movements which undermined their one-party system. During the year to come, free multiparty elections were held. Many similarities can be seen in these events. Popular movements used nonviolent means to put pressure on their political leadership and the Soviet Union hesitated to come to the aid of the communist establishments. All of the old communist leaderships found themselves in difficult situations that they could not cope with. They did not know how to respond to the lack of violence from the protesters as they had trained their police and military troops to handle violent uprisings. With international television the price became much higher than they could afford.

Nonviolent actions from an organized civil society played an important role in the following countries: Hungary, East Germany, Czechoslovakia, Bulgaria, Moldavia, Mongolia, Lithuania, Tajikistan, Azerbaijan, Estonia, Latvia and Russia.

Wave three: sub-Saharan Africa

In sub-Saharan Africa a similar wave of massive nonviolent actions removed the old regimes in country after country. The opposition in Benin had been growing for a long time and drew further inspiration from the dismantling of the Berlin Wall. With the break-up of The Soviet Union in 1991, several of the francophone countries saw the possibility of following the path of Benin. The student movement in China in 1989 and the bicentennial of the French revolution gave extra energy to new movements. Nonviolent and relatively well-organized oppositions forced the former marxist regimes to open up for more pluralistic political systems. In countries like Burkina Faso, Guinea, Senegal, Mali and Malawi, similar waves of democratization as in Benin followed. And the most well-known case, South Africa, got rid of the apartheid system after a long and mainly nonviolent struggle in 1994.

In 2001, President Ratsiraka of Madagascar faced a well-organized opposition that did not accept the official results of the elections. Large-scale demonstrations, strikes and peaceful protests forced him to resign in 2002.

Wave four: Serbia, Georgia, Ukraine, Kyrgyzstan and Lebanon

The next wave is still going on. With the massive bombing by NATO of Serbia in 1999, the opposition against Slobodan Milosevic was weakened. But the experiences from nonviolent opposition during 1996–7 became the base for a new and better organized opposition, aiming for the removal of Milosevic in the elections in autumn 2000. Following a number of demonstrations opposing the official results of the elections, close to a million people gathered in Belgrade on 5 October. They filled the city, occupied the government-controlled TV station and parliament and Milosevic resigned. The student movement Otpor was crucial in this revolution. Activists from Otpor later trained students in other countries and have worked as consultants for similar movements in Georgia, Ukraine and Kyrgyzstan. These three countries went through similar revolutions during 2003–5. A similar revolution took place in Lebanon in 2005. And for several of the former Soviet states oppositional movements are organizing for analogous revolutions.

What was the role of nonviolence in these cases?

Each of the revolutions mentioned above is unique. But they also have several common aspects. All of them include a pragmatic nonviolent strategy, with large masses of people gathered at central places. The aim is to show strength, unity and power. In most cases an election was part of the process – either the opposition successfully demanding an election, or an election taking place and the opposition accusing the old regime of fraud to stay in power. Most of these cases have an element of external support of some sort. That could be political and/or moral support for the opposition or it could be practical help in organizing, training and accomplishment of the protests. One of the most debated forms of assistance is financial transferences from foreign states or foundations to local opposition groups.

This discussion is obviously important and is one which will need more attention in the years to come. Some of the questions are: To what degree will external funding influence the agenda of the opposition? Will external funding have a different function in these conflicts depending on who the funders are?

The role and impact of financial, practical, political and moral support have not yet been sufficiently researched. Neither are there many studies of external forces intentionally creating problems for an opposition and trying to hinder them to achieve their goals. One crucial question is, if some intervention from abroad is important, necessary or sufficient for local movements to be victorious. Another important and disputed question is to what degree external support influences the agenda of the incoming power-holders once they are in power. These are all important tasks for research on nonviolent revolutions in the years to come.

Not enough to remove the old regime

The long list of successful nonviolent political revolutions all have one problematic consequence: they have been more successful in removing a regime than in replacing it with something better. Only a few of them have had a well prepared strategy for building a new and better society when the old one falls. Some changes are identifiable in the majority of cases:

- They introduce multiparty elections.
- Their foreign policies are more friendly towards the US and the EU.
- Neo-liberal market economies are introduced.

The new economic system with extensive privatization and liberalization results in a growing economy. The surplus gets bigger and bigger. In principle there is more wealth available for each citizen. But since the market economy doesn't include a system for a fair distribution of the surplus it ends up in the hands of the few. The gap between rich and poor tends to be deeper and wider than before. That results in a deadly form of structural violence, with serious consequences for the weakest ones in these societies. In summery: it is a tendency that the modern nonviolent revolutions end up with more structural violence.

This side of the nonviolent revolutions is not anything unique to them. Almost all states worldwide have been included in the new global economy and are facing similar problems. That the changes of societies only occur 'at the surface' by changing the people at the top level and that no profound social changes occur was also the result when Gandhi evaluated the liberation of India. His firm belief was that it was a consequence of too much non-cooperation and too little 'constructive work'. Gandhi's conclusion was that for a country to change into a nonviolent society it is necessary to start building the new nonviolent society long before the 'takeover' and, in addition to changing the political structures, it is essential to change the social structures as well. In addition to that, Gandhi eagerly argued that without an 'inner revolution' there could never be a nonviolent society. To change the attitudes and spirits of each individual was, according to Gandhi, not done sufficiently during the struggle against British rule and that is why the liberated India become a quite ordinary state, ridden by internal violent conflicts, was partitioned, and never came even close to a nonviolent state.

If the 'total revolution' in the Gandhian tradition includes changing the political power, the social structure and the inner transformation of each individual, then the waves of nonviolent revolutions presented above are only a fraction of what is needed for a nonviolent society to materialize.

The future

Peace research on nonviolence has never received the same resources and attention from the leading universities and institutions as studies on weapons, wars and other forms of violence. But after some interest in the early days of modern peace research there is a renaissance in the early part of the twenty-first century. More books are published and more studies carried out today than ever before. An impressive amount of work has been done by committed individuals in academia as well as by activists. Most of it focuses on the more pragmatic understanding of nonviolent means. Evaluations and case studies of the growing number of practitioners dominate. When it comes to developing new theories, production is still relatively meagre.

Mohandas Karamchand Gandhi is the most well known among those who have developed the nonviolent theories and techniques further. He is the 'greatest' in many respects and since he passed away in 1947 none have been able to move the field forward in the same way as he did. His life, practice and ideas have served as inspirations for many who have taken up these means and used them in their practical struggles. His autobiography is called *My Experiments with Truth* and points to the leading methodology in his life. He experimented with a diverse variety of political actions, diets, forms of communities, partner relations and constructive campaigns.

Probably there will never be anyone who can match Gandhi, but there are many who can follow the same path and do 'experiments with the truth'. To use creativity and empathy to develop new nonviolent tools; test them in conflict situations and build up a record of well-documented experiences is the most important job for those interested in nonviolence in the years to come. In this work there are tasks for academics and activists from all parts of human activities.

Notes

1 The Analects of Confucius – supposedly sayings of Confucius, but the text was not collected and edited until some 400 years after Confucius' death. Also called 'The four books'.
2 Five works traditionally attributed to Confucius that form the basic texts of Confucianism. The collection of writings by Confucius and his disciples is often referred to as 'Four Books and Five Classics'.
3 A Sanskrit poem that is part of the Indian epic known as the Mahabharata.
4 (Arabic, al-Qur'an) The primary holy book of Islam.

5 The second part of the Christian Bible, which contains 27 books that form the basis of Christian belief. The New Testament canon as it is now was first listed by St Athanasius, Bishop of Alexandria, in 367. That canon gained wider and wider recognition until it was accepted by all at the Third Council of Carthage in 397. Later, certain books continued to be questioned.
6 The Jewish name for the Hebrew Bible. It is the sacred scripture of Judaism and the first part of the Christian Bible.
7 A compilation of Jewish oral law and rabbinical teachings that is separate from the scriptures of the Hebrew Bible.
8 (The Way and Its Power) The basic text of the Chinese philosophy and religion known as Taoism.
9 The holy texts for Sikhs. The texts contains the actual words from the founders of the Sikh religion and various other saints from other religions, Hinduism and Islam included.
10 The sacred scripture of Hinduism of which the Upanishads form the final portion.
11 Gandhi, M. K. (1970) *Collected Works of Mahatma Ghandi*, Vol. 37, New Delhi: Publications Division, Ministry of Information and Broadcasting, Government of India.
12 Hindu men (and some women) who have devoted their entire lives to the quest for moksha (liberation from the chain of lives). These holy men renounce worldly concerns and live on alms.
13 According to the code of Manu, a Kshatriya is a member of the military or reigning order, one of the four varna within the Vedic caste system.
14 'Constructive Work' was to start building the future liberated India while the British still ruled the country as a colony. To be independent of British textiles by spinning, weaving and sewing your own clothes was one of several campaigns Gandhi included in the struggle for an independent state.
15 Jayaprakash Narayan (1902–79).
16 The founder of Sampoorn Kranti Vidyala (Institute for Total Revolution).
17 A very good explanation and discussion on these terms can be found in *Satyagraha and Group Conflict* by Næss (1974).
18 On the ashrams of Gandhi and Vinoba Bhave, the first seeds of Shanti Sena, the Peace Army, developed. In the 1920s, Shanti Sena became a part of the Indian struggle for independence and fostered fearless and impassioned co-workers.
19 This term indicates that there are only two actors in a conflict. This common misunderstanding is based on very superficial views on conflicts. A better term would be 'n+1 party'.
20 One major reason for this was the demand from the Soviet Union to send large quantities of meat from Warsaw Pact countries to Moscow prior to the Olympic Games. They wanted to prove false the Western rumours that there was a lack of meat in the Soviet Union.
21 That was the maximum agreed in the round table discussions.

References

Desai, N. (1980) *Handbook for Satyagrahis: A Manual for Volunteers of Total Revolution*, New Delhi: Gandhi Peace Foundation.

Galtung, J. (1969) 'Violence, peace, and peace research', *Journal of Peace Research*, 6, 3: 167–91.

Galtung, J. (1990) 'Cultural violence', *Journal of Peace Research*, 27, 3: 291–305.

Galtung, J. (1996) *Peace by Peaceful Means: Peace and Conflict, Development and Civilization*, Thousand Oaks, CA: Sage.

Galtung, J. and Næss, A. (1955) *Gandhis politiske etikk*, Oslo: Grundt Tanum.

Gier, N.F. (2004) *The Virtue of Nonviolence: From Gautama to Gandhi*, Albany: State University of New York Press.

Hunter, A. (2003) *Forgiveness in Jainism*, Coventry: Centre for Peace and Reconciliation Studies.

Kubik, J. (1994) *The Power of Symbols Against the Symbols of Power: The Rise of Solidarity and the Fall of State Socialism in Poland*, University Park, PA: Penn State University Press.

Næss, A. (1974) *Gandhi and Group Conflict: An Exploration of Satyagraha – Theoretical Background*, Oslo: Universitetsforlaget.

Narain, J.P. (1978) *Towards Total Revolution*, vol. 1, Bombay: Popular Prakashan.

Sharp, G. (1973) *The Politics of Nonviolent Action*. Boston, MA: P. Sargent Publisher.

Vinthagen, S. (2005) Ickevåldsaktion. En social praktik av motstånd och kontsruktion [Nonviolent Action – A Social Practice of Resistance and Construction], *PADRIGU*, Gothenburg: Gothenburg University.

11

Human rights and peace

Jim Ife

The aim of this chapter is to examine the field of human rights, to identify some areas of debate and controversy about human rights at the beginning of the twenty-first century, to suggest some ways in which these might be overcome, and to relate these ideas to the field of peace studies.

If understood at a superficial level, the aims of peace and human rights can be seen to be at times in conflict. It might be argued that in some cases too great a concern for human rights can lead to processes that prevent the achievement of peace; an example is the case of East Timor, where peace with Indonesia can perhaps only be achieved if at least some of the human rights violations committed by the Indonesian military between 1975 and 1999 are quietly forgotten, and those responsible for the violations are allowed to go unpunished. Similar arguments might be made in the case of Bosnia, Kosovo, Rwanda, Burma, and in other parts of the world, suggesting that 'human rights' should be sacrificed in the interests of peace. Similarly, if 'peace' is regarded as synonymous with 'security', then the argument that human rights must be sacrificed in the interests of peace is heard consistently in the rhetoric of the so-called 'war on terror'. From this perspective, attempts to achieve peace can be seen to be stifling human rights, and attempts to achieve human rights can be seen to be stifling peace.

This chapter sees such a view of a conflict between human rights and peace as being fundamentally flawed, and based on inadequate understandings of both peace and human rights. Rather, the position taken in this chapter is that peace and human rights are necessary for each other: peace cannot be achieved without human rights being protected and realized, and human rights cannot be achieved in the absence of peace. Peace without human rights would be a weak and flawed peace. People cannot be said to be living in peace if their human rights are violated, as the structural and institutional violence inherent in human rights abuse is the antithesis of peace, as understood in other chapters of this book. Similarly, human rights cannot be realized in the absence of peace; war is itself a human rights abuse, for both the military personnel involved and for civilians, and it also creates other human rights abuses, from censorship and the denial of civil liberties, to torture, rape and summary executions. The abuse of human rights in times of war, when narrowly defined ideas of 'national security' and 'the national interest' are seen as trumping human rights imperatives, are well documented. Indeed, labelling the current concern with 'terrorism' as a 'war on terror' has allowed human rights guarantees to be eroded in a number of western nations, in the form of 'anti-terror' legislation. War and human rights violations belong together, and in the same way their opposites – human rights and peace – also belong together, and neither can be achieved without the other. To work for one involves also working for the other, and the two are necessarily connected.

It is therefore necessary to understand both peace and human rights at a more sophisticated level, so that they will not be seen as in conflict. Other chapters of the book deal with peace and peace studies, and this chapter will develop ideas of human rights that are not only compatible with ideas of peace, but that also reinforce peace studies and peace advocacy.

Conventional discourses of human rights

This chapter takes the view that 'human rights', as conventionally understood in the dominant Western discourse, is a limited construction, with significant inadequacies. This contributes to the apparent conflict between peace and human rights mentioned above, and, while there is no doubt that the idea of human rights has led to significant and positive change for many people, the conventional human rights discourse is inadequate for the needs of the twenty-first century, in a post-colonial and postmodern world.

The intellectual origins of 'human rights'

At one level, human rights are as old as humanity, as they are about how human beings treat each other. There are ideas that might be equated with human rights in many different traditions, including ancient Greece and Rome, Chinese and Arabic cultures, the Jewish, Christian, Muslim, Buddhist, Hindu and Shinto traditions, and Indigenous spiritual and cultural traditions from different parts of the world (Hayden 2001; Ishay 2004). On the other hand, while human rights can be said to be as *old* as humanity, they are, in another sense, as *new* as humanity. This is in the sense of the idea of the 'human' and of something unique called 'humanity' having emerged from the Western Enlightenment tradition, in the discourse of 'humanism', only in the period since the European Renaissance (Carroll 2004). The humanist project, while so pervasive in contemporary thought, is in fact of recent historical origin, and human rights, in the form in which they are commonly understood, are firmly embedded within this worldview.

This is at one level hardly surprising. Almost every social and political idea with which we are familiar has been profoundly affected by Western Enlightenment thinking, with its associated strands of humanism, liberalism and modernism. This includes community, society, democracy, liberty, justice and the nation state, as well as ideas of humanity and of rights. To say that human rights are a product of Enlightenment modernist thinking is really to state the obvious, and 'human rights' is in good company in this regard. The question is whether 'human rights' is so embedded within this world view that it has no relevance in the world of postmodernity, where other worldviews are competing with Western liberalism, so that human rights will inevitably remain a part of the colonialist project. However just because something is defined in Western liberal terms is not a sufficient reason for it to be abandoned. To take a couple of trivial examples, Western domination of food production and consumption does not imply that we should abandon eating, and Western domination of clothing styles does not mean we should stop wearing clothes. Rather, the need is to deconstruct the Western domination of the human rights discourse, and reconstruct one or several views of human rights that are more inclusive of different intellectual, cultural and spiritual traditions. That is the aim of this chapter.

The dominant contemporary discourse of human rights has its philosophical origins in the works of Hobbes, Locke, Rousseau and Mill (Hayden 2001; Herbert 2003). These writers concentrated on the relationship of the individual to the state, where some individual sovereignty is ceded to the state in return for protection of basic rights, as part of the social contract. Although these writers offer different interpretations of this contract, there are common themes of individualism, and the protection of individual freedoms, in their work. From this tradition, it is unsurprising that ideas of human rights developed with a primary emphasis on individual liberties. These are sometimes referred to as 'negative rights', namely rights which need to be protected, rather than rights which need to be provided; the latter are referred to as positive rights, examples being the right to education, to healthcare, to employment, to social security, etc. Positive rights require a stronger role for the state; they require the state to take positive action to ensure that various services and programmes are *provided*, rather than simply providing legal mechanisms to ensure that rights are *protected*. The emphasis on negative, civil and political rights is seen in media reporting of human rights; a country with a 'poor human rights record' is one where individual liberties are under threat, rather than one with a poor health system or inadequate education facilities.

Along with the emphasis on negative rights arising from the Enlightenment tradition, it is also important to acknowledge the emphasis on individualism. Ideas of collective rights have little place in the works of Locke and Mill. The emphasis is on the individual, the 'rights of man [*sic*]' (Hayden 2001; Mill 1969; Paine 1994). And as the language indicates, those ideas of human rights were also gendered, with women's rights being excluded from the discourse, though it should be noted that there has always been an opposing voice articulating women's rights within this perspective, beginning with Mary Wollstonecraft's 1792 publication, *Vindication of the Rights of Woman* (Wollstonecraft 1983).

Another feature of the liberal Enlightenment tradition of the construction of human rights is that the distinction between the human and non-human is both implicit and rigid. The humanist tradition, in privileging the 'human' as at the centre of the world, forces a separation of the human from the non-human, resulting in 'human rights' being seen as a different category from animal rights or rights which might be attached to nature. This is a characteristically Western view, and is not replicated in all cultural traditions; indeed in many Indigenous cultures people are seen as so interconnected with other life forms, with nature, with animals, rocks, trees, rivers, etc. that the Western tradition of separating 'man' from the rest of nature simply makes no sense. Seen this way, 'human rights' simply perpetuates the separation of humans from the rest of the world, and is part of the same thinking that has led to increasing environmental destruction, as people have come to see the rest of the world as simply serving the needs of humans, rather than as being interconnected with humans in such a way that they share a common experience and a common destiny (Eckersley 1992).

A further important characteristic of the Western construction of human rights is the emphasis on rights rather than on duties or responsibilities. Rights are defined, and then the responsibilities of others to protect or realize those rights are consequently inferred: these responsibilities vary and include, for example, the responsibility of the state to ensure that the rights to education and healthcare are met, the responsibility of the individual to ensure that others are treated with dignity, the responsibility of the community to achieve inclusiveness, etc. However the important point to note is that the thinking begins with an assumption of rights, and then proceeds to define the implied duties or responsibilities. In this way, the Western secular tradition differs from other ethical traditions where it is the duties to others that are defined initially, and any understanding of rights then emerges as implied from the *a priori* duties. This is a reversal of the conventional human rights discourse, and is one of the reasons why people from other cultural or religious traditions often find it difficult to engage in a discussion of 'human rights', especially if human duties are unacknowledged in the debate.

The final characteristic of the Western liberal understanding of human rights is the idea of universality. Human rights are seen as deriving from our humanity, and they therefore apply to all human beings anywhere, regardless of context. This universality has been a central characteristic of the human rights discourse, and at the same time is one of its most problematic elements. In a world of diversity, where different cultural contexts result in people defining 'reality' in very different ways, the imposition of a single 'set' of universal human rights on the entire global population is controversial – yet to question this universality may be seen to weaken the power of human rights and to endorse the actions of those who seek to justify human rights violations on the basis of cultural relativism.

The ideas discussed in this section represent, in summary, the 'intellectual baggage' of human rights. In order to develop an approach to human rights that can truly serve the needs of humanity, it is necessary first to understand that human rights have been constructed from within this particular worldview, which is not the only way of seeing the world, nor is it a world view which is compatible with many belief systems and cultural traditions. Then it is necessary to deconstruct these assumptions and to seek ways in which human rights might be understood in a more intellectually robust way. This in turn will establish an approach to human rights which is more compatible with ideas of 'peace', and this is the aim of the second half of this chapter. First, however, it is important to examine some further characteristics of conventional constructions of human rights, which also affect the dominant discourse of human rights in the contemporary world.

The political origins of 'human rights'

Human rights emerged as a significant global discourse after the Second World War, specifically as a reaction to the experience of the Holocaust (Ishay 2004; Lauren 1998; Sellars 2002). The significance of the Holocaust in shaping modern ideas of human rights must not be underestimated. There had been other large-scale human rights abuses, but the Holocaust, unlike others, was perpetrated by Westerners on other Westerners, and therefore could not be easily ignored. The recognition of human rights abuse, on a massive scale, as something that could happen in a so-called 'civilized' and archetypically white European nation, the home of Bach, Beethoven, Goethe, Schiller, and the origin of half the royal houses of Europe, demanded attention in a way that previous abuses did not. The 'human rights movement' thus formed at a particular historical moment, in part at least to restore the reputation of 'Western civilisation'. This is not to underestimate the power or significance of that achievement, but rather to recognize its cultural and political significance. As a consequence, it is hardly surprising that one of the criticisms of human rights has been that they have been used as part of the colonialist project, as an apparently benign form of spreading the gospel of Western superiority to the remainder of the world. Despite, and at the same time because of, the genocide that was committed by a major Western power, the West was able to use the idea of human rights to reassert its moral superiority.

The Universal Declaration of Human Rights was adopted by the United Nations in 1948, and is seen as the foundation statement of human rights. Despite the criticisms of its being a device to restore the reputation of 'Western civilization', it nevertheless represents an amazing achievement for the nations of the world to sign and affirm such a document, and it remains as one of the great human achievements of the twentieth century. Subsequently the UN established the Covenant on Civil and Political Rights and the Covenant on Economic, Social and

Cultural Rights, which are the legal documents giving effect to the ideals of the Universal Declaration, and which impose obligations on signatory parties to enact legislation to give effect to the terms of the Covenants, and to report to the UN Human Rights Commission on their compliance. This division of human rights into two categories – civil/political rights and economic/social/cultural rights – reflected the Cold War thinking of the time. The West, and especially the US, emphasized civil and political rights while giving less attention to economic, social and cultural rights, while the reverse was true of the Soviet bloc. Thus the way in which human rights were defined represented the two dominant political discourses of the time; the split between the two categories of rights became enshrined in human rights thinking, and remains powerful even in the post-Cold War period. As a result of the critique of conventional human rights as individualist, further reinforced by the so-called 'Asian critique' of human rights (Bauer and Bell 1999), which maintains that conventional individual human rights are less important for the more collective societies of Asia, a number of writers refer to a 'third generation' of collective rights, to sit alongside the other two, though this has not been enshrined in UN conventions.

This 'three generations' approach to human rights has become conventional human rights wisdom, but this has served to limit and confuse understandings of human rights rather than to clarify them. The three 'generations' have been labelled as 'first generation' (civil and political), 'second generation' (economic, social and cultural) and 'third generation' (collective). This suggests an order of priority, assuming that first generation rights are somehow more significant, or that their satisfaction is a precondition for the other generations to become important. This is clearly not so – indeed many of the survival rights, such as the right to food, clothing, shelter and healthcare, which are included in the second generation, might be seen as needing to be realized before rights to freedom of expression or of assembly become of any great importance. On the other hand, some people have been prepared to die rather than give up such freedoms. There can be no clear and uncontested order of priority for human rights, and indeed the priority afforded to different rights will vary with cultural context. Any categorization that suggests that some rights are more important or fundamental than others is unhelpful. The categories of 'first', 'second' and 'third' generation rights carry those names simply because that is the order in which they emerged as important in modern Western thought. To use such terminology is simply to reinforce the dominance of Western thought in the framing of human rights. A further problem with the 'three generations' approach is that defining the third generation as collective rights assumes that the other two generations are, by contrast, individual rights. This forces an individualist focus onto these rights, rather than allowing them too to be understood collectively. Yet many, perhaps all, first and second generation rights can be understood collectively as well as individually: for example, the right to freedom of expression for ethnic or cultural minorities, the right to healthcare for Indigenous People, the right to education for people with disabilities, and so on. It would surely be preferable to develop a schema of human rights that enables all rights to be seen as having both individual and collective aspects. There are other criticisms of the 'three generations', to the effect that economic rights, social rights and cultural rights are sufficiently different to warrant separate categories, the need to allow for survival rights to be treated separately, and so on (for further elaboration of these arguments, see Ife 2005). However, the main point for present purposes is that the 'three generations' framework has serious conceptual problems. It reflects the political reality of the mid to late twentieth century, but is not particularly useful as a framing for human rights in the twenty-first century.

Legal dominance of the human rights discourse

One of the important characteristics of the conventional approach to human rights has been that it has been defined primarily within legal discourse. The law is seen as the principal way in which our human rights can be protected, and hence legal mechanisms and processes, courts, legislation, and the work of lawyers are given prominence in human rights. Sometimes human rights are simply equated with law, and sometimes it is even argued that the only rights that should count as 'human rights' are those which are justiciable, i.e. that can be defined and protected through laws and legal practices. This is a very limited, and limiting, view of human rights. The law has its limitations, and many of the rights most people would claim as human rights, such as the right to be treated with dignity, the right to freedom of expression and the right to be free from intimidation or discrimination can only be partially protected though the courts. Human rights, if they are about how people respect each other and behave towards each other, require more than merely legal procedures in order to be protected and realized. The way we treat each other has as much to do with cultural norms and expectations, media constructions of reality, parental influences, educational experiences and peer pressure as it does with what the law says we can and cannot do. The danger of a legalistic construction of human rights is that it can lead to the idea that once a UN declaration has been ratified and legislation passed, problems such as racism, child abuse, age discrimination or gender discrimination have been solved, and human rights have been protected. While such legislation is important, indeed necessary, it is far from sufficient if human rights are to be guaranteed. A society that protects and realizes human rights must have those rights embedded in its culture, not merely codified in its laws. Working for human rights is not the sole prerogative of lawyers; it is also the task of teachers, community workers, health workers, religious leaders, politicians, and indeed it is the task of all citizens, in their various roles of parent, child, relative, supervisor, colleague, workmate, community member, lover and friend.

The dominance of the legal discourse of human rights has contributed to the emphasis on civil and political rights, or negative rights, as these are the rights that are most readily justiciable. The importance of laws, the rule of law, legal rationality and the power of the legal profession have served to reinforce this legalistic view of human rights – human rights are what the law says they are – and this has limited our understandings of the way we can work for human rights. Legal work is important, of course, but the perspective of this chapter is much broader, and sees the law as only one part (though an important one) of understanding and achieving human rights.

Human rights and the public/private divide

Another characteristic of the conventional understanding of human rights is that it has been seen largely as applying within the public domain. Rights such as the right of freedom of expression, freedom of association and the right to be free from discrimination or harassment are typically understood as applying within the public sphere, even though they are also important in the private or domestic sphere. Typically, freedom of expression is understood as applying to the right to express one's views in public, in civil society. For many people, however, and especially for women and children, the right of freedom of expression is much more important within the family than in the public sphere, and the same can be applied to other rights, such as the right to an adequate income, the right to be treated with dignity, the right to safety and the right to freedom from discrimination. This has led to a powerful feminist critique of human rights organizations such as Amnesty International, which have been seen as operating largely in the public domain and thereby protecting the human rights largely of men, while ignoring human rights violations against women which typically take place in the private domain. In recent years Amnesty has responded to this criticism and has specifically included issues such as domestic violence within its mandate, but the fact remains that the traditional public construction of human rights has tended to work in a gendered way. Part of the reason for this has been the domination of legal frameworks for human rights, as discussed above. The law has always been less adequate in dealing with the private domain, and can only intervene in extreme cases of, for example, child abuse or domestic violence. More subtle human rights violations in the family, such as denial of the right of freedom of expression, or continuing humiliation and degradation, do not lend themselves well to legal action, but are better dealt with through other means. The law is, in many ways, a blunt instrument that is useful for dealing with extreme cases of human rights violations, but that is unable to deal effectively with the subtleties and nuances of human rights abuse as experienced by many people in their daily lives.

Expanding the boundaries of human rights

Thus far, this chapter has explored the conventional understandings of human rights, as derived from the Western intellectual tradition and the politics of the second half of the twentieth century. A number of critiques of the conventional discourse have been suggested, but it needs to be emphasized that these are not sufficient to invalidate the idea of human rights. There is no doubt that, despite these problems, human rights has been a powerful ideal, and has been the motivation for much that has been progressive over the past 50 years. The world would be a much poorer place without the Universal Declaration of Human Rights, the many other international declarations and human rights covenants, the UN Human Rights Commission, Amnesty International, Human Rights Watch, the bills of human rights which have found their way into the constitutions or statute books of most nations, and the actions of many citizens and community groups who have used 'human rights' as a driver for their various campaigns. Human rights are important, and the purpose of this chapter is not to demolish the idea of human rights, but rather to suggest ways in which the idea of human rights can be strengthened, and to link it to the idea of peace. There is active and engaged debate within the human rights literature around these issues, and through this debate the idea of human rights is being transformed into something more robust and appropriate for the world of uncertainty and diversity in an era of post-modernity.

Universalism and relativism

As mentioned earlier, the problem of universalism and relativism has been an ongoing theme in discussions of human rights (e.g. Bell et al. 2001). For some, it has been an insurmountable obstacle, preventing human rights from being taken seriously, as human rights might be seen as only having value if they are universal, yet such universality is clearly invalid in a world characterized by diversity. While diversity is arguably under threat from increasing globalization, it nevertheless seems likely that cultural diversity will remain a characteristic of the global village, especially if we accept the view of those who claim that globalization, in the form we know it, is only a passing phase (Saul 2005). There is no space in this chapter to consider the important issue of globalization, but for present purposes we will assume that cultural diversity will remain an important reality in the twenty-first century, and that if human rights are to remain a powerful ideal they must be understood in a way that embraces such diversity.

It is clear that a naïve universal position, and a naïve relativist position, are both untenable in relation to human rights. A naïve universalism would seek to impose a uniform human rights regime across different cultural contexts, and becomes little more than another exercise in Western colonialism, as the universal view of human rights that it imposed is inevitably Western in its orientation. A naïve relativism, on the other hand, leaves one powerless to act in the face of human rights abuses, as they can always be justified as 'cultural' and therefore sacrosanct. What is needed is a more sophisticated and nuanced position, which seeks to incorporate both the power of universalism and the diversity of relativism. While there is insufficient space in this chapter to deal with this issue in detail, three approaches will be briefly discussed. The first is to draw on the distinction between rights and needs.

Rights and needs are inevitably linked. A traditional way of understanding human rights has been to attempt to derive them from some notion of universal human needs (Doyal and Gough 1991). However, needs are far from universal. What we 'need' in order to satisfy our 'right' to education, to housing, to freedom of expression or to freedom from discrimination will be very different in different contexts. Seen in this way, rights can be regarded as universal, but the corresponding needs will vary from place to place, and over time. Hence the universal *right* to education is translated into very different educational *needs* (e.g. for classrooms, for computers, for books, for radios, for teachers) in different contexts. In this sense we can think of rights as universal, and those rights will necessarily be very general, while the definition and meeting of specific needs becomes the way in which those rights are contextualized differently. We can argue about the definition of needs (what is *really* needed) as a way of thinking about context, without questioning the validity of the right to which the needs are attached.

It should be noted in passing that the connection between rights and needs can be applied to the relationship between human rights and peace. The ideal of peace can be represented as a human right (the right to peace) or perhaps more appropriately as a set of human rights, including the right to security (both individual and collective), the right to safety, and the right to various freedoms. An overall right to peace might therefore be seen as implying more context-specific needs so that the right to peace can be realized, and these include needs for security, but also the need for the prerequisites for positive peace (e.g. health, education, income security, food security) which are also regarded as positive human rights and are identified as such in the UN Covenant on Economic, Social and Cultural Rights.

A second way to understand universalism is to think of the universality of rights as aspirational rather than empirical. If I define something as a human right, I am saying that I wish it to apply to all of humanity, regardless of culture or location. Someone in a different context may have a very different view of 'human rights'. But each of us is expressing a universal wish, something we each believe, from our own value systems, should apply to all people, everywhere. The universality therefore lies in the expressed wish of the right definer rather than in the 'existence' of the right universally, and it exists alongside relativism, in that each right definer is defining the right from her or his own cultural context. This is a different kind of universalism, which opens up the possibility of dialogue, because if different people are defining their universal aspirations for humanity, there is the capacity for them to share their ideas and learn from each other. This is in contrast to the conventional view of universalism, which is criticized for imposing one view of human rights on others in the name of 'humanity'.

A third approach to the problem of universalism and relativism is to see each as existing alongside the other, and as necessary for the other. Whenever we make a universal value statement, such as a statement about a 'universal human right', we do so in a context, as it is only our own lived experience that gives that statement any meaning for us. Universals are thus always derived from personal, and partial, experience and cannot claim any universal empirical validity. Dialogue can broaden the base of the personal experiences on which a universal statement is grounded, but a universal value statement cannot escape from its contextual basis. Similarly, whenever we make a statement about a particular context, we can only do so by making reference to some more general experience; for example, to define a particular culture as 'materialistic' only makes sense if we have broader understandings of other cultures and an understanding of materialism and its alternatives that transcends any single cultural understanding. Understood in this way, it is simplistic to talk about either universals or specifics in isolation from the other. Each is reliant on the other to give it meaning, and hence we need to understand universalism and relativism as occurring together and as dependent on each other, though of course one or the other may be foregrounded at any one time. Thus human rights are neither purely universal nor purely contextual. To assume either of these positions is to miss half the picture. Rather they are both, and human rights always reflect the tension between the two.

Collective and individual rights

Just as the distinction between the universal and the contextual needs to be deconstructed, and seen not in terms of a simple dichotomy, the same can be said of individual and collective rights. As argued above, the so-called 'three generations' typology of human rights has served to reinforce this distinction, and the very term 'collective rights' suggests that rights held collectively are somehow different from rights held individually. However, as suggested above, all human rights can be understood both individually and collectively, and while some cultural traditions such as the West may emphasize individual understandings, and others such as the Confucian may emphasize the collective, it is important to emphasize that the two need not be differentiated or seen as mutually exclusive. It is only by understanding all human rights as both individually and collectively held that we can move beyond the limited Western liberal view that has dominated the mainstream human rights discourse.

Rights and responsibilities

There is a natural link between rights and responsibilities or duties. This is obvious: my claiming a 'right' implies that there are others who have responsibilities to ensure that my right is either protected, in the case of negative rights, or provided, in the case of positive rights. However, this link has not always been emphasized, usually for ideological reasons. Those on the political right have often been reluctant to talk about rights, seeing them as dangerously socialist (except in the case of individual property rights, e.g. Kristol 1989), and have preferred to emphasize citizenship responsibilities and obligations rather than citizenship rights. Those on the political left, by contrast, have been happy to talk about rights, but reluctant to engage in too much talk about responsibilities, as this sounds too coercive. Thus the natural link between rights and responsibilities is broken, for reasons of ideological convenience, when in reality the two belong together and each makes little sense without the other.

Any discussion of rights and responsibilities must be undertaken from within an analysis of power. Talking about 'my/our rights' and 'your/their responsibilities' can be selfish and coercive if articulated by those in power, for example by managers talking about their workforce. However, if articulated from a position of disadvantage, for example by workers talking about managers, or the poor talking about the rich, it becomes a position of resistance or liberation. Similarly, talking about 'your/their rights' and 'my/our' responsibilities, if articulated from a position of advantage, represents a humanitarianism or an altruism, but if articulated from a position of disadvantage it represents submission and acceptance of injustice. It is important therefore always to look at who is defining rights and who is defining responsibilities, whether for themselves or others, and at the power relationships involved. Human rights do not exist in a political vacuum; discussion of rights and responsibilities can be coercive and oppressive, but it can also be liberating and transformative; it depends on the political, social and economic context. It is significant to notice, in this regard, who is seen to have rights and who is seen to have responsibilities; in countries influenced by neo-liberalism, for example, it is common for the advantaged to be seen to have 'rights' – the rights of shareholders, of managers, of elites, of media owners, etc. – while the disadvantaged are seen as having responsibilities and obligations, which they have to meet in order to benefit from state programmes and services.

Responsibilities might be regarded as the hard side of human rights work. It is often easy to obtain agreement about people's rights, but the question of who is responsible for protecting or meeting those rights is more problematic. It is important to emphasize that there are different locations where responsibility for meeting human rights can lie. The person or group claiming a right has a responsibility to exercise that right responsibly, as for example in the case of freedom of expression not being used as an excuse for racial vilification. Also the person's family and immediate social network have responsibilities, as does the person's employer, the community and the state. For example, the right to health imposes obligations on the individual to take reasonable care of their own health, on the family to provide a healthy environment, a balanced diet, etc., on the employer to provide a safe working environment, on corporations to sell safe and healthy products, and on the state to provide adequate health services. Thus a single right implies a range of different responsibilities, and this applies to all human rights.

Like rights, responsibilities must be understood both individually and collectively. By accepting that it is necessary to look at both rights and responsibilities, and by accepting that each can be understood both individually and collectively, we can derive Figure 11.1, which identifies four ideological traditions of rights and responsibilities.

The dominant Western individual discourse emphasizes the liberal tradition, of individual rights and associated individual responsibilities, but this is only one of four possibilities. An emphasis on individual rights and collective responsibilities to meet those rights is characteristic of the socialist tradition, with its emphasis on a strong welfare state to act collectively to meet people's needs. The Confucian tradition, by contrast, emphasizes the rights of the collective, and the responsibilities of individuals to contribute to the collective good. Finally, the communitarian tradition seeks to emphasize both collective rights and collective responsibilities.

Of course, reality is always more complex than such a simple figure suggests, and none of these traditions exists in a pure form, to the exclusion of all others, in any actual political or

		Rights	
		Individual	Collective
Responsibilities/ Duties	Individual	LIBERAL	CONFUCIAN
	Collective	SOCIALIST	COMMUNITARIAN

Figure 11.1. Rights and responsibilities: individual and collective

social order. Nor is it necessary to engage in a discussion of whether one or other of the four traditions is preferable. Rather, the value of the figure is that it identifies a range of ideologies of rights and responsibilities, and in encouraging each to be recognized as legitimate it provides a more inclusive framework to incorporate cultural and political traditions other than the Western, in understanding human rights.

The community of rights and the culture of rights

The connection between rights and responsibilities, and the incorporation of collective as well as individual understandings of rights, suggest that human rights need to be embedded in some idea of human community. Human rights make no sense in a purely individual world, as a single person on a desert island has no 'rights', because there is no one to meet the corresponding responsibilities. Rather than assertions of rights being assertions of individuality, they are more properly understood as assertions of our interdependence, as they imply an interlocking set of rights and responsibilities that tie people together in human community. This argument has been made by Gewirth (1996), who has put forward the idea of a 'community of rights' which derives from the very nature of human rights. In this sense, building human rights involves building human community, where it is not 'independence' but rather our inevitable *interdependence* that is emphasized and reinforced. There is thus a natural link between human rights and community development, and it can be argued that each needs the other. Indeed, human rights workers like to talk about realizing our 'common humanity' while community development workers talk about realizing 'human community', and the two terms are etymologically the same.

Such an approach to human rights is analogous to the idea of developing a 'culture of human rights'. This view suggests that it is not sufficient for human rights to be enshrined in constitutions and in legislation, but that they also have to permeate the culture, and become entrenched in cultural norms and cultural practices. In this way human rights achieve a sense of ownership across the community, and affect the way people treat each other in a much more complete way than is possible through legislation alone.

Human rights from below

The above discussion about broadening the idea of human rights, beyond the traditional Western, individual, legal frameworks, can best be summarized as an argument for 'human rights from below' as opposed to 'human rights from above'. The conventional idea of human rights accepts the view that human rights are defined in conventions, whether at UN level or in national constitutions or legislation, and that achieving human rights is simply a matter of applying these principles. It is therefore important to consider who drafted these conventions; in other words, who has taken on the task of defining human rights for the global population. The definers of human rights are an elite group; a small number of politicians, lawyers, academics, public intellectuals and human rights leaders have in effect defined human rights for the rest of us. This, it can be argued, represents a human rights abuse, in that the vast majority of the world's population has been denied any participation in the definition of their rights. The criticism that this elite is exclusively white and male is no longer true; women, and people from different cultural traditions, are actively engaged in formally constructing human rights. But it remains an elite group, representative only of the political, intellectual and legal elite, rather than of the global population as a whole, and those whose human rights are routinely violated – the poorest and most disadvantaged – are the least likely to be represented. This is *human rights from above*, and, however well-intentioned the definers of human rights, it remains a discourse of the powerful about the powerless.

To rectify this, it is important to develop a view of *human rights from below*, and this has been the thrust of much of the preceding discussion, with its emphasis on moving beyond the narrowly legal view of rights and developing ideas of a community of rights and responsibilities, and a culture of human rights. In this sense, human rights are embedded in human community, and indeed in our daily actions. In their day to day lives people work on certain assumptions about how to treat others, and about what they can expect from others. This represents a tacit understanding of human rights and responsibilities, not in the sense of universals defined in the Universal Declaration, but arising out of people's own lived experience and the way they negotiate their dealings with others. The approach of human rights from below works with these understandings, and encourages people to define human rights, and responsibilities, from their own experience, culture, moral and religious traditions.

Human rights from below allows for different understandings of human rights and responsibilities in different contexts, but then opens up the possibility of dialogue where individuals or groups can learn from each others' wisdom. It has the potential to develop a culture of human rights and responsibilities, and is linked to ideas of developing strong human community, in whatever form that may take. There are different ways in which people and communities can be involved in the definition and ownership of rights and responsibilities, drawing on community development principles (Ife 2002), but which are outside the scope of this chapter. The important thing for present purposes is to see this as an alternative vision for human rights and responsibilities, which overcomes many of the problems associated with conventional human rights discourse. This is not to deny the value of human rights from above – human rights conventions have been used to achieve significant outcomes in the improvement of human rights, and will continue to do so – rather it is to suggest that human rights from below need to sit alongside human rights from above, if the power and the potential of human rights are to be fully realized.

Human rights and peace

The argument above for 'human rights from below' as an alternative to more traditional formulations of rights, can similarly be applied to peace. In doing so, a view of human rights and peace emerges which is a way of moving beyond the apparent conflicts between peace and human rights identified at the beginning of this chapter. The aims of human rights work and of peace work become the same, and in the process the methods of peace work and human rights work also coalesce. Human rights and peace, indeed, cannot be separated, each is heavily dependent on the other. The three dimensions of any practice are knowledge, values and skills, though of course the relationships between them are problematic. With human rights work and peace work there is considerable overlap in the knowledge drawn on by each. The values of each, it might be argued, are identical, or at least so overlapping that it is hard to make any distinction between them. And the skills required to practise both human rights work and peace work are common.

It is clear that if peace is only achieved 'from above' it will only be a partial peace, that can leave many conflicts and tensions unresolved. True peace can only be achieved if 'peace from below' can be realized alongside 'peace from above', and peace-building is as much about community development with the powerless as it is about seeking peace agreements among the powerful. This chapter, by making the same case for 'human rights from below', has demonstrated the strong parallels between peace work and human rights work, as both depend on developing and sustaining strong, inclusive communities, within which human rights and human responsibilities can be constructed. Far from peace and human rights being in conflict, as was suggested at the beginning of the chapter, they actually reinforce each other, and at the community level the agenda is a common one. At this level, peace workers can only gain from an understanding of human rights studies, just as human rights workers can only gain from an understanding of peace studies. At a more conceptual level, the challenge remains of how to integrate ideas of peace and human rights in research and scholarship in each field. The broader understanding of human rights developed in this chapter, however, which expands the boundaries of the conventional human rights discourse, provides a framework within which this more theoretical integration can also be achieved.

References

Bauer, J. and Bell, D. (eds) (1999) *The East Asian Challenge for Human Rights*, Cambridge: Cambridge University Press.

Bell, L., Nathan, A. and Peleg, I. (eds) (2001) *Negotiating Culture and Human Rights*, New York: Columbia University Press.

Caroll, J. (2004) *The Wreck of Western Culture: Humanism Revisited*, Carlton, Australia: Scribe Publications.

Doyal, L. and Gough, I. (1991) *A Theory of Human Need*, New York: Guilford Press.

Eckersley, R. (1992) *Environmentalism and Political Theory*, New York: SUNY Press.

Gewirth, A. (1996) *The Community of Rights*, Chicago: University of Chicago Press.

Hayden, P. (ed) (2001) *The Philosophy of Human Rights*, St Paul, MN: Paragon Press.

Herbert, G. (2003) *A Philosophical History of Rights*, New Brunswick, NJ: Transaction Publishers.

Ife, J. (2002) *Community Development: Community-based Alternatives in an Age of Globalisation*, 2nd ed, Sydney: Pearson.

Ife, J. (2005) 'Human rights beyond the three generations', in E. Porter and B. Offord (eds) *Activating Human Rights*, Oxford: Peter Lang.

Ishay, M. (2004) *The History of Human Rights: From Ancient Times to the Globalization Era*, Berkeley: University of California Press.

Kristol, I. (1989) ' "Human rights": the hidden agenda', in W. Laqueur and B. Rubin (eds) *The Human Rights Reader*, New York: Meridian.

Lauren, P. (1998) *The Evolution of International Human Rights: Visions Seen*, Philadelphia: University of Pennsylvania Press.

Mill, J.S. (1969) *On Liberty*, Oxford: Oxford University Press.

Paine, T. (1994) *The Rights of Man*, London: David Campbell.

Saul, J. (2005) *The Collapse of Globalism and the Reinvention of the World*, London: Penguin.

Sellars, K. (2002) *The Rise and Rise of Human Rights*, Stroud: Sutton.

Wollstonecraft, M. (1983) *Vindication of the Rights of Woman*, Harmondsworth: Penguin.

12

Reconciliation

Joanna Santa-Barbara

Humans are an intensely social species, highly dependent for their well-being on good social relations with those around them. But the goals of normal individual humans are constantly conflicting with those of others, and in pursuit of our goals we frequently do harm to each other, in sharp words, in physical violence, stealing, cheating and so on. And what we do as individuals is multiplied when we act as organized groups. When we have harmed someone or some group we need or must live alongside, how do we restore the good relationship?

Further, there seems to be a deeply embedded and early manifested tendency to require reciprocity in behaviour, good for good and bad for bad, the latter being known as revenge. It can be seen in quite young children 'hitting back'. How do we forestall revenge when we have done bad things or forego revenge when we have suffered harm?

These might seem peculiarly human problems, but they are not. The other primate species squabble at least as much as we do, and also need each other at least as much.

They, like us, have ways to reconcile when they have harmed each other. Primatologist Frans de Waal describes events after a screaming, chasing quarrel between two dominant males in a chimpanzee colony, Nikkie and Yeroen:

> I have seen Mama, the oldest female, effectively mediate conflicts between the two coalition partners. On one occasion she went first to Nikkie, to put a finger in his mouth, a common gesture of reassurance among chimpanzees. While doing so, she impatiently nodded her head to Yeroen and held out her other hand to him. Yeroen came over and gave Mama a long kiss on the mouth. When she withdrew from between them, Yeroen embraced the still-screaming Nikkie.

The outstretched hand, the kiss and the hug are all part of the primate reconciliation repertoire, and so, for some species, is sex (de Waal 1989).

Reconciliation, then, is a very fundamental process. We might expect it to be mentioned in ancient religions, and it is. We focus here on the issue of reconciliation with fellow humans, rather than with the deity:[1]

- In *Hinduism*, forgiveness (a component of most reconciliation) is considered a virtue, and there are divine exemplars (for example, the Goddess Lakshmi) in the scriptures. There is the concept of karma, in which accounts will be settled in further lifetimes, requiring no human agency.

- In *Buddhism*, the believer is encouraged to forego attachment to the self, including ideas of being wounded or offended, to let go of anger against others and to move towards compassion for an offender through deep understanding. It is forbidden to harm another. There is also the concept of karma.
- In *Judaism*, the believer is expected to forgive a repentant offender. The Day of Atonement focuses on forgiveness and reconciliation with others. Repentance is an important concept.
- In *Christianity*, forgiveness is a central concept, and is rewarded by God's forgiveness of the sins of the one who forgives. 'Forgive us, as we forgive those who have trespassed against us' is part of the prayer prescribed by Jesus.
- In *Islam*, also there is the idea of extending forgiveness to others in order to attract Allah's forgiveness for one's own sins. Moderate revenge is permitted, but forgiveness is preferable.

While religious references have mainly to do with forgiveness and reconciliation between individual persons, in this chapter we will consider these concepts at all levels, between persons, between small and large groups, between nations, states and civilizations.

Definitions

Having established that reconciliation has always been with us, and is a pervasive and fundamental concept in human societies, let us try to pin down more precisely the meanings of relevant terms. Our starting point is a *relationship* between two or more entities (persons, states, etc.). If this is a *peaceful relationship* the entities will at least do no harm to each other, and at best will maintain a harmonious, cooperative and mutually beneficial relationship. When conflicts inevitably arise, they will be resolved nonviolently. When this state of affairs persists over time, *trust* is established. This means that there is a reliable expectation of benign, nonharmful behaviour from one entity to the other. But humans being humans, situations arise in which *harm* is done to one or both or all members of the relationship, very often in the course of pursuing conflicting goals. The harm may be to the body or to the mind – the construction of oneself and others and one's future. It may be the large-scale harm to human life and social infrastructure of war and genocide. The relationship is no longer peaceful, and trust diminishes or disappears. The victim is likely to regard the offender as morally in debt to them.

What is to be done? One possibility is *revenge* – where the victim of harm deliberately causes harm to the offender, reciprocating bad for bad, cancelling, they imagine, the debt. We will shortly examine the problems of this course of action. Another possibility is to end the relationship, to *move away*, physically or emotionally, but this is often not desirable or possible. States cannot move away from neighbouring states. Finally, there is *reconciliation*. Reconciliation can be thought of as the *restoration of a state of peace to the relationship, where the entities are at least not harming each other, and can begin to be trusted not to do so in future, which means that revenge is foregone as an option*. The word *reconcile* means *to come back together into council*, that is, to work harmoniously together. The processes to accomplish this transformation of a relationship are complex; we will examine them. A central one is *forgiveness*; we have seen its importance in religious prescriptions. Forgiveness means that *the moral debt is cancelled; anger and resentment are dropped; there will be no revenge*.

Harm

Harm inflicted by one entity on another can be physical: pain, injury, disease, death or deprivation of sufficiency of life support systems. It can be mental: damage to the construction of the self and its place in society, or to culturally valuable objects, the grief of loss of loved ones, the induction of fear, the loss of hope for the future. Such harms can be inflicted on individuals or even within an individual, and multiplied a millionfold, on populations. In the case of large-scale violence, there is damage to the physical infrastructure of society (schools, water treatment systems, health clinics), to the social infrastructure (judiciary, healthcare) and the cultural infrastructure (as when refugees cannot or are not permitted to maintain their cultural practices).

There is harm to the offender in causing suffering to others. The offender may or may not experience this as guilt or social disapproval. In a Buddhist formulation, they have contaminated their karma. From a Western perspective, we know that many soldiers who have committed atrocities suffer from mental illness subsequently.

There is harm to the relationship between the entities. The shattered trust may be particularly serious if the entities are living in close proximity.

Beyond any objective appraisal of the degree of the harm, Johan Galtung (no date) points out that the meaning to the victim will be much affected by certain dimensions of the harm done. The *intentionality* of the harm is very important, recognized in most moral systems and in law. The degree of anger and resentment will increase according to whether the harm caused by an offender was completely accidental (child runs on to road, hit by car), whether it was caused through ignorance or thoughtlessness without intention to hurt (driver distracted on mobile phone hits child on road), or whether the offender wished to harm the victim (malevolent driver aims car at child). The *irreversibility* of the harm may affect the difficulty of reconciliation, death being the prime example. The harm can never be undone. No reparation, no matter how penitent the offender, can reverse it. Finally the degree of *personalization* of the harm, the degree to which it is directed to a particular person or group will be a dimension relevant to the difficulty of reconciliation. There is a very big difference between the meanings of losing a limb to a terrorist bomb through being in the wrong place at the wrong time, through being a member of a targeted group or through being specifically targeted as an individual person.

Humans exist in social networks. When one suffers direct harm (dies, loses a leg to a landmine, is imprisoned) the network reverberates with the harm. One can imagine that at least ten people are seriously affected, and depending on the meaning of the harm (intentionality, etc.), the attitudes of hundreds may be affected. In this way, the offender whose harm breaks social norms, for example in criminal violence, is considered to have a 'debt to society'. The harm to society's members may be considered as moral offence at the breaking of social norms, the weakening of those norms, and the diminution of personal security of everyone from harm by dint of that weakening.

We might consider the debt to global society incurred by harm done by breaking international law, for example in the war against Iraq waged by the United States, the United Kingdom and other states. In going to war the Charter of the United Nations was infringed. In the conduct of the war – targeting civilians, use of chemical weapons, treatment of prisoners-of-war, the Geneva Conventions were flouted. Beyond the extreme harm suffered by Iraqis, there is the harm of global moral outrage, of the weakening of international law and of the consequent diminution of personal security of everyone, everywhere. There is a debt to global society.

A further harmful outcome of serious and repeated events is the distortion of the identity of the victim around the fact of victimization. The victim identity is a stance of permanent aggrievedness, even when threats are no longer evident. This 'scar' may become so intrinsic to the identity that it becomes impossible to relinquish by processes of reconciliation.

What is to be healed?

The harm suffered by the victim (both or all sides may have been harmed).
The offender's propensity to hurt others and themselves.
The relationship between the entities.
The relationship between the offender and broader society.

Galtung (no date) has used '3Rs' to designate the tasks to be addressed after an episode of large-scale violence: *Reconstruction* of physical, social and cultural infrastructure and rehabilitation of persons; *Reconciliation* of relationships; *Resolution* of the conflict that erupted in violence. Here we focus on reconciliation of the relationship, and this will facilitate the other peace-building tasks.

How does healing take place? The processes of reconciliation

There is some consensus that the following processses are relevant (Galtung no date; Kriesberg 2001; Lederach 1997), although not all elements are present in every situation:

- Uncovering the truth of what happened.
- Acknowledgement by the offender(s) of the harm done.
- Remorse expressed in apology to the victim(s).
- Forgiveness.
- Justice in some form.
- Planning to prevent recurrence.
- Resuming constructive aspects of the relationship.
- Rebuilding trust over time.

Truth

Uncovering the truth about harms done may be very simple ('You stepped on my toe.' 'Oh, how careless of me. I didn't mean to.') or very difficult, contentious and dangerous to the truthteller.[2] Powerful interests may be threatened by the revelation of the truth. An important function is served by those who record truths of atrocities in the face of interests wishing to suppress this knowledge. The records of genocide kept by the Documentation Centre of Cambodia[3] will be important in the justice process now begun in that country and the hoped-for future reconciliation process. What needs to be uncovered goes far beyond an objective appraisal of harms done, as above. There needs to be an understanding of who did what, for what reasons, with what intentions. In simple cases, the revelation that the harm caused was accidental, not intentional, is all that is needed to effect a reconciliation. In complex cases, elaborate chains of causality can be mapped, taking into account the influence of violent structures, violent cultures and misinformation on the harmful behaviour of individuals and groups. This may need to be understood for two or more parties causing harm to each other. One formulation for this is 'mapping the contribution system, avoiding the "blame game" ' (Stone et al. 1999). The 'blame game' assumes that the responsibility for the harm falls entirely on one party. The other party will see the situation in the opposite way. Mapping contributions accepts that in many situations, each or all parties may have contributed to what went wrong. However, there are situations in which the 'victim' is entirely blameless.

Exposing players on each side to the 'truth' of the other is a crucial step in eliciting understanding that may contribute to reconciliation. Beginning with an attempt to record the conflicting narratives of two sides to make them available to each other, as Uri Avnery has done in his document 'Truth vs Truth' (2003), it may eventually be possible to go on to write a unified history of a conflictual period, as was facilitated by UNESCO in the aftermath of The Second World War. This in itself would seem to be an instrument of reconciliation.

Acknowledgement

There needs to be a sincere acknowledgement to the victim by offending parties of their responsibility for the harm caused, or their contribution to the complex causes of the harm. 'Your child died of a water-borne disease in Baghdad. This was an appalling loss for you. I flew the plane that dropped a bomb on the water-treatment plant. I contributed to your loss.' The acknowledgement needs to include more than the objective facts of the harm, but also the emotional meaning of the harm. It is hard to overstate the importance of such acknowledgement for victims. It is that the reality of their suffering has been recognized. Someone has taken responsibility for it. Physicians in litigious societies have learned that often the principal motivation for patients' court cases against them for mistakes and malpractice is to wring from them acknowledgement of and apology for an error and the suffering it caused. This is more important to many patients than financial compensation.

Apology

There needs to be a sincere apology by the offender to the victim for the harm caused. It should contain the following meanings. 'I regret what I did. I wish I hadn't done it. You should not have suffered this harm. I won't do it again.' In apology the offender goes beyond acknowledgement of responsibility. They admit falling below certain standards of human behaviour, standards they now agree should apply to them. They affirm the victim's right to expect such standards from others. They agree to adhere to such standards in future. They acknowledge a moral debt to the victim. Apology may include expressions of guilt (falling below one's own moral, etiquette or practice standards) and possibly of shame (awareness of falling below society's standards).

To move from a point of inflicting harm to a point of regretting it and experiencing guilt over it may involve a great deal of difficult inner work by the offender. Such work may be facilitated by those who represent the behaviour standards of society, by religious leaders, therapists or peaceworkers.

This great load of meaning in an apology tells us why it is so hard to wring an apology from people when it seems warranted. In addition, it may be feared that a moral debt will be interpreted as a monetary debt.

Special cases arise when there are historical harms that have been perpetrated by an institution such as a government or a church. The present leaders of the institution have had no personal part in these wrongs, but find themselves in the position of making an apology on behalf of the institution. This has been done with grace and sincerity on many occasions now, for example, then-Prime Minister Willy Brandt's apology for the crimes of the German government under Hitler. It seems meaningful to the recipients and contributes to reconciliation.

On the part of a victim, an apology may be accepted or rejected. Rejection would be likely if the apology were regarded as insincere or contained inadequate acknowledgement of the harm.

Forgiveness

An apology is often followed by, or implies, asking for forgiveness. 'Will you forgive me?' means 'Will you cancel my moral debt to you? Can we put this matter behind us?' Implied, but not often explicit is, 'And will you agree to forego revenge?' Forgiveness can be granted or withheld by the victim. As has been pointed out in the course of the South African Truth and Reconciliation process, *only* the victim can forgive.[4] This is relevant when there are third parties such as church or state attempting to facilitate reconciliation, and who might ardently desire expressions of forgiveness from people not ready to grant them. But there are many victims beyond the primary recipient of the violence, and forgiveness may be relevant for all who suffered.

Forgiveness is a complex inner process for the victim, involving moving from anger, resentment, believing a moral debt is owed by the offender, wish for revenge, conducting the relationship with the offender contaminated by all of these feelings and beliefs, to a position of letting go anger, cancelling the debt, foregoing revenge and, if proceeding with the relationship, dropping any reference to the wrongs previously committed. Many who go through this process experience it as liberating in the sense of discarding burdens of anger, resentment or fantasies of revenge. One woman, a victim of years of incest, described to me decades of being locked into a resentful, bitter conceptual relationship with her long-dead father. She then described the release provided by her arrival at forgiveness, and the liberation in an attitude of 'benign indifference'. Such a process may be supported by religious principles such as mentioned earlier in this chapter, or exemplified by iconic figures such as Nelson Mandela. It may also involve leaving behind a 'victim identity' as described above, opening the way for more creative identity developments.

Forgiveness thus accomplished may be a unilateral process. The offender may be dead or departed, there may have been no remorse or apology, but the victim will still benefit from leaving behind the burdens of resentment. Bilateral forgiveness involves conveying the inner changes in the victim to the offender. When the relationship is to continue, this sets the stage for resumption of a benign, cooperative way of proceeding, cleared of resentments and apprehensions.

Can groups forgive? This question is addressed by Trudy Govier in *Forgiveness and Revenge* (2002: 78). Desmond Tutu (1999) makes strong exhortations for political forgiveness in South Africa and beyond. Govier argues that we commonly regard groups as moral agents (Greenpeace protested nuclear weapons testing) and courts clearly treat them as such (tobacco company on trial for contributing to lung cancer and other diseases). Groups can suffer harm as groups – this seems obvious (Palestinians suffer from Israeli occupation of their land; Israelis suffer from suicide bombings). The distribution of suffering is likely to be uneven, but those who do not suffer death, injury, loss, displacement, etc. will suffer stress through empathy with those who suffer, and anxiety that they may be next. Govier argues that groups can have beliefs, attitudes and feelings, including forgiveness, and that, when these are expressed by legitimate leaders, they can be regarded as valid in the absence of evidence of widespread dissent. Theoretically, it would also be possible to test this by public opinion polls. Although there are many examples of public apologies by leaders representing groups, it is hard to find examples of expressed group forgiveness. The political demeanour and absence of revenge in post-apartheid South Africa is possibly one.

In cases of serious harm, the arrival by the victim at a state of forgiveness assumes that the active harm has ended and may require a perception that some justice has been done. We now turn to that difficult topic.

Justice

Concepts of justice are so fundamental to our moral functioning that it is quite difficult to find adequate definitions for our context. Perhaps we might try: *the fair distribution of goods and bads.* What is fair? This will be culturally defined. The simplest answer is *equal, or adjusted according to need* (for example, some people need more healthcare than others). Many cultures believe it is fair to allocate fewer goods to women. For example, in Afghanistan the 'good' of 'credibility as a witness' is halved for women. Courts require two women to equal the credibility of one man. But concepts of the universality of human rights challenge such beliefs more and more. Not only goods, but 'bads' should be fairly distributed, for example taxes in societies, chores in families.

In interpersonal relationships, there seems a rough idea of reciprocity. You invite me to dinner, I should some time invite you. You borrow money from me, I have the right to ask you for a loan some time. In those serious 'bads' we are considering here, where harm is inflicted by one entity on another, we tend to feel there should be some balancing – the offender should suffer some bad. They should not 'get away with it'. Current discourse deplores the 'culture of impunity'. The most obvious and primitive form of balancing 'bads' is revenge.

Revenge

Revenge is the deliberate infliction of harm in retaliation for harm received. Some urban youth gangs cultivate a system of revenge. In some areas of the world, 'blood feuds' continue to be the system of (attempted) justice, where insults to 'honour' of members of one family are avenged by sometimes fatal assaults on members of another family, even if the individual assaulted had nothing to do with the original offence. After the attack by terrorists on the World Trade Towers and on the Pentagon in the United States in 2001, it was clear that President Bush would seek vengeance, though unclear how there could be retaliation against the shadowy organization that possibly committed the violence. Bush chose to attack Afghanistan on the basis that some of the terrorists had trained there and their leader, Osama bin Laden, lived there at the time. This revenge attack was widely supported in the US.

Govier outlines the moral case for revenge (Govier 2002: 11): the offender 'pays' for their wrongdoing, that is, some kind of justice is achieved; the victim has stood up for themselves, asserted their worthiness and restored their damaged self-respect; some kind of equality has been restored to the relationship; there may be a specific deterrent effect on this offender, and a general deterrent effect on other potential offenders.

Revenge is also supported in the Koran, as long as it is moderate, that is, the harm inflicted is no greater than the harm received. But therein lies a considerable problem, and it is fortunate that the Koran suggests that forgiveness is morally superior to revenge. The problem is a well-known bias in human perception, whereby we inflate the value of the wrongs we suffer, and minimize the value of those we ourselves inflict. This then sets the scene for a long cycle of escalating revenge, as each party with biased perception attempts to 'get even' with the other.

Govier points out a very fundamental moral problem with revenge. Based on an ethic of respect for persons and not using persons as instruments for our satisfaction, revenge becomes objectionable. It is the deliberate infliction of harm to achieve personal satisfaction. It requires the cultivation of something evil in ourselves – the desire, even relishing of another's suffering and purposeful acts to cause it. The avenger becomes offender. As for the argument of deterrence – there is something preposterous about it. A culture of vengeance is likely to apply both ways. An act of revenge seems more likely to provoke another in retaliation, unless the power differential makes this too dangerous. In this case smouldering resentment will bide time, possibly centuries, waiting for conditions to change.

Such a system seems profoundly destructive. Innocent people are killed, the roots of the problem are never dealt with, the latest victim preoccupies himself with the next possibility of revenge, and the latest avenger lives in fear of attack. Reconciliation is unattainable. Successfully cutting across such a system in Albanian families some years ago, Johan Galtung suggested the feuding families join forces against a common enemy – the system of blood feuds itself.

Retributive justice

Many societies, presumably recognizing the problems with revenge, have invented more elaborate arrangements to deal with wrongdoers. A court of some kind is interposed between victim and offender. There are measures to ensure innocent people are not accused, that there is reasonable evidence of wrongdoing, that victim and offender have the benefit of experts in law, that they can be judged by 'peers' rather than a harsh upper class, and that 'the punishment fits the crime'. There have been attempts to move the system away from punishment and towards rehabilitation, especially in the case of young offenders. There has been a global effort, on the bases of fundamental moral principles concerning the state as murderer and also on the significant proportion of mistaken convictions in all courts, to abolish death as a punishment for any offence. This system, however, continues the fundamental idea of returning bad' for 'bad'.

The extension of this system to address the crimes and atrocities of war, ethnic cleansing and genocide takes shape in tribunals under the aegis of the United Nations, and the International Criminal Court. There are merits to these developments. They convey the idea that it is not acceptable to local or global society to commit these massive crimes, and that there will be accountability for them. Certain powerful and very destructive players may be removed from the field of political action through arrest for war crimes.

There are problems too. It is very hard to bring to trial the most powerful – state or militia leaders who are protected by armies. Those brought to trial are more likely to be middle-level people. Trials, to follow procedures of formal justice, are time consuming and expensive. This is especially a problem when there are huge numbers of people who have been involved in atrocities, as in the Rwandan genocide. The fact that attribution of blame is loaded on to certain designated offenders tends to simplify and distort the 'contribution system', and to exonerate people, structures and cultures that were and possibly still are part of a destructive system. In addition, victors in wars are never tried, although they always commit atrocities.

The victim is largely left out of the transactions in most organized justice arrangements. There may be a 'victim impact statement' whereby a victim's suffering is exposed to court and offender. Reconciliation does not enter into this transaction at all. However, the testimony of victims may be a very important and liberating step for some and may secure widespread acknowledgment of previously hidden atrocities.

Metaphysical retribution

In some cultures people are urged to refrain from personal revenge, and to understand that there will be punishment at a metaphysical level. There is the belief that God will punish the wrongdoer in theistic systems: they will burn in hell. The wrongdoer has contaminated their own karma in nontheistic systems, and will have more suffering cycles of birth and death to traverse. Such beliefs may serve to inhibit the taking of personal revenge. It is hard to see, however, that they do anything to foster reconciliation of broken relationships, although Buddhist compassion may extend to trying to improve the karma of wrongdoers.

Restorative justice

Some cultures have developed justice systems which seem far more based on the idea of healing than on the idea of returning 'bad' for 'bad'. Many indigenous societies have evolved such systems, and they go by several names – ho'oponopono in Hawai'i, healing circles in North American native communities, victim–offender mediation in other settings. These attend closely to some version of the formulation we began with – what is to be healed?

- The harm suffered by the victim.
- The propensity of the offender to do harm.
- The relationship between victim and offender.
- The relationship between offender and their society.

The processes brought into play seem well designed to address these tasks. First, there may be a lengthy period of preparation, before any attempt to move towards a resolution. In this period, the victim may receive input to enable them to assert themselves in relation to their need to be treated with respect, and may receive physical and mental healing for the damage they have suffered. The offender may receive moral and psychological counselling, possibly from elders, intended to assist them in acknowledging the harm they have done, the causes of that violence in themselves, locating ways to address those problems, developing an apology to the victim, and considering modes of reparation to the victim.

Then a circle is convened. It will include all those affected by the event, and who may themselves have influenced what happened, together with concerned community members. It usually begins with some form of ritual reminding people of their orientation to the good of the community rather than to their selfish interests, and refreshing their dedication to the central moral principles of the community. There is a first 'round' of accounts of what happened, including an account by the victim of the effects of the violence on them. Then there is discussion of the causes of what happened, with development of a 'contribution system' as described above, rather than attribution of all blame to the designated offender at whose hand the harm was committed. The victim is asked what they need for their healing. The offender is asked what they can do to contribute to the victim's needs, and all members of the circle are invited to contribute to this process. The conditions for resumption of relationship with the victim and with society are laid out. Various community members take responsibility for aspects of the process.

In Canada and Australia, judges from the state justice system may attend, integrating the indigenous justice into the state system. This has led to a movement to move the state justice system towards reparative justice, because of its many merits. Another motive force in such a movement has been the apparently independent generation by Ontario Mennonites of similar ideas of reparative justice (Forget 2003). Particularly in relation to young offenders, they developed 'victim–offender mediation' in which reparation was an element in the process, and reconciliation was a possible outcome. Variations and hybrid versions of such processes are becoming more widespread. In a case in the US in 2005 in which a woman killed a child through careless driving, the perpetrator received the following sentence: she must pay the funeral expenses for the child, and for ten years, on the anniversary of the child's death, she must spend the day in jail, presumably contemplating the gravity and the causes of her crime. This incorporated acknowledgement, reparation and an unusual form of punishment. The parents expressed considerable satisfaction with this sentence (CBC News 2005).

In general, reparative processes generate more satisfaction for those involved than punitive ones. People in indigenous communities in particular favour the restorative justice process for its community-healing functions. If retributive justice were to be applied, the perpetrator might be sent away to jail for years and be lost, perhaps forever, to the community. In a restorative process, the perpetrator remains in the community, working to restore the trust of others, and to compensate for the harm done. The process itself is victim-centred, unlike retributive processes, and has far more possibility of healing and compensation for the victim.

Can such processes be applied to the large-scale wrongs of war, ethnic cleansing and genocide? In such situations, for example Afghanistan and Bosnia-Herzegovina, wrongs may have been committed by multiple parties. In both these countries, reconstruction is held back by the absence of reconciliation, and the risk of further outbreaks of violence adds to the stress of living in such a society and again detracts from the resources that could be applied to reconstruction. The 'problem-solving workshops' of Kelman and others (Estrada-Hollenbeck 2001) have shown that with influential political players (though not top leaders), it is possible to accomplish part of this process, for example in the Middle East conflicts. With skilful leadership, members of such groups have been able to acknowledge the narratives of suffering of the 'others', and to generate constructive ideas to address the suffering. They have, to my knowledge, not been able to address the issues of reparations for wrongs and of just settlements, or to move much beyond personal reconciliation towards political reconciliation.

The TRANSCEND approach, developed by Johan Galtung (2000), lays great emphasis on the preparatory phase of the process, before parties are brought together. It has been largely applied to the conflict resolution phase of a violent conflict, but would seem to have much to offer the reconciliation phase in its attention to preparatory work, to complex understandings of causality rather than simple ones, and to the elicitation of creativity from players. Creativity is much needed in the generation of feasible reparations (for example in poverty-stricken settings) and in creation of security for both sides (How can we be sure you mean what you say when you say you won't do it again?).

The South African Truth and Reconciliation process was a remarkable moral invention in which amnesty from state punishment was granted for full disclosure of truth about wrongs committed. Genuine remorse at times elicited forgiveness. Reparation was supposed to be part of the process, but was not well implemented. Restoration of reconciled relationships seems to have been effected at a societal level, as judged by the absence of vengeance. For some victims, however, there seemed an insufficiency of the 'balancing' sense of justice.

How could the US make restitution for its debt to global society for weakening international law in the war against Iraq? We might consider the possibility of constructive reparation – strengthening international law, for example, by US accession to the many instruments of international law it has declined, such as the Universal Declaration on the Rights of the Child.

Planning to prevent recurrence

If an apology has been made, a promise of no recurrence is explicit or implicit, but is that enough for a victim who has suffered serious harm? The promise may be insincere, it may be glibly made, with no serious plans to make it operational, it may be made with insufficient understanding of the factors that went into determining the harmful event in the first place. The victim may decide not to risk a recurrence, that the process has gone as far as reasonable, and that reconciliation of the relationship is not desirable. For victims of spousal abuse, this is often the most moral decision. What about large political or ethnic groups in a country recently in civil war? We know that in the first five years after such an episode, there is a 44 per cent risk of recurrence (Collier et al. 2003: 83). What factors can protect against this? Messages of reconciliation from the leadership are important, both verbal and symbolic. Further investment in the military would send the wrong signal. Investment in health for all, with a unified accessible health system would send the right signal, and in fact, is known to be followed by investment of other kinds, as it signals justice and stability (Collier et al. 2003: 155). A truth and reconciliation process seems important. Peace and reconciliation education in schools would be a constructive contribution. Signals of positive valuing of the diverse population components, for example in cultural festivals, may be useful. Northern Ireland is emphasizing this currently. Aspects of institutional structures and aspects of culture may need to be scrutinized for their contribution to the violence, and measures taken to revise them.

Resuming constructive aspects of the relationship

Exchange of goods and services is the most obvious way we express our interdependence, and resumption of such activities may be the first in reconciled relationships. Galtung mentions the possibility of joint reconstruction work, joint mourning of losses and joint conflict resolution as strengthening reconciliation.

Rebuilding trust over time

Shattered trust is rebuilt by experiencing benign, trustworthy behaviour over time. The only shortcuts are acts of uncommon generosity or sacrifice signalling great respect for and valuing of the formerly disrespected other. Promises must be kept; there must be transparency of process, especially in a situation of low trust. Benign intentions must be acted on. Incrementally, trust builds up. It can be rapidly depleted by adverse events, but perhaps not back to zero. Exposure to each other's humanity revises dehumanization and joint accomplishment increases trust.

Timing and intertwining elements in reconciliation

The sequence described above may seem the most logical one, but in fact many variations occur. Apology may be stimulated by and follow forgiveness, rather than the other way around. Justice provisions of some kind may have to play out before any possibility of forgiveness can be considered. It may be necessary to leap to the last element of joint action before anything else can be attempted. Derek Evans (2004) describes attempting to mediate reconciliation between contending sides in north-east Sri Lanka. There was no possibility of respectfully listening to each other's experiences, much less moving to any of the further elements of reconciliation. However, both sides agreed that their populations would greatly appreciate resumption of refuse removal services in urban areas. They worked out an intricately cooperative plan to accomplish this, and success in this area led to further closeness of the opposed sides.

Some cultures value suppression of suffering, and prefer not to talk about terrible events of the past. Decades may pass before the horrors can be processed. Cambodia began only in 2005 to publicly deal with its horrifying period of war and genocide after a quarter of a century of relative silence.

What helps and hinders reconciliation?

When one needs or cannot avoid a relationship with another who has harmed one, there is a strong incentive to engage in reconciliation. One cannot walk away. Conversely, if the harm is done by an entity one will likely never encounter again, there seems little reason to engage energy in the process of reconciliation.

Other factors likely to favour reconciliation are: strongly endorsed cultural values of forgiveness, sometimes based on religious beliefs; complex understanding of causality, with 'blame' distributed in many players; an aspiration to inner peace or psychological healing after harm, coupled with the belief that forgiveness will foster that peace.

Can outsiders help reconciliation processes? An impartial outside party may mediate a reconciliation in a process analogous to conflict transformation. This happens at an individual level, and also at the levels of states riven by civil war. The United Nations was relatively successful in playing this role in Central America and Cambodia, according to Keating (2003), because it was impartial, whereas the US may have hindered reconciliation in Haiti because it favours certain sides in the political process.

There are many other factors that can hinder reconciliation. If the values of revenge and retribution are strong in a culture, and particularly if they are linked to masculinity, reconciliation will be a 'hard sell'. Another cultural element that may hinder the process is that of suppression of painful memories. This is said to be related to the slowness of progress to reconciliation in Cambodia.

If one party is so strong in a military or economic sense that it can continue to derive benefit from a relationship it has harmed (that is, exploit the other party) without acknowledging or in any way processing the harm it has caused, it may do just that. It will avoid adopting the supplicant position of making an apology.

The process may stall at any of its elements. The harm-doer may not be 'cured' of their potential to do harm, in which case it would be foolhardy to expose oneself to further harm. In this case it is possible that the victim may unilaterally forgive, but not reconcile. One or other party may remain too angry to engage in any healing process. The victim may not see any benefit in relinquishing their victimhood; this may apply to an individual or a group. It may be considered that the crimes are unforgivable, as for many, the Nazi Holocaust was.

The offender may refrain from confessing in the belief that they can escape culpability, or, at least, liability for the wrong. Retributive justice systems, in which blame tends to be an all-or-nothing phenomenon, fosters this problem. The offender may wish to avoid the shame of acknowledgement, or the 'loss of face' in apologizing. The victim is lost to a reconciliation process in the retributive justice system. The focus is all on the perpetrator and their relationship with the state, as represented by the court.

Finally, in large-scale reconciliation processes, there may be deliberate 'spoilers' of the process – people who see their interests served by continuing absence of a peaceful relationship. They may foment an incident that once again shatters trust and undoes anything that has been achieved.

Some of these problems are best dealt with by the slow process of cultural change, facilitated by peace education at all levels. 'Peace literacy' of those involved will leave the process less vulnerable to the machinations of 'spoilers'.

Conclusion

Peace is the state in which humans can maximize use of their resources, physical, mental and cultural, and which gives the most chance for happiness for most people. Knowledge and skill in reconciliation after harm has been done is one of several areas of peace studies vital to the future of humans on this stressed planet.

Notes

1 For more on this topic, see Rye, M.S. et al. (1999) 'Religious perspectives on forgiveness, in M.E. McCullough, K.I. Pargament and C.E. Thoresen (eds) *Forgiveness: Theory, Research and Practice*, New York, London: Guilford Press.
2 For example, Israeli citizen Mordechai Vanunu was imprisoned in Israel for 18 years for providing evidence of that country's capacity to threaten surrounding states with nuclear weapons. Now out of prison, he continues to suffer threats to his freedom.
3 Documentation Centre of Cambodia: http://www.dccam.org.
4 For an extended discussion of this issue, see Govier, T. (2002) *Forgiveness and Reconciliation*, USA and Canada: Routledge, 92–5.

References

Avnery, U. (2003) 'Truth against Truth', at: http://www.gush-shalom.org/Docs/Truth_Eng.pdf.
CBC News (2005) 'Woman receives 10 one-day jail terms', 14 December.
Collier, P., Elliott, V.L., Hegre, H., Hoeffler, A., Reynal-Querol, M. and Sambanis, N. (2003) *Breaking the Conflict Trap: Civil War and Development Policy*, Washington, DC: World Bank and Oxford: Oxford University Press.
Estrada-Hollenbeck, M. (2001) 'The attainment of justice through restoration, not litigation: the subjective road to reconciliation, in M. Abu-Nimer (eds) *Reconciliation, Justice and Coexistence*, Lanham, MD: Lexington Books.
Evans, D. (2004) *Before the War: Reflections in a New Millenium*, Kelowna, Canada: Northstone.
Forget, M. (2003) 'Crime as interpersonal conflict: reconciliation between victim and offender', in C.A.L. Prager and T. Govier (eds) *Dilemmas of Reconciliation*, Waterloo, Canada: Wilfred Laurier Press.
Galtung, J. (2000) *Conflict Transformation by Peaceful Means*, United Nations Disaster Management Training Programme, at: www.transcend.org.
Galtung, J. (no date) 'The three Rs: Reconstruction, Reconciliation, Resolution', published online by TRANSCEND: a Peace and Development Organization, at: www.transcend.org.
Govier, T. (2002) *Forgiveness and Revenge*, New York: Routledge.
Keating, T. (2003) 'What can others do? Foreign government and the politics of peacebuilding', in C.A.L.

Prager and T. Govier (eds) *Dilemmas of Reconciliation*, Waterloo, Canada: Wilfred Laurier University Press.

Kriesberg, L. (2001) 'Changing forms of coexistence', in M. Abu-Nimer (ed.) *Reconciliation, Justice and Coexistence*, Lanham, MD: Lexington Books.

Lederach, J.P. (1997) *Building Peace: Sustainable Reconciliation in Divided Societies*, Washington, DC: United States Institute for Peace.

Stone, D., Patton, B. and Heen, S. (1999) *Difficult Conversations: How to Discuss What Matters Most*, New York: Penguin Books.

Tutu, D. (1999) *No Future Without Forgiveness*, London: Rider Books.

De Waal, F. (1989) *Peacemaking among Primates*, Cambridge, MA: Harvard University Press.

13

Peace as a self-regulating process

Dietrich Fischer

A brief history of self-regulating systems

Homeostasis, the maintenance of a desired internal state under adverse external conditions, made possible by self-sustaining processes, is the essence of life. Living organisms constantly must adjust to changes in their environment and maintain a certain equilibrium of nutrition, temperature, acidity, etc. to survive. Such mechanisms have developed in nature through evolution since the early origins of life on earth, and we can learn a great deal by studying them.

One of the earliest engineering applications of an automatic control system was James Watts' addition of a 'governor' to the steam engine in 1788. Others had invented steam engines before, but they sometimes overheated and exploded. Watts' main contribution was to add a pair of rotating weights which open a valve to let steam escape automatically if the machine begins to overheat and rotate too fast. Only with this control system was it possible to build safe, usable steam engines.

The popular belief is that space travel was made possible by the invention of big and powerful rockets. But a far more critical technology is computers and automatic control. For a space probe to reach its destination, such as a distant planet, many small course corrections are required along the way, by rapidly calculating the probe's current path from observations and firing small booster rockets to correct deviations from its desired path. Without such control systems, space travel could not succeed.

Harold Chestnut (1986) pointed out that insights from systems control theory, which have long been applied successfully to many engineering tasks, have rarely been used to address social problems. Of course, social problems are far more complex and difficult than technical problems, but given the enormous problems we face, on which human survival may depend, we should be open to anything that can provide new insights. A systems approach allows the integration of contributions from many different disciplines into a coherent framework. It looks systematically at threats to peace and surveys potential corrective measures, exploring where a minimum intervention can have a maximum effect.

No claim is made that this is the best way to address such issues. It is only one of many angles from which to look at problems. New insights often emerge when methods of one discipline are applied to questions from another, and vice versa. This chapter seeks to apply some notions from automatic control theory to the problem of maintaining or restoring peace.

A comprehensive concept of peace

Peace includes the absence of war, but much more. It is the absence of violence in all of its forms and the presence of mutually beneficial cooperation and mutual learning. Galtung (1992) has offered the following comprehensive definition of peace, with eight components.

Human needs can be grouped into four basic categories: survival, economic well-being, freedom and identity (the opposites of death, misery, oppression and alienation). They are threatened by four forms of violence: direct violence (hurting and killing people with weapons), structural violence I (the slow death from hunger, preventable diseases and other suffering caused by unjust structures of society), structural violence II (deprivation from freedom of choice and from participation in decisions that affect people's own lives) and cultural violence (the justification of direct and structural violence through nationalism, racism, sexism and other forms of discrimination and prejudice). There is also a broad correspondence between these four forms of violence and the four basic forms of power: military, economic, political and cultural.

Peace has then eight components (see Table 13.1) – the absence of these four forms of violence ('negative peace'), and the presence of activities to bring relief for past or present violence and to prevent future violence ('positive peace'). I will use here the terms survival, development, freedom and peace culture. This chapter will examine how peace can be maintained through self-sustaining regulatory processes. To this end we need some basic concepts from regulatory feedback systems.

Table 13.1. Eight components of peace

	Negative peace	*Positive peace*
Survival: absence of direct violence caused by military power	Absence of direct violence: ceasefires, disarmament, prevention of terrorism and state terrorism, nonviolence	Life-enhancing cooperation and prevention of direct violence: peace-building, conflict transformation, reconciliation and reconstruction
Development: absence of structural violence I caused by economic power	Humanitarian aid, food aid, alleviation of poverty and misery	Building a life-sustaining economy at the local, national and global level in which everyone's basic needs are met
Freedom: absence of structural violence II caused by political power	Liberation from oppression, occupation, dictatorship	Good governance and participation, self-determination, human rights
Peace culture (identity): absence of cultural violence caused by cultural power	Overcoming prejudice based on nationality, race, language, gender, age, class, religion, etc.; elimination of the glorification of war and violence in the media, literature, films, monuments, etc.	Promotion of a culture of peace and mutual learning; global communication and dialogues; development of peaceful deep cultures and deep structures; peace education; peace journalism

Positive and negative feedback loops

In a positive feedback loop, a trend gives rise to forces which increase the trend. For example, if a country's population grows at a fixed annual rate, the annual increase is proportional to the current population, producing exponential growth. In a negative feedback loop, a trend gives rise to counter-forces which hold it in check. An example is the 'governor' that prevents a steam engine from spinning out of control.

It is often assumed that 'stability' based on negative feedback loops is desirable, and 'instability', or uncontrolled growth resulting from a positive feedback loop, is undesirable, as in the two examples just given. But sometimes growth can be desirable. For example, if food is scarce, exponentially growing agricultural production is highly desirable. A positive feedback loop can be called a *virtuous cycle* if it reinforces a desirable trend, or a *vicious cycle* if it reinforces an undesirable trend. A negative feedback loop that keeps a variable under control is not necessarily always desirable. It is said to cause *stability* if it retards an undesirable trend (such as inflation), or *stagnation* if it retards a desirable trend (such as economic growth). Neither positive nor negative feedback mechanisms are in themselves desirable or undesirable. What is necessary is to reinforce desirable trends and to restrict undesirable trends. Table 13.2 lists a number of examples of vicious cycles, virtuous cycles, stability and stagnation, discussed further below.

During the 1920s, a number of European countries experienced hyperinflation, because their governments mistakenly believed they could control inflation if they increased the money supply faster than prices rose. Today we consider that belief absurd. Yet some governments still believe that they can achieve security by producing nuclear weapons faster than their rivals, leading to an escalating arms race that makes everyone less secure. As US President John F. Kennedy said, we need to abolish nuclear weapons, or they will abolish us.

Another example of a vicious cycle is the great depression. After the 1929 stock market crash some companies went bankrupt. This reduced tax revenue. US President Herbert Hoover was advised to balance the budget by cutting public spending. This increased unemployment further, reduced private consumption, led to more bankruptcies and still lower tax revenue. Hoover kept cutting public spending further, aggravating the crisis, until unemployment reached more than 25 per cent. This vicious cycle was broken only when President Franklin Delano Roosevelt initiated the New Deal, providing jobs to the unemployed to build schools, hospitals, roads and hydroelectric dams, putting income into people's pockets, so that they could buy goods again. Firms could rehire the workers they had dismissed earlier, further reviving the entire economy and increasing tax revenue. But the failed remedy of cutting public spending, even for child

Table 13.2. Some examples of positive and negative feedback loops

	Positive feedback loops	*Negative feedback loops*
Undesirable	**Vicious cycles** Hyperinflation Great depression Environmental degradation Arms races	**Stagnation** Poverty trap Political repression Intellectual conformity
Desirable	**Virtuous cycles** Economic growth Political rights International cooperation	**Stability** Trade balance Market prices Equalization of wages

nutrition and other essential services, despite very high levels of unemployment, is still practised in poor countries today at the insistence of the International Monetary Fund (Stiglitz 2002).

A third example of a vicious cycle is environmental degradation. Once the environment's capacity to abate pollution begins to be strained to its limits, that capacity rapidly deteriorates and pollutants begin to accumulate to unhealthy levels.

Examples of virtuous cycles are economic growth (provided it does not damage the environment) and the expansion of human rights. If there is free expression and impression (the right to hear other opinions than the official one), abuses of power will be discovered and bad governments replaced through democratic elections. International cooperation is another example. The more agreements have already been concluded and found in every member country's interest, the easier it is to reach additional agreements, in a type of desirable 'peace race'.

An example of undesirable stagnation is the poverty trap. If people live near or below the subsistence level, they can hardly extricate themselves from misery. They need everything they earn to feed their family. Poor nutrition can stunt children's physical and mental growth. They cannot afford education and medical care. Children remain unskilled and trapped in poverty.

Dictatorships are often hard to dislodge because free expression is suppressed by imprisonment, torture or executions. Abuses of power cannot be criticized and remain uncorrected. There is a false facade of unanimous, even enthusiastic support for the government, out of people's fear for their lives and also because they are misinformed by false propaganda.

Even in societies where there is no violent repression, there can be tendencies towards intellectual conformity. Those who agree with the prevailing intellectual paradigm are rewarded with university teaching positions, tenure, promotion, research grants, publication of their papers and favourable reviews. Those who think new and independent thoughts, which contradict long-held, cherished beliefs, may find it more difficult to be heard, published or to obtain grants to pursue their research. In a climate where conformity is rewarded and originality penalized, the result is intellectual stagnation.

An example of a mechanism producing desirable stability is trade balance. If a country imports more than it exports, accumulating a foreign debt, its currency tends to decline in value. This makes its exports cheaper and its imports more expensive. Exports increase, imports decrease and the country's trade balance will automatically tend to return close to zero over time. Government interventions (such as manipulations of the exchange rate, protectionism, and raising interest rates to attract financial flows) may either strengthen or weaken that natural balancing mechanism.

Another example of a stabilizing mechanism is market prices. If a good is in short supply, this will drive its price up, encouraging more producers to enter that lucrative market and driving the price down again. If a good is oversupplied, its price will drop, some producers will shift to other more profitable goods and the price will gradually rise again. Such a market mechanism keeps supply and demand more or less in balance. However, the market mechanism does not guarantee that basic human needs are met. There have been cases where food was exported despite a domestic famine, because foreigners could afford to pay more.

A third example producing desirable stability is the mechanism that tends to equalize wage rates across borders. If a company opens a new plant, it will choose the location where wages are lowest, to minimize its production costs, provided other conditions are equal. Thus demand for labour in low-wage countries will gradually increase, raising wages, while the demand for labour in high-wage countries will decrease and reduce wages. Similarly, consumers tend to buy goods with the lowest price, if quality is equal, and give poorer countries a competitive advantage, leading to a reduction of inequality over time.

It is not necessary that wages drop in some countries to increase in others. A policy of expanding production to meet human needs, such as the New Deal, can raise effective wages in rich and poor countries alike.

The tendency toward greater income equality is impeded because richer countries can afford to invest more in the latest technology and automation. Its workers tend to be healthier and better educated. The infrastructure tends to be superior, lowering transportation costs. The legal system may be more reliable, which removes uncertainty. The country may have greater political stability, which reduces the risk that the company's assets may be seized with a change in government. Many such obstacles help maintain large wage differentials over prolonged periods of time, or may even exacerbate them.

Adam Smith emphasized the benefits of the free-market mechanism that makes entrepreneurs serve the public good out of self-interest. Karl Marx emphasized the growing accumulation of wealth in fewer and fewer hands in a capitalist economy. Who is right? Both! These two mechanisms and many others are simultaneously at work in the world economy. Similarly, in nature, gas in a bottle tends to disperse, with equal pressure everywhere, whereas thin cold gas in the universe tends to be attracted by gravity to points of higher density, forming stars. Our challenge is to promote economic mechanisms that support growth and have an equalizing tendency, and to hold in check mechanisms that retard economic development and/or produce growing inequality.

Positive feedback loops, which produce exponential growth, are desirable if they help satisfy the basic needs for survival, development, freedom and a culture of peace. They are undesirable if they promote war and violence, misery, oppression and alienation. Negative feedback loops, which prevent change, are desirable if they preserve peace and the satisfaction of human needs, and undesirable if they preserve war, poverty, repression and despair.

War as a self-sustaining system

Violence breeds more violence. Without deliberate interventions to promote peace, the world can degenerate into a jungle where Hitler's dictum 'might makes right' prevails. Defeat in war breeds the desire for revanche (to change the outcome in one's own favour) and revenge (to hurt those who have hurt us). Conversely, victory nurtures the desire for more victories.

Arms races are a typical example of vicious cycles. One country's acquisition of arms, supposedly to increase its own security, is seen as a threat by its adversaries, who then also increase their arms, producing the so-called 'security dilemma' (Jervis 1976). This exacerbates fear and the feeling of insecurity in the first country, leading to more arms purchases, etc., in a growing spiral. Such vicious cycles can be broken, even unilaterally, with a purely defensive military posture, which allows a country to resist aggression, but not to carry out aggression (Afheldt 1976; Fischer 1984a; Galtung 1984; UNIDIR 1990).

Arms races tend to lead to war. Michael Wallace (1982) found that among 99 cases of 'serious dispute or military confrontation' from 1820 to 1964, 23 of the 28 preceded by an arms race ended in war, whereas only three of the 71 not preceded by an arms race ended in war.

The remainder of this chapter focuses on negative feedback loops that help preserve peace. Many of these mechanisms already exist and can be strengthened. Indeed, most countries have been at peace most of the time, war is an exception and can be eliminated.

Peace and regulatory feedback systems

It is rare to find people who openly advocate war, poverty, oppression or prejudice. Why do we have so much of all of these? Is it due to human selfishness, shortsightedness, inadequate legal systems or simply ignorance? All of these factors play a role, and several more.

It is interesting that all of these problems can be regarded as various ways in which a regulatory feedback system can break down (Fischer 1993). Any viable system needs a number of regulatory feedback mechanisms to maintain or restore a healthy state and to adapt to a changing environment. A feedback system has three main components:

1. Agreement on a desirable goal state.
2. Methods to detect deviations from the goal.
3. Mechanisms to move the system closer to the goal if it has deviated.

An example from nature is the human immune system. The desirable state is a healthy body that is not under attack by an excessive amount of disease germs. White blood cells both detect disease germs, and eliminate them if found. Another essential feedback mechanism in our body is the nervous system. The feeling of pain ensures that we protect injured parts of our body until they can heal. Leprosy, a disease of the nervous system, has the consequence that patients no longer feel pain. Therefore, they do not notice minor injuries to their limbs, keep using them and ultimately lose them. If a government is insensitive to the suffering of its population, that society suffers a pathology analogous to leprosy.

An example of a regulatory feedback system in human society is the legal system, which is designed to deter crimes, aggression and other harmful behaviour. Laws define what is acceptable behaviour, the desired state. Courts determine whether someone has violated a law, detecting deviations from the desired state. And the police and corrections system are there to enforce the laws, moving society closer to a desired state.

A negative feedback loop is also the essence of quality control: through dialogues with the end users, an entrepreneur must find out what the users wish. Then the manufacturing process must be adjusted constantly to meet the users' wishes, and any deviations need to be corrected. Other examples include market mechanisms: rising prices indicate shortages and encourage more production and less consumption, to restore an equilibrium between supply and demand. Independent news media can expose abuses of power, and democratic self-regulation can replace oppressive or corrupt governments, fulfilling a role analogous to that of white blood cells in the human body. Table 13.3 lists various ways in which a feedback system can break down, with possible remedies.

Table 13.3. Six defects of a feedback system, with possible remedies

		Defect	*Possible remedy*
1	No goal	Lack of agreement on goals	Conflict transformation
2	No feedback	Lack of information about deviations from the goal	Better observation and communication
3	Distorted feedback	Externalities, i.e. others are affected by our choices	Ethical behaviour (concern for others) and proper incentives
4	Delayed feedback	The consequences are noticed too late, when a problem is beyond repair	Future planning and early preventive action

	Defect	Possible remedy
5 Rejected feedback	Pathological behaviour, due to prejudice, hatred, megalomania, etc.	Understanding psychology and culture to be able to change them
6 Lack of knowledge and resources	Even if people are aware of a problem and wish to correct it, they may not know how or lack the necessary resources	Research and education, economic development

The following sections provide some examples of how these six defects can contribute to direct violence, structural violence I (misery), structural violence II (oppression) and cultural violence, and what strategies may help overcome these problems to contribute to peace with survival, development, freedom and a peace culture. It is necessary that all six of these possible defects of a regulatory feedback system be overcome simultaneously. If even only one defect is present, the whole system may fail.

Peace with survival

Agreement on goals

Violence and war are typically the result of untransformed conflicts. Therefore the first step to prevent war is to seek common goals, or at least agreement on how to deal with differing interests in a peaceful way. Methods of peaceful conflict transformation with many case studies are described in Galtung (2004) and elsewhere in this handbook.

Conflicts that can lead to war concern border disputes, disagreements about who has the authority to govern a people, over the sharing of natural resources, over the allocation of taxes and spending, and sometimes over whose ideology or religion is the correct one, including respect for other religions.

A good example of how a border dispute was resolved peacefully is the way in which the Danish–German border was drawn in 1920. The people in every community of Schleswig-Holstein could vote whether they preferred to belong to Denmark or Germany. In the north, most voters preferred to join Denmark. In the south, the majority preferred to belong to Germany. Somewhere in the middle it was 50–50. That is where the border was drawn, and it has remained stable ever since.

Self-determination is a good way peacefully to transform conflicts over the authority to govern. The Good Friday Agreement of 1998, which foresees that the people of Northern Ireland can decide their future in a referendum, brought a considerable reduction in violence. A possible civil war between a French-speaking Catholic minority in the Jura region of the Canton Bern in Switzerland and the German-speaking Protestant majority was avoided by holding a referendum in 1978 and allowing those communities in the French-speaking region who wanted to form their own canton Jura to do so. There is no guarantee that people will always make the optimal choice, they can make mistakes as well as governments, but if they discover that they made a wrong choice, they have nobody else to blame and will do better at the next opportunity. However, if they are forced by a government to do something they do not want, and suffer as a consequence, they will naturally be angry at that government. Therefore, the right to self-determination can help avoid many conflicts.

What is the optimal level for self-determination? Generally the smallest unit that includes all those affected by the decision (subsidiarity principle).

Cooperation on mutually beneficial projects is an effective way to build mutual trust, which makes it easier to transform any emerging conflicts peacefully. Today's close cooperation of the Nordic countries, which fought many wars with each other for centuries, is a good example, as well as the European Union, which gradually emerged from the modest beginnings of the European Coal and Steel Union, conceived by Jean Monnet and Robert Schumann and established in the 1952 Treaty of Paris.

Observation

Numerous ceasefire agreements have been broken, with each side accusing the other of having started to shoot first, claiming they acted only in self-defence. If UN observers are present and can identify who was responsible for breaking the ceasefire, this puts pressure on both sides to adhere to the agreement.

If violations of disarmament agreements, and preparations for aggression such as the massing of troops and tanks along a border, can be detected early, this gives time to protect the potential victim, and to seek a diplomatic solution. A useful instrument for that purpose would be an International Satellite Monitoring Agency (ISMA), proposed by France in 1978 at the First Special Session of the UN General Assembly on Disarmament, endorsed by 123 nations and opposed only by the two superpowers. By making its findings available to the global community, such an agency could help prevent surprise attacks. Countries with purely defensive intentions have no reason to hide them. In fact, if preparations for defence are secret, they will be useless in dissuading a potential aggressor. Only someone with aggressive intentions has an interest in hiding them.

Incentives

Oskar Morgenstern, co-founder of game theory, pointed out that if those who make decisions about war or peace had to fight at the front-line in case of war, there would be fewer wars. Top military and political leaders usually protect themselves far behind the front-line, sending instead young people to their deaths.

The millions of citizens who are involuntarily held as nuclear hostages by the governments of the nuclear powers have never been consulted if they wish to play that role. If they had a right to choose, it is doubtful that they would consent.

Collier and Hoeffler (1998) found through correlation analysis that an important factor in civil wars is economic incentives: the availability of 'lootable' resources (diamonds and other precious stones, minerals, oil, timber, opium, etc.) and high unemployment, especially among youth, which makes it cheap to raise an army, often without paying them anything, simply promising them that they can keep what they can loot. Therefore, it is important to make sure that those who initiate war do not get rich from it. Another pernicious factor is arms manufacturers and merchants. They profit at the expense of other people's lives, as slave traders and slave owners used to do.

As long as aggression is rewarded, it will continue. A standing international peacekeeping force that could intervene rapidly at the first signs of aggression could help make it clear to any would-be aggressor that aggression does not pay.

To be effective, a peace agreement must be mutually acceptable and sustainable. It should be so attractive for all parties that none has any incentive to resort to war.

Foresight

So as not to delay corrective action until it is too late, it is important to foresee that vindictiveness tends to provoke a desire for revenge. Brams (1985) called the naive belief that if we gain an advantage over an opponent, this will not provoke any reaction, the 'fallacy of the last move'. John Maynard Keynes, who was a member of the British delegation to the 1919 Versailles peace talks, warned that assigning the guilt for the First World War to Germany alone and imposing huge reparations payments on it for 50 years would prepare the way for another round of war. When his advice was ignored, he resigned. The Versailles treaty indeed was a condition that made it easier for Hitler to gain power with the promise to abrogate it. If it had been revised, say after five years, this might have helped prevent the Second World War, with 60 million deaths. Acts of omission are as serious as acts of commission.

Early intervention in a conflict, before it has erupted in violence, is much less costly than seeking to end a war after it has begun. For example, during the 1980s, the greatest fear of a war in the Balkans focused on Romania, where 1.6 million ethnic Hungarians live among 23 million Rumanians. Romania and Hungary were enemies in both world wars, and tensions remain. Allen Kassoff and colleagues organized two mediating sessions of three days each in 1992 and 1993 with four representatives each from the Rumanian government and the Hungarian minority. They reached a mutually acceptable agreement, which allowed the Hungarian minority to use the Hungarian language in school lessons and local newspapers, in return for a promise not to seek secession, thus avoiding another possible civil war such as that in former Yugoslavia.

In 1995, Galtung (2004) met one of Ecuador's chief negotiators in the border talks with Peru. Peru and Ecuador had fought three wars over an uninhabited 500 square kilometre territory where the border was defined by a watershed that kept changing position. Galtung suggested to make the disputed border territory into a 'binational zone with a natural park', attracting tourists to benefit both countries. This proposal became the basis of the 1998 peace treaty signed in Brasilia, and has since spun off other similar peace zones elsewhere. A highway is being built along this 'border of peace'. Since this agreement produces income and benefits for both countries, it is self-reinforcing and sustainable. This peace initiative cost nearly nothing compared to a military intervention to end a war. The Gulf War of 1991 to expel Iraq from Kuwait cost $100 billion, not counting the destruction it caused. Most of all, peaceful conflict transformation can save many lives.

Newspapers today write extensively about war, but rarely about successful peace initiatives. People need to hear also about creative peace proposals. It is time to have not only 'war correspondents', but also peace journalists who report about ideas for conflict transformation, peace-building and reconciliation.

The world should place more emphasis on preventive diplomacy, as UN Secretary General Boutros Boutros-Ghali (1992) has advocated. The United Nations Secretary General has played a valuable role as mediator on a number of occasions, but he is overburdened. The International Peace Academy, the one organization affiliated with the UN system with the task of solving conflicts before they lead to war, has only 26 staff members, and only a few who are trained in mediation. Compared with the millions of men under arms, this is totally inadequate and not nearly enough to address the nearly 100 potential conflicts simmering simultaneously around the world that could erupt in war at any time. We need a UN Agency for Mediation, with several thousand professionals, comparable to the World Bank or IMF in size, who can detect emerging conflicts early and help transform them peacefully before they lead to war (Fischer 1993). That would be an excellent investment for a more peaceful world.

Mikhail Gorbachev (1987) proposed creating a commission of about 100 former heads of state, scientists, writers and creative thinkers who could deliberate about various dangers facing humanity and ways to avoid them, free from the daily pressure to respond immediately to the latest crisis. To support such a commission would cost a small fraction of the millions of troops kept under arms, but it could do a great deal more to avoid future catastrophes.

Most governments wait until a conflict erupts in war and then intervene with military force, instead of seeking a peaceful solution long before it leads to violence. Such a policy is comparable to driving with closed eyes, waiting until we hit an obstacle and then calling an ambulance, instead of anticipating dangers and avoiding them.

Rejected feedback

Even the best feedback cannot help if a decision-maker chooses to ignore it. Leaders suffering from megalomania or paranoid fears of conspiracy have often led their countries into war, against the best advice. According to attribution theory (Jones 1973), most people tend to attribute good motives to themselves and bad motives to those they see as adversaries. Jervis (1976: 170) writes, 'One tends to see what one believes.' Kull (1988) interviewed nuclear strategists in East and West and found them convinced – unchecked by experience – that an opponent would yield to threats, but that they themselves would never do so. Such misperceptions can lead to the escalation of conflicts. Being made aware of such inconsistencies is the first step toward overcoming them.

Knowledge and resources

Peace research is a young field, barely half a century old, compared with research about military strategy. More research on creative ways to transform conflicts peacefully and broad-based education is urgently needed.

In 2004, annual military spending by all states amounted to $950 billion, $466 billion for the United States alone, more than the next 25 countries combined (www.globalsecurity.org. military_world_spending.htm 2006). By contrast, world expenditures for peacekeeping in 2004 amounted to only $3.645 million (www.globalpolicy.org.finance.tables.pko.expend.htm 2006). Even so far less is spent on peaceful conflict transformation. To deter or reverse aggression, a standing United Nations Peacekeeping Force can play an important role, at considerably lower costs than if each country maintains its own armed forces. It would be equally wasteful if all home owners in a town maintained individual fire engines, instead of combining their resources to form one fire company that can be deployed wherever and whenever needed.

Even better than sending armed peacekeepers after a war has begun is to help mediate in conflicts around the world before violence has erupted, and to promote reconciliation after war, to prevent its recurrence. TRANSCEND, a global peace and development network founded in 1993 by Johan Galtung, is doing high-level mediation in numerous conflicts and training people around the world in peaceful conflict transformation. Even better than curing people from an illness is to teach them how to stay healthy.

The resources available for such efforts are minuscule compared with the billions spent for war and weapons. Yet the people who fought against slavery in the nineteenth century had no foundation support, they made personal sacrifices and took risks, while the slave traders and slave owners accumulated big fortunes. Still, the anti-slavery movement prevailed, because it was morally right. For the same reason, it can be expected that war will be abolished as an accepted institution, in the same way as slavery and colonialism.

Peace with development

Agreement on goals

In 2000, the UN General Assembly agreed on the Millennium Development Goals that include universal primary education, halving extreme poverty and halting the spread of HIV/AIDS by 2015. Such an agreement is a first necessary step toward achieving those goals, but so far the implementation is lagging far behind. Most governments have also signed conventions guaranteeing the right to adequate nutrition for all of their citizens, yet about 840 million people suffer from hunger and malnutrition. Those who have the power and resources to remedy that problem must be persuaded to do so.

Observation

If information about people's suffering does not reach those who can help, help will not be forthcoming. For example, a famine in China during 1958–60, from which an estimated 10 to 20 million people died, was long hidden from the outside world because of censorship. There were enough grain reserves in the world, and if pictures of starving people had been shown around the world, aid could have been mobilized to save them.

One of the main obstacles to development is corruption. As long as it is easier to get rich by controlling the army and police than by producing goods, it is more tempting to plot coups than to develop business enterprises that can meet people's needs and provide employment. Corruption thrives in a climate of secrecy, where officials can make arbitrary decisions that are not subject to public scrutiny. Openness and competition render corruption impossible. For example, if an official of the central bank can allocate scarce foreign exchange arbitrarily, there is great temptation to give it to friends, or to those who offer the highest bribe. If the available amount is auctioned to the highest bidders, there is no room for corruption. Openness, transparency, glasnost is one of the best remedies against corruption.

Incentives

If companies that run a deficit receive state subsidies and those that operate efficiently must hand over their profits to the state, as in some former centrally planned economies, there is little incentive to be efficient. Efficiency and creativity ought to be rewarded.

Unequal income distribution distorts the reflection of true needs in a market, so that it is more profitable to produce food for pets of the rich than for children of poor people, or more profitable to develop new tranquilizers than life-saving medicine against tropical diseases, from which most sick people suffer, because they have no purchasing power. Such distortions need to be corrected, through income redistribution, or by subsidizing essential goods and taxing luxury items. At the January 2006 Social Forum in Caracas, the proposal was made for a tax on world trade to raise revenue for development.

One source of distorted incentives is what Garrett Hardin (1968) has called the 'Tragedy of the Commons'. Common resources accessible to everyone, such as fish in the ocean or firewood, tend to be overused. The reason is simple. If I have a privately owned fish pond, I will not want to catch all the fish at once because there will be no more left that can regenerate the fish population for the future. But if everyone has free access to the pond, and I catch only a limited quantity to leave some for the future, they will not remain for the future because someone else will catch them. For this reason, many fish species in the Atlantic Ocean have become nearly extinct. It is necessary to allocate quotas and enforce them, to prevent the extinction of ocean fish, or the clear cutting of forests, which leads to irreversible soil erosion.

Foresight

Mohammad Yunus (1988) has discovered that a small investment – in some tools, farm animals to produce milk or eggs, or an initial stock of goods to open a shop – can help lift a person out of misery. Traditional commercial banks refuse loans to the poor because they have no collateral. So Yunus founded the Grameen bank, initially in Bangladesh and now around the world. It operates as a self-help organization, where groups of people put away small savings every week, and as soon as they have saved enough for the first two small loans, the group chooses the two most promising and deserving projects. Once those people have repaid their loan, the next two get their projects funded. Social pressure to repay replaces the threatened loss of collateral, such as land or a building. This method is very effective. The Grameen Bank of Bangladesh has an astonishingly high repayment rate of 98 per cent, compared with only about 30 per cent for agricultural loans and 10 per cent for industrial loans for commercial banks in Bangladesh (Kamaluddin 2006).

The market often operates too slowly as a regulating mechanism. For example, if there is a shortage of doctors, the price of their services will rise, and this may encourage more students to enter medical school. But by the time they have passed through medical school, completed their practical training and can help relieve the shortage, half a generation may have passed. That adjustment mechanism is too slow. It is necessary for governments to engage in some long-range planning to meet society's future needs. This does not mean that particular individuals need to be told to enter medical school, but additional fellowships can attract more students to medical school in time, before a shortage of doctors begins to hurt, while still leaving individuals free to choose any field of study.

Rejected feedback

Even when economic cooperation would be mutually beneficial, it may not come about because of old enemy images. Building confidence by starting with small but visibly successful joint projects may be the most likely path toward overcoming such prejudice.

Companies may fail to hire the most qualified employees because of racial or class prejudice. Laws prohibiting discrimination can help overcome such unfair practices.

Knowledge and resources

The greatest obstacle to development is probably a lack of knowledge and resources. Sharing technology can go a long way toward reducing world poverty, but there is also a need for massive transfers of financial resources to meet people's most urgent needs and to build necessary infrastructure. Tinbergen (in Tinbergen and Fischer 1987: 157–8) proposed the creation of a World Treasury. He observed that to almost every ministry at the national level, there is some corresponding international organization, except for the treasury. Yet without a treasury, which collects taxes to finance the other ministries, any government would soon collapse.

Funds for a World Treasury could initially be raised by auctioning a portion of the rights to mineral exploration on the deep seabed, outside of any national jurisdiction, to the highest bidder. In this way, the richer countries would automatically tend to pay a higher share of global revenue, without the need for long and difficult negotiations about national assessments. In addition to raising revenue, such an orderly allocation procedure could also help prevent future wars over those resources. The revenue thus raised could be used to support development projects to meet the basic needs of those most in need, for peacekeeping, and protection of the global environment.

Disarmament and economic conversion could make substantial resources available for development (Dumas 1986; Leontief and Duchin 1983). A tax on currency exchanges, proposed by Tobin (1974), could help dampen the high volatility of international exchange rates and help increase international trade and investment by making it less risky, in addition to raising revenue.

Another potential source of global revenue is a carbon tax to stem global warming. Contrary to a widespread belief, pollution taxes do not increase overall taxes, but help reduce them. This is easily seen through a thought experiment: if we did not pay for petrol at the pump, people would consume a lot more petrol. Someone would have to pay the annual petrol bill anyway, which means that everybody's taxes would have to be increased. Since more is consumed, this tax increase would be considerably more than we now pay for petrol. The same applies to pollution. If we do not charge polluters directly for the damage they cause, we get more pollution, and end up paying much more to clean it up, or to pay for the cure of cancer and other illnesses it causes.

Voltaire said that freedom is the only good that is used up when it is not used. This is also true of knowledge and wisdom. If it is not applied, it tends to be forgotten. And unlike physical resources, which must be taken from someone to be given to someone else, knowledge, once discovered, can be copied without any limit at almost no additional costs. For that reason, it is perhaps the most under-utilized resource to promote peace, development, a clean environment, human rights and a culture of peace. If the least resource-, energy- and labour-intensive and the least polluting production technology known anywhere were available throughout the world, everybody could be much better off. Knowledge that can be used to produce more and better food, shelter and clothes, to give health to people or new methods of education, should be made openly available to everyone. Since it is a public good, for which the cost of production is independent of the number of users and non-payers cannot be excluded from using it, the production of basic knowledge is not profitable for private enterprise, and needs to be funded from public revenue.

Peace with freedom

Agreement on goals

Agreement on goals is a basic precondition for the solution of problems confronting humanity. For this reason, the adoption of common standards, such as the Universal Declaration of Human Rights, is of great importance. It does not guarantee, by itself, that these rights will indeed be respected, but without agreement on principles, it is much more difficult to point out violations and mobilize pressure to correct them.

An important step preparing the end of the Cold War and bringing greater freedom to Eastern Europe and some (not yet all) former Soviet Republics was the 1973–5 Helsinki

Conference on Security and Cooperation in Europe. Finnish President Urho Kekkonen had the wisdom of simply inviting all the European governments to such an open-ended conference, with all issues on the table. If he had asked the UN Security Council for permission, the proposal would probably have been vetoed. Fifty-nine of the 60 European governments (except Albania) came. They reached agreement on three baskets of human rights: Basket I includes security, human rights and freedoms, the principle of coexistence, the pledge that frontiers should be changed only by peaceful means and that states should cooperate and refrain from intervention in the internal affairs of other nations. Basket II deals with economic, technical, and scientific cooperation, problems of trade and the environment. Basket III deals with human contacts, emigration rights, cultural and educational exchange, free movement of people and information. This gave NGOs like Helsinki Watch the opportunity to press governments to fulfill the obligations they had signed.

Observation

Reliable information about political prisoners and torture is a precondition to mobilize world public opinion to stop such abuses. Amnesty International carefully checks that its reports of human rights violations are accurate, and has built a reputation of impartiality and reliability that governments cannot deny. Its reports have saved many political prisoners' lives.

Incentives

The Nuremburg Principles have established the principle of individual responsibility, making clear that receiving illegal orders is no exoneration for crimes against humanity. Human rights violations are often committed by governments, which also control the national courts and do not prosecute them. Therefore, the creation of the permanent International Criminal Court in Rome in 1998 is an important step. It must have the authority to investigate crimes against humanity without permission from the government in whose country the crime occurred, otherwise it would be rendered meaningless.

Foresight

We sometimes fail to resist encroachments on our freedom early enough, when it is still possible, hoping that the danger will pass on its own. That can be an illusion. Martin Niemöller warned: 'When the Nazis arrested the Communists, I said nothing; after all, I was not a Communist. When they locked up the Social Democrats, I said nothing; after all, I was not a Social Democrat. When they arrested the trade unionists, I said nothing; after all, I was not a trade unionist. When they arrested the Jews, I said nothing; after all, I was not a Jew. When they arrested me, there was no longer anyone who could protest.'

Rejected feedback

The denial of freedom and equal rights to various groups is often based on racism, sexism or other types of irrational prejudices and enemy images. It reflects a lack of tolerance for anyone who thinks or looks differently or speaks a different language. Education plays a central role in either creating or avoiding such harmful bias.

People sometimes ignore warnings of impending danger to their lives and freedom. Elie Wiesel (1982) tells how an old man who was able to escape from a Nazi concentration camp returned to his village to warn his family and neighbours of the horrors he had seen, urging them to flee while they still could. To his great disappointment, nobody believed him and all were later deported into concentration camps.

Knowledge and resources

People whose rights have been violated often do not know how to seek legal recourse or may lack money to hire a lawyer. Lawyers who defend political prisoners free of charge perform an important service.

Peace culture

The preamble of the Charter of UNESCO states, 'Since war begins in the minds [of people], it is in the minds [of people] that the defenses of peace must be built.' Our ways of thinking, conscious and subconscious, are at the root of whether we are able to keep peace, and indeed survive the nuclear age.

Agreement on goals

An international group of specialists, based on the latest scientific findings, has written the 1986 Seville Statement on Violence, which emphasizes that aggression is not part of human nature, but a learned behaviour, and it is equally feasible to teach children nonviolent behaviour and the skills to transform conflicts peacefully.

War has long been justified by the glorification of victory in history books. Boulding (1978) pointed out that the glorification of victory in duelling ended when guns became more accurate and duelling almost inevitably lethal. Modern weapons have made the glorification of war equally obsolete.

UNESCO has brought together historians from countries that used to be at war, to write common history textbooks, which are not nationally biased and omit the vilification of 'enemies'. This can help break the cycle of hostility passed from generation to generation.

It would be useful to have also a truly global press service and television network, not based in one country, where voices from every different culture and political perspective can be heard, in an ongoing dialogue of civilizations, not as a replacement of national news services, but as an addition.

Observation

Some gifted writers have pointed out social problems and thus inspired movements to overcome them. *Uncle Tom's Cabin* (Harriet Beecher Stowe 1852) awakened many people to the inhumanity of slavery, mobilizing them against it. Rachel Carson (1962), the perceptive biologist and gifted writer, woke up the world to the looming environmental catastrophe with her *Silent Spring*. Jonathan Schell's (1982) *The Fate of the Earth* energized the anti-nuclear movement. Metta Spencer (2006) pointed out that the film *Gandhi*, released in 1983, influenced the peaceful revolutions in the Philippines 1986, Eastern Europe 1989 and Russia 1991.

Journalists also influence people's thinking. Galtung (1998) pointed out that during the nineteenth century 'disease journalism' described in detail where people had died from epidemics and how they died, but little was known about cures and little written. Today, most newspapers publish regular 'health pages' with information about new cures and ways to prevent various diseases, which are very popular. Yet most reporting about conflict today must still be characterized as 'war journalism', which reports in detail how many people were killed in war, where and who appears to be winning. Journalists could make a major contribution to help end or prevent wars if they also reported about various groups' ideas for solutions, and in addition to asking about the number of dead and wounded, would ask 'What is this conflict about?' and 'What are possible solutions?' People are thirsting to know this.

Incentives

The freedom of expression (and impression, the right to hear dissident views) is fundamental to a free and healthy society. Government censorship is often a first step to establishing a dictatorship. Yet the freedom of expression does not give the license to shout 'fire' in a crowded theatre. Openly advocating murder, as Nazi propaganda and the Rwandan hate radio did, should not be seen as a legitimate expression of opinion. Neither does the freedom of movement permit us to enter someone else's house. Freedom ends when it encroaches on the freedom, or indeed the right to survival, of others. Even those countries that have constitutional guarantees of free expression do not permit the deliberate and malicious publication of lies about a person, prosecuting it as 'libel'.

We need a broad public debate about what is covered by free speech, and what crosses the border of advocating violence. This is as different from government censorship as democracy is from dictatorship. It is a paradox that showing the human body on television is strictly prohibited in many countries, but showing war and gruesome murders is permitted, and children have seen tens of thousands of murder scenes on average by the time they grow up.

Maybe prizes and public recognition for the best reports and programmes, which help promote a culture of peace instead of a culture of violence, could help improve the content of what is disseminated by the media.

Foresight

It is important to recognize early signs of potential atrocities to follow. The anti-semitic propaganda, followed by the harassment of Jews in Germany in the 1930s should have been taken as a warning of the enormous danger posed by Hitler and the Nazis, and earlier efforts to stop Hitler's aggression and the Holocaust should have been made. The broadcasts of radio Mille Collines in Rwanda in early 1994, which called Tutsis roaches that need to be exterminated and openly called on Hutus to kill Tutsis, should have been recognized as the looming threat of genocide that followed. Romeo Dallaire (2003), the commander of the 1500 UN peacekeepers sent to Rwanda in 1993, estimates that if he had obtained the requested reinforcement to 5,000 troops, he could have prevented the genocide, but he was ordered to withdraw his troops.

Rejected feedback

Education, particularly early education, strongly influences whether children are open-minded and interested in learning about various cultures and ways of thinking, or indoctrinated to despise and hate anyone who thinks differently. Many rigid doctrines insist they are the only true belief, for everybody for all times. Global Education Associates, founded in 1973 by Patricia and Gerald Mische (1977), now has over 2,500 active members in 90 countries. It seeks to expose children from an early age to a wide variety of cultures and viewpoints, to awaken their interest in mutual learning. Through dialogue, in which we truly seek to learn about different points of view and understand them, we can all increase our knowledge and insights. Dialogues are very different from 'debates', where one 'wins' by catching the opponent in a contradiction.

Knowledge and resources

The world has enough resources to give a good education to every child, not only in reading, writing and mathematics, but also in the moral teachings common to all great religions. But many families cannot afford to pay school fees. It was the great contribution of reformers like Heinrich Pestalozzi in Switzerland, John Dewey in the United States, and others, who introduced the idea that every child has a right to free education, not only the children of the rich who can afford to hire private teachers. It is time to extend that overdue reform worldwide.

Table 13.4 summarizes some of the obstacles to peace in all of its aspects, and some potential remedies.

Table 13.4. Some potential remedies against the six basic defects in social feedback systems

Source of problems	*Examples*	*Potential remedies*
Conflict over goals	Border conflicts; conflicts over distribution of resources; human rights violations; nationally-biased textbooks and news	Peaceful conflict transformation, self-determination, mutually beneficial cooperation, reconciliation; focus on the satisfaction of basic needs of those most in need; UN conventions; dialogue of civilizations
Lack of feedback	Miscalculations as cause of wars; lack of information about poverty, famines and ecological disasters; corruption thriving in secrecy; censorship	Verification of peace and disarmament agreements; increasing public awareness of problems; transparency; free press; peace journalism
Distorted feedback, externalities	War is profitable for some, lethal for others; undemocratic forms of government; security dilemma; inequality; tragedy of commons; impunity; glorification of violence in the media and arts	Ethical norms, moral education; democratization; nonoffensive defence; law; taxes and incentives; greater equality; income redistribution; resource conservation; International Criminal Court; promoting peace culture
Delayed feedback	'Fallacy of last move' as cause of arms races and aggression; failure to transform conflicts at an early stage; low saving and investment; apathy toward denials of freedom and hate propaganda	Planning for the future; foresight; UN Agency for Mediation; increased savings and investment; long-range planning; intergenerational ethics; vigilance against emerging dictatorships and hostility
Rejected feedback	Megalomania, hatred, prejudice, racism, discrimination as causes of civil and international wars; job discrimination; oppression of minorities	Expanding international contacts at all levels; global education to improve the understanding of other cultures and to overcome prejudices; equal opportunity; minority rights
Lack of knowledge and resources	Shortage of resources for peace-building; unequal distribution of income and wealth; insufficient sharing of useful knowledge; military spending	Standing UN Peacekeeping Force; disarmament and economic conversion; more research; development assistance; greater sharing of science and technology; disarmament; world treasury; universal free education

The future of peace as a self-regulating process

Given the vast theoretical knowledge about effective control systems, and their widespread successful application to technical problems, these methods should gradually find their way to be applied also to the prevention of violence and the promotion of peace in all its forms, including better protection of human survival, the reduction of poverty and disease, environmental protection, the promotion of human rights, the elimination of dictatorships, and the emergence of a global culture of peace.

Since early actions to prevent a disaster require much less effort than interventions after violence has erupted on a large scale, it is anticipated that we will steadily improve our ability to foresee potential problems early, and eliminate them before they become intractable.

Ignoring regulatory feedback signals can be dangerous. In 1986, the director of the Chernobyl nuclear power plant wanted to conduct a new experiment, but automatic controls repeatedly indicated that some variables were outside of the safe range and kept shutting down the reactor. So he ordered his technicians to switch off the control instruments. After that, the plant exploded, spewing radioactive waste across Europe and beyond.

How vital self-regulating systems are to maintain peace or health becomes obvious when they are absent. If the human immune system, which constantly searches for disease germs and eliminates them before they can multiply and spread throughout the body, is weakened, as in AIDS patients, they become vulnerable to all kinds of diseases, and eventually die. If the immune system stops functioning altogether, at the time of death the body is rapidly consumed by microbes. Similarly, a healthy, peaceful society needs good government at all levels and a vibrant civil society that constantly searches for potential sources of violence, misery, denial of freedom, intolerance and lies, including cases of corruption or abuse of power on the part of the government, and helps overcome them nonviolently. Without such feedback systems that constantly detect deviations from a desirable goal state and correct them, in the body and at various levels of human society, life becomes miserable or impossible.

Modern science and technology have given humanity the opportunity to overcome age-old problems of hunger, disease and poverty. But they have also made it possible to destroy ourselves. The late physicist Richard Feynman once met a Buddhist monk who told him: 'Humanity possesses a key that can open the gates to heaven. But the same key can also open the gates to hell.' The choice is ours.

References

Afheldt, H. (1976) *Verteidigung und Frieden*, München: Hanser.

Boulding, K.E. (1978) *Stable Peace*, Austin: University of Texas Press.

Boutros-Ghali, B. (1992) *Agenda for Peace. Report of the United Nations Secretary General to the United Nations Security Council*, New York: United Nations.

Brams, S.J. (1985) *Superpower Games: Applying Game Theory to Superpower Conflict*, New Haven, CT and London: Yale University Press.

Carson, R. (1962) *Silent Spring*, Boston, MA: Houghton Mifflin.

Chestnut, H. (ed.) (1986) *Contributions of Technology to International Conflict Resolution*, Oxford: Pergamon Press.

Collier, P. and Hoeffler, A. (1998) 'On economic causes of civil war', *Oxford Economic Papers*, 50, 4: 563–73.

Dallaire, R. (2003) *Shake Hands with the Devil*, Toronto: Random House of Canada.

Dumas, L.J. (1986) *The Overburdened Economy*, Berkeley: University of California Press.

Fischer, D. (1984a) *Preventing War in the Nuclear Age*, Totowa, NJ: Rowman & Allanheld.

Fischer, D. (1984b) 'Weapons technology and the intensity of arms races', *Conflict Management and Peace Science*, 8, 1: 49–69.

Fischer, D. (1993) *Nonmilitary Aspects of Security: A Systems Approach*, Aldershot: Dartmouth.

Galtung, J. (1984) *There Are Alternatives! Four Roads to Peace and Security*, Nottingham: Spokesman.

Galtung, J. (1992) 'The coming one hundred years of peacemaking: visions of peace for the 21st century', a lecture given at the Centenary Conference of the International Peace Bureau in Helsinki, 30 August.

Galtung, J. (1998) 'High road, low road: charting the course for peace journalism', *Track Two, Constructive Approaches to Community and Political Conflict*, 7, 4: 7–10.

Galtung, J. (2004) *TRANSCEND AND TRANSFORM: An Introduction to Conflict Work*, London and Sterling, VA: Pluto Press.

Gorbachev, M. (1987) *Perestroika: New Thinking for Our Country and the World*, New York: Harper & Row.

Hardin, G. (1968) 'The Tragedy of the Commons', *Science*, 162: 1243–8.

Jervis, R. (1976) *Perception and Misperception in International Politics*, Princeton, NJ: Princeton University Press.

Jones, E. (1973) *Ingratiation: An Attributional Approach*, Morristown, NJ: General Learning Press.

Kamaluddin, S. (2006) 'Lender with a mission – Bangladesh's Grameen Bank targets poorest of poor', at: www.gdrc.org/icm/grameen-article4.html.

Kull, S. (1988) *Minds at War: Nuclear Reality and Inner Conflict of Defense Policy-Makers*, New York: Basic Books.

Leontief, W. and Duchin, F. (1983) *Military Spending: Facts and Figures, Worldwide Implications and Future Outlook*, Oxford: Oxford University Press.

Mische, P. and Mische, G. (1977) *Toward a Human World Order*, New York: Paulist Press.

Schell, J. (1982) *The Fate of the Earth*, New York: Knopf.

Spencer, M. (2006) *Two Aspirins and a Comedy: How Television Can Enhance Health and Society*, Boulder, CO: Paradigm Publishers.

Stiglitz, J. (2002) *Globalization and its Discontents*, London: Penguin.

Stockholm International Peace Research Institute (SIPRI) (2004) *SIPRI Yearbook*, Stockholm: SIPRI.

Tinbergen, J. and Fischer, D. (1987) *Warfare and Welfare: Integrating Security Policy into Socio-Economic Policy*, Brighton: Wheatsheaf.

Tobin, J. (1974) *The New Economics One Decade Older*, Princeton, NJ: Princeton University Press.

UNIDIR (1990) *Nonoffensive Defense: A Global Perspective*, New York: Taylor and Francis.

Wallace, M. (1982) 'Armaments and escalation', *International Studies Quarterly*, 26, 1: 37–51.

Wiesel, E. (1982) *Night*, New York: Bantam.

Yunus, M. (1988) 'Grameen Bank: organization and operations', paper presented at the World Conference on Support for Micro-enterprises, 6–9 June, Washington, DC: World Bank.

Part 3

Supporting peace

14

Gender and peace

Towards a gender-inclusive, holistic perspective

Tony Jenkins and Betty A. Reardon

Introduction: toward a new phase of the inquiry into gender and peace

The authors of this chapter are peace educators who believe that peace knowledge in all its forms constitutes one field from which multiple forms of learning relevant to the tasks of educating and acting for peace can be gleaned. We have drawn upon all of them, the fruits of peace research, the substance of university peace studies, the methodologies of peace education and practical peace action in the development of the pedagogies we practise. We adhere to educational methods consistent with the values of justice and nonviolence that inform the pursuit of peace knowledge. These are built upon a verifiable knowledge base, informed by sound theories, and directed toward developing the capacities of learners to make normative judgements based on the values, apply the knowledge and verify or refute the theories through inquiry and communal learning. These methods imbue the approach we take to gender and peace as considered in this essay as well as in our professional practice. They reflect adherence to principles of holism in inquiry into problems and in exploration of possible resolutions of or means to transcend the problems of peace that we take in sum to be the problematic of violence.

These are the premises that underlie the following discussions that will reflect upon the possibility that gender, the social roles of and social distinctions between men and women, when fully perceived, is not only as the United Nations refers to it, a cross-cutting issue, affecting most problems and areas of concern to peace knowledge, but also one possible core of a holistic study of the central problematic of violence. Because of this cross-cutting character and the universality of gender concerns, might not gender also serve as an organizing concept around which to build studies not only of gender equality and peace, but as the potential core of a systematic inquiry into the possibilities for the transformation of the present violent world order? We also ask whether such a transformation is possible without recognizing, dismantling and forswearing various institutions and habits of patriarchy that we perceive as integral to the present global culture of violence, a major factor affecting such problems as denial of human rights, economic inequity, ecological deterioration and armed conflict. Taken as a whole these problems comprise all that we have come to consider as the war system, those pervasive habits and institutions of political, economic, social and cultural violence that are a major impediment to peace and human security. We hope that others concerned with the role of gender in the creation and dissemination of peace knowledge would join in an inquiry into the illumination of contemporary forms of patriarchy as a complement and extension to what has gone before in the evolution of the field of gender and peace. We define patriarchy, as does Joshua Goldstein, as the 'social organization of men's control of power'.[1] The topic as presented in this volume is classified as knowledge supporting peace; we, however, ask is not this problematic of gender as constitutive to peace knowledge as are conflict studies or any of the other topics here categorized as central to the substance of peace studies?

Overview of some significant developments in the field

The field of gender and peace has evolved through various phases, each with a perspective based on the concerns of its time. All phases, however, found some roots in the problematic of patriarchy, a social and cultural construct that has not only privileged men over women, but can be seen as a paradigm for other forms of authoritarianism, hierarchy and inequality. It is precisely the 'patriarchal privilege' as it is termed by Michael Kaufman,[2] that is the common thread that runs through the development of the field as it does through women's and men's struggles for gender justice. Through this century we see the field as evolving over the following chronology on which scholarship responds to and influences social movements for gender equality.

This chronology is developmental rather than uniquely event based. It underlies an organic view of the evolution of the field in which all realms of peace knowledge interact around the 'cross-cutting issue' of gender. Peace action, research and education on the subject of gender evolved in a process of reciprocal influence that illustrates the holistic nature of peace knowledge that informs our approach to peace education. The periods delineated below are not discrete, nor do the developments, even when viewed from a global perspective, evolve simultaneously in all areas of the world. We offer it here as a general framework for the narrative which will, by nature of the topics addressed, weave in and out of the various developmental phases we designate as follows.

The years 1900–45 were decades of the articulation of the problematic of women's subordinate social and political status, and in the years preceding both world wars of the articulation of intuitions regarding women's lack of political power as an obstacle to peace. Women's primary political activities were devoted to achieving suffrage. From 1945 to 1970, attention was focused on the ongoing subordination of women and the limitations on their legal rights that existed, in some cases, even where women had the vote. The United Nations established a Commission on the Status of Women and later a more proactive agency, the Division for the Advancement of Women. A number of foundational works in modern feminism were published.

From 1970 to 1985, the activism of women directed toward the realization of equality in all spheres, both public and private, energized the United Nations to launch efforts to set standards and goals for women's equality. These efforts were significantly advanced by the International Decade for Women (1975–85) and three international conferences, held in 1975, 1980 and 1985, organized around the themes of 'Equality, Development and Peace'. A major landmark of the period was the adoption of the Convention on the Elimination of All Forms of Discrimination against Women (CEDAW). These were also the years of the first academic inquiries into women and peace and the emergence of what was to become a significant body of literature on the topic.

The final developmental phase of the century occurred from 1985 to 2000. There was intense interest and activity around the denial of the human rights of women, resulting in campaigns to implement and augment CEDAW, one result of which was the Declaration on the Elimination of All Forms of Violence against Women. The 1995 Beijing Fourth World Conference on Women set a range of standards to assure that women's rights were recognized and implemented as universal human rights. Feminist theory on women and peace was further developed and was complemented in the 1990s by the initiation of masculinities studies, making an actual gender perspective on the peace problematic possible. The culminating development of this phase was the adoption of Security Council Resolution 1325 on 'Women, Peace and Security'.

The first decade of the twenty-first century saw the beginning of inquiry and action around the vestiges of traditional patriarchy that continue to pose significant obstacles not only to gender equality but to a range of problems addressed by the fields of peace knowledge. The Patriarchy Project we describe in the last section of the essay was launched at the UN Conference on Racism held in 2002 in Durban, South Africa and carried to global civil society at the World Social Forum held in Rio de Janeiro, Brazil in 2004. It is carried on by a worldwide network of scholars and activists, committed to the achievement of universal gender justice and an end to war.

In the first sections of our essay we offer a selective account from our own particular perspective on issues and developments in action, research and education that have influenced the place of gender in the realms of peace knowledge. Starting with some consideration of women's resistance to war, we will move to noting how taking a political perspective to women's secondary status in most societies led feminists to proposing integral links between women's exclusion from policy-making and continued recourse to war as a mechanism for the conduct of international conflict. Next, we will observe how international attention to the status of women led to the development of international agreements intended to achieve gender equality. Then, we take note of how the international cooperation among women that produced the agreements bought about an even wider view of the relationship between gender inequality and gender violence and a more holistic gender analysis of the problematic of the global culture of violence currently being informed by masculinities studies. These sections of our chapter serve as a preface to a statement of the new more inclusive dimension we hope to see integrated into this essential field of inquiry into the conditions of peace as a means to more fully illuminate the problematic of patriarchy.

We place our account in the framework of the twentieth-century international women's movement and peace actions interacting with scholarship on gender and peace. While taking this international view, we acknowledge that our own experiences, knowledge and interpretations derive primarily from developments in the United Nations, the United States and various international civil society initiatives. The global movement that contributes to knowledge about gender and peace we know to be far wider and more varied than our limited account. We see this chapter as an invitation to exchanges with others that might broaden and deepen gender and peace knowledge so that we may be more effective inquirers into the conditions and consequences of patriarchy and some alternative approaches to transcending them.

From the mid-twentieth century to the last decade, the academic field evolved primarily out of the theoretical frameworks of feminist scholarship introduced into international relations, peace studies and peace research, and United Nations policies. The earlier phases (1945–70) were focused on legal and political and later economic equality of women, dealing with the manifestations more than the causes of women's subordination, and seeing remedy primarily in the changing of women's legal status. Feminist perspectives that focused more on the underlying structural and cultural causes came in the later decades of the century as the term gender came to replace woman as the descriptor of the problematic. The recent addition of masculinities studies, addressing the consequences of men's socialization for peace issues and the consequences to men of the expectations and responsibilities that devolve to them in the war system, now gives validity to 'gender and peace' as the designator of a field, still referred to in some cases as 'women and peace' or 'women and world order'.[3]

The roots of the field lie, as noted, in women's experience of and response to war, documented in literature and history as the experience of loss, mourning, heroic maternal sacrifice and – most important to the field – dissent and resistance. Study of these universal experiences and responses came out of concern with women's secondary position in human society, noted as a problematic since the outset of Western democratic experiments with representative government. The relevance of the status of women to peace was somewhat acknowledged when raising the status of women was undertaken as a task for international society in the mid twentieth century by the United Nations, largely at the behest of a few women diplomats, such as Helvi Sippila of Finland who became chair of the first UN World Conference on Women in 1975 and Margaret Bruce of the UK who served in the 1970s as director of the UN Division for the Advancement of Women together with women's NGOs. Feminist discourse around the connections between women's political status and war, however, date to the early decades of the century in Europe and the United States, and while neither vigorous nor prominent, it laid the foundation for the scholarship that gained attention with the new mid-century interest in the status of women. This interest inspired an outpouring of critiques of the gender blindness of the established field of international relations and the emerging field of peace knowledge, comprising research, studies, education and action.[4]

The gender blindness was first attributed to the limited participation of women in these fields, in policy-making, scholarship, and, especially from the lack of women's perspectives in the research and teaching of the two interrelated but distinct fields, international relations and peace studies. Largely as a consequence of the two UN declared International Women's Decades (1975–95), these critiques brought about attempts to remedy gender bias through a set of international standards set forth by the United Nations. These standards were introduced into the substance of a growing body of research and courses in women's studies. Some of them included issues related to women, war and peace and violence against women. While it was in the area of human rights scholarship that this body of normative standards – including references to violence against women and women in armed conflict – received most academic attention, some scholars began to integrate feminist theories with peace theories into work that ultimately became a sub-field in peace studies and a major pedagogical influence on peace education. These standards are an essential component of the inclusive, integrative approach to gender and peace we, the authors, now take in our research and teaching.

Feminist arguments, bolstered by international human rights norms, gave public validation to assertions concerning the negative effects of women's exclusion from analysis and policy-making on matters of peace and security. Taken up by scholars who explored the ways in which gender arrangements contributed to the perpetuation of the social and political uses of violence and the rationalization of war as an instrument of national policy, the links among women's secondary status, war and gender violence became more widely accepted as a given of the problematic of war, and a body of literature on these connections began to emerge and continues to grow. However, there was at first only minimal integration of the work done by feminist scholars and activists working on peace with that of those focusing on human rights. The mainstream women's studies, for the most part perceived these particular inquiries as somewhat more specialized than their own more general study of women's issues and women's history.[5]

One of the most politically effective aspects of the international women's movement focused on the human rights of women and the use of the international standards to defend and implement them. Efforts were led by the Rutgers University Center for Women's Global Leadership and its executive director, Charlotte Bunch. It was from these efforts, mainly on the part of women scholar-activists, that intensive public attention was brought to violence against women.[6] Inquiry into issues of pervasive social and cultural gender violence and later into the effects of armed conflict on women by feminist scholar-activists in the human rights movement contributed to the articulation of a more general theory of violence, encompassing multiple forms and arenas of violence from interpersonal and domestic violence to organized warfare. The gendered aspects of violence became an important area of inquiry for a number of feminist scholars who sought to develop theories addressing male aggression as a factor in cultures of violence and the inclination toward war. Some argued that male aggressivity was socially and culturally cultivated in men and problematized male dominance in science – among them, Brian Easlea and Evelyn Fox Keller – as well as politics as a major causal factor in the origins and continuation of the arms race.[7]

Inquiries on social and gender violence, a significant aspect of the emerging field of the study of masculinities, have increased the numbers of male scholars in the field and led to the conceptualization of an inclusive gender perspective now taking hold. Recent developments have deepened and extended the arguments advanced on the issue of gender violence by feminist scholarship through the twentieth century to the present day in which institutionalized patriarchy itself is becoming more widely viewed as a central problematic.

We see this latest development to be infusing new possibilities for the transformational learning pursued by the education realm of peace knowledge. We would suggest that this currently developing phase of the field could integrate masculinities studies with human rights norms and concepts in a framework of inquiry into patriarchy. We have a particular interest in issues of gender inquiry of this type because of its relevance to the fundamental elements in the puzzle of peace as well as the transformative learning possibilities it offers. The gender issue itself is at once challenging, comprehensive and, we believe, highly amenable to positive change through learning facilitated by the critical and reflective pedagogies practised in peace education.

Gender refers to the culturally defined, socially sanctioned and usually separate roles in human affairs played by men and women and the characteristics attributed to each that have rationalized these roles. Gender here is construed as it has been defined by the United Nations in the Beijing Platform for Action, the Swedish report on patriarchal violence quoted below, and in such documents as those calling for gender mainstreaming – including a gender perspective in the consideration of all issues and in all programmes addressed and conducted by the world body. We believe that the systematic nature of patriarchal gender designations and roles constitutes a highly significant and much neglected aspect of the study of gender and peace. Because we perceive gender aspects in virtually every issue and problem addressed by peace and conflict studies, we are attempting to integrate elements of these issues into all our work in peace education.[8]

This concept of gender and our assumptions about the connections of gender violence and patriarchy were articulated by the government of Sweden. In a 2005 report of a survey 'Patriarchal violence – an attack on human security', identified as a major global issue, they define gender as:

> The totality of ideas and actions that combine to create social gender identity in individuals. A cultural process that collectively attributes traditionally male/masculine or female/feminine

qualities to individuals. Also used in queer theory, which to a greater extent emphasizes gender as a diverse concept in which heterosexuality is seen as the basis of the gender order.[9]

Lysistrata to Greenham Common and Okinawa: women's resistance to war and militarism

The Lysistrata phenomenon, our designation of women's resistance to war – taken from the classical work by the Greek playwright Aristophanes – gave rise to discussion of some gender concepts that have been largely repudiated as essentialism, the notion that there are essences or essential characteristics within each sex that significantly influence how they respectively view the world and behave in it. Women's purported tendency to avoid or prevent violence is one such characteristic, sometimes attributed to the perceptions that women have less physical strength than men, and are therefore more timid and fearful of violence. As recent experiences of the men of the Christian Peacemakers Team held hostage in Iraq in 2005 attest, nonviolence is not an exclusively 'womanly' behaviour.[10]

Women's resistance has involved a range of strategies of active nonviolence, which while not intended to harm those whose power, policies or ideas are being resisted, involves significant risks on the part of the resisters.[11] Withholding sexual access in a patriarchal society risks the wrath of the patriarchs who control the destinies of the women resisting. The strategy is largely based on the essentialist assumption that men cannot or will not live without sexual gratification. While this strategy is said to have been employed by pre-colonial Native American women, and maybe others in addition to women of ancient Greece, it is not credited with ending any particular war and certainly has not limited or weakened the institution of war. However, such actions have helped to feed the essentialist notion that women are more 'civilized' or morally developed than men, and that this quality rather than a considered judgement on the political efficacy of war has accounted for women's resistance.[12]

Resistance as a strategy to avoid or end war has continued to be practised in other forms by women peace activists, often in highly visible forms such as the Greenham Common Women, encamped around the US military bases in the UK during the early 1980s to demonstrate their opposition to the presence of the bases, and to the nuclear weapons stored beneath the common. Within this particular initiative there were strong separatist elements that rejected men's participation in the resistance. There were elements of radical feminism, one school of which, articulated by Andrea Dworkin, held that misogyny and the binary gender designations that came from the assumption of heterosexuality as 'normal' served to perpetuate patriarchal control over women and children as it oppressed and repressed all other forms of sexuality and gender identities.[13] Those who held these views insisted that women's actions should be separated from men's actions (indeed, that it was the behaviours of men that formed the problematic) in various women's acts of resistance to war. This position was reinforced by women's relegation to secondary or auxiliary roles in many peace movement activities, by the lack of acknowledgement of women's taking primary responsibility in the organizing of major peace campaigns and actions, and by the exploitation of women's efforts by some men in the peace movement – such as the major anti-base manifestations in Okinawa, and one of the largest peace marches in history in New York on 12 June 1982 – and by instances of sexual harassment experienced by some women in the movement.

The experience of the marginalization, even the exclusion, of women was not unknown in the other realms of peace knowledge and peace action. While the first efforts to introduce the question of the relationship of women's status to peace into the International Peace Research

Association (IPRA) were undertaken in 1975, it was not until a decade later that the Women and Peace Commission was established, officially recognizing the topic as a field of peace research. In Okinawa, women who sought to call attention to the gender security problems posed by the long-term presence of US military on that island were rebuffed as distracting from the goal of base removal by male activists who could not understand the repeated gender violence against women committed by US service personnel as another argument to place before the Japanese government to induce it to request base closings. These women organized Okinawa Women Act Against Military Violence (OWAAM) in 1995 in launching protests about the rape of a twelve-year-old girl by three US servicemen. This and subsequent actions of resistance and opposition were taken within an analytic framework that placed this gender violence, which OWAAM termed military violence – violence committed by military against civilians or outside the realm of combat – within a framework of patriarchal militarization. A similar analysis of the militarization of society informed the resistance efforts of the Israeli women who organized New Profile.[14] Both groups continue to resist as the Israeli occupation of Palestinian territory continues, and US bases, while somewhat changed by moving forces from one base to another, still occupy large, formerly agricultural areas of Okinawa.[15] New Profile also facilitates men's nonviolent resistance in its support of conscientious objectors' refusal of service in the occupied territories of Palestine.

Accounts of Greenham Common and similar encampments in other countries were widely admired by the international women's peace movement that proliferated along with the proliferation of nuclear weapons during the Cold War, and so were included in some peace studies as well women's studies courses. These actions along with the 'gender gap', a phrase used to describe the purported tendency of women to vote for more peace-oriented candidates and policies while men tended to support policies of 'strength' and armed force, were included among other such types of evidence to explore the sources of these differences. The notion that women's experience as mothers, if not their reproductive biology per se, accounted for these manifestations of resistance, or that women were by nature more peaceful than men was, as noted, rejected by most feminist as essentialism, reducing the phenomenon to the reproductive difference between the sexes. Some, such as Christine Sylvester, argued that women had warrior capacity and political inclination equal to that of men.[16] These manifestations took on political forms such as the women's delegation to European leaders on the eve of The First World War that attempted to persuade them to continue to follow the diplomatic path to spare their countries the inevitable suffering that any war brings.

The 'motherhood' rationale for resistance was articulated during the mid-nineteenth century in the wake of the American Civil War when the 'Mothers Proclamation', pledging to raise sons who would not take the lives of other mothers' sons was promulgated, and Mothers' Day declared as an anti-war holiday. It continued into the twentieth century and found its manifestations in such movements as the US Women Strike for Peace, a movement initiated to protect children from the health consequences of nuclear testing that brought about the 1963 Test Ban Treaty and the Soldiers' Mothers' Movement in Russia through which women resisted their sons' serving in the armed conflicts in Chechnya in the 1990s.[17] More recently, in 2006 the organizers of Code Pink, a women's group organized in opposition to the Iraq war, circulated the Proclamation in observance of the third anniversary of the American invasion of Iraq, reminding the public that Mothers' Day had political significance beyond the commercialism and sentimentality that it has come to manifest.[18]

While it was evident that the motherhood concept was an organizing principle for such actions, feminist peace scholars and educators generally refuted it as being inconsistent with the theory of gender as a socially or culturally constructed category of human identity as indicated in the definition used in the previously cited report from the Office of the Swedish Government. While not uncontested, this argument gained ascendancy in the growing field of peace knowledge that focused on women's roles in and perspectives on war and peace. We, the authors, do not deny the differences in behaviours and inclinations that research suggests may be biologically based. So, too, we find interesting and potentially useful toward our own purposes of challenging the patriarchal paradigm of enforced heterosexuality, male dominance and militarized security, the theoretical propositions published by Myra J. Hird of Queens University in Canada:

> In contemporary society, the conceptual division between 'sex' as the biological differences, and 'gender' as the social, cultural, economic and political differences is largely taken for granted . . .
>
> . . . current concern with the fragmentation of identities is crucially linked to questions concerning the continued viability of [this differentiation]. . .
>
> Nature . . . offers shades of difference and similarity much more often than clear opposites.[19]

As peace educators, we find this discourse on diversity in sex and gender promising of new possibilities into the many forms of diversity which we believe must be understood and defended against the onslaughts of fundamentalist reductionisms in the realms of gender, culture and religious and political ideology. In fact, we expect that wider and deeper inquires into the political valences of gender will offer possibilities to educate for a humanly diverse as well as a more just and less violent global order.

With regard to the issues raised by the relevance of motherhood to gender and peace, we tend to believe it is the experience rather than the biological fact of motherhood, the learned caring and nurturing more than the biology of reproduction that influences mothers' pleas and actions for peace.[20] The biological factors under discussion indicate that the evident differences between men and women in regard to war and peace are far more complex than either of the two explanations of biology or social construction of gender or men's and women's actual roles in conducting war can account for.[21] This complexity, as we will see below in the account of the emergence of masculinities studies, is what gives this area of peace knowledge its special cogency for peace education. The multiple concepts and constructions of masculinities in various cultures and during different historic periods, not only continue to challenge biological determinism and essentialism, they illustrate that human behaviour and characteristics are susceptible to the influence of context and circumstance and, we believe, can be affected by intentional education as much as by traditional socialization.

Peace education is concerned with developing pedagogies that enable learners to think in terms of complexities beyond the standard curricula on controversial issues that usually teach students to consider little more than the two major opposing positions involved in the public discourse on the issues in question. It also seeks to enable learners to confront and explore some highly charged social issues that have personal valence for most people in as deeply reflective and socially responsible a manner as possible. Gender and the contending theories about its formation and significance is such an issue.

It is well known that the peace education has been influenced by Freirean pedagogy.[22] The Brazilian educator, Paulo Freire, advocated practice of a dialogic pedagogy of reflection and action that was one of the foundations of critical pedagogy practised by many peace educators. But it is not so widely known that feminist pedagogy that addresses the significance of the personal dimensions to classroom discussion and learning has also had a profound effect on the work of many peace educators. In this regard, the work of Belenky et al. described in *Womens' Ways of Knowing* and the work of Carol Gilligan on gender differences in moral decision making are very relevant to peace education practice.[23] Gender differences in ways of learning and knowing, which we believe to be, largely but not entirely, the consequence of gender relations and the differences in the socialization experiences of boys and girls, provide some of the multiple ways of thinking that are essentially human. They offer the same possibility as cultural differences for broadening the learning and knowing repertoire necessary to understanding and analyzing the complexities of the challenges of overcoming violence and achieving peace. Gender differences are a primary basis for understanding both multiple ways of knowing and varying perspectives on peace problems.

For feminist peace scholars these complexities were further evidence of the need to include in the growing 'canon' of peace studies the issues and perspectives they had argued to be integral to addressing the central purposes of the field, developing the knowledge necessary to reduce violence and advance justice. They argued that the failure to include these considerations militated against achieving the purposes for which peace knowledge was being produced and advanced through research and education. It took over a decade of professional discussions and arguments to gain general recognition of the cogency of the feminist arguments. Some specifics of these developments will be noted below as we discuss some of the political dimensions of gender and peace.

Connecting women, war and political participation

The national and military valorization of motherhood was poignantly evident during the two world wars of the twentieth century. The value that patriarchal, nationalist popular culture placed on motherhood and its vital contribution to the maintenance of fighting forces served as a means to deflect the potential influence of the more political anti-war arguments women were advancing and to impede the drive for women's suffrage, seen as a way for women to have more political influence over war, peace and other public matters. Lack of the vote, however, did not prevent the American, European and Japanese women's active political involvement, not only in forms of passive resistance, but in instances of political intervention such as the aforementioned international women's campaigns to avert the First World War that produced the Women's International League for Peace and Freedom (WILPF). Launched in this Euro-American peace initiative, WILPF now has national chapters throughout the world, with significant leadership from developing countries.[24]

WILPF, in a framework of values of justice and peace, made a significant contribution to the development of the integrated, holistic approach that the international peace education movement began to advocate in the 1980s. From its earliest days WILPF made clear connections between what later became recognized as the integral relationship between peace and human rights and contributed to the growing belief that more democratic governments would be less likely to engage in warfare.[25] This argument advanced by others has also been put forth by feminists who argue that the extreme underrepresentation of women in most spheres of government documented in UN studies precludes claims of the majority of states to be democracies.[26] Interpretations of the rationale for the Second World War, which saw the Western democracies allied in the war, tended to strengthen rather than undermine the argument since the popular interpretation was that these nations had taken up arms to defend democracy against dictatorship. This argument, along with the 'gender bending' contributions women made to the successful conduct of the war, was taken up by some in the women's movement in the post-Second World War period in a new phase of feminism. What was to become the international women's movement along with anti-colonialism and anti-racism movements, arose to demand the fulfilment of the promises of the avowed purposes of the war, to defend democracy, and in the aftermath, to assure human rights as one means to prevent further wars.[27]

The issues of anti-colonialism and to some extent issues of racial justice found their way onto the research agendas and into the syllabi of peace scholars, but such was not the case with feminist or women's issues. Well into the 1970s questions that we now refer to as gender issues were considered by all but a very few peace researchers – those few were mainly feminists – to have little or no relevance to peace. In the first three editions published in 1972, 1978 and 1981 of the compendium of peace studies syllabi, Peace and World Order Studies, no courses on women's or gender issues or approaches were included. The next issue, published in 1983 – the only one edited by a woman – contained five syllabi on the topic in the section with the least entries of any of the topics included. In the edition of 1989, the topic is one of four sections containing only three syllabi – the other three being: ecological balance, alternative futures, education and teacher training, all topics which gender perspectives on peace education considers integral to the holistic approach it favours.

Through these two decades of the 1970s and 1980s feminists and activists with WILPF in the lead insisted on a significant, undeniable interrelationship among the various justice issues of the post-war era that ultimately became the domain of positive peace. One of the unifying concepts was exclusion from and marginalization in politics of disempowered groups. Most of the groups becoming engaged in struggles to achieve a voice in policy-making, participation in their own governance, their places on research agendas and in university and school curricula previously had been for the most part excluded from all these policy realms. Some saw this exclusion as the intentional dominance of the powerful over the powerless to maintain their privileges, rationalized by their greater capacity for the exercise of power. But others began to take a more system-based view, suggesting that the international power-based system itself was the major impediment to justice and peace, bringing the question of alternatives and system change into classroom inquiries and to the design of research projects.[28] The questions that formed this inquiry lead to theorizing the links among these forms of exclusions, the economic and political oppressions they rationalized and the institution of war, and, ultimately, to a more systematic analysis of patriarchy and its hold on so many social and institutional systems from school curricula, to church hierarchy, to the corporate world, governmental structures and the security establishment

Advances in international standards: women's equality and peace

WILPF, along with various other women's organizations, took a leading role in the activities surrounding the United Nations' International Decade for Women from 1975 to 1985. Under the general themes of equality, development and peace, concerted efforts were made by the UN and associated NGOs to advance women's legal equality, political participation and involvement at all levels of economic development from planning through assessment. It was in the arena of development that the negative consequences of gender inequality and gender-biased cultural practices became so evident. Issues of advancing the roles and participation of women in the UN system and setting standards to increase their participation in the politics and economies of the member states achieved wider public attention. They were also given more consideration in the field of peace knowledge by those who believed that the UN diagnosis of the relationship between gender and development and the assessments of the consequences of women's marginalization in the development process vividly illustrated the concept of structural violence.

Severe critiques of the almost total lack of attention to the actual effects of prevailing development policy on women – similar to criticisms still raised today about globalization and the economic burdens it imposes on the poor, especially women – were most acutely evident in such basic practices as the UN accounting system that failed to include the unpaid work of women that formed the very foundations of a society's capacity for economic production.[29] Especially forceful criticisms came from scholars of women's productive activities. A pioneering work in this field was Ester Boserup's 1970 study on women in development.[30] The research on women's economic impoverishment and exclusion from economic policy-making was to become a significant factor in both feminist and human rights arguments on the definitions of human security and what comprises it that arose in the 1990s.

For our purposes of illuminating the peace knowledge consequences of these exclusions, the most significant critiques came from feminist political scientists and international relations scholars. We find the most relevant to our perspective to be the works of Cynthia Cockburn of the UK and Anne Tickner and Cynthia Enloe of the US who argue that much of what peace research and the peace movement consider wrong headed and destructive policies and practices in the international system derives from an exclusively masculine perspective. They suggest that the failure to give adequate consideration to alternatives to the politics of force can be attributed to a significant degree to the limitation on and in many cases exclusion of women and women's perspectives from the security policy discourse.[31] These assertions informed the efforts of UN-associated NGOs to convene the October 2000 open session of the Security Council that issued Security Council Resolution 1325 (SC 1325), calling for the equal representation of women in peace and security negotiations and policy-making.

Gender exclusion refers not only to lack of women's participation, but also and especially ignoring the human consequences of gender-blind policies as they are experienced by both men and women. Such exclusion has also negatively impacted men, especially those at lower levels of political power, a problem not yet systematically addressed. Recognition of the impact of gender exclusion set into motion innovations in UN policy and norm setting that reciprocally affected and were affected by women's studies and a bit later by feminist scholarship such as that noted above.

The most significant of UN normative gender standards were the Convention on the Elimination of All Forms of Discrimination against Women (CEDAW 1980), the Declaration on the Elimination of All Forms of Violence against Women (1993), the Beijing Platform for Action (1995) and Security Council Resolution 1325 (2000).[32] These documents constitute a line of awareness and assertion of public responsibility for the achievement of women's equality in political, economic, social and cultural arenas, complementing and extending the preceding major emphasis on legal equality – although this still remains a significant and controversial issue in various societies. With the latter two documents, protection of women from gender-based violence, including and especially military violence, was designated as a fundamental human right. The inclusion of women in peace and conflict negotiations and security policy-making was declared by the UN to be essential to democracy and the achievement of this right. SC 1325 has become an important basis of action to implement all these gender relevant international norms, serving as a political tool for international peace groups as well as women's NGOs. It is also a powerful example of collaboration between NGOs and the UN, and between women and men. The developments making the resolution possible were set in motion in 1999 by Anwarul K. Chowdhury, who was then the UN Ambassador from Bangladesh and president of the UN General Assembly. His words quoted below attest to his commitment to its purposes:

> The potential of Resolution 1325, its implications and impact in real terms are enormous. That

> women make a difference when in decision- and policy-making positions is no longer in dispute. When women participate in peace negotiations and in the crafting of a peace agreement, they keep the future of their societies in mind. They have the broader and longer-term interest of society in mind. Whereas, historically in post-conflict situations, men are interested in ensuring that the peace process will give them the authority and power that they are seeking. A lasting peace cannot be achieved without the participation of women and the inclusion of gender perspectives and participation in peace processes.[33]

Thus, through this human rights route over the terrain of positive peace, the issue of gender as it relates to negative peace, the actual gendered experiences and consequences of war and peace within the sphere of traditional concepts of security became an important focus of the international gender discourse. With a particular focus on the multiple forms of sexist violence suffered by women in most societies and the effects of armed conflict on women, came recognition that these multiple forms of violence both in times of apparent peace as well as in times of war were interconnected in a global culture of violence. These trends illuminated and brought wider attention to the gender inequality–war interconnections. Understanding the interconnections in turn led more feminist scholars, researchers and peace activists, among them those in the Peace Education Commission of the International Peace Research Association, to adopt as a working premise the assertion that gender violence is one component of an essentially violent patriarchal international system. These interconnections were integral to a statement from the 1983 consultative meeting of what was to become IPRA's Women and Peace Commission. The statement identified the interconnections as 'a continuum of violence which links the violence against women to the violence of war.' The consultation also asserted that there were, 'connections between patriarchy, militaristic structures and values and direct violence. . . .'[34] The assertion was that patriarchy has been maintained through the monopoly on power held by the men at the top of the hierarchical order rationalized by a claim of male superiority. The power is manifest in the hierarchy's control of force. These assertions were later to become a subject of further analysis by masculinities scholars in exploration of the connections between masculine identities and aggressivity. Some of their conclusions will be elaborated on later in this chapter. Similar assertions were also echoed in a statement from a preparatory meeting for the Beijing Fourth World Conference on Women organized by the United Nations Division for the Advancement of Women in December 1994.[35]

During the 1980s when there was a quantum leap in literature on women, peace and security there was also a wider acknowledgement that violence, the institutions, habits of mind and behaviours that perpetuate it comprise what had been defined as the war system.[36] We now argue that war is an essentially patriarchal institution. But patriarchy itself was not the subject of wide study for some years to come. Only now is it emerging as a central focus among scholars in masculinities studies, feminist peace and human rights activists whose analytic attention has turned to a more concentrated and systematic consideration of patriarchy as it manifests in contemporary institutions, policies and phenomena.[37]

We use the phrase 'apparent peace' above to describe the context in which violence against women occurs outside actual war and to call attention to the on-going conditions of structural violence endured by vulnerable groups under the present global economic system, also, and especially, to take note of the gendered nature of the social and cultural violence that has been described as 'the war against women'.[38] This war rages in most times and places whether or not societies are engaged in armed conflict. We would argue that there has been an invisible theatre of combat in this gender war, 'the war against men'. Patriarchy is an 'equal opportunity' destroyer of both women and men. As we recommend below, an inclusive gender perspective that takes into account patriarchy's disadvantages to both men and women offers a unique opportunity to engage in transformational learning toward a peaceful, just and gender equal global order. We believe that a transformation process would require the extension of human rights standards intended to achieve gender justice to include all men and women of all sexualities, gender orientations and identities.[39]

Violence against women: gendered link between human rights and peace

CEDAW, the Convention on the Elimination of All Forms of Discrimination Against Women, the 1980 'women's human rights convention', was a culmination of the campaign for equality women's groups have been waging since the founding of the United Nations. It comprises a review of most of the forms of discrimination and oppression of women as they had been perceived and studied to that point. Its emphasis on the economic, social and cultural factors underlying the lack of legal and political equality echoed the concerns of the larger human rights movement that this sphere of rights had too long taken a back seat to civil and political rights. The separation between the two spheres of human rights impeded the holistic view of the field that a growing number of human rights advocates argued to be essential to the institutionalization and realization of universal human rights. It became the preferred framework for the UN's human rights efforts when it was noted as constitutive to the field in the final document of the 1993 International Conference on Human Rights held in Vienna.

As peace educators, we advocate this holistic perspective as a comprehensive framework for the study of positive peace, arguing that the realization of human rights is the most practical means to the achievement of positive peace. We also consider that a holistic human rights perspective is integral to a truly inclusive gender perspective that in the mode of holism includes the whole spectrum of sexualities, heterosexual, transsexual, bisexual and homosexual, all gender identities. CEDAW is not adequate to the fulfilment of human rights as they would pertain to all these groups; nor does it address the problem of gender violence of any type, not even that perpetrated against women that became a focus of a women's human rights campaign in the next decade.

The origins of the Declaration on the Elimination of Violence against Women, issued by the Vienna International Conference on Human Rights in 1993, initially lacked systematic focus on the institution of war, but it achieved a major breakthrough in demonstrating that the phenomenon of gender violence was global, pervasive and constituted a long-ignored gross violation of human rights. It eliminated the distinction between women's rights and human rights that had ghettoized gendered aspects of both the discourse on human rights and the struggle for their universal realization. The Beijing Platform for Action, the product of the 1995 Fourth World Conference on Women, viewed as a human rights document made the connections that irrevocably integrated the issue of war into the analysis of and action on issues of gender equality. It paved the way for the campaign organized and conducted by women's NGOs for an open session of the Security Council on 'Women, Peace and Security', which in Resolution 1325 called for the representation of women in all matters concerned with peace and security official UN policy.[40]

The declaration and the resolution are clear illustrations of the ways in which women's movements have bridged the gap between civil society and the interstate system, and achieved a Freirean integration of research, education and action. In the early 1990s, the statistics on violence against women became the subject of even the popular press, producing some governmental response among Western states. Grassroots women's organizations throughout the world gathered multiple thousands of signatures calling for the international legal acknowledgement that gender violence was in serious contradiction of the international human rights norms.[41] The signed petitions were delivered to the UN Secretary General and facilitated the agreement to the declaration by the Vienna Conference on Human Rights, further strengthening the claim that women's rights are human rights, articulated in the 1995 Beijing Declaration that introduces the Platform for Action (BPFA). In recent years there has been the discussion of the development of a legally binding international convention on gender violence, so that its prohibition would be established within the body of international human rights treaty law.

The Global Framework of the Beijing Platform is organized around 12 areas of critical concern, three of which provided the precedents that made possible SC 1325. The areas of concern referring to violence against women, women and armed conflict, and women in power and decision making make up the main substance and imperatives put forth in that Security Council resolution that in terms of gender and peace is the most significant international document issued to date. The Platform offers an illuminating definition of violence against women, bringing specificity to the more abstract definition of the Declaration on Violence against Women. For peace educators it is a useful tool for demonstrating how conceptual definitions of problems such as gender injustice can and should be derived from and help to explain the lived realities of those who suffer the problems.

With the two short and simple statements quoted below, the Beijing Platform for Action demonstrates international acceptance of an inclusive concept of gender as a social construct, indicating it is a requisite factor of consideration in all areas of critical concern:

> . . . the differences between women's and men's achievements are still not recognized as the consequences of socially constructed gender roles rather than immutable biological differences.[42]

An even more significant statement supporting our assertion of the inseparable integral interdependence between gender equality and peace first argued as between women's equality and peace by one of the authors is articulated in the Platform quote below:[43]

> The maintenance of peace and security at the global, regional and local levels, together with the prevention of policies of aggression and ethnic cleansing and the resolution of armed conflict, is crucial for the protection of the human rights of women and girl-children, as well as for the elimination of all forms of violence against them and their use as weapons of war.[44]

The assertion reflected in this quote, as it is in SC 1325, is that viable peace in the absence of democratic politics, providing equal participation to all citizens, is not possible. The unequal representation of women in policy-making is a serious obstacle to peace as indicated in this quotation. Without significant representation of women in the political process abuses listed are not likely to be adequately addressed. The emergence of these concepts that linked women's situation to peace and violence against women to the larger systems of structural and armed violence and the developments that introduced them into the actions of international civil society and the policies of the UN system were – to an extent that may not exist around any other global issue – informed by the involvement of feminist scholars and peace researchers. A symbiotic partnership among the UN agencies such as the Division for the Advancement of Women, UNIFEM (the women's development agency), UNESCO, women's organizations and the academy, produced problem-relevant policies, sharpened research questions, enriched courses with contemporary international developments, and gave this arena of peace research significant valence in international politics. As noted above, these years, the 1980s in particular, saw a plentiful harvest of literature on women, war and peace and women's human rights that brought a number of scholars together as participants in international civil society, further internationalizing the field, strengthening its global perspective and enriching courses in women's studies and peace studies with research and theorizing around the long-neglected sphere of gender and peace. It also offered particularly fruitful substance for pedagogical developments in peace education, especially among those practitioners who perceived human rights as essential and integral to the field.[45]

From our perspective, this literature's relationship to developments in international civil society and their combined relevance to peace education and the deconstruction of patriarchy, especially, as noted, the feminist critiques of prevailing international relations theory and peace research perspectives, are the most significant. When viewed in terms of the consequences of the lack of women's perspectives and consideration of women's experiences in the analyses and prevailing theories of international relations and interstate conflict since the end of the Second World War, these critiques significantly compromised the conclusions and paradigms in which international security policy was made, analyzed and assessed.[46] While there are now various critiques of the realist school of international politics, feminist scholar Jane Tickner offered a groundbreaking perspective that remains relevant to our concerns:

> In realism's subject matter, as well as in its quest for a scientific methodology, we can detect an orientation that corresponds to some of the masculine-linked characteristics . . . such as the emphasis on power and autonomy and claims to objectivity and rationality. But among realism's critics, virtually no attention has been given to gender as a category of analysis. Scholars concerned with structural violence have paid little attention to how women are affected by global politics or the workings of the world economy, nor to the fact that hierarchical gender relations are interrelated with other forms of domination they do address.[47]

Feminist criticisms such as Tickner's were among the most challenging leveled at the realist school of international politics. This work was prescient, anticipating criticisms that now are voiced even in mainstream discourse. Similar interpretations of the international significance of hierarchical gender relations later emerged in masculinities studies. Together they have made a significant place for gender in the global peace movement. The Hague Agenda for Peace and Justice in the 21st Century, issued by the end of century civil society peace movement conference held in the Netherlands in 1999, put an inclusive gender perspective in a prominent place in a statement that echoes many similar criticisms of the realist – we would say patriarchal – paradigm of international relations:

> The costs of the machismo that still pervades most societies are high for men whose choices are limited by this standard, and for women who experience continual violence both in war and peace. The Hague Appeal for Peace supports the redefinition of distorted gender roles that perpetuate violence.[48]

Towards an inclusive gender perspective: the emergence of masculinities studies

From the earliest days of women's striving for equality there have been men who accepted the arguments, sympathized with the goals, and some few joined in the efforts. Clearly, without cooperation from a significant number of men in the respective systems, women's national political rights would never have been legally established nor would any of the international gender equality norms been introduced into the body of international human rights standards. While some men ridiculed, reviled and resisted, some also publicly and vigorously assisted. While some men sought to understand and respond to men's violence against women, others felt threatened by changes bringing a wider range of life choices to women.

These challenges produced several distinct responses, some of them referred to as men's movements. In the US, phenomena such as 'Iron John' encouraged men to reclaim their traditional 'male values' of courage, assertion and leadership. Other American initiatives such as the 'Promise Keepers' and the 'Million Man March' called for re-assuming the responsibilities of fatherhood and family. These developments were largely in response and reaction to what were seen as the social and cultural dislocations brought about by women's movements in general and feminism in particular. They focused on men's self image and to some degree on reclaiming male pride of place in traditional society. Such projects we would describe as masculinist.[49] Masculinism is the reassertion of the masculine characteristics and values of the patriarchal gender order. Australian scholar R. W. Connell writes of the way in which that order is now global and profoundly affected by globalization in a way that reflects present power relations in the international system:

> Clearly, the world gender order is not simply an extension of traditional European-American gender order. That gender order was changed by colonialism, and elements from other cultures now circulate globally. Yet in no sense do they mix on equal terms, to produce a United Colors of Benetton gender order. The culture and institutions of the North Atlantic countries are hegemonic within the emergent world system. This is crucial for understanding the kinds of masculinities produced within it.[50]

As so much of the women's movement focused on women's distinct and separate experience, some men's approach to gender issues also emphasized the injustices integral to gender roles focusing on the particular experiences of men. As noted, one strand of the men's movements was related to perceptions that loss of exclusive right to certain social functions and positions was imposing inequality on men. But only masculinities studies worked within a relational or systemic framework that provides an inclusive gender perspective. As Connell states, 'Masculinities do not first exist and then come into contact with femininities; they are produced together in a process that constitutes a gender order.'[51]

Another strand of men's response to the gender problematic, the White Ribbon Campaign, a Canadian organization, responding to the growing body of data and policy concern with violence against women, took an approach of acknowledging individual responsibility for and societal acceptance of violence against women in North America.[52] Some masculinities scholarship, as did some feminist theory, contextualized gender violence within a framework of violence in a male-dominated hierarchy. Michael Kaufman describes interrelationships among forms of men's violence:

> Men's violence against women does not occur in isolation but is linked to men's violence against other men and to the internalization of violence that is a man's violence against himself . . . male dominated societies are not only based on a hierarchy of men over women but some men over other men. Violence or the threat of violence among men is a mechanism used from childhood to establish that pecking order.[53]

Other male activists and scholars looked to the socialization of men, in the framework of gender as a social construction, undertaking research that became the foundation of masculinities studies. The social construction theory provided a foundation for masculinities studies to explore the cultural, social and biological influences in the formation of masculine identities. They inquired into influences from historical myths, cultural messages, family, biological assertions, ritual, laws, customs, media and sports on male assertiveness and claims to power. Taken together, these messages formed expectations of how a man should behave.

Peace scholars were particularly concerned with the dominant masculine identities that reinforced social hierarchies and the exertion of power by men at the upper levels of hierarchies over women and other men. Gender identities such as the warrior, breadwinner or adventurer, and characteristics such as valour and toughness, served to inspire violent approaches to dealing with conflict and legitimated militarized approaches to peace and security.[54] During the world wars joining the army was a rite of passage to full American manhood – a phenomenon not unique to the US, as has been documented by Turkish and Israeli scholars.[55]

The manhood myth of the warrior was confronted during the Vietnam War as the anti-war movement decried sending a generation of young men to die in an unjust war. This issue, along with the mandatory military conscription, opened a small window for challenging the valorization of war in forming men's identities. It also manifested another problem as US military recruitment practices began targeting poor, urban and rural youth, particularly African Americans, demonstrating hierarchies among men based on race and socio-economic status.

Over the 1990s and the first decade of this century, scholars began to consider the concept of 'multiple masculinities' in which gender could be seen as constructed differently in different contexts, cultures, historic periods, and under unique circumstances. Multiple masculinities were defined establishing alternatives to the concept of the masculine ideal as the warrior. Especially in times of war, masculinity norms are strongly influenced by patriotism and military service, nurturing strong hero and protector identities, and denigrating male war resistors as less masculine, often meaning humanly inferior. Even in less conflict-plagued times, hierarchies exist among masculinities, and in most contexts a hegemonic or most desired form of masculinity emerges.[56] Within the hierarchies privileged exemptions from the ideal are possible. During the Vietnam War, for example, white middle-class American men could forestall, even avoid going to war by going to college. Upon graduation, the privileged were more likely to gain important positions in society. The poor who served in the military often returned to a jobless civilian life. Hierarchies among masculinities involving race and class as manifest in military service, are further evidence that gender is as rooted in social constructs as it is in biology. The Vietnam war also made more evident the relationship between gender and the institution of war and demonstrated the possibility that both gender inequality and war are amenable to change through socialization and education.

Most masculinities studies were undertaken in the light of the social construction theory of gender. The gendered nature of various institutions and other social arrangements was illuminated, exposing the power and subordination arrangement of patriarchy as one that exists and is sustained largely through the unequal status of men and women. Gender inequality, as asserted earlier by feminist scholarship, an assertion now shared by masculinities studies, pervades virtually all formal and informal institutions, playing a significant role in sustaining the gendered world order and the institution of war. Therefore, any approach to the transformation of the war system will require taking into account the gendered nature of the entire system, inclusive of all the component institutions, social, economic and political. In sum, it calls for a broad and critical social education. We advocate for the inclusion and mainstreaming of gender in all social education, as has been advocated for UN policy and programmes. Gender mainstreaming is:

> . . . assessing the implications for women and men of any planned action, including legislation, policies and programmes, in any area and at all levels . . . making women's as well as men's concerns and experiences integral [to education as well as policy-making] . . . so that woman and men benefit equally. The ultimate goal is gender equality [and positive peace].[57]

Especially in the realms of peace studies and peace education, a focus on developing new thinking about gender should become integral to all study and inquiry, cultivating learning that will enable men and women to understand how their gender identities are informed by and sustain the larger system of violence in which war and all forms of gender violence are imbedded. A major task is raising awareness regarding the gender and peace problematic and how all are implicated in it. Women need not perceive themselves as subjects of discrimination or oppression to understand their subordination in the patriarchal hierarchy. Most men do not identify themselves, nor do they perceive their actions, as sustaining gender disparities. Education should elicit understanding of the complex realities of gender inequality. Men do not need to directly contribute to or behave in ways that sustain patriarchal society to be the beneficiaries of male privilege. Building awareness of the patriarchal structures that account for gender disparities and male privilege are core learning goals of an inclusive gender perspective in peace education.

We think it noteworthy that it was in the field of education that some of the earliest and most significant work on gender disparities was conducted. It is, therefore, not surprising that some of the leading scholars in masculinities studies are from the discipline of education. Indeed, as noted earlier, the first formal discussion of these issues within the International Peace Research Association were initiated and introduced to peace researchers by IPRA's Peace Education Commission. One of the first works in the field was by the distinguished Norwegian educator Birgit Brock-Utne, a member of that commission who had concluded that the socialization of boys in ways that promoted cooperation and care for others as valorized in girl's socialization had significant potential as a means to educate for peace.[58] Male socialization became a fruitful area of inquiry pursued as well by American educators and introduced into international research and policy discussion by UNESCO.[59]

Reflection on the insights and knowledge produced by masculinities studies and their potential integration into an inclusive gender perspective in peace studies and peace education is one of the main tasks that should be high on the agenda of peace knowledge professionals. We need to take into account all of the complexities constitutive to gender and peace. Peace education could utilize the framework of patriarchy to illuminate various forms of hierarchy and to reveal the relational view of gender in which masculinities and femininities – as described above in the quotation from Michael Kimmel – are defined in terms relative to each other in a social construct built into institutions, cultures, power relations and social arrangements. In this context gender construction can be seen as varied, active and dynamic, an example of possibilities for truly significant change in the human condition. Whereas gender roles were formerly defined as dichotomous and static, they may now be conceived as mutable and subject to intentional, normative change. As social constructs, gender roles and relations are revealed to be the product of masculine and feminine identities being formed in parallel social processes. Neither these qualities and identities nor attitudes toward violence and war are formed in isolation from their social and cultural contexts. To understand the contexts toward changing them, it is essential to understand gender and the gender order conditioned by patriarchy.

Moving toward an inclusive gender perspective requires institutionalizing democratic practices and relations that promote tolerance of a range of sexual and gender identities, understanding the significance of gender to the social order and recognition of the potential peace contributions of what have been previously defined as masculine and feminine qualities. Peace education can play an important role in fostering this perspective through developing critical inquiry that examines various gender identities for both the positive gender attributes that can contribute toward nurturing a culture of peace, and the negative attributes that sustain and promote a culture of violence. Through such a process, conducted in open discourse, respectful of difference, learners may gain confidence in their own critical abilities and a sense of personal responsibility for the achievement of a just social order that could enable them to challenge the gender orders that have so long stifled the aspirations of men and women. As growing awareness of and action on the subordination of women produced historic strides toward gender equality, study of the consequences men suffer in a system of inequality can bring about new strides toward the authentic and inclusive human equality we are denied by patriarchy.

Challenging the patriarchal paradigm: gender equality and human security

Peace educators and peace researchers favouring holistic and integrated approaches to the tasks of building and transmitting peace knowledge have for some time focused attention on paradigms as heuristic devices to clarify characteristics and components of systems of thought, the cultures that produced them and the institutions that sustain them. Until the advent of the concept of a culture of peace, promulgated by UNESCO, the objective had been to develop knowledge to facilitate change in peace and security policies and institutions that would reduce violence and increase justice. Among some of the feminist scholars and activists who have recognized gender equality as a requisite for peace, the premise of the social construction and cultural derivation of gender is now leading to a more focused inquiry into patriarchy itself and how, as we have noted, it is manifested in various contemporary institutions, in cultural practices, both traditional and contemporary, and in social behaviours and relationships. This inquiry – like that which led to the normative and policy changes regarding gender violence and women's political participation – has been taken up mainly by feminist human rights activists. They argue that the achievement of full and authentic gender equality calls for an inquiry into assumed, enforced and encoded inequalities of the patriarchal paradigm within which neither men nor women are fully free human beings. The patriarchal system is not only a source of gender violence and inequality but of many egregious human rights violations, oppressive to both men and women. We would add to that argument that it also constitutes the most fundamental impediment to peace at all levels of the social order. The failure to name it as such, to fully analyze it as a primary obstacle to the kind of just global order that most would agree to be peace, is what keeps us caught in the war system and mired in the global culture of violence which it nurtures and by which it is nurtured.[60]

A major action research project to remedy this failure is being undertaken by the People's Movement for Human Rights Education (PDHRE), an NGO that advocates for human rights learning as the means to capacitate populations to achieve social justice, economic equity and political agency. In a document circulated to NGOs and UN agencies, PDHRE states a rationale for the project to which we would adhere and which we would augment:

> Throughout recorded history in most human societies some form of patriarchy has prevailed,

> reinforced by cultural values derived from systems of male dominance. It has been so commonly and continually practiced as to appear natural rather than a humanly constructed social order that is both changing and changeable. In its present forms patriarchy has become more an ideology and belief system than the explicit social and political systems of earlier times. Even in countries where legal equality of women and men has been established, the deep psychological and cultural roots of patriarchy survive as a belief system in the minds of many women and men. [It] asserts the superiority of all males to all females and arranges this fundamental inequality in a hierarchal order in which middle aged men now hold primary power over all others, controlling economies, militaries, educational and religious institutions. Men in general are more powerful and advantaged than women. Western men have more power in the global order than men from other world regions. Women of higher economic class have power over both men and women of lower income and poverty status. At the very bottom of this hierarchy are the vulnerable and oppressed of the world, most the aged, all children, and women; with most vulnerable being aged, poor women. [Global] threats are made the more complex and difficult to address because of the limits imposed on human capacities and creativity by the gendered power divisions that comprise [patriarchy.] [It] is the antithesis of the ideology of human rights . . . human rights is the core of an alternative belief system that can transcend the limits [patriarchy] imposes on the realization of human possibilities and the enjoyment of human dignity.[61]

This statement comprises the normative core of an alternative to the patriarchal paradigm. Human rights, as we have seen, are the inspiration and the practical tool for confronting and overcoming injustice. They have provided the most significant progress to date in gender equality. But, in and of themselves human rights, even under stronger possibilities for enforcement, cannot transcend the violence problematic of patriarchy. Patriarchy maintains itself not only through the patriarchal mind set that has prevailed through centuries, but also and more evidently through the power of armed force, most especially that which is controlled by the hands of the state, exercised through police and military, mirrored in the use of force by non-state actors. Clearly the state itself is a patriarchal institution, and those who aspire to its powers also manifest patriarchal characteristics such as control, force used in self-interest and disregard for the humanity of others. So, an alternative paradigm must elaborate an alternative to military security, pursue the reduction of violence through the reduction of armed forces and weaponry and seek to assure the human dignity of all.

If human rights can be the instruments of progress as it has, even within the patriarchal paradigm, under an effort to simultaneously reduce the primary tools and means of violations while advancing the realization of human rights, the international norms and standards are far more likely to provide actual human security. As peace educators, we endeavour to introduce consideration of these possibilities and to pose elements of the kind of inquiry PDHRE now invites civil society groups throughout the world to engage in as a form of human rights learning. Human rights learning and study of the conditions and possibilities for human security are central to peace education.

We believe that gender can serve as the conceptual core of a comprehensive study of these issues, exploring the problems, the possibilities, the institutions, the values, the concepts and the human experiences that comprise the complexities of the peace problematic. We hope that the field of gender and peace will become central to all realms of peace knowledge, and that all who seek ways to peace through these realms will join in a global inquiry into possible alternatives to the patriarchal paradigm. This paradigm conflates hierarchy with order and command of armed force with virtue as it coerces others into its own image. An alternative human equality paradigm rests on authentic democracy, nonviolent approaches to conflict and assurances of the human dignity of all.

Notes

1 Goldstein, J. (2001) *War and Gender*, Cambridge: Cambridge University Press.
2 Kaufman, M. (1999) *The Seven P's of Men's Violence*, at: http://www.whiteribbon.ca.
3 As it is referred to in a series of compendia of peace studies course outlines, see: Thomas, D. and Klare, M. (eds) (1989) *Peace and World Order Studies: a Curriculum Guide*, 5th edn, New York: World Policy Institute. This is the final of five editions issued by several publishers.
4 For distinctions among the realms of peace knowledge, see: Reardon, B. (1998) 'The urgency of peace education: the good news and the bad news', *Japan Peace Studies Bulletin*, 17, at: http://wwwsoc.nii.ac.jp/psaj/05Print/e_newsletter/1998/reardon.html.
5 The master comprehensive work in women's history by a peace researcher is: Boulding, E. (1976) *The Underside of History*, Boulder, CO: Westview Press.
6 This work led by the Center for Women's Global Leadership at Rutgers University was disseminated through the annual trainings on the human rights of women they conducted for women activists from the global south and women's NGOs associated with the United Nations.
7 Such arguments inform: Easlea, B. (1983) *Fathering the Unthinkable: Masculinity, Scientists and the Arms Race*, London: Pluto Press, and Cohn, C. (1987) 'Sex and death in the rational world of the defense intellectuals', *Signs*, Winter: 687–718; and Fox Keller, E. (1983) *A Feeling for the Organism*, New York: W.H. Freeman and Co.
8 Course syllabi demonstrating this inclusive, integrative approach developed by the authors are available at: www.tc.edu/PeaceEd/portal.
9 Gerd Johansen-Latham, translated by Stephen Croall (2005) *Patriarchal Violence – An Attack on Human Security*, Stockhdm: Government Offices of Sweden.
10 The four peace activists were kidnapped on 26 November 2005.
11 See especially: McAllister, P. (1991) *The River of Courage: Generations of Women's Resistance and Action*, Philadelphia, PA: New Society Press.
12 Harvey Mansfield, the author of the recently published *Manliness* in a radio interview with New York Public Radio's Leonard Lopate on 21 March 2006, opined that it is women's task to civilize men. Mansfield, H. (2006) *Manliness*, New Haven, CT: Yale University Press.
13 Dworkin, A. (1974) *Woman Hating*, New York: E. P. Dutton & Co., Inc.
14 Members of both of these movements informed one of the authors that their frameworks were consistent with the arguments and analysis put forth in: Reardon, B. (1995) *Sexism and the War System*, New York: Syracuse University Press.
15 New Profile (2006) at: http://www.newprofile.org/default.asp?language=en. For more on Okinawan Women Against Military Violence, see: Akibayashi, K. (2001) 'Okinawa women act against military,' unpublished doctoral dissertation, Teachers College, Columbia University.
16 Sylvester, C. (1989) 'Patriarchy, peace and women warriors', in L. Rennie Forcey (ed.) *Peace: Meanings, Politics, Strategies*, New York: Praeger Press.
17 See: Swerdlow, A. (1993) *Women Strike for Peace: Traditional Motherhood and Radical Politics in the 1960s*, Chicago: University of Chicago Press; and Zdravomyslova, E. (1999) 'Peaceful initiatives: the Soldiers' Mothers Movement in Russia', in Breines, I. et al. *Toward a Women's Agenda for a Culture of Peace*, Paris: UNESCO.
18 Code Pink, at: http://www.codepink4peace.org.
19 Hird, M.J. (2005) *Sex, Gender and Science*, New York: Palgrave Macmillan, 24–5.
20 See: Ruddick, S. (1995) *Maternal Thinking: Towards a Politics of Peace*, Boston, MA: Beacon Press; Noddings, N. (1993) *The Challenge to Care in Schools: An Alternative Approach to Education*, New York: Teachers College Press; Noddings, N. (1984) *Caring, a Feminine Approach to Ethics and Moral Education*, Berkeley: University of California Press; and Hamburg, B. and Hamburg, D. (2004) *Learning to Live Together*, New York: Oxford University Press.
21 A relevant discussion of testosterone and aggression is found in Goldstein, op. cit., 148–53.
22 Freire, P. (1970) *Pedagogy of the Oppressed*, New York: Herder and Herder.
23 Belenky, M.F., McVicker Clinchy, B., Rule Golberger, N. and Mattuck Tarule, J. (1986) *Women's Ways of Knowing: The Development of Self, Voice, and Mind*, New York: Basic Books. See also: Gilligan, C. (1993) *In a Different Voice: Psychological Theory and Women's Development*, Boston, MA: Harvard University Press.
24 Foster, C. (1989) *Women for all Seasons: The Story of the Women's International League for Peace and Freedom*, Athens: University of Georgia.

25 The integral and essential relationships among peace, human rights and gender equality are foundational to the UN Charter and the Universal Declaration of Human Rights.
26 See: Gierycz, D. (1999) 'Women in decision-making: can we change the status quo?', in I. Breines et al. (eds) *Toward a Women's Agenda for a Culture of Peace*. The argument that democracies don't wage war on each other has been advanced by Rudolf Rummel, author of Rummel, R.W. (1994) *Death by Government*, New Brunswick, NJ: Transaction Publishers.
27 How the society reneged on this promise and the meaning of the war work experience to the modern women's movement is dealt with in Honey, M. (1984) *Creating Rosie the Riveter: Class, Gender and Propaganda During World War II*, Amherst, MA: University of Massachusetts Press.
28 Notable among these was the World Order Models Project. Most active during the 1970s and 1980s, it brought together an international team of scholars to research and propose alternatives to the existing order.
29 See: Waring, M. (1988) *Counting for Nothing*, Wellington, New Zealand: Bridget Williams Books Limited.
30 Boserup, E. (1970) *Woman's Roles in Economic Development*, New York: St Martins Press.
31 The work of Cynthia Enloe, J. Anne Tickner and Cynthia Cockburn have been especially helpful. Their arguments are among the influences leading to our advocacy of the inclusion of gender perspectives in the study of and inquiry into all issues of peace, security and other related topics of the peace problematic. See especially, Enloe, C. (1989) *Bananas, Beaches, and Bases: Making Feminist Sense of International Relations*, Berkeley: University of California Press; Enloe, C. (2000) *Maneuvers: The International Politics of Militarizing Women's Lives*, Berkeley: University of California Press; Cockburn, C. (1998) *The Space Between Us: Negotiating Gender and National Identities in Conflict*, London: Zed Books; and Tickner, J.A. (1992) *Gender in International Relations*, New York: Columbia University Press.
32 We do not list the documents issued by the UN women's conferences of 1980 and 1985 for we do not find that they made substantive contributions to either the knowledge or normative base of an inclusive, holistic approach to gender and peace. The 1985 Forward Looking Strategies, however, did note that violence against women was an obstacle to peace (paragraph 258).
33 Anwarul K. Chowdhury, United Nations Under-Secretary General, Presentation at the 816th Wilton Park Conference, Sussex, England, 30 May 2005.
34 International Peace Research Association (1983) *Conclusions of the Consultation on Women, Militarism and Disarmament*, Hungary: Gyor, 3.
35 United Nations Division for the Advancement of Women, 'Report of the Expert Group Meeting on Gender and the Agenda for Peace', United Nations Headquarters, New York, 5–9 December 1994.
36 Reardon, *Sexism and the War System*, op. cit.
37 The first and definitive work on patriarchy was by historian Gerder Lerner. Lerner, G. (1986) *The Creation of Patriarchy*, New York and Oxford: Oxford University Press. It is Lerner who made the clearest distinction between sex as biologically determined and gender as a cultural construct.
38 French, M. (1992) *The War against Women*, New York: Summit Books.
39 We recognize that this chapter does not deal with human rights violations and violence against persons of other than heterosexual identities, but we believe it is a significant manifestation of gender violence, also largely attributable to patriarchy.
40 An open session of the Security Council is one in which non-member states and UN staff may address the Council. These sessions are often preceded by preparatory non-formal sessions in which Council members who wish to do so hear from NGOs qualified in the subject of the open session. The People's Movement for Human Rights Education (PDHRE) developed a workbook using the comprehensive framework of the BPFA that demonstrates the holistic nature of human rights as a tool for action in the achievement of full equality (PDHRE (2003) *Passport to Dignity*, New York: PDHRE); this issued Resolution 1325 on Women, Peace and Security. See: United Nations (2000) *Security Council Resolution 1325*, at: http://www.peacewomen.org/un/sc/1325.html.
41 See: Heise, L. (1994) *Violence Against Women: The Hidden Health Burden*, Washington, DC: World Bank.
42 Beijing Platform for Action, Global Framework, para 27.
43 Reardon, *Sexism and the War System*, op. cit.
44 Beijing Platform for Action, Global Framework, op. cit., para 12.
45 See: Reardon, B. (2005) 'Peace and human rights education in an age of global terror', *International House of Japan Bulletin*, 25, 2.
46 See especially the work of Spike Peterson and J. Anne Tickner. Peterson, V.S. and Runyan, A. (1999)

Global Gender Issues, Boulder, CO: Westview Press; and Tickner, J.A. (1992) *Gender in International Relations*, New York: Columbia University Press.

47 Tickner, op. cit., 14.

48 Hague Agenda for Peace and Justice for the 21st Century: Root Causes of War/Culture of Peace Agenda, at: http://www.haguepeace.org/index.php?action=resources.

49 We take this term from the language of the Japanese scholar, Kinheide Mushakoji, who used it in summarizing the gender perspective assertions regarding male dominance made in an international scholars' statement to the Independent Commission on Human Security in 2003. It is also used by many masculinities scholars.

50 Connell, R.W. (1998) 'Masculinities and globalisation', *Men and Masculinities*, I, 1: 3–23.

51 Connell, op. cit., 7.

52 The White Ribbon Campaign was launched in Canada to build awareness and responsibility among young men.

53 Kaufman, op. cit., 1.

54 An excellent study on how men form their gender identities and how those identities influence their behaviour was conducted by peace educator, Ian Harris. Harris, I. (1995) *Messages Men Hear*, London: Taylor and Francis.

55 Altinay, A.G. (2004) *The Myth of the Military-Nation: Militarism, Gender, and Education in Turkey*, New York: Palgrave Macmillan; and Gor, H. (2003) 'Education for war in Israel: preparing children to accept war as a natural factor of life', in K. Saltzman and D. Gabbard (eds) *Education as Enforcement: The Militarization and Corporatization of Schools*, New York: RoutledgeFalmer.

56 R.W. Connell has been influential in the development of masculinities and gender studies, particularly through contributions to theories of multiple masculinities. See: Connell, R.W. (2000) *The Men and the Boys*, Berkeley: University of California Press.

57 United Nations, Economic and Social Council (1997) *Draft Agreed Conclusions on Mainstreaming the Gender Perspective into All Policies and Programmes in the United Nations*, Paris: UNESCO.

58 Brock-Utne, B. (1989) *Feminist Perspectives on Peace and Peace Education*, 1st edn, New York: Pergamon Press; and Brock-Utne, B. (1985) *Educating for Peace: A Feminist Perspective*, New York: Pergamon Press.

59 See: Miedzian, M. (1991) *Boys will be Boys: Breaking the Link Between Masculinity and Violence*, New York: Lantern Books; Breines, I., Connell, R. and Eide, I. (2000) *Male Roles, Masculinities and Violence: A Culture of Peace Perspective*, Paris: UNESCO; and Reardon, B. (2001) *Education for a Culture of Peace in a Gender Perspective*, Paris: UNESCO.

60 A fundamental aspect of the core argument in Reardon's *Sexism and the War System* regards the relationship of reciprocal causality that exists between women's oppression and war.

61 People's Movement for Human Rights Learning (2006) *Transforming the Patriarchal Order to a Human Rights System: A Position Paper*, New York: PDHRE.

15

Peace business

An introduction

Jack Santa-Barbara

Overview

This chapter will briefly outline why and how peace businesses is emerging – from historical, ecological and moral perspectives; will identify the key characteristics of the ideal 'peace business'; and give some examples of movements in the direction of this ideal. Some of the obstacles to implementing peace business will be discussed, as well as approaches to minimizing these obstacles.

Assessment of current field

Peace business is in its early stages. There are a wide variety of activities underway in various sectors, each contributing to the emergence of peace business. Currently, the dominant focus is restricted in terms of peace business ideals – focusing on the reduction of direct violence, and some of the very worst offences regarding structural violence. While there is widespread support for the ideals of peace business, there remains limited opportunities for organized expressions of these ideals. However, the organizations addressing these issues are relatively new, and their sophistication and effectiveness is increasing with experience.

The future of peace business

The obstacles to universal implementation are formidable. However, circumstances surrounding the imminence of peak oil[1] will generate significant changes in the current business paradigm, making the argument for the transition to peace business all the more immediate and compelling. Whether peace business fully emerges will depend on how effectively and quickly values shift. There are considerable dangers and opportunities regarding the future of peace business. The dangers involve clinging to current economic and business models, especially as peak oil begins to have an impact. Attempts to continue a profit-oriented, economic growth paradigm may well lead to further ecological degradation, violent conflict and social inequities. Moving to a peace business paradigm will reduce violent conflict, as well as restore and maintain both ecological sustainability and social justice.

A brief history and overview of peace business

The term 'peace business' has at least three distinct uses. It is sometimes used to refer to the 'business' of peacemaking or peacekeeping.[2] It also refers to the role of business in reducing or preventing violent conflicts. Our interest here is with the broadest use of the term, to describe business models based on the principles of nonviolence, social justice and ecological sustainability[3]. In the ideal, peace business not only avoids contributing to any kind of violence against people or nature, but actually exemplifies nonviolence, social justice and ecological sustainability as part of normal business operations (see Galtung and Santa-Barbara in press).

Throughout history, war and business have been intimately connected (e.g. Black 2002). Wars were often fought to preserve or expand national business interests (including those of the crown in pre-parliamentary times). The business of colonialism was spread and maintained by force of arms. During the two great wars of the twentieth century, some firms profited from trade with belligerents of all persuasions, providing armaments and provisions which allowed the conflicts to continue.[4]

Business interests have also played a positive role with respect to reducing violent conflict. The emergence of the European Coal and Steel Company after the Second World War was the brainchild of diplomats who foresaw an end to war in Europe based on economic connections among its major nations. This effort evolved into the European Union and considerable political and economic cooperation among its member nations. Several decades later when the IRA expanded its bombing campaign to the streets of London in the 1990s, certain business interests successfully lobbied the British government to negotiate a resolution to the conflict.

Violent conflict can be good for some businesses (armaments, security, provisioners of all kinds, and those involved in reconstruction of damaged areas post-conflict). Today, some armies contract out many non-combatant and even some combatant roles to the private sector. The Second World War is said to have brought the world out of the Great Depression, and stimulated an unprecedented level of economic growth. While the 'military-industrial complex' that President Eisenhower warned about continues to function, the global economy is now so large that military spending (still large in absolute terms) is a smaller proportion of the global economy than it was several decades ago.

The growth of business activity expanded dramatically in the twentieth century, based largely on the availability of cheap energy in the form of fossil fuels. Corporations grew in size, profitability and influence, many now having a global scope of operations and revenues larger than many nations. Operations in foreign and undeveloped areas led to many human rights abuses and much ecological degradation.

As in the past, many corporations had connections with violent conflicts – providing armaments, supporting repressive regimes through various natural resource concessions, allowing or encouraging the removal or even eradication of Indigenous peoples, the use of slave labour, or laundering money from these same repressive regimes. Military force has been used to protect the interests of national business operations on foreign soil (e.g. Butler 2005).[5] Today's military actions in the Middle East are attributed to protecting the business interests of foreign powers (Clark 2005; Klare 2001, 2004; McQuaig 2004).

The kinds of connections between military actions and business interests which characterized international relations from colonialism through much of the twentieth century were not new. What was new was the organized opposition to some of these actions by civil society organizations. These organizations, focusing on social justice, human rights, development, peace and environmental issues, have grown significantly in numbers and sophistication over this period. These civil society organizations focused a spotlight on the most serious business abuses, and embarrassed corporations into changing some aspect of their operation that was perpetrating violence of some sort against people or nature.[6]

With experience, many of these organizations became respected for their content expertise, as well as for their ability to work with the corporations they were exposing to public scrutiny. Moving beyond the simple identification of undesirable business practices, these organizations began negotiating with the businesses and governments involved, and played a role in shaping the reform process.[7]

The most forward thinking businesses began inviting these civil society organizations into their planning activities. This led to some businesses and business organizations, often with the involvement of civil society organizations, formulating social responsibility codes which they publicly endorsed. There are now several dozen Corporate Social Responsibility (CSR) codes of various kinds (Jenkins 2001).[8] Most do not explicitly address the issue of peace and violent conflict. Some codes are more socially oriented; some are more environmentally oriented. All share the characteristic of being voluntary, and thus relatively weak.

Aside from the involvement of some few businesses supporting or promoting military actions for their own benefit, many more find themselves operating in zones of conflict. It is now well understood that the very presence of legitimate businesses can have a positive or negative impact on the course of a violent conflict. Consequently, a variety of recent initiatives has addressed some of these issues. International Alert, a civil society organization based in London, recently published *Conflict Sensitive Business Practices: Guidance for the Extractive Industries* (Banfield et al. 2005). This is part of a broader UN initiative under the Global Compact,[9] 'Business Guide to Conflict Impact Assessment and Risk Management', which involves an ongoing dialogue among businesses, civil society organizations, academics and UN representatives (UN Global Compact 2004).

The Organization for Economic Cooperation and Development (OECD)[10] has adopted Guidelines for Multinational Enterprises (OECD 2000) as a means of promoting corporate adherence to UN Security Council decisions and international conventions. And yet another recent Global Compact project has released a report entitled, 'Enabling Economies of Peace: Public Policy for Conflict Sensitive Business' (Ballentine and Haufler 2005).

These UN-sponsored and -related activities focus on the role of business in violent conflict situations. While this is an essential characteristic of peace business, it deals primarily with the issue of direct violence. The concept of structural violence was introduced (Galtung 1969, 1980, 1996) to address the issue of how various institutions and organizations cause harm to others as a normal consequence of the way they are structured and operate. This type of structural violence can be as deadly and disruptive as direct violence and likely accounts for greater mortality and morbidity than direct violence (Galtung and Santa-Barbara in press).

There are significant limitations associated with the existing CSR codes. Their voluntary nature means that most businesses are not involved. There is continuing debate over the comprehensiveness or adequacy of the existing codes, especially ones established by a corporate sector with little or no input from civil society organizations. In some cases there are competing codes in the same sector – one stimulated by civil society input and the other by corporate interests. Often the codes do not contain any monitoring mechanism, or means of dealing with violations.

Independent reviews of some codes question their current value and call for establishing mandatory regulations so that all businesses must respect the values the codes embody, and adhere to the standards they establish (e.g. Jenkins 2001; OECD Watch 2005).

There are a variety of international frameworks which support peace business, such as the UN Charter forbidding war and the UN Declaration of Human Rights. Related UN declarations deal with the rights of the child, of women, of labour practices, the slave trade and racism. In some few cases civil society actions for reform have resulted in national regulations or international agreements.

Many nations now have environmental protection agencies of some kind and there are a wide variety of international agreements in which civil society organizations, as well as related businesses, have been involved (business interests often but not always opposing the reforms, e.g. Leggett 1999). These include peace-related (e.g. various nuclear disarmament treaties, the banning of chemical and biological weapons, the International Land Mines Treaty, etc.) and environmental agreements (e.g. the Montreal and Kyoto Protocols, the Convention on Biodiversity, the Basel and Stockholm Conventions, etc.). All of these treaties have significant impacts on the way businesses can legitimately operate, curbing structural violence in a variety of ways.

These successes are especially important considering the dominance of neo-conservative public policies promoting government deregulation and downsizing, and the dominance of a global free market over the past half century.

Particular international agencies are also responding to pressures from civil society. The World Health Organization recently barred a life sciences industry association of food, chemical and pharmaceutical companies from participating in setting global standards protecting food and water supplies because its members have a financial stake in the outcome.[11]

The financial services sector has played an important and not always positive role in violent conflict situations, often contributing to structural violence of various kinds (e.g. Henry 2003; Perkins 2004). The UN has convened an international group of major financial institutions to address the role of the finance sector in situations of violent conflict. The result is the document 'Who Cares Wins' (UN Global Compact 2004), which establishes guidelines for the financial sector regarding how to integrate environmental, social and governance issues in their asset management and security brokerage activities. Broader restraints on loan practices have met with only partial success (e.g. Rainforest Action Network 2005).

The micro-credit and micro-banking movements have found ways of making small amounts of capital available to the poor, allowing them to use their talents to enter the market economy (Yunus 1999).[12]

Along with these international and intergovernmental reforms, other sectors are also involved. A variety of certification programmes have emerged as a result of civil society efforts, ranging from forestry (e.g. Forest Stewardship Council) and fisheries (e.g. Marine Stewardship Council) to restaurants[13] and cemeteries (Grant 2005). These programmes certify business operations as following a set of explicit standards, many of which are independently reviewed as part of the certification process.

The Ethical Investment movement is also having an impact. There are now well over $2 trillion dollars[14] invested in these funds in the US alone (Social Investment Forum 2006), and a variety of ethical investment indices have emerged to guide investor behaviour (e.g. Dow Jones Sustainability Index[15]). Some shareholder groups have gone further and put forward shareholder resolutions to reform various aspects of corporate behaviour in the direction of peace business, and many have been successful.[16] Various studies have shown that ethical investing is as least as successful as general investing, and in some cases provides a slightly higher return.[17]

In addition to promoting investment in ethical companies, a variety of consumer strategies have also been aimed at corporate reform. Numerous boycotts have been organized (e.g. against French wines to protest France's nuclear testing in the Pacific; against South African goods to protest apartheid; against General Electric for its building of devices used in nuclear weapons;

against Exxon Mobil for the high lead content of its petrol; against Shell Oil for its actions in Nigeria; and recently, against Coca-Cola for its water use in India).[18]

Consumer activities also support corporations who have adopted a green or ethical procurement policy, whereby ethical or green purchases are preferred. Studies of ethical consumers have found significant numbers of general consumers favouring green or ethical purchases, and a willingness of many more to do so with some minor incentives (Harrison et al. 2005).

The Fair Trade movement is another example of making it possible for consumers to express their values. An increasing number of goods are coming within the Fair Trade circle, as well as an increasing volume of trade.[19]

The investor and consumer activities are important tactics for promoting peace business. However, they are limited by the amount of time and energy investors or consumers put into examining the ethical and green consequences of their purchases.

One of the most significant activities from the perspective of eliminating violence against nature has been the sustainable business movement (e.g. Hawkens 1993; Hawkens et al. 1999; Weizsacker et al. 1998; see also the World Business Council on Sustainable Development[20]). This development seeks to redesign all business operations so that energy and resource productivity is dramatically increased, so that renewable resources replace non-renewable ones, and so that wastes are reduced or eliminated (especially toxic wastes). The overall objective is to greatly reduce the ecological footprint of business operations so that they remain within the regenerative capacities of global ecosystems.

In summary, peace business has grown significantly over the twentieth century, encompassing a wide variety of tactics and strategies. It should be noted that many of the activities identified above have not necessarily been conducted within an explicit peace business framework. They have nonetheless contributed to both the formulation and development of this framework, and can arguably be considered part of the emergence of peace business. One of the most significant developments is the expansion of the concept of peace business from a focus on the role of business in violent conflicts, to the structural violence against both people and nature perpetrated by legitimate businesses as a normal part of their operations (Galtung and Santa-Barbara in press). Despite the wide variety of activities outlined above, peace business activities remain the exception rather than the norm, and few if any businesses would meet all the criteria for the ideal peace business.

Need for peace business

The need for peace business extends far beyond a moral imperative to do good. Eliminating direct violence and all its attendant miseries is clearly one of the motivations for peace business in a narrow sense. From a business perspective, there is immediate self-interest for the majority of businesses to eliminate violent conflict; conflicts disrupt normal business operations. Unfortunately, those businesses that profit from violent conflict are often closely linked to governments and can influence government decisions. These divergent interests between the few businesses which profit from direct violent conflict and the majority of businesses for whom violent conflict is an obstacle, are not often addressed.

There are also longer-term issues of self-interest for businesses to move to a comprehensive peace business paradigm, but only a few visionary business leaders seem to appreciate these needs. The current business paradigm has not only produced great material and financial wealth but also enormous social inequities, injustices and ecological degradations. While some 400 plus people enjoy the status of billionaire, their combined wealth exceeds that of the 40 per cent of humanity at the bottom of the wealth pyramid. Much of the wealth in the upper 10 per cent of the wealth pyramid has been accumulated at the expense of the majority world (Krugman 1992; Ponting 1993).

Structural violence is expressed in many ways: as displacement of Indigenous peoples for development projects, as appropriation of peasant lands for export crops, as mining or forestry concessions interfering with traditional lifestyles and despoiling the environment, as structural adjustment programmes, as refusals to forgive the poorest nations' debts, as the exporting of wastes (including toxic wastes) to poor nations or areas, and a host of other legal business-related practices, have enriched the few at the expense of the many (see Galtung and Santa-Barbara in press).

It is also legal for businesses to cause considerable ecological degradation in the normal course of their operations. Resource depletion is an important but not sole example. Not only are businesses depleting non-renewable resources at an accelerating pace (e.g. petroleum), but also resources that should be renewable (e.g. forestry and fishery practices; soil degradation resulting from industrial agriculture). In the normal course of business activities biodiversity is being destroyed, to the point where biodiversity loss is now 100 to 1,000 times the pre-industrial level (Ehrlich 1995). This occurs as a normal part of industrial agriculture, of urban expansion, and the extractive industries, to name just a few (Czech et al. 2000; Foley et al. 2005; McDaniel and Borton 2002).

There are also numerous examples of businesses knowingly providing products or services that affect the health of purchasers (e.g. the exposure of the auto industry by Nader (1972); the chemical industry;[21] the tobacco industry,[22] and even the healthcare sector, e.g. by Epstein (2005)).

Almost all businesses use fossil fuels in some way. It is clear that emissions from these fuels are altering global climate patterns that in turn will reduce biodiversity, cause diseases to spread, change precipitation and wind patterns, cause a rise in ocean levels, create more frequent and intense weather events, and generally disrupt all the human activities dependent on predictable weather patterns (e.g Schneider 1997).

The cumulative impact of business activities is now so great that they are challenging the ability of many natural ecosystems to continue providing the life support services necessary for human civilization as we know it (Millennium Ecosystem Assessment 2005).[23] We have gone beyond the mere act of fouling our nest, and are now actually destroying it.

These direct consequences of social inequities, injustices and ecological degradation are no less real for being unintentional.[24] These practices are ecologically and, ultimately, economically unsustainable. Inequities and injustices inevitably lead to conflict which can turn violent. Ecological degradation is reaching the point where some global ecosystems may be altered beyond the point of rehabilitation (Millennium Ecosystem Assessment 2005). Both extremes of inequity contribute to this ecological degradation, the high end through waste and over consumption, and the low end through unsustainable practices to eke out a meagre living in the short term. More violent conflict will increase the inequities, injustices and ecological degradation.

Unfortunately, the greatest obstacles to peace business becoming the norm are the values of the current economic and business paradigms. To the extent that the problems of inequity and ecological degradation are acknowledged by mainstream economics and businesses, the mainstream answers to these twin threats are more economic growth and business development – the very causes of the problems.

The trickle-down theory of economic development continues to be promoted despite its abysmal failure to decrease inequities and ecological degradation over the last century. Never has there been so much financial and material wealth available; and never have there been such inequities and ecological threats to human well-being. The solutions will not be found in the causes of the problems, and until this irony is appreciated, peace business will remain marginalized.

In sum, peace business is not simply a nicety to salve a few consciences, but rather a social and ecological imperative if human civilization is to endure in a manner which provides for the basic needs and well-being of humanity.

Obstacles and future directions for peace business

The major obstacle to peace business is the cultural violence perpetrated by the current economic and business paradigms.[25] Cultural violence involves the values and beliefs embedded in institutions which support the direct and structural violence of those institutions (Galtung 1969, 1996). There are a variety of values and beliefs of the current economic and business systems which support and maintain the direct and structural violence common to many contemporary business activities (Galtung and Santa-Barbara in press). The dominance of the economic growth ideology is central to this value set, just as the 'civilizing mission' was central to the expansion of colonialism in centuries past.

Economic growth requires individual businesses to operate profitably and grow. Continuous economic growth assumes a limitless or substitutable supply of natural resources and technological innovation to overcome any ecological degradation caused by business activities. Considerable evidence is now available to indicate that accumulated global economic activities are stressing global ecosystems to the point where they are unable to continue providing the life supports upon which modern civilization depends (Meadows et al. 1972, 1992, 2004; Millennium Ecosystem Assessment 2005; Odum and Odum 2001; Smil 2003; Speth 2004; Wackernagel 2002; Wackernagel and Rees 1996).[26]

Growth in the economic sphere is expressed in business as profit. Business profits drive economic growth. However, when profit is the overwhelming business motive social equity and ecological sustainability goals are ultimately put aside, even in corporations that pride themselves on their contribution to the poor and their protection of workers (e.g. Bakan 2004; Lapierre and Moro 2002).

Another belief common in business operations is the notion that whatever is not explicitly forbidden by law is allowed. Consequently, if creating negative externalities for people or nature are not illegal, then at least some businesses will permit such externalities. In a competitive market where cost reductions are crucial, others will follow. In the process, a living wage, worker health and safety, and environmental protection are easily lost. In the extreme, even what is illegal is pursued; greed for profit can and does provoke violent conflict, some illegal and some state sponsored (Bacher 2000; Berdal and Malone 2000; Klare 2001, 2004; McQuaig 2004; Renner 2002).

There are a multitude of avenues for the expression and reinforcement of these values and beliefs about the importance of economic growth and profit. They range from economic theories which place growth at their centre, to the process of creating money which requires profit for the money supply to grow (Anielski 2000), to laws which require corporations to do everything legally within their power to maximize a return to shareholders, to the glorification of consumptive lifestyles in advertising and the media, to name just a few. Their pervasiveness makes these values and beliefs appear as givens which are inevitable and for which there are no alternatives.

There are indeed alternative values and beliefs upon which an economic framework and peace business paradigm could be based (Polanyi 2001). An economic framework has been articulated which recognizes the biophysical limits required for healthy ecosystem functioning, and which advocates fair distribution as a key goal of economic activities (Carley and Spapens 1998: Daly 1997; Daly and Cobb 1989; Daly and Farley 2004). These approaches place ecological sustainability and fair distribution as pre-eminent goals of economic activities.

Efficient allocation of resources, the pre-eminent goal of neoclassical economics and measured by level of profitabilty, is relegated to third place. This framework argues that efficient allocation can only be considered once limits are established that ensure both ecological sustainability (which involves fair distribution for future generations) and fair distribution for current generations.

Translating these concepts from the realm of economics to the level of business operations involves establishing regulations that limit the behaviours of each business in such a way as to ensure ecological sustainability and social justice. The roles for economics and business become ecological sustainability and meeting basic human needs, rather than unfettered growth and profit. Adherence to such priorities would also reduce the incidence of violent conflict to secure resources.

Economic growth and the generation of profit over the last century would have been impossible without the availability of cheap energy, primarily in the form of fossil fuels, especially oil. The imminence of peak conventional[27] oil (Campbell 2002/3; Campbell and Laherrere 1989)[28] means that less energy will be available post-peak, requiring a major reformulation of the economic growth paradigm and business models based on use of cheap and abundant energy to increase productivity and generate profit (Heinberg 2004, 2005). Much of the values and institutional frameworks underlying current economic and business thought will have to adapt to the decline in energy availability. Failure to make these adaptations by clinging to the current values and institutions will likely lead to more violent conflict, greater social inequities and ecological disaster.

The ideal peace business framework

Even without peak oil there is an urgent need to reduce the social inequities which exist in today's world, to reverse the process of unprecedented ecological degradation and to eliminate violent conflicts. Normal business activities make significant contributions to worsening each of these major challenges. Conflicts over how to create a new global energy regime once peak oil occurs could worsen all of these issues; for example, violent conflicts over remaining resources; the use of abundant but environmentally harmful sources of energy (e.g. coal); continued emphasis on economic growth; or greater inequities as remaining energy supplies are appropriated by the powerful. A peace business paradigm would make a positive contribution to each of these challenges.

It is worth noting that in the current paradigm business is regarded as the means of solving many of our most serious problems – poverty, hunger, inequity, ecological degradation, overpopulation, disease, etc. Generating profit for individual businesses is believed to be the best way of raising living standards for everyone. The assumption is that the profit that is reinvested can be put to use solving these other difficulties. Unfortunately, the facts do not support this assumption. Greater global financial and material wealth has invariably led to great social inequities and ecological degradation. A new model is needed.

Peace business requires a broad policy framework which views the role of business alongside that of the informal economy and the role of government in providing public goods. Much of what is important to human well-being and happiness is not the result of business activities, but of services provided by friends and family in the informal economy, and by the state in the form of public goods such as education, healthcare, basic infrastructure, environmental protection, health and safety standards and so on (Lane 2000; Layard 2005).

The informal economy is based on mutual support and cooperation, and involves a wide range of services from child and eldercare to advocacy for various rights and protections. It is not based on profit or personal benefit, yet constitutes a large portion of what contributes to quality of life.

Governments are responsible for a variety of public goods, especially those which are non-market goods and services. Exactly what goods and services should be included in market transactions is part of an ongoing political debate. However, it is clear that goods and services which are non-excludable[29] and non-rival[30] (such as peace and security, climate stability and atmospheric ozone protection) cannot be part of the market system because of their inherent qualities – they cannot be owned, and one person's use does not detract from another's use (Daly and Farley 2004). These non-excludable and non-rival goods and services are nonetheless essential for human well-being.

Businesses evolved to provide exchange opportunities for people to meet their basic human needs. Exchanges in a peace business paradigm would focus on goods and services which meet these needs, where the exchange is equitable, and transparent, and where negative social and environmental externalities are eliminated. The provision of luxury goods and services while the majority of the human population is not able to meet their basic needs would not be part of a peace business paradigm. Given that the cumulative impact of global business activities currently threatens ecological sustainability, what is needed in a peace business paradigm is a more equitable distribution of the benefits of economic and business activities.

A peace business paradigm requires an economic framework where economic growth is focused on meeting the needs of those whose basic human needs are not yet met. Where such needs are more than adequately met, economic and business activities would seek to maintain basic levels of services, and focus on improving the quality of services provided to people, rather than to expand them in quantity.[31] Such priorities are distinctly different from current ones, where the greatest profits are sought in marketing highly profitable luxury items afforded by the minority, while the majority's basic needs are left to governments, civil society and chance. Relying on ever-increasing levels of general economic growth will not achieve equitable distribution.

Another distinction involves the attention given to maintaining a level of material throughput[32] that meets existing needs rather than continuing to increase the level of throughput in business expansion and economic growth. Ecological sustainability requires that the use of energy and resources in economic and business activities does not exceed ecosystems' capacities to regenerate. Ultimately, all our wealth derives from nature, from the ecosystem services that provide our food, materials for clothes and shelter, and all the other goods required to meet basic human needs. If our use of these resources exceeds ecosystems' capacities to regenerate, the essential services provided by these ecosystems will degenerate to the point where they can no longer function.[33] Considerable evidence is accumulating that such ecological thresholds have already been breeched (Millennium Ecosystem Assessment 2005).

To avoid such unsustainable use of nature, economic and business activities must remain within the level of throughput that respects the biophysical limits of ecosystems. This requires economic growth and business expansion to stop at some point, and evidence is accumulating that we have reached that point on a global scale (Daly 2005). The goals of economic and business activities must therefore shift from growth and expansion to sustainable use and fair distribution (e.g. Carley and Spapens 1998).

In practical terms, this means that developed nations make a transition from a growth paradigm to one of a steady state – an economic and business paradigm where material throughput is sustainable in terms of ecosystem services. This means an end to increasing the physical size of the economy, focusing on maintaining sustainable levels of throughput, and working on increasing the qualitative aspects of economic and business activities (Czech 2000; Daly 1991; Czech and Daly 2004).

Areas of the world where human needs are not yet being met may require some continued economic growth and business expansion. However, the global level of material throughput must remain within certain limits for ecological sustainability to occur. Given the current stresses on global ecosystems, this may well mean that the levels of throughput must actually decrease in developed nations if all of humanity is to have its needs met, and the global economy is to remain within sustainable limits.[34]

These criteria for ecological sustainability and social equity require major reorientations for global business operations. If businesses are to meet these challenges, the principles and practices of sustainable business activities will have to become the norm: radical increases in resource productivity; radical decreases in energy use; weaning from non-renewable resources and energy sources to renewables; and elimination of wastes, especially toxic wastes. In addition, it will require a focus on providing goods and services that meet basic human needs for all peoples before turning to luxuries.

Peace business rests on the values of nonviolence to people and nature (including structural and cultural violence as well as direct violence), a focus on meeting basic human needs (rather than profit from whatever will sell) and a fair distribution of the benefits of business activities (rather than the accumulation of great wealth by the minority). These values translate into a variety of economic and business-oriented public policies that are dramatically different from the current system (Galtung and Santa-Barbara in press). Behaviours which support and reinforce these values will have to be regulated by national and international agreements, as the serious limitations of voluntary codes and programmes are now clear (Jenkins 2001; OECD Watch 2005). The fact that some of these policy instruments have already been implemented with positive results indicates the peace business approach is indeed practical and realistic (Galtung and Santa-Barbara in press).

The key characteristics of peace business have been elaborated elsewhere, as well as numerous examples of actual business which are moving in this direction (Galtung and Santa-Barbara in press). Table 15.1 provides a comparative summary of peace business and traditional business paradigms.

Aspiring to nonviolence of all kinds means that business operations have to avoid contributing to structural and cultural as well as direct violence. It also means avoiding any contribution to violence against nature as well as against people. Nonviolence, broadly understood, is the fundamental value of peace business and from which the other values derive. Nonviolence against people requires social equity: that business operations do not deprive anyone of their heritage, their health and safety, their dignity, their source of livelihood, their culture or their future.

Nonviolence against people requires that the equity principle be respected in all interactions: between those who own or rely on the resources of interest to business; between employer and employee; between business and consumer; between business and the general public. No party to any of these transactions should extract an advantage (not even a small one, as the cumulative effect amongst billions of people is highly relevant) at the expense of the other.

Table 15.1. Traditional and peace business paradigms

Dimension of comparison	*Traditional paradigm*	*Peace business paradigm*
Cultural values	Profit driven; growth oriented; externalize costs whenever possible (including those associated with violent conflict); do whatever is not explicitly forbidden (push boundaries)	Nonviolence; equity; ecological sustainability; development oriented (growth only for the poor); maintenance oriented; internalize all costs; strive for expression of core values (push boundaries)
Products and services	Whatever will sell; high mark-up, luxury items	Meet basic human needs; cover legitimate costs; compostable or recyclable
Production cycle	Efficiency first; externalize costs if possible; the more value added the better; deplete resources as efficiently as possible	Life cycle analysis of impacts (social and environmental); recycle or compost all products and wastes; restrict use to ensure sustainability
Structure	Corporate charter (limit liability); global if possible; hierarchic; secretive/proprietary; monopoly, if possible; high salaries and perks for senior management; push suppliers; exploit customers; crush competitors; community involvement for PR purposes	Corporate charter only in limited circumstances (tbd); flat hierarchy; open and transparent; local or regional in scope; collaborative with staff, suppliers, customers and community
Profit	Maximize; capture for CEO and senior management; expense personal benefits	Limit profit (fix ratio between highest and lowest salaries); share with colleagues, community; restrict expenses to group benefits (e.g. pensions, health and social benefits, R&D, etc.)

In practical terms, this value orientation means that the products and services provided by businesses should meet basic human needs, rather than create unnecessary artificial needs through advertising and other means that are then met at a profit to the business and detriment to the consumer or wider community.

Incorporating the notion of no violence against nature into this process requires that the accumulated material throughput of global business activities do not exceed the capacity of ecosystems to continue providing essential life support services. To destroy a critical ecosystem's[35] capacity to continue functioning is an example of violence against nature, and is not acceptable in a peace business paradigm. The destruction of the atmospheric ozone layer by the use of innovative gaseous compounds in the 1930s is one of many examples (see Speth 2004).

In summary, peace business has to do with the production and exchange of goods and services which meet basic human needs in an equitable and ecologically sustainable manner. The challenge is one which will require considerably more cooperation between sectors that currently do not work well together, or more often, do not work together at all. The goals of nonviolence, social justice and ecological sustainability essential for peace business require collaboration among not only the leaders in the sustainable business movement, but also those concerned with oil depletion and energy use, economic reforms, development and democracy, human rights and the environmental movement. The alternatives to peace business involve continued and likely escalating violence to people and nature, both of which are morally repugnant and unsustainable. Peace business is an ideal everyone has a stake in, and as this simple fact becomes more widely accepted, it will succeed.

Notes

1 Peak oil refers to the peak extraction of conventional oil which many geologists are predicting will occur on a global basis sometime within the next ten years or so (Campbell 2002/3; Campbell and Laherrere 1989). The implication is that once this occurs less energy will be available as there are no energy substitutes which have a net energy anything close to conventional oil (Hall et al. 1986). Business and economic growth require energy, and less energy will trigger changes in both these areas.
2 This use will not be considered in this review.
3 These goals reflect the values in the UN Charter which focus on peace, development and the environment.
4 See also: http://www.wealth4freedom.com/Elkhorn2.html.
5 Smedley D. Butler wrote this book after retiring as a Major General from the United States Marines.
6 See the following for examples of CSR codes: http://web.worldbank.org/WBSITE/EXTERNAL/WBI/WBIPROGRAMS/CGCSRLP/0,,contentMDK:20719568~pagePK:64156158~piPK:64152884~theSitePK:460861,00.html; and http://www.eldis.org/dbtw-wpd/exec/dbtwpcgi.exe?QB0=AND&QF0=QSET@ELDNO&QI0=ethical+business&MR=50&TN=a1&DF=f1csr&RF=s1csr&DL=0&RL=0&NP=3&MF=eldismsg.ini&AC=QBE_QUERY&XC=%2Fdbtw-wpd%2Fexec%2Fdbtwpcgi.exe&BU=http%3A//www.eldis.org/search.htm; both viewed 28 December 2005.
7 The tactic of engaging the corporate targets of concern has been adopted by many civil society organizations, just a few examples of which include: the Rainforest Action Network (www.ran.org); Greenpeace International (www.greenpeace.org); and Earth Economics (www.eartheconomics.org); Friends of the Earth (www.foe.org); Oxfam (www.oxfam.org); and International Alert (www.international-alert.org).
8 See Note 6.
9 See www.unglobalcompact.org.
10 The OCED is an organization composed of some 30 highly industrialized nations, and describes itself as 'fostering good governance in the *public service* and in *corporate activity*. It helps governments to ensure the responsiveness of key economic areas with sectoral monitoring. By deciphering emerging issues and identifying policies that work, it helps policy-makers adopt strategic orientations' (from the OECD website, at: http://www.oecd.org/about/0,2337,en_2649_201185_1_1_1_1_1,00.html, viewed 28 December 2005).
11 Environmental News Service (2006) 'WHO shuts life sciences industry group out of setting health standards', 2 February.
12 The micro-credit movement is very different from the attempts to 'sell to the bottom of the pyramid' (see Prahalad 2004). The micro-credit movement provides the poor with credit to start their own micro-business, generally providing necessities to other poor people. The approach by Prahalad and others involves corporations marketing to the poor with business models which allow for profits to accrue by greatly increasing the number of consumers.
13 See http://www.dinegreen.com/startupcontract.asp.
14 Ethical investing now constitutes almost 10 per cent of total investing, and is one of the fasting growing areas in the investment sector (Social Investment Forum 2006).
15 See http://www.sustainability-index.com/.
16 The Investor Responsibility Research Center (IRRC.org) calculates that commercial bank shareholders have filed 33 resolutions on climate change issues in 2005, up from 25 in all of 2004.
17 See www.sristudies.org.
18 See http://www.ethicalconsumer.org/boycotts/boycotts_list.htm for a list of current boycotts.
19 See Fair Trade Federation (http://www.fairtradefederation.org/); and the Fairtrade Foundation (http://www.fairtrade.org.uk/).
20 See www.wbcsd.org.
21 See http://www.truthout.org/docs_05/011905X.shtml for a recent example.
22 See http://www.tobacco.org/resources/documents/documentquotes.html, viewed 28 December 2005.
23 See also www.sustainablescale.org.

24 These consequences of normal business operations are also no less real due to the cumulative nature of the activity (e.g. generating greenhouse gases). While no single business may be responsible for climate change, every business that uses fossil fuels contributes.

25 An additional and important obstacle to peace business is the very affluence created by business activities. The material consumption provided by affluent societies provides many immediate benefits that are difficult to consider relinquishing. However, many of the psychic benefits of material consumption are fleeting, requiring ever more consumption (Kasser 2002). Much empirical research now demonstrates that material consumption beyond a low level by affluent standards (but high by the standards of the world's poor) does not contribute to personal happiness or objective measures of well-being (Lane 2000; Smil 2003). In other words, much of this material consumption is wasted in terms of contributing to happiness or well-being, although it does make a relatively few very wealthy.

26 See also www.sustainablescale.org.

27 The peak of conventional oil does not mean that there is no more oil in the ground. The significance of peak conventional oil means that this unique resource, which has a very high net energy return, will begin to decline. If demand for oil is to be maintained or grown, the shortfall from the peak of conventional oil means that unconventional sources will need to be extracted (i.e. arctic and deep ocean sources, as well as tar sands). Unfortunately, the net energy of these unconventional sources is many times less than that for conventional oil. The implication is that the shortfall in conventional oil may not be easily replaced, leaving a considerable and growing gap between the demand and supply for this vital resource. Such scarcities of vital resources are a potential source of violent conflict.

28 See also the Association for the Study of Peak Oil, at: http://www.peakoil.ie/newsletters/aspo59.

29 Non-excludable goods are those which can be used by anyone because they are either not protected by patents, or because no one can be excluded from using them because of their physical properties (e.g. the illumination provided by a street light).

30 Non-rival goods and services are those which can be enjoyed by one person without reducing the amount available to anyone else (e.g. a beautiful vista).

31 Qualitative improvement is considered to be development, as distinct from growth, which is a quantitative increase (Daly and Cobb 1989). This distinction is important from an ecological sustainability perspective, as development so defined can occur without material growth. In other words, benefits to human well-being can occur without growth of the physical economy.

32 Material throughput refers to the physical dimensions of any and all economic activities; economic activity is impossible without some level of material throughput – use of resources or energy (Daly 1997; Daly and Cobb 1989; Daly and Farley 2004). All use of material throughput has an impact on ecosystems, either in the process of extracting the resources, in their use, or their extrusion as wastes. Any level of material throughput which exceeds the ability of ecosystems to regenerate the services they provide is unsustainable (Daly 2005; see also www.sustainablescale.org).

33 Clearly, the size of the human population is an important factor in this relationship between levels of material throughput and ecological sustainability. With a smaller human population, a higher level of per capita material throughput is possible while remaining within ecological limits.

34 See Note 33.

35 A critical ecosystem is one which is essential to human well-being and for which there is no substitute if lost (Ekin 2003; Ekin et al. 2003a, 2003b).

References

Anielski, M. (2000) 'Fertile obfuscation: making money whilst eroding living capital', Pembina Institute, at: http://www.pembina.org/pubs/pubs.php.

Bacher, J. (2000) *Petrotyranny*, Toronto: Dundurn Press.

Ballentine, K. and Haufler, V. (2005) *Enabling Economies of Peace: Public Policy for Conflict Sensitive Business*, New York: UN Global Compact Office.

Bakan, J. (2004) *The Corporation: The Pathological Pursuit of Power*, Toronto: Viking Canada.

Banfield, A., Barbolet, R.G. and Kilick, N. (2005) *Conflict-Sensitive Business Practice: Guidance for Extractive Industries*, London: International Alert.

Berdal, M. and Malone, D.M. (eds) (2000) *Greed and Grievances: Economic Agendas in Civil Wars*, Boulder, CO: Lynne Rienner Publishers.
Black, E. (2002) *IBM and the Holocaust: The Strategic Alliance Between Nazi Germany and America's Most Powerful Corporation*, New York: Three Rivers Press.
Butler, S.D. (2005) *War is a Racket*, at: http://lexrex.com/enlightened/articles/warisaracket.htm.
Campbell, C.J. (2002/3) 'Forecasting global oil supply 2000–2050', *Hubbert Center Newsletter*, M. King Hubbert Center for Petroleum Supply Studies.
Campbell, C.J. and Laherrere, J.H. (1989) 'The end of cheap oil', *Scientific American*, March, 78–83.
Carley, M. and Spapens, P. (1998) *Sharing the World: Sustainable Living and Global Equity in the 21st Century*, London: Earthscan.
Clark, W.R. (2005) *Petrodollar Warfare: Oil, Iraq and the Future of the Dollar*, Gabriola Island, BC: New Society Publishers.
Czech, B. (2000) *Shoveling Fuel for a Runaway Train*, Los Angeles: University of California Press.
Czech, B. and Daly, H.E. (2004) In my opinion: the steady state economy – what it is, entails, and connotes, *Wildlife Society Bulletin*, 32, 2: 598–605.
Czech, B., Krausman, P.R. and Devers, P.K. (2000) 'Economic associations among causes of species endangerment in the United States', *Bioscience*, 50, 7: 593–601.
Daly, H.E. (1991) *Steady-state Economics*, 2nd edn, Washington, DC: Island Press.
Daly, H.E. (1997) *Beyond Growth: The Economics of Sustainable Development*, Boston, MA: Beacon Press.
Daly, H.E. (2005) 'Economics in a full world', *Scientific American*, September: 100–7.
Daly, H.E. and Cobb J.B., Jr. (1989) *For the Common Good: Redirecting the Economy toward Community, the Environment and a Sustainable Future*, Boston, MA: Beacon Press.
Daly, H.E. and Farley, J. (2004) *Ecological Economics: Principles and Applications*, Washington, DC: Island Press.
Ehrlich, P. (1995) 'The scale of the human enterprise and biodiversity loss', in J. H. Lawton and R. M. May (eds) *Extinction Rates*, Oxford: Oxford University Press.
Ekins, P. (2003) 'Identifying critical natural capital: conclusions about critical natural capital', *Ecological Economics*, 44: 277–92.
Ekins, P., Folke, C. and de Groot, R. (2003a) 'Identifying critical natural capital', *Ecological Economics*, 44: 159–63.
Ekins, P., Simon, S., Deutsch, L., Folke, C. and de Groot, R. (2003b) 'A framework for the practical application of the concepts of critical natural capital and strong sustainability', *Ecological Economics*, 44: 165–85.
Epstein, S.S. (2005) *Cancer-Gate: How to Win the Losing Cancer War*, New York: Baywood.
Foley, J.A., DeFries, R., Asner, G.P., Barford, C., Bonan, G., Carpenter, S.R., Chapin, F.S., Coe, M.T., Daily, G.C., Gibbs, H.K., Helkowski, J.H., Holloway, T., Howard, E.A., Kucharik, C.J., Monfreda, C., Patz, J.A., Prentice, C., Ramankutty, N. and Snyder, P.K. (2005) 'Global consequences of land use', *Science*, 309.
Galtung, J. (1969) 'Violence, peace and peace research', *Journal of Peace Research*, 6, 3: 167–91.
Galtung, J. (1980) 'The basic needs approach', in K. Lederer, D. Antal and J. Galtung (eds) *Human Needs: A Contribution to the Current Debate*, Cambridge, MA: Oelgeschlager, Gunn and Hain: Konigstein: Anton Hain.
Galtung, J. (1996) *Peace by Peaceful Means: Peace and Conflict, Development and Civilization*, London: Sage.
Galtung, J. and Santa-Barbara, J. (in press) *Peace Business: The Role of Business in Reducing Violence, Inequity and Ecological Degradation*.
Grant, D. (2005) 'At rest in nature', *Medical Post*, 41, 23.
Hall, C., Cleveland, C. and Kaufmann, R. (1986) *Energy and Resource Quality: The Ecology of the Economic Process*, Toronto: Wiley.
Harrison, R., Newholm, T. and Shaw, D. (2005) *The Ethical Consumer*, London: Sage.
Hawken, P. (1993) *The Ecology of Commerce: A Declaration of Sustainability*, New York: HarperCollins.
Hawken, P., Lovins, A. and Lovins, L.H. (1999) *Natural Capitalism: Creating the Next Industrial Revolution*, Boston, MA: Little Brown and Company.
Heinberg, R. (2004) *Powerdown: Options and Actions for a Post-Carbon World*, Gabriola Island, BC: New Society Publishers.
Heinberg, R. (2005) *The Party's Over: Oil, War and the Fate of Industrial Societies*, Gabriola Island, BC: New Society Publishers.

Henry, J.S. (2003) *The Blood Bankers: Tales from the Global Underground Economy*, New York and London: Four Walls Eight Windows.
Jenkins, R. (2001) *Corporate Codes of Conduct: Self Regulation in a Global Economy*, New York: United Nations Research Institute for Social Development, Technology, Business and Society, Programme Paper Number 2, April.
Kasser, T. (2002) *The High Price of Materialism*. Cambridge, MA: MIT Press.
Klare, M.T. (2001) *Resource Wars: The New Landscape of Global Conflict*, New York: Henry Holt.
Klare, M.T. (2004) *Blood and Oil: The Dangers and Consequences of America's Growing Dependency on Imported Petroleum (The American Empire Project)*, New York: Henry Holt.
Krugman, P. (1992) 'The right, the rich, and the facts', *American Prospect*, Fall: 22.
Lane, R.E. (2000) *The Loss of Happiness in Market Democracies*, New Haven, CT: Yale University Press.
Lapierre, D. and J. Moro, J. (2002) *Five Past Midnight in Bhopal*, London: Scribner.
Layard, R. (2005) *Happiness: Lessons from a New Science*, London: Penguin.
Leggett, J. (1999) *The Carbon War: Dispatches from the End of the Oil Century*, London: Penguin.
Mastny, L. (2003) 'Purchasing power: harnessing institutional procurement for people and the planet', *Worldwatch Paper* (166), Washington, DC: Worldwatch Institute.
McDaniel, C. and Borton, D. (2002) 'Increased human energy use causes biological diversity loss and undermines prospects for sustainability', *BioScience*, 52, 10: 929–35.
McQuaig, L. (2004) *It's the Crude, Dude: War, Big Oil and the Fight for the Planet*, Toronto: Random House.
Meadows, D., Randers, J. and Meadows D. (1972) *Limits to Growth*, New York: Universe Books.
Meadows, D., Randers, J. and. Meadows, D. (1992) *Beyond the Limits*, White River Junction, VT: Chelsea Green Publishing Co.
Meadows, D., Randers, J. and Meadows, D. (2004) *Limits to Growth: The Thirty Year Update*, White River Junction, VT: Chelsea Green Publishing Co.
Millennium Ecosystem Assessment (2005) *Ecosystems and Human Well-being: General Synthesis*, Washington, DC: Island Press.
Nadeau, R.L. (2003) *The Wealth of Nature: How Mainstream Economics has Failed the Environment*, New York: Columbia University Press.
Nader, R. (1972) *Unsafe at Any Speed: The Designed-in Dangers of the American Automobile*, New York: Grossman.
Odum, H. and Odum E. (2001) *A Prosperous Way Down*, Boulder, CO: University Press of Colorado.
OECD (2000) *The OECD Guidelines for Multinational Enterprises*, Paris: OECD.
OECD Watch (2005) *Five Years On: A Review of OECD Guidelines and National Contact Points*, Paris: OECD Publications.
Perkins, J. (2004) *Confessions of an Economic Hit Man*, San Francisco, CA: Berrett-Koehler Publishers.
Ponting, C. (1993) *A Green History of the World: The Environment and the Collapse of Great Civilizations*, New York: Penguin.
Polanyi, C. (2001) *The Great Transformation*, 2nd edn. Boston, MA: Beacon Press.
Prahalad, C.K. (2004) *Fortune at the Bottom of the Pyramid: Eradicating Poverty Through Profits*, Upper Saddle River, NJ: Wharton School Publishing.
Rainforest Action Network (2005) *First investment bank joins growing ranks of global financial institutions addressing urgent environmental and social issues*, at: http://www.ran.org/ran_campaigns/global_finance/goldmansachs_victory.html.
Renner, M. (2002) 'The anatomy of resource wars', *Worldwatch Paper* (162), Washington, DC: Worldwatch Institute.
Schneider, S. (1997) *Laboratory Earth*. New York: Basic Books.
Smil, V. (1990) *The Earth's Biosphere*, Boston, MA: MIT Press.
Smil, V. (2003) *Energy at the Crossroads*, Boston, MA: MIT Press.
Social Investment Forum (2006) *2005 Report on Socially Responsible Investing Trends in the United States: 10 Year Review Executive Summary*, Washington, DC: Industry Research Program.
Speth, J. (2004) *Red Sky at Morning*. New Haven, CT: Yale Univesity Press.
United Nations Global Compact (2004) *Who Cares Wins*, New York: United Nations Global Compact.
Wackernagel, M. (2002) 'Tracking the ecological overshoot of the human economy', *Proceedings of the National Academy of Sciences*, 99, 14: 9266–71.
Wackernagel, M. and Rees, W. (1996) *Our Ecological Footprint*, Gabriola Island, BC: New Society Publishers.

Weizsacker, E.V., Lovins, A. and Lovins, H.L. (1998) *Factor Four: Doubling Wealth, Halving Resource Use*, London: Earthscan Publications.

Yunus, M. (1999) *Banker to the Poor: Micro-Lending and the Battle Against World Poverty*, New York: Public Affairs, Perseus Book Group.

16

Peace Journalism

Jake Lynch and Annabel McGoldrick

Peace Journalism has emerged, since the mid-1990s, as a new field within Peace and Conflict Studies. It offers both a form of critical analysis of existing war reporting, and a set of practical plans and options for journalists. Peace Journalism does not just mean 'reporting peace'. In essence, it entails the application of insights from Peace and Conflict Studies – the sum of what is known and has been observed about conflict, its dynamics and the potential for transformation – to the everyday jobs of editing and reporting the news.

It is now under development by journalists, university researchers and others in many countries, following an original definition by Johan Galtung. As the authors of this chapter, we are professional journalists, with 30 years' experience between us. We have been at the forefront of this work since running a Peace Journalism Summer School in the UK in 1997.

This chapter:

- Explains what is at stake in news about conflict.
- Contrasts Peace Journalism and War Journalism.
- Considers War Journalism and Peace Journalism in a case study – reporting in the UK press of the 'Iran nuclear crisis'.
- Demonstrates why Peace Journalism is more accurate and more responsible.
- Shows why the distinctions between them are the important ones.
- Uses framing theory to show why journalism is so receptive to war propaganda.
- Applies the ideas of eminent researchers in Peace and Conflict Studies.
- Shows how to build in peace perspectives to stories about violence.
- Maps out future directions for the development of Peace Journalism.

News about conflict – what's at stake?

'The only battle we might lose was the battle for hearts and minds. The consequence would have been NATO ending and losing the war' (Campbell 1999). These are the reflections of Alastair Campbell, then press secretary to British Prime Minister Tony Blair, after the bombing of Yugoslavia in 1999.

This battle has become increasingly important as wars have become increasingly mediated. Nearly 3000 media workers accompanied NATO forces when they entered Kosovo at the end of Operation Allied Force. For comparison, a generation before, 500 were on hand to witness the peak of the action in Vietnam (Knightley 2000).

To narrow the timeframe a little further, even by 1991, just 22 overseas journalists were in Baghdad for Operation Desert Storm. By contrast, during the invasion of 2003, in the words of one senior reporter: 'We used to bang on about this thing called "the New World Information Order", which was going to be imposed by UNESCO. It has in fact been created by technology. There were two Indian TV stations there, there was a Bangladeshi reporter for a newspaper, Philippines television was there, everybody was in Baghdad. The rest of the world was not depending on European and American broadcasters and newspapers anymore, so that is a real change, something new and very important' (Hilsum 2004).

Technology has also enabled non-Western-owned media to transcend their national boundaries in the form of satellite broadcasting, with rolling television news services, led by al Jazeera, now available on screens around the world. And a different set of technologies – for the targeting and guiding of missiles and shells – have been used to attack it, with the organization's offices hit in Kabul, Basra and Baghdad. The International Federation of Journalists said, 'it is impossible not to detect a sinister pattern of targeting' (White 2004: 25).

A memo of a conversation between Blair and George W. Bush, leaked to a British newspaper, seemed to suggest that the American president wanted the station's headquarters in Doha to be bombed.[1] Months before, Defense Secretary Donald Rumsfeld had blamed al Jazeera for 'promoting terrorism'.

At the same time, the Pentagon was spending millions of dollars on 'psy-ops', hiring private firms to '[translate] rosy articles written by the US military and pass them off as independent news stories by Iraqi journalists, some of whom allegedly paid newspapers to run them' (Baxter 2005).

News representations of conflict now form 'a key site for the exercise of power, seen as such by "primary players" and many others besides' (Lynch and McGoldrick 2004, 2005: xvi). This awareness, too, is shared by many beyond the traditional elite.

According to an influential critique of reporting of the Great Lakes crisis of 1996–7, journalists should 'understand from the start that warring factions, even if their soldiers wear gumboots, have now acquired a sophisticated military doctrine and techniques for fighting low-level information warfare using manipulation, disinformation, misinformation and obstruction'.[2] The crisis itself stemmed from the Rwandan genocide two years earlier, in which media played a sinister role.

It is within this context that Peace Journalism has been more and more widely discussed, developed and carried out – whether known by that name or not – among journalists, media and development workers and within universities, around the world, since about the mid-1990s.

The country involved in the highest number of international armed conflicts of any in the world, between 1946 and 2003, according to the Liu Institute's inaugural *Human Security Report*,[3] was Britain, with 21 (France came next, with 19 – the US third, with 16). At the same time, 'the journalism of professional editors, reporters and producers [in Britain] has a strong claim to be considered the best in the world' (Lynch and McGoldrick 2005: 1) – a reputation attributable partly, though by no means only, to the BBC.

Indeed, with Reuters News Agency, the *Financial Times* and the *Economist* all headquartered in London, along with choice assets of Rupert Murdoch's global empire, the Europe bureaux of many US media and CNN's biggest office outside Atlanta, it could be considered the world's most influential media capital.

So it seems as good a place as any to open a discussion about news representations of conflict and what is at stake. And after several rounds of violence in Iraq, the invasion and occupation of Afghanistan, armed intervention in Sierra Leone, the Good Friday Agreement in Northern Ireland and, of course, the bombing of Yugoslavia, Britain's next frontier, at the time of writing in early 2006, seemed to be the escalating dispute with the Islamic Republic of Iran.

Iran – the next frontier

When Iranian revolutionaries stormed the American embassy in Tehran, in November 1979, and took approximately 70 hostages, the incident occurred almost exactly halfway through a history of conflict between Iran and the US.

But it was the British who involved their American allies in the first place. Twenty-six years previously, in 1953, London had called in the CIA to help overthrow the elected government of Mohammed Mossadegh. His crime? To nationalize the Anglo-Iranian Oil Company, following failed negotiations in which Iran sought higher royalty payments from Britain. And 26 years later, in 2005, President Bush, on a trip to Israel, warned that 'all options are on the table' in 'dealing with Iran's nuclear ambitions'.[4]

Blair mused, at a European Union summit he was hosting in London, 'the question people will be asking us is – when are you going to do something about Iran?' A favoured journalist, Trevor Kavanagh, veteran political editor of Murdoch's popular *Sun* newspaper, told his readers: 'We are now to all intents and purposes at war with Iran' (Kavanagh 2005).

To represent the formation of this conflict as we have briefly done here is to apply some of the principles of Peace Journalism. The term and the concept were coined by Johan Galtung, founder of Peace and Conflict Studies, and one of its trademarks is to report conflicts as occurring in 'open space, open time, [with] causes and outcomes anywhere, also in history/culture'.

Peace Journalism is the counterpart and corollary of War Journalism, which tends to report conflicts as if they are confined to the present day and to the 'conflict arena' where violence is taking place, or might potentially take place. Galtung's original and now classic table, setting out the characteristics of each form, is reproduced as Table 16.1. Key questions are:

- Why should these be the important distinctions?
- Why does the reporting of conflict according to these respective plans merit the terms War Journalism and Peace Journalism?
- Can the latter claim to be any better than the former?
- If so, how and why?

Case study: the 'Iran nuclear crisis' and the British media

The remarks by Bush and Blair, quoted above, were reported in the context of the 'Iran nuclear crisis'. This had been brewing at least since 2002, with Bush's State of the Union Address in which Iran was labelled as part of the 'Axis of Evil' along with Iraq and North Korea. Months later, Russian technicians started to build the country's first nuclear reactor.

To answer the questions listed here, in the context of this important story, we will consider the practical implications of reporting it as though confined to the conflict arena, in the present

Table 16.1. Galtung's table

Peace/Conflict Journalism	*War/Violence Journalism*
I. Peace/conflict-oriented	**I. War/violence-oriented**
Explore conflict formation, x parties, y goals, z issues	Focus on conflict arena, 2 parties, 1 goal (win), war
General 'win, win' orientation	General zero-sum orientation
Open space, open time; causes and outcomes anywhere, also in history/culture	Closed space, closed time; causes and exits in arena, who threw the first stone
Making conflicts transparent	Making wars opaque/secret
Giving voice to all parties; empathy, understanding	'Us-them' journalism, propaganda, voice, for 'us'
See conflict/war as problem, focus on conflict creativity	See 'them' as the problem, focus on who prevails in war
Humanization of all sides; more so the worse the weapons	Dehumanization of 'them'; more so the worse the weapon
Proactive: prevention before any violence/war occurs	Reactive: waiting for violence before reporting
Focus only on visible effect of violence (killed, wounded and material damage)	Focus on invisible effects of violence (trauma and glory, damage to structure/culture)
II. Truth-oriented	**II. Propaganda-oriented**
Expose untruths on all sides / uncover all cover-ups	Expose 'their' untruths / help 'our' cover-ups/lies
III. People-oriented	**III. Elite-oriented**
Focus on suffering all over; on women, The aged, children, giving voice to voiceless	Focus on 'our' suffering; on able-bodied elite males, being their mouth-piece
Give name to all evil-doers	Give name to their evil-doers
Focus on people peacemakers	Focus on elite peacemakers
IV. Solution-oriented	**IV. Victory-oriented**
Peace = nonviolence + creativity	Peace = victory + ceasefire
Highlight peace initiatives, also to prevent more war	Conceal peace initiative, before victory is at hand
Focus on structure, culture, the peaceful society	Focus on treaty, institution, the controlled society
Aftermath: resolution, reconstruction, reconciliation	Leaving for another war, return if the old flares up again

day, on the one hand; and as something which is taking place in open time and space, on the other.

US political leaders and diplomats took a lead in convincing many allies that Iran was in breach of its obligations under the nuclear Non-Proliferation Treaty (NPT) of 1970. For many years, the country had, indeed, concealed its nuclear programme from the international community.

But the NPT was a grand bargain of world diplomacy, with reciprocal obligations on the 'haves' and 'have-nots'. Non-nuclear armed states would have the right to develop civil nuclear power plants, on condition that they renounce any ambitions to nuclear weapons. The declared nuclear-armed states of the day – the US, the then USSR, China, France and Britain – undertook to 'pursue good-faith negotiations on effective measures relating to nuclear disarmament'.[5]

After the NPT entered into force, a succession of arms control agreements followed between the superpowers – the Strategic Arms Limitation Treaty, or SALT, in 1972; SALT II in 1979 and three rounds of the Strategic Arms Reduction Treaty, or START, with negotiations continuing into the 1990s.

Latterly, though, the US in particular had been increasingly criticized for reversing this progress, both through the development of new nuclear weapons – as a 'fortuitous' consequence of care and maintenance programmes of existing stockpiles (Kimball 2005) – and for changes in its nuclear doctrine which widened the range of circumstances in which a first strike would be contemplated (Norton-Taylor 2005). In the UK, the government of Tony Blair had already been thinking aloud about commissioning a like-for-like replacement for its own fleet of Trident nuclear submarines.

In UK media, where the story 'hotted up' during the later months of 2005, War Journalism tended to concentrate on 'expos[ing] "their" untruths' – chiefly by referring to 'suspicions' or 'fears' that Iran's nuclear power programme was a cover for its real ambition of developing a military capability.

In the comment quoted above, Blair continued: 'Can you imagine a state like that . . . having nuclear weapons?' According to Kavanagh's article, the prime minister now faced a 'nightmare . . . fuelled by certain knowledge that nothing – apart from unimaginable military action – can now stop the mullahs acquiring nuclear power and then nuclear weapons. Worse, there is every prospect they will use them.'

Was military action 'unimaginable'? If so, that would have been bad news for a president determined to remove no options from the table – a line echoed by Blair himself.[6]

Kavanagh had built up his legendary reputation with a long series of 'insider' political scoops, as a conduit for information his sources intended to reach the public sphere. The sources' aim in such cases is usually to influence public opinion, 'to shape perceptions, manipulate cognitions and direct behaviour' (Jowett and O'Donnell 1999: 6) – a quote taken from a widely-used definition of propaganda. To keep a military option on the table, *war* propaganda has to convince publics that force is justified.

The restriction of time and space in representing the conflict is a key part of such propaganda. Detailed 'public interest polling' carried out in the US shows that public approval for the use of force depends on the case being made passing six 'screens' (Kay 2000):

- Rogue leaders.
- Evidence tying them to heinous crimes.
- Non-military means exhausted.
- Military allies (to share the risk and cost).
- A 'visionary' objective (e.g. turn an enemy into an ally or bring long term peace to a region).
- Early non-military intervention tried in good faith, but confounded.

Underpinning all these factors is a proposition that the prospective target for ultimate military action is where 'the problem' is to be found – a country aberrent from acceptable norms of behaviour inscribed in such formulations as 'the international community'. Targeting this country can therefore be presented as a way to 'solve the problem', being made steadily more imaginable in the process.

In the case of Iran, the 'rogue leader' duly arrived, in mid-2005, in the shape of newly elected President Mahmoud Ahmadinejad. At the summit, Blair was responding to journalists' questions about his remarks, interpreted in the West as a call for Israel to be 'wiped off the map'. The 'heinous crimes' can be prospective rather than actual – summoning up the spectre of a nuclear-armed 'Maniac plot[ting] World War III', as a front-page headline in the mid-market *Daily Express* put it.[7]

Another definition of propaganda is 'a partial account or representation which is not, on closer inspection, a lie' but which is 'a deliberate attempt to mislead' (Lynch and McGoldrick 2005: 115–16). To shape perceptions and manipulate cognitions, then, relies on the omission of certain parts of the picture. It works by *framing* issues in such a way as to exclude or eclipse countervailing facts and perspectives. Specific pieces of evidence, for example that, for all the 'fears' and 'suspicions', Iran was not secretly developing nuclear weapons after all.

In August 2005, results were announced of a two-year investigation by a team of scientists into what was, on the face of it, the most incriminating 'exhibit for the prosecution' – traces of highly enriched uranium, found on centrifuges seized from an Iranian laboratory by international inspectors two years earlier. Iran said at the time these must have been on the centrifuges when it bought them from its nuclear-armed neighbour, Pakistan – an explanation supported by the scientists' conclusions. Iran had, on this charge at least, been found 'not guilty' (Linzer 2005).

Shortly afterwards, the US National Intelligence Assessment concluded that the country was ten years away from acquiring the bomb – putting it in the same category as any other state with a nuclear power plant, certainly including South Korea and Brazil, for instance, if they were so minded. There was, in other words, in the consensus view of all the American intelligence agencies, no *specific* evidence against Iran.

The International Atomic Energy Agency reported Iran to the UN Security Council, in February 2006. But the IAEA's inspectors did record numerous examples of Iranian compliance with their requirements under an additional protocol to the NPT, which provided for unannounced snap inspections – an onerous burden, and one never applied to any other signatory state.[8]

What if Iran did harbour secret ambitions to acquire nuclear weapons? States have done so with the express purpose of deterring attack, and Iran might well infer, from recent events, that deterrence still works. Of the three members of the Axis of Evil, named by President Bush in 2002, the one with nuclear and long-range missile capabilities – North Korea – was met with multilateral negotiations. The one without them – Iraq – sustained invasion and regime change.

By late 2005, US or US-allied troops were stationed in many of Iran's neighbouring countries – central Asia as well as Turkey, Iraq and Afghanistan. Israel had its own nuclear arsenal, outside the provisions of the NPT, and also boasted US-supplied warplanes capable of bombing Iran and returning to base without refuelling – a capability it acquired in 1998, when it took delivery of the latest variant of the F15.

So these would be some of the elements to restore to the frame for the Iran story if war propaganda were to be effectively supplemented with a representation of the conflict as taking place in open time and space. Peace Journalism was further 'operationalized', for an exercise in empirical content analysis, in the form of five criteria, applied to 211 articles in the UK press between August 2005 and January 2006 (Lynch 2006):

1 Does the article mention the Non-Proliferation Treaty?
2 Does it report, as a fact – as distinct from something Iran 'claims' or 'insists' upon – that this gives Iran the right to develop civil nuclear power?
3 Does the article mention 'our' nuclear weapons and/or failure to engage in disarmament negotiations, as a factor to be taken into consideration when assessing Iran's behaviour under the NPT?
4 Does the article mention any of the evidence that Iran is not, in fact, engaged in a process of developing nuclear weapons?

5 Does the article mention Iran's possible reasons for seeking a nuclear arsenal, if it were to do so, in terms of deterrence against threats from outside?

The study found that, on these criteria, the 'Peace Journalism quotient' of the UK press at this time was just 15.4 per cent, though some publications did significantly better, notably the *Financial Times*, which covered the story most frequently of all, on 22.2 per cent.

Conclusions? Some Peace Journalism is apparent, at least in this one aspect of this one story, but it is a minority pursuit. And the distinctions in the table *do* have a strong claim to be considered the important ones when reporting conflict because they foreground the key framing issues in war propaganda. They effectively map out the contested territory.

Peace Journalism more accurate

The other claim of Peace Journalism is that it provides what Lynch and McGoldrick call 'anchorage' for editors and reporters:

> When covering conflicts, Peace Journalism proposes, we can tread down to find solid ground beneath our feet, by studying and applying what is known and has been observed about conflict. . . . We can use this knowledge to help us decide for ourselves what is important, and to identify what is missing from what we are told by interested parties. Key findings include:
>
> - *Violence is never wholly its own cause.* Conflict is made up of structure, culture and process – the context, without which no explanation for a violent event is complete or, indeed, correct.
> - *Non-violent responses are always possible.* There is always more than one way of responding to conflict. Many people, in many places, are devising, advocating and applying non-violent responses.
> - *More than two sides.* There are always more than two parties to any conflict – some, whose involvement or interest is hidden, need putting on the map. Others, presented as a solid aggregate of view, may contain important internal divisions, and they need *dis*-aggregation.
> - *Every party has a stake.* Parties to conflict should be seen as stakeholders, pursuing their own goals, needs and interests – some openly acknowledged, but almost invariably some hidden as well.
>
> (Lynch and McGoldrick 2005: xviii)

Only if a conflict is represented as taking place in open time and space can proper weight be given to context, including structure, culture and process; space be created to acknowledge and consider possible nonviolent responses; or the parties and their goals, needs and interests be correctly identified.

The alert reader will have picked up on the normative nature of the claims here – 'proper' weight; 'correctly' identified. Peace Journalism has been presented to journalists as a way to make their coverage of conflicts 'more accurate and more useful' (Lynch and McGoldrick 2005: xv).

How come? All over the world, professional editors and reporters define their job as bringing readers and audiences the answers to 'five w's and an h' – who, what, where, when, why and how.

Peace Journalism proposes that, when it comes to conflict, the answers to be found in news reports can usefully be assessed by comparing them with the answers furnished by researchers in the field of Peace and Conflict Studies. These have been assembled under the normal safeguards of academic rigour in social science: openness about – and preparedness to justify – starting assumptions for both observation and interpretation; and peer review. Built into social science, moreover, is the principle of the participant-observer – as soon as you start to observe something, you cannot avoid changing it.

Peace and Conflict Studies is further distinguished, in terms of content, by acknowledging the potential for creative transformation of conflicts, and by the insight most readily associated with the Australian peace researcher, John Burton, that behaviour in conflicts cannot be explained solely in terms of power – power gradients, or the struggle for power. There is an irreducible role for human needs (Burton 1993: 55–64). In all these respects, it offers accounts of *relationships* in conflict that journalism generally ignores – and, without which, the representations it makes are bound to be flawed, both by incompleteness and by a lack of critical self-awareness.

Journalists' six questions correspond roughly to what peace researchers call 'conflict dynamics'. According to Diana Francis, any statement of the dynamics of a conflict must identify 'its history, recent causes and internal composition – the different parties, the nature of their involvement, their perspectives, positions and motivations, and the different relationships between them in terms of power, allegiance and interest' (Francis 2002: 28).

Crucially, this means that any representation of a conflict which omits or occludes any of these factors is inaccurate. In the UK press study, those publications with a higher quotient of Peace Journalism, on the criteria applied, were reporting the 'Iran nuclear crisis' more accurately than those with a lower score.

Clearly, the analysis was fairly 'lenient' since, to answer fully the questions posed by Francis about the conflict between Iran and the US, journalists would have to explore further back in its history than 1970, to include the events briefly alluded to here about the overthrow of the Mossadegh government – which none of the articles did. Neither did they open up the question of motivation by the US, for its close concern with developments in the world's main oil-producing region.

This important claim to accuracy can also be made for Peace Journalism on other counts than the openness in time and space. To quote another peace researcher, John Paul Lederach:

> I have not experienced any situation of conflict, no matter how protracted or severe, from Central America to the Philippines to the Horn of Africa, where there have not been people who had a vision for peace, emerging often from their own experience of pain. Far too often, however, these same people are overlooked and disempowered either because they do not represent 'official' power, whether on the side of government or the various militias, or because they are written off as biased and too personally affected by the conflict.
>
> (Lederach 1997: 94)

Lederach writes about reconciliation in societies divided by years, even decades of war, but his remarks could equally apply to international conflicts. Johan Galtung's proposal for a Conference on Security and Cooperation in the Middle East (Galtung and Fischer 1998), to repeat the Helsinki Process of the 1970s and its eventual success in bringing down the 'Iron Curtain', has been aired around the fringes of the news media by two British university researchers – Mary Kaldor in the context of Iraq (2003) and Timothy Garton Ash in the context of Iran (2006).

And an avowedly alternative news service, Alternet, reported on a peace proposal (Daley et al. 2006) in the 'Iran nuclear crisis' which commended the principle adopted by Mikhail Gorbachev to end the Cold War – 'mutual security':

> If you threaten your adversaries, they'll threaten you back. If you make your neighbors more secure, you make yourself more secure. The basis of peace is understanding the fears of others.

According to the authors of this proposal, the US should say to Iran:

> We don't expect you to endure the nuclear double standard forever until the end of time. The NPT doesn't just impose non-proliferation obligations on you, it also imposes disarmament obligations on us. We understand that you will not forever forego nuclear weapons if we insist on forever retaining nuclear weapons. Nuclear weapons won't protect you, and nuclear weapons don't protect us. We know that eventually we must abolish these abominations, or they will abolish us.

Such visions and the people who create them – not to mention their actions to bring it about, or to alleviate the worst effects of conflict and violence – are generally absent from the dominant discourse of War Journalism, with its elite orientation and focus on 'elite peacemakers'. Peace Journalism creates space for 'people peacemakers' too – not 'either/or' but 'both/and'. In doing so, it is a better match for what is known and has been observed, both about individual conflicts and about conflict *per se*. It therefore has a strong claim to be more accurate in its representations.

Peace Journalism more responsible

Definitions

> Peace Journalism is when editors and reporters make choices – of what stories to report and about how to report them – that create opportunities for society at large to consider and value nonviolent responses to conflict.
>
> Peace Journalism:
>
> - Uses the insights of conflict analysis and transformation to update the concepts of balance, fairness and accuracy in reporting.
> - Provides a new route map tracing the connections between journalists, their sources, the stories they cover and the consequences of their journalism – the ethics of journalistic intervention.
> - Builds an awareness of nonviolence and creativity into the practical job of everyday editing and reporting.
>
> (Lynch and McGoldrick 2005: 5)

With more Peace Journalism, according to Galtung, 'the conflict in and over Northern Ireland [for example] would have entered a more peaceful phase long ago . . . focus on non-violent outcomes, empathy with all parties and creativity is more likely to bring peace' (Galtung 1998).

Large claims, which raise a further set of questions – how do opportunities arise, for society at large to consider and value nonviolent responses, as a result of 'journalistic intervention'? Do War Journalism and Peace Journalism affect the course of events in a conflict, and, if so, how?

Further, what ethical implications follow from these questions and any answers we may propose? A publicity leaflet for an early Peace Journalism event in the UK promised to discuss 'what difference journalism can make. And if it can [make a difference], should it?'[9]

Most discussion about the effect in conflict of news representations, or patterns of news representation, has focused on source behaviour – the actions and motivations of parties to conflict. Journalists in most places go through their working life with a rough-and-ready assumption that 'we just report the facts'. But facts, in this highly mediated world, are ever more likely to have been presented, assembled or even created – at least partly – in order to be reported.

How can sources know what facts to create, and how to present them, to be reported so as to lead readers and audiences – they suppose – to respond in a way that will help their cause? Only on the basis of their experience of previous reporting (or the experience of expert advisers – as in the old gag, politicians don't watch television, they hire people to watch it for them).

It's a feedback loop of cause and effect, and it means the facts of tomorrow bear a slight residue, or imprint, of the reporting of today. It may be impossible to separate out 'media strategy' and quantify it as a proportion of motivation for parties to conflict to speak and act as they do. This is, after all, complex social behaviour. But, like one of the original colours in a tin of mixed paints, it is clearly visible, in countless cases – and it brings journalists a new ethical dilemma, one that can be seen as an artefact of a media-savvy age.

The challenge is to devise a workable teleological ethic, from the Greek *telos*, meaning goal or outcome. Traditionally, in British and other Western media, journalistic ethics are deontological, from *deon*, meaning duty. Reporters are not generally supposed to consider the consequences of reporting before or as they do it – merely to 'report the facts without fear or favour'. But this becomes harder to sustain as the consequences become more foreseeable. Hence the widely observed exceptions to the rule – don't report suicides or bomb scares. It is not difficult to guess the likely consequences if these were routinely publicized.

An awareness of conflict dynamics, attentive to the insights of Peace and Conflict Studies, cannot help but set the bar higher. 'Report incidents of political violence without context, for example, and you are likely to incentivize a "crackdown" in response.'

How so? By omitting context, War Journalism renders conflicts 'opaque', as the Galtung table says. In a feedback loop, the way a problem is diagnosed, in news reports about a conflict, conditions what is likely to be presented – to the same reporters from the same news organizations – as an appropriate remedy. If the original reports do not show anything that could be *set right*, in order to remove the causes of violence, all that is left is more violence – to punish or corral the perpetrators. If parties to conflict wish to be reported as 'getting to grips with the problem' then they may feel they have to be seen to 'crack down'.

At times of stress, the workings of this feedback loop can speed up, as with the '7/7' London bombings of July 2005. Prime Minister Tony Blair used a televized news conference in Number Ten Downing Street to launch a 12-point plan, including an extension of the list of proscribed organizations, detention of 'terrorist suspects' for up to 90 days before charge and giving police powers to close down mosques suspected of breeding 'extremism'.

By force of iteration, Blair sought to quash suggestions that the bombs were a form of 'blowback' from Britain's foreign policy, notably its part in the invasion of Iraq. Not a bit of it, he insisted – such acts were entirely attributable to 'an evil ideology'. The appropriate response was, therefore, not to reconsider the consequences of such adventures – or to attend to the circumstances, historical and material, in which such an ideology could attain its persuasive power – but to 'send a clear signal out that the rules of the game have changed'.[10]

The preoccupation of Blair's government with its media image has been well-attested by many insiders, and his response here came after some extravagant rhetoric in popular newspapers had turned to impatient criticism that 'more was not being done'. The following day, the biggest of them hailed the initiative with the front-page headline, 'Victory for *Sun* over new terror laws'.[11]

In practice, most of Blair's proposals were either abandoned or watered down, having proved impossible to legislate for, impractical to implement, or both. Leaked official documents showed he was warned, both by the Home Secretary (Interior Minister) and the security and intelligence services, that several of the measures were unworkable (Bright 2006) – but the imperatives of media strategy, deduced from previous coverage, evidently overrode such objections.

Propaganda, framing and objectivity

Inscribed in the definition of propaganda we have used here is a clear concept of agency. Perceptions are deliberately shaped, and cognitions manipulated 'to achieve a response that furthers the desired intent of the propagandist' (Jowett and O'Donnell 1999: 6). The notion of 'framing', in disciplines including sociology, psychology and communications, as well as Peace and Conflict Studies, is actually somewhat less specific. A definition from the Frameworks Institute:

> Framing refers to the construct of a communication – its language, visuals and messengers – and the way it signals to the listener or observer how to interpret and classify new information. By framing, we mean how messages are encoded with meaning so that they can be efficiently interpreted in relationship to existing beliefs or ideas.[12]

War Journalism can be seen as an exercise in framing, without implying that journalists are actively conspiring in some kind of plot to bamboozle the public into supporting wars.

News conventions combine to construct communication about conflicts in such a way as to lead us – or leave us – to overvalue violent responses and undervalue nonviolent ones. They classify new information according to three key signals about its meaning:

- A bias in favour of official sources.
- A bias in favour of event over process.
- A bias in favour of dualism.

The first cuts out the grassroots peacemakers documented by John Paul Lederach, and can leave the impression to prevail, by default, that noone is talking about peace, or 'doing peace', so further violence is all we can expect.

The second means that news often tells us, to quote the catchphrase of US news anchor Walter Cronkite, 'the way it is' – without helping us to see how it came to be that way. It excludes, for example, any account of the circumstances – material, everyday and historical – in which three young British Muslims could be so swayed by an ideology as to decide to end their lives in acts of mass murder.

The third means that conflicts are conceptualized as dual, a zero-sum game of two parties; ultimately a tug-of-war in which each faces only two alternatives, victory or defeat. Defeat being unthinkable, each has a ready-made incentive to try harder to win – to escalate the conflict.

So these three key framing factors all merit the term, 'War Journalism'. They acquired the status of conventions as news developed into a mass communication industry, and sought a register in which to address all its potential consumers, whatever their own opinions about the affairs of the community and the world around them. This register is commonly known as 'objectivity'.

Officials can be accepted as a source for news – whether you agree with the particular official being quoted, or not – by virtue of their officialdom. Lead the news on the 'visions for peace' of people from outside this charmed circle and you risk the response Lederach himself noted – that they will be written off as biased or too personally affected by the conflict. A reporter from the *Times of India* recounted her experience of building in such sources to her articles, and being greeted with the response, from editors: 'What is their claim to fame, exactly?' (Boga 2003).

Event and process? Report that a bomb has gone off and no one will give you an argument. It has, incontestably, taken place. Reach into context, to give an account of the process leading to the incident, and you automatically risk objections – why this bit of context, and not that?

Then, dualism does the work of objectivity because of 'its close resemblance, in shape and structure, to so much of the story-telling we already take for granted' (Lynch and McGoldrick 2005: 210). Think of politics, divided into left and right, interiority into conscious and subconscious, the temporal and the spiritual realms of the universe, and so on. A decision to tell a story, to frame a conflict, as two-handed, is a familiar way in which journalists insulate themselves against allegations of bias ('on the one hand . . . on the other'). It's a decision, indeed, that can easily slip by without announcing itself as such. It can pass itself off as 'common sense'.

The combined effect of all three conventions is to produce a form of news that is unexceptionable to potential consumers 'of all political views and none' (Lynch and McGoldrick 2005: 203), at least within the likely range of views held by those with enough money to buy it. But it is also a form of news predisposed towards the War Journalism column in the table.

In the context of Peace and Conflict Studies, it brings us to the question posed by yet another peace researcher, Friedrich Glasl: 'Do we have a conflict? Or does the conflict have us?' (Glasl 1999: 22–3).

War Journalism and war propaganda should be seen as coterminous. The conventions of news are always already there, built in to the actions and motivations of parties to conflict. The tug-of-war effect, in particular, ensures that anything which is not unequivocally 'winning' risks being reported as 'losing'. At one critical stage in the 'Iran nuclear crisis', the *Financial Times* reported:

> The European Union has 48 hours to decide one of the biggest foreign policy issues confronting it: whether to report Iran to the United Nations over its nuclear programme and risk an increase in Tehran's nuclear activities; or delay and face charges of a climb-down on nuclear proliferation.
>
> (Dombey 2005)

It means that War Journalism has to be *reckoned with*, as a hazard lying in wait for anyone seeking to build and sustain a case for patience, empathy or mutual confidence-building. They may find themselves being reported as having 'climbed down', or worse – Trevor Kavanagh's doom-laden article, quoted above, titled 'Why the West is paying for going soft on Iran', likens the European Union's attempts to negotiate an agreement to the appeasement of Hitler in the 1930s.

To use Glasl's words, this is a symptom of 'self-infection' (Glasl 1999: 24), in which the original conflict is exacerbated by a 'conflict about the conflict' and even a 'conflict about the conflict resolution'. As the conflict between Iran and the US and its allies descended down what Glasl calls the 'levels of escalation' (Glasl 1999: 85), the quotient of Peace Journalism in the UK press also fell (Lynch 2006) – not one before the other, but together in a feedback loop of cause and effect.

Such are the foreseeable consequences of War Journalism – consequences which demand, by virtue of their foreseeability, a workable teleological form of ethics for journalists to take some responsibility for their interventions in conflict dynamics. Whatever form that takes, in particular media at particular times and in particular places, could be defined as 'Peace Journalism'.

Building peace perspectives into reports of violence

Editors and reporters work within various commercial and structural constraints, but this is not the place to discuss them in detail. Suffice to say, for present purposes, there is some Peace Journalism so there could be more. Contained within the conventions of news are easily enough anomalies, boundaries, shifts and divisions to permit considerable scope to move along a 'sliding scale' towards the Peace Journalism side of the table.

Sometimes, the War Journalism paradigm is exposed by particular developments in conflict in such a way as to invite inspection from the outside. The categorical claims by official sources in the US and UK about Iraq's 'weapons of mass destruction' were proved wrong – either deceitful or mistaken, according to choice – so a form of newsgathering which elevates those sources to a position of primacy is bound to come into question. Indeed, the *New York Times* and *Washington Post* felt bound to publish apologies for their misleading coverage.

In another case, Indonesian journalists were relishing their newfound freedoms after the fall of President Suharto's 'New Order' regime, in 1998, and the abolition of his Ministry of Information. Then they realized their coverage of so-called 'horizontal conflicts' that flared up in the new atmosphere of political uncertainty might be unwittingly fuelling them – hence their hunger for Peace Journalism, or *Jurnalisme Damai*: 'There was, before the advent of *Jurnalisme Damai* as such, a *Jurnalisme Damai*-shaped hole in Indonesian journalists' professional repertoire' (Lynch and McGoldrick 2004: 142–3).

Such developments create the potential for Peace Journalism, and there are as many different ways of practising it as there are journalists. All are valid and useful – but some are more important than others.

In our opening discussion of what is at stake in media representations of conflict, it was noted that US 'psy-ops' tactics included writing favourable accounts of events in Iraq and passing them off as news stories. It is news – as distinct from features, comment, sidebar pieces or 'alternative' websites, say – that is still widely seen, not as a source of perspectives but as the factual basis on which competing perspectives can be assessed:

> Television journalists: know your place. The overwhelming view of the public is that the job doesn't involve creative decisions, because 'news is news', according to ITC [Independent Television Commission] audience research. 'What do you mean, what should they cover?' a young woman from London asked a researcher. 'They have to cover the news. What has happened, what is going on, there is not a lot of deciding to do about it.'[13]

'That notion of journalism as a record – a reliable account of what is really going on – is built in to many of our assumptions about the world and the way it works' (Lynch and McGoldrick 2005: xv). Hence the top priority for Peace Journalism is to influence and transform the way news is reported.

This is the significance, to our discussion here, of John Burton's often misunderstood suggestion that Peace and Conflict Studies should be seen as not merely interdisciplinary but 'adisciplinary' – its job being to penetrate key categories in every other discipline. So too with Peace Journalism – rather than being sequestered away as a separate form of media activity in itself, it must inscribe context, empathy and the potential for transformation in the categories of 'what has happened' and 'what is really going on' if it is to create opportunities for society at large to consider and to value creative, nonviolent responses to conflict.

In practical terms, that often means working from the 'top line' of a story that is not conducive to an account of conflict dynamics as Peace and Conflict Studies would understand it. One would not begin to describe the Israel–Palestine conflict, for instance, with a suicide bombing in Jerusalem, but that is often what the journalist is called upon to do, such are the enduring conventions of news.

Lynch and McGoldrick (2005: 162) examine a story from the English-language *Jakarta Post* newspaper, about a series of bombs planted in the Indonesian city of Palu, Central Sulawesi. The province, which has a mixed Muslim and Christian population, saw several rounds of inter-religious clashes in the early 2000s, centred on the nearby town of Poso. The bombs can be seen as a form of 'propaganda by deeds', or provocation, aimed at re-igniting the violence.

Participants in workshops in Indonesia, the Philippines, Norway, Sweden and Australia, among others, have all carried out the exercise of weaving into this story testimony from two local characters, a Muslim refugee and the leader of a Christian lay association, both loosely based on real people. It involves practising one of the most important skills for Peace Journalism, creating a 'framework of understanding' (Lynch 1998: 24) in which the relevance of such sources, to the 'main' story, can be made clear to readers.

To do so requires particular techniques to 'turn the corner' from one narrative direction to another. In this example, the italicized section of Peace Journalism is dovetailed so as to follow on from a chunk of the *Post*'s original story:

> Asked whether rioters were moving to Palu as the nearby conflict-torn town of Poso was under tight security, [the police chief] said the provincial police were investigating possible links between the two incidents.
>
> Poso has been the site of religious fighting since 2000, with thousands of people killed in clashes. Muslim and Christian leaders signed a peace deal last December but it appeared to be ineffective with the renewed outbreaks of violence.
>
> *Civic leaders have raised fears that refugees from conflict-torn areas of Indonesia might bring the contagion of inter-communal strife to Palu. One of them, Mrs Hidayat, was forced to flee her home in Poso, two years ago.*
>
> *She lost her husband and one child, but despite her tragic story, she is very firm that her two teenaged sons should not seek revenge or join in the violence . . .*
>
> (Lynch and McGoldrick 2005: 166)

(Hidayat describes how she and other local mothers gather to compare notes on 'lines to use' with their children to dissuade them from hanging about with local gangs – again, based on real grassroots peacework reported from Maluku as well as Poso.)

Another example:

> *If the bombers' aim was to sow discord between followers of different faiths, however, then, according to some local religious leaders, they were destined to fail. Jotje Yulianto, the head of a local Christian lay association . . .*

(Yulianto is quoted on the extensive practical peacework he and other leaders, both Christian and Muslim, are doing to build trust and mutual understanding between sections of the community.)

Development and future directions

The effect of Peace Journalism and War Journalism, as different patterns of representation of conflicts, has been discussed here as something that impacts on the course of events in a conflict by feeding back into source behaviour – the actions and motivations of parties to conflict.

This depends not on audience response as such but on suppositions, by those parties, about the likely audience response, to media frames. Propaganda, as an exercise in framing, may be intended to bring about short-term shifts in public opinion, and the record from particular episodes testifies to its effectiveness – in Britain in the weeks leading up to the invasion of Iraq, for instance (Lynch and McGoldrick 2005: 2).

But it leaves the question of whether the suppositions can be justified – how, why and to what extent does it make a difference, to audience responses, to alter the frame – in favour of more Peace Journalism, say? How do media frames interact with individual frames? After all, communications researchers once believed that 'campaigns do not influence people; their major effect is the reinforcement of existing attitudes. Even for those who do actually change their minds, the effects are minimal' (Scheufele 1999: 105).

This orthodoxy has since been replaced by social constructivism, as an account of how media and individual frames combine into a strong effect: 'Media discourse is part of the process by which individuals construct social meaning, and public opinion is part of the process by which journalists . . . develop and crystallise meaning in public discourse' (Gamson and Modigliani 1989: 2).

Recently, researchers in Peace and Conflict Studies have begun to investigate this process using the distinctions in representation that we have been discussing here – potentially one of the most important avenues for future development in Peace Journalism.

Wilhelm Kempf (2005) found significant differences between cognitive responses, among the same subjects, to German newspaper articles containing elements of content categorized as 'escalation', and to three re-written versions: '(a) with increased escalation-oriented framing, (b) with moderate de-escalation oriented framing and (c) with more determined de-escalation oriented framing of the events'.

Samuel Peleg and Eitan Alimi (2005) investigated 'the structuring of comprehension and interpretations to political reality in the context of the Israeli–Palestinian conflict, focusing on one particular facet: the possibility of an independent Palestinian state'. The research involved showing subjects the same articles, only with different sets of cross-headings inserted between blocs of text, and experimented with the effects of only minor changes of nomenclature; for the Palestinian leader, for example, as 'Abu Mazen' or 'Palestinian President Mahmoud Abbas'. Significant differences, in subjects' opinions about the likelihood and desirability of statehood for the Palestinians, were discerned.

These writers are members of a group of international scholars and practitioners, with a broad range of interests, convened from 2004 by the Toda Institute for Peace and Policy Research to advance research projects and curriculum development for Peace Journalism on a global scale. Together with ongoing training and dissemination, it completes the picture of what is now an organically growing field within the subject of Peace and Conflict Studies.

Notes

1 Maguire, K. and Lines, A. (2005) 'Exclusive: Bush plot to bomb his Arab ally', *Daily Mirror*, 22 November.
2 Nik Gowing, *Lessons Learned*, quoted in Jake Lynch et al. 'Peace Journalism and the Kosovo Crisis', Transnational Foundation for Peace and Future Research, at: http://www.transnational.org/features/2000/LynchPeaceJourn.html.
3 Accessed via http://www.humansecurityreport.info/figures/Figure1.3.pdf.
4 Bush: 'All options are on the table regarding Iran's nuclear aspirations', Associated Press, Jerusalem, 13 August 2005.
5 Retrieved from US State Department website, at http://www.state.gov/t/np/trty/16281.htm.
6 In interview with James Rubin on *World News Tonight*, Sky News, 24 October 2005.
7 *Daily Express*, 29 October 2005.
8 IAEA document, 'Developments in the Implementation of the NPT Safeguards Agreement in the Islamic Republic of Iran and Agency Verification of Iran's Suspension of Enrichment-related and Reprocessing Activities', update brief by the Deputy Director General for Safeguards, January 2006, at: http://www.campaigniran.org/heinonen31012006–2.pdf.
9 What are Journalists For? Conflict and Peace Forums, Taplow Court, Bucks, 3–7 September 1998.
10 Blair quoted by Anthony Barnett in Introduction to Peter Oborne (2006) *The Use and Abuse of Terror*, London: Centre for Policy Studies, v.
11 *Sun*, 6 August 2005.
12 'The Frameworks Perspective: Strategic Frame Analysis', The Frameworks Institute, at: http://www.frameworksinstitute.org/strategicanalysis/perspective.shtml.
13 Quoted in Jake Lynch, *Reporting the World*, Conflict and Peace Forums, Taplow, UK, 2002, 21.

References

Baxter, S. (2005) 'Oxford socialite linked to Iraq propaganda row', *Sunday Times*, 11 December.

Boga, D. (2003) 'Peace building media'. Centre for Peace and Conflict Studies, Sydney.

Bright, M. (2006) 'Losing the plot', *New Statesman*, 30 January.

Burton, J.W. (1993) 'Conflict resolution as a political philosophy', in D. Sandole and H. van der Merwe (eds) *Conflict Resolution Theory and Practice: Integration and Application*, Manchester and New York: Manchester University Press, 55–64.

Campbell, A. (1999) 'Kosovo: communication lessons for Nato, the military and the media', speech to the Royal United Services Institute, London, 9 July.

Daley, T., Evans, J. and Kennedy, M. (2006) 'The Peace Movement's plan for Iran', Alternet, 6 March, at: http://www.alternet.org/story/33062/.

Dombey, D. (2005) 'Moment of truth looms for Europe on Iran', *Financial Times*, 22 September.

Francis, D. (2002) *People, Peace and Power*, London: Pluto, 28.

Galtung, J. (1998) 'High road, low road – charting the course for Peace Journalism', *Track Two*, 7, 4, Centre for Conflict Resolution and Media Peace Centre, Cape Town, South Africa, December.

Galtung, J. and Fischer, D. (1998) 'Towards a comprehensive peace settlement in the Middle East', TRANSCEND peace column, 23 February, at: www.transcend.org.

Gamson, W.A. and Modigliani, A. (1989) 'Media discourse and public opinion on nuclear power: a constructionist approach', *American Journal of Sociology*, 95: 2.

Garton Ash, T. (2006) 'We need a European approach to supporting democracy in Iran', *Guardian*, 9 March.

Glasl, F. (1999) *Confronting Conflict* (translated by Petra Kopp), Stroud: Hawthorn Press, 22–3.

Hilsum, L. (2004) Diplomatic Editor, Channel Four News, quoted in Jake Lynch, 'Reporting Iraq – what went right? What went wrong?', in A. Biressi and H. Nunn (eds), *Mediactive*, 3, *Mediawar*, London: Barefoot.

Jowett, G.S. and O'Donnell, V. (1999) *Power and Persuasion*, London: Sage, 6.

Kaldor, M. (2003) 'Regime change without war', *Red Pepper*, April.

Kavanagh, T. (2005) 'Why the West is paying for going soft on Iran', *Sun*, 12 October.

Kay, A.F. (2000) 'When Americans favor the use of force', *International Journal of Public Opinion Reasearch*, 12: 182–19

Kempf, W. (2005) 'Experimenting with de-escalation oriented coverage of post-war conflicts', paper presented to 3rd International Conference on Communication and Mass Media, Athens Institute for Education and Research, Athens, 23–25 May.

Kimball, D.G. (2005) 'Replacement nuclear warheads – buyer beware', *Arms Control Today*, Arms Control Association, May at: http://www.armscontrol.org/act/2005_05/focus.asp.

Knightley, P. (2000) '*The First Casualty*, London: Prion Books, 504.

Lederach, J.P. (1997) *Building Peace – Sustainable Reconciliation in Divided Societies*, Washington, DC: United States Institute of Peace Press, 94.

Linzer, D. (2005) 'No proof found of Iran arms program', *Washington Post*, 23 August.

Lynch, J. (1998) *The Peace Journalism Option*, Taplow: Conflict and Peace Forums, 24.

Lynch, J. (2006) What's so great about Peace Journalism?', *Global Media Journal Mediterranean Edition*, 1, 1: 74–87.

Lynch, J. and McGoldrick, A. (2004) 'Reporting conflict – an introduction to Peace Journalism', in T. Hanitzsch, M. Loffelholz and R. Mustamu (eds) *Agents of Peace*, Jakarta: Friedrich Ebert Stiftung, 142–3.

Lynch, J. and McGoldrick, A. (2005) *Peace Journalism*, Stroud: Hawthorn Press, xvi.

Norton-Taylor, R. (2005) 'As the US lowers the nuclear threshold, debate is stifled', *Guardian*, 5 October.

Peleg, S. and Alimi, E. (2005) 'Constructing political discourse in the Israeli print news media – an experimental design', *Conflict and Communication Online*, 4, 2.

Scheufele, D.A. (1999) 'Framing as a theory of media effects', *Journal of Communication*, Winter: 105.

White, A. (2004) *Justice Denied on the Road to Baghdad*, Brussels: International Federation of Journalists, 25.

17

Peace psychology

Theory and practice

Antonella Sapio and Adriano Zamperini

> Peace Psychology requires a profound re-thinking of psychology itself . . . peace is a social construct with direct political implications.
>
> (G. Jovanovic)

Peace psychology is a cross-disciplinary subject which has only recently developed both its theoretical framework and methodological practice. Therefore, peace psychology is a new discipline, not only because of the novel contents of its thematic field (conflicts, peace, etc.), at least as far as its collective dimension is concerned, but also because of the distinctive novelty of the thinking framework on which it is based.

Contrary to what many authors seem to think, peace psychology is not a mishmash of psychological knowledge taken from different fields, such as social and dynamic psychology, interpersonal psychology, to be then applied to Peace Studies. If that were the case, this discipline would only be an attempt to produce a different pattern out of the same jigsaw pieces: referring to 'Peace' would thus only be a means to create a new sub-discipline of psychology. On the contrary, it is worth stressing that here the very pieces of the jigsaw are profoundly different from the outset.

In addition to the original nature of its thematic field, which traditional psychology did not properly take into account, at least until the period of the so-called 'Cold War', Peace psychology proposes above all a new form of psychological practice which, similarly to nonviolence and active peacemaking, challenges the traditional frameworks of thought.

The approach centred on the 'care' of the 'patient' and interventions for the most part individual or concerned with restricted situations within relational dimensions defined as 'therapeutic' undergo a sort of 'Copernican revolution' in the perspective of nonviolence, in that questioning power relationships as deviant tends to undermine the very basis of the therapeutic relationship, which counts structural violence among its intrinsic components. According to a nonviolent reading, people's suffering is not a 'minus' which ends up confirming, by means of its own exclusion, the 'sanity' of the context, but is, on the contrary, the genuine and direct product of a structural form of suffering, of which it becomes the epiphenomenon.

In this sense, it might be useful to introduce peace psychology by way of the concepts of nonviolence and active peacemaking, which provide the background for the discourse as well as the reasons for the distinctiveness of such an approach.

The notion of 'active peacemaking' refers to that transformative social process which is able to identify, question and modify the violent structural components within a system, which may be, mostly indirectly, a cause of suffering for individuals. Such a process may be activated and sustained through knowledge tools and practices pertaining to various disciplines, including psychology; however, when applied in a peace-psychological context, such tools do not remain unchanged. Seen in the perspective of an evolutional social dynamic, psychology, though starting from the expression of subjective suffering, affirms and activates the possibility of change, conferring on the subject himself the power and ability to elaborate experience, according to a 'bottom-up' procedure.

The object of traditional care, be it the individual or the community, if rendered passive and located within a process of change which 'encysts' the discomfort, runs the risk of becoming 'nonsense' in a social context; and therefore merits a kind of thinking-action specifically designed to regulate and discipline it. On the other hand, if it is this same discomfort that becomes a source of collective experience, by means of an emergent subjectivity modelled by it, this may itself become an expression of a new sense which is an advantage to the collective.

Summarising, peace psychology may be said to be:

- A cross-disciplinary field which deals with human suffering, both individual and collective, through psychological perspectives and instruments which consider the subjects as actors of their own change.
- A body of knowledge and practices aiming at the nonviolent transformation of conflicts, at micro-, medium- and macro-levels.
- A new approach to psychosocial issues, based on 'facilitating and sharing experiences' rather than on therapeutic interventions.
- A critical contribution to post-constructivism, aiming to enrich the practical work of collective psychology.

Peace psychology premises

The first systematic applications of psychology to overcome collective issues may be traced to Dewey's and Mead's attempts to act upon social reforms in Chicago at the beginning of the twentieth century. By the 1930s, in the United States, the foundation movement of the Society for the Psychological Study of Social Issues made possible new perspectives for the application of psychological knowledge (Collier et al. 1991). In the following years, this brought about the involvement of psychologists during and after the Second World War, in accordance with Lewin's indications (1948). During the 1950s, psychology reverted to experimental laboratory practices. However, the crisis of the 1960s and 1970s stimulated the demand for applied psychology, in the sense of research and intervention in the context of the real world, with a view to understanding human behaviour and finding a solution for social problems.

While the path of Western psychology is pretty well known, the same cannot be said for a movement that contributed to laying certain foundations – important, though little acknowledged – for the construction of a psychology of peace. We are referring to Liberation Psychology. Born in Latin America, this new perspective arose out of the consciousness of how little psychology had to offer, as science and praxis, towards solving the problems of the Latin American peoples. Therefore, Liberation Psychology developed as an answer to the 'crisis of

Western psychology' during the 1970s. It proposed a serious re-examination of the epistemological foundations of psychology itself, by means of contributions towards social commitment, reflections of an ethical nature, ecological observation and field research.

In the context of this scenario, three types of problem emerged in Western psychology, problems of particular importance to peace psychology:

1 *A lack of social relevance*. Psychology seemed to have become incapable of producing any knowledge directly rooted in many social problems.
2 *Local knowledge accompanied by claims to universal validity*. Psychology depended on research based on population samples selected in artificial contexts, yet aspired to validity outside of these.
3 *A levelling out in the direction of scientific neutrality*. This involved the consequent abandonment of the ethical dimension.

Psychologists therefore began to feel acutely uncomfortable with regard to the quality, meaning and usefulness of their work. They began to question themselves as to what was its purpose and recognized that certain theoretical explanations, which had been accepted as an appropriate means of studying and understanding reality, either failed to produce any answers or appeared irrelevant and useless (Montero 1991). Wherever these problems sprang from a background of widespread social injustice, as in Latin America, there was a growing awareness of the need to elaborate a psychology not merely theoretical, but also and primarily practical. As a first step, however, this involved a break with its own 'enslavements' and with uncritical recourse to the traditional ideologies. In other words, the realization of a Liberation Psychology required, in the first place, the liberation of psychology itself by means of a revision of the traditional way of thinking and practising psychology. A contribution in this direction came from social constructivism, thanks especially to the attention paid to both the critical and anti-realistic vision of knowledge and the historical-cultural specificity and intimate correlation between knowledge and action (Burr 1995; Kvale 1992).

Peace psychology was therefore born as an 'Alternative Psychology', starting with its use of non-conventional terminology. Linguistic expressions such as 'application' and 'intervention', conveying as they do the implicit representation of psychological work as performed 'on' someone, are henceforth abandoned for the very good reason that the basis of the operation is to work 'with' someone: the interlocutors are not 'objects of care' but rather 'participant citizens'. To gain a thorough understanding of this change – plainly not a mere word-game, but the very foundation of an ethics of participation – it is advisable to enlarge the scope of our analysis, passing from a psychology of 'objects of study' to a psychology 'of problems'. Peace, therefore, is not a 'new object of study' but the foundation stone of a different epistemological approach, and one which challenges the thought and practice of traditional psychology.

The globalizing thought of traditional psychology and psychiatry

Traditional psychology (starting with psychoanalysis) has relied on the assumption (here called in question) that the object of 'care' is a 'patient' with some form of psychic disturbance, and that care practices take place within a therapeutic relationship involving a 'therapist' and a 'patient'. There is an intrinsic imbalance of power in this relational axis, since only the caregiver possesses the instruments required to direct the relationship. In our belief the 'vertical' nature of this relationship is in itself an ambiguous preconditioning to the construction of an independent personal identity, since it is the 'need for care' which binds a person to his own difficulties. The clinical model of the therapeutic relationship, even though updated on the basis of more humanizing approaches, presupposes fixed positions ('therapist' and 'patient') which render the relational space artificial, and often leave the field of interaction unchanged. Likewise, the globalizing way of thinking which at present marks our era, in the sense of an imaginary common thinking capable of annulling the differences within vertical power relationships between rich societies and very poor ones, is a direct expression of that same consumerist thinking that years ago produced psychoanalysis and its infinite number of derivatives.

If we consider that the increasing degree of discomfort in Western societies is a direct consequence of lifestyles and relationships which are not responding to people's authentic needs, it is clear that the response to this discomfort can no longer be represented by individual psychological readings which, by reconfirming and reinforcing 'goodness' of the sociocultural patterns, end up by cauterizing the aberrations present. Is it therefore possible to imagine calling in question those very patterns of thought and of sociocultural functioning which lead people towards passivity and impotence, and thereby to depression and alienation? Engaging in a critique of Western consumerist thinking also implies an analogous critical look at the various forms of traditional psychology and at ways of thought regarding globalization. What does it mean today to put forward a real alternative to the degradation of consumerist culture, one capable of persuading the West to overcome its discomfort and give rise to a genuine dialogue with cultural differences? How is it possible to imagine psychological work that does not run the risk of reproducing vertical power relationships that are, in any case, inauthentic?

Peace psychology may thus be put forward as a field of study and practice which aims to develop new forms of sharing people's suffering, over and above the traditional 'therapeutic spaces' and in profound empathy with all that pertains to the direct life experience of the individual. From a theoretical point of view, there is a shift between relying on the 'analytic judgement of clinical psychotherapy', which separates the people involved in a relationship, and sharing experiences in a way that puts the relationship itself at the heart of a possible change in a person's own life story.

In this sense, peace psychology represents an alternative approach with respect to traditional psychology, which in virtue of its specific vocation is able to deal with social conflict, with a distinct leaning not towards the solution of dissentions, but towards the transformation of the most unjust of conditions in which people live (Zamperini 1998).

It is clear, therefore, that traditional psychology, when dealing with conflict, tends to regard this as something to be 'solved' in the light of a process of pacification whose aim is composing the differences. This psychological approach, directed at a sterile 'mediation between parties', indifferent to the outcome and for the most part neutral and equidistant with respect to the subjects involved, corresponds fully to the traditional approach, in that it solves the conflict without actually touching the basic framework of the system. Peace psychology, on the contrary, does not aim at pacification, but at transforming the interactions and distinguishing features of the conflict into newer and more authentic forms of relationship and conditions of life (Table 17.1 illustrates the differences between traditional psychology and peace psychology).

The TRANSCEND approach, proposed by Galtung, is actually understood, within the ambit of mediation contexts, as a pathway that does not aim at a sterile 'pacification', but rather gathers the suggestions of conflictuality to orient them towards a sort of creative and creating transcendence which allows individuals themselves to transform their own conflict reality. The general formula for the TRANSCEND approach is the tripartite 'mantra' of empathy, nonviolence and creativity (Galtung 2007 this volume). In this sense, the mediating function takes the

Table 17.1. Differences between traditional psychology and peace psychology

Traditional psychology	*Peace psychology*
Globalizing approach	Awareness of difference
Conflict resolution as 'pacification'	Conflict transformation leading to change
Search for compromise solutions in controversies	No compromise is sought without a previous change in suffering
Intervention practices modelled on vertical power relations	Intervention practices modelled on authentic sharing experiences
Negative or passive peace, easy 'peace' [not interfering with the structure]	Active peacemaking, nonviolence, 'uneasy' peace [clashing with resistance to change]
Peace as an 'internal, inward dimension'	Peace as a 'collective dimension'
Aims at 'individual well-being'	Aims at the collective good through socio-emotional sharing practices
Peacemaking and mediation practices	Peacebuilding and facilitating practices

perspective of a polysemic view, capable of enriching context reality with several meanings through access to a transcendent thought (Galtung 1996).

Psychological knowledge may tackle the issue of peace in two different ways:

- By leaving intact its own theoretical framework and adapting it to the study of peace.
- By calling in question the traditional approaches and proposing a form of differential psychological knowledge to encourage the evolution of the individual and of society in all its expressions (thought, behaviour, relationships), according to an integrated cross-disciplinary perspective.

In the first case, we consider the use of the term 'peace' to be ambiguous, since it refers to a process of pacification of the individual, and not to a collective process. 'Peace' in the sense of quiescence, pacification, passivity is an individual phenomenon, which in interpersonal relationships emerges on the basis of a conflict perceived as contextual to the histories of the individuals concerned. In such cases we prefer to us the term 'pacification', in so far as what we are dealing with is a specific and contingent action directed *ad hoc* at a specific problem (Sapio 2004). However, when 'peace' is defined as an entirely collective phenomenon we arrive at meaningful objectives of social change, starting with an individual transformation in a position to question one's passive adherence to the functional context. In such a case, therefore, not only is there no 'pacification', but the conflict itself becomes valuable ground for the social transformation of conditions considered and perceived to be unjust. In the first case, therefore, the intervention will aim to allay the suffering of the individual and render it functional to social adjustment, without acting upon the social context in which the person belongs. But, in the second case, the intervention will be specifically directed at supporting the suffering with a view to modifying the existing context, and it will do this by means of the techniques of facilitation. In our view, not only is the first approach to be considered wrongheaded, but we maintain that, on account of the existing conceptual ambiguities in the matter, it is necessary for the scientific community to differentiate between the terms 'pacification' (in the sense of passive, negative peace) and 'peace' in the real semantic and conceptual meaning of the word.

Psychology has usually been far from clear about the relation between the interruption of the process of subjective alienation and that of society, between individual control and collective power, between the liberation of the individual and that of a whole population, thus helping to obscure the relation between personal alienation and social oppression, and thereby loading a large part of social discomfort onto the shoulders of individuals. Although social psychology has contributed to the understanding of individual and group processes underlying stereotypes, prejudices and racism, in the light of worldwide phenomena such as the globalization of merchandise and human beings, it appears increasingly urgent today to recognize and inquire into how far structural sociocultural operations can produce modifications at the psychological level. The social psychology of the last century, during the 1920s and 1930s, at the time of the Great Depression in the United States and the rise of Nazi and Fascist totalitarianism in Europe, shifted attention onto three basic arguments – poverty, prejudice and peace – placing the study of psychological and social problems within the context of economics. Later psychosocial research lost touch with this attitude with a few exceptions, for example the study in which the increase in xenophobic sentiments in adolescent males in ex-East Germany proved to be connected to the interiorization of the values championed by capitalism (Boehnke et al. 1998). Today, although globalization and the free market are glorified in the West, it is (contrariwise) only too easy to see to what extent they create new social divisions, priming and encouraging attitudes of intolerance.

A similar awareness must accompany psychologists in selecting their objects of research. For example, the concepts of aggressiveness and homeostasis have often been wrongly understood. Aggressiveness, read as associated with antisocial behaviour, has obscured the sort of 'legitimate aggressiveness' put into action by socially victimized groups, such as the peasants' revolts caused by sheer poverty or the workers' struggles to obtain a decent wage. The concept of homeostasis – very widespread in systematic psychology, as well as that of cognition and of personality – has led to a reading of change in terms of lack of balance, which in turn has led to negatively evaluate everything that represents rupture, conflict and crisis. With this perspective in view, it is unlikely that the imbalances inherent in the social struggle can fail to be interpreted as personal disorders, and that the conflicts generated by a rejection of any given collective system are not considered to be pathological. Non-conformity in the face of domination is hence seen as a subjective symptom of mental unbalance.

The necessity of not falling into the traps of individual psychology when faced with collective phenomena such as war has been particularly stressed by the psychologists of liberation, above all by Ignacio Martín-Baró (1994). Individual work is necessary, but if psychology were to confine itself exclusively to the period of treatment, it would become a mere palliative within a situation which generates and multiplies pathologies. One cannot, for example, go no further than the question of what treatment is most effective in curing post-traumatic stress; indeed, the analysis must extend to the very roots of such traumas, and therefore to war itself as a psycho-pathogenetic social situation. In this context Liberation Psychology speaks of 'psycho-social trauma' rather than 'psychic trauma'. The latter term in fact emphasizes the individual, acute and unexpected nature of trauma, but appears inadequate to describe the collective and often chronic nature of the trauma undergone by those with first-hand experience of war and oppression. Psycho-social trauma constitutes, in individuals, the concrete crystallization of aberrant and dehumanizing social relations, such as those prevailing in civil war or situations of prolonged social injustice. Psycho-social trauma may be considered as a normal consequence of a social system based on exploitation and oppression.

Peace psychology therefore starts with the assumption that psychologists are capable of thinking in terms which are critical of the ideological and scientific frameworks in which they find themselves operating, continually posing themselves questions as to their ability to see problems from the point of view of the victims and the oppressed. This leads us to a psychology that is 'from the viewpoint of' and not 'for' those who customarily are 'objects of intervention': a psychology of education from the viewpoint of the illiterate, a psychology of work from the viewpoint of the unemployed, a clinical psychology from the viewpoint of the social outcast, a psychology of the community from the viewpoint of the immigrant. And so on. To the change of perspective must be added praxis, that is, an activity that transforms the present situation and makes it possible to know it not only as what it is but also as what it might become. Here there is an evident link between peace psychology and community social psychology, which had its beginnings in the 1960s. It had various objectives in view, such as social promotion, economic development, anti-poverty programmes, quality of life and human rights, and it imposed a constant check on the degree of coherence between the demands of the population and the nature of the projects to be implemented, the guiding principle being that social change cannot really and truly come about without the direct participation of the people involved.

Peace-thinking as difference-thinking

By the term peace-thinking we mean that specific type of difference-thinking which is capable of questioning those dominant sociocultural frameworks of thought which impose conformity in cases where we find aspects of structural violence that cause suffering to people. Intrinsic to difference-thinking is a creative and critical attitude towards questioning the formal aspects and the fixed sociocultural parameters which inhibit the free and authentic expression of life, and may therefore be applied to an infinite variety of fields of knowledge and social living. Attitudes towards critical difference-thinking, and therefore also creative thinking, have been extensively studied in psychological literature (Zamperini and Testoni 2002). In particular, we should mention Lerner's 'just-thinking theory' (1980; for further developments, see Montada and Lerner 1996) and, in general, the studies on obedience, which, starting with Milgram (1974), have continued to enliven the scientific debate on the issues of conformity and dissent.

Peace psychology therefore proposes:

- A new and cross-disciplinary type of difference-thinking, capable of a critical reading of the factual situation, as well as of activating the resources which may transform it in a positive sense.
- A non-traditional psychological approach which in itself establishes authenticity of interaction with otherness according to horizontal types of relationship (psycho-social facilitation).

The values promoted by peace psychology are not those of a sterile neutrality (being 'strictly impartial'), but involvement; not a 'distancing' from suffering, but a 'closeness' to it; not the vertical relationship of the 'top-down' therapeutic setting, but the ability 'to be' in a situation through experiences of sharing and full reciprocity, which in turn are able to facilitate evolutional changes both at the personal and (even more) at the contextual level.

In this sense, rather than 'mediation' practices for the most part based on neutrality, equidistance, etc., which indeed may be categorized as 'peacemaking', peace psychology – far from being neutral – promotes practices of 'facilitation' which, based on the full sharing of the pain experienced by the suffering party or parties, may lead to the nonviolent persuasion of the opposing party. If instead of an interpersonal relationship we are dealing with social relations and types of suffering caused by structural damage on the part of penalizing social systems (as, for instance, in the case of conflict between individuals and institutions), there is an even more evident difference between mediation practices, which tend to 'resolve' problems in a contingent manner, without seeking to modify the structural framework, and practices of social facilitation which, on the contrary, cannot avoid questioning those aspects of violence or structural damage which lie at the roots of that conflict, starting with a transparent and openly declared 'proximity' to the party subjected to a vertical power relationship, which is in itself the source of structural, and often cultural, damage (Sapio 2004).

An interactive-emotional model for the nonviolent transformation of destructive interactions, from the micro to the macro level

With reference to studies on the non-innate nature of human destructiveness (cf. Krahé 2001 for a review), it is to sociocultural aspects of the matter that we attribute the taking root of 'false destructive beliefs' in the practical life of social relations; beliefs quite capable of steering human interactions towards violent modes of behaviour. This is due to social images which legitimize competitive styles of relationship. We in fact maintain that at the very base of violent behaviour, whether interpersonal or collective, reaching even to the tragic heights of war and genocide, we always and in every case find that same image of competitive human relationship which, on a less extreme level, directs the choices of politico-social cultures based on economic exploitation and the affirmation of vertical power relationships.

Aggressiveness, we know, may have both a positive, constructive reading, defined as 'benign', and a destructive reading related to the exercise of vertical power relationships at the expense of others. In Western cultures the social acceptance of destructive interactions, implicit in both economic and simply human relations, is openly denied only when it assumes an explicitly violent form, becoming damaging to the person. This is so unless the violent behaviour may be justified in terms of a need for equilibrium and for protection of the social system, as in the case of war. The recent international events which led to the Iraq war bear striking witness to how easily such cultural mechanisms may be validated and reinforced, especially when destructive actions are made to serve priority political and economical interests, even to the point of becoming instrumental in seeking political election.

However, it is difficult to achieve an awareness of the continuum existing between 'war' or 'destructive interactions' and those cultural mechanisms which underlie or justify the expression of violence, starting with the false beliefs that orientate any vertical power relationship.

The approach made by peace psychology is distinctive in that it takes as its central point the epistemological question of the value of horizontal human relationships and aims at a new awareness of those forms of structural violence, implicit and indirect, which are present in the workings of certain sociocultural systems, proposing as it does a new key to understanding how to overcome destructive patterns of thought and behaviour.

Figure 17.1 illustrates the three possible modes of behaviour in reply to an aggression (Sapio 2004). We believe that these explain different cultural mechanisms which create both interpersonal and collective social relations, and that the adoption of any one definite mode of interaction is, in its unconscious patterns, culturally oriented. Destructiveness, passivity and assertiveness (or affirmativeness) underlie the behavioural choices which a person may act upon in reply to an 'attack'.

In the first case, the 'attack–defence' diagram, the type of relation proposed by the aggressor is reproduced in thought and behaviour in a counter-reactive and specular-symmetrical manner. The aggressor may be a fully aware person, an agent unaware (or only slightly aware) of the

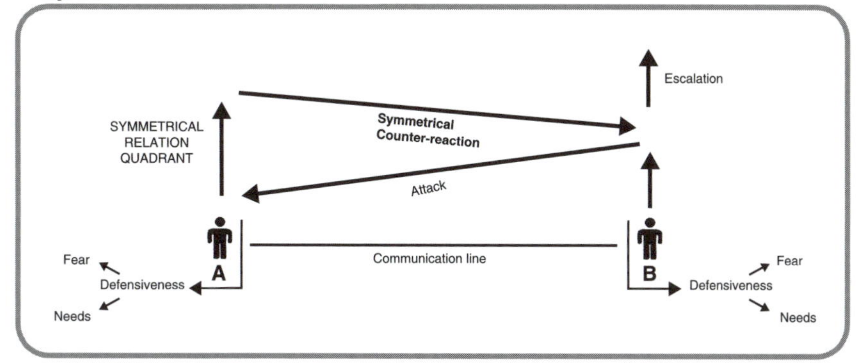

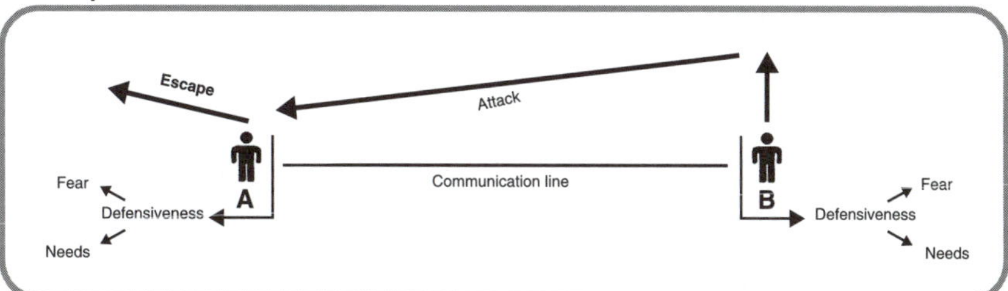

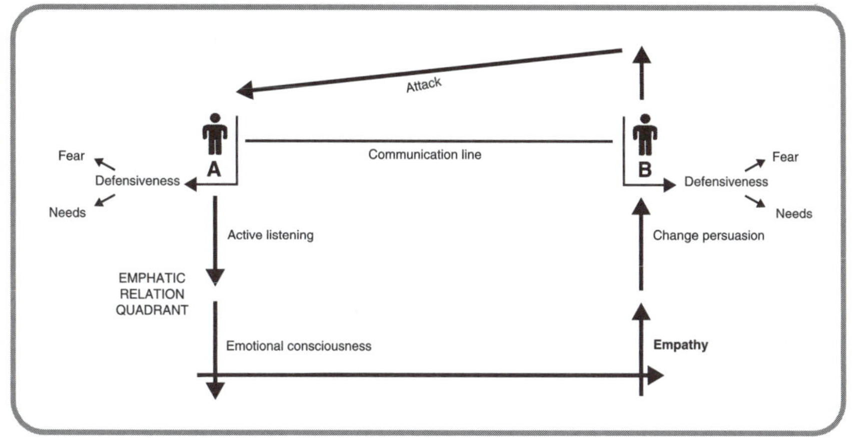

Figure 17.1. Three interactional responses to an attack

damage being inflicted, or a social system which acts indirectly to the detriment of people. The type of relation inherent in this last mode of behaviour is very widespread in our culture, on account of being socially accredited. The symmetrical–conflictual pattern of interaction is among the most common interactions of a highly contentious nature. In the case of collective phenomena it is easy to imagine an evolution towards tragic forms of escalation.

In the second case, a passive behavioural reaction leaves the type of destructive interaction unaltered and can cause the condition of the offended party to take a turn towards serious psychic compromises. In the case of collective phenomena, we have no trouble in recalling the difficult history of downtrodden peoples who have had long experience of foreign occupation or pitiless domestic dictatorships. In this case also, the tendency towards the adoption of passive and non-transformative behaviour is culturally induced (Sapio and Zamperini 2003).

In the third case, on the other hand, the choice of thought and behaviour tends towards the transformation of the type of relation in the light of a possible constructive evolution of the conflict, one capable of bringing positive changes to the existing context. This possibility lies at the very heart of the proposal of nonviolence, which, from interpersonal relationships to collective phenomena, discerns a specific evolutional psycho-social development in the search for genuine relationships supported and upheld by profound respect for the Other, and in the possibility of the constructive transformation of structurally violent situations.

In Figure 17.1, the letter B represents the cause of the (more or less unconscious) injury, while A stands for the person who receives the injury but is also in a position to transform his own experience and that of others. It will be seen that the attack–defence pattern shown in the upper quadrant illustrates the kind of damaging interaction applicable to all those destructive relational forms and conditions of life, counter-reactive in character, which can constitute conflictual experiences that have not been worked out. If, for example, the cause of an injury is an unjust social system, any change whatever requires specific activation, starting with a forceful shift towards the containment of counter-reactive destructive impulses, the 'disarmament' of the defensive psycho-relational or social framework and the sharing of experiences of suffering with a view to transforming the conditions which brought them about. In this regard, the type of interaction can be transformed in the direction of genuine relationships in the case of interpersonal conflicts, or into experiences shared collectively. This, however, requires a conscious adoption of choice, inevitably connected with the possibility of attempting to overcome both the awkwardness of the relationship and the unpleasantness of the emotions present; which, once they are conscious, can in interpersonal interactions be expressed in words and in collective relations simply shared. It is obvious, according to this line of thought, that there can be no transformation of the type of relationship without deliberate activation by one of the two parties.

The model which we present in Figure 17.2 is a diagrammatic synthesis of how symmetrical counter-reactive reactions lead to escalation; or else, if that does not occur, simply to destructive interactions which may well remain at levels of low tension. According to this model, passive behaviour patterns can often be even less useful than symmetrical reactions, in so far as they can, according to the context and circumstances, encourage the aggressor (Gandhi 1951). The transformation of the conflictuality therefore requires a conscious activation leading to full contact with the unpleasant emotions induced by the aggression, in the light of a profound understanding of the fears and needs concealed by the defensive mechanism, which has in any case been stiffened by the attack. This 'disarmament', whether personal or collective, originates and takes form within the possibility of acquiring new awareness of one's own emotional world, an awareness which can enable one to interact with an aggressor by putting into the field the forces of newly-acquired awareness rather than the defensive–destructive mechanism. The working out of a number of 'false beliefs' with regard to the efficacy of one's own social behaviour is indispensable in working for peace because otherwise one would run the risk of acclaiming values (for example, unilateral disarmament) which it would be difficult to realize even within oneself and in one's social relationships, on account of the rigidity of the defence mechanism. Opting for nonviolence today, therefore, means defusing the central destructive patterns, repetitive as they are and very deep-rooted, on which Western culture is based, and developing a conscious change of heart which leads to the transformation of the quality of social relations, and thereby also to that of our politico-economic systems.

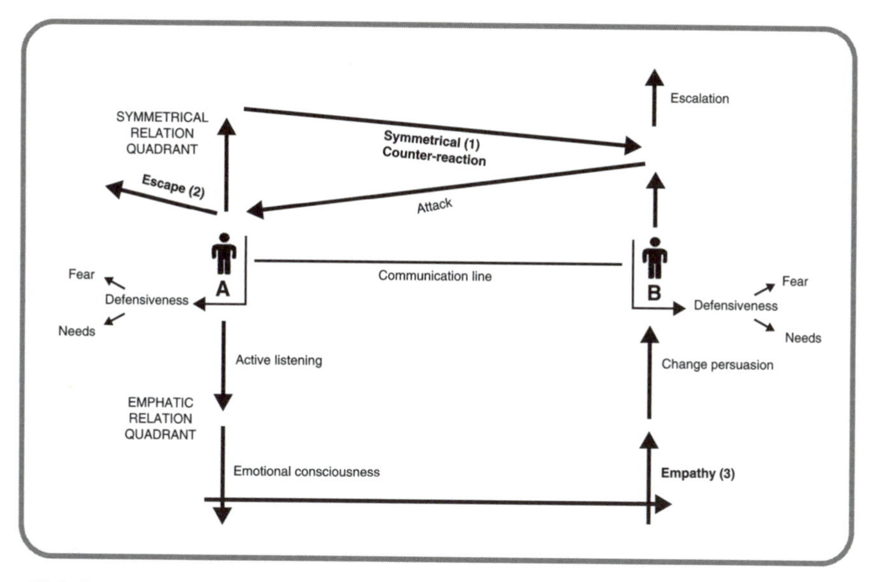

Figure 17.2. Interactive-emotional model

The process indicated in the lower quadrant of Figure 17.2, which we define as the Empathetic Relation Quadrant, must be activated by subject A who, restraining the impulse to counter-react and paying attention to his own unpleasant emotions, becomes aware of the emotional exchange in progress and, in the explicit communication of his needs and fears, pursues an authenticity of the rapport that in itself leads to a transformation of the conflict. Such a position can bring about radical change as long as the other party, convinced of the genuineness of the experience undergone, receives the other's contribution as part of their interaction. The reading of collective phenomena, and therefore of complex entities interacting according to parameters difficult to assess in terms of 'aggressor' and 'victim', can nonetheless be included in the framework here traced out in so far as it is possible to identify Subject A simply as that party (or that complex entity) which is capable of activating any change.

Training groups

One of the practical methods used by peace psychologists is group training. These groups are by nature formative and are aimed at achieving personal and collective evolution towards nonviolence.

The training groups are not psycho-therapeutic, nor are they directed towards 'well-being' or 'treatment'. Their aim is to achieve the conscious activation of a person's nonviolent potential for purposes of transformative social commitment (Euli 1999). Since we maintain that the growing discomfort and social suffering in Western societies owe a large part of their origin to the poor quality of socio-affective relationships, on account of destructive 'central thought patterns', we think that trajectories of personal growth and education in nonviolence are in themselves experiences in the reading of sense and also the transformation of individual suffering (Sapio 2004).

These training groups take place at regular intervals, in a medium to short timescale agreed on with the participants themselves. The activities are experiential in character, and deeply involve the participants with regard to such things as manner of interaction, false relational beliefs, stereotypes and prejudices, categorical patterns, social images, emotional situations, the elaboration of suffering and capacity for transformation, empathy and authenticity, and empowerment. Work with training groups may reveal some aspects of personal crisis that possibly require work with the individual running parallel with the group. This often turns out to be very useful in sustaining the fragility of a person by means of collective work.

Other modes of collective work for peace psychologists include: narration groups (largely centred on the stories of individuals), groups for the stimulation of awareness (directed at shared problems) and empowerment groups (for the transformation of social conflictuality).

Psycho-social facilitation

As we have suggested above, social facilitation is to be seen in the context of 'peace-building' operations based on the work of local communities. Psycho-social facilitation is a practice involving interventions aiming to transform the aspects of violence or damage structural to a social system, starting with experiences of sharing with the most fragile social groups, and continuing with an evolutional change which is at the same time capable of enriching the resources of the local community itself (Zunes et al. 1999).

Psycho-social facilitation is a recent acquisition in fieldwork, an up-to-date instrument based on experience drawn from the study and practice of community work. Unlike the modes of operation previously used in work in the field, connected with institutional matters, and also questions of social mediation, these also being located within the institutions however much they may be projected towards the fact of conflict, social facilitation does not claim for itself any institutional position, which would be in evident contrast to the very meaning of its mandate.

Psycho-social facilitation is therefore a form of 'participatory presence' in the field, which:

- Flanks those who are experiencing forms of suffering by means of genuine sharing (it is therefore not neutral, nor equidistant, nor 'strictly impartial', as mediation is).
- Is by nature decidedly non-institutional.
- Is recognized in its 'function' by the local community that supports its work.
- Activates processes of democratic participation from 'the bottom up'.
- Supports processes of empowerment in the community.
- Pursues aims of the transformation of violent socio-cultural attitudes by means of nonviolent forms of persuasion and conviction shared by the opposing party.

The techniques of facilitation have as yet been little tested and little noticed, and the literature on the subject is therefore not very abundant. We would like to affirm, however, that operations in this field are a great deal more substantial than scientific comment might lead us to believe.

From psychology to peace psychology

In comparison with psychology as generally understood, peace psychology gives priority to the problem of social change, and this aspiration on its part is solidly buttressed by a system of values. For example, the subjects of solidarity and tolerance are not relegated to the outer edge of interpersonal and inter-group dynamics, but extended to social processes, with particular attention being paid to the ideologies of exclusion and oppression. School, for example, rather than being the place where a person is educated in openness towards others, can – and often does – become the place where we see above all the dominion of the strong over the weak, of conformity over diversity, of the rich over the poor, of the norm over the abnormal. In addition, though we have stressed how deep-rooted prejudice is in interpersonal exchanges and group processes, we should not fail to mention the role of speech habits and therefore the vocabulary adopted by every society to regulate collective relations, in the folds of which may be hidden whole linguistic repertories which tend to justify and accredit exclusion and dominion. In this case, recourse is often made to scientific narratives (we need only mention the ideological exploitation of biology) to legitimize social injustices, giving a natural appearance to what is really a cultural construction. Finally, as we have pointed out, peace psychology does not fail to stress to what extent political economies which accentuate social inequalities both instigate and facilitate xenophobic sentiments and other forms of intolerance.

When action aimed to reduce intolerance and promoting solidarity takes place at a micro-level, the problem essentially regards psychological change: what inner renewal is needed and how should we act to bring it about? This question, which invests both theory and practice, is central to peace psychology for the purposes of preventing violence, achieving reconciliation after racial and political conflicts, promoting multi-ethnic community living, and controlling conflicts of long standing (the so-called 'intractable conflicts'), just to mention a few. Studies in social psychology on the subject of tolerance have enabled us to recognize a number of strategies, such as overcoming negative interdependence to arrive at a positive interdependence (superordinate goals), the hypothesis of that contact which enables one party to personalize the other, the re-categorization which leads to a richer knowledge of oneself and others, thus demonstrating that individuals endowed with more complex cognitive images of their own group tend to be more tolerant with members of other groups. On the macro-level of analysis, light has been shed on the role of those ideologies and collective beliefs that nourish intolerance and fortify indifference.

Only recently has psychology inserted among the priorities on its agenda the study of the strategies of social mobilization and those pro-social acts directed at challenging the 'oppressive narrations' of the closed and exclusive structures which produce them, and in particular bringing about a revision of the strictly negative connotation connected with deviation. Society does, in fact, have a need for dissidents – both individuals and groups – who are capable of pointing out alternative ways of reaching goals which the majority would never manage to attain. The introduction of the concept of active minorities replaces such terms as deviance and anomia – central to the traditional approaches to social influence – with those of conflict and antinomy, thus redesigning the identity of deviant groups (Moscovici 1976). These last are no longer seen negatively as socio-pathological, but appear rather as groups endowed with a code of their own which is proposed to the majority as an alternative model. We are therefore no longer in the presence of 'residual bodies' situated at the very edge of the majority, but rather as active and innovatory subjects able to influence the majority from within a dynamic social process.

In conclusion, psychology is certainly more at ease when acting on the interpersonal and inter-group level, but we must bear in mind how many sociocultural elements there are which can influence the positive outcome of work on the micro-level to the point of thwarting them completely. For example, the promotion of solidarity clashes openly with the celebration of the culture of narcissistic individualism in the new environments delegated to the formation of personality, such as the television studios have become. The growth of human solidarity and of a culture of peace, on both the micro- and the macro-level, cannot but demand that the symbolic patrimony which constitutes the traditional categories (of religion, race, sex, customs and the like) be superseded by means of the elaboration of new codices of thought and language, capable of providing access to a genuine philosophy of difference, and thereby to authentic experiences of united social co-existence.

References

Boehnke, K., Hagan, J. and Hefler, G. (1998) 'On the development of xenophobia in Germany: the adolescent years', *Journal of Social Issues*, 54: 585–602.

Burr, V. (1995) *An Introduction to Social Constructionism*, London: Routledge.

Collier, G., Minton, H.L. and Reynolds, G. (1991) *Currents of Thought in American Social Psychology*, New York: Oxford University Press.

Euli, E. (1999) *Reti di formazione alla nonviolenza* [*Networks for Non-violence Training*], Torino: Pangea.

Galtung, J. (1996) *Peace by Peaceful Means: Peace and Conflict, Development and Civilization*, London: Sage.

Galtung, J. (2007) 'Peace by peaceful conflict transformation: A TRANSCEND model', in C. Webel and J. Galtung (eds) *The Handbook of Peace and Conflict Studies*, London and New York: Routledge.

Gandhi, M.K. (1951) *Non-Violent Resistance*, New York: Schocken Books.

Krahé, B. (2001) *The Social Psychology of Aggression*, Hove: Psychology Press.

Kvale, S. (ed) (1992) *Psychology and Postmodernism*, London: Sage.

Lerner, M.J. (1980) *The Belief in a Just World: A Fundamental Delusion*, New York: Plenum Press.

Lewin, K. (1948) *Resolving Social Conflicts: Selected Papers on Group Dynamics*, New York: Harper.

Martín-Baró, I. (1994) *Writings for a Liberation Psychology*, Cambridge, MA: Harvard University Press.

Milgram, S. (1974) *Obedience to Authority: An Experimental View*, New York: Harper and Row.

Montada, L. and Lerner, M.J. (eds) (1996) *Current Societal Concerns about Justice*, New York: Plenum Press.

Montero, M. (1991) *Psicologìa de la liberacion* [*Liberation Psychology*], Caracas: Universidad Central de Venezuela – Mimeografiado.

Moscovici, S. (1976) *Social Influence and Social Change*, London: Academic Press.

Sapio, A. (2004) *Per una Psicologia della Pace* [*For a Psychology of Peace*], Milano: F. Angeli.

Sapio, A. and Zamperini, A. (2003) 'Passive bystanders in front of violence and injustice: from inertia to change in social thinking', in G. Chiari and M. L. Nuzzo (eds) *Psychological Constructivism and the Social World*, London and Milan: EPCA-Angeli.

Zamperini, A. (1998) *Psicologia sociale della responsabilità* [*Social Psychology of Responsibility*], Torino: UTET.

Zamperini, A. and Testoni, I. (2002) *Psicologia sociale* [*Social Psychology*], Torino: Einaudi.

Zunes, S., Beth Asher, S. and Kurtz, R.L. (1999) *Nonviolent Social Movement*, Oxford: Blackwell.

18

Rethinking peace education

Alicia Cabezudo and Magnus Haavelsrud

Introduction

This chapter will discuss three components within which major choices are made in designing peace education practice. Peace education will be discussed in terms of its content and communication form in relation to the contextual conditions within which the educational action takes place. Choices made in these two components are decisive in defining the substance of any education – including education for peace. Differing conceptions of the substance of peace education are related to the implicit or explicit choices made within each component.

The history of peace education shows differing opinions concerning which principles should guide the selection of content and also which principles should guide the selection of methods of learning and teaching. In the following, principles of content selection and form preferences are discussed separately before they are seen in relation to each other and in relation to contextual conditions. It is to be expected that selected content and form are very much related to specific contextual conditions for the simple fact that some contextual conditions exclude the possibility of selecting specific contents and forms. It is therefore important to keep in mind that peace education is not limited to formal systems of education but also to informal education in the home and non-formal education in various voluntary organizations. So contents and forms may be quite different in these three educations depending upon contextual conditions. What may be impossible in the formal system may very well be possible in the home and in the non-formal sector including adult education. This realization is central to the field of political socialization, which has demonstrated how political preferences are developed in the home and in the school – sometimes with very discrepant results (Haavelsrud 1999: 55–80).

It seems obvious that participatory peace education of the kind we are going to discuss here presumes some fundamental rights and guarantees, i.e. democratic contextual conditions must prevail in order to secure that peace education occurs in relation to its role of creating social change. Therefore links between content, form and contextual conditions will be discussed as an integral process for setting adequate learning conditions that lead to social transformation.

Participation and democracy are described together as a challenging scenario where society must perform if it wishes to implement political, social and economic processes which lead to peace learning. Therefore peace education is to define a vision which will allow the setting of a course to be steered and collective objectives to be identified. There are twin objectives upon this happening: democratic society defines the dream it wishes to become a reality and it motivates actors to explore ways of making this come about. That is to say peace education in action.

Searching for the content in peace education

It is necessary to define what peace is in order to discuss the content of peace education. The following three approaches (Haavelsrud 1991) towards the discussion of the concept of peace are made in order to better understand the principles from which content may be selected. First, peace is seen in terms of what it is and what it is not. Peace is seen as the opposite of violence and three forms of violence are discussed, viz. direct, structural and cultural. Secondly, the concept of peace is discussed in relation to different levels, ranging from the individual to the global or expressed in another way: in terms of close, intermediate and distant realities as seen from the perspective of the individual. Third, peace is seen as a relatively permanent structure which enhances peace values but also as a process of interaction within structures which might be more or less peaceful or violent.

Content related to negative and positive peace

The idea that peace as the absence of war and/or any other form of organized physical violence has a long history and is quite predominant in common sense definitions of peace. The idea has also been incorporated into scientific definitions. Negative peace seems easy to exemplify and define. Negative peace certainly applies to cases where there is an absence of war between nations and civil war within a nation.

Positive peace is when social justice has replaced structural violence. In contrast to negative peace, positive peace is not limited to the idea of getting rid of something, but includes the idea of establishing something that is missing. While getting rid of structural violence or social injustice, positive peace implies the presence of social justice. Galtung has defined structural violence as the distance between the actual and the potential. This definition allows for many interpretations based on differing opinions about what is actual and potential. And such subjective understandings of present as well as future realities are important to recognize in peace education content.

On the other hand, scientific research can greatly help to transcend the level of subjective opinion about what 'is' (in existence) and what 'could be' (potential). The scientific monitoring of human society produces systematic studies of the quality of life in any given society. Thus, we have data on drop-outs from school, infant mortality, unemployment, social security recipients and juvenile crime. Social science research also shows how conditions of life vary from nation to nation and across social groups within one nation. Such empirical data on actual conditions are seen in the light of social theories which, to varying degrees, help explain the causes of such empirical findings.

Thus, our knowledge of the actual constitutes a large body of research. In contrast to the great emphasis in social science upon problems of the actual, our knowledge of the potential is less extensive. Questions about what 'could be' have not been dealt with in social science to the same degree as what is actually in existence.

This first approach in searching for the content of peace education points towards the importance of understanding the consequences in human suffering from both direct and structural violence. It is apparent that both types of violence often produce the same results in terms of death and human suffering. In a sense, one might argue that direct violence is worse than structural violence because its victims are often people who are not directly involved in any manifest conflict, but who are at the receiving end of a global structure of violence which oftentimes is hidden to its victims. This first approach in searching for the content of peace education also poses questions about the relationship between direct and structural violence and how they interact in support of each other.

The study of violence is an important part of the content of peace education. Hiding violence in pedagogical work will serve to legitimate it and make it difficult to develop an understanding of the causes of violence, including the cause that pedagogical preferences might conceal the study of violence and its causes. This latter phenomenon is an example of cultural violence – a third type of violence especially relevant to education as this education itself could be violent if it helped legitimate direct and structural violence. All cultural agencies in a society, including education to varying degrees, may choose to expose issues of peace and violence (religious institutions, mass media, universities, schools, etc.).

Content from micro- and macro-levels

In this second approach in discussing the concept of peace in the search for the content of peace education, Figure 18.1 is useful.

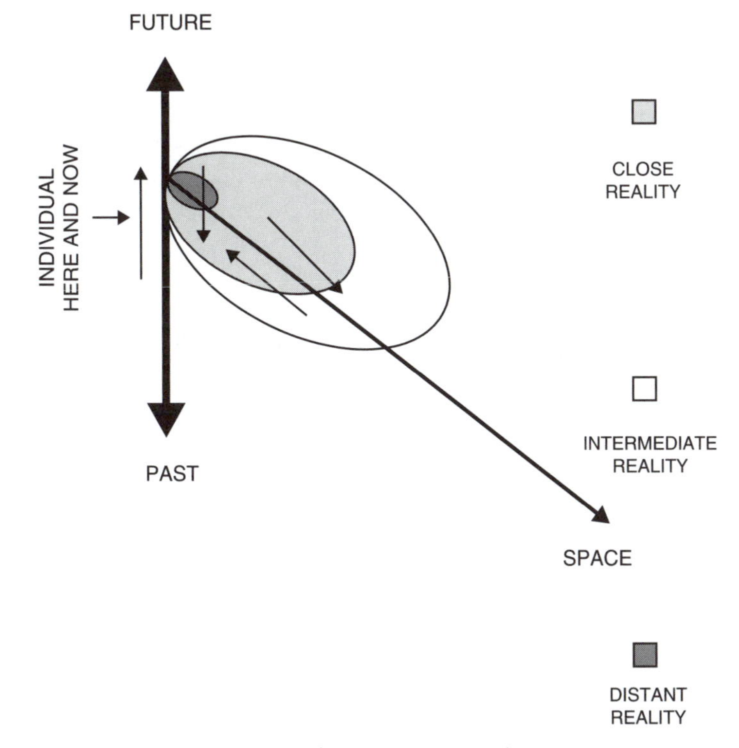

Figure 18.1. Relationships in time and space (Haavelsrud 1996: 55)

The space axis is horizontal and the time axis is vertical. Their crossing point illustrates the 'here and now context' of each individual. This context is constantly changing as time progresses and as situations outside the 'here and now' develop. The figure thus puts each individual in the centre of time and space.

Time can be visualized in terms of the past, the present and the future. The past is indefinite and so is the future. The present may be defined in terms of measurable time such as seconds, hours, days, weeks or months. The limits of 'the present' may be drawn by individuals in reference to events such as change of location (e.g. moving from home to school), change of activity (e.g. getting up in the morning means to change one's behaviour (from sleeping to eating breakfast) or change of social context (e.g. a guest arrives or leaves). 'The present' may also be a moment of *kairos* (Galtung 2004) in which only a few moments may seem like an eternity (e.g. waiting to get out of a catastrophic situation or a moment of deep love).

Departing from such 'now' contexts, the time axis stretches towards the past as well as the future. In Figure 18.1, three points in both directions are indicated to illustrate that time can be seen in terms of its distance to each individual, viz. close, intermediate and distant. The two arrows along the time axis illustrate causality over time. The arrow pointing upwards illustrates that the context at one time will influence the context at a later time. The arrow pointing downwards illustrates the idea behind the self-fulfilling prophecy: expectations, aspirations, hopes and visions of the future influence human behaviour at earlier time points (e.g. visions of the future influence our present tactics or strategies for transforming the present towards our visions).

The extreme left is the position of the individual, and the arrow pointing to the right signifies indefinite space in physical terms. As human life (with only a few exceptions) is limited to our planet, the crossing point of the outer circle and the space axis points out the physical limits for global society. Thus, this point represents planet earth in physical terms and the social, cultural, economic and political characteristics of global human society.

The arrow pointing to the left along the space axis illustrates the influence of society upon individuals living in it. The arrow pointing to the right along the space axis illustrates the fact that society is a human product. Thus, the figure points out that there is a dialectical relationship between world society and each individual. Each individual is involved in an everyday context which has linkages to contexts that are outside this context. 'Outside' contexts have been called intermediate and distant realities in the figure.

Space can be measured in physical terms (e.g. metres and kilometres) but also in terms of societal dimensions, such as social, cultural, economic and political realities. As we know, there is a great variation in these realities from context to context. Each individual is closely interwoven with specific realities and distantly separated from others. Whatever dimensions are used, everyday reality of individuals and groups varies in terms of social, cultural, economic and political facts. In a comparative perspective, specific realities can be seen in terms of their similarity or dissimilarity with other realities.

Although dissimilarity between everyday contexts seems to increase as a function of physical distance, there is no simple relationship between physical distance and type of social, cultural, economic and political characteristics of two or more everyday contexts. In one and the same geographical location, e.g. in a large city, there may be greater dissimilarities between two contexts than between two locations on different continents. Thus, there may be more corresponding characteristics between the contexts of upper-class families in New York and London than between these two contexts and the contexts of poor families in Harlem and East London. The latter pair may have more in common with each other than with their upper-class counterparts in the same city.

In this discussion on how micro and macro realities find their place in the content of peace education it is important to keep in mind that each specific and everyday context in which people are in direct interaction with each other has certain links to the higher levels of some society which has, in its turn, certain social, cultural, economic and political characteristics. This is illustrated by the space axis in the figure. Everyday contexts are embedded in larger and political contexts.

When time and space are seen together, it becomes apparent that there are possible causal chains arriving at each individual from any time in the past and future and from any place along the space axis. In turn, there are possible causal chains departing from each individual to any point in the future. This possible influence is not restricted to the individual's own future, but includes the future of society and of the world. Thus, the individual can potentially influence the future world as well as any part of it. Thus the area of influence lies in the area above the space axis, i.e. in the future. Past and present have already been created and cannot be changed. Only our understanding of the past and present realities can change, not the realities themselves.

As the past interactions among individuals, social groups and institutions have created present society, it seems clear that one important relationship is that macro produces micro. If micro contexts can be seen as resulting from the macro contexts, one might argue that macro is in micro. This means that every time direct, structural or cultural violence is manifested in a specific close reality it is more than probable that causes of this violence are to be found outside that micro reality.

This leads to the impact of micro upon macro. The characteristics of the larger context are dependent upon the existence of similar characteristics in the micro context. Without the existence of attitudes, opinions and valuations among people at large in the multitude of micro contexts in everyday life, the idea of gender equality, for instance, would simply be an abstract idea without any roots in people's existence. Such roots in the micro are a necessary condition for the continual maintenance of the characteristics of the larger macro society. Thus, the trunk, branches and leaves of the societal tree would fade away without the support of energy flowing through the roots. In this sense, each small root is a mediator of the energy necessary for the tree as a whole to continue its existence. In other words, micro produces macro. This production can be limited to reproduction, but it can also be production (or creation) when new roots are established from seeds that have fallen off the old tree. In both cases, one might argue that the influence of micro upon macro is such that micro is present in macro.

The content of peace education may be found in all contexts because violence as a phenomenon is not isolated to only some everyday realities. Some everyday realities have more violence than others but oftentimes the search for the causes of violence in one specific everyday reality may have to be done in other everyday realities. The specific manifestation of violence (direct, structural and cultural) in the everyday life of people is therefore part of the content of peace education. But the content stretches to other close realities where the causes of this violence may originate. The links of violence between one close reality and another are to be traced in the search for that content. The concept of peace is relevant to all times and all places (contexts). If peace is limited to a specific time and context (place), the result would be that the relationships between micro and macro as suggested above would be excluded from consideration. Such exclusion might lead to a distorted view of peace, because it is more and more difficult if not impossible to find a context which is completely isolated from the rest of the world. Just like weather systems develop in constant interplay with each other, it would seem that the content of peace education would have to open up for both micro and macro perspectives in the perception of violence in micro realities and the search for the causes of this violence. Without such thorough diagnosis of the problem, is it going to be possible to develop content about a realistic vision of peace and the road towards this vision?

Content about peace as structure and process

A third way of searching for the content of peace education is to see peace as a structure as well as a process. A peace structure is by definition a structure that has institutionalized values of peace, i.e. absence of violence and presence of social justice, participation and diversity. Just like any building, its basic features would allow for certain interactions and make other interactions difficult or impossible. To stick with our example from architecture, one extreme type of building might be the one that is designed for individualism. This building would have no common rooms and each individual unit would be separated from the others. The singles condominium might be the closest example in the real world. Another extreme might be the commune, which is designed according to the value of collectivism. This structure would have large areas for common experiences and few, if any, rooms for individual or private activity. In between, there are all kinds of structures that allow for certain interactions and exclude others. A most common structure is the core family home.

A structure is taken to mean the presence of relatively permanent relations between specific units (Mathiesen 1981). The units can be any social actors ranging from the individuals and groups on the micro-level to the nations and transnational organizations such as the UN on the macro-level. A structure for peace would be a structure that enhances peace values, both those values that enhance negative peace (absence of direct violence) as well as those values that affirm peace (social justice, participation and cultural diversity). In order to test whether a specific structure secures peace, an investigation of the interactions among two or more units within the structure is necessary. Looking closer at interactions of this kind it is possible to find out the extent to which the values of peace are realized over time. If peace values are strengthened, we are witnessing a peace process.

As the discussion on peace as structure has already shown, a structure is defined in terms of interaction over time between specific units. The structures established through interactions can be maintained or changed through new interactions. Therefore, a non-peaceful structure can be changed to a peaceful structure through new interactions. Such peaceful interactions can occur within a non-peaceful structure. If such peaceful interactions are allowed to develop over time into new patterns, they will in the end become structures of peace within the overall structure of non-peace. At this moment, the new structures may be so powerful that their confrontation with the violent structure may lead to an overall peaceful structure. The opposite might also be the result, viz. repression of the peaceful structure by the violent structure.

History is abundant with examples of such processes. Actually, it seems that most interactions based on the value of independence and autonomy during the decolonization period have led to new structures that in the end were successful in dismantling the status quo. Today, we are witnessing liberation movements on the part of women, ethnic minorities, groups suffering from human rights violations, the working class and the poor all over the world. Such interactions among various groups are often based on values of peace and have started as interactions among members of these groups beyond the control of those in power. Such interactions will, if continued over time, involve more and more people, and in the end become structures of peace confronting existing violent structures.

In searching for the content of peace education, it is important to consider peace as both a structure or a building as well as a process. A peace structure means the presence of relatively permanent relations between structural units that enhance peace values. The idea of 'relative permanence' implies that peace is a structure, as opposed to a process. But peace is also the process of interaction between specific units as long as the interaction is geared to the enhancement of peace values.

Communication form in peace education

In Figure 18.2, the integration of the world of practice and the world of reflection is highlighted. Everyday life may be characterized by habitual behaviours adapting to contextual conditions that may be both violent and nonviolent. The embodiment of oppressive elements in such habitual behaviour is one factor that sustains the oppression. Cultural preferences in everyday life may support violence and inhibit peace. At the same time, cultural preferences are part of the identity of the person and can only be changed according to the will of the person, even though external pressures for such change are strong. It is contended here that the cultural style of the learner is an important factor to take into account in any learning process. It is argued that the practical subjective preferences manifested in everyday life are always places to start the learning process in spite of the fact that the subject might be a violent actor in that context.

The voice of all learners in the dialogical process is therefore necessary in peace education. These voices blend into a chorus of dialogical communications. Most false tones in this chorus will hopefully sooner or later be corrected in the educational process. Some may remain, hopefully without dominating the dialogical harmony. Dialogical learning (Freire 1972: 45–9) is characterized by codification and de-codification processes in which the world of practice in everyday life is put on the agenda for discussion in the educational interactions. This discussion may reveal challenges of everyday life that become themes for further dialogue. The description of a learner's own reality is codified by the teacher in order that the learner may then de-codify the teacher's attempt at mirroring the discussion. If accepted by the learners, the description or theory coming from the participants themselves and codified by the teacher may become a critical light on the initial practice so that this practice is transformed to another practice based on the insights of the initial discussions. This transformation from practice to praxis implies that the practical world of everyday life has been understood in a theoretical light coming from the discussions of the participants themselves and accepted as a guide for changes in everyday life. If the codification is not accepted, a new dialogue takes place in order to arrive at a better insight into the world of everyday life and its possible transformation.

Figure 18.2 has the form of a large arrow. This illustrates the continuous development of dialectics between theory and practice – it is never static. The numbers illustrate the different

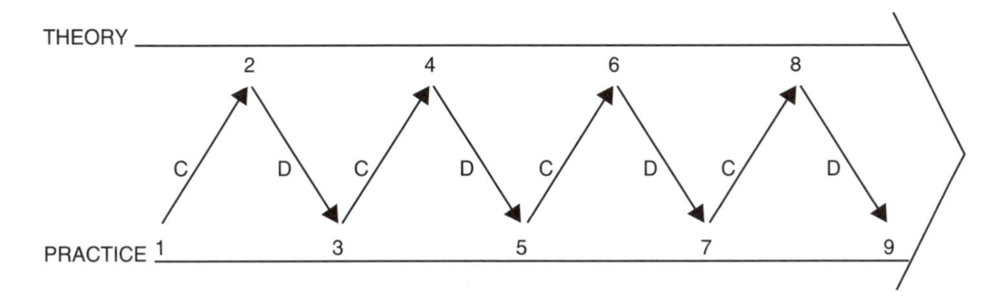

Figure 18.2. The dialectics between theory and practice

phases in this development. The number 1 signifies the first phase in the dialogical process. In this phase the initial meeting of the group and its teacher/facilitator/coordinator takes place in order to select the generative theme for continued content development. The discussion about a generative theme constitutes the materials to be used in the teacher's codification (C). The codification represents a bridge between the concrete and the abstract. In the de-codification (D), the more abstract description of the practice or initial theoretical understanding of the practice is tested in reference to that part of the empirical reality that is known to the participant. At this stage the theory may be changed, some subjective perceptions accepted and others refused. After a new phase of codification new de-codifications follow. C and D are positioned in the middle between the two lines illustrating theory and practice. The distance between the two processes of codification and de-codification, as well as between theory and practice, is dependent upon many things – not the least of which is how far the participants have reached in the development of theory starting from their own practice.

The process of development of theories departing from social practices – codification – and returning to practices with new knowledge from theory – de-codification – in order to apply and enrich the reality in a new turn leads Paulo Freire to define education as a practice of freedom. Freedom of practices, freedom of thinking and freedom to build interconnections in order to create new thoughts in a transformative path. And so works peace education.

Peace education would be – as well – a liberalizing process in which people – not as recipients but as knowing subjects – achieve a deepening awareness both of the sociocultural reality which shapes their lives and of their capacity to transform that reality. Hence peace education would be a practice of freedom and not domination – also a conscious act, one of choosing rather than one of being given – an act of cognition rather than mere transfer of information.

Peace education is also a dialogical act – at the same time rigorous, intuitive, imaginative and emotional. The educational process has to create conditions for horizontal dialogue; but dialogue applied towards the concept of pedagogic strategy. It is a truth criterion and it includes communication and intercommunication. Dialogue is not only a generous act of human understanding of the other. It is an ontological and epistemological need for knowing the truth and searching with the others. Peace education needs a dialogical, communicative rationality and the acts of knowing and thinking are directly tied to one another as knowledge requires communicative expression (Morrow and Torres 2004: 69). Dialogue does not exclude the conflict as truth does not come from the conformation of my vision with the vision of 'the other'. Confronting other visions, it is necessary to arrive at the common understanding of problems and building solutions. This confrontation does not mean that dialogue within those who think and dream differently has to be divided or segregated. There is no democratic growth in society, no civic learning – therefore no peace learning – without the co-habitance of different groups enjoying the same rights. Rights to struggle for their dreams and hopes interacting with others with different dreams and hopes in a challenging process of 'crossing borders' in an individual and collective dimension (Giroux 1997).

If dialogue is the main form in which peace education builds knowledge and understanding as a learning process for approaching contents and 'the others', participation is the practice by which this dialogue is embedded along the whole process.

Participation is a fundamental right of citizenship, the means by which a democracy is built and a standard against which democracies should be measured. Participation means that all the groups of society (the whole) are able and are invited to gather, to discuss and to exchange ideas not only in policy-making decisions but also in planning issues related to their daily life, needs and hopes. They should be able to plan and decide their learning themes and issues according to their needs and realities, which is to say, according to their contextual conditions.

So in a way contextual conditions 'dictate' the themes and at the same time 'condition' the themes for analysis, discussion and research. In this process, the passing from 'silent-voting objects' to 'participative subjects' is a pre-condition for the development of a democratic society with rights to all and duties to accomplish (Cabezudo forthcoming).

So the participative component of the peace learning process is also a practice of freedom itself, and a praxis where reflection and action occur.

This process initiated as a participative one through dialogical communication (see Figure 18.2 – position 1) implies the ability to detach oneself from reality and look at it critically – codification. This process is to be followed by de-codification – the ability to envision possible futures and possible strategies for social change. The ability to think about one's situation with an eye on social change is crucial for peace education.

Therefore peace education by applying processes of codification and de-codification in its methodology comes to be a training for critical thinking itself.

Man has the capacity to look at reality critically through a process of detachment for which man is endowed. If we adapted this to peace education, we would say that it is a challenge to the human being to recognize and analyze the causes of discord, the conditions of personal and structural violence and to search for possibilities to bring about change. Trying to relate the issue of peace to the experience of people is useless unless it is preceded by an effort to build certain tools which will enable them to lead a critical process for understanding and creating alternatives, which means reinstall hope in societies.

The peace learning process creates a space for meeting, for talking about common issues and problems, as well as challenging the actors in this process to find new ideas tackling borders by confronting solutions for their individual and collective hopes–needs–dreams.

The practice of dialogic communication and participatory decision involves a collective democratic process. And this is one of the main goals in peace education.

On content and form in peace education

As it has been discussed here, peace education is not just concerned with different concepts of peace and what you teach but also with how you teach and the contextual conditions within which you teach. In fact, there is a desirable unity between the content, the form and the context where the learning process takes place.

If peace education is the pedagogy that has to deal with the goal of change in order to set up an education that does not reproduce the system but envisions social transformation, it is evident that content and form are linked components of its substance where changes have to be made. At the same time, they would produce changes in the contextual conditions due to their dialectical dynamics.

Hence it is highly possible that peace education might improve the reality through its practice as an alternative pedagogy. A conceptual view that is based on the critical pedagogical understanding of knowledge as a social product – legitimated and distributed – that expresses particular interests and values – is never 'objective' per nature. So the role of practices is fundamental in feeding theories and building new actions where these theories can be contrasted and rebuilt.

According to this assumption educators would be forced to confront the relation between knowledge, power and control and include transformative action in their practices. These pedagogical practices should offer procedures for reflexive consciousness raising and demystification of the officially handed-down discourse. Figure 18.2, previously depicted, shows how this process occurs.

Often contents are selected and presented as abstract structures with obscure concepts, and with poor contact with daily life and real problems. A structure with its own codes for selected chosen people – the only ones able to de-codify the meanings for others – who depend on 'de-codification experts' in order to understand 'the world', the society, the reality . . . no matter if it is close or far.

Peace education contents will not start from abstract categories but from people's needs, captured in their own expressions. The traditional concept of content as a summing up of different themes is replaced by the analysis of micro-reality, the selection of problems, connections with the macro and the emerged dialogue among them. So in the learning process students deepen into roots and causes and share ideas on possible solutions in a dynamic exercise of 'crossing borders'. Gender, class, ethnic, religious, social-economic and cultural differences will flow through dialogue, will be part of the discussed problems – and at the same time part of the solution.

According to this process to know is not to accumulate knowledge, information or data regarding certain themes or problems only. To know implies everyday knowledge, taking care of small things and thinking about the local and the global in a linked understanding so that the outer world will be part of everyday life as well. (See the earlier section on the relationships between the micro and the macro.) There is no division within instructive significance and everyday educative significance. It is the everyday knowledge of the social group that incorporates individual and collective 'learnings and understandings'. And while people incorporate knowledge through dialogue, other meanings are incorporated such as 'how we know', 'how we produce knowledge' and 'how society uses knowledge'. To know is also changing attitudes, learning to think critically, establishing relationships and creating links.

This learning process would depart from collective discussions on significative themes for people, would continue searching for solutions to close problems with a reference to macro structures, use existing practices as useful background and try to shape solutions as a reflective social construction – the praxis.

The links within form and content are evident. The way dialogue is created and themes are selected builds a particular dynamic that feeds and enriches both. Hence peace learning acquires a particular significance itself as a dimension of a transformative tool for change in all the actors of this process, not only in their own 'insides' but also for their potential 'outside' actions – in the closer and far realities.

> *Content becomes form, in a way form is the content. And both – acting as agents for change – have the powerful chance – the challenge – to transform contextual conditions.*

On contextual conditions

Important assumptions underlying peace education initiatives need to be discussed critically in light of the realization that the whats, hows and whys of peace learning are all problematic in that there is no absolute answer to be found without reference to the contexts in which learners live their lives and how these contexts relate to the outside world. The experience of living provides the learner with the possibility of 'reading the world' so that they can: (1) observe and diagnose violence (physical, structural, cultural) in their own context and in its external relations to other contexts; (2) search for root causes of such violence, both internal to (including the self) and external to their own context; (3) formulate visions of nonviolent alternative futures; (4) reflect upon appropriate means of change; and (5) act with skill towards the creation of new peace processes and buildings. Let these five components serve as an informal guide on how a peace education process directs learners from an initial point of observation and diagnosis of violence towards practical actions in order to transform that reality to peace and nonviolence.

Important contextual conditions for peace education comprise the types and levels of violence manifested in the context and how that violence is caused by both micro- and macro-forces as explained in the time-space diagram. Contextual conditions also relate to the possibilities present for transcendence of violence involving the development of desirable visions of the future and possibilities for action, for transforming present violence to nonviolent futures. Contextual conditions are therefore both internal and external to the context. In reference to the above discussion about the relationships between micro and macro, contextual conditions may be seen as both internal and external at the same time.

This reflects a main idea in Bourdieu's (1984) theory: the habitus of the human being and objective and material structures in the larger society seek harmony. This means that the lifestyle and personality of each human being has been influenced by the outside world at the same time as the human being is challenged to transform the outside world to fit cultural preferences. This force towards harmony between cultural expressions or lifestyles and the outside world makes changes in both habitus and the outside world possible.

Contextual conditions relate to micro- as well as macro-realities. Such realities can be described in terms of social, political, cultural and economic aspects and how these relate to each other. Understanding contextual conditions therefore involves nothing less than understanding both micros and macros and their relationships. This means beginning to develop an understanding of the relationships between close and distant realities and how different forms of violence at different levels interact in space and time. To develop a conception of this is a requirement for finding effective spaces for new interactions in the peace process.

A highly relevant part of contextual conditions would be the educational policies selected by the authorities. The formal education system in most countries is characterized by division of knowledge into specific subjects, teachers with specific competencies in these subjects, the grouping of students into classes and the division of time into periods and breaks. These basic characteristics – others could be added such as evaluation procedures and discipline codes – are important structural components, which allow for certain types of initiatives for introducing peace education into the curriculum and exclude other types. Thus, curriculum preferences may make it possible to change the content of a specific subject in such a way that it would deal more with peace issues. Such change in the content might not have any significance for the other components, such as the methods employed, the division of knowledge into subjects and the division of time into periods and breaks.

If, however, the form of education is regarded as a problem, as well as the way knowledge has been divided into subjects, the peace educator runs into other problems of a structural nature, i.e. the peace education project might contradict the basic characteristics of the structure in which it is introduced. If, for instance, a peace education project is based on the principles of problem orientation and participatory decision making it could not, without problems, be introduced into a school system which rigidly practises the division into subjects, classes and periods.

It would be extremely difficult to realize problem-oriented and participatory education through a prescribed plan for a subject, carried out by a teacher in a rigidly structured classroom situation with 30 students, in periods of 45 minutes each. Apart from the rigidity imposed by these three components (subject, class, time), the greatest barrier for peace education projects might be the rules laid down in educational systems concerning evaluation of the students, through which students are sorted into categories according to their achievement in school subjects focusing on what is known but not on what is not known.

Through this discussion about contextual conditions with examples from the structure of the formal school system, it should be clear that a peace education project might be in harmony or disharmony with it. Therefore, it is possible that so many disharmonies exist that the structure itself must be changed before peace education can be introduced.

The question then arises whether the structure can be changed through changes in form and content, or whether this is impossible until changes are brought about in the contextual conditions in society, which has produced the educational structure.

On content, form and contextual conditions

The analysis of how structure can be changed through form and content or whether structure can be transformed after changes if contextual conditions occur leads the discussion to a consideration of *the appropriate scenario* for this process; that is to say, a scenario to develop peace education in desirable conditions. These conditions should privilege dialogical form, allow discussion on contents by all the actors engaged in the learning process and build critical thinking. Simultaneously actors should develop practice in reality by operative and practical actions.

This scenario is without any doubt that of democracy – at micro- and macro-level – where guarantees for freedom of thinking and action help the start of transformative processes at individual and collective level. Therefore a question arises immediately on what is the substance of democracy related to peace education (Gadotti 2004)

Let us discuss it in a macro-framework first. A democratic scenario for transformation means a scenario where a 'civilizing process' can be developed in contradiction to the 'uncivilizing process' characterized today by the erosion of legitimacy of political authority, combined with the impact of globalization and the emergence of powerful transnational economic forces. This kind of scenario originates an explosive combination in the creation of structural and cultural violence with linked consequences on direct violence. Contextual conditions do not help peace learning – content and form reflect this non-peaceful environment – and the emerged interactions probably create a new spiral of violence (Kaldor and Luckham 2001: 52–7).

The key to building a democratic peace – that is to say, desirable contextual conditions for peace learning – is to break through the vicious cycle of violence and to reconstruct relations based on dialogue, agreed rules and mutual understanding. Ending violence is very difficult without democratization of structures and it is a huge challenge for peace education to consider that isolated changes on content and form within certain contextual conditions would provoke transformation itself.

Many times democratic contextual conditions are not present *and change happens all the same.* Certainly it was not in the space of the formal system – that reproduces goals, subjectivities and policies of the macro political structure – but in the diverse spaces of the non formal and informal learning settings. Having in mind peace education goals, non-formal and informal agendas goes across almost every issue, showing a tension between explicit and hidden sides and enriching the possibilities of learning and developing concepts/practical skills in 'real life situations', which means learning in the broadest sense of the word. The search for a harmonious interaction within formal, non-formal and informal education is one of the most difficult challenges for education and certainly an issue that must be considered very seriously in the field of peace education. A pedagogic attempt to explore, analyze, study and search for possibilities to solve this complicated link related to our field is a contemporary issue that needs to be accomplished.

Non-formal and informal learning challenge structures by creating opportunities for skipping the 'rules' of non-democratic formal systems and allowing them to build peace and nonviolent learning as ways of resistance through creativity and imagination. These learnings will confront non-democratic, hard realities by developing liberatory strategies rooted in social and collective experiences and actions.

Non-formal and informal education bring alternative spaces for peace learning when a specific context created by structures does not allow the development of free and critical thinking through constructive autonomous procedures. The process of learning and exchanging knowledge as a social practice is one of the most important means non-formal and informal education offer to peace education. And the potential of its strength was challenged many times under non-democratic contexts resulting in transformative social learnings. Social practices and learnings created in this process operate as a tool for resistance in those contextual conditions where education is manipulated, denying critical thinking, emancipation and freedom.

Peace education in non-formal contexts considered as a strategy and a tool for resistance departs from the assumption that: (a) education is a social production and not merely knowledge transmission; (b) education for freedom is a precondition to a democratic life – meaning a life with autonomy, sovereignty and real decision-making power in daily life; and (c) education implies refusal of authoritarianism, manipulation, hierarchical relationships and exacerbation of power control ideology from specific individuals/groups over others (Cabezudo forthcoming).

Resistance is the path and the way to promote transformation in violent contexts where those conditions do not allow change or actions towards change. The Nobel Peace Prize Laureate Adolfo Perez Esquivel described the concept of resistance as a 'state of consciousness' (Perez Esquivel 2004) that strengthens work in difficult contextual conditions where violence prevails; a state of consciousness that leads to active participation within close or far realities creating new social conditions through practice.

When contextual conditions block positive changes in society, collective and individual resistance operates as a motto that feeds actions and works as a strategic tool towards transformation. Departing from difficult – often violent – 'presents' dreams and visions on diverse 'futures' helps to lead concrete transformative actions into reality and pave the way to liberation. Isn't this a practical peace learning?

Resistance is also a collective strategy for being seen and heard in circumstances when the context is not interested or does not allow certain people/groups/problems to be seen or discussed at social or political levels. Resistance has been the path, as well, that led many countries to freedom and democracy like South Africa and most of the present Latin American republics. Latin-American contextual conditions along the 'wave' of dictatorships between 1960 and 1985 are a model sample of how non-formal education assumes peace learning when the formal system turns back. During this period the rule of law disappeared; civil, political and social freedoms did not exist. Peoples from almost all countries of the continent – Brazil, Paraguay, Chile, Argentina, Uruguay, Bolivia, Peru – lived under the horror of being kidnapped, murdered or tortured due to their beliefs, their hopes or their dreams for justice and social change. In Central America and Colombia, the same period was characterized by 'open war' within national parties. The whole region was opposite to a desirable scenario where contextual conditions would produce transformation and change. The formal system – functional to the macro political structure – turned schools, universities, colleges and teachers into reproductive tools of the dominant ideology.

But change occurs . . . People understood those contextual conditions *as a challenge and not as a defeat.* People reacted against 'domestication' of their lives by 'others' in a certain space and time – the place where they live and the time where they live. They reacted to contextual conditions where the future is manipulated in a predetermined way. The future is something inexorable – something that will necessarily occur but decided by 'others'. In refusing the domestication of time and space, the importance of the role of subjectivity in history was recognized. Therefore challenges for change broke fixed a priori concepts of possible 'defeats', and visions of hope and nonviolent contexts prevailed. Inexorable futures handled by obscure forces were transformed into desirable futures towards which society struggles (Cabezudo forthcoming). Isn't this a peace learning lesson?

On this assumption non-formal and informal education settings brought the spaces where nonviolent and peace actions at micro-level could work as alternatives. Those alternatives were built in 'non-domesticated places and times' confronting hard macro-contextual conditions in a devastating struggle for autonomy, freedom and democracy.

A true struggle for peace against structural and cultural violence (Galtung 1998).

Along with this process social movements, civil organizations and individuals develop resistance – nonviolent forms in communication and action. These forms reach other people's minds and souls and society/individuals shape collective visions for change that with time will become realities and not merely utopian 'futures'.

Resistance works and it is a peace learning process interesting to study and research in other contextual conditions different to those exemplified here by the Latin American case.

After dictatorships the process of democratization works out as an educative path in which the transformation of contextual conditions – due to the passing from dictatorships to democracies – brings changes in the ways of thinking, acting and reconstructing the reality. This process is a good example of how context interacted with content and form in terms of transformation. Internal and external conditions flowed from the democratization process breaking pre-existent structures and 'liberating' people at individual and collective level. Therefore these internal and external 'new' contextual conditions strengthen processes of economic and social change.

Formal systems and peace education have to take good note of these kind of processes as educative and transformative strategies for their own disciplinary fields.

Working on a micro- or macro-level, the centrepiece of any peace strategy has to be the restoration of trust and confidence in ourselves and towards others. It has to counteract fear and hate with a strategy of hearts and minds. Contextual conditions have very much to do with this. It should be stressed, however, that any such strategy is very difficult and likely to be of long duration. Education and peace education is a long-term process whose goals will be accomplished in realities sometimes rather far from the departing point.

Therefore if we think of education as a continuum of practices in reflection and action producing daily-life praxis and building knowledge by ourselves and with others, it does not matter when we achieve the prescribed goals. What matters is the process itself and the significance of its path. What matters indeed is the development of critical thinking, the analysis and discussion of problems, and how new alternatives are created in a democratic process. At the same time, the dynamics of the process itself provoke changes in contextual conditions.

The transformative condition in the substance of peace education has moved from a potential to a real-world status setting, changing and creating new ways of thinking and acting.

Peace education is a tool for transforming internal–external contextual conditions and building – at the same time – a liberatory and creative process in both dimensions.

Peace education as a transformative social process in democracy

We have noted that peace education in a democratic social system would develop successful processes which would bring it to a state which is to be attained and maintained. Democracy and peace education as a whole learning participatory process takes place at both social and individual levels. Democracy is not confined only to the way the state exercises its power and to citizens' participation. It is also the way people communicate with each other in the family, at school, within association groups, as well as religious or ethnic communities and society as a whole. Early socialization through family interaction and local educational policies promoting active dialogue and participation creates a democratic atmosphere for a transformative process in education. The correct application of the representative democratic systems and the participatory democracy model as well as the strategies of participatory budgeting in the development of public policies open spaces to reflect on new perspectives of the concept of peace education related to democracy and its capacity to build transformation at social and political levels working on individual and social grounds.

Peace education has to identify appropriate teaching–learning activities, new contents and transformative strategies for the settlement of peace learning pedagogies coming from political and social praxis as well as new tools and forms developed in non-formal practices.

With this picture in mind, peace education is a suitable field for discussing and selecting, in a dynamic way, a whole kit of contents to develop alternatives for transforming violence and conflictive situations. It is – as well – the field for practising dialogue as a basic form of communication. Dialogical democratic form as peace learning praxis. Peace education – like true democracy – has an inclusive view of who in the community should be involved in the decision-making process. Room is made for every person's input and interaction. Participation is not mandatory but expected and provided for. Responsibility then lies with the individual to take advantage of a political peaceful process designed to make participation by the ordinary citizen as easy as possible.

Assuming education as practice for freedom, the concepts of democracy and peace education appear complementary in the sense that they work in a dynamic synergy facing the risk – and the challenge – of crossing borders 'for reading the world' – the micro and macro worlds – more completely. Inviting social actors – the whole population – in different spaces of formal and non-formal education to reflect and act over structural and cultural violence.

Borders are always surrounding us. Academics and educators who occupy very narrow borders do not realize that they also have the capacity to capture and block our minds for better understanding. Many times borders work as mechanisms of structural and cultural violence at macro-level and micro-contextual experience (see Figure 18.1).

We assume here peace education as a learning process that would allow the linking of interactions crossing borders towards direct and structural violence as well as cultural confrontation or misunderstandings. According to this assumption the practice of dialogue and participation in democratic structures work as strategic tools for change, transformation and more justice.

Hence the generation of conditions for peace education; in other words, the building of this capacity in the social system, is the primary task of democratic public policies related to the educational field. This might be a main issue in the agenda of democratic governments since it aims to identify the conditions to be attained and proposes criteria of evaluation that will assist in the preparation of a plan for action and follow-up for the creation and strengthening of peace education programmes in the formal system and non-formal policies.

In such terms, peace education and peace learning ceases to be a theoretical dissertation of a vague purpose, and it acquires the dimension of an action plan, with the possibility that goals can be defined by it, results evaluated by qualitative methods and status constantly monitored, so that alarm bells will ring when the condition in which it takes place is not secured.

Based on the lessons learned particularly from African and Latin American contexts, it is assumed that democratic social systems have the conditions to make their purposes viable as a whole and in each particular project. The process is part of an objective and contributes to it, if there are individuals or organizations with the capacity to influence society as a whole, if the strategic actors use their capacities positively, if individuals take part in the various stages of the process and if the process has a positive effect on the transformation and change of society.

In sum, to develop peace education as a transformative process in democracy certain requirements must be met:

- The construction of a collective vision of nonviolent and transformative development which reflects some collective purpose to be achieved and which stimulates a large rank of social actors.
- The recognition of individual or collective leadership with the capacity to call upon the commitments of society to the promoted educational process.
- The development of constructive relations between actors committed to the process. The importance of the identification of the actors, their roles and their potential contributions presupposes a precise definition of how the public and private national and sub-national factors of power interact, the obtaining of consensus, legitimacy and leadership.
- The building of institutional capacity to ensure that the public policy required by a peace education process – formal and non formal – is effective. This aims to deepen discussion of the instruments of administrative efficiency, transparency in public administration, innovative practices and financial sustainability of experiences.
- Civic participation in the various steps of the peace education planning and ongoing process. With due regard to the importance of democratic governance, it will be necessary to define its scope and especially its status as a tool. There need to be definitions and discussions of the risks of applying it, the way in which those risks can be faced and its limitations.
- The obtaining of results through indicators which reflect transformation towards non-violent conditions, collective learnings and changes within societies where the process of peace education and peace learning takes place.

The notion of building and practising peace learning in democratic environments entails the notion of a democratic citizenship where social actors are responsible and able to participate, choose their representatives and monitor their performance. These are not only political but also peace learning pedagogical practices. The construction of a democratic citizen implies the construction as well of a pedagogic subject committed to nonviolent practices and peaceful means ready to interact with others and with the close/far reality. And this process of construction of the democratic pedagogic subject – individual or collective – is not only a process of cultural nurturing, but it also involves principles of pedagogic and democratic socialization where peace education has a vital role to accomplish.

How is the constitution of this pedagogical democratic subject is related to peace learning processes? How do the content, form and contextual conditions on which this process occurs affect the constitution of a peaceful democratic subject open to transformation, solidarity and change by nonviolent means?

This is the dilemma of the present world and present time. Here and now.
And this is the main question we have tried to discuss and reflect on in this chapter.

Conclusion

This chapter has intended to explore the substance of peace education and its nature as it is essentially political in the sense that it calls for the analysis of power and authority within the structures and processes. In other words, peace education and the praxis and learning that it entails, is a challenge across genders, generations and cultures and an important part of life-long leaning. Peace education – peace learning – takes place in informal, non-formal and formal settings. It involves cultural action for peace and this organic set of actions helps shape the way in which peace is defined and generated in different contexts.

Even in those situations where conflict is not evidently present, the dynamics and interaction generated from living together in harmony are a lesson we have to underline and learn as a wise peace education praxis. It is therefore evident that we need peace-minded leadership and vision, but such leadership can only be effective and sustainable if public opinion supports and actively promotes the visions and strategies that make peace real and nearer. This requires that we look at the transformation of conflicts through peaceful means. This, in turn, requires a dialogically-oriented praxis, and a peace learning approach by all actors directly involved in the transformation, as well as actors who are marginal to the epicentres of direct violence.

Peace education should help build visions of peaceful futures in a world in which diversity and plurality can be celebrated without fear and threat. These visions need to be realistic enough so that it is possible to find the road map to the vision and as that road may be long or short it would have certain milestones along the way for verifying that the direction is correct. But as we have pointed out, no diagnosis, no vision and no road map would be sufficient if all of this reflection is not combined with action founded on a conception of the knowledge that we have summed up in the concept of praxis. Without the realization of this combination of reflection and action it is believed that peace education would end up in either verbalism or activism.

The main goal of this chapter is to demonstrate how peace education can contribute to the process of change at the micro- and macro-level by developing critical thinking, dialogue across borders, social attitudes favouring voluntary restraints on the use of force, settlement of disputes without resorting to direct violence, acceptance of the rule of law and multicultural understanding.

The challenge to peace education is not to adapt to contextual conditions that contribute to violence but to develop knowledge supporting alternatives to violence, whether that happens in formal, informal or non-formal education. A state may leave few options for the selection of both content and form in peace education in the formal education system. A state may choose to control the non-formal sector. But so far no state has been able to control informal education in the everyday life of family and friends. And under the most violent conditions the power of the people has been effective in the struggle for their rights and envisioned world of hope and justice. The knowledge, processes, strategies and mechanisms through which this struggle towards a more desirable world finds its form and the transformative consequences of actions taken – praxis – is the main content of peace education in the present world.

This chapter has intended to demonstrate that an alternative peaceful future is defined not only as the absence of open hostilities or negative peace but as the presence of peacemaking processes and contextual conditions likely to ensure a durable, just and positive peace. It implies a state of well-being, a dynamic social process in which justice, equity and respect for basic human rights are maximized and violence, both physical and structural, is minimized.

Peace education will not achieve the changes necessary for peace. Rather, it prepares learners to achieve the changes. It aims at developing awareness of social and political responsibilities, guiding and challenging people to develop their own learning from individual and collective actions. It encourages them to explore possibilities for their own contribution to resolving the problems and achieving better conditions for living their lives by themselves and with others.

The approach to peace education in this chapter has emphasized a critical dimension, questioning existing structures, power, norms and educational values. While we were aware of the limitations of peace education, we have seen that it arouses hope by demonstrating that people are capable of acquiring the required skills and by illuminating creative learning moments.

> *Peace education can definitively help to provide the requisite inspiration and direction to move beyond a culture of violence to envisioning and working toward a better world for all.*

References

Bourdieu, P. (1984) *Distinction*, Cambridge, MA: Harvard University Press.

Cabezudo, A. (forthcoming) *Learnings from Democracy Culture of Peace and Human Rights: A Challenge of Our Time*, for Fundación Cultura de Paz, Madrid: International Project on Education for a Culture of Peace: Asia, Africa, America and Europe.

Freire, P. (1972) *Pedagogy of the Oppressed*, Harmondsworth: Penguin.

Gadotti, M. (2004) 'Paulo Freire. Pedagogy and Democratization Process in Brazil: Some Views of his Theory, Method and Praxis to Introduce a Debate', presentation at the World Social Forum, Porto Alegre, Brazil.

Galtung, J. (1998) *Conflict Transformation by Peaceful Means (the Transcend Method): Participants' Manual, Trainers' Manual*, New York: UN Disaster Management Training Programme.

Galtung, J. (2004) *Transcend and Transform*, London and Boulder, CO: Pluto and Paradigm Press.

Giroux, H. (1997) *Pedagogy and the Politics of Hope. Theory, Culture and Schooling: A Critical Reader*, London: Westview Press.

Haavelsrud, M. (1991) *Fredslæring (Peace Learning)*, Tromsø: Arena.

Haavelsrud, M. (1996) *Education in Developments*, Tromsø: Arena.

Haavelsrud, M. (1999) *Sources of Political Socialization*, in J. Calleja and A. Perucca (eds) *Peace Education: Contexts and Values*, Lecce: UNESCO and Pensa Publishers.

Kaldor, M. and Luckham, R. (2001) 'Global transformation and new conflicts', *IDS Bulletin*, 32, 2.

Mathiesen, T. (1981) *Law, Society and Political Action*, London: Academic Press.

Perez Esquivel, A. (2004) La *Gota de Agua: Relatos de experiencias de Lucha y Resistencia*, Buenos Aires: Amorrortu Editores, English version forthcoming.

Part 4

Peace across the disciplines

19

Peace studies as a transdisciplinary project

Chadwick F. Alger

The titles of the chapters that have preceded this one, and those that follow, make it very obvious that peace studies flows across many disciplines. Chapter titles include various dimensions of conflict formation and transformation, and human rights, gender, journalism, psychology, education, business, and peace movements. Other chapters focus on political science, international law, health, religion and language. Of course, authors of these chapters draw on many other disciplines.

No doubt readers of this chapter have a diversity of perspectives on the transdisciplinary aspects of peace studies. Their approach has been shaped by the path that they took into peace studies. It is likely that most readers of this chapter began their education and personal inquiry in a specific discipline. Eventually they became concerned with a specific peace and conflict issue and found a specific dimension of peace studies relevant to the issue that was challenging them. Quite likely this aspect of peace studies also led them to relevant literature in other academic disciplines.

For example, I was educated as a political scientist with a speciality in international relations. I developed a research focus on the UN and was seeking understanding on how inter-state violence might be avoided. My search for insight led me to Johan Galtung's distinction between negative peace (elimination of direct violence) and positive peace (elimination of constraints on human potential due to economic and political structures) (Galtung 1969). Relevant also was my 1967 attendance at a conference of the International Peace Research Association in Sweden, where scholars from Africa, Asia and Latin America offered analyses of structural violence. What an eye-opener it was to learn that people around the world define peace differently, depending on what it is that is preventing them from fulfilling their potential. Will it be caused by quick death from direct violence, or the much more prevalent slow and painful death from structural violence?

Is peace and conflict studies a discipline?

Of course, peace studies has made great progress in the 40 years since I became aware of its emergence. In 2006, the Peace and Justice Studies Association (PJSA) and the International

Peace Research Association (IPRA) Foundation compiled a *Global Directory of Peace Studies and Conflict Resolution Programs* (Seventh Edition). It profiles over 450 undergraduate, masters' and doctoral programmes and concentrations in over 40 countries and 38 US states. No doubt some readers of this chapter acquired their first knowledge about peace studies with one of these programmes and may consider peace studies, or peace and conflict studies, to be a discipline. But at the same time they too must recognize that they are dependent on relevant knowledge emerging from a range of linked disciplines.

Whether or not peace studies is considered to be a discipline, there is no doubt that research in the past couple of decades has produced a great advance in understanding of the causes of war and other forms of seriously disruptive conflict. At the same time, there has been a remarkable development in knowledge about preventative measures, particularly with respect to strategies for long-term peace-building. Some of these contributions are a result of a distinguishing characteristic of the research of some peace researchers. The research mainstream of much of social science – certainly this is true of international relations – is focused on explaining what caused certain aspects of human conditions that now exist. On the other hand, the agenda of many peace researchers is to acquire knowledge that can be applied in developing strategies for achieving a vision of a more peaceful world in the future.

Unfortunately, the results of this research are not reaching most social science students because of the disciplinary organization of most colleges and universities. Most scholars who have a broad background in peace studies do not have the disciplinary qualifications, particularly publication in mainstream disciplinary journals, that is required for appointment to a position in political science, sociology, psychology, anthropology, history, etc. Thus, unless there is a department or programme of peace studies, or peace and conflict studies, scholars with degrees in one of these disciplines tend not to be appointed when the main focus of their teaching and research is peace studies. At the same time, they may receive little credit for their publications in peace research journals, such as the *Journal of Peace Research*, the *International Journal of Peace Studies*, *Peace and Change*, *Peace Review* and *International Journal of World Peace*.

In writing an essay on 'Peace studies as a transdisciplinary project', our first approach was to provide information on the contributions to peace research in each relevant discipline. We quickly decided to take another approach because of the difficulty of giving a disciplinary identity to research that almost always flows across disciplinary boundaries. This would have required frequent discussion of the boundaries that we were applying because there is great diversity in the definition of disciplinary boundaries by different individuals, disciplinary departments and journals. Meanwhile, as we reviewed the literature, we became ever more aware that current research is revealing how people everywhere, no matter what their profession or occupation, are involved in creating conditions that are leading toward peace or toward disruptive conflict. Therefore, we decided that it would be most useful to provide the reader with concrete examples of the vast range of human involvements in activities that have an impact on peace and conflict conditions.

While reviewing the literature for this essay we also reached the conclusion that peace research does have the qualities of a discipline. It is certainly important that peace research is one dimension of virtually all disciplines. On the other hand, it is vitally necessary that the various dimensions be assembled, as is the need in efforts to develop long-range peace-building strategies. As with all other disciplines, the peace research discipline will always have a need to continually be linked to, and apply, the insights of other disciplines. But, at the same time, other disciplines need the insights that the peace research discipline can offer them with respect to how the dimension of peace research that is an aspect of their discipline fits into a more holistic view of peace.

An indication of the emergence of peace studies as a discipline has been the emergence of peace studies textbooks. David P. Barash, with disciplinary roots in psychology, wrote *Introduction to Peace Studies* in 1991. A revised version, written jointly with Charles P. Webel, *Peace and Conflict Studies*, appeared in 2002. The chapter titles in this 577-page textbook reveal that the peace research on which it is based reaches across all social science disciplines. The textbook opens with chapters on the meanings of peace, peace movements, the meaning of wars and the special significance of nuclear weapons. Following are chapters on these 'levels': individual, group, state, decision-making, and ideological/social/economic. These are followed by chapters on negative peace that include diplomacy/negotiations/conflict resolution, peace through strength, disarmament/arms control, international organizations, international law, world government and ethical/religious perspectives. Chapters on building positive peace include human rights, women's rights, ideological well-being, economic well-being, nonviolence, and personal transformation and the future.

Another recent, somewhat shorter, textbook of 407 pages, *Peace and Conflict Studies: An Introduction* (2000), was written by Ho-Won Jeong, who has political science disciplinary roots. After providing nine chapters of background necessary in a textbook, Jeong divides a concluding section on Strategies for Peace into nine topics: control of military power, conflict resolution and management, human rights, self-determination, development, environmental politics, global order and governance, nonviolence, and peace movements. Of the 91 sections in the nine topics, at least 80 offer a peace strategy. These topics in the Environmental Politics chapter reflect the disciplinary range: building global consensus, international policies, management of the global commons, international organizations and coordination, nongovernmental organizations, struggles in indigenous communities, sustainable development and prospects for future cooperation.

It is very important to recognize that the impressive growth in peace studies knowledge has taken place in two primary arenas of human activity. One is research institutes and universities. The other is knowledge acquired by those working in organizations attempting to cope with seriously disruptive social conflict. In this chapter we will primarily focus on the impact of research on the interdisciplinary spread of peace research. But it is also necessary to briefly indicate how practitioners who are coping with challenges in the 'real world laboratory' have also made significant contributions.

Emergence of peace tools in the UN System

Because I have for years focused much of my attention on the UN System, my understanding of learning about peace-building through practice has been significantly shaped by the quest for peace in these organizations. In many respects this is a quite appropriate 'laboratory' because of the growth of the United Nations to a membership of 191, including virtually all states. This means that agendas, debates and dialogue are open to contributions from all states, increasingly supplemented by contributions from civil society around the world, thereby enhancing the global relevance of results. The evolving emergence of peace tools presented in Figure 19.1 is obviously a very simplified version of a very complicated process. Nevertheless, Figure 19.1 offers a useful perspective on the emergence of a growing array of peace activities that reach across ever more academic disciplines.[1] Peace researchers who examine this figure will quickly become aware that there have been times when strategies for long-term peace-building emerged through practice long before they received significant attention from researchers.

Before the League of Nations was founded, *diplomacy* (1) and *balance of power* (2) were the

	19th century	1919	1945	1950–1989	1990–	
NEGATIVE PEACE	Diplomacy (1) Balance of Power (2)					
	I	League Covenant	UN Charter	UN Practice	UN Practice	NGO/People Movements
		Collective Security (3)	Collective Security	Collective Security	Collective Security	
				Peacekeeping (9)	Peacekeeping	
		Peaceful Settlement (4)	Peaceful Settlement	Peaceful Settlement	Peaceful Settlement	Track II Diplomacy (17)
		Disarmament/ Arms Control (5)	Disarmament/ Arms Control	Disarmament/ Arms Control	Disarmament/ Arms Control	Conversion (18)
		II			Humanitarian Intervention (15)	Defensive Defence (19)
					Preventive Diplomacy (16)	Nonviolence (20)
POSITIVE PEACE			Functionalism (6)	Functionalism	Functionalism	Citizen Defence (21)
			Self-determination (7)	Self-determination	Self-determination	
			Human Rights (8)	Human Rights	Human Rights	Self-reliance (22)
			III	Economic Development (10)	Economic Development	Feminist perspective (23)
				Economic Equity (NIEO) (11)	Economic Equity (NIEO)	Peace education (24)
				Communication Equity (12)	Communication Equity	VI
				Ecological Balance (13)	Ecological Balance	
				Governance for Global Commons (14)	Governance for Global Commons	
				IV	V	

Figure 19.1. Emergence of peace tools in the League of Nations and the UN system (Alger 2006: 10)

primary available peace tools. Because of the tendency of balance of power to result in arms races that ended in wars, the League Covenant attempted to replace it with *collective security* (3), through which military aggression would be prevented by the threat of response with overwhelming military force by members of the League. The Covenant made an effort to strengthen diplomacy by adding procedures for *peaceful settlement* (4) of disputes (through mediation, conciliation and the World Court). The League also created procedures for *disarmament and arms control* (5). These approaches emphasized the use of, and control of, violence in the pursuit of peace, sometime referred to as 'negative peace'.

Practice under the League and some of the lessons of the First World War, contributed to the drafting of the UN Charter in 1945. Significantly, these three approaches were again incorporated into the UN Charter in 1945. The greatest difference between the Covenant and the Charter is three peace strategies added to the latter by those assembled at San Francisco: *'functional' cooperation* (6) on economic and social issues, *self-determination* (7) and *human rights* (8). These approaches, in contrast to the earlier three, emphasize the creation of peaceful economic, social and political relationships – sometimes referred to as 'positive peace'. The new Economic and Social Council (ECOSOC) was based on growth in functional activities of the League during its brief history. The Trusteeship Council continued League supervision over the treatment of colonies seized by the victors in war, but it was the Declaration Regarding Non-Self-Governing Territories (Chapter XI) that opened the way for future self-determination advances under the Charter. And the mention of human rights seven times in the Charter, including the second sentence of the preamble, was a dramatic departure from the League Covenant.

As our most significant peace 'laboratory', the present UN System of organizations reflects very significant learning since its founding. We have learned that collective security – actually a form of deterrence – is as dangerous as any other deterrence strategy if it fails. The application of collective security in the Korean War, in which we tottered on the edge of the Third World War, taught us this. On the other hand, *peacekeeping* (9) forces are a useful new invention.

Functional collaboration has flowered as the UN System has developed agencies that cope with a broad array of global issues, such as health, refugees, labour, education, clean water, communications, balance of payments and housing. Self-determination has been one of the United Nations' greatest success stories, as it has assisted a multitude of states in Africa, Asia and the Caribbean to independence and immediate UN membership.

With respect to human rights, under UN auspices the states assembled have drafted standards for human life on the planet through the Universal Declaration of Human Rights, and covenants on civil and political rights and economic, social and cultural rights, and an array of other treaties on genocide, women's rights, elimination of racial discrimination, rights of children, rights of labour, environment, hunger and malnutrition, religious discrimination, and many others.

With the attainment of self-determination by states created by colonialism, the number of member states in the United Nations with widespread poverty grew rapidly. Difficulties in achieving successful functional cooperation in a United Nations in which wealth and resources are so unequally distributed among members soon became apparent. Thus began the effort to narrow the gap through *development* (10) programmes in the poorer countries. Despite significant successes in some locations, the gap between the rich and the poor of the world has continued to grow, at the same time that the world economy has become increasingly interdependent.

As worldwide systems for exploitation of resources, production, marketing and communications reached ever more intrusively into the most distant human settlements and rural areas, the peacelessness of population explosion in urban shantytowns in cities in the poorer countries provoked a searching dialogue on the meaning of development. This debate shifted the focus from development projects in the poorer countries to the inequities in the international economic system. A debate that began in the General Assembly grew into a UN Conference on Trade and Development (UNCTAD), to an UNCTAD organization, to a demand for a new international economic order (NIEO). In 1974, this campaign for *international economic equity* (11) produced a declaration for a NIEO, a plan of action for a NIEO, and a Charter of the Economic Rights and Duties of States.

Frustration over the unwillingness of the industrialized countries to conduct global negotiations over a NIEO contributed to demands for *international communications equity* (12) and emergence in the 1980s of the demand, centred in UNESCO, for a new international information and communications order (NIICO). The domination and control of worldwide communications by media corporations based in cities in the industrialized countries mirrors that of transnational corporations for resource exploitation, production and marketing. As a consequence, leaders in the poorer countries complain that control of worldwide communications by corporations in Europe and North America prevent the people in the industrialized countries from learning about the actual condition of people in the poorer countries and the reasonableness of demands for a NIEO.

Questions of *ecological balance* (13), too, can be seen as evolving out of global debate on the meaning of development. Ecological problems became a prominent issue on the agenda of the UN System beginning with the UN Environment Conference in Stockholm in 1972. The initiative came from the industrialized countries, and at first the environment was perceived to be their issue. Initially, many in the poorer countries even suspected that environmental initiatives from the industrialized countries were a covert strategy for preventing their development. But by the time of the UN Conference on Environment and Development (UNCED) in Rio de Janeiro in 1992, environmental issues were perceived to be a concern of people from all parts of the world. A new UN Commission on Sustainable Development (CSD) is leading the search in the early twenty-first century for meanings of development that can include ecological balance. At the same time, the squalor, disease and death that result from destruction of the human habitat are increasingly judged to have the moral equivalence of similar peacelessness produced by weapons of war.

As new technology has enabled humankind to exploit more extensively the depth and the breadth of the commons (atmosphere, space, oceans and the two polar regions), this activity becomes an ever greater threat to peace – threatening war, environmental disaster, inequitable sharing of resources of the commons and inequitable access to the transportation and communications potential of the commons. Thus *governance for the global commons* (14) has emerged as a significant dimension of peace. Some consider the drafting of the United Nations Convention on Law of the Sea (1982) to be the most significant event in the struggle to develop peaceful governance for the commons. The Convention sets territorial limits and provides regulations for ocean transit, for sharing of resources in and under the oceans, for control of pollution, and for scientific research. This was followed by the creation in 1994 of the International Seabed Authority, with its headquarters in Kingston, Jamaica, and the International Tribunal for Law of the Sea in Hamburg, Germany. Both have 145 member states.

The more recent emergence of *humanitarian intervention* (15) offers a striking example of how the emergence of new peace tools gradually reinterprets the UN Charter. Article 2.7 states: 'Nothing contained in the present Charter shall authorize the United Nations to intervene in matters which are essentially within the domestic jurisdiction of any state.' Nevertheless, emerging human rights standards have been used to justify UN intervention in places such as Kosovo and Somalia. At the same time, interventions in the 'failed states' of former colonies reveal how the achievements attained under one tool, in this case *self-determinism* (7), may lead to conditions that require the creation of another tool, such as humanitarian intervention.

At the same time, the recent emergence of *preventive diplomacy* (16) reveals a striking demand from many quarters for preventive measures that take a long-term perspective and thereby overcome the tendency to respond to threats of violence too late to prevent it. This has been accompanied by a remarkably rapid development of academic works that offer relevant insight. The efforts of these researchers and others to make their work useful for policy-makers are striking.

Our brief overview has revealed remarkable progress in fashioning tools that are now available for enhancing peace and well-being in the twenty-first century, as well as reflecting the escalating involvement of more and more disciplines in peace studies. Not only have functionalism, self-determination and human rights been supplemented by economic development, economic and communications equity, ecological balance, and governance for the commons, but these new themes have deepened our insight on neglected dimensions of earlier approaches. We now understand better the full meaning of self-determination, as we have learned about its economic and communications dimensions. We now have insights on the ecological aspect of human rights. At the same time, new conflict resolution institutions, such as the International Seabed Authority and the International Tribunal for Law of the Sea, have been created.

As practitioners in the UN System have introduced an ever larger array of peace tools, they have created an increasing number of organizations that apply these tools. The names of these organizations offer readers a quick view of the disciplinary range of these organizations. In Table 19.1 we have developed this view by taking key words out of the names of

Table 19.1. Functions appearing in names of UN Systems agencies (Alger 2006: 6)

Number	*UN Systems agencies*	*Number*	*UN Systems agencies*
1	Agriculture (sa)	25	Investment guarantee (sa)
2	Atomic energy (ro)	26	Indigenous issues (ecosoc)
3	Banking (sa)	27	Intellectual property (sa)
4	Civil aviation (sa)	28	Labour (sa)
5	Children (ga)	29	Maritime (sa)
6	Chemical weapons (ro)	30	Monetary fund (sa)
7	Climate change (sa)	31	Meteorology
8	Crime prevention (fc)	32	Monetary (sa)
9	Criminal tribunal (sc)	33	Narcotic drugs (fc)
10	Culture (sa)	34	Nuclear test-ban (ro)
11	Development (ga) (fc)	35	Peacekeeping (sc)
12	Disarmament (ga)	36	Population (fc) (ga)
13	Drug control (ga)	37	Postal (sa)
14	Education (sa)	38	Reconstruction (sa)
15	Environment (ga)	39	Refugees (ga)
16	Finance (sa)	40	Science (sa) (fc)
17	Food (sa) (ga)	41	Settle investment disputes (sa)
18	Forests (ecosoc)	42	Social development (ga)
19	Health (sa)	43	Staff college (ga)
20	High technology	44	Statistics (fc)
21	HIV/AIDS (ga)	45	Sustainable development (fc)
22	Human rights (fc)	46	Telecommunications (sa)
23	Human settlements (ga)	47	Tourism (sa)
24	Industrial development (sa)	48	Trade (ga)

Continued overleaf

Table 19.1. (Continued)

Number	*UN Systems agencies*	*Number*	*UN Systems agencies*
49	Trade and development (ga)	52	Volunteers (ga)
50	Training and research (ga)	53	Women (fc) (ga)
51	University (ga)	54	World trade (ro)

Notes
ecosoc Other bodies under ECOCOC
fc Functional Commission, under ECOSOC
ga Under General Assembly
ro Related organization
sa Specialized Agency
sc Under Security Council

54 organizations in the organization chart of the UN System (www.un.org/aboutun/chart.html) and placing them in alphabetical order. When reading this list it is virtually impossible to think of a discipline without a reason to include one or more of these organizations in its research agenda. It also appears that members of all professions may be involved in the UN System.

The disciplinary and professional scope of peace studies has also been extended by the escalating involvement in the UN System of NGOs/civil society, local authorities and business. The final column in Figure 19.1 lists eight peace tools that have been largely developed by NGOs/civil society: Track II Diplomacy (17), Conversion from military to civilian production (18), Defensive Defence, development and employment of strictly defensive weapons and strategies (19), Nonviolent movements for social change (20), Citizen Defence, deployment of nonviolent techniques for national defence (21), Self-Reliance, development rooted in the satisfaction of individual human needs, (22) Feminist Perspectives with respect to social relations and visions of alternative futures, (23), and Peace Education (24) (Alger 1999: 30–9).

The International Union of Local Authorities was founded before the League of nations, in 1913. Since the Second World War other worldwide associations of local authorities have been created with a special issue focus, including peace, the environment and the challenges confronted by larger cities. Now there is a World Association of Cities and Local Authorities Coordination (WACLAC), a UN Advisory Committtee on Local Authorities and projects assisting the economic development of cities in UNEP, UNDP, UNICEF, the World Bank and the UN Human Settlements Programme (Alger 2003: 98–103).

The UN website states that, 'The business community has played an active role in the United Nations since its inception in 1945. A number of UN organizations have a successful history of co-operating with business. Recent political and economic changes have fostered and intensified the search for collaborative arrangements' (www.un.org/partners/business). In 1999, Secretary General Kofi Annan challenged business leaders to join an international initiative – the Global Compact – that would bring companies together with UN agencies, labour and civil society to support ten universal principles in the areas of human rights, labour, the environment and anti-corruption. There are now Global Compact Offices in six UN agencies: UNHCHR, UNEP, UNDP, UNIDO and the UN Office on Drugs and Crime. A recent volume by Andreas Wenger and Daniel Mockli, *Conflict Prevention: The Untapped Potential of the Business Sector* (2003), perceives that there is potential for business to play significant roles in preventing disruptive international conflict.

Emphasis on multi-track and multiple methods

The growing disciplinary range of peace research is dramatically reflected in peace research trends. Limited space makes it necessary to illuminate these trends with only five examples: emphasis on multiple tracks and multiple methods, the growing range of activities with respect to peacekeeping and NGO/civil society, post-conflict peace-building, preventive long-term peace-building and concern for local arenas of conflict within states.

An excellent example of the multiple track approach is Louise Diamond and John McDonald's *Multi-Track Diplomacy: A Systems Approach to Peace* (1996). Their multi-track approach builds on 'second track diplomacy' that is sometimes referred to as 'citizen diplomacy' because the second track has often involved people who are not government officials. Diamond and McDonald find a need to identify these nine tracks because of the diversity of the professions and activities now included in the 'second track': Government (peacemaking through Diplomacy), Nongovernment/Professional (peacemaking through Professional Conflict Resolution), Business (peacemaking through Commerce), Private Citizen (peacemaking through Personal Involvement), Research, training, and Education (peacemaking through Learning), Activism (peacemaking through Advocacy), Religion (peacemaking through Faith in Action), Funding (peacemaking through Providing Resources), Communications and the media (peacemaking through Information). Their description and analysis of each track includes very informative lists of participating individuals and organizations. This volume offers important insight on the challenges confronted by participants in increasingly significant multi-track diplomacy. They are challenged to have knowledge of an array of peace-building processes, of the ways in which activities in their track are linked to these processes and of the interdependence of their actions and those in the other eight tracks.

Another recent trend has been emphasis on the development of peace strategies consisting of multiple peace tools. This is overcoming a tendency in the past by many to emphasize one or two approaches, such as disarmament or human rights. One example of the multiple peace tool approach is Ho-won Jeong's *Peace and Conflict Studies: An Introduction* (2000). After providing nine chapters of background necessary in a textbook, Jeong divides a concluding section on Strategies for Peace into nine topics: (1) control of military power, (2) conflict resolution and management, (3) human rights, (4) self-determination, (5) development, (6) environmental politics, (7) global order and governance, (8) nonviolence, and (9) peace movements. Of the 91 sections in the nine topics, at least 80 offer a peace strategy. These topics in the Environmental Politics chapter reflect the disciplinary range: building global consensus, international policies, management of the global commons, international organizations and coordination, nongovernmental organizations, struggles in indigenous communities, sustainable development and prospects for future cooperation.

The growing disciplinary range of peace research is dramatically revealed in peace research trends that are reflected in the scope of Barash and Webel's textbook, *Peace and Conflict Studies* (2002). Limited space makes it necessary to illuminate these trends with only five examples: emphasis on multiple tracks and multiple methods, the growing range of activities with respect to peacekeeping and NGO/civil society, post-conflict peacebuilding, preventive long-term peacebuilding, and concern for local arenas of conflict within states. William Zartman's edited volume on *Peacemaking in International Conflict: Methods and Techniques* (2006) is another example that reflects the multiple-tool approach to peacemaking. It describes an array of tools and skills for peacemaking and assesses their usefulness and limitations. Included are chapters on negotiating, mediation, adjudication, social-psychological dimensions of international conflict, problem-solving discussions between unofficial representatives of groups of states engaged in violent protracted conflict, roles for religion in peacemaking, the contributions education and training can make to peacemaking, the economic tools of peacemaking, and the role of force in peacemaking.

Growing diversity of peacekeeping and NGO/civil society activities

Another perspective on the growing multidisciplinary range of peace studies can be gained by examining the growing diversity of activities involved in two kinds of peace activities: peacekeeping operations and non-governmental organization (NGO)/civil society activities. Peacekeeping, invented by UN practice, first consisted primarily of lightly armed UN forces patrolling a ceasefire line. It tended to be highly successful in preventing violence but rarely successful in resolving the conflict that led to violence. More recently, peacekeeping forces have been employed in 'humanitarian intervention' before conflicting parties have achieved ceasefires. In addition, missions have been expanded into what Ratner calls *The New UN Peacekeeping* (1995), that include domestic police forces, supervision of elections, overseeing transitions to new governments, monitoring referenda on self-determination, supervision and delivery of humanitarian assistance and development aid, supervision of the disarming of conflicting parties, creating and training new police forces, protection of refugees, and protection for NGO/civil society organizations involved in a diversity of economic, social and political activities. Thus peacekeeping has been extended to evolve into what is now frequently called peacemaking.

The relevance of NGOs/civil society to peace studies now ranges from their local to global activities. Jackie Smith (1997: 47) has selected 631 NGOs which she classifies as Transnational Social Movements (TSMOs), and indicates the issues on which they are focused: human rights (27 per cent), environment (14 per cent), women's rights (10 per cent), peace (9 per cent), world order/multi-issue (8 per cent), development (5 per cent) and self-determination-ethnic (5 per cent). The 31 kinds of activities of these TSMOs can be grouped into six types: (1) they create and mobilize global networks; (2) they participate in inter-governmental organization (IGO) conferences; (3) they are involved in meetings of the UN Security Council, Economic and Social Council and Security Council; (4) they facilitate inter-state cooperation outside these meetings and at other places around the world; (5) they engage in activities within states; and (6) they enhance public participation in a variety of ways (Alger 1997: 262).

Useful insight on the diversity of NGO/civil society roles is illuminated by the roles that they play in peace-building in the field. They are extensively discussed in *Peacebuilding: A Field Guide* (Reychler and Paffenholz 2001: 75–442). They participate in selecting the type of mediation, in identifying the key actors in the mediation, and in designing the mediation process. They are involved in monitoring an array of peace-building activities. They are involved in relief aid and development cooperation. They train local participants in peace-building. They are involved in promoting media coverage and endeavour to insure that it is compatible with their aims. They attempt to diminish the impetus of conflicting parties to seek revenge and punishment. They offer images of a peaceful future. They attempt to bring weapons of violence under control.

Post-conflict peace-building

Two approaches in the development of peace strategies reflect more recent emphasis on combining a broad array of peace tools in long-term strategies: post-conflict peace-building and preventive long-term peace-building. In *Peacebuilding and Postconflict Societies: Strategy and Process*, Hon-Won Jeong (2005) provides a broad overview of this emerging field. The concerns that led to post-conflict peace-building are illuminated by Robert Rothstein in an edited volume, *After the Peace: Resistance and Reconciliation* (1999). He emphasizes that a peace process is not so much what happens before an agreement is reached but what happens after it and illuminates this conclusion with several case studies and contributions from eight other scholars. The present significance of post-conflict peace-building is reflected in a February 2006 speech in Addis Ababa by UN Secretary General Kofi Annan, when he called for urgent support for post-conflict peacebuilding:

> In recent years, the international community has come to recognize that conflict resolution calls for a comprehensive approach in which parties emerging from conflict require assistance not only in negotiating peace agreements, but also in building and consolidating peace. That means providing humanitarian and reconstruction assistance, ensuring security and security-sector reform, promoting good governance, and in the broadest sense demonstrating to people that peace brings real dividends – improvements in their standards of living, in their sense of opportunity, and in the way their societies function. The recent establishment of a new United Nations Peacebuilding Commission is an important step in this regard.
>
> (UN, SG/SM/10347)

Necla Tschirgi (2004: 9) has listed the ten 'operational principles of post-conflict peace-building' in a document prepared for a conference jointly sponsored by the International Peace Academy and WSP International (formerly the War Torn Societies Project): (1) Has political, social economic, security and legal dimensions. (2) Security is key. (3) Requires a holistic approach guided by a hierarchy of priorities in response to the needs of each specific case. (4) The people of the war-torn society must own the process and be actively involved. (5) Support from external actors is necessary but mechanisms must be established so that external and internal actors work within a coherent strategy. (6) A commitment to local capacity building from the earliest stages is vital. (7) Rapid response is vital but reconstruction is a long-term process that may take a generation. (8) Adequate, predictable and flexible funding is essential. (9) Reconstruction requires local, national, regional and international responses. (10) Accountability is vital. Commitment to 'do no harm' is essential.

Numerous volumes have analyzed the significance of one peace tool in the pursuit of post-conflict peace-building. We have space for only a few examples. Frishna Kumar has edited two volumes. One is *Rebuilding Societies After Civil War: Critical Roles for International Assistance* (1997). Kumar has particular concern for how more effective policies and programs can be designed and implemented for food, security, health, human rights, military demobilization, resettlement and local reconciliation. The other is *Post conflict Elections, Democratization and International Assistance* (Kumar 1998). The book is rooted in the belief that election monitoring is important because elections are the cornerstone of creating a democratic political system. The focus is on planning and conduct of elections in eight countries (El Salvador, Haiti, Nicaragua, Cambodia, Ethiopia, Angola, Mozambique and Liberia), the technical and political success of those elections and their consequences for democratization.

Good Intentions: Pledges of Aid for Post Conflict Recovery (1999), edited by Shepard Forman and

Stewart Patrick, focuses on the consequences of failure to fulfil pledges of aid in 'post-conflict' situations. The six case studies in this volume contribute to concluding insights on how delays and failures in aid follow-through can undermine peace settlements. They offer insight on how delays and failures in aid follow-through can threaten vulnerable polities whose collapse would endanger regional peace and security.

Birgitte Sorenson, in *Women and Post Conflict Reconstruction: Issues and Sources* (1998), notes that women have broad local participation and serve as a reserve labour force in wartime, but then is puzzled by the fact that they are expected to withdraw when the war is over. Also, women rarely participate in formal peace negotiations. She believes that reconstruction efforts would be significantly strengthened if women were given roles in all aspects of post-war reconstruction.

The potential that forgiveness provides for moving on to build post-conflict relationships has recently received wide attention. We will mention three quite different works on forgiveness. The first is an empirical study, 'The Propensity to Forgive: Findings from Lebanon', – an effort to apply psychological research on forgiveness to conflict among Catholics, Maronites and Orthodox in Lebanon (Azar 1999). A sample of 48 Catholics, Maronites and Orthodox were asked to respond to brief stories about events in the Lebanese 'civil' war. It was found that all respondents 'were to a certain extent willing to forgive, at least under some circumstances' (Azar 1999: 177). Educated people were more prone to forgive than the less educated. Surprisingly, 'the participants expressed practically equivalent propensity to forgive whether the offender was a member of their religious group or a member of another religious group.' Very significant is the finding that 'when remorse and apologies were present, it was easier to forgive; especially for less educated people' (Azar 1999: 180). The authors caution that this self-reporting data requires a follow-up based on actual forgiveness behaviour.

The second work, Henderson's *The Forgiveness Factor: Stories of Hope in a World of Conflict* (1996), presents 13 case studies 'of morally compelled actors and their effects in various parts of the world over fifty years' since the establishment of a centre of reconciliation and change by the Swiss Foundation for Moral Re-Armament. The case studies range across North Africa, Japan, Cambodia, South Africa and the South Tyrol. In an introduction, 'Science and faith come together', Joseph Montville (editor of *Conflict and Peacemaking in Multiethnic Societies*) asserts that these cases are 'raw data for a rigorous new theory of personal and political conflict resolution that had its origin in spiritual experience and is being studied at diverse secular research institutions' (Montville 1996: xiii–xviii).

In the third work, *An Ethic for Enemies: Forgiveness in Politics* (1995), Donald Shriver discusses German–US, Japan–US relationships and race in America, seeking to understand the implications of Christian faith: 'The principal purpose of the whole study is to identify both the need and the actual presence of forgiveness in political history, and thus to encourage readers, as citizens, to consider the political wisdom inherent in this neglected virtue. Is forgiveness indispensable for turning political enmity into political neighbourliness?' (Shriver 1995: 11). Shriver offers a penetrating analysis of the problems created for the future by the insistence on revenge for past deeds. Then he takes up the diverse facets of apology and forgiveness and the difficulties confronted in mobilizing and implementing them in political contexts involving large numbers of people.

Closely related to these volumes focusing on forgiveness is the Truth and Reconciliation strategy applied in South Africa after the demise of apartheid. No doubt this approach to 'post-conflict' peace-building will be the focus of extensive inquiry in the near future. Useful for future inquiry will be *A Brief Evaluation of South Africa's Truth and Reconciliation Commission:*

Some Lessons for Societies in Transition (Simpson 1998). In considering transitions from authoritarian to democratic rule, he places the TRC somewhere between two extremes: the prosecutions of 'war criminals' in post-Second World War Germany, and the blanket amnesties for gross violators of human rights in post-Pinochet Chile. Simpson sees the high level of violent crime in South Africa today as rooted in 'experiences of social marginalisation, political exclusion and economic exploitation which are slow to change in the transition to democracy' (p. 29). He concludes that in order for the rhetoric of reconciliation to become reality it is necessary 'to tackle those deep rooted social imbalances, which – at the most fundamental structural level – underpin the culture of violence' (p. 30). In other words, we might say that he concludes that the TRC approach can only be effective if it is creatively combined with other peace-building tools.

The growing significance of post-conflict peace-building in practice, and its disciplinary and professional range, is reflected in the number of organizations in the UN System that explicitly consider post-conflict peacemaking to be a dimension of their traditional missions. We will offer very brief examples of the involvement of UNEP, IMF, the World Bank, UNESCO, FAO, WHO, ILO and UNAIDS. The approach of the Post-Conflict Assessment Unit (PCAU) of the UN Environment Programme (UNEP) is 'to demonstrate the linkages between environmental degradation, public health and sustainable development in order to identify risks and promote sustainable resource use. Following assessment activities that reflect local circumstances and realities, a series of workshops and seminars are provided to help build capacities for environmental management and protection, and to ensure that environmental considerations are integrated into the reconstruction and recovery process' (www.unep.org).

In 1995, the policy on emergency assistance of the International Monetary Fund (IMF) 'was expanded to cover countries in post-conflict situations. This assistance is limited to circumstances where a member with an urgent balance of payments need is unable to develop and implement a comprehensive economic program because its capacity has been damaged by a conflict, but where sufficient capacity for planning and policy implementation nevertheless exists. IMF financing can help a country directly and by catalyzing support from other sources, since Fund support must be part of a comprehensive international effort to address the aftermath of the conflict' (www.imf.org). The IMF has a table on its website, that indicates that it provided Post-Conflict Emergency Assistance from 1995 to 2005 to 12 member states (www.imf.org/external/np/exr/facts/conflict.htm).

The World Bank explains the inclusion of post-conflict peace-building in its traditional mission in this way:

> Conflict prevention and post-conflict reconstruction are critical to the World Bank's mission of poverty reduction. Many of the world's poorest countries are locked in a tragic vicious circle where poverty causes conflict and conflict causes poverty. Eighty percent of the world's 20 poorest countries have suffered a major war in the past 15 years. On average, countries coming out of war face a 44 percent chance of relapsing in the first five years of peace. Even with rapid progress after peace, it can take a generation or more just to return to pre-war living standards.
>
> Through assessment of the causes, consequences and characteristics of conflict and the transfer of lessons learned, the Conflict Prevention and Reconstruction Unit works to design development efforts specific to conflict-affected countries. The Post-Conflict Fund provides financing for physical and social reconstruction initiatives in post-war societies. The Bank is playing a significant role in Afghanistan, Africa's Great Lakes region, the Balkans, Iraq, Liberia, Nepal, Sierra Leone, Timor Leste, the West Bank and Gaza, and other war-torn areas.
>
> (www.worldbank.org)

UNESCO has linked its mission to preserve the 'world heritage' to post-conflict peacebuilding through a 'Heritage and Post-Conflict' emphasis, as expressed in these words:

> As world events unfold, we have witnessed the tragic destruction of cultural heritage, for the heritage can become a prime target, especially in intra-State conflicts for reasons of symbolism, identity, aggressiveness, misunderstanding and rejection. In the last decade or so, UNESCO has played a leading and high-profile role internationally in coordinating complex operations to safeguard heritage damaged or threatened by conflicts, with the assistance of many different partners, both public and private.
>
> (www.unesco.org)

The Food and Agriculture Organization (FAO) has posted a paper on 'lessons learned' concerning 'post-conflict land tenure and the sustainable livelihoods (SL) approach', along with a consideration of the SL approach in a post-conflict case study. It also describes some of the primary critical issues that may require further attention, so as to tailor both post-conflict assessment and the SL approach to post-conflict settings (www.fao.org).

The World Health Organization (WHO) has posted a 'Post-conflict strategic framework for WHO in Sudan'. There is also a programme 'designed to assist in re-establishing health services in a context of political and economic instability'. A 'guide to health workforce development in post-conflict environments provides practical information and tools for rebuilding a health workforce, as well as examples from post-conflict countries' (www.who.org).

The International Labor Organization (ILO) has an Action Programme on Skills and Entrepreneurship Training for Countries Emerging from Armed Conflict. On the ILO website there is a paper on 'Training and Employment Promotion for Sustainable Peace ILO Action Programme on Skills and Entrepreneurship Training for Countries Emerging from Armed Conflict'. Section IV describes 'ILO's historical Role and comparative advantage in Post-conflict reconstruction'. Another paper discusses the relevance to ILO of 'Gender issues in complex conflict and post-conflict reconstruction and peace-building processes' (www.ilo.org).

UNAIDS, a joint programme of ten agencies in the UN System, has declared that 'the relationship between conflict and the spread of HIV is complex, unpredictable and poorly understood. It is influenced by such factors as population mobility, existing prevalence of HIV infection, and level of sexual interaction. The post-conflict period of reconstruction is also a period of heightened vulnerability to infection. AIDS prevention needs to be an integral part of all humanitarian programmes to assist populations caught up in conflict' (www.unaids.org).

Long-term peace-building

An exceedingly significant advance in current peace research is the present emphasis on prevention of seriously disruptive conflict through preventive long-term peace-building.[2] Louis Kriesberg has offered a valuable foundation for preventive efforts in *Constructive Conflicts: From Escalation to Resolution* (1998). It is Kriesberg's intent to 'develop an empirically grounded understanding of how people prevent or stop destructive conflicts, but instead wage relatively constructive conflicts' (1998: xiii). This volume challenges those engaged in 'prevention' to attempt to devise procedures for clearly distinguishing between potentially violent/disruptive conflicts and those that are constructive. It certainly is necessary to seek the termination of some conflicts, but, in the interest of long-term peace, others should be converted into constructive conflicts.

Also offering a valuable foundation for prevention of violent/disruptive conflicts is research on risk assessment and early warning. Here, a significant contribution is Davies and Gurr's edited volume on *Preventive Measures: Building Risk Assessment and Crisis Early Warning* (1998). They are attempting to develop the capacity to diagnose 'failures' far enough in advance to facilitate effective international efforts at 'prevention or peaceful transformation'. Contributors to this volume examine potential early warning indicators in different situations and attempt to judge their effectiveness according to various models.

Different emphases are suggested by the varying terminology employed by scholars emphasizing prevention. Bloomfield and Moulton (1997) wish to 'manage' international conflict. The Carnegie Commission (1997) desires to 'prevent deadly conflict'. Cahill (1996), Jentleson (2000) and Lund (1996) place their efforts under the rubric 'preventive diplomacy'. Also useful contributors in this vein are Bauwens and Reychler (1994), Cortright (1997), Peck (1998), Reychler (1998) and Vayrynen (1997). We choose to mention them separately because I believe they significantly err in asserting that it is their goal to 'prevent' conflict, thereby making a mistake widely encountered in the literature. It is quite obvious, in the light of the contribution of some forms of conflict to useful social change, that these insightful scholars really mean 'transformation' most of the time.

Some of the volumes on prevention encompass a wide array of approaches and tools. Lund, in *Preventing Violent Conflicts: A Strategy for Preventive Diplomacy* (1996), develops a broad 'preventive diplomacy toolbox' that includes military approaches (restraints on the use of armed force and threat or use of armed force), diplomatic measures (coercive – without use of armed force and noncoercive), and development and governance approaches (promotion of economic and social development, promulgation and enforcement of human rights and democracy, and national governing structures to promote peaceful conflict resolution). This is indeed comprehensive because these three categories embrace more than 50 individual tools. For example, the noncoercive diplomatic measures are divided into judicial or quasi judicial and nonjudicial. Included in nonjudicial are 12 tools with a diversity of approaches, such as third-party mediation, propaganda and fact finding.

Kevin Cahill, a medical doctor, asserts in his edited volume on preventive diplomacy (1996), that 'it is only natural for me to think of clinical and public health models in contemplating the disorders now threatening the health of the world community'. Thus he has sections on 'interrupting a global epidemic', 'causes and local remedies', 'signs, symptoms and early intervention' and 'establishing trust in the healer'. There are also chapters on early warning, fact finding, economic sanctions, human rights, peacekeeping, the media and education.

After examining why deadly conflicts occur, the Carnegie Commission, in *Preventing Deadly Conflict* (1997), distinguishes between operational prevention and structural prevention. Operational prevention strategies range across early warning and response, preventive diplomacy, economic measures and 'forceful' measures that include peacekeeping, preventive deployments and a rapid reaction 'fire brigade'. Structural prevention, employed as a synonym to peace-building, addresses root causes of deadly conflict and includes security (from violence), economic well-being and justice. Responsibilities are laid out for states and their leaders, civil society (religion, science, media and business), the UN and regional arrangements. A concluding section, 'toward a culture of prevention', provides tasks for the mass media, religious institutions and the United Nations.

Although prevention necessarily involves a diversity of approaches and tools, some volumes focus their efforts on one kind of activity. In a volume on 'sustainable peace', Connie Peck (1998) asserts that the most sustainable means is good governance because good governance offers groups a voice in resolving grievances at an early stage. In *The Price of Peace: Incentives and*

International Conflict Prevention (1997), edited by David Cortright, the focus is on incentives, rather than on coercion, deterrence and sanctions. These positive inducements of an 'economic, political or security character' can be focused on deterring nuclear proliferation, armed conflict and defending human rights.

In *Do No Harm: How Aid Can Support Peace – or War*, Mary Anderson (1996) asserts that the impact of aid is not neutral. She asks, how can humanitarian or development assistance be 'given in conflict situations in ways that rather than feeding into and exacerbating the conflict help local people to disengage and establish alternative systems to deal with the problems that underlie conflict?' Her response includes concern for the implicit ethical message of aid and the impact of resource transfers on conflict. She would use aid in developing local capacities for peace through food for work, village rehabilitation, working with children in the context of civil war and coping with poverty. In a Bock and Anderson article (1999), the focus is on how aid agencies can defuse intercommunal conflict. Here, aid would be used to 'inculcate a sense of belonging among a large, more inclusive group' and to 'support/strengthen interconnection structures and systems, rather than competitive ones' (p. 336).

Also offering insight on links between aid and peace is the Prendergast (1996) study of humanitarian aid and conflict in Africa. He offers ten commandments for avoiding 'good intentions on the road to hell', i.e. providing aid without sustaining conflict. His commandments involve deep analysis based on a diversity of information sources, independent monitoring and evaluation, integrating human rights monitoring, advocacy and capacity building and making aid conditional upon acceptance of humanitarian principles and conflict resolution. He concludes that humanitarian aid is the most important avenue of contact among the international community and conflicting parties; thereby aid offers one of the best policy instruments for preventing escalation of conflict and promoting long-term peace-building (Prendergast 1996: 143).

In the light of the prominent use of religious differences by leaders as a basis for waging conflict and war, research advocating the use of religion as a peace tool is an increasingly important response (Alger 2002; Groff and Smoker 1996; Smock 1995). Appleby, in *The Ambivalence of the Sacred: Religion, Violence and Reconciliation* (1999), asserts that religion's ability to inspire violence is intimately related to its equally impressive power as a force for peace. He identifies what religious terrorists and religious peacemakers share in common, what causes them to take different paths in fighting injustice and the importance of acquiring understanding of religious extremism.

Johnston and Sampson, in *Religion, the Missing Dimension of Statecraft* (1994), opens with a foreword by Jimmy Carter asserting that, 'we all realize that religious differences have often been a cause or pretext for war. Less known is the fact that the actions of many religious persons and communities point in another direction. They demonstrate that religion can be a potent force in encouraging the peaceful resolution of conflict' (1994: vii). After six case studies of reconciliation, the volume concludes with implications for the foreign policy community and implications for four religious communities: Buddhist, Islamic, Hindu and Christian.

There are other works provoking thoughts of how religion can be used as a peace tool. These include Sampson, who informs us of the institutional moves within some religious communities toward developing 'an increasingly intentional and systematic approach to peacebuilding' (Sampson 1996: 304). Johansen (1997) has contributed 'Radical Islam and Nonviolence: A Case Study of Religious Empowerment and Constraint Among Pashtuns'. Reychler (1997) asks for a serious study of the impact of religious organizations on conflict behaviour that includes a comparative study of the peace-building efforts of different religious organizations. He asserts that the world cannot survive without a new global ethic and that the religious ties of parties, passive bystanders, peacemakers and peace-builders will play a major role.

Local conflict within states

Recently, the peace research field has become linked to a larger field that has focused on local arenas of conflict within states, including schools, local communities, business and courts. One example is the Ohio Commission on Dispute Resolution and Conflict Management: 'Focused on four program areas – educational institutions, state and local government, courts, and communities – the Commission works to positively affect the lives of all Ohio citizens by providing dispute resolution and conflict management training, consultation and technical assistance in designing dispute resolution programs, and facilitation and mediation services' (www.disputeresolution.ohio.gov).

Together with the Ohio Department of Education, and other educational organizations, it works to provide Ohio schools with constructive, nonviolent methods for resolving disputes. Through these efforts the Commission helps to build partnerships among communities, courts and schools throughout Ohio. Currently, there are more than 75 community and court programmes serving more than one-half of Ohio's 88 counties. Together with the Ohio Department of Education, the Ohio Board of Education and other educational organizations, the Commission works to provide Ohio schools with constructive, nonviolent methods for resolving disputes.

These kinds of dispute resolution and conflict management activities now exist in other states in the United States and in other countries. Although many that are involved see them only as a means for coping with local conflict, nevertheless they do see an advantage in sharing knowledge and experiences with those involved in other countries. On the other hand, some involved in the peace research field with a global focus perceive that knowledge and experience acquired in coping in local dispute resolution and conflict management activities enhance the ability of people to cope with these issues in larger geographic arenas. In response to both of these concerns, an International Network (IN) for Conflict Resolution (CR) and Peace Education (PE) has been created. CREPE sees its role as 'prevention of conflict by stakeholders at all levels including international organizations, governments, education administrators, teachers, and faculty, parents, students and members of the local community'. The Ohio Commission on Dispute Resolution and Conflict Management is a member of CREPE. Included in the goals of CREPE are conducting research to illustrate the effectiveness of PE and CRE and networking across groups including government, non-governmental and civil society organizations and educational institutions. The functions of the network include creating an inventory of resources such as curriculum and training materials, providing opportunities to share knowledge and expertise, offering a clearinghouse of existing legislation and policies related to PE and CRE, conducting/supporting forums and conferences, providing samples of best practices, and supplying access to existing research and evaluation (www.disputeresolution.ohio.gov).

Conclusion

In conclusion, the expansion of the functions of the UN System, and the growing diversity of the participants, reveal that virtually all professions are now involved in peace-related activities. We have illuminated the expanding disciplinary range of peace research by examining five themes: emphasis on multiple tracks and multiple methods, the growing range of peace activities associated with peacekeeping and NGOs/civil society, post-conflict peacemaking, preventive long-term peace-building, and local arenas of conflict within states. We have found that virtually all organizations have peacemaking and peace-building potential: governmental, NGO/civil society and business. In all categories this includes organizations that range from local to global.

Peace researchers are now providing ever more empirical evidence in support of Johan Galtung's conclusion 26 years ago: 'There are tasks for everybody' (Galtung 1980: 396). The General Assembly of UNESCO reached the same conclusion when it issued a Declaration on a Culture of Peace in 1999:

> The Declaration defines the culture of peace as a set of values, attitudes, traditions, modes of behaviour and ways of life based on respect for life, ending of violence and promotion and practice of non-violence through education, dialogue and co-operation; commitment to peaceful settlement of conflicts; respect for and promotion of the right to development, equal rights and opportunities for men and women, the rights of everyone to freedom of expression, opinion and information; and adherence to the principles of freedom, justice, democracy, tolerance, solidarity, co-operation, pluralism, cultural diversity, dialogue and understanding at all levels of society and among nations.
>
> (www.unesco.org/education)

In *Cultures of Peace* (1999), Elise Boulding has provided illuminating descriptions of widespread cultures of peace that now exist throughout the world, in families, communities, regions, states and organizations that range from local to global. Because media coverage tends to emphasize violence and seriously disruptive conflict, it is difficult for many people to have a vision of peace. But a distinguishing attribute of many involved in peace research is their devotion to acquiring knowledge that can provide the path to their vision of a more peaceful world. Elise Boulding's volume, and other studies of peaceful cultures, is making an essential contribution to the ever more significant peace research discipline by making it easier for ever more people to have a vision of a peaceful world.

Notes

1 Table 19.1 and its description are extracted from Alger (2006: 6–15).
2 This section is extensively extracted from Alger (2000: 6–9).

References

Alger, C.F. (1997) 'Transnational social movements, world politics, and global governance', in J. Smith, C. Chatfield and R. Pagnucco (eds) *Transnational Social Movements and Global Politics*, Syracuse, NY: Syracuse University Press, 260–78.

Alger, C.F. (1999) 'The expanding tool chest for peacebuilders', in H.-W. Jeong (ed.) *The New Agenda for Peace Research*, Aldershot: Ashgate, 13–44.

Alger, C.F. (2000) 'Challenges for peace researchers and peace builders in the twenty-first century: education and coordination of a diversity of actors in applying what we are learning', *International Journal of Peace Studies*, 5, 1: 1–13.

Alger, C.F. (2002) 'Religion as a peace tool', *Global Review of Ethnopolitics*, 1, 4: 94–109.

Alger, C.F. (2003) 'Searching for democratic potential in emerging global governance', in B. Morrison (ed.) *Transnational Democracy in Critical and Comparative Perspective*, Aldershot: Ashgate, 88–105.

Alger, C.F. (2006) *The United Nations System: A Reference Handbook*, Santa Barbara, CA: ABC-CLIO.

Anderson, M.B. (1996) *Do No Harm: How Aid Can Support Peace – Or War*, Boulder, CO: Lynne Rienner Publications.

Appleby, R.S. (1999) *The Ambivalence of the Sacred: Religion, Violence and Reconciliation*, Boston, MA: Rowan and Littlefield.

Barash, D.P. and Webel, C.P. (2002) *Peace and Conflict Studies*, Thousand Oaks, CA: Sage.

Bauwens, W. and Reychler, L. (eds) (1994) *The Art of Conflict Prevention*, London and New York: Brassey's.

Bloomfield, L.P. and Moulton, A. (1997) *Managing International Conflict: From Theory to Policy*, New York: St Martin's Press.

Bock, J.B. and Anderson, M.B. (1999) 'Dynamite under the intercommunal bridge: how can aid agencies help defuse it?', *Journal of Peace Research*, 36, 3: 325–38.

Boulding, E. (2000) *Cultures of Peace: The Hidden Side of History*, Syracuse, NY: Syracuse University Press.

Cahill, K.P. (1996) *Preventive Diplomacy: Stopping Wars Before They Start*, New York: Basic Books.

Carnegie Commission on Preventing Deadly Conflict (1997) *Preventing Deadly Conflict: Final Report*, Washington, DC: Carnegie Commission Preventing Deadly Conflict.

Cortright, D. (ed.) (1997) *The Price of Peace: Incentives and International Conflict Prevention*, Boston, MA: Rowan and Littlefield.

Davies, J.L. and Gurr, E.R. (eds) (1998) *Preventive Measures: Building Risk Assessment and Crisis Early Warning Systems*, Boston, MA: Rowan and Littlefield.

Diamond, L. and McDonald, J. (1996) *Multi-Track Diplomacy: A Systems Approach to Peace*, 3rd edn, West Hartford, CN: Kumarian Press.

Forman, S. and Patrick, S. (eds) (1999) *Good Intentions: Pledges of Aid for Post-conflict Revcovery*, Boulder, CO: Lynne Rienner Publications.

Galtung, J. (1969) 'Violence, peace and peace research', *Journal of Peace Research*, 6, 3: 167–91.

Galtung, J. (1980) *The True Worlds: A Transnational Perspective*, New York: Free Press.

Groff, L. and Smoker, P. (1996) 'Spirituality, religion, culture, and peace: exploring the foundations for inner–outer peace in the twenty-first century', *International Journal of Peace Research*, 1, 1: 57–114.

Henderson, M. (1996) *The Forgiveness Factor: Stories of Hope in a World of Conflict*, London: Grosvenor Books.

Jentleson, B.W. (ed.) (2000) *Opportunities Missed, Opportunities Seized: Preventive Diplomacy in the Post-Cold War World*, Lanham, MD: Rowan and Littlefield.

Jeong, H.-W. (2000), *Peace and Conflict Studies: An Introduction*, Boulder, CO: Lynne Rienner Publications.

Jeong, H.-W. (2005) *Peacebuilding in Postconflict Societies: Strategy and Process*, Boulder, CO: Lynne Rienner Publications.

Johansen, R.C. (1997) 'Radical Islam and nonviolence: a case study of religious empowerment and constraint among Pashtuns', *Journal of Conflict Resolution*, 34, 1: 53–72.

Johnston, D. and Sampson, C. (1994) *Religion, the Missing Dimension of Statecraft*, New York: Oxford University Press.

Kriesberg, L. (1998) *Constructive Conflicts: From Escalation to Resolution*. Boulder, CO: Rowan and Littlefield.

Kumar, K. (1997) *Rebuilding Societies After Civil War: Critical Roles for International Assistance*, Boulder, CO: Lynne Rienner Publications.

Kumar, K. (1998) *Postconflict Elections, Democratization, and International Assistance*, Boulder, CO: Lynne Rienner Publications.

Lund, M.S. (1996) *Preventing Violent Conflicts: A Strategy for Preventive Diplomacy*, Washington, DC: US Institute of Peace Press.

Montville, J.V. (1996) 'Foreword', in M. Henderson, *The Forgiveness Factor: Stories of Hope in a World of Conflict*, London: Governor Books, xii–xviii.

Peace and Justice Studies Association (PJSA) and the International Peace Research Association (IPRA) Foundation (2006) *Global Directory of Peace Studies and Conflict Resolution Programs* (seventh edition), San Francisco, CA: PJSA.

Peck, C. (1998) *Sustainable Peace: The Role of the UN and Regional Organizations in Preventing Conflict*, Boulder, CO: Rowan and Littlefield.

Prendergast, J. (1996), *Frontline Diplomacy: Humanitarian Aid and Conflict in Africa*, Boulder, CO: Lynne Rienner Publications.

Ratner, S.R. (1995) *The New UN Peacekeeping: Building Peace in Land of Conflict After the Cold War*, New York: St Martin's Press and Council on Foreign Relations.

Reychler, L. (1997) 'Religion and conflict', *International Journal of Peace Studies*, 2, 1: 19–38.

Reychler, L. (1998) 'Proactive conflict prevention: impact assessment', *International Journal of Peace Studies*, 3, 2: 87–98.

Reychler, L. and Paffenholz, T. (eds) (2001) *Peacebuilding: A Field Guide*, Boulder, CO: Lynne Rienner Publications.

Rothstein, R.L. (ed.) (1999) *After the Peace: Resistance and Reconciliation*, Boulder, CO: Lynne Rienner Publications.

Sampson, C. (1996) 'Religion and peacebuilding', in I. Zartman and J. L. Rasmussen (eds) *Peacemaking in International Conflict: Methods and Techniques*, Washington, DC: US Institute of Peace Press, 273–315.

Shepard, F. and Patrick, S. (eds) (1999) *Good Intentions: Pledges of Aid for Post-Conflict Recovery*, Boulder, CO: Lynne Rienner Publications.

Shriver, D.W. (1995) *An Ethic for Enemies: Forgiveness in Politics*, New York: Oxford University Press.

Simpson, G. (1998) *A Brief Evaluation of South Africa's Truth and Reconciliation Commission: Some Lessons for Societies in Transition*, Johannesburg: Centre for Study of Violence and Reconciliation.

Smith, J. (1997) 'Characteristics of the modern transnational social movement sector', in J. Smith, C. Chatfield and R. Pagnucco (eds) *Transnational Social Movements and Global Politics: Solidarity Beyond the State*, Syracuse, NY: Syracuse University Press, 42–58.

Smock, D.R. (1995) *Perspectives on Pacifism: Christian, Jewish and Muslim Views on Nonviolence and International Conflict*, Washington, DC: US Institute of Peace Press.

Sorenson, B. (1998) *Women and Post Conflict Reconstruction: Issues and Sources*, Geneva: UN Research Institute for Social Development and Programme for Strategic International Security.

Tschirgi, N. (2004) *Post-Conflict Peacebuilding Revisited: Achievements, Limitations, Challenges*, New York: International Peace Academy.

Vayrynen, R. (1997) 'Toward effective conflict prevention: a comparison of different instruments, *International Journal of Peace Studies*, 2, 1: 1–18.

Wenger, A. and Mockli, D. (2003) *Conflict Prevention: The Untapped Potential of the Business Sector*, Boulder, CO: Lynne Reinner Publications.

Zartman, I.W. and Rasmussen, J.L. (eds) (2006) *Peacemaking in International Conflict: Methods and Techniques*, revised edn, Washington, DC: US Institute of Peace Press.

20

The spirit of war and the spirit of peace

Understanding the role of religion

Graeme MacQueen

Many people are confused about the relationship of religion to war and peace. They are perplexed by the fact that the world's religions typically announce themselves as favouring peace while contributing in major ways to war. They seek an interpretation that will make sense of the situation. Perhaps all religions, for example, are inherently inclined to peace but are subject to manipulation by malevolent non-religious forces, which use them to promote or legitimize war? This common solution to the problem is, unfortunately, simplistic. In this chapter I want to suggest, through definitions, proposals and distinctions, a more fruitful approach.

It is not my intention to summarize or catalogue the historical attitudes of world religions toward war or peace. My aim is to encourage an approach that is informed by both Religious Studies and Peace Studies and that may help these disciplines to carry on a more interesting conversation than they have in the past.

I will begin by explaining what I mean by religions. I will then suggest a methodological approach to the 'spirit of war' and the 'spirit of peace' that is deliberately anti-modern and will, therefore, challenge our thinking. I will follow this with an account of the difference between national religion and autonomous religion. I shall then briefly discuss two post-Napoleonic developments in the West that the preceding distinctions help illuminate and that were crucial to the emergence of modern war and of the movement for peace. I shall conclude by situating the origin and development of Religious Studies as a discipline within the same historical moment that encouraged the growth of peace spiritualities.

Definitions

No definition of religions has won universal acceptance within Religious Studies. I find this lack of unanimity healthy. The definition I put forward here is a working definition, adapted from one by Gavin Flood (1999) and offered for the sake of clarity and to encourage a conversation between two disciplines.

I shall define a religion as a system, incorporating grand narrative as well as action both ritual and ethical, which binds people to each other and to trans-human realities.

'Grand narrative' refers to a narrative or quasi-narrative that deals with issues of great importance for human beings (such as human destiny or the nature of the cosmos) and has a position of dominance in relation to a society's other narratives and symbols, which it grounds and integrates. As a category, grand narrative includes what are usually called religious myths, but it may include many other sorts of narrative, such as Emancipation through Science, or Fulfilment through National Glory. When I suggest that a grand narrative may be a mere quasi-narrative, I mean that it will not always be a complete, explicit story in the way that most traditional myths are. It may be brief, suggestive or fragmentary like the life narratives of most individuals.

'Trans-human realities' includes the various gods, spirits and immortal powers and conditions of traditional religions, but it may include under some circumstances such entities as History, the Unconscious, Society and the Nation.

Religious Studies accepts the need for two complementary forms of interpretation: emic interpretation, which employs the categories of the people being studied, and etic interpretation, whereby the observer uses an interpretive framework independent of the people being studied. Most people professing modern ideologies and nationalisms have not wished to use the term 'religion' for what they are doing, and emic interpretations have honoured this self-understanding. I believe that an etic moment is now called for, and that nationalisms and ideologies must be called religion when they fully exhibit the characteristics listed above, whether or not they have traditionally been called religions and whether or not those professing them are happy with the label.

In this essay I shall concentrate on nationalism's relation to religion, but an analysis similar to the one given here could also be carried out for modern ideologies.

Methodological proposal: two spirits

Instead of adopting either methodological atheism (the assumption, common in the social sciences, that gods, spirits and immortal conditions are all inexistent), or methodological monotheism (the assumption, common among Christian theologians and in popular Western culture, that there is but one God), I propose that we imaginatively enter the worldview of the majority of historical human societies and adopt a position of methodological polytheism. Let us assume that there are numerous gods, spirits or immortal Powers and that some are warlike while others are peaceful.

How does such an interpretive frame aid our understanding? Methodological atheism fragments each of the traditional Powers, denying its integrity; weakens these Powers and denies their strength; reduces them to dependent status as shadows of other realities. In brief, it takes them lightly and is therefore at a loss when they demonstrate their power and resilience. Methodological monotheism, having reduced the Powers to idols and replaced them with one God, has no adequate means for recognizing religious multiplicity and complexity.

As methodological polytheists, we will expect multiple, coherent Powers, and we will expect that individuals or societies will be moved to war or to peace depending on which Power enters them or forms an association with them.

The word 'enthusiasm' is derived from the Greek and literally means 'possessed by a god'. To be enthusiastic about war will mean, from our methodological perspective, to be possessed by a warlike god or spirit. To be enthusiastic about peace will mean to be possessed by a peaceful spirit. The apparent paradox of religion's complex relation to war disappears in the face of the diversity of trans-human realities and of grand narratives dealing with these powers.

But we will also understand, by adopting this point of view, that attention must be given to the means by which the Powers are invoked, placated, defended against and put to rest.

When, at the outbreak of war, the Roman consul took hold of the sacred spears of Mars, the Roman war god, and shook them, saying, 'Mars vigila!' ('Mars, wake up!') both the act of awakening and its effects were real. Polybius speaks of the injunction to 'kill everyone they met and to spare no one' after the taking of a city, and he comments that, 'one can see in cities captured by the Romans not only human beings who have been slaughtered, but even dogs sliced in two and the limbs of other animals cut off' (Keegan 1993).

In modern societies it is not easy for human beings without serious pathology to enter into such a destructive condition. There is no reason to believe it was easy for the Romans (Grossman 1995: 145–6). Indo-European warriors – whether Roman legionnaires or Greek hoplites – often fought by methods associated with very high battlefield mortality, and it was understood that if men were to face this experience attention had to be paid to the induction of enthusiasm. 'The whole sequence of rites leading up to battle expressed what men desired, the ideal outcome being the collaboration of gods with men at every step' (Janeson 1991: 220).

But we will not be interested only in how the warrior becomes possessed by the spirit of war. We will want to know how, after the conclusion of war, the warrior becomes dis-possessed and reintegrated to society. We will want to know whether a person or society can resist possession by, or bonding with, a warlike deity. And we will also ask, How does one become possessed by, or bound to, a peaceful deity? After all, when the eighteenth-century Quaker, John Woolman, said, 'Remember, O my soul, that the Prince of Peace is thy Lord' (Steere 1984: 217) he was referring to a particular relationship he had experienced between a Power (the 'Prince of Peace') and his psyche (soul). The reader of his journal will find a detailed account of his communion with this Power and of his attempts to manifest its nature in his life – to abolish slavery, to resolve disputes nonviolently, and so on. What are the methods of invoking gods of peace?

How much latitude does an individual or society have in deciding whom to be possessed by? Are warlike deities more powerful than peaceful ones? What is the relation of the various Powers to nation, state and society? If war is a characteristic of immortal Powers, does this mean it is itself immortal and can never be abolished?

As we allow ourselves to settle into this interpretive frame, we perceive a host of interesting questions. Although we cannot pursue them here, we can see that they would provide a somewhat different perspective on the human relationship to war and peace than is customary in modern Western studies.

But are we actually to pretend we are polytheists? If not, of what use is this interpretive frame to us in the twenty-first century West?

The point of the method is not to force ourselves to pretend commitment to a metaphysical position we cannot entertain. The point is to ensure that even if we feel a need to honour the present, Western cultural moment by locating the Powers in places that feel appropriate to us – the Unconscious, for example, or even the Brain; or perhaps Society or Culture – we will not be quick to dismiss them. They belong to the deep experience of humanity. Let us study these Powers according to the methods that seem most fruitful, whether these be group psychology or decision theory, but let us not take them lightly, let us not expect them to yield readily to rationality, and let us not assume they will be in harmony with each other.

Two forms of religion

I wish to begin the next stage of analysis by examining two statements composed during twentieth-century international conflicts. Both statements are original productions inspired by Christian creeds (statements of faith). The second is modeled closely on an actual creed, while the first is looser in its construction but uses creedal rhythms and makes ample reference to Christian artifacts and forms of worship. The official church creeds on which these pieces are based are often recited in unison within a sacred context, so these statements evoke, for a Christian reader, the affirmation of both the divine and the worshiping community.

The first statement, 'Credo for France' by M. Henri Lavedan, was composed in France during the First World War (Lasswell 1938: 56–7):

> I believe in the courage of our soldiers and in the skill and devotion of our leaders. I believe in the power of right, and in the crusade of civilization, in France, the eternal, the imperishable, the essential. I believe in the reward of suffering and the worth of hope . . . I believe in the blood of wounds and the water of benediction, in the blaze of artillery and the flame of the votive candle; in the beads of the rosary . . .
>
> I believe in women's prayers, in the sleepless heroism of the wife, in the calm piety of the mother, in the purity of our cause, in the stainless glory of our flag. I believe in our great past, in our great present, and in our greater future. I believe in our countrymen, living and dead. I believe in the hands clenched for battle, and in the hands clasped for prayer. I believe in ourselves, I believe in God. I believe, I believe.

This creed skilfully weaves together two distinct forms of religion: national religion and autonomous religion. A national religion, as I shall use the expression, is a religion in which the trans-human realities honoured are a nation or are Powers uniquely bound to that nation. (By 'nation' I mean any sizable group that considers itself intimately linked through origins, history and customs.) An autonomous religion is a religion in which the central trans-human realities are not a nation and not Powers uniquely bound to a nation.

By speaking of 'autonomous' religion I do not wish to suggest that a religion can ever be hermetically sealed from its historical or cultural context, but I do suggest that it can have relative autonomy from the nation and from national culture. What we call the 'world religions' – Islam, Christianity, Buddhism, and so on – are in this sense autonomous. It is necessary to make this point because it is frequently assumed today that religion is part of culture. If we are using 'culture' in the broadest sense to refer to everything humans think, say and do that is not a direct product of biology or environment, then religion is certainly part of culture. But if we are using the term in a narrower sense, as when we speak of French culture or Melanesian culture, then it is misleading to say that all religion is part of culture. When Muslims gather at Mecca during the Hajj, what unifies them is not so much culture – their cultures are extremely varied – but Islam, which transcends these cultures as an autonomous system. When Hsuan-tsang made his way overland from China to India in the seventh century CE it was Buddhism, as an autonomous religion transcending the cultures of China, India and Central Asia, that inspired him. He was aware of the national cultures he experienced on his journey and in his writings he often describes them, but these cultures were not his primary interest (Beal 1968).

Lavedan's creed plays with these two forms of religion, alternating them (blaze of artillery and flame of votive candle; hands clasped for battle, hands clasped for prayer) and having the autonomous religion of Christianity lend its power to the national religion of France.

But it is clear which form of religion is uppermost in his creed. The Christian deity is worshipped only in order that France may be worshipped. The nation is the central trans-human reality ('France, the eternal, the imperishable, the essential'); the grand narrative is the story of this divinity ('our great past . . . our great present . . . our greater future'), and the actions taken by the religious person, whether ritual actions ('hands clasped for prayer') or ethically charged actions ('hands clenched for battle') are pure and holy to the extent that they are devoted to the nation.

Lavedan's creed is useful for us because it explicitly states what modern pledges of allegiance, as well as national anthems and ceremonies, usually affirm less directly. Lavedan wants to say that during war the nation must be worshipped. Although he draws on Christian symbols where they are helpful, he does not pretend that Christianity itself is adequate to the task. War is not an ordinary act of the people-as-nation but the central act of the Nation-as-God. In the practical and ritual act of going to war, the nation is transformed from a collection of individual subjects into a transcendent, unitary Subject. 'I believe in ourselves.'

Lavedan's creed did not, of course, come from the blue. It expressed formally the already existing French national religion. Ritual and symbol already functioned to make the divinity visible and audible. In the Tricolor, France is seen; in the Marseillaise, France is heard. These visions and auditions are primarily communal: France descends into the flag and the anthem when participants partake of these elements with others. Participants of the cult thereby become bound to each other and to the trans-human reality they worship.

The second statement, 'Profession of Faith', was composed in the United States by John LaForge in 1982 during the Cold War against the Soviet Union (LaForge 1982):

We believe in one God,
the Pentagon, the Almighty,
destroyer of heaven and earth,
of all that is seen and unseen.

We believe in one Lord, the Bomb,
the only son of the Pentagon,
continually begotten of the Pentagon,
Bomb from Bomb, Flash from Flash,
true War from true War,
profitable, not sane, one in being with the Pentagon.

For us and for our cremation
the Bomb came down from heaven:
by the power of the multinationals
the Bomb was born of fear and became death.

For our sake the Bomb was exploded over Hiroshima
where people still suffer, die, and are buried.
On the third day it was exploded again
in fulfillment of a war game;
its mushroom cloud ascended into heaven
and its fallout is seated at the right hand of all people.

The Bomb will come again in gore
to vaporize the living and the dead
and its devastation will have no end.

> We believe in the threat of the Bomb, the taker of life,
> which proceeds from the Pentagon and its contractors.
> With the Pentagon and its generals
> the Bomb is worshipped and glorified.
> It has spoken through the Joint Chiefs.
> We believe in one Holy anti-Soviet and apocalyptic foreign policy.
>
> We acknowledge multiple preemptive strikes
> for the forgiveness of socialism.
> We look for the resurrection of the Right,
> and the death of the world as we know it.
>
> Boom.

This creed is presented as a statement of faith in a national religion but it is, of course, ironic. LaForge's implied reader is Christian, and the piece draws its power from the contrast between the Christian grand narrative familiar to the reader, and the grand narrative the American citizen is supposedly being asked to subscribe to by the state. The detailed rewriting of the Apostle's Creed uses parallels that, even when apparently spurious (for example, the exploding of the atomic bomb again on the third day paired with Christ rising on the third day), powerfully contrast what the author evidently regards as a beautiful and life-affirming profession of belief with one he regards as monstrous and necrophilic.

LaForge understands that the human mind is easily led from kratophany (the manifestation of power) to theophany (the manifestation of Power, or of the divine), so that it is relatively easy for a cult to elevate a device of mass destruction, the explosion of which is accompanied by a huge mushroom cloud, to the level of the sacred. And he recognizes the connection that exists between the Power the destructive device has become and the Power the nation becomes in its warlike manifestation ('the Bomb' is 'the only son of the Pentagon'). He understands as well that nuclear war is 'true War' in a sense that Clausewitz would at once have acknowledged: it knows no restrictions or restraints and is pure violence.

Instead of worshipping the Nation-as-God like Lavedan, LaForge attempts to evoke disgust with this god, but he agrees with Lavedan that national religion is real religion. There is much evidence to support this belief. National religions are not quasi-religions that have evolved through a mimicking of the 'real' autonomous religions. Historically, it is at least as likely, as Durkheim suggested almost a century ago, that the autonomous religions developed out of national religions (1915: 493).

National religion was a major feature of the ancient and classical worlds. Yahweh was the god of the Hebrew people; moreover, in the Hebrew Bible, and arguably in the New Testament as well, we encounter the belief that every nation has its own distinct spiritual Power or Angel (Wink 1992: 26ff.). Rome promoted a national religion while keeping a careful eye on the autonomous religions of its day, which it suspected of subversion. One of the charges against Socrates was that he had failed to honour the traditional gods of the city.

This analysis does not require us to regard all nationalisms as religions. Although we need not expect to be confident about the precise point at which a nationalism becomes a national religion, there are obvious signs to look for. The term 'trans-human' in my definition of religion is intended to imply that these realities are not merely of a different nature from humans but are above humans, and that to be bound to them implies honour or reverence. So, in a controversial case we will ask: Are such trans-human entities present? How and to what degree are they honoured? Are they worshipped? We will also want to look for grand narratives that centrally incorporate these trans-human realities and that situate human beings in relationship with trans-human realities in time and space. We will look to see whether the narratives and the honouring are connected to ritual action and ethical action. And so on. Each instance of possible religion will need to be examined in its own right.

What is the relationship of these two forms of religion, national and autonomous, to war and peace? The relationship is complex, and I am not proposing the simple formula: NR = war, AR = peace. Today, as in the past, autonomous religions often reveal themselves to be deeply implicated in war-making. To use the language developed earlier, every autonomous religion has at some point played host to the spirit of war. (The reader interested in the intricate relationship of the autonomous religions to war is advised to consult the Routledge *Encyclopedia of Religion and War*, Hollar 2004.) Moreover, not all national religions are equally warlike. Although they all establish and sanctify the separation of the national in-group from out-groups, this need not involve demonization of out-groups, nor need it involve celebration of war and violence. It is nonetheless true that although autonomous religions have a mixed record in their stance toward war, they have stimulated some of humanity's most impressive critiques of war, and they have played host to the spirit of peace more frequently and more sincerely than national religions.

But the chief usefulness to Peace Studies of the AR–NR distinction is that in the modern period, as war has increasingly been viewed as a rational instrument of the state, national religion, usually with fragments of coopted autonomous religion, has come to be regarded as more dependable to the state than autonomous religion and to that extent has superceded it as a means of invoking the spirit of war.

Clausewitz and the spirit of war

When he sat down in 1816 to begin his classic, *On War* (Rapoport 1968), Carl von Clausewitz, Prussian soldier and philosopher, tried to distill the essentials of war from his experiences in the just concluded wars against Napoleon. His analysis and recommendations became extremely influential in the formation of the institutions and strategy of subsequent European war-making and contributed powerfully to two world wars.

Clausewitz was an Enlightenment man and had no interest in promoting traditional European religious wars of the sort that had ended with Westphalia in 1648. He believed in war as a means for the rational implementation of state policy. But he had personally witnessed Napoleon's entry on the European stage as 'the very God of War himself' (Rapoport 1968: 373), sweeping away everything in his path, and he knew that Bonaparte's power came from a massive, united body of citizens and soldiers fired by patriotism. For the first time, Europe had seen a nation fully mobilized, institutionally and emotionally, for war. 'All these events,' he wrote, 'have shown what an enormous factor the heart and sentiments of a Nation may be in the product of its political and military strength . . . it is not to be expected that [governments] will let them lie idle in future Wars' (Rapoport 1968: 295). He realized he must build into his model of war the popular zeal that had been kindled by the French Revolution and captured by Bonaparte.

Clausewitz's model is, therefore, based on what he called 'a wonderful trinity' (p. 121). Successful war requires reason to determine war's goal; skill to deal with the forces of chance; and feeling to fuel the enterprize. These factors belong to different social groups. Reason belongs to government, skill to the leaders of the armed forces, and feeling to the people.

Clausewitz did not portray himself as promoting religion. (When he referred to Bonaparte as 'the very God of War himself' he was using a metaphor, which is a means of incorporating insights from other worldviews while simultaneously maintaining distance.) But the challenge faced by the European nations seeking to emulate France's battlefield success was serious. How could they achieve the French fervour without the French revolution?

Now, even the French revolutionaries had lost no time, whatever their anti-clericalism, in constructing a national religion to promote and guide the spontaneous fervour of the people (Kertzer 1988: 151ff.). The Marseillaise, adopted as the national anthem in 1795 – though temporarily banned by Napoleon because of its revolutionary potential – remains to this day a primary text for the study of modern national religion. The crucial factors as it sets them forth include: a passionate thirst for glory and self-sacrifice; a desire to demonstrate masculinity; a willingness to be marshalled and to find strength in armed unity; and a potent mixture of devotion to the pure Nation and hatred of the impure Other – expressed in the Marseillaise as the desire to fertilize the fields of the Fatherland with the impure blood of the enemy. It is no surprise, therefore, that Europe, having finished with traditional wars of religion, honoured the Napoleonic and Clausewitzian breakthrough by preparing for a new phase of religious wars, this time wars of national religion. National anthems rang out, flags were unfurled, national worship services were elaborated and the young were inducted into the cult with verses from national religions of the classical world (Parker 1987: 99).

The new wars were not generally considered wars of religion, of course, but of rational patriotism. National religion was remarkably successful in shielding its true nature and its irrationalities from Enlightenment critique while, all around, autonomous religion was being forced to defend itself. In fact, despite national religion's appalling record in twentieth-century wars, in which it created havoc by wedding itself to unprecedented firepower, it has remained surprisingly resilient.

It is not fair, of course, to blame the resurgence of national religion equally on all people, for Clausewitz's model is hierarchical, and the responsibility for initiating and directing a war, and for ensuring that the people are enthused, is given to government. To government and the associated elite groups belongs the burden of responsibility for the perfection of national religion in the modern period. Fortunately, some citizens were prepared to resist being inducted into national enthusiasm, and to this recalcitrance we owe the modern movement for peace.

The early nineteenth century and the spirit of peace

Wars provoke new thinking about military strategy but they also stimulate new thinking about the promotion of peace. Thus it was that while Europe struggled to recover from the Napoleonic wars and while the United States struggled to recover from its war of independence and the subsequent war of 1812, a new form of organization was created, the peace society. The first such group was formed in 1815 (Brock 1991: 3). While Clausewitz was pondering ways by which war could be made manifest in its true and absolute form, these other thinkers were meeting in living rooms in the United States and England (and soon in other countries) to plan a campaign for the abolition of war.

The peace societies were the offspring of two parents, the Enlightenment and Christianity. Let us take these one at a time.

The peace societies must be sharply distinguished from the groups of sectarian Christian pacifists of an earlier period. The new societies wanted to change the world, not witness to it; they wanted to be able to convince by rational argument and evidence instead of merely by the use of scriptural or ecclesiastical authority. Their discussions, public speaking tours and published tracts can be seen as continuous with the eighteenth-century Enlightenment, and their attempts to get rid of war can be viewed as reactions to perceived superstition and irrationality. Since they are ancestors of both the modern peace movement and peace studies in the West, it may be useful to consider three of the terms they used in the rational de-legitimation of war.

Firstly, they sometimes referred to war as a *system* (Dodge 1972: 63, 79; Dymond 1973: 2, 4, 29, 82–3). While we must not read modern systems theory back into their tracts, they clearly saw war as more than an act or series of acts of violence. They saw it as an enduring relationship among different elements in a society and culture. War has its overtly violent periods, but even when overt violence is low, as a system it is part of the fabric of society, drawing out economic resources for military institutions and threatening society's highest ideals and values with antithetical military ideals and values.

Emphasis on the systemic nature of war enabled these thinkers to see beyond certain limitations of just war theory and traditional notions of offence and defence. For example, they perceived that, however just a military act might be within the world's existing war system, its execution would participate in, and likely strengthen, the entire system, and in the long term would legitimize the system and guarantee its continuance.

In opposing the war system, the peace societies encouraged what would today be called a 'culture of peace' – to be spread through education – and recommended the use of international arbitration as well as the establishment of an international congress of nations and an international court (Brock 1991: 30ff., 53). These values, practices and institutions formed the rational basis of the peace system they wished to see replace the war system.

Secondly, they said that war was a *custom* (Mott 1972: 5–6; Worcester 1972). Although ancient and deep-rooted, this custom could be replaced by other customs. They pointed out that human slavery, another ancient and deep-rooted custom, was, in their time, being gradually abolished (Brock 1991: 19; Dodge 1972: 21–2; Mott 1972: 5–6; Worcester 1942: 3–4). They watched this fight against slavery – carried out by one of the first successful, international humanitarian social movements in history – and they also participated in it. There was significant overlap in the two abolition movements (Brock 1991: 58ff.). They also compared war to other customs they considered barbaric and irrational, such as human sacrifice (Worcester 1972).

Thirdly, they repeatedly spoke of the *spirit of war* (Dodge 1972: 4–6, 18–19, 33; Mott 1972: 20; Worcester 1972: 4, 10, 12; Dymond 1973: 39). They were writing before the publication of Clausewitz's work but could foresee, based on what they had witnessed in their lifetimes, where the spirit of war would fit within the model he would soon propose. They could see that the decision to go to war would continue to lie in the hands of a small number of men who, having made their decision according to their own interests, would make 'powerful exertions . . . to excite what is called the *war spirit*' (Worcester 1972: 5) in the population in order to overcome people's natural aversion to war. They recognized the danger the war spirit thus excited would pose to civil rights ('to inflame a mild republic with the *spirit of war* is putting all its liberties to the utmost hazard'; Dodge 1972: 32) and they laid stress on the connection between this spirit and the spirit of the nation. Dodge said, 'the great object in times of war is to rouse up what is styled the spirit of the country,' (p. 32), while Worcester described the 'armies meeting under the influence of enmity, artificially excited, to plunge their bayonets into the breasts of each other; and thus to offer human sacrifices by thousands, to some idolized phantom' (1972: 6).

It would be easy to conclude from the way these authors dealt with the noxious 'spirits' that they were, as true heirs of the Enlightenment, adopting a position of methodological atheism. Worcester, for example, at one point in his writing reduces the spirit of war to 'a deleterious compound of enthusiastic ardor, ambition, malignity and revenge' (1972: 10). Yet his reference to the spirit of the nation as an 'idolized phantom' should alert us to the dual parentage of the peace societies. The Enlightenment thinker speaks of a phantom; the Christian sees an idol. Methodological atheism and methodological monotheism walk hand in hand.

We must remember that the members of the earliest peace societies were mostly Protestant Christians writing for other Protestant Christians. They were heir to two moments of religious upheaval in which the good 'spirit' was central. The first was seventeenth-century England, the 'world turned upside down' in which Quakerism and various other radical religious and political spirit-filled movements began (Hill 1975). The second was the Evangelical Revival of eighteenth-century Europe and North America, in which experiences of the spirit were common and were often felt to impel the enthused person to enter social movements for human betterment (Brock 1991: 21).

Although the spirits of war and the nation may have been phantoms and idols, no such reduction of the spirit of Christ was carried out in the early peace societies. On the contrary, this spirit, associated closely with the spirit of peace, was considered absolutely real and experientially knowable (Dodge 1972: 1, 5; Worcester 1972: 5, 17). But affirming the reality of one spirit while denying reality to the spirits of war and of the nation required a difficult theological manoeuvre. The part of the Bible that Christians refer to as the Old Testament is permeated by war and by God's approval of it. How could this be dealt with? The authors of the tracts typically explained rather curtly that the new covenant that came with Christ had superceded the old (Dodge 1972: 87ff.; Dymond 1973: 52ff.; Mott 1972: 14ff.) Not surprisingly, they supported their anti-war position largely through quotations from the New Testament. Their difficulty was this. They wished to see war abolished. They therefore had to take the position that war was not an aspect of the divine. If it were an aspect of the divine it neither could nor should be abolished. They tried to solve the problem within the parameters of mainstream Protestant Christianity of their day. They did not, for example, like Marcion in the second century CE (expelled from the church as a heretic), conclude that the Old Testament and the New Testament were devoted to entirely different gods.

As they emphasized the peaceful nature of the divine, these thinkers participated in the general evolution of Western Christian theology as well as the growing popularity of the idea of peace. But it is striking how unprepared the peace societies were when the spirits of war and of the nation were again invoked. When the American Civil War broke out in 1861 the chief US peace societies collapsed (Brock 1991: 56, 117ff.). Most members abandoned their anti-war position to support the military efforts of the northern states. From one point of view this was both morally and rationally consistent with their previous position. They strongly opposed slavery, and many of them had come to feel that institution could not be abolished without military force. The abolition of war would simply have to stand in line until this other abolition could be accomplished. However, there was more at work than rationality and ethics. Many members of the peace societies had themselves become caught up in the 'spirits' of war and of the nation. They were suddenly enthusiastic about what they had previously denounced (Brock 1991: 56, 117ff.). As methodological polytheists we cannot help but wonder whether methodological atheism and methodological monotheism failed these peace societies, leading them to underestimate the Powers against which they struggled. The same failure has haunted the subsequent movement for peace. At the outbreak of the First World War, for example, the anti-war rhetoric of socialists, feminists, labour activists and various other proponents of peace was largely cast aside as members of these movements jostled to support the war efforts of their nations. There is danger in underestimating the Powers.

The Christian spirituality of the early peace societies imposed additional limitations on the movement for peace. Their religious language and scriptural references left little room for secular humanists committed to peace. And what about people in societies where Christianity was not the religion of the majority? The fact is that when the early peace society members spoke of the system of peace with which they wished to replace the war system they were sometimes referring to Christianity (Dodge 1972: 63ff.; Worcester 1972: 17ff.). But in this case the spread of peace to the world would require the spread of Christianity. The references in the early tracts to people of the 'Hindoo' and 'Mahometan' faiths, and of other non-Christian religions, are largely negative (Worcester 1972: 3, 19). It was apparently assumed that these faiths would eventually melt away before the Christian gospel.

Of course, we must be fair to these writers. They, and the Western public generally, knew little about non-Christian religions, especially religions from Southeast Asia and the Far East. By the late nineteenth century this would change.

During what is sometimes called the Oriental Renaissance (Schwab 1984), beginning roughly in the middle of the nineteenth century, missionaries, orientalists and functionaries of European colonialism brought back to Europe masses of religious texts from Asia, which they translated and made known to European society. The Western public picked up these texts and ideas with great interest. When Edwin Arnold published his versified life of the Buddha, *The Light of Asia*, in 1879, it was an immediate success, and it eventually sold between half a million and a million copies in over 83 separate printings (Wright 1957: 74–5). Western peace proponents realized they had a new ally when they heard the Buddha say in Arnold's poem, 'My chariot shall not roll with bloody wheels/From victory to victory' (Arnold 1890: 150).

During the decades that followed, readers in the West discovered that in north India Buddhism and Jainism had worked out complex institutions of nonviolence five centuries before Christianity began. They discovered that among the 'hundred schools' of thought in ancient China, two of the dominant ones, Confucianism and Taoism, had worked out distinctive theories and methods to limit the proclivities of rulers for war, and that in the fifth century BCE the Chinese philosopher Mo Tzu had already begun estimating the economic losses war brought to his society and had proposed that wars of aggression be criminalized (Watson 1963). They learned that Islam had helped create great and sophisticated societies that often displayed more religious tolerance than contemporary Christian ones. They learned that Hindus had found ways to accommodate enormous diversity of belief and practice without holy war. They came to see that Judaism was neither static, locked in the 'Old Testament', nor a mere prelude to Christianity, but a religion that had evolved, like all other religions, and that had a subtle set of mechanisms for balancing old tradition and new realities. They saw, in short, that the global resources for the creation of a peace spirituality and a peace system were much richer than they had previously thought.

The knowledge of this richness and the use of it in dialogue between peace advocates in the West and the East distinguish major peace proponents of the end of the nineteenth century from those at its beginning. Unlike people such as Worcester and Diamond of the early peace societies, Leo Tolstoy was familiar with Asian thought, and while he was close to the early writers in his view of war and his high regard for the Sermon on the Mount, he was able to say that the 'law of love' that opposed the 'law of violence' was known in all religions and was, in fact, accessible even to those without any religious involvement (Tolstoy 1987). Mohandas Gandhi, meanwhile, enthusiastically mixed ancient Indian asceticism and English vegetarianism, Hinduism and anarchism, the Sermon on the Mount and the Bhagavad-Gita, and gave to his teachings on nonviolence a universal rather than a national appeal. Tolstoy and Gandhi – especially Gandhi – brought forth through this synthetic and creative process a form of nonviolence that went beyond the earlier Christian forms of 'non-resistance' and was able to demonstrate enormous power in the world of politics. This nonviolence began to answer the dilemma posed by wars, as it showed that in some cases justice and security could be achieved better through unarmed methods than through resort to arms.

The discovery of the religions of India and China was also good news for secular humanists who had felt left out of the movement for peace. The West now had access to religions with non-theistic forms of inner cultivation. In Confucianism such cultivation was based on the essentially non-mythical concept of the fundamental goodness of human nature. According to the Confucian philosopher Meng Tzu, for example, the development of civilization and peace would take place through the careful nurturing of the four 'incipient tendencies' in all human beings: the ability to feel compassion, shame and respect, and the ability to make ethical distinctions (Lau 1970: 82–3). Likewise, Buddhists felt that a human being did not need the divine in order to become 'a binder together of those who are divided, an encourager of those who are friends, a peacemaker, a lover of peace, impassioned for peace, a speaker of words that make for peace' (Rhys Davids 1899: 5). For Buddhists, the development of the mind and heart took discipline and inward exploration, but the trans-human Powers that existed in the universe were regarded as, at best, helpers in this process.

I have argued elsewhere that it is legitimate to use the word 'spirituality' for these diverse traditions of inner cultivation and that it is appropriate to use the term 'peace spirituality' for any form of spirituality in which peace and peacemaking are accorded very high value (MacQueen 1999). One of the most important developments of the twentieth and early twenty-first centuries has been the maturation of numerous peace spiritualities and their increasing communication and cooperation with each other. It is now possible to glimpse a global peace system that incorporates diverse but harmonious peace spiritualities.

Religious studies and peace studies

One of the benefits of the Oriental Renaissance was the stimulation of a new academic discipline devoted to the study of religion. The religious texts that poured into the West during the late nineteenth century provoked reflection on the common factors in the world's religions and the need for new ways of studying these. One of the first persons to propose the establishment of a science of religion was the nineteenth-century Orientalist Max Müller, who edited *The Sacred Books of the East*, published in 51 volumes between 1879 and 1904 (Müller 1879–).

Since the late nineteenth and early twentieth centuries, the study of religion as a distinct academic discipline (usually known simply as Religious Studies today) has evolved in a way that has made it an increasingly important contributor to respectful religious and cultural dialogue. This evolution has been gradual and has mirrored similar developments in other academic disciplines.

In the earliest stages of the study of religion, the excitement with which Western scholars greeted the texts and traditions of Asia was often overwhelmed by a threefold arrogance:

- *Scientific arrogance.* The West considered itself the land of reason and science, and many Western scholars held that all religions, but especially non-Western varieties, were the product of primitive superstition, infantilism and simple error. A great deal of energy was expended speculating about the historical origins of religion (understood as the origin of error), and these attempts were as notable for their disdain for evidence as for their ingenuity.
- *Monotheistic arrogance.* Most of the scholars studying Asian religion were Christian, and many thought it obvious that their form of religion was the most rational and the most

ethically noble. Comparative studies often concluded that Christianity was the highest form of religion, with the religions of tribal peoples generally assigned the lowest rung of the ladder.

- *Civilizational and imperial arrogance.* Many of those in the West taking up the new study of religion assumed that not only in science and religion, but in philosophy, political and economic theory, and the study of history, the West had the oldest, soundest and certainly most up-to-date systems, with the very concrete implication that non-Western societies should allow themselves to be both tutored and governed by the West.

The development of Religious Studies since those early days can be viewed as a progressive abandonment of these three forms of arrogance. The process is well advanced but far from complete.

In this evolutionary process, perhaps the most important school of thought has been that of the phenomenology of religion (Flood 1999; Kunin 2003; Smart 1973), the key methodological characteristics of which are: (i) 'bracketing' – the suspension of judgements of truth and falsity so that the *meaning* of religious phenomena within a particular religion and within the wider reality of religion per se can be discerned; (ii) attending, during the determination of meaning, to the meaning of religious phenomena for the religious practitioners themselves, not merely for observers, with a resultant emphasis on the need for imagination and empathy on the part of the observer; and (iii) creating typologies, on the basis of wide-ranging study, which allow the central categories of religion (traditionally thought to include such things as ritual, myth and scripture) to be isolated and described in general terms.

From the point of view of civilizational dialogue, the phenomenology of religion has represented a great leap forward. It has eroded each of the three forms of arrogance and made stereotyping of the religions of others much more difficult. The teaching of Religious Studies in colleges and universities during the past few decades has been greatly influenced by the phenomenology of religion, and hundreds of thousands of young people have in this way had their horizons broadened and their prejudices challenged.

Of course, this school of thought has had its critics, and to those annoyed by its 'liberalism' and 'relativism' has now been added the voice of post-modern scholars, who regard it as more a method than a theory of religion, who regret its search for 'essences' beyond the particulars of history, and who feel its imaginative empathy is inadequate for the task of truly listening to the voice of the Other (Flood 1999). In the best possible future, these post-modern scholars will further erode the three forms of arrogance that have prevented Religious Studies from reaching its potential as a force for peace and justice. In the worst possible future, post-modernism will undercut the phenomenology of religion only to succumb to its own elitism, obscurantism and naive philosophical nominalism.

From the point of view of Peace Studies, the challenge is surely clear. Whatever its methodological stance, Religious Studies must rise to the intellectual and moral challenges of a diverse and fragile world, helping to create the deep global dialogue without which the system of peace required to replace the war system cannot fully emerge.

References

Arnold, E. (1890) *The Light of Asia: Being the Life and Teaching of Gotama, Prince of India and Founder of Buddhism*, Chicago, IL: Rand McNally.

Beal, S. (ed. and trans.) (1968) *Si-Yu-Ki: Buddhist Records of the Western World*, London: Kegan Paul, Trench, Trubner.

Brock, P. (1991) *Freedom from War: Nonsectarian Pacifism 1814–1914*, Toronto: University of Toronto Press.

Dodge, D. (1972) 'War inconsistent with the religion of Jesus Christ', in P. Brock (ed.) *The First American Peace Movement*, New York: Garland Publishing.

Durkheim, E. (1915) *The Elementary Forms of the Religious Life*, New York: Allen & Unwin.

Dymond, J. (1973) *War: An Essay*, New York: Garland Publishing.

Flood, G. (1999) *Beyond Phenomenology: Rethinking the Study of Religion*, London: Cassell.

Grossman, D. (1995) *On Killing: The Psychological Cost of Learning to Kill in War and Society*, Boston, MA: Little, Brown and Company.

Hill, C. (1975) *The World Turned Upside Down: Radical Ideas During the English Revolution*, Harmondsworth: Penguin.

Hollar, B. (ed.) (2004) *The Routledge Encyclopedia of Religion and War*, New York: Routledge.

Jameson, M. (1991) 'Sacrifice before battle', in V. Hansen (ed.) *Hoplites: The Classical Greek Battle Experience*, London: Routledge.

Keegan, J. (1993) *A History of Warfare*, New York: Alfred A. Knopf, New York.

Kertzer, D. (1988) *Ritual, Politics and Power*, New Haven, CT: Yale University Press.

Kunin, S. (2003) *Religion: The Modern Theories*, Baltimore, MD: Johns Hopkins University Press.

LaForge, J. (1982) 'Profession of Faith', *The Other Side*, 27 (out of print).

Lasswell, H. (1938) *Propaganda Technique in the World War*, New York: Peter Smith.

Lau, D.C. (1970) *Mencius* (transl.), Harmondsworth: Penguin, 82–3.

MacQueen, G. (1999) 'Spirituality and peacemaking', in *Encyclopedia of Violence, Peace, and Conflict*, San Diego, CA: Academic Press.

Mott, J. (1972) 'Lawfulness of war for Christians, examined', in P. Brock (ed.) *The First American Peace Movement*, New York: Garland Publishing.

Müller, M. (ed.) (1879–) *The Sacred Books of the East*, Oxford: Clarendon Press.

Parker, P. (1987) *The Old Lie: The Great War and the Public-School Ethos*, London: Constable.

Rapoport, A. (ed.) (1968) *Carl Von Clausewitz: On War*, Harmondsworth: Penguin.

Rhys Davids, T.W. (trans.) (1899) *Dialogues of the Buddha [Digha Nikaya]*, vol. 1, London: Oxford University Press.

Schwab, R. (1984) *The Oriental Renaissance: Europe's Rediscovery of India and the East, 1680–1880*, trans. G. Patterson-Black and V. Reinking, New York: Columbia University Press.

Smart, N. (1973) *The Science of Religion and the Sociology of Knowledge: Some Methodological Questions*, Princeton, NJ: Princeton University Press.

Steere, D. (ed.) (1984) *Quaker Spirituality: Selected Writings*, New York: Paulist Press.

Tolstoy, L. (1987) *Writings on Civil Disobedience and Nonviolence*, Philadelphia, PA: New Society Publishers.

Watson, B. (1963) *Mo Tzu: Basic Writings*, New York: Columbia University Press.

Wink, W. (1992) *Engaging the Powers: Discernment and Resistance in a World of Domination*, Minneapolis, MI: Fortress Press.

Worcester, N. (1972) 'A solemn review of the custom of war', in P. Brock (ed.) *The First American Peace Movement*, New York: Garland Publishing.

Wright, B. (1957) *Interpreter of Buddhism to the West: Sir Edwin Arnold*, New York: Bookman Associates.

21

International law

Amid power, order and justice

Richard Falk

Introductory considerations

The history of international law has been decidedly mixed. It has functioned for several centuries both as a sword for the strong and a shield for the weak. It has developed over the course of the Westphalian Era, stretching back to the Peace of Westphalia in 1648, as a regulatory and cooperative framework for the interplay of sovereign states. Throughout this history the juridical logic of equality that is embodied in international law has been consistently subordinated to the geopolitical framework of world politics based on the logic of relative power. The same ratio of law to power pertains today. This means that the quality of world order is very dependent on the prudence, wisdom and legitimacy of the global leadership provided at a given time and in various settings by the main geopolitical actors.

During the early stages of the Cold War this leadership was provided mainly by the United States, with the Soviet Union in a defensive and reactive pattern. Under this leadership the United Nations was established, the Numerberg/Tokyo war crimes trials were held, and the Universal Declaration of Human Rights (UDHR) was adopted. Each was a major *geopolitical* acknowledgement of the importance of strengthening the relative role of the normative side (that is, law plus morality) of international relations. This strengthening related to three major world order deficiencies that had been disclosed by the great devastation of the two world wars, and the human suffering associated with oppressive regimes: ending the discretionary status of war by UN Charter prohibition on recourse to force except in self-defence (Articles 2(4) and 51), holding political leaders accountable for crimes of state (Nürnberg and Tokyo Judgements, as supplemented by the Genocide Convention), and challenging a central tenet of the Westphalian ethos, which holds that whatever takes places *within* the territory of a state is a matter of sovereign right and not subject to external review. Such initiatives were tentative and provisional steps, but opening wide horizons of possibility, which unfortunately have not been successfully implemented. These initiatives were from the outset subject to major qualifications and regressive moves in geopolitics that occurred throughout the Cold War. At the same time such steps gave grounds for hope that future world order could be an improvement on the past, and that the essence of this improvement would be a greater effort to reconcile international law with global justice. This hope, while often crushed by persisting geopolitical

Machiavellianism, has remained important as an inspiration and source of legitimation for normatively inclined governments and visionary elements of civil society. Even when states have cynically cast aside or defied these normative promises of the Charter, Nuremberg and UDHR, civil society actors have done their best, especially in war/peace and human rights situations, to fulfil these higher expectations. The sad truth remains, that international law operates as an essentially *voluntary* system of constraints for major states, and is selectively, and often unfairly, enforced in relation to weaker states. The non-proliferation regime governing development and possession of nuclear weapons illustrates both sides of this dynamic: exemptions for the powerful; enforcement for the weak.

The United Nations Charter and practice is a major arena within which these tensions were expressed. For instance, the Charter affirms sovereign rights in rather unconditional terms, famously declaring that the UN shall refrain from intervening in matters 'essentially within the domestic jurisdiction of any state' (Article 2(7)), which effectively nullifies any prospect that international human rights will be implemented in relation to abusive governments. Going further, it seems clear that the only reason that the UDHR could be agreed upon in the first place was the tacit understanding among participating governments that it would *not* be enforced. But civil society took more seriously the norms contained in the UDHR, and found ways to convert this instrument from the statist intention to compile a list of pieties into a viable political project. This political project took hold as a result of pressures exerted by an array of trans-national human rights organizations founded and funded by civil society, and given historical relevance in the course of a variety of struggles against oppressive rule, including in East Europe, in the form of the promotion of the right of self-determination in the movement against colonialism, and at the core of the global anti-apartheid movement. In this sense, states, including geopolitical actors, *rediscovered* human rights as a useful instrument of world order *after* these norms of political behaviour had been first taken seriously at the level of civil society.

In a sense, the same dynamic is manifest with respect to the legacy of the Nuremberg/Tokyo tradition. This tradition always suffered from the taint of victors' justice, exempting from legal scrutiny such wartime atrocities of the winning side as the indiscriminate bombing of German and Japanese cities, and the initiation of the Nuclear Age with the atomic bombs dropped on Hiroshima and Nagasaki. At Nuremberg it was declared that the standards used to judge the defeated Germans would only be vindicated if in the future those who sat in judgement accepted accountability by reference to the same legal constraints on the behaviour of sovereign states. This 'Nuremberg Promise' was repeatedly broken by the subsequent official crimes of the Second World War victors. But the promise was not forgotten by representatives of civil society. In the course of the Vietnam War, in the United States many acts were committed by anti-war Americans based on their reading of Nuremberg that were seeking to implement over the heads of the geopoliticians norms of limitations associated with the prohibition of aggressive war and the obligations of international humanitarian law with respect to the conduct of war. The impact of these acts of civil resistance is hard to assess, but it would seem at the very least that they contributed to the delegitimation of the Vietnam War, and when coupled with battlefield failures, led to its eventual repudiation even by policy-making elites. With a similar effect was the Bertrand Russell War Crimes Tribunal set up in 1967 on the basis of civil society concerns about the criminality of the Vietnam War, engaging the participation of the leading European intellectuals of the day (Jean-Paul Sartre, Simone de Beauvoir) and later inspiring the formation of the Permanent People's Tribunal in Rome that has for 20 years relied upon the progressive elements in international law to assess the injustices, wrongdoing and crimes of leading geopolitical actors that are met with silence by the state system and even by the United Nations.

The Charter itself embodied the contradictory impulses of international law and geopolitics. On the one side, principles of non-internvention, self-determination and equality of states are affirmed, as well as the prohibition of all non-defensive uses of force to resolve international disputes. On the other side, there is imposed no legal obligation to disarm or to submit disputes to the International Court of Justice, and the five permanent members of the Security Council (picked from the winners of the Second World War plus China) are given a veto power, which in effect exempts them from the Charter. Such deference to political realism is an explicit acknowledgement that international legal authority cannot be imposed upon leading political actors. In practice this exemption, combined with the geopolitical stalemate in the Cold War and the refusal of either superpower to go forward with the Chapter VII (Articles 39–49) efforts to establish procedures and capabilities to provide collective security in the face of aggression, doomed the effort to end recourse to discretionary war by geopolitical actors and their friends. Again to the extent that this normative expectation has been kept alive, it has been a result of the action of world citizens and peace movements that base their demonstrations and other initiatives on an unconditional acceptance of the outlawry of aggressive war for all states, big and small alike.

What is evident, then, over the course of the last century is a long struggle to curtail the primacy of geopolitics and territorial sovereignty as the pillars of world order. This struggle has had ebbs and flows. Its positive results often depend on some sort of convergence between the demands of civil society and either the moderation or weakness of geopolitical forces. Its negative experiences usually reflect the impact of extremist geopolitical orientations and militarist orientations toward the fulfilment of geopolitical world order goals. This pattern has been given great prominence in the period since the end of the Cold War. The next section examines the optimistic mood of the 1990s associated with the first normative 'revolution' in world politics that raised hopes as the millennium approached despite some discouraging aspects. The third section focuses on the return to regressive geopolitics as a consequence of the American approach to the pursuit of grand strategy goals in the aftermath of the 9/11 attacks. A final section discusses prospects as of the early twenty-first century for reviving the normative revolution, taking some account of three impinging trends: the growing dysfunction of war and militarism as geopolitical instruments; the tightening energy/ecological squeeze that will require transition to a post-petroleum world economy by stages during the decades ahead, requiring painful adjustments; and the growing need for a more institutionalized form of global governance to cope effectively and fairly with the growing complexity and fragility of the world.

Notes on the normative revolution of the 1990s

The period immediately following the Cold War seemed to present strong opportunities for global reform, giving the West lots of political space to take initiatives to make the world safer and more equitable. It was a moment of liberal capitalist global ascendancy in the aftermath of the Soviet collapse, with a virtually worldwide acceptance of only those forms of political governance based on a combination of a strong market economy and constitutional democracy. Additionally, there was a virtual completion of the decolonization process, with only South Africa and Palestine remaining important remnants of the colonial era at the start of the 1990s. The United States emerged as the undisputed global leader, claiming for itself a special role as 'indispensable nation' given the geopolitical background of unipolarity. In such a favourable context there were several promising world order initiatives that might have been encouraged by the US either on its own or in concert with other leading governments: serious nuclear disarmament and negotiated demilitarization (e.g. a worldwide 1 per cent of GNP ceiling on military expenditures for national security); a UN peace force and independent revenue base; limitations on the use of the veto and mandatory reference of contested policy issues to ICJ for resolution; serious and balanced diplomatic efforts to promote a fair settlement of the Israel–Palestine conflict. But instead, the geopolitical preoccupation of major states was devoted to global economic growth along neo-liberal lines, producing both a prevailing sense that 'globalization' was the true new world order and an anti-globalization backlash by those social forces around the world being victimized by this latest phase of predatory world capitalism. The intergovernmental basis for reformist action lacked any forward energy. The supposed 'new world order' proclaimed by the first George Bush was an opportunistic packaging of recourse to war to legitimize a coalition formed under a UN mandate in 1990 to push Iraq out of Kuwait. It was never meant to be anything more than a temporary effort to mobilize support within the US and the world for a dubious war that was intended to be controlled from Washington but backed by the United Nations. In this sense, rather than the *new* world order, it was a dramatic reminder of the resilience of the *old* world order, with the geopolitical ventriloquist making use of its UN puppet.

Despite this disappointing failure to take advantage of the global setting to introduce needed changes, the 1990s did produce some notable developments that were based on the potentially constructive contributions of international law to global justice and humane global governance. In all instances, and this is a dramatic expression of the rise of non-state, civil society actors, these developments depended on the rise of global civil society as a political force, acting either autonomously or in collaboration with those statist forces that wanted to restrict sovereign rights and geopolitical discretion, which historically were the two main sources of human wrongs and warmaking within the Westphalian framework. International law played a central role in giving substance to these undertakings and confidence to activists. Several of these initiatives can be mentioned to show a continuity with the global reformist surge evident after 1945: to restrict warmaking, to hold leaders criminally accountable for violations of fundamental rules about the use of force and with respect to the treatment of persons under sovereign control, and to move toward the *international* protection of the fundamental human rights of vulnerable peoples subject to severe abuse from territorial governments. Despite the forward movement in each domain, there were also major setbacks, and contradictory tendencies, but overall there was a widespread appreciation that these efforts to globalize liberal legality were improving the quality of world order.

Several significant legal developments involved moves to restrict certain tactics in relation to warfare over the opposition of geopolitical actors. Two illustrations can be given. 'A new internationalism' involving a coalition of civil society actors and moderate governments managed to produce a treaty that was rapidly negotiated and widely supported by most governments to ban the use of anti-personnel landmines. Such a move was impressive symbolically as it suggested a certain space for global reforms without geopolitical backing in the face of American opposition to this move. At the same time, the success was of only marginal relevance to modern warfare as the dependence on anti-personnel landmines was mainly a matter of cost efficiency, and military substitutes existed to achieve similar battlefield results.

More challenging was an initiative of the General Assembly, responsive to well-orchestrated civil society pressures, to refer to the World Court the question of the legality of nuclear weapons. Once again, with greater resolve than in relation to landmines, the US government energetically used its political leverage to oppose this reference, and again failed. This failure was reinforced when the World Court in 1996 issued its legal opinion, which cast grave doubt on the legality of almost every contemplated use of nuclear weapons, casting legal doubt on strategic thinking in the nuclear weapons states, and unanimously reminded nuclear weapons states of their solemn obligation under Article VI of the Non-Proliferation Treaty to pursue in good faith nuclear disarmament. This set of World Court directives, while completely ignored by the nuclear weapons states, did contribute to the general climate of illegitimacy, even criminality, associated with any future threat or use of nuclear weapons. In this respect the gap between an objective reading of international law requirements and the attitude of nuclear weapons states suggests two lines of interpretation: the inability of international law to overcome the priorities of geopolitical actors with respect to the most urgent of war/peace issues; and the importance of future collaborations between non-nuclear weapons states and anti-nuclear civil society forces in seeking the implementation of international legal standards with respect to these weapons of mass destruction if the Preamble of the UN Charter 'to save succeeding generations from the scourge of war' is ever going to take on entrenched militarism that continues to dominate the grand strategy of geopolitical actors.

Perhaps of more immediate substantive impact was the effort to revive the Nuremberg tradition of accountability of leaders. The victims of the Pinochet regime in Chile were particularly active around the world in seeking some kind of justice in response to years of abuse. In 1998, Pinochet was detained in Britain because of a request for extradition that came from Spain where a prosecutor was prepared to indict the former Chilean dictator for torture and other international crimes. The litigation in British courts that followed focused world attention on this issue of criminal accountability of heads of sovereign states. Although Pinochet was eventually allowed to escape prosecution in Spain and returned to Chile because he was deemed unfit to stand trial, there was great enthusiasm generated in civil society for moving toward the establishment of an international criminal court, as well as to extend the authority of domestic courts throughout the world to enforce international criminal law, what is called by international lawyers 'universal jurisdiction'. Again, a global coalition of civil society actors and moderate, reform-minded governments was effective in generating a process that has led to an international treaty that brought the International Criminal Court into being in 2002. Whether such an institution and accountability can operate effectively in the face of intense American opposition remains to be seen. This opposition has taken various forms. One of the most obstructive of these is for the US government to negotiate a large number of bilateral agreements with governments to exempt its citizens from ever being turned over for prosecution. It requires only a touch of irony to appreciate that it is American policy-makers and commanders that would stand in the greatest jeopardy of indictment and prosecution if an international criminal procedure of the sort foreshadowed at Nuremberg were allowed to go forward in the early twenty-first century and have the capacity to extend its reach to those who acted on behalf of *all* states, and not just, as at present, the leadership of weak or defeated states. As the criminal trials of Slobodan Milosevic and Saddam Hussein show, the US government is not opposed to the Nuremberg legacy if narrowly confined, but only to its extension to the activities of dominant geopolitical actors.

A third kind of initiative during the 1990s was associated with 'humanitarian intervention' in circumstances where a vulnerable population faced catastrophe. The first major attempt to move in this direction involved the break-up of former Yugoslavia, with some earlier half-hearted and pathetic efforts under UN auspices to avoid ethnic cleansing in Bosnia in the early 1990s. A second early humanitarian effort involved Somalia, where the UN was tasked with the job of alleviating a massive human crisis brought about by governmental collapse. Its role was to provide emergency food and medical assistance, and the mission enjoyed initial success. However, when followed by a more ambitious UN peacekeeping undertaking, led by the US, to restructure the country politically, armed resistance ensured, the operation was rather abruptly ended and international forces were withdrawn to avoid any deeper involvement in factional struggles that were ripping Somalia apart, and making the goal of restoring stable governance seem unattainable. The difficulties encountered in Somalia that led to failure contributed to an American-led unwillingness to allow protective action by the UN to prevent, or minimize, a set of genocidal developments in Rwanda in 1994, and this show of global apathy was followed by the ignominy of UN peacekeepers standing by while Muslim males were slaughtered in the thousands in the supposed UN safe haven of Srebrenica in 1995.

Humanitarian concerns converged with some geopolitical priorities a few years later, generating political backing for humanitarian intervention in Kosovo under NATO command in 1999. The undertaking, although criticized for bypassing the UNSC and thus contrary to international law, was politically supported by most European governments, seemed welcomed at the time by the overwhelming majority of the Kosovar population, and did successfully avert what appeared to be a new cycle of ethnic cleansing in the region. The effectiveness of this response, as compared to Somalia and Rwanda failures, is certainly associated with the geopolitical commitment to the use of sufficient force that was based on giving NATO a new set of security roles after the Cold War, showcasing the continuing seriousness of American involvement in European affairs, and reinforcing the message that military force under American leadership can achieve desired political results at acceptable costs. In other words, the geopolitical stakes associated with the post-Cold War credibility of NATO combined with the display of a continuing American commitment to European issues ensured that the humanitarian concern would not be shortchanged if difficulties emerged.

There were also some serious criticisms of the NATO approach: it undermined the proper UN role with respect to global peace and security; the aerial bombardment from high altitudes shifted the burden of risk to the civilian population of Serbia and Kosovo; inadequate steps were take in the immediate post-conflict setting to protect Serbs from Albanian acts of revenge; and insufficient resources were devoted to enable a successful reconstruction effort. The Kosovo War remains a normatively ambiguous experience in which the role of global civil society was marginal, partly because civic attitudes were not unified, and the geopolitical stakes overshadowed the humanitarian challenge.

The Kosovo precedent is also ambiguous with respect to international law. It definitely seemed to authorize an evasion of the supposedly total authority of the UNSC over non-defensive uses of force, setting an unfortunate precedent that looks worse in retrospect. At the same time, the effect of the NATO undertaking was to rescue a vulnerable population from probable imminent catastrophe, and to induce the return from refugee camps of hundreds of thousand of Kosovars who had fled in fear across borders. It also illustrated the degree to which the convergence of normative and geopolitical priorities has the capacity to produce effective action.

The 1990s gave rise to additional efforts to improve the quality of world order. There were an unprecedented number of efforts to redress historic wrongs either by apologies, commissions of truth and reconciliation, and reparations and compensation. Long suppressed issues involving the victims of Japanese and German abuses during the Second World War (slave labour comfort women, confiscated assets) or the dispossession of indigenous peoples in various settings around the world suddenly received meaningful official attention. There seemed to be a definite set of moves designed to bring international law into closer conformity with the requirements of global justice, as well as to set limits on the sovereign rights of states. At the same time, these moves toward normative revolution were preliminary, and as subsequent developments have made clear, quite reversible due to adverse geopolitical developments in almost all respects. The

1990s did nothing to displace the central observation that world order continues to be shaped by geopolitical actors. This role is inconsistent with aspirations to achieve a bottom-up, more democratic world order, but it is not necessarily malevolent. It depends on the orientation and behaviour of the dominant geopolitical actors. Compare the relatively constructive role of the US in the period immediately following the Second World War and its role after the 9/11 attacks. One dimension of this comparison can be made by emphasizing the degree of congruence between global reform and the strengthening of international law and institutions in 1945, and the hostility toward such goals since 2001. This latter pattern is the focus of the next section.

American lawnessness in the twenty-first century

The US government has long adopted double standards when it comes to respecting international law, especially in the setting of national security issues. It promotes a generalized respect for the rule of law in world politics, is outraged by violations of international law by its enemies, and chooses selectively when to comply and when to violate. This pattern can be traced far back in American history, but it is convenient to take note of American violations of international law in the setting of the Vietnam War, as well as periodic interventions in Central and South America. I would argue that this pattern has diminished America's global reputation and capacity for leadership, as well as worked against its own national interests.

It seems clear that the US, and the American people, would have benefited over the years from a foreign policy carried out subject to the discipline of international law. If the US government had abided by international law, the dreadful experience of the Vietnam War would never have occurred. More recently, an observation that will be discussed further below, upholding international law would have avoided the fiasco of the Iraq War. Contrary to popular belief, respecting the restraints of international law better serves the national interest of a powerful country at this stage of history far better than does an attitude, so prevalent in neo-conservative circles and since 9/11, that international law poses inconvenient, unnecessary, unwise and removable obstacles on the path toward national and global security.

It is important to understand that the restraints embodied in international law have been voluntarily developed on the basis of international experience and changing attitudes toward war by representatives of sovereign states acting to uphold the realist interests and professed values of their governments. The intent of international law, even with respect to warmaking, is practical rather than aspirational or idealistic. The core principles of international law encode the wisdom of diplomacy accumulated over the course of the last several centuries. International law is of particular importance in relation to uses of force as an instrument of foreign policy, and more generally, as it bears upon issues relating to security, especially war and peace. The US Constitution declares in Article VI(2) that, 'duly ratified treaties are the supreme law of the land'. This puts the key rules and principles of international law on a par with Congressional acts within the American legal system. The Supreme Court has ruled that in the event of an unavoidable clash between these two sources of legal authority, the last in time should prevail, but that to the extent possible both forms of legal authority should be validated by interpretative flexibility.

The basic argument in support of a foreign policy that is respectful of the constraints of international law deserves to be expressed vigorously: in a globalizing world of great complexity it is overwhelmingly in the interest of all states, large and small, that their relations be reliably and peacefully regulated by international law. This observation is uncontroversially applicable to the daily operations of the world economy and many other types of international behaviour, including maritime safety, environmental protection, tourism, immigration, disease control and criminal law enforcement. The stability of international life depends on a closely woven fabric of law as providing a needed foundation of reliability for almost all activity that partly or wholly takes place outside the borders of a sovereign state.

What is a cause for deepest current worry is that the US government has seemed to abandon this elementary understanding of the relevance of law to the establishment of world order. As suggested, this tendency is not entirely new. It runs like a great river throughout the entire course of American history, but it has taken a serious turn for the worse during the Bush presidency, especially in the aftermath of the 9/11 attacks. Even prior to the attacks, the foreign policy of the Bush administration made it a point of pride to disclose its disdain for widely respected international treaties. The Bush White House contended that existing and pending treaties limited its military and political options in undesirable ways. In the early months of the Bush presidency, the White House announced its opposition to the Comprehensive Test Ban Treaty prohibiting nuclear weapons testing, its withdrawal from ABM Treaty design to avoid an arms race in space, its unwillingness to submit for Senate ratification the Kyoto Protocol regulating greenhouse gas emissions, and its defiant and gratuitous withdrawal of its signature from the Rome Treaty establishing the International Criminal Court. Such a pattern of unilateralist and undisguised hostility to international treaties and multilateral cooperation was unprecedented in American history. It led to a strong negative reaction at home and abroad. Normally friendly governments were clearly disturbed by this strident display of unilateralism and international nihilism by the new American president. This American repudiation of widely endorsed multilateral treaty arrangements upset large segments of world public opinion. These treaty arrangements dealing with important matters of global policy were generally viewed as important contributions to a peaceful world, making their repudiation seem contrary to common sense, as well as dangerous for the overall well-being of the peoples of the world. These expressions of unilateralism by the US to global policy issues did not involve violating existing international law. What was exhibited was a diplomacy based on an outmoded and ultra neo-conservative opposition to almost any form of multilateral undertaking in the security area other than by way of alliance relationships such as NATO or the aggressive partnership with Israel. This unilateralism dysfunctionally limits the capacity of America to make constructive use of its status as the sole remaining superpower in the aftermath of the Cold War, as well as privileges excessive reliance on military approaches to problem-solving and wasteful expenditures on over-investment in unusable military hardware.

The US Congress, and American public, are also not exempt from blame on these counts. It was in Congress even before George W. Bush came to Washington in 2001 that militarist pressures were brought to bear in such a way as to oppose beneficial multilateral treaty constraints on US policy. The Senate refused to ratify the Comprehensive Test Ban in the Clinton years, in addition to being so strongly opposed to the International Criminal Court and Kyoto Protocol that there was no prospect for such treaties to be approved by the required 2/3s vote if submitted to the Senate for ratification. What mainly distinguished the Bush approach to international law were two developments: its alignment of the Executive Branch with an anti-internationalist set of policies; and its avowedly ideological and emphatic repudiation of treaty instruments in order to signal a unilateralist approach to foreign policy premised upon military dominance and interventionary diplomacy. It was this geopolitical posture by the Bush leadership that frightened world public opinion. Before 9/11 a rising crescendo of domestic and international opposition to the Bush policies led to mounting criticism of this approach to world affairs, which hardened the perception that Bush's credentials as president were already unusually weak given his contested electoral mandate. Many observers who scrutinized the results in 2000 believed that a fair count of the votes in Florida would have resulted in Bush's defeat, and victory for Al Gore.

This concern and opposition has dramatically intensified outside the US since 9/11 because the Bush White House has moved from this earlier hostility to multilateralism to a posture of pronounced unwillingness to abide by fundamental international legal rules and standards that this country, along with other constitutional democracies, had previously accepted and applied as a matter of course. These rules include humane treatment of prisoners taken during armed combat, unconditional prohibitions on torture and assassination of political opponents, and the duty to protect civilians in any foreign territory under occupation. The most important of all these legal restrictions on foreign policy is the rule of international law prohibiting non-defensive uses of force without a mandate from the UN Security Council. In his 2004 State of the Union Address, President Bush told Congress that the US would never seek 'a permission slip' in matters bearing on its security. But it is precisely a permission slip that international law, and the UN Charter, requires if force is used outside the scope of self-defence *against a prior armed attack*. This strict limitation on recourse to war was written into the Charter largely at the behest of the US government after the Second World War. The basic idea was to bind the states of the world to a legal framework that unconditionally prohibited wars of aggression, what has more brashly been recently called 'wars of choice'. German and Japanese leaders were sentenced to death at war crimes tribunals in 1945 because they had initiated and conducted aggressive wars, a precedent not entirely lost on the peoples of the world.

The Iraq War is a notorious example of an aggressive war (or war of choice) that violates this fundamental rule of international law set forth authoritatively in Article 2(4) of the United Nations Charter. As such, according to the Nuremberg Principles embodied in general international law after the conviction of German leaders for their criminal conduct, the invasion of Iraq in 2003 constitutes a Crime Against Peace. The American prosecutor at Nuremberg, Justice Robert Jackson, famously said to the tribunal, '. . . let me make clear that while this law is first applied against German aggressors, the law includes, and if it is to serve a useful purpose it must condemn, aggression by other nations, including those which sit here now in judgement.' It is this Nuremberg Promise that is being repeatedly and defiantly broken by the US and Israel, thereby undermining any prospect for peace and normalcy in the world.

The pattern of illegality associated with the Iraq War, and subsequent occupation, continues to shock the conscience of humanity. American officials have strained to redefine 'torture' so as to permit what the rest of the world, and common sense, understand to be 'torture'. The abuse of prisoners detained in Guantanamo, Abu Ghraib and elsewhere has severely damaged America's reputation in the world, as well as discredited a genuine and necessary struggle against extremist enemies engaged in terrorism. Government lawyers and their neo-conservative supporters in society have argued in favour of assassinating terrorist suspects in foreign countries, and have justified under the terminology of 'extraordinary rendition' deliberately handing over suspects to foreign governments notorious for their reliance on torture as their normal mode of prisoner interrogation. The detrimental impact of American lawlessness on the protection of human rights worldwide and within the US has been set forth in great detail by such respected organizations as the American Civil Liberties Union, Amnesty International and Human Rights Watch. This record of American abuse has badly undercut the capacity of the US government to exert pressure on other governments to protect human rights, rendering such pressure suspect and hypocritical.

It is notable to observe that the events of 9/11 produced a patriotic surge within the US that has given the Bush administration the political space needed to embark on a foreign policy aimed at 'geopolitical preeminence', and only incidentally concerned with the defeat of Al Qaeda and the containment of transnational terrorism. Such an ambitious priority was stated clearly before 9/11 in the report of the Project for a New American Century published in September 2000 under the title of 'Repairing America's Defenses', and endorsed by many individuals who later became leading advisors to the Bush presidency. This wider grand strategy was explicitly embraced, and set forth in detail, subsequent to 9/11, in the important White House document entitled, 'The National Security Strategy of the United States of America' (2002), which has been itself updated by a new document released by the White House in 2006 with the same title. In other words, violating international law, especially embarking on wars of aggression, has been integral to the realization of pre-existing American global ambitions that were politically non-viable before 9/11. To sustain a climate of acquiescence within the US it has been necessary to rely upon a manipulative politics of fear and anger associated with the 9/11 experience that has largely led to a suspension of mainstream criticism by the media, an absence of debate reinforced by the passivity of the opposition Democratic Party, and by the US Congress. In this crucial respect, Congress is failing in its constitutional duties by its unwillingness to exert principled pressure on the Executive to uphold the rule of law by demanding compliance with international law. The public outrage associated with the derelictions of governmental duty in the setting of Hurricane Katrina in 2005 seemed temporarily to have finally opened a space for challenging the legitimacy of the present government, but then the critical mood vanished, despite the fact that the Bush presidency has been steadily losing popular support. There is still no indication that Congress or the public is willing to cancel the blank cheque issued to the Bush presidency in the setting of foreign policy in the feverish atmosphere following 9/11. And despite all that has happened, it appears to remain politically viable for the US government in collaboration with Israel to move toward a new aggressive warfare in the Middle East.

This focus on American behaviour obscures the larger framework of argument. It has become a requirement of a constitutional democracy in the twenty-first century for a government's foreign policy, as well as its domestic behaviour, to be conducted in a manner consistent with the discipline of international law. In a globalizing world the extension of law to international activity almost always serves the national interest of even powerful states. The constraints of international law keep the leaders of democratic states from embarking on dangerous geopolitical ventures that would not be supported by an informed citizenry. The refusal of one state, particularly if it is seen to be a leading state, to abide by international law creates a precedent that gives other states a reciprocal right, as well as political encouragement, to violate their legal obligations.

Finally, adherence to international law in matters of war and peace is in the interest of the peoples of the world. There may be humanitarian emergencies or dangerous threats of attack that might justify recourse to war as the UN Secretary General's report 'In Larger Freedom' and as the UN High-level Panel on Threats, Challenges and Change recommends, but such recourse to war is only legally valid if it is authorized by the Security Council. America and the world will be better off when non-defensive warfare requires in every instance the issuance of 'a permission slip'. The bad American example should not confuse political leaders around the world. It will be beneficial for the peoples of the world to strengthen the global rule of law, and to encourage a pedagogy of peace and security that emphasizes the relevance of international law to a peaceful and equitable world order. Perhaps the disadvantages of American lawlessness in this period can stimulate a global swing by other political actors back toward lawfulness, thereby emulating the broad tendencies toward law-oriented global policies associated with the European Union. It would be helpful if leaders in global civil society would give attention to the importance of effective legal regimes to regulate many sectors of international life, and move to reinforce efforts to hold criminally accountable those who are responsible for aggressive warfare and abusive conduct. The world is now morally sensitive and politically integrated to ignore or tolerate the commission of Crimes Against Peace or Crimes Against Humanity.

Concluding comments

International law remains subordinate to geopolitics, and is shaped to a considerable extent by the priorities and prudence of the leading political actor at a given historical interval. But such an overview is not the entire story. International law, especially as embodied in Nuremberg, the UN Charter and the UDHR, as well as the many recent rulings by the World Court, also offers and encourages resistance to geopolitically driven projects destructive of human values and to particular abuses of sovereign rights. The emergence of global civil society actors represents a further geopolitical challenge in a number of domains of international life. The World Tribunal on Iraq, organized as a civil society undertaking in 2005, held in Istanbul, confirmed the unlawfulness of the American and British invasion of Iraq and its subsequent occupation, as well as implored global institutions to hold those responsible for these policies criminally accountable in the Nuremberg sense. Such a decision by a civil society tribunal, now spread to all parts of the planet by virtue of the Internet, definitely contributes to a climate of illegitimacy surrounding the persisting war policies of the US and Israel, despite being unable to implement its 'legal' findings in a manner that would alter behaviour.

There are several developments that suggest an important potential role for law in shaping the future of humanity on a global scale:

- Accepting the practical need for agreed patterns of order amid the complexity and fragility of many aspects of trans-national activity.
- Acknowledging the growing evidence that warfare and military expenditures are dysfunctional means by which to pursue political ends, and that adherence to legal standards and procedures offer promising alternatives.
- Meeting the challenge of globally delimited problems such as global warming, polar melting, mass migration, energy and water shortages.
- Recognizing the success of the European Project in providing a model of post-Westphalian political order on a regional scale that relies on regional law, procedures and institutions to address conflict, and has managed to instill a culture of peace among the participants.

At the same time, this potential role can only become actual if the US as rogue hegemon changes its approach toward these issues, becoming less unilateralist, abandoning the pursuit of global empire, and growing to appreciate the benefits of a law-oriented foreign policy in which self-discipline accomplishes much of what law enforcement requires. The prospect of an American defeat in Iraq, and the frustration of the main plan to bring 'democracy' to the Middle East by freely elected secular leaders who rush off to Washington to pledge allegiance once in control, may open enough space for alternative visions of world order to become relevant. Before such an adjustment occurs, we are likely to experience a downward spiral that will diminish still further respect for the core norms of international law. In the summer 2006 regional crisis, Israel, with the backing of the US, used large-scale border-crossing military action to punish the whole of Lebanon for allowing Hezbollah, claiming falsely that this is 'self-defence' as understood in international law. Of course, it was nothing of the sort. The media went along with the confusion caused by affirming that a state subject to attack enjoys a right of response, but unless the attack is of a scale to qualify as 'an armed attack' across a border it does not give rise to a right of self-defence by the attacked government, but only a legal option of retaliation in kind, limited and focused. What is discouraging, although not surprising, is that Turkey took advantage of what its foreign minister called 'Israel's precedent in international law' to frame an argument about a comparable Turkish right to intervene militarily in northern Iraq to deal with an allegedly mounting Kurdish threat.

But civil society actors need not be merely reactive with respect to international law. It would seem quite appropriate to frame a future world order by two different, although complementary, legal directives: (1) the affirmations in Articles 25 and 28 of the UDHR that everyone enjoys 'the right to a standard of living' adequate to meet basic human needs' and that 'everyone is entitled to a social and international order' that realizes all of the specific enumerated human rights. Such normative affirmations are almost too good to be true, but provide civil society actors with official criteria by which to legitimate their struggles to achieve global justice and humane global governance; and (2) to articulate and act upon a new globalist ethos of human solidarity that informs a concept of responsible global citizenship, mindful of specific national and regional identities, but dedicated to the *whole* rather than to its *parts*, whereby 'global law' comes to anchor world order rather than Westphalian 'international law'.

22

The language-games of peace

Anat Biletzki

Introduction

From antiquity and on through the Enlightenment, peace has been posited as a worthy end to human endeavour; indeed, as that aspect of human existence which is to be pursued by all rational beings. Modern times – the twentieth century and onwards – have seen this construct mobilized both socially and institutionally. Its unequivocally positive status has made it the rationale for discourse and action in numerous frameworks – education, media, politics and academia (among others). We thereby encounter, in our modern Western culture, the establishment of educational peace projects, teaching and learning peace programmes; journalists and writers working for peace; political movements and organizations for whom peace is both motivation and aim; and academic work devoted to the issues of peace (usually, but not always, known as 'peace studies').

This chapter will attempt to look more critically at this burgeoning phenomenon. Beyond the naively optimistic viewpoint which welcomes multiple and diverse activities under the aegis of 'peace', and alongside sincere efforts to develop tools, infrastructures, organizations and legal means for the attainment of peace, there has developed, in recent decades, a certain new discourse of peace that is a veritable language-game all on its own. Intimately, and now automatically, associated with other familiar concepts (such as 'democracy', 'dialogue', 'empowerment', and soon), the term 'peace' has given rise to a linguistic institution which has rules, players, moves, audiences, speakers and aims. In a sense, however, the aims of this new game seem to have become internal rather than external; in other words, the rules of this current language-game of peace seem to constitute peace as the aim which the game itself defines, rather than to regulate the game to an already existent aim – 'peace' in its classical meaning.

Following such a description of the language-game of peace is the more problematic question of the use which is made of it. Here there are two levels of critique: first, such an 'industrialization' and 'capitalization' of the field (of peace) raises the spectre of a cheapening of the concept, making it a useful tool rather than an end in itself. But this gives rise to a second, more challenging question: If the term 'peace' is available for use, then what is to ensure that it is not to be used cynically, i.e. in collaboration with those who would promote war?

Consider the conventional truisms voiced in many a famous quote: 'Peace cannot be achieved through violence, it can only be attained through understanding' (Ralph Waldo Emerson); 'There never was a good war or a bad peace' (Benjamin Franklin); 'In peace the sons bury their fathers, but in war the fathers bury their sons' (Croesus); 'For everything there is a season, And a time for every matter under heaven . . . A time for war, and a time for peace' (Ecclesiastes 3:1–8); 'We must pursue peaceful ends through peaceful means' (Martin Luther King, Jr.); 'Peace is not the absence of war; it is a virtue; a state of mind; a disposition for benevolence; confidence; and justice' (Spinoza); 'Give peace a chance' (John Lennon); 'Peace starts with a smile' (Mother Teresa); 'Peace, like charity, begins at home' (Franklin D. Roosevelt); 'The purpose of all war is ultimately peace' (Saint Augustine); 'Peace begins when the hungry are fed' (Aquinas) . . .

This haphazard list could go on and on. Whether creatively imagined or culled from innumerable sources, it is easily recognized by any able reader as a list of familiar statements, almost clichés, purporting to guide us in both conceptual and practical dealings with peace.

And consider the following: Help Increase the Peace Program (HIPP); UNESCO Culture of Peace Programme; Peace Corps; Madonna Frequency Planetary Peace Program; Food for Peace Program; World Peace Project for Children; Everest Peace Project; Partners for Peace; International Interfaith Youths Conference on Peace (IIYCP); '2 Billion Voices for Peace' project, Australia; United for Peace; Women's International League for Peace and Freedom; Peace Now; CodePink Women for Peace; Women in Black; Peace Boat; Grandmothers for Peace International; Canadian Peace Alliance, Peacebuilding and Development Institute, National Peace Foundation . . .

This coincidental list of institutions is a miniscule representation of any comprehensive summation of schools, groups, organizations, conferences, workshops and programmes claiming a hold on peace. Although not 'endless' in the mathematical sense, it is a mushrooming list, one that would have been virtually non-existent if put together in the nineteenth century, became somewhat more weighty in the twentieth century, and, towards its end and now in the twenty-first century has become an exponentially growing cadre of 'peace institutions'.

In attempting to put order into these lists – order in the sense of tracking, indeed constructing, a meaningful categorization of things said about peace and institutions dealing with peace (not to mention the various connections between the two lists) – one might travel several paths. The historical/chronological path would place quotes in their date-context and identify institutions (perhaps even quantifying them as we attempted above) by their historical presence. The sociological way to go could dig into those quotes and those institutions that focus on the social perspectives gleaned in them; alternatively, the sociological way could operate on a meta-level providing sociological analysis of any of these quotes and institutions. A very natural, probably the most popular, setting would be the political perspective, i.e. one that would emphasize the elements and factors of states and ideologies that go into peace-dealings. And then, some additional roads could go down more traditionally 'scientific' angles, thereby bringing into the (peace-studying) fold disciplines such as biology, economics, linguistics, medicine or geography. All of these have been ably done in that venerable field of peace studies.

What would a philosopher do? Viewing philosophy as the game (in the Wittgensteinian sense of 'game') of conceptual analysis, and adopting the (Wittgensteinian) adage of 'meaning as use', this philosopher will attempt to describe (again, in Wittgensteinian manner) the appearance of the concept of 'peace' in its classical, that is to say 'modern', usage and to then investigate the current usage – some of which is epitomized in the two lists above – of that same concept. An essential change in use, if apparent, will then hint at a change in meaning. My hypothesis will not be so unequivocally radical but I will, in hypothesizing, point to the vagaries of current 'peace-talk' (in politics, in the media and even in academia), which lead from use to abuse and from naivety to cynicism.

The tradition

'War and Peace' is the ultimate posit which grounds the concept of peace in a dichotomous definition. In the effort to define, explain, explicate, illustrate and finally understand peace it is natural to ask what peace is not. Along with 'war', one encounters 'conflict', 'struggle', 'battle', 'confrontation', 'fight', 'feud' and various other synonyms and related concepts. This binary, even exclusionary, use of both terms, 'war' and 'peace', constitutes their meaning, almost of necessity, and guides the political conversation which is at the core of our discussion.[1] Furthermore, the tradition, both classical and modern, is sometimes straightforward, even simplistic, sometimes more sophisticated, in making a lucid value judgement concerning the dichotomy: war and its relations are negative, peace is positive. Very clearly Plato tells us that '. . . the best is neither war nor faction – they are things we should pray to be spared from – but peace and mutual good will'. The move to sophistication, however, has to do with two aspects of this value-laden discussion on peace (and war): (a) the means vs ends division, and (b) the rationality clause.

'Peace is good, and therefore also the way or means of peace are good,' we are told by Thomas Hobbes. A positive evaluation of peace is not simplistic when it is recognized that the way to achieve peace is not necessarily or automatically through peaceful means. Given that peace is perceived, deeply and essentially, as a desired end and given that war and its cognates are allegedly opposed to this end, a certain complexity of thought is required in order to accept that war might be a means to the desired end which is its diametrical opposite. Yet this awareness is obvious throughout the history of philosophical and political thought. From Aristotle – 'We make war that we may live in peace' – via Cicero, Augustine, Siddhartha Buddha to Eisenhower, Reagan and Kennedy – 'It is an unfortunate fact that we can secure peace only by preparing for war' – this sophistication is abundant at both the conceptual level and the rhetorical level. At the conceptual level one is obligated to give a satisfactory account of why it is that we require (the concept of) war to do the needed work on (the concept of) peace. The rhetorical level is, surprisingly perhaps, more pertinent to our enterprise for it is there that peace is mobilized for the (perhaps interim) end of war. In other words, the double-play between war and peace, their obvious opposition, the consensual presupposed preference for peace, and mostly the practical realities of the human race's need and desire for war have come together in a discourse which pays lip service to peace while advocating war. One could say that, from as early as Thucydides, we meet explicit recognition of the possibility of a language-game which uses the concept of peace for ulterior motives. It is, in a way, a harbinger of the language-game which will be at the crux of our discussion.

A different form of complexity in the traditional discussion on peace arises in connection with the rational–irrational dichotomy, part and parcel of the discussion but not simplistically parallel to the one of peace–war. Interestingly enough, the tradition tolerates both arguments: that which adduces rationality in the progress from war to peace, pointing to the fulcrum of a rational human being who makes that rational choice[2] and that which sees the rational human being as concentrating on war.[3] The sophistication spoken of here has to do, again, with an elusive to and fro between rationality and irrationality, now moving under the auspices of war and peace and tantalizing us in our indecision as to which is the manifestation of rationality.

Supposing a positive value-judgement of both rationality and peace, it behoves a philosopher who juxtaposes war and rationality to ponder the divorce between peace and rationality. Similar to the above recruitment of war as a means to peace, one can identify the machinations that go into explaining a predilection for peace with or without rationality.

These complications notwithstanding, it is a straightforward assertion that puts the discourse on peace from Plato onwards, but most emphatically and explicitly in the modern philosophical era, in a rationalistic, progressive, positivistic and universal context. Whether analyzed in a means–end framework and recognized as the obvious and positive condition that human beings should strive for or described as a point to be reached via rational procedure, peace is the ultimate construct which philosophical thought can adhere to in its modernistic discourse. This philosophical ambience of peace is further buoyed by the history and politics of modern times: since the French Revolution, with the rise of liberal and democratic nation-states, the parlance of peace as a positive ideal to be aspired to by peoples, nations and the international (now called global) community has acquired backing from the praxis of politics on ground-level. That is to say, the language used by laymen and professionals, individuals and groups, informal speakers and institutions, is informed by the theoretical and conceptual insights that constitute the concept of 'peace' in modern philosophy and the day-to-day political conversation which is, and has been for more than two centuries (at the least), conducted by all these speakers. Its fundamental principles are expressed, aptly, by any and all of the quotes adumbrated above – peace is based on universal human reason, which is, in turn, a fundamental assumption of modernity. Striving for peace is therefore assumed to be a self-evident proposition in any condition that is not the final, perpetual peace, formulated by Kant and the philosophers.

Current sophistication

So the tradition of peace-talk was a clear-cut one. A term conceived from antiquity as referring to the ultimate human condition[4] was used in both personal and social-political discourse in exclusively positive connotation. The personal – that which speaks of the familiar 'peace of mind', 'go in peace' and so on, is not our point; the social-political term – that which speaks to a relationship between peoples, societies, nations, or states, was consistently and continuously touted as the end to which humanity in general should strive and local communities, in particular, should endeavour. This is not to say that the tradition itself was simplistic or superficial. Instead, the undeniable affirmation of peace as a worthy end did not belie the recognition of its complexities – in the quagmire of human emotions (which could be warlike) and the tensions of human relationships (which could be ambiguous), but, most importantly, in the reality of political intercourse which is never naive. A reading of texts having to do with peace – and war – throughout the tradition exposes the sophistication alluded to above: peace is to be sought, safeguarded and cherished but that does not mean that war is to be naively ignored or that the complex of rational action can be easily mapped out. The study of peace is, consequently, a necessary and difficult study. Still – it studies an undeniably worthy end.

When does sophistication become cynicism? When does use become abuse? And when does a worthy end become a tool in the hands of powers who are not necessarily in search of that end? In lieu of trying to sketch out a theory of cynical use, specifically of the concept of 'peace', let us describe the uses of words. These descriptions turn to a family of concepts, 'family' being utilized here in its Wittgensteinian sense, in order to identify a set of words that have become related in current political discourse, words that exhibit a Wittgensteinian family resemblance with 'peace', such as 'democracy' and 'dialogue'. Recall, again, the programmes listed above, and add to them hundreds of others – institutions and slogans of and about peace, democracy, dialogue, reconciliation and on and on. These can all be categorized and put into various contextual compartments of current society and culture: education, media, academia and politics, among others. In all but the first, one can ascertain a sophistication that follows the death of naivety; innocence, if authentic, is encountered mostly in the area of education. The educational mission is still intent, it appears, on working, at least with children, in the traditional rubric of peace (or democracy or dialogue) as a clear, uncomplicated and surely positive purpose of study and activity. Self-reflection, in this context, is present for purposes of further support of the project, not for sceptical challenge. This is one contemporary language-game of peace. In media, in academic discussion and, not surprisingly, in political institutions there is, it seems, a modicum of a different sort of self-reflection. Work being done there, in other words, on and for peace (or democracy or dialogue), is work conscious of not only the desirability and difficulty of attaining peace but also the need to reflect more critically on peace and its complexities. These are additional, currently popular, language-games of peace.

So first – education. In a myriad of contexts and frameworks the idea that children, and sometimes adults, must be *educated* for peace is developed, both theoretically and practically. This is an interesting idea precisely due to the fact that 'peace' seems to be a simple and single-minded term that children learn to use exclusively as a basic positive word in their linguistic repertoire. It is, indeed, unassumingly heartening to behold the oft-produced books, exhibits, shows, pageants and other venues that present children's dealings with the term. Given such popularity of a word, why, we could ask, would it be necessary to educate for peace? And it is here that naive optimism is tempered by an understanding of the need for more than a poster-idea of peace. Considering the mostly peace-less surroundings enveloping children in today's world – in the supposedly peaceful 'Western' world, in the post-1989 'Eastern' arena, in the poverty-ridden Third World and, undoubtedly, in the geographical points of real warfare – educators are well aware of the mockery which is inherent in postcard 'peace'. It is a worthwhile project, that which is taken up by teachers, schools, whole school-systems and extra-curricular activists, in their educational enterprise of training for peace rather than just singing, drawing, acting-out and celebrating peace. And it is a difficult one – that which is attempted by these optimists, in programmes that teach how to engage in real dialogue, since it must move the children themselves from the superficial (and always childish?) use of 'peace' as a smiley icon to peace as a difficult form of life. Difficult, but not at all pessimistic.

We move on to the media. Mainstream media[5] is entrusted with reportage of and comment on events. We cannot, here, go into the troublesome moral quandaries of the journalistic field nor shall we elaborate on the differential ethics of the reporter vs. the publicist (though these may be relevant to our point). Suffice it to point to the consensus, identified above, in media at large, concerning the desirability of peace and the positive evaluation accorded to subjects and objects – of report or opinion – who are perceived as promoting, supporting or working towards peace. Here, however, as opposed to the context of education, the conversation of peace is necessarily more sophisticated for the simple reason that any story and any opinion piece must be written or broadcast from a certain perspective under a certain 'roof' – that of the media person. We have graduated, long ago, from the modernistic illusion that a story can be told in objective neutrality; try as it may, the media cannot hold on to its ideal of non-partisanship.[6] It is, therefore, instructive to investigate what the media says about peace and, more so, what the media says about what it says about peace. There is, here, a subtle point of emphasis and interest: the headline-grabber is, understandably, news about war rather than peace. The reportage on peace is therefore moved to backstage – either as quotes by leaders, politicians and generals who pay lip service to peace while waging war, or as accounts of peace 'happenings', be they conventions, treaties, ceremonies, parties or other happenings. Of more interest to our conceptual project are those media personages who aspire to commentary and analysis; these play a multi-faceted game. They report, as just mentioned, on the discourse of peace, which takes place in the society and in our culture, and they do so under the auspices of the general, universalistic and positive consensus. That is not to say that all pundits agree (in estimates of heroes or interpretation of events); but it is to note that a certain routine defines them all, an adherence to certain clichés seems to bind them to the accepted discourse on peace. Happily, though, as befits intellectual exercises, the media, even the mainstream media, is involved in a certain critique which, in some rare cases, leads to self-reflection on its own role in the game of peace. Thus we now see courses and seminars at schools of journalism attending to these issues, and there is no dearth of conferences, organized by political groups, universities or sometimes even the media itself, addressing the role of journalism in (war and) peace.

On to academia. It should come as no surprise that academic work is imbued with analysis, reflection, self-reflection and critique. I do not mean to aggrandize the academic stage above all others but to point out the (idealized) demands made of academic parlance in general, and that relating to peace in particular. Systematized examination of peace can and does come up in various disciplines: political science – the first usual suspect – and then international relations, economics, philosophy, history, literature, the list is long and predictable, and can sometimes lead to the less predictable – biology, medicine, etc. In all these areas one can expect to meet, again, a consensual, though not necessarily a single-minded, discourse which is, even if less clichéd than media-talk, a language-game conducted under well-defined rules. These include the presupposition that peace is a desired, even if eventual, end and go on to instruct the listener or reader in the ways of its attainment (in political science), its description (in literature and art), its rational analysis (in economics and international relations), its conceptual and normative character (in philosophy), and so on.

The more interesting point in the academic arena are the programmes of study, sometimes even the institutional departments, institutes, conferences and think-tanks that have been established to deal expressly and exclusively with peace. This is a relatively novel phenomenon which should engage us, and legitimately so. I submit that the general trend now manifested institutionally as 'Peace Studies' is the epitome of what I have been calling a sophisticated attitude towards peace which marks the current, though several years' old, ambience of the discourse of peace. Its defining characteristic is still the traditional, i.e. modernistic, turn to peace as a rational end of human striving but now accompanied by the need to grasp, with full consciousness, the problematics that accrue to its realization in a complex and variegated world. Importantly, though, such full consciousness also entails work being done – looking inwards and asking if the very study of peace, which uses the conventional language of peace, does not need to provide its own critical analysis of this talk. Nothing could embody more aptly, the reflective, self-reflective and critical nature, i.e. the sophisticated nature, of language-games of peace.

This survey of the contexts of peace-talk, that is to say, of diverse language-games of peace, cannot be complete without the most glaring context within which peace is touted – politics. It is a trite observation, and surely clichéd in itself, to identify peace-talk as a part of political discourse and action. Notice, again, the usual suspects of terms, which serve the political havoc having to do with peace: 'peace process', 'peace treaty', 'peace agreement', 'peace settlement', 'peace protocols', 'peace-keeping forces', 'just peace', 'peace-building', etc. Observe also the facile manner with which politicians of all bents can appropriate peace to their different, ofttimes contradictory, agendas. And finally, make note, nevertheless, of the conceptual consensus that is carried over from the tradition: peace is always to be desired, never to be shunned.[7] This is now the context, which propels us forward from sophistication to cynicism and from language-games of good intent to a convoluted one of unclear design.

Cynical convolution

We see that the uses of 'peace' in peace programmes, peace projects and peace studies can be divided into those that are (perhaps intentionally) naive and those that are (perhaps unintentionally) sophisticated. The further, analytical step that I wish to take here is risky: I venture that in the current cynical environment of globalization, rampant capitalism, ruthless power struggles and interest-laden politics, peace is being used in the service of anybody and everybody. The new language-game of peace has developed rules of use, which can be exercised by all – those who are sincerely in pursuit of peace, but, just as well, by those who are in pursuit of other ends, even war. Let us tread gingerly here, though.

The enlightenment, and in its wake the modernistic world-view lasting until well into the twentieth century, extolled the rationality and logic which went into a constructive view of peace and its realization. There is no reason to think of this world-view as necessarily naive or simplistic. Contrariwise, the ability to ponder complexities of concept and reality is no stranger to modern philosophy or modernistic culture; it is, in fact, this ability that we have been calling 'sophistication' and that makes possible the questioning of peace in various, reflective and self-reflective, ways. Now let us call, for the moment, 'postmodern' that intellectual and cultural milieu that has made a point of critiquing the adulation of a single-minded rationality and logic and an attendant recognition of an a priori, universalistic, objectivist theory of meaning involved in the modernistic world-view. This type of criticism has made it possible to move from puzzling over the complexities of peace (e.g. is war a necessary means to peace? Is peace a condition of rationality?, etc.) to wholeheartedly questioning its consensual meaning and the manifestations of its supposedly universalistic sense. On postmodernism's heels we are now lambasted with the demand that we should recognize the relative worth of differing perceptions of peace, the contingency of our traditionally accepted struggles for peace, and the indeterminacy of any specific language of peace. Put differently, it is a current mode of critique to identify a certain 'discourse' of peace, call it the modernistic discourse, and to emphasize that it is, indeed, no more than a *certain* discourse, which should be exposed for its contextual, cultural and political interests.[8]

Well, one can say, let the intellectual elites play their game of highfalutin conceptual analysis; we, on the ground, will continue to do our peace work while speaking our language of peace in the traditional, up-to-now affirmative, language-games. Our speakers will be leaders, activists, teachers, human rights workers, participants in dialogue groups, academics, journalists and even politicians. Our audiences will be states, individuals, grant associations and the public at large. The rules of our language-games will include the constitutive rule that peace is an end to be (actively) sought after and the regulative rule (among others) that peace-talk must be conducive to that end. In other words, the language-games of peace on the ground will continue to exhibit traditional, modernistic parlance, albeit one that can house countless multifarious and diversified sub-games.

It is here that we pause to descend from the heights of theory and tell some concrete stories, very current stories, troubling stories of the language-use of peace (and its cohorts: dialogue, humanitarian aid, etc.).[9] First is the story of the children of dialogue. 'Dialogue' is a close second to peace in the current ambience of peacemaking and conflict resolution. In hundreds of educational programmes and cultural events one encounters not only the ideational construct of 'dialogue' but worked-out, sometimes almost algorithmic, programmes of dialogue – all geared to producing, developing and enhancing the capabilities of (warring) parties and their constituents to engage in dialogue. In the 1990s, during the 'Oslo years' of the Middle East, when it seemed that the Oslo accords had seen the beginnings of a real 'peace process', dialogue became a popular activity for those in the business of peace. There were the Jewish–Palestinian Living Room Dialogue Group, the Israeli–Palestinian Dialogue Group, organizations such as Getting to Know the Other, The Bereaved Families' Forum for Peace, Building Bridges for Peace – Seeking Common Ground, Hand in Hand, Hope Flowers School, Peace Child Israel, Seeds of Peace – just for a start. This was the epitome of positivism and optimism, where one could naively believe that dialogue would be an efficacious part of a (road to a) real peace. What could be wrong with such activity in such an atmosphere? Two things: first, it soon became a boon of satire and joke to talk of dialogue – 'dialogue, schmialogue' – in the Israeli general public, not to mention comedians and intellectuals, deriving ironic pleasure from the perceived futility of dialogue as a substitute for real peace; 'dialogue', literally in laugh-quotes, became a specific language-game in substitution for real peace-talk. More painful were the thoughts of some of the 'graduates' of dialogue programmes, especially the children from both sides, who had grown up in the meanwhile. For, as these children said, a week, or a month, or a summer of 'dialogue camp' had created friendships and relationships; but many of these friends had found themselves, at the end of the day, on different sides of a wall and a war: one occupying the other, one victimizing the other, one even killing the other. That these dire consequences were the result of a failure of the peace process is, perhaps, a factor which should be taken into consideration when thus demeaning the idea and concept of dialogue; but that dialogue comes out a weak practical construct is a consequence of note as well.

Very similar in character, though arising in a far more sophisticated context, is the idea of joint peace work by academic groups, and others, on both sides of a conflict. Several such groups and organizations have been established and continue to promote mutual projects all over the world. In Israel–Palestine, again during the Oslo years, such initiatives gained support and force from academic institutions (e.g. the Van-Leer Institute or the Truman Institute in Jerusalem), from politically oriented research organizations (e.g. Israel/Palestine Centre for Research and Information (IPCRI)), or from established funds and foundations (e.g. the Bronfman Fund or the Economic Cooperation Foundation). The more subtle point to notice now, however, is groups of individuals who refuse to partake in such projects or even some who have, in the past, participated in some of these and are now adamant at ceasing to cooperate in (what they term) a farce. This is the reluctance of the educated (Palestinian, in this case) to use words that sound like 'peace' when peace is nowhere to be found; doing so means collaborating with the powers that be, the stronger power, and accepting the terms of talk and engagement that that power dictates. In contrast to the *post-factum* realization of the children of dialogue that their dialogue did not usher in peace, the refusal to engage in joint peace projects *ab initio*, or even abstention in *medias res*, is born of frustration and authenticity: frustration at the hypocrisy of such projects, pretending that there is, or could be, a communality, symmetry or camaraderie between warring parties; and authenticity which requires that said parties admit to the evil and injustice of war (or occupation) instead of engaging in a show of joint ventures and normalization. So, paradoxical as it may seem, there are honest and committed workers for peace who refuse to do their work in conjunction with counterparts on 'the other side'. Is this subversive of peace work, or rather a call for a more genuine version of it (and what would that be?)?[10]

These two cases, of thwarted or frustrated missions of peace, are instructive precisely because of their convolution. We have said, above, that vouchsafing the modernistic use of 'peace' is a defence against postmodernistic denigration of the concept as an empty idol and that, to be sure, this use is the accepted guiding principle in some current language-games of peace. It now appears, however, that the real, down-to-earth, practicalities of peace-talk have spawned the very results that we were defending against. The clear-headed misuse of 'peace' perpetrated by cynical politics and consequently pulled off in the public arena by the media is a simple case of abuse based upon the consensual meaning that all are assumed to adhere to. In public discourse, full of superficiality and clichés, it is no wonder that those with political or public power make use of a term approved by all to further their interests. Far more worrisome, however, is the complication that arises from the gargantuan industrialization of peace that we are witness to now in the twenty-first century; industrialization and capitalization of peace, of dialogue, of human rights, even of 'democracy', point not to a modern, but rather to a postmodern condition. With or without intentional cynicism, but also with no clear design, the new language-game of peace has metastasized into a veritable business, replete with owners, workers, technology, capital and a programme of action which does not adhere to a clear meaning of the word 'peace' since its use has become so commercial, political and fictitious.

Conclusion

Can one talk of peace without talking about war? There is now, in this heyday of peace studies, an honest attempt to draft uses of 'peace' that do away with the need for peace-talk to be conditioned, either theoretically or practically, upon war. Thus, for example, peace is accorded a positive rather than negative definition and peace journalism is taught as a way of changing the perspective of reportage on human affairs – from emphasis on the negative, warlike character of events to a positive one of peace. For the essentialist philosopher the question would be – what is peace 'in itself'? For the Wittgensteinian philosopher the answer would be a rendition of a specific language-game of peace that attempts to track the uses of the word itself (and seeing if the rules of use obligate us to also and always use 'war' in such games).

We have tracked these uses, and thereby the meaning, of 'peace' in peace-talk, pointing to an overriding agreement, throughout the ages, as to its affirmative desirability coupled with the intricacies of its attainment. In other words, in Wittgensteinian manner, we have located a certain ordinary meaning of 'peace', residing in the traditional language of the Enlightenment. And we have, furthermore, seen that this discourse is common to several areas of human action, viz. education, media, academia and politics. In all of these, peace is propagated as an ultimate end; the means to this end are then worthy of discussion, research, investigation, argument and toil.

What happens when 'peace' itself, that is to say, the word, the term, the concept of 'peace', becomes a means? And the following question is, of course, a means to what? We have touched on this question only tentatively by questioning one current use of this construct, when it has become not only pervasive but also industrialized, commercialized and altogether established. We venture that instead of rejoicing at its universal acceptance (which was part of its meaning to begin with), one should be wary of a postmodern turn in the attitude towards peace. Put differently, one should realize that the exploitation of contingency, relativism and, most importantly, power leads to a cynicism in the use of the word by those in established authority – and authority can be had in education, in academia, in media and in politics – and to despair in those who strive for it.

This has been, then, an exercise in philosophical analysis. But speaking of meaning as decided by use is a philosophical (Wittgensteinian[11]) ploy; perhaps, since there are limits to philosophy as a critical tool, what is needed is more than philosophical criticism.[12] Whether and how we play the language-games of peace is a philosophical query, but perhaps the important question is whether and how peace, in its old, traditional, authentic sense, can be achieved.*

Notes

1 Clearly distinguished from this necessary duality is a different use, and thereby a different meaning, of 'peace', alluding to the spiritual, perhaps even psychological condition described by the proverbial 'peace of mind', 'inner peace', 'at peace', and similar phrases and expressions. This meaning is, admittedly, a stand-alone use of 'peace', but is irrelevant to our purposes. Whether it can, or should, be connected to the meaning that is vexing us is fodder for a different, semantic analysis.

2 Such a 'rationalistic' tradition can be seen as early as the Stoics and Plato, for whom war is a shortcoming of the body and the emotions, and goes on to, e.g. Locke and, of course, Kant.

3 Most (in)famously, in this camp, is Clausewitz (*On War*, 1833).

4 In religious thought, that ultimate condition is sometimes reserved for salvation; in both Christianity and Islam, however, there is ample use of 'peace and salvation'.

5 I make note here of the distinction between mainstream media and alternative media. Mainstream media is owned by corporate powers and is always and constantly caught in the dilemma of serving the public in its right to full information and serving its own masters in upholding and promoting their interests.

6 There is reason here to ask about the explicit partisanship adopted by alternative media; and to, subsequently, evaluate these two types of media differently perhaps by speaking about admitted partisanship (in alternative media) vs unrecognized partisanship (in the mainstream).

7 Or almost never. In these very realistic political times we do meet, in concrete and pragmatically oriented institutions, argument pointing to the inability to achieve (a real) peace and therefore to the desirability of changing our aims to something other than peace (e.g. conflict management, dispute resolution, etc.). These are other language-games – but not of peace.

8 See especially Ilan Gur-Zeev's (2001) article 'Philosophy of peace education in a postmodern era', *Educational Theory*, 51, 3: 315–36.

9 These 'stories' are rooted in the Middle East conflict, but parallel narratives and happenings are to be found in all other contexts where similar circumstances abide.

10 Also tricky and challenging is the criticism being waged against the work of humanitarian and human rights organizations – to the tune of 'collaboration' with the powers of evil. This argument is analogous to the one against (certain) peace organizations and thereby a part of the quagmire of peace-talk. The magnitude and speed of expansion of the human rights and humanitarian 'industry' have led to its being accosted as a tool in the hands of the strong (occupiers, victimizers) who pretend to attend to the (humanitarian) needs of the weak (occupied, victims).

11 The term 'language-game' must be made to do more analytical work. In order to justify our hypothesis that this is a *new* game, its constitutive rules must be elaborated, thereby giving a new meaning to the construct 'peace' itself (and thereby, perhaps, also explaining why one might be deluded, misled, or manipulated into thinking it is the same game).

12 That the *Stanford Encyclopedia of Philosophy* has an entry on 'War' but is lacking one on 'Peace' is a telling sign.

* I owe deep thanks to colleagues at Boston University, including Juliet Floyd, Aaron Garrett, Charles Griswold, David Lyons, and David Roochnik, who challenged me on many ingredients of this article.

23

Peace and the arts

Patrick McCarthy

Amor's the god of peace
it's peace we lovers worship
the hard fight I have with my lady's
enough for me.
Sextus Propertius, early Roman poet[1]

During the dark days of the Second World War, Picasso and Matisse ran into each other walking along a street in Paris. 'None of this would have happened if people did their job as well as we do ours,' one great artist said to the other.

Working artists do not begin wars. It is the last thing on their minds. And if wars happen during their lifetime, and wars have happened nearly everywhere, they often do their best to carry on with their appointed mission. But many times this becomes impossible, and artists, like everyone else, are drawn into the fray. They must choose. They must change. They take a position. Ethics impacts, and can even override, aesthetics, and looking back on their production during brutal, enveloping wars, it is easy enough to see the effects that human slaughter has had on artistic styles.

Picasso was a tough guy, like many artists of his day. They say he spoke French 'like a cop'. But he could be a tenderhearted man as well. *Guernica* was his astonishing response to the malevolent bombing of a small village in Spain by fascist forces. This huge painting is often regarded as the greatest painting of the twentieth century. What a century it was: to be symbolized by Picasso in a black and white, hectic, tableau of homicidal fury.

Matisse, the other giant of painting in the last century, has no Guernica in his catalogue. He preferred to concentrate on colour, harmony, light and grace. His intellectual attitude over his long lifetime kept him aloof and his eye fixed on what he deemed timeless beauty. He sought an art that would offer a 'calming influence on the mind, something like a good armchair that provides relaxation from fatigue'.[2]

Which artist best represents an artist's proper calling? Must an artist use his or her vocation to further peace on earth? Or is being an artist enough?

Artists are masters of experiencing, interpreting, valuing and expressing emotion. Tolstoy believed that art is the transmission of a feeling. When an artist looks at a picture of a child crying against a backdrop of a shattered, war-torn city he must be stirred to an intolerable degree. As sensitive instruments they register the slightest impressions and transform these subtle experiences into sharable realities – more than a politician, a scientist or philosopher. (Santayana, when considering the scale of death in the First World War, blandly said it was just as well, since many of those who died would not have contributed anything useful to society had they lived.) What will be the artist's response? A poem, a song, a sculpture or a film? Or will it be business as usual? It varies.

When an artist enlists in a cause, outside of art itself, the results can be striking, and even puzzling. The French novelist Stendhal greatly admired Napoleon, and his fictional heroes take on some of the antisocial characteristics of a cold-blooded conqueror. Julien Sorel, the anti-hero of *The Red and the Black*, saw himself being at war with the whole of society. Other artists go even further. Ilya Ehrenburg, a Russian revolutionary poet, wrote some of the most bloodthirsty propaganda ever penned when he urged the Red army to defeat the Nazis:

> Now we understand the Germans are not human. Now the word 'German' has become the most terrible curse. Let us not speak. Let us not be indignant. Let us kill. If you do not kill a German, a German will kill you. He will carry away your family, and torture them in his damned Germany. If you have killed one German, kill another.[3]

Although this frenzied screed goes against the popular idea of a poet as a rather dreamy, ineffectual sort, it points out some of the differences in the relationship of artists to modern warfare. It's not surprising that amongst creative types, it is the writers that have most often been tempted to be supportive of war. They actually have the least to lose, in a practical sense. A book may be burned, but another copy always remains. However, painters, sculptors and architects are not so fortunate. When the bombs are dropped, rockets launched, buildings shattered, homes invaded, vandalized, looted and razed, just imagine what certain artists feel about the fate of their own productions.

Ehernburg's violent prose certainly transmits a feeling. A feeling of murderous revenge and the desire for retaliation in the name of justice. So according to Tolstoy's aesthetic, his countryman is being a first-rate artist in his wartime essays. But Tolstoy was a pacifist who believed in nonviolence and Christian love and forgiveness. So we have a paradox here, and perhaps a flaw in the famous author's definition of art.

Art is transmission of a feeling. Not always a peaceful feeling. Nor only a soothing, serene feeling. Yet the feelings evoked by art are categorically different from the feelings elicited by other means. For example, I may walk outdoors and notice the sunshine. I say to myself: I feel hot. The sun has caused this feeling. I cut my finger, and think, 'this feels painful'. Or I walk down the street and see a homeless person sleeping on the pavement. He makes me feel sad. In these three situations I have chosen to feel something, but it is not an aesthetic response. Art is a conscious attempt to stir another person's emotions by means of a specialized technique. Without an artist there can be no art, hence no transmitted feeling. Art, in Tolstoy's opinion, is like a meeting of mentally affected bodies through triggered sensations.

Propagandistic art, while still being art, will nevertheless aim to unleash homicidally jingoistic emotions. Artists, then, can use their gifts to promote love or hatred, life or death.

Is anti-war art essentially different from propaganda? And if so, does it ever rise to the level of universal greatness? Anti-war art has a long history, going back at least as far as Aristophanes, whose drama *Lysistrata* deals with women rebelling against their lovers who abandoned them to go off to battle. In the modern era, Goya's *El Tres de Mayo de 1808 en Madrid*, a representation of a massacre, is as great a painting as exists during that period, and even by today's formal standards qualifies as a powerfully moving work, even more significant than his *Disasters of War* engravings, which are still able to shock and horrify.

The turbulent previous century spawned an enormous number of highly important works in all media: film, painting, novels, poetry and even sculpture. A few of the best: Otto Dix, George Grosz and John Heartfield in the visual arts; films like *Johnny Got His Gun*, *Grand Illusion*, *Coming Home* and *Elvira Madigan*; novels such as *All Quiet on the Western Front*, *Catch-22* and *Night*; the poems of Rupert Brooke, Ruben Dario, Robert Graves and Wilfred Owen; sculpture by David Smith (his anti-war bronze medallions), and even Giacometti, whose ravaged, skeletal figures appeared after the photos of the concentration camp atrocities.

Most Western art about war is against war, at least in some standard, moralistic way. There are exceptions, such as the government-sponsored works under the fascists and Third Reich, which glorified war and made it central to their political agenda.

Anti-war art is different to propaganda in at least one significant way. Propaganda is not so much against war as it is against a particular 'enemy'. Propaganda is anti-foe art. By limiting itself to building enthusiasm for conflicts against an officially sanctioned out-group, nation, race, religion or culture, it actually puts itself in the service of violence instead of peace. The best anti-war art attacks the essence of war; all war, at all times and all places.

What is the difference between pro-peace art and anti-war art? It often comes down to the difference between positivity and negativity. An utterly pacifistic work of art deliberately and conscientiously banishes all negative aspects in both form and content. It will not even hint at the existence of barbarism and savagery. A passage from Baudelaire, speaking of his 'spiritual room', writes of an 'encompassing atmosphere of mystery, silence, perfume, and peace'.[4] This massively affirmative description reduces the question of war to nothingness. The same could be said of certain paintings by Mattisse, Vermeer, Monet, Renoir, Bonnard and Leonardo, poems by Yeats and the English Romantics, and nearly all classical instrumental music. Peace in art is shot through and through with a plentitude of overflowing serenity. By the utmost concentration of creative power towards building an image of an everlasting peacefulness the artist sabotages a world-view of life as an incessant psychological and political battlefield of contending forces.

The opposite of peace is traditionally regarded as war, yet other possibilities exist. Peace could be contrasted with anxious restlessness. Or wild panic. Nor should war be predominantly thought of as nations battling nations, or even guerilla struggles within a state. War, like power, is spread across the cultural horizon, and arises from below. As power unites factions, and tangled, complex groups under regional control, it attains a centralized sovereignty that represents multiple, smaller interests. But these units are relatively isolated elements characterized by divided, and often conflicted, goals, aspirations, beliefs and conduct. That is, the origins of war and peace, nonviolence and violence, harmony and cacophony, order and chaos, love or hate, begin with the individual, even at nearly imperceptible, physiological levels.

War and peace, then, must be analyzed both microscopically as well as macroscopically. And the relationship of art to these twin states requires the same kind of rational explication. That is, the history of art and artists can be examined on the one hand, and the structure and nature of art itself must also be taken into account, on the other, if a full understanding of their true relationship to peace is to be attained.

This question of the role of an artist in society, whether he advances culture towards a higher realization, or manages to weaken and even degrade a culture, is an age-old issue. It goes back at least as far as Aristotle, who tried to interpret the peculiar pleasure humans experience when watching the performance of a tragedy.

Are artists, because they hunger for perfection in their art, and this perfection is out of reach in spite of unremitting efforts, doomed to a life of frustrated longing? There are numerous examples to support this conclusion: the 'peintre maudit' (accursed painter) of the School of Paris, such as Modigliani, Utrillo and Soutine. Not to mention Van Gogh, Cezanne, Rimbaud, Hart Crane, Lautrec, Caravaggio, Mayakovsky and Munch: all apparently suffered intensely throughout their lives. Happy, fulfilled artists are perhaps not as common as the dejected ones, but they do exist. Brancusi, in referring to his sculptures, states it simply: 'I give you pure joy.'[5]

What makes the difference between the two? Does a realized painting make one artist happy, but another less so, even much less so? Take Van Gogh's famous painting of his bedroom at Arles. It is the bedroom of a single man, a lonely man, a man anything but effective as an emotionally satisfied, socialized human being. The two pictures on the wall, the two chairs, and the two pillows: all very heartbreaking. The work is a masterpiece but isn't it something of a vicarious pleasure for the artist himself? Isn't art a substitute for direct, fully engaged, first-hand experience? There are cases where this could be so.

But for a wealthy and highly celebrated man like Rodin, his bronze sculptures do not seem to be a way of evading life's problems, or merely a runner-up prize. Rodin used art differently to Van Gogh. Rodin's art managed to attract the world to his door. Nor did this make his work any less beautiful and timeless.

Without art, there really isn't a 'high' culture. The only thing left from otherwise ancient, vanished cultures are their artifacts, and their art. Some shards of pottery, a bead or two, some roughly shaped pebbles.

Art always accompanies humanity, and even defines humanity. A human being is the animal that makes art. The animal that is driven to embellish his world, to enhance his life, to cover the depressing nakedness of a barren horizon.

Art satisfies a fundamental human craving. Early humans can fill their bellies through hunting, gathering and planting; fulfil their curiosity about their environment through crude tool making; their reproductive urges through sex; and their frightened awe of hidden forces through religion. But why is art so important to these so-called primitive tribes? Flutes have been unearthed that are 9,000 years old. Masterly cave paintings, 35,000 years old, have been discovered. Small carved ivory animals and female figurines have been dug up, some dating back to possibly a 100,000 years ago.

Does early collective history somehow reflect early individual history? Is art one of our first and primordial experiences? As far back as we trace civilization we discover art, and as far back as we examine the single human existence we detect a subtle form of behaviour that could qualify as artistic creativity.

The oceanic bliss of very early infancy is the inalienable legacy of being human. The mother–child bond, the inter-uterine state of pure sufficiency, is a potent reality whose influence dies hard. This rich source of hazy, glimmering unity haunts many of us, consciously or unconsciously, for the rest of our lives. Out of this primary, luminous swirl, a thousand mythic tales are spun, pictures are painted, dances are danced, poems are written and songs are composed.

All authentic art is like a pleasurably baffling memory, pointing to some barely glimpsed world just out of reach. Genuine art is known by the risky personal attempt to make concrete the strongest of inner sensations.

Each calling arises from some influence, but art stems from the earliest of early experiences. But doesn't everything, every field of endeavour, stem from early childhood? What makes art different from anything else? Or is everyone an artist?

Again and again, the artist returns to this inexhaustible source for inspiration. If we all are potential or actual artists does that mean you can play the violin, or sing an aria? Art is a way of doing something, and as such differs from other vocations. You aren't a scientist if you don't adhere to a scrupulous scientific method. And art, too, has a method, but unlike science, not a single method. Art is non-formulaic, anti-algorithmic. The method of art is to have no set method, but rather to battle all attempts at codifying and regulating creativity. As such it would be correct to say that art is a never-ending revolution.

Freud saw artists as types who skilfully regressed only to a pragmatic degree, as if dipping into a richly evocative psycho-history in order to express it for the rest of the world. The artist exploits his infancy and is smart enough to realize that all adults have experienced this primordial sweetness, this paradise lost. Taking a page from the medieval alchemists, Freud theorized that the technique for artists was sublimation, that is, manipulating the dross of instinct into the gold of art. Raw, unmediated emotion, pulsing with erotic aggressiveness cannot lead directly to great art. It must undergo a sublimation, metamorphosis, transformation, and transmutation, even a transfiguration.

The artist toils to recreate a common experience of embryonic fusion, a state of Edenic perfection. Out of each individual's undifferentiated, all-satisfying condition of pure, half-recollected, infancy, art is born. For the infant – all is in all. For the adult mystic there is no separation between self and other, background and foreground, ego and world – only an overwhelming unity with brilliantly distinguishable elements. The mystic can perhaps duplicate in his own specialized way the infant's original maternal bond. This primordial state is a recollection that cannot be wholly eclipsed, a lamp that can never be completely extinguished.

The American 'folk' artist, Edward Hicks, a devout Quaker, painted a series of magnificent canvases called *The Peaceable Kingdom*. In these compositions a radiant child is surrounded by docile animals, even lions and leopards, in a depiction of benign harmony. What are we to make of this transcendent scene?

Why does an established religion insist on a 're-birth' experience? And the need to become again as a 'little child' to enter the 'kingdom of heaven'? For an artist, this is elementary. The artist will endlessly re-identify with the child-like wonder of his infancy, long before a second-hand, ready-made world will be foist upon him. While others are content with prefabricated interpretations of life, the artist seeks to personally structure his own version of existence.

The French poet Verlaine's work evokes this nostalgic imagery of gently embracing, but nevertheless baffling, harmony:

> I often have this dream, strange and penetrating,
> Of a woman unknown, who loves me,
> And who's never, each time, the same exactly,
> Nor exactly different, she knows me, she's loving.[6]

But not every artist is given over to such reveries. Many seem to be more captivated by loss, dread and sorrow. Some, like Ehrenburg, adopt a cause, or take up arms. Others use their gifts as tools of a regime, even a cruel, reactionary one. Knut Hamsun, Celine, Ezra Pound and others fell under the Nazi spell of simplistic, and massively homicidal violence against others. Not to mention exceptionally talented artists like Arno Breker or Leni Riefenstahl who allowed themselves to be seduced by diabolic Hitlerian schemes.

The question of artists and their relationship to the ideals of a progressive, humanistic democracy is not as clear-cut as one might expect. Artists are often as foolish in their ethics as they are wise in their aesthetics. But even if this is so, their art can surprisingly evade the most severe judgements of their time. A painting can be beautiful even if it's been done by a murderer.

The insane British artist Richard Dadd killed his father, but his paintings are quite entrancing. In this particular case, it would obviously have been better to have symbolically worked out his aggressive rage on canvas instead of directly assaulting his father. Dadd's rare, elaborately executed paintings do, in fact, point to psychological conflicts that betray both his real and phantasmagorial violence towards his father. Here we have an example of both successful and failed sublimation in the same person.

By imaginatively, reflectively, contemplatively and intellectually returning to this first condition, one can confidently advance emotionally, as well as artistically, in life. Prior to all disappointment, sorrow, dismay, anger, fear and misery, everyone experiences his own Peaceable Kingdom. By relentlessly backtracking, by sincerely searching, by an effort of the entire person, one can re-identify with one's distinctive origins. This innocent realm is permanently devoid of violence, of the every-man-for-himself style, which unfortunately can appear later in life. As a re-purposed, re-directed, 're-born' adult, new answers are available and gradually understood. A regenerative undertaking is perhaps more important to creative workers than anyone else.

Building upon, while expanding, Freud's ideas, the psychologist Melanie Klein turned her thoughts to the area of art and creativity. She theorizes that the first few months of infancy lay the groundwork for an aesthetic development. The infant is submerged in a thoroughly encompassing situation he denominates as 'phantasy':

> Unconscious phantasies are not the same as day dreams (though they are related to them) but an activity of the mind that occurs on deep unconscious levels and accompanies every impulse experienced by the infant. Klein gives the example of a hungry baby who temporarily deals with his hunger by hallucinating the satisfaction of being given the breast, and being held and loved by the mother. But she adds that the unconscious phantasy also takes the opposite form of being deprived and persecuted by the breast that refuses to give this satisfaction. Phantasies – becoming more elaborate and referring to a wider variety of objects and situations – continue throughout development and accompany all activities. Indeed, Klein stresses that 'the influence of unconscious phantasy on art, on scientific work, and on the activities of every-day life cannot be overrated'.[7]

Phantasy, then, makes the world go round, ruling our lives from the womb to the tomb.

Phantasies may take many forms, and express themselves in many ways, some of which, according to Klein, are very aggressive, hostile, destructive and sado-masochistic. The mechanisms involved include schizoid splitting, projection and dissociation, among others, all of which are involved in artistic expression, or the lack of it.

Why are we all artists at birth, or right before birth? Because the process of separation and differentiation is a creative act. The original parent is neither father nor mother, but a union of both. The child then begins to create duality out of oneness. Fusion leads to diffusion, oneness to greater and greater multiplicity. The early creativity is authentically personal, but over time, it diminishes and the child is integrated into an alienatealienating world, a given, hand-me-down environment instead of a self-made one.

But even if this is so, how does the artist differentiate himself from others, all of whom have entered this world in nearly the same way?

Kleinian aesthetic theory sees artists as those people who have made it their vocation to repair the psychic splitting of their deepest 'phantasies' into symbolized dramas from early childhood. They understand that they themselves as well as their non-artist brethren are unhappy, aggrieved, frustrated, relentlessly nostalgic, confused and hurting. The creative types are driven to reconcile in a specialized manner this universally depressing situation. They seek to re-present the primal inner conflict, in a seductively objectified manner.

But even to the most casual observer most art is not an illustration of paradise regained. How is it possible to explain tragedy, or presentations of violence and murder, by tracing art back to infantile impressions? The origins of violence must be examined. How it enters a person, and what happens after that.

But what do we mean by violence? The etymology of the word is like the phenomenon itself: somewhat ambiguous, contradictory and mystifying. Basically, violence derives from the Latin 'vis', which gives us the English vim, meaning vigour, energy, force. Violence can be grouped in a category that contains many similar, but often opposing terms, such as virtue, vice, via, vision, vital, wise and others. All cluster around the Latin 'vita', or the French 'vie' meaning life – as if life itself is defined in pre-moral, pre-religious, pre-scientific terms. Life is a kind of activity, peaceful and restrained, as well as overpowering and war-like. In order to live one must kill, even if it is nothing more than an edible plant, not to mention an animal. Living viruses attack us, and we fight back. But on a higher plane we reject murder and use of force, saying in our hearts, 'this is not life'. Yet, in a way it is, and we are tempted to conclude that life is a sort of peaceful violence, or violent peacefulness.

The irreducible ambiguity of the nature of violence reveals much about its place in our world, our attitudes, our beliefs, and the facts of history.

A philosopher like Nietzsche, after studying the roots of language, and the history of cultures, came to the conclusion that modern Judeo-Christian morality has it all wrong. That power, strength, vim and vigour, and, yes, violence, have actually been cunningly devalued and wrongfully displaced in Judeo-Christian society. He sought to restore vigour, energy, vitality, strength and power to its former Dionysian glory. We all know how that turned out. Not very pretty, after the fascists and Nazis twisted his philosophy to suit their own criminal plans.

Nietzsche mocks Aristotle's concept of catharsis. Far from feeling pity and sorrow at the portrayal of a tragic death, people actually take a dark pleasure (*schadenfreude*) in it. But since society has become so hypocritical and timid, people now merely pretend to be compassionate and sympathetically moved to tears. Nietzsche is a very acute psychologist and he uncovers some embarrassing truths about human motivation and our secret fantasies.

The connection between the violent and the 'sacred' is another thorny problem to solve. Original violence over time becomes ritualized, and part of a religious ceremony. 'This is my body, and this is my blood.' As civilization progresses and the old rites fade in memory, sacred practices become secularized and transformed into theatre. Everything is softened and organized. Ghastly human sacrifices become harmless ball games. Instead of a conquered chief's head being kicked around an open clearing we now throw an inflated pigskin down a scrupulously measured gridiron. A real-life murder in ancient Denmark becomes *Hamlet*.

The savage human pre-history may leave its traces, but isn't the indispensable psychological foundation of art the beautiful primordial unity between an infant and a mother? In the West, aren't the earliest statues dug up by archeologists crudely fashioned female figurines, with pronounced maternal features? Is violence in art an aberration, an error in judgement and a clear example of faulty taste?

The scream of pain pierces every art form of the last century; the poetry of Rimbaud, The Beats and Bukowski, the novels of Celine, Camus, Hemingway and hard-boiled detective fiction, the countless horror, gangster and action films, all contemporary urban rap music, the paintings of Munch, Bacon, Golub, the German expressionists like Beckmann, Dix and Grosz, the photographs of Diane Arbus, the aesthetics of the Italian futurists and European surrealists.

> Art, in fact, can be nothing but violence, cruelty, and injustice.
> (Marinetti (1909) *Manifesto of Futurism*)[8]

Violence has not only insinuated itself into the arts, but it has made itself at home and even flourished. Nor is this merely a recent innovation.

But a need for clarification arises. First of all, art and life are separable. Art does not necessarily imitate life, but in fact generally imitates other art. And, another consideration: life imitates art as much as the reverse. Nor even in the most unsophisticated person is art identical to life. If this were so, then people would rush the film screen to save the victim. But they do not. In addition, not only is there in Coleridge's famous words, a 'willing suspension of disbelief' in the aesthetic experience, but also there is *a willing suspension of belief.* Even children notice the difference between a play and playing. The hue and cry over violence in art is generally based on a naive misunderstanding of both life and art. It is well to keep in mind that art is nearly an autonomous, self-reflexive, parallel dimension, complete with its own laws, its own techniques for deployment, its own facts, meanings and values.

Also, which would be more preferable: a peaceful world with violent art, or a violent world with peaceful art? Obviously, the first situation would be better. Examples in history support this. Dramatic, even bloody, art flourished in Periclean Athens, Augustan Rome, Elizabethan England, and perhaps even now in Western Europe and the US. And it is no coincidence that each era (excepting perhaps our own) has received high marks for its degree of civilization. On the other hand, the Nazi period was stupendously violent yet produced sentimentalized kitsch. There is evidently something to be learned from this.

How does violence, this snake in the grass, enter the home, even the nursery? And once inside, how does it grow from there?

The human life begins peacefully enough, floating in the all-comforting warmth of the womb. But what happens next is one of the most useful keys to the appearance of violence. The traditional family, with its complicated patterns, its seething emotions, and endlessly adjusted rules and regulations, is the dense ground from which desire and aversion, peace and violence will spring. The breast-feeding child will become more harmoniously strengthened through the loving interaction with a caring, nourishing mother. But eventually the child must be weaned, and the rude shock of not being able to experience uninterrupted pleasure at the breast of the mother will set up the first drama in a person's life. This crucial disappointment will start the wheels inside the brain turning. According to Kleinian theory, primal love will now lead to primal anger. The stunned baby will begin to bawl and squawk. The mother will return, but this return is no longer under the infant's control. The child then develops ambivalent feelings towards the mother, and by extension, towards the father, or any other person who seems to be vying for the mother's attention.

Love begins to alternate with rage. The initial cry of the child is perhaps the beginnings of a special kind of art. Poetry is often described as a 'cry from the heart'. (Read *Howl* by Allen Ginsberg.) The infant learns how to regain the presence of the mother through his bodily activity, through crying, reaching out, wriggling. All of which can evolve into multiple, highly complicated, categories as the infant grows and turns into an adult. But so many attitudes, emotions, responses and beliefs can be traced to the earliest strategies for existence. They are all there compacted into a vivid, gradually unfolding, microcosm.

Each human responds differently to often nearly identical stimuli. The complex interaction between a mother and a child will give us either an Einstein or a Hitler, and everything in between. The child begins to understand itself by interpreting cues from the mother, who in turn understood herself from cues from her mother, and this regresses ad infinitum.

The initial love, the narcissistic experience of pure pleasure, will become either a bitter memory, or a goal to recapture. Immature humans can never get over the primordial rupture, and go through life angry and ready to harm anyone or anything that somehow resembles their mother. But because of the consciousness of original love they can never quite feel pure hatred for the woman who gave birth to them, and so they punish themselves, causing a variety of ills, in order to atone for their guilt-ridden hostility. They then victimize themselves as well as anyone else who gets in the way.

So much adult violence in contemporary society is the maladjusted response to childhood trauma, which is generally little else than the unresolved shock of not being able to feel unceasing pleasure. The consciousness that one is not the centre of the universe, that one has limits, that love is more subtle and more widely distributed than one imagines, can lead to an enraged reaction. The infant can only throw a bottle out of his crib, but a traumatized adult with political power can hurl deadly missiles at an imagined enemy.

According to Kleinian theory, the psychic splitting of the original source of love into Good Mother (one who feeds and gives pleasure) and Bad Mother (one who withholds food and causes pain) will set in motion the very complicated apparatus of symbolism. Neutral objects will take on a colouring, an attitude, a value. Instead of a purely concrete stand-alone existence, the human will project a metaphorical, poeticized, elaborate system of interrelated signs, images and words. The shift goes from mother to maternalized things, such as Holy Mother Church, alma mater, matrimony or mother country, and will flesh out an adult's 'phantasy' life, which is now mistakenly regarded as unconditioned external reality. The superficial identification with symbolically fetishized objects can lead to life and death situations. People will kill and be killed in order to defend the 'motherland' (or fatherland).

A few years ago the world watched in great disgust as the Taliban regime, composed of religious fanatics, used canons to blast into powdered dust monumental, priceless, ancient statues of Buddha carved from a mountainside in Afghanistan. Many times a year vintage film clips of Nazi book-burnings are still shown on television. But before so-called Enlightened countries take pride in their attitudes about art they should recall similar events in their own culture. Literary masterpieces banned from high school English courses and provincial libraries, nude statues in government buildings in Washington, DC prudishly hidden behind drapery, WPA murals by great painters like Diego Rivera whitewashed, art exhibitions closed and savaged in the press by hack politicians and televangelist frauds; new, revolutionary music or comedy pulled from the radio.

'When I hear the word culture, I reach for my gun,' Goebbels joked, even though in the end the laugh was on him. Violence against art is second only to violence against the people themselves. The poet Heine remarked prophetically: 'wherever they burn books they will, in the end, burn human beings.'[9]

The child, who is already traumatized by early development issues, is coerced into greater and more thoroughly indoctrinated forms of alienation. His own creative power is daily and ruthlessly minimized and denied until it becomes a feeble memory. This theft of a person's artistic potential can leave a smouldering, lifelong sensation of bitter, twisted resentment. A prime example is the life of Hitler, who started out as an artist, a painter of sorts, but after disappointing results, turned to politics, and became a sworn enemy of all authentic art. The blockage of creativity may open the gates of destruction.

Whether an emotionally deprived human chooses to become a one-man crime wave, enlist in an established army or join up with a bloody revolution, the end result, psychologically and artistically speaking, is the same. There exist individuals, as well as entire groups of people, who will not use violence in any case, even obstinately going to the extreme extent of refusing to engage in personal self-defence, not to mention repudiating the quest for 'justice'. Revolutions can be either bloody, or bloodless. When human beings embrace violence, no matter what the cause might be – righteous, legal, just – the fertile, productive, creative aspect of a well-adjusted human is temporarily, if not permanently, blunted and replaced with empty, homicidal, aggressive destructiveness.

In the British Museum there is a great painting by Botticelli of Mars and Venus. Mars, the god of war, is a sleeping man, while Venus is a beautiful woman who sits upright awake. That is, love comes to life when war-like behaviour fades into unconsciousness, and vice versa.

An ancient Roman poem by Sextus Propertius makes a similar point. After spending the night with his difficult mistress, the poet declares:

> . . . even one night may make any man a god. If all men longed to pass their
> lives like this, with bodies held down by cups of wine, there would be
> no vicious swords, or ships of war . . .[10]

Love and war are mutually exclusive. Where one is, there will not be the other. Love is the desire to do good towards others, to identify with, protect, nourish and willingly accept the existence of the non-self. War seeks to destroy, annihilate and reduce to nothingness certain others. The political philosophy of fascism glorified war, but it would be wrong to say that a fascist 'loves' war. A fascist chooses war, seeks war, exalts conquest and domination, but this conduct has nothing in common with the nature, essence and definition of love.

The poet says that his behaviour, his lovemaking and his wine drinking, 'offended no gods'. But wholesale murder, rape and pillaging are not as innocent in the eyes of either mortals or immortals.

The American psychologist James Prescott, after a lifetime of practice in the field of childhood development, comes to this conclusion about the origins of violence:

> The reciprocal relationship of pleasure and violence is highly significant because certain sensory experiences during the formative periods of development will create a neuropsychological predisposition for either violence-seeking or pleasure-seeking behaviors later in life. I am convinced that various abnormal social and emotional behaviors resulting from what psychologists call 'maternal-social' deprivation, that is, a lack of tender, loving care, are caused by a unique type of sensory deprivation, *somatosensory* deprivation. Derived from the Greek word for 'body,' the term refers to the sensations of touch and body movement which differ from the senses of light, hearing, smell, and taste. I believe that the deprivation of body touch, contact, and movement are the basic causes of a number of emotional disturbances, which include depressive and autistic behaviors, hyperactivity, sexual aberration, drug abuse, violence, and aggression.[11]

Art is one of the safest possible havens for society's accumulated, explosive rage. Stepping back from violence, re-framing, re-channeling, sublimating and imaginatively transforming wrath into a work of art will go a long way towards ameliorating the evolutionary traits of aggression.

Artists are image-makers. And an image should not be confused with the reality it represents. This fact works to the benefit of the image-makers as well as the audience for the image itself. An image is an effigy. And it is undeniably better to hang or burn an effigy, rather than the person himself. Nor would it be right to hang the maker of the effigy if one is offended by such an act, as was the case of Salman Rushdie, who was placed under a death threat for his allegedly satirical writings against a religion.

At one level, art has always functioned as social criticism, and it is one of the healthiest ways to release accumulated societal tensions. Art can be a safety valve for the world's destructive fury, and as such must be protected and fostered. The iconoclasts took out their rage on statues, but even this is better than smashing living humans to pieces. If art offends, get used to it, and consider oneself the better for it. Even children learn to take out their frustrations on some inanimate object rather than a fellow playmate.

The world is a mixed bag. Good and evil, truth and error, beauty and ugliness, violence and nonviolence, are blended into a dappled wholeness. This mixture is partly organic and possibly indissoluble. Yet there are ways of handling it, ways of making it work for everyone. Art can help by using its two greatest tools: first, Aristotelian catharsis for dealing with undeniably primitive, brutally violent sensations, and second, by imaginative depictions of primordial unity, for the sake of intensifying memories of a paradisiacal fusion, where consciousness is held in the grip of a distinguishable oneness.

Creativity has its deepest reservoir in two extreme states, both of which could be regarded as hypothetical realities since they are not so easily demonstrated, but rather experienced and haltingly expressed. That is, on the one hand, the pre-conscious embryonic unity of the womb and the earliest months of infancy, and, at the opposite end of the spectrum, the highly conscious adult re-imagining the original, relative fusion. See Figure 23.1.

A human being is both centre and circumference. This dualistic interpretation explains the alternating currents of violence and creativity in the same person. If the scientists who made the first atomic bomb were also highly cultivated, even creative, men, then at that phase of their weapon production they were more identified with their belligerent, physical, destructive

Figure 23.1. *Paradise Now* (McCarthy 2005), silkscreen and paint on canvas

perimeter and not their pacifistic, centred, creative selves. We are not all of a piece. We can be both creative and destructive. The prisons are filled with convicts who spend their time painting and writing poetry.

If the world seems to be in an aggressively conflicted rut, try not to blame it on the artist. He daily, hourly, works perpetually to heal life's multiple fractures and vividly enhance both the collective and particular human adventure.

Oscar Wilde, while visiting a saloon in the American Wild West in 1888, noticed what he called 'the only rational method of art criticism' he ever discovered. It was a posted sign:[12]

PLEASE DO NOT SHOOT THE PIANO PLAYER
HE IS DOING HIS BEST

In conclusion, it appears as if art has a strong, necessary, but as of today only partial, identification with both inner and outer peace. The tormented artist, such as a Dostoyevsky or Van Gogh, manages to construct a strangely beautiful, often peaceful, world that is both inside and outside of what passes for 'the' world. The artist says no to life for the sake of revealing, explaining, and enhancing life. An individual no resulting in a collective yes. Art is more than a mirror of life; it is a newly created life surrounding life, like an extra layer of quivering consciousness, extending and deepening our vision as it re-defines life according to its own discoveries, obsessions, anxieties and fabrications. By expressing the violent peacefulness of human existence, art manages to make life both more intelligible and endurable.

Notes

1 http://www.tkline.freeserve.co.uk/Prophome.htm.
2 Flam, J. (2004) *Matisse and Picasso*, Boulder, CO: Westview Press, 65.
3 http://www.sovlit.com/bios/ehrenburg.html.
4 Baudelaire, C. (1970) *Paris Spleen*, New York: New Directions, 6.
5 www.seniorwomen.com/ca/cw/04/cult072004.html.
6 http://www.tonykline.co.uk/PITBR/French/Verlaine.htm#_Toc9225478.
7 http://human-nature.com/free-associations/glover/chap2.html.
8 Apollonio, U. (ed.) (1973) *Futurist Manifestos*. New York: Viking Press, 23.
9 Heinrich Heine, 'Almanasor: a Tragedy', 1823. Used as an inscription on a memorial at Dachau concentration camp.
10 http://www.tkline.freeserve.co.uk/Prophome.htm.
11 http://*www.violence.de*/prescott/bulletin/article.html.
12 Oscar Wilde, 'Impressions of America, Leadville', 1888, at: http://www.catbirdpress.com/firstchaps/usa.pd.

24

Peace through health?

Neil Arya

Introduction: war, violence and health

War and violence are known to have a devastating effect on human health and well-being. Project Ploughshares (1996) estimates at least 110 million deaths from war in the last century (Elliot 1972). Each year over 1.6 million people worldwide lose their lives to direct violence, which is among the leading causes of death for people aged 15–44 years worldwide, accounting for 14 per cent of deaths among males and 7 per cent of deaths among females (Krug et al. 2002). Garfield and Neugut (1997) suggest that the percentage of civilians killed due to war has increased from 14 per cent during the First World War to 75 per cent during the 1980s and to even 90 per cent in some conflicts taking place during the 1990s. By 2020, the World Health Organization and the World Bank predict that war will be the eighth leading cause of disability and death (Murray and Lopez 1996). For every person who dies as a result of such violence, many more are injured and suffer from a range of physical and mental health problems.

Malnutrition and under-nutrition occur with increased frequency during and after wars. Disruption of infrastructure allows waterborne cholera, dysentery and typhus. HIV/AIDS may be spread as soldiers engage in unsafe sexual practices with multiple partners. New diseases such as Ebola 'emerge' with greater frequency and diseases such as measles, malaria and tuberculosis are difficult to reduce as a direct result of war (Connolly and Heymann 2002; Diamond 1997; Holdstock 2002). Epidemics often spread; the extent of the Spanish flu epidemic of 1918, for instance, is thought to be related to the concentration of otherwise healthy young men in the trenches in close proximity to very sick ones (Orent 2005). A major barrier to the campaign to eliminate polio has been the pockets of wild polio virus remaining in areas of active armed conflict such as Sierra Leone, the Democratic Republic of Congo and Angola (Guha-Sapir and van Panhuis 2002; WHO 2001). The continuation of an African belt of meningococcal meningitis Type A (CDC website) may likewise be related to conflict in the zone.

War impacts on the basic rights of all (UN 1948). Children may be forced into slavery, early employment or combat, violating their right to being '*protected against all forms of neglect, cruelty and exploitation*' (UN 1959; UNICEF 2005). Women may suffer from sexual and physical abuse, and be at increased risk of sexually transmitted diseases including HIV/AIDS, increased reproductive complications and death and mental health issues (Shanks and Schull 2000). Refugees and internally displaced persons (IDPs) suffer from increased mortality, disability and psychological distress (Santa-Barbara 1997). Damage to the physical environment may have consequences for many generations (Ashford and Gottstein 2000; Leaning 2000).

Violence costs countries billions of US dollars each year in healthcare, law enforcement and lost productivity. The Inter-American Development Bank in Latin America has estimated the direct and indirect cost of (direct) violence for Latin America at US$140–170 billion per year, up to 15 per cent of GDP (GIIS 2001); in Colombia, some claim figures up to 25 per cent of GDP (Vieira 1998).

Countries at war tend to be lower socio-economically (UNDP 2005); those with increased military expenditure often have decreased spending on education and healthcare (Levy and Sidel 1997; Sivard 1996). Zwi and Ugalde (1989) found a strong correlation between infant mortality rates and the proportion of GNP devoted to military expenditure. The cost of the arms trade to many Third World countries which can ill afford such expenditure, may reduce security (Sidel 1995).

Interestingly, a nation's ill health may also be a risk factor for war. As a nation's childhood mortality exceeds 100 per 1000, the probability of it becoming engaged in an armed conflict increases substantially (Hotez 2001). Such a relationship also exists between the incidence of other infections such as tuberculosis and conflict. Speculation as to the mechanisms of such links include reduced gross national product, increased population pressures forcing migration and urbanization, increased competition for resources, loss of confidence in government leadership to manage epidemic situations, depletion of skilled administrators as a consequence of disease and flight of capital (Moodie and Taylor 2000).

Defining health

Yet as ill health and disease are linked to war and violence, so too is health linked to peace. Peace and health have many parallels in definition, both negative and positive, as human rights at least for children in terms of their determinants and ways of promotion (Arya 2004a). The Constitution of the World Health Organization (WHO) defines health as 'not merely the absence of disease or infirmity', but more holistically as a 'state of complete physical, mental and social well-being' (WHO 1946). Governments reaffirmed this in 1978 at the Alma Ata Conference (WHO 1978), promising 'Health for all in the Year 2000'. In 1986, public health specialists and health promoters determined that the fundamental conditions and resources for health were (in this order): peace, shelter, education, food, income, a stable eco-system, sustainable resources, social justice and equity, in what became known as the Ottawa Charter (WHO 1986). Not only is 'peace' the first prerequisite cited to provide a 'secure foundation' for health, but war affects each of the other conditions. Subsequent efforts in public health and health promotion (e.g. People's Health Charter 2000) and United Nations Millennium Development Goals (MDG 2000) place some emphasis on reducing structural violence and eco-system damage and improving social cohesion and human rights to promote health.

The message is clear: to truly improve the health of our patients, it is our professional responsibility to reduce both direct and structural violence.

How poorly done health work in war zones exacerbates conflict[1]

Those on the ground working in war zones often are too busy dealing with acute illness to think about abstract concepts such as peace. But such concepts have a very practical impact on decision-making. These health and aid workers face difficult choices.

Will they try to be neutral or impartial? Will they cooperate with governments? Will they work in solidarity with populations? How will they secure their aid so it can be delivered? 'Positive' developmental or health outcomes might produce 'negative' peace-building consequences, which may in turn impact their health work (Anderson 1999; Anderson and Olson 2003).

By working through existing power structures in order to gain access to people in need, international assistance agencies can prolong oppression by authoritarian regimes. By adopting policies of solidarity with groups fighting for their legitimate rights, international donors can contribute to the will of the people to engage in violent conflict over prolonged periods of time. When agencies hire armed guards to protect their delivery of goods to needy recipients, they 'buy into' the terms of existing conflicts.

The health sector often receives significantly greater resources than other peace-building efforts. Aid is not always good for peace. It can lead to centralization of power and authority and reinforce structural or overt violence, thereby disempowering local people. Introducing external resources into a conflict-prone, resource-scarce environment may distort local economic activities, changing income and employment opportunities differentially, increasing competition and suspicion, thereby worsening divisions among warring parties. Further, these additional resources might free up internal ones to be used in pursuit of war. When more than one agency works in an area, they may even become participants in competition and the furthering of inter-group suspicions.

After the genocide in Rwanda, NGOs were puzzled to find food failing to reach the most needy, in refugee camps in Goma, Zaire. After several months, MSF stopped working in Goma when they found militias had taken over aid distribution and the same people who had organized the genocide now were being strengthened by NGOs (Rachel Monroe-Blanchette, cited in Peters 1996).

The health sector, which is relied on for information, may find this being manipulated or selectively communicated. Humanitarian agencies circulating pictures or stories of war-based atrocities as a means of enlisting support for their work may fuel the cycle of accusation and counter-accusation perpetuating conflicts among groups.

Health work for peace?

But can we in healthcare professions actually act to mitigate the effects of violence and help create conditions for peace? The Nobel Peace Prize Committee in Oslo certainly seems to think so. In 1901, it awarded its first Prize to Henri Dunant, founder of the Swiss Red Cross. Dunant, a Swiss businessman, won not only for founding the medical relief organization, but for developing the first of the Geneva Conventions, regulating the rules of war and the care of combatants. Since then, the International Committee of the Red Cross (ICRC) has won the Nobel in 1917, 1944 and 1963. So have individuals such as Albert Schweitzer (1952), who won for his work at the Lambaréné Hospital in Gabon, and organizations such as International Physicians for the Prevention of Nuclear War (1985) and Médecins sans Frontières (1999). The International Campaign to Ban Landmines (1997) won with a medical message – to stigmatize a weapons system because of its disproportionate effect on civilian non-combatants. But the power of the health sector in peacemaking and peace-building has failed to reach much of the peace studies community. In their model of multi-track diplomacy, Joseph Montville and Louise Diamond do not even mention health as a sector to create help peaceful environments (Montville 1990). Let us examine some of the efforts in the health sector to contribute to peace.

Nuclear war

International Physicians for the Prevention of Nuclear War (IPPNW) proved very effective in changing public discourse around nuclear weapons, going from its formation in 1980 to the Nobel Peace Prize in 1985. In *Perestroika*, Mikhail Gorbachev credited the organization with changing his thinking with regard to the utility of nuclear weapons. As such, Gorbachev was able to make agreements that his generals thought compromised security:

> The International Physicians for the Prevention of Nuclear War has come to exercise a tremendous influence on world opinion in quite a short period of time. . . . For what they say and what they do is prompted by accurate knowledge and a passionate desire to warn humanity about the danger looming over it.
>
> In the light of their arguments and the strictly scientific data which they possess no serious politician has the right to disregard their conclusions.
>
> (Gorbachev 1987)

What were these conclusions? In short, in the event of a nuclear attack, don't bother to call your doctor! The 98 per cent of medical personel who live and work in the centre of cities would be dead. Bernard Lown, the renowned inventor of the implantable defibrillator, was also an author of a 1962 study (PSR 1962) showing that an attack on Boston would lead to unimaginable horror, with bones shattered and internal organs ruptured by gale force winds. There would not be enough burn beds in all of the US to deal with the victims from just this city and radiation would continue to cause cancers years after an attack (Sidel et al. 1962). Using epidemiological knowledge to show the destruction of the medical and civilian infrastructure, they gave lie to the claim that there could be a meaningful medical response to such an attack. Lown's friend and fellow expert on Sudden Cardiac Death, Evgeni Chazov, was the cardiologist for much of the aging Soviet leadership. United in friendship and concerned about the hearts of the world, the pair asked how they could be working together to save lives while their two nations be planning to blow up tens of millions of their families, friends and compatriots? Nuclear war was 'unwinnable' by any side, should never be fought, nor contemplated nor prepared for, but only prevented by abolition. Nuclear war moved from the realm of the military and political to a public health problem. Psychiatrist Robert J. Lifton, who had studied both victims in Hiroshima and Nazi mass murderers, showed how 'psychic numbing' might be responsible for people prepared to commit the genocide that pushing the nuclear button entailed (Lifton and Markusen 1990) and paediatrician Helen Caldicott, immortalized in Academy Award winning film 'If You Love this Planet', became perhaps the most effective spokesperson for the movement. IPPNW asked why the superpowers would need to develop tens of thousands of bombs and spend trillions of dollars to develop these arms, when they only led to more insecurity? IPPNW continues research, education and advocacy for nuclear abolition in the post-Cold War era where the dangers of accidents (Forrow et al. 1998) and of terrorism remain (Helfand et al. 2002).

Landmines

In 1992, Handicap International, Human Rights Watch, medico international, Mines Advisory Group, Physicians for Human Rights, and Vietnam Veterans of America Foundation united to form the International Campaign to Ban Landmines (ICBL). Using pictures of injured children and postcards describing how every 22 minutes someone was killed or maimed corresponding to a human death toll of 10,000 deaths per year (Stover et al. 1997), it showed that any military utility was far exceeded by disproportionate and indiscriminate damage to civilian non-combatants. Basing its argument on this medical burden of suffering and illness – physical, psychological and rehabilitative – and the depletion of resources (they were designed to maim resources devoted to treatment), often lasting years after a war, it galvanized a civil society effort to ban these weapons.

Medical groups continue to be involved in treatment and in social projects providing employment opportunities and rehabilitation. Landmines explode into tiny particles, inevitably contaminating wounds and leading to major blood loss and amputations. IPPNW (a member of the ICBL) has chosen to highlight the damage of landmines by producing both documents on the geopolitical damage and burden of illness as well as a treatment primer. An estimated nine million landmines are scattered throughout Cambodia, where they cost less than $10 to plant and $300 to clear (Cahill 1995; Human Rights Watch 1991; Stover et al. 1994).

The ICBL is now a network of more than 1,400 organizations in over 90 countries. Though cluster bombs continue to be used in Afghanistan and Iraq, and though many major producers refuse to sign on, even non-signatories have been shamed by the norms established by the Ottawa Convention (officially 'The 1997 Convention on the Prohibition of the Use, Stockpiling, Production and Transfer of Anti-Personnel Mines and on Their Destruction') into modifying their behaviours.

Using lessons from the landmines campaign, other organizations have tried to use international humanitarian law to restrict weapons that cause damage disproportionate to war aims. The International Committee of the Red Cross was less successful in attempting to replicate the success of the ICBL in launching the SirUS project to ban all weapons deemed to cause 'superfluous injury and unnecessary suffering' and tried to define these medically (ICRC 1999). A lesson learned is that in addition to good epidemiological data, it is essential to have bold images to sway partners, policy-makers and the general public.

Small arms

The public health damage related to small arms and light weapons (SaLWs) is far greater than that of landmines because of their physical, psychological, social and economic costs. One estimate has them killing about 500,000 annually – 300,000 in armed conflict situations and 200,000 in peace (Cukier 1998). This would rank on the scale of that of the major public health issues of HIV/AIDS (2.9 million), tuberculosis (1.6 million) and malaria (1.1 million) (WHO 2001). Public health models are being used to address gaps in our knowledge, to standardize databases and collection methods, to propose areas for research, to ponder educational and advocacy strategies and to evaluate the effectiveness of preventive approaches (Arya 2001, 2002a; Arya and Cukier 2005).

IPPNW has used 'One Bullet Stories' to personalize the damage of war with stories of each victim (IPPNW student). IPPNW is part of the International Action Network on Small Arms (IANSA), a coalition of victims' groups, medical and humanitarian organizations, researchers and policy-makers united to reduce the damage. In El Salvador, the IPPNW affiliate,

MESARES, examined the damage of small arms along with medical students through hospital, police and coroners' data. Engaging in advocacy, they received much press coverage, enabling a meeting with political leadership helping convince them to tighten up legislation on small arms (IANSA 2004). They are extending this work in partnership with the UNDP, PAHO and WHO.

Epidemiologists have compared rates between the geographically close and demographically similar Canadian and US cities of Vancouver and Seattle (Sloan et al. 1988), examined the lethality of handguns compared to knives and ropes (Chapdelaine et al. 1991) and compared households with and without small arms in terms of homicides, suicides and accidents (Kellerman et al. 1992, 1993). In Afghanistan, Meddings showed that, despite the end of hot war, when social conditions remained unchanged and weapons weren't removed, morbidity and mortality due to small arms could remain high (Meddings 1997).

Medical reasons for opposing war and sanctions

The two major wars of this millennium led by the US have each been opposed by many medical organizations in the Western world. The first, on Afghanistan in the immediate aftermath of 11 September, was considered by many activists as arguably 'just' or legal, but certainly unwise and not a last resort (Arya 2002b). Delegates to the first Peace through Health Conference called for an end to military activity in the immediate aftermath of the US invasion (Sibbald 2002). The American Public Health Association led by Public Health officials in New York, also opposed a military response to the World Trade Center attacks (APHA 2002). These cautions seem well advised four years later as the war continues: Afghan President Karzai is unable to travel outside of Kabul without US military escort, in the rest of the country fundamentalists and warlords are often in charge, in practice women have few more rights than under the Taliban, the opium trade has resumed and cluster bomblets continue to maim children.

Health professionals were critical in highlighting the damage of the wars and sanctions in Iraq. The cost of the first (1990–1) Gulf War turned out to be far greater to the Iraqi people than was obvious from the nightly 'videogame' shows by the US military during the war, including a precipitous fall in GDP at a cost of $170 billion. This included the deliberate targeting of infrastructure, including water supply (MacQueen et al. 2004). But more damaging than the war, in terms of direct and indirect health consequences, was a decade of sanctions targeting civilians. Chlorine, for instance, was considered 'dual use' – of potential military utility it was prohibited for years and then severely restricted, and households were left without any work income, restricting access to food, many basic medicines and immunizations. This caused an increase in deaths due to malnutrition and a resurgence of infectious disease such as cholera, typhoid, hepatitis and malaria. In the end sanctions were responsible for the deaths of at least one and a half million, including over a half a million children under age five (Arya and Zurbrigg 2003). US Secretary of State Madeleine Albright said the price was worth it, ironically and tragically in the end, to fight weapons that had been destroyed or never existed.

While UNICEF and the ICRC highlighted the humanitarian tragedy during the decade (ICRC 1999; UNICEF 1999), it was remarkable that the damage had been forecast by an international study led by the Harvard School of Public Health immediately after the first Gulf War and published in the *New England Journal of Medicine* (Ascherio et al. 1992). Throughout the 1990s, physicians from various organizations, including IPPNW, went on humanitarian missions to Iraq (Gottstein 1999). They took supplies and came back reporting on 98 per cent of childhood leukemics dying because of lack of chemotherapeutic agents, that had cured

90 per cent before the war, of diabetics not receiving insulin and of the malnourished and under-nourished, personifying the otherwise invisible Iraqi plight (Johnson 1999; PGS 2001).

With the second (2003) Gulf War, even before the war began physicians were prepared to oppose its effects with evidence. Using a medical approach, in an article entitled, 'Ask the Right Questions', I asked: 'How imminent and credible is the threat? What would the war do for the Iraqi people? What would it do for countries and peoples of the region? Would it enhance our own security? What would it do to international institutions and international law?' and 'Might there be more cost-effective ways to make us more secure?' (Arya 2003a). A prediction of a $200 billion price tag of the war, considered by the US Administration at the time to be a wild overestimate (National Priorities Project website), now turns out to be an underestimate. Including indirect costs, Nobel Prize winning economist, Joseph Stiglitz calculates the figure 'conservatively' as being over $1 trillion (Bilmes and Stiglitz 2006).

Four months before the outbreak of the second Gulf War, Medact, the British affiliate of IPPNW, released a report, predicting between 48,000 and 250,000 deaths (Salvage 2002), though was unable to predict the conduct of the war. Another International Study Team and the WHO published similar figures (Hoskins et al. 2003). Such data was used throughout the world by medical journals, organizations and even students to oppose the war on medical grounds (Clark 2002; CMAJ 2003; Lee 2002; Ottawa Citizen 2002).

Eminent epidemiologists and public health officials in Coalition countries have called for an accounting of the dead so that we can evaluate the success of this venture. Donald Rumsfeld claimed that the US military did not 'do body counts' and US forces, in fact, tried to put a halt to an Iraqi Health Ministry survey of civilian casualties and prevented release of any data collected (*Toronto Star* 2003). Academics, led by British psychologist John Sloboda, sprang up to fill this apparent void using documentary evidence from credible media to establish direct deaths due to the conflict, which now are greater than 30,000 (Iraq Body Count website). US President George Bush now appears to acknowledge these figures (Baker 2005). The Iraqi Ministry of Health, in spite of US opposition, privately continued to keep figures, which showed that 60 per cent of both conflict-related civilian deaths and injuries in Iraq in the last half of 2004 were caused by the US-led coalition and Iraqi security forces (*Toronto Star* 2005).

Immediately prior to the 2004 US election, at a time when Iraq Body Count reported 10,000 direct deaths (Iraq Body Count 2004), a retrospective study by Johns Hopkins University showed 100,000 excess deaths, with general mortality being 2.5 times greater than pre-war and violent death 58 times greater (Roberts et al. 2004).[2] Medact continues to issue follow-up reports using secondary sources to highlight the public health consequences of war. And the media and general public continue to turn to physicians for an opinion on the merits of the war (Arya 2003e).

Humanitarian ceasefires[3]

In the early 1980s, Central America was plagued with civil war and children were dying in great numbers, not because of direct violence, but in fact because of a lack of sanitation and low rate of immunization. From 1981 to 1985, El Salvador, Guatemala, Honduras and Nicaragua, suffering from the effects of war, had infant mortality levels about 80 per 1,000 while their neighbours at peace, Panama, Costa Rica and Belize, had levels just below 25 per 1,000 live births (Rodriguez-Garcia 2001). UNICEF, under Executive Director James Grant, the Pan American Health Organization (PAHO), and the Roman Catholic Church together brought these facts to the attention of the Duarte government and the FMLN rebels in El Salvador and brokered a series of ceasefires beginning at Christmas 1985 allowing children throughout the country to be immunized. Soon numerous other national and international organizations including Rotary International and the International Committee of the Red Cross joined in the planning and the implementation of the ceasefires and the 'days of tranquility' were expanded to three times a year. Almost 300,000 children were immunized annually at several thousand sites until peace accords were signed in 1992 and the incidence of measles and tetanus dropped dramatically, while polio was eradicated. While a major success as a health venture, this effort is thought to have facilitated an atmosphere of trust and allowed the identification of common goals, setting the stage for the peace accords.

With the help of intermediaries such as the ICRC and WHO, similar efforts were replicated in Lebanon in 1987, the Philippines from 1988 to 1993, Afghanistan from 1994 to 1997 and again in 2000–1, the Democratic Republic of the Congo in 1999 and 2000 and Iraq/Kurdistan from 1996 onward.

In Sudan in 1989, UNICEF's James Grant again achieved an agreement with the Sudanese government and the SPLA to allow 'corridors of peace' to deliver relief supplies to the desperate people of southern Sudan in what became known as Operation Lifeline Sudan. This has been credited with increased commercial activities in these regions, resulting in a more stable environment and a zone of 'almost peace' without a real ceasefire occurring.

Though temporary pauses in fighting have been arranged in at least 19 countries since 1985, and while humanitarian ceasefires, days of tranquility and corridors of peace meet significant health needs, how can they be part of larger peace-building processes? They represent a space of tranquility, reminding people of what peace is really like and can inspire them with hope and strengthen their commitment to work for peace. They may be seen to empower people to overcome the sense of isolation that war brings. Negotiations for ceasefires and corridors also help to make communities aware of their basic human rights to receive food and medical care. They can draw a wide range of parties at the local, national and international level into dialogue, and help to shed light both nationally and internationally on the effects of the war on all people, especially children. They might develop new channels of communication and foster the creation of an environment of confidence in negotiations to end the armed conflict.

In the case of Sudan, the picture is not so rosy as ceasefires also allowed rearming, repositioning of forces and smuggling in of weapons. NGOs delivering aid were forced to sign agreements with the government or rebels, which severely limited their independence, so much so that the ICRC refused to participate (Hendrickson 1998; Macrae 1998). What makes the difference between efforts paving the way to lasting peace and those which merely provide a temporary lull in fighting? Mary Anne Peters (1996) attempted to find part of the answer.

Firstly, the ability to strike *common ground* between warring factions. Intervenors have to help parties identify a concern or goal of value to all sides. The well-being of children is an ideal super-ordinate goal transcending all issues of the conflict. Another might be dignity and respect for human life. The benefits of the humanitarian operation must be delivered *impartially and transparently*, with assistance focused on the civilian population. There must be *agreement on standards and monitoring*: time limits have to be defined; the parties must establish a minimum code of conduct; and there must be an ability to apply pressure to adhere to these rules. For example, a clear identification of vehicles used and an assurance that no arms will be transported or military information passed may be helpful.

The choice of intermediaries is important. *International governments can apply pressure and international non-governmental organizations*, with their capacity for neutrality and their ability to act without the constraints of governments and official agencies, are often helpful. Ultimately in internal wars, it is local groups or civil society that can maintain such a peace. Community participation is important, with the *voices of women and children* being strongly represented. If possible, *local NGOs* of the country or the region, with an understanding and respect for indigenous cultures and political realities, are the best vehicles for providing aid.

The *military and militias* must be made part of the solution and an attempt to address political and strategic questions must recognize that they and their families are often the victims of war. *Local human rights and legal organizations* can make clear reference to international agreements and laws to safeguard the peace. *Education* and communication are important and the *media* can play a vital role in peace education. Distance education through radio teaching or correspondence courses can complement standard education. Training of *community healthcare workers* can strengthen the outcomes of these initiatives but health workers must make use of the peace-building potential through building partnerships with many outside of the health sector.

The World Health Organization and Health as a Bridge for Peace[4]

PAHO initiated the concept of Health as a Bridge for Peace (HBP) in the 1980s, based on the principle that '*shared health concerns can transcend political, economic, social and ethnic divisions among people and between nations*'. Later this developed into a multi-country, multi-agency process, with cross-border surveillance of populations, joint procurement and the exchange of medicines and vaccines among Central American countries. The leadership role of PAHO was essential in bringing health to the forefront of the peace-building agenda, while the actions of UNICEF, the ICRC and NGOs were important in coordinating efforts at the field level. The involvement of the international community (OAS, Spain, US, other European countries, UN agencies) was also integral to the conceptualization and implementation of HBP efforts and invested between $50–100 million in this project in the late 1980s.

The WHO has embraced the concept of Health as a Bridge for Peace (WHO HAC website) and even facilitated training workshops on HBP in the Caucasus/Russia in 1998, in Sri Lanka (1999–2000) and Indonesia in 2001; but HBP remains minimally operationalized and funded within the WHO. Let us look at some of the WHO-supported activity in the field in the name of HBP.

In 1996–7 in Eastern Slavonia, the largely ethnic Serbian part of Croatia, the WHO led an effort to reintegrate health services according to principles of the Dayton, Paris and Erdut agreements. Chairing the Joint Implementation Committee (JIC), it involved governments, civil society leaderships and health NGOs to bring together Croat and Serb health workers in confidence-building activities. These included joint health situation analysis, planning and implementation. In the public health domain, ethnic Croatians and Serbs worked together on the organization of a sub-national immunization day against polio and provision of essential drugs, along with epidemiology and other health research. The administrative reintegration of the health sector included physical rehabilitation, mental health and health information systems. By providing a safe space for dialogue on technical issues, the WHO hoped to create a basis for mutual understanding and cooperation within the health sector. This included emphasizing the respect for both sides' roles as health professionals, and their traditional neutrality and impartiality in situations of conflict. While it seemed to increase the number of Serb and Croat health employees working together and to provide for more equal opportunities for local Serb health workers, few Serbs were employed by the Croatian administration, none were selected for key positions in the health system, and only half of the Serb population were covered by the Croatian National Insurance System.

During the 1992–5 war in Bosnia-Herzegovina, government buildings, civilian homes, hospitals and other public institutions on all sides were targeted and destroyed; a severe refugee crisis ensued, with hundreds of thousands fleeing to Croatia and the rest of Europe and many others being internally displaced. As the war ended, the health sector remained divided and the WHO again worked to unify staffing, service provision, training and healthcare delivery. With European partners, it facilitated 'decentralized cooperation' (DC), a community empowerment bottom-up initiative to link local communities (institutions, health and social services, professionals and lay people) in Europe, primarily in Italy, with 22 diverse towns in Bosnia-Herzegovina (particularly Croat and Muslim) to create and/or consolidate long-term cultural, technical and economic partnerships. The WHO assisted in the coordination of preliminary meetings, needs assessments, planning exercises and training sessions, and provided technical assistance meant to strengthen the trend towards reconciliation. The importance of the WHO and health sector and ultimate success of this venture is still not clear.

When a military junta overthrew the democratically-elected Haitian government of Jean-Bertrand Aristide and ruled from 1991 till 1994, the WHO and international NGOs were torn as to whether or not they should cooperate with it in order to deliver needed aid. Some in the international community (supported by many in Haitian civil society) felt that the best response was strict non-cooperation, enforcement of sanctions and evacuation of foreign personnel. In the end a decentralized strictly apolitical Health/Humanitarian Assistance Programme (HAP), involving Haitian professionals of different backgrounds, and targeted to most vulnerable segments of the population, contributed to the development and stabilization of the health sector. Opponents of such an approach would argue that maintaining relations with the de facto government may have legitimated it and weakened civil society (Böck-Buhmann 2005).

The WHO also tried to help integrate health systems in Mozambique and Angola. From 1992 to 1996, cooperation of the government and RENAMO in Mozambique led to a comprehensive effort to re-train RENAMO health workers to re-integrate them within the National Health System and to increase the accessibility to basic healthcare for demobilized soldiers and their families in order to defuse political tensions. After the signing of the Lusaka protocol, UNITA and the Angolan government worked with UNICEF and the WHO to disarm and demobilize soldiers from armies on both sides of the conflict. The latter brokered arrangements for the development and implementation of a health programme. This included joint data collection activities, designing common protocols between groups, the adoption of national guidelines on priority health issues (sleeping sickness, malaria, TB) and a common simplified health information system (early warning system). Integrated activities, meant to promote dialogue, trust and common goals, included in-service training, working with communities to develop public health programmes and setting up a joint medical team to assess and classify disabilities supporting a legal basis for institutionalizing benefits to disabled war victims and demobilized soldiers. When fighting broke out again in 1998, Days of Tranquility once again allowed for immunization.

The WHO has identified the following characteristics as important for success: working with health authorities and professionals on all sides openly and transparently according to geographical boundaries (not political) to create a safe space for health (neutral environments), addressing human rights and ethics through health, fostering and empowering responsibility for health and environment with action based on best available information and flexibility to correct when necessary. However it has not been able to properly evaluate the success of the above measures nor really developed a framework for assessment. Is such an effort worthwhile or indeed possible? This will be examined later in this chapter.

Peace through Health at McMaster

McMaster academics articulated an engaged theory of health initiatives promoting peace processes and developed study tools to systematize such knowledge (Peters 1996; MacQueen and Santa-Barbara 2000; MacQueen et al. 1997, 2001; Santa-Barbara 2004; Yusuf 1998). In addition, McMaster projects included field studies and interventions in former Yugoslavia, Sri Lanka and Afghanistan. These projects demonstrated the desirability of the health sector to cooperate with other sectors of society, including teachers and artists.

Designed 'to promote trauma healing, non-violent conflict resolution, peaceful living, human rights, and reduction of ethnic bias in Croatian children affected by war' (Woodside et al. 1999), a school-based project trained fourth- and fifth-grade teachers in modules discussing emotional reactions, flashbacks, 'bias and prejudice' conflict skills, nonviolence and communication skills.

Afghan Canadian physician, Seddiq Weera, led a series of workshops in partnership with Afghan University in February 2001 in Peshawar, Pakistan, where much of the Afghan refugee community took shelter. Intellectuals, opinion leaders, political leaders, journalists, writers, educators and NGOs (across the political spectrum, with a special effort to promote the participation of women) all participated. After the Taliban fell, given Weera's access to the new Afghan leadership, Western governments and international agencies, a psychosocial model of conflict transformation and a peace education curriculum were developed for Afghan school children ages 10–15. Major transferable outputs included a training manual and a storybook demonstrating peaceful principles; the latter has been adapted for a puppet show (Centre for Peace Studies, CPS website).

In the Tamil-speaking ethnically mixed eastern Batticaloa district of Sri Lanka (two-thirds ethnic Tamil and one-third Muslim), there had been massacres, kidnappings and displacements. There the study showed that of 170 children, 41 per cent had experienced personal exposure to war-related direct violence (home attacked shelled, being shot at, beaten or arrested); 53 per cent had a direct family member suffering a violent death; 95 per cent reported events placing them at risk for PTSD; and 20 per cent showed severe levels of post traumatic psychological distress (Chase et al. 1999).

In searching for a 'health initiative' to respond to the needs of children identified in the survey project, medicalized models of trauma (PTSD) and treatment with drugs or counselling were found to be stigmatizing and not accessible locally. The focus on children living amidst conflict shifted explorations towards models of resiliency, the capacity to positively cope with adversity and traumatic stressors. Rob Chase, lead physician in this Health Reach study, helped facilitate an exploratory visit to Sri Lanka by artist Paul Hogan. Together with Jesuit father, Paul Satkunanayagam, a qualified counsellor and educator, and a multi-ethnic committee of local representatives, in partnership with schools, religious and tribal leaders, they opened the Butterfly Peace Garden (the Butterfly Peace Garden Media Unit website). The Garden itself would provide sanctuary, a space to honour children. The animators possessing a 'contemplative, respectful spirit' were meant to accompany children and through personal engagement and using imaginative play involving earthwork, artwork and heartwork ultimately help heal the trauma of war and promote resilience. They planted herbs, cared for abandoned animals on site, designed costumes, developed stories, played music, worked with clay and paint.

The teachers initially sent the most troubled children aged 9 to 14 from surrounding villages half Hindu, half Muslim and half male, half female. Soon the programme developed to 150 students a year. The Butterfly Garden assisted in meeting each of the child's basic needs – physiological, safety belonging and love needs and esteem needs as defined by Maslow. The peace-building components of the Garden project include repair and transformation of damaged relationships, reconciliation, trust-building and maximization of mutual understanding (Wetmore 2005).

Peace through Health as an academic discipline

As an academic discipline Peace through Health is relatively new, yet Peace through Health education efforts have already taken place in many countries (see the section References to this chapter). The WHO Report on Violence includes direct macro-level violence along with suicides and domestic violence. Peace through Health practitioners have generally chosen to concentrate interventions on direct violence at a macro-level, though they recognize the relationship between community violence, family violence and violence to the self with macro structural, cultural and ecological violence. Academics in Norway, Canada, Holland and Britain, however, include in their analyses the ability of health sector action to promote human security and to mitigate structural (including poverty, malnutrition and illiteracy) and ecological violence (Arya 2004b).

As opposed to disciplines of eco-system health, health and human rights, social determinants of health, medical ethics and global health, Peace through Health is more designed at interventions and while projects are often at a micro-level (individual or interpersonal), the objective is macro-levels of violence.

A new paradigm: development of a model of Peace through Health activities

MacQueen et al. (1997) made the first significant attempt to classify PtH work. Medical professionals participating in organizations such as the ICRC and MSF dare to tread where few outsiders might venture. They assist with *Communication of Knowledge*.

By their very presence, as one institution persisting throughout a conflict, they contribute to *Strengthening of Communities* and can develop, foster or sustain a structure for post-conflict rebuilding. They might help with *Healing of the Individual and Society* (physical, psychological and at times even spiritual). They *Extend Solidarity* merely by their presence; that is, by risking their own lives to treat people in war zones. Such gestures can give hope to the relatively powerless side of a conflict, strengthening their struggle for fundamental human rights. They *Broaden the Concept of Altruism*, treating victims impartially, when military and other civilian personnel are propagandized into believing that people on the opposite side of a conflict have and deserve fewer rights as they are different. While opposing war leaders who seek to diminish, depersonalize and dehumanize the 'enemy', they seek to *Personify the Enemy*. For example, IPPNW used common professional contacts and friendships during the Cold War to show that the consequences of war for 'real people' on the other side would be as real and catastrophic as they were for 'us' in the 'free world'. *Construction of Super-ordinate Goals* such as the well-being of their children allowed the warring factions to find a common goal in El Salvador. The refusal of medical personnel to participate in what are considered unjust war campaigns of their governments, such as Israel in the Occupied Territories, the US in Vietnam and Iraq, or Russia in Chechnya, or to oppose weapons systems such as nuclear weapons, is an example of *Non-cooperation and Dissent*. IPPNW, MSF, UNICEF, ICRC and PAHO have all

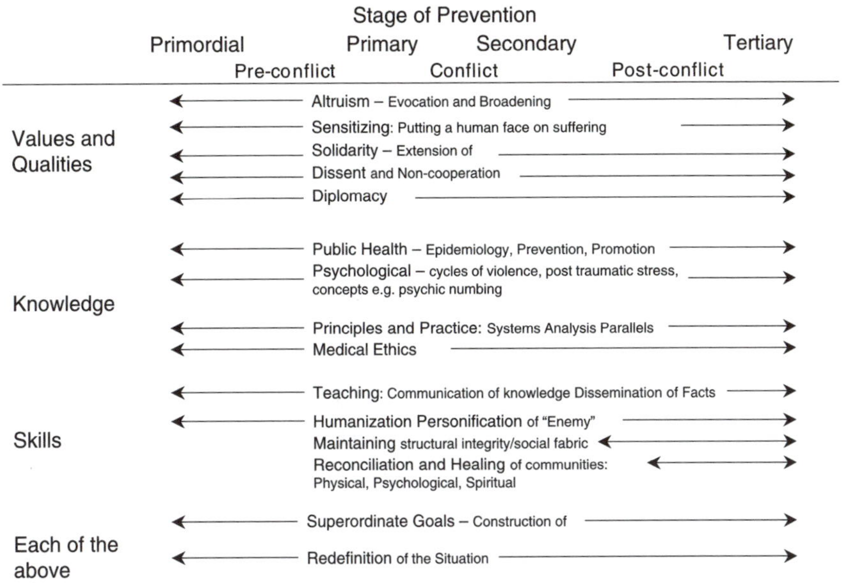

Stage of Prevention
Primordial Primary Secondary Tertiary
Pre-conflict Conflict Post-conflict

Values and Qualities
- Altruism – Evocation and Broadening
- Sensitizing: Putting a human face on suffering
- Solidarity – Extension of
- Dissent and Non-cooperation
- Diplomacy

Knowledge
- Public Health – Epidemiology, Prevention, Promotion
- Psychological – cycles of violence, post traumatic stress, concepts e.g. psychic numbing
- Principles and Practice: Systems Analysis Parallels
- Medical Ethics

Skills
- Teaching: Communication of knowledge Dissemination of Facts
- Humanization Personification of "Enemy"
- Maintaining structural integrity/social fabric
- Reconciliation and Healing of communities: Physical, Psychological, Spiritual

Each of the above
- Superordinate Goals – Construction of
- Redefinition of the Situation

Figure 24.1. Peace through Health working model

used credibility and fame to engage in *Diplomacy* at the highest levels. The final category identified by MacQueen et al. – *Redefinition of the Situation* – may be the most interesting. IPPNW turned what ostensibly was a military and political issue, nuclear war, into a medical one, as the bombs would indiscriminately target civilians and a disproportionate number of healthcare personnel to which traditional medical responses were useless. The International Campaign to Ban Landmines (ICBL) similarly de-legitimized the use of landmines as an instrument of war.

The assets of the MacQueen et al. classification have been incorporated into a knowledge–skills–values paradigm used in many disciplines, including medicine in a model used by the author in Figure 24.1 (adapted from Arya 2004a). This has also been of interest to other sectors of society.

Assets of health workers: a knowledge–skills–values paradigm

Knowledge assets

Among the major assets of physicians in zones of conflict is *epidemiology* – measuring death and disease and determining causality. As such, they can measure effects of war and violence as they impact on health directly, including mortality and morbidity, but also the indirect health effects via epidemic illness, refugee movement, infrastructure damage, deprivation of basic needs and effects on mental health. Such efforts have been made on issues ranging from nuclear weapons, small arms and landmines to effects of militarism and economic sanctions and war. Further, the *mental health* expertise of health professionals in diagnosis, treatment and rehabilitation of trauma and stress has been invaluable in projects. Traditional tenets of *medical ethics* to gain trust and confidence of parties in conflict include confidentiality, impartiality, beneficence and non-malefiscence (Hippocratic Oath website). The recent Medical Professionalism Charter accepted by the American College of Physicians and the European Federation of Internal

Medicine and promoted by many other medical bodies (ABIM) considers the primacy of patient welfare, patient autonomy and social justice leading to important professional responsibilities.

The Responsibility to Protect report (ICISS 2001) produced by the International Commission on Intervention and State Sovereignty, composed of former military, political and diplomatic leaders from around the world including former heads of states, international legal experts, NATO generals and UN officials, was meant to develop criteria to prevent genocides. It seems to have reflected such ethical principles from the medical world as Autonomy, Beneficence, Non-Maleficence, and Altruism and Primum non Nocere (first of all, do no harm) (Arya 2003c). Other criteria for outside military intervention, including Right Authority, have Right Intention, use force only as a Last Resort and, with Proportionate Means, in the case of Incapacitance of the patient State, seem very familiar to medical practitioners. These principles might be used to guide any outside intervention in world affairs (Arya 2005). Finally, lessons from the realm of medicine such as the failure of a simplistic 'hard power' approach might have analogies in world affairs (Arya 2006).

Practice skills

The name 'doctor' is derived from Latin 'docere' to teach. Educating is important for adherence to treatment recommendations and allied professionals such as nurses, physiotherapists, occupational therapists, social workers, psychologists and pharmacists may be even better adapted and trained in teaching. Health professionals can contribute to healing of individuals and communities, development of a civic identity and maintenance of structures, giving a sense of order to people's lives when all else is in disorder thereby facilitating post-conflict rebuilding. They can communicate knowledge about war zones, daring to go where no one else will. James Orbinski, who had been the MSF physician in Kigali, chose to use MSF's Nobel Prize acceptance speech (Orbinski, Nobel website) to highlight the effect on the civilian populations of Grozny, Chechnya, due to bombing. Orbinski claimed that the humanitarian act is 'to relieve suffering, to seek to restore autonomy, to witness to the truth of injustice, and to insist on political responsibility'. Political and military leaders try to dehumanize 'the enemy' be they Jew in Nazi Germany, Soviet during the Cold War, or Iraqi, Libyan or Serb in the recent past (Keen 1986). Doctors in practice must personify their patients, including the 'undesirable' and marginalized in society, whom they treat as individuals worthy of respect with dignity and human rights (patient-centredness).

Values and qualities

Physicians, whom society sees as bright, altruistic individuals, and perhaps having power over life and death, have disproportionate access to leadership allowing them to engage in diplomacy as well as to the media allowing them to engage in dissent and non-cooperation. In working with individuals, the sense of solidarity is meaningful to people with whom they work and they can sensitize both political leaders and media to such suffering.

Stages of war

The second element to the model adapted by the author from McMaster work refers to stages of war. Yusuf et al. (1998) describe how war may be viewed as analogous to a disease. As such, it has risk factors and may allow preventive manoeuvres or interventions during pre-war, during and post-war stages at the primordial, primary, secondary and tertiary stages paralleling a medical model of prevention, treatment and rehabilitation.

Primordial prevention involves looking at not just proximate causes of disease, but root causes, the underlying disease conditions, preventing the 'risk factors' for conflicts from developing in the first place. These would include poor governance, human rights deficits, education deficits, economic and social inequalities, ecological degradation, community and cultural disintegration. Primary prevention refers to modification of these risk factors and concerns prevention of war from breaking out when a situation of conflict already exists, or from escalating to more dangerous levels. 'Peacekeeping', limitation of arms, combating propaganda and diplomacy are examples of such efforts. Secondary prevention refers to the situation where war has already broken out (the disease has manifested itself) and where the effects of war can be treated. These efforts might be termed 'peacemaking'. Once the damage has taken place, health workers can be involved in Tertiary prevention, and analogous to rehabilitation in medicine and ecological restoration for environmentalists would be post 'hot' war 'peace-building' (Melf 2004).

The knowledge – skills – values framework and the stages of action are incorporated into the model shown in Figure 24.1.

Deficits of knowledge, skills and values in health workers

Despite the major assets possessed by health workers, to truly work effectively for peace, they must incorporate the efforts, knowledge, skills and values of other professionals, often in a team. What, then, are some of the deficits of health workers?

Knowledge deficits

The biomedical focus of medical training on the pathological basis of disease, leaves physicians with major deficits even when trying to deliver healthcare in war zones. Nurses and other allied health professionals seem better equipped to approach problems more holistically. Understanding nonviolence, violence and conflict analyses, reconciliation and conflict resolution/transformation are among the many parts of Peace Studies that might be useful for health workers to act constructively in war zones. So are knowledge of intercultural communication, peace processes, international human rights norms, humanitarian law, human security and codes of conduct.

Skills deficits

These include the ability to monitor events and effect continuous political analysis, conflict resolution, negotiation and mediation. From anthropology case studies, key informants, participant observation and focus group interviews may help to understand the nature of conflict and its resolution and in the design of culturally appropriate and sensitive interventions. The Butterfly Garden in Sri Lanka shows how other professionals' expertise may be incorporated and how resilience may be fostered rather than merely treating trauma in a medical way.

Values deficits

These are important as the knowledge, skills and access of physicians in particular makes them even more dangerous without a firm moral compass. Complicity with torture in military dictatorships, with apartheid and currently in Abu Ghraib and Guantanamo occur when physicians forget professional obligations for individual gain in terms of what they see as a greater good (Marks 2005; Miles 2004). In the fictional media, bad apple physicians, the Hannibal Lecters and Dr Evils of the world, can represent the highest form of evil. Self-assured physicians occupying positions of leadership such as Radovan Karadic may perpetrate tremendous evil. Where things go wrong, they can go wrong on a large scale from Harold Shipman to Josef Mengele.

Seidelman (1995), quoting Kater (1983), recounts that of all occupational groups in Germany at the time, the medical profession had the largest membership in the Nazi party (44.8 per cent of all licensed physicians were party members). Nazi racial policies derived from the medical profession itself. Public population health, or 'Volksgesundheit', provided a scientifically legitimate vehicle for the achievement of their political goal of racial purification or hygiene, and sterilizations of those with hereditary conditions or deemed 'unfit' were performed in hospital under general anaesthetic and later using radiation. The rationalizations and ability to perpetrate genocide continues in the nuclear age (Lifton and Markusen 1990). The Nuremberg Code (1949) was meant to standardize the ethical role of physicians towards research subjects.

Critique of the model

This evolving model has been critiqued as too biomedical and reductionist in design rather than a more holistic, ecological 'systems' approach. Further it may be Eurocentric, and focusing on outsiders, neglecting local capacities and internal resources. Some would say that the deficit/asset model may not be promotional for either health or peace. Finally it is focused on health professionals, especially doctors. Each of these criticisms has some validity, but the model is not meant to encompass all of the peace productive capacity of societies, nor is it meant to be static, but as a tool to explore mechanisms for those outside immediate zones of 'hot' conflict to contribute to its prevention, mitigation and resolution.

Mitigating conflict through the Peace through Health model?

A critical part of this model is to establish at what point in the conflict organizations should work. IPPNW has been a *primary prevention* organization designed to prevent nuclear war and later all war, while MSF has primarily been active during and after conflict to help societies rebuild (*secondary and tertiary prevention*). The ICRC assists victims during wars and with rehabilitation afterwards (*secondary and tertiary prevention*). To a far lesser extent, they try to help in *primary prevention* and with root causes (*primordial prevention*). The International Society of Doctors for the Environment (ISDE) and Physicians for Human Rights (PHR) are examples of medical organizations with an international scope, but with specific foci related to root causes (*primordial prevention*), only peripherally related to prevention of war. IANSA and the ICBL often use a health, humanitarian or human rights message as a central focus for advocacy work. Both work on *primary prevention* of violence and war by reduced access to weapons and on tertiary prevention with victim assistance and rebuilding post-war. The McMaster University Peace through Health group has restricted its field activities in Croatia, Sri Lanka and Afghanistan to primary and *tertiary prevention* mental health work, meant to prevent resumption of conflict, and generally avoided presence during active conflict. These types of activities are demonstrated in Figure 24.2. Rodriguez-Garcia et al. (2001), from

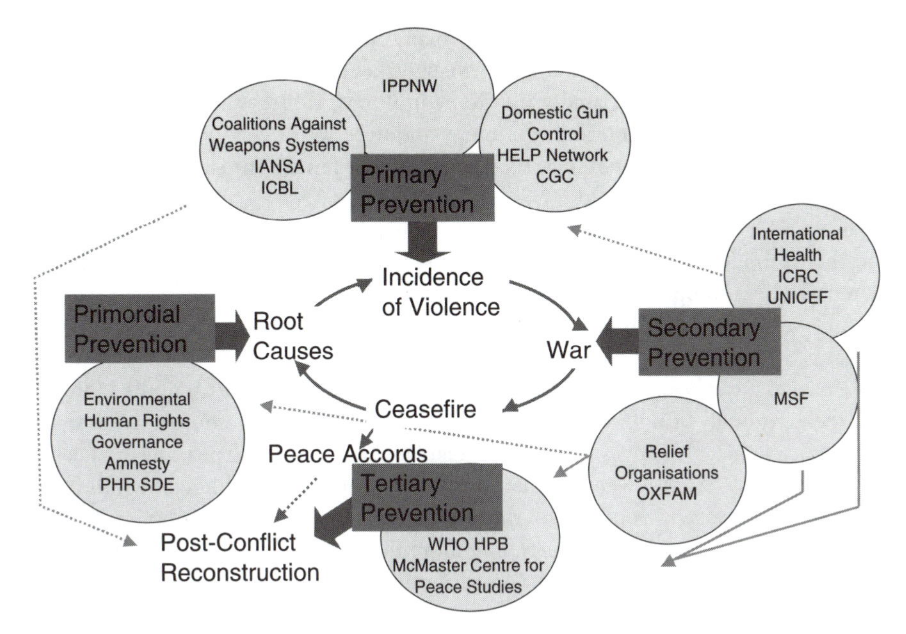

Figure 24.2. Breaking the chain of war: medical peace action in a framework of prevention

George Washington University, have described how organizations may work at various stages of conflict.

The model suggests that we should restrict activity to those where our knowledge, skills and values make us credible. For instance, in anti-nuclear activism, IPPNW cannot be credible if it concentrates efforts on legal, economic, political or military aspects. Coalitions and partnerships may assist in addressing peace knowledge and deficits. This model could be applied to other sectors of society not currently identified by the multi-track model, such as legal professionals, human rights workers, engineers, scientists, artists, athletes and musicians, and help them develop frameworks for their work using their unique characteristics (knowledge, skills and values) at various stages of conflict.

While it is true in general that activities might be restricted, the highly successful MSF campaign for essential drugs (MSF website), which targets globalization and trade indirectly while concentrating on basic health needs, shows how we can operate outside of these parameters. The WHO and the ICRC, with greater resources and staff, are able to participate in all stages, but each division must restrict its foci to its area(s) of expertise.

Dilemmas in PtH

Issues related to aid such as funding being short term and inflexible, oblivious to changing conditions on the ground, evaluations and goals which are inappropriately Western centric, and difficulties transitioning between humanitarian relief work and development work are well known among practitioners. Less well described are, 'Can work in war zones be apolitical or impartial?' 'Do our models of intervention in mental health designed in the West really work for trauma?' Are locals willing to work within these Western frameworks for added resources?' 'Are some of the most needy people avoiding seeing mental health professionals because of stigma?'

The bio-medicalization of trauma concerns many in the Global South, particularly those from traditional cultures where healing normally takes place in communities and within religious traditions. Stigma associated with biomedical practitioners and the neglect of family, school and community both in terms of etiology and in terms of healing, neglect of the social meaning of suffering, development of agency and resilience remain the subject of heated debate (Giacaman et al. 2005; Summerfield 1998).

The ICRC, UN and nation states stick to principles of neutrality or non-interference, often to the frustration of many of their field workers. Yet James Orbinski asks, 'Can rape be considered merely a complex gynaecologic emergency?'

How do we look at collaboration and partnership where there is a tremendous power differential as between Israel and Palestine?

The Canadian International Scientific Exchange Programme (CISEPO) of the University of Toronto seeks to build bridges to peace in the Middle East with a cooperative hearing aid project and academic exchanges to train paediatric cancer specialists, trying to keep work 'below the politics' (CISEPO website). Such work (Skinner et al. 2005) has drawn the criticism that one cannot stay outside of politics in the area (Jabbour 2005). In fact, politics prevented the congenital hearing loss project from screening more than 1,000 Palestinians, while 8,000 each of Israelis and Jordanians were screened. Most Palestinian academic institutions have called for public boycotts of all Israeli universities as arms of the state (Santa-Barbara 2005a). It is unclear how this model seeks to address disparities of conditions, issues of structural violence (social justice, equity) and dignity. The programme itself is not well known and therefore has faced organized opposition. If there were greater success, how might this be addressed?

The 'Healing across the Divides' project, led by Norbert Goldfield, with two decades of work in the region, is designed 'to assist Israeli/Palestinian health care organizations to improve the health of Israelis and Palestinians via increased health professional mediated health and human rights improvements and policymaker decisions.' Choosing its partners carefully, it acknowledges the difference of conditions, seeks to address inequalities and capacity building while contributing to the dignity of all sides. It is currently engaged in a diabetes study in Israeli and Palestinian villages, largely working with civil society partners (Healing Divides website).

Evaluation tools

A major shortcoming of this discipline is that evaluation of PtH projects in the field is not yet well developed (Vass 2001). This may be true for Peace Studies generally. How do we bring intellectual rigour to such a field? Health studies may offer some methodologies.

Mary Anderson describes some resistance to evaluation by those on the ground. Often field workers say it is: 'Too soon'; 'Too complicated'; 'Too intangible'; 'Unnecessary'; 'A donor agenda' (Anderson and Olson 2003). But the positives seem to outweigh the negatives. These include ensuring effectiveness and accountability, avoiding wasting resources on ineffective efforts, answering stakeholders, increasing support for a programme and contributing to the scientific knowledge base.

Evaluation may be done at any stage. Formative evaluation is meant to gain information to guide or improve programme development, while summative evaluation is meant to render a summary judgement about critical aspects of a programme performance vis-à-vis specific goals and objectives. We might assess theoretical components, conceptualization and design, do a 'needs' assessment, look at process operations, implementation and delivery and finally impacts or outcomes, cost effectiveness or efficiency.

Evaluation tools include: Components (groups of closely related programme activities); Inputs (programme resources); Activities (identifiable programme tasks); Outputs (products of programme activities); Goals (general statements about desired programme direction (objectives and indicators); and Outcomes (short term and long term). Such evaluation planning may help identify underlying assumptions, reveal stakeholder expectations, describe cause and effect relationships and serve as a starting point for discussion and the resolution of differences. The Peace through Health model identifies some of the unique inputs available to health professionals.

Outcomes

Anderson's Reflecting on Peace Practice (RPP) approach suggests positive outcomes at a peace writ large, macro-level might include not just stopping direct violence, but building a just and sustainable peace predicated on creation of reform of institutions, prompting participants to increasingly resist provocation to violence, and causing them to develop their own initiatives for peace (Anderson 1999, 2003).

Joanna Santa-Barbara (2005b) suggests PtH projects may look at more concrete impacts such as the abolition of war as an institution, prevention of specific outbreaks of violence, limiting harm and ending episodes of violence when they occur, rehabilitation of people and social systems after violent conflicts with a goal of preventing further violence, addressing structural and cultural causes of direct violence such as poverty, and stimulation of other sectors of society (e.g. education, media, justice systems) towards parallel action as viable goals.

Ken Bush (2003) determined six macro-level outcomes: dismantling the culture of war; living with compassion and justice; building intercultural respect, reconciliation and solidarity; promoting human rights and responsibilities; living in harmony with the earth; and cultivating inner peace.

Each of these indicators are certainly reflective of the Galtung definition of peace. Violence, according to Galtung, may be considered avoidable insults to basic human needs including survival needs; well-being needs; freedom needs; and identity needs (death, misery, repression and alienation), with war being an extreme form of collective violence impacting on each. A typology of violence might include *direct* acts, not only physical violence, but psychological (e.g. verbal threat), social (act of exclusion) and spiritual (act of desecration), i.e. reduction of human potential bodily, but also mentally, socially and spiritually, *structural* hidden 'violent processes' built into the social system expressing itself in unequal opportunities (i.e. inequality in the distribution of income, education opportunities, etc.), *cultural* (religion, ideology, language, art, science) and *ecological*. Peace, by contrast, can be defined as not merely the absence of direct, cultural and structural violence (negative peace), but a state of complete loving, harmonious acts to elicit the good in each other (direct peace), of complete equitable, horizontal relations (structural peace) and of complete positive culture, which promotes peace and non-violence (cultural peace) (Galtung 1996). Perhaps it is this definition which should be used to measure outcomes.

Outputs

At a field level, Bush's Peace and Conflict Impact Analysis (PCIA) (Bush 1998, 2003) is intended to evaluate project outputs. Bush feels that pre-assessment location (infrastructure), timing (opportunity), political, military and socioeconomic context (stability/structures) and environmental context are all important considerations to determine dynamics and risk. Areas of potential Peace and Conflict Impact (PCI) include: conflict management capacities and peace-building; military and human security; political structures and processes; economic structures and processes; social reconstruction and empowerment. Post-project, Bush feels that we might measure changes in access to individual or collective material and non-material resource effects on socioeconomic tensions, effects on privilege, hierarchies and dependencies, changes in political economy and governance challenges. But how objectively measurable are these paths to peace and project outputs?

Anderson cautions that goals at a programmatic level must not worsen divisions, increase danger of local participants, reinforce structural or overt violence, divert human and material resources from productive peace activities, increase cynicism or disempower the local people from a local peace-building perspective. Insiders and outsiders each play a role and projects can be directed at the interpersonal or structural level and can try to involve more people or key people. Knowing where we are and who our target audience is, is of utmost importance for a programme (Anderson 2004).

Anne Bunde Birouste and Anthony Zwi, of the Health and Conflict Research Project of the University of New South Wales School of Public Health (UNSW 2004), have developed a concise, yet comprehensive set of filter questions on such issues relevant to outputs. These have been field tested in Sri Lanka, the Solomon Islands and East Timor, and are to be used at the design, monitoring and assessment phases of health projects in areas of armed conflict. Questions are in five major categories of Cultural Sensitivity, Conflict Sensitivity (trust and conflict awareness and responsiveness), Social Justice (equity and non-discrimination, gender), Social Cohesion (community cohesion, psychosocial well-being), and Good Governance (community capacity building and empowerment, sustainability and coordination, transparency and accountability).

Efficiency

Even if we could measure and compare these categories, would it allow determination of cost-effectiveness? I would argue that the model in Figure 24.1 demonstrates many of the capacities (knowledge, skills and values) of health workers for peace and are key to determining efficiency. Other efforts to define efficiency among health workers for peace in the Global South include a project called Peace Works. Funded by a Reebok human rights award, young Filipino physician Ernest Guevarra has gathered together health and peace workers from Timor, Chechnya, Chiapas and Rwanda (Santa-Barbara 2004).

What is in store for Peace through Health in the next 20 years?

Peace through Health will need to improve in terms of evaluation. It is one thing to propose an alternative discourse, another to justify it with evidence. Peace through Health practitioners are increasingly sought after for training. From the former Yugoslavia to El Salvador, communities developing social reconstruction are seeking training in nonviolence, reconciliation and conflict analysis from Peace through Health academics and practitioners.

Medicos Salvadoreños para la Responsabilidad Social MESARES, and the IPPNW Medical Students Chapter (E-MESARES), hope to incorporate Peace through Health training in partnership with PtH practitioners and academics in Canada. In the 1980s, more than 160,000 Central Americans died in wars or civil violence, and many more were wounded. Over two million people fled their homes, often to neighbouring countries at peace such as Costa Rica, stressing the social fabric even of these peaceful countries (Guerra de Macedo 1994). Going beyond the documentation of health effects of small arms (Paniagua et al. 2005) and the achievement of policy changes with regard to small arms, the project is meant to build capacity, especially among youth, to formulate proposals to help resolve violence. Using medical students trained in peace-building education and field application to act as facilitators, they hope to improve individual and community mental health, and to help empower communities to develop their own individually managed violence prevention projects, built on the Problem Solving for Better Health (PSBH) model of the Dreyfus Health Foundation. The PSBH or Solpromesa model is an innovative and flexible approach viewing violence as an individual and group responsibility, requiring coordination with local authorities and community leaders. It is aimed at strengthening local capacities with the optimal use of existing internal resources as it seeks health solutions to problems of violence.

Many view Peace through Health as an overall paradigm for their health work. I expect that in the next few years we will see a convergence of: (a) work that we consider as health as a bridge for peace, (b) work on social determinants, and (c) work on environmental and eco-system health, as the linkages between each become apparent. Peace through Health may influence other health disciplines as we realize concrete ways to act on non-biomedical determinants of health. Work on humanitarian assistance and development from the Global North will become more obvious as self-interest and one might hope that a model of solidarity will develop. Unlike many other parts of peace studies, Peace through Health ventures and interventions are often student-led, including the Nuclear Weapons Inheritance Project (NWIP), which is bringing students together in nuclear weapons states, and ReCAP, which is doing Peace Education in Palestinian refugee camps (IPPNW Students website).

One could anticipate an expansion of the role of epidemiology to stimulate social change. Physicians and epidemiologists will continue to use their projections such as represented by the Harvard Study Team, Collateral Damage and Johns Hopkins team in Iraq to predict and document the effects of war and social violence, gaining credibility and respect beyond that of politicians and generals (Murray et al. 2002). We hopefully will be able to offer more peaceful but also cheaper, more effective and sustainable alternatives to war.

In our most optimistic dreams we would see governments and medical practitioners recognizing the mistakes of the past. We might hope that governments could move beyond the traditional 'realist' security agenda, past a human security agenda (Arya 2003c) to seeing their role as health promoters with health and well-being explicitly accepted as the overriding goal of governments (Arya 2003d, 2005). To achieve this will require them to embrace peace in all its forms: direct, structural, cultural and ecologic. Perhaps we can transform the realm of medicine from a pathogen, hard-power, threat-based, 'realist' model to a more holistic, eco-system approach.

Rudolf Virchow, one of the giants of medicine, said, 'If medicine is to fulfil her great task, then she must enter the political and social life.' 'Politik ist weiter nichts als Medizin im Grossen' – Politics is nothing more than medicine on a grand scale (Virchow 1848). Virchow would have been pleased to see medicine and health entering the realm of peace.

Appendix: web links

Education

Peace through Health

University of Waterloo
http://www.grebel.uwaterloo.ca/pacs301

http://www.fes.uwaterloo.ca/ers/faculty/narya.htm
Contact: Neil Arya narya@uwaterloo.ca

McMaster University
www.humanities.mcmaster.ca/peace-health
http://www.humanities.mcmaster.ca/peace-health/PtHCourse/PtHCourse.htm
Contacts: Joanna Santa Barbara Joanna@web.ca Neil Arya narya@uwaterloo.ca, Rob Chase chaser@cc.umanitoba.ca

Tromsoe University
Medical Peace Work
http://uit.no/sih/7665/1
www.medicalpeacework.org
Contact: Klaus Melf Klaus.melf@fagmed.uit.no

Erlangen University
Krieg. Trauma. Gesundheit: Ärztliche Verantwortung in Gewaltprävention und Friedensförderung
http://www.gesch.med.uni-erlangen.de/eth/lehre/gte_5.html#gast
Contact: Stephan Kolb s.kolb@klinikum-nuernberg.de

International organizations

Health as a Bridge for Peace http://www.who.int/hac/en/
Violence and Injury Prevention www.who.int/violence_injury_prevention/violence/en/
Health and Human Rights www.who.int/hhr/en/
PAHO http://www.disaster-info.net/catalogo/English/dd/Ped/helidcat.htm
UNICEF http://www.unicef.org/

Non-governmental organizations

International Physicians for the Prevention of Nuclear War www.ippnw.org www.ippnw-students.org
Doctors Without Borders http://www.msf.org/
International Committee of the Red Cross http://www.icrc.org/
Physicians for Human Rights http://www.phrusa.org/

Acknowledgements

Caecilie Buhmann, Rita Giacaman, Emperatriz Crespin, Rob Chase, Rob Stevens, Klaus Melf, Ryan Marks and Joanna Santa-Barbara all kindly helped with reviewing the manuscript and making suggestions. Amelie Baillargeon continued to be generous with her time, assisting with critical editing and reference checks.

Notes

1 Concepts in this section on perils of humanitarian aid are largely derived from Anderson (1994) and Peters 1996.
2 A follow-up study by the Hopkins group conducted in 2006 showed an excess mortality of the 650,000 Iraqi casualties in the 40 months post-invasion, with increasing rate annually to 2006 (Burnham et al. 2006). This time the Iraqi Minister of Health acknowledged at least 150,000 civilians (Hurst 2006), still more than 3 times the estimate of Iraq Body Count, had been killed since 2003.
3 Source material for this section and good references on humanitarian ceasefires include Galli (2001), Guerra de Macedo (1994), Hess and Pfeiffer Large (1997), Manenti (2001), Peters (1996), Rodriguez-Garcia (2001), UNICEF (1996) and WHO (1997).
4 Further recommended reading and source material on WHO Health as a Bridge for Peace includes Large (1997), Manenti (2001), Peters (1996), Rodriguez-Garcia (2001), and WHO (1997)

References

ABIM Foundation (2002) 'Medical professionalism in the new millennium: a Physician Charter', *Annals of Internal Medicine*, 136, 3: 243–6, at: http://www.annals.org/cgi/content/full/136/3/243.

American Public Health Association (APHA) (2002) *Association News*, at: http://www.apha.org/legislative/policy/2002/2002–11-oposwar.pdf.

Anderson, M.B. (1994) 'Ten ways that international assistance can worsen conflict, adapted from "International assistance and conflict: an exploration of negative impacts" ', Case Studies Series #1, Cambridge, MA: Local Capacities for Peace Project.

Anderson, M.B. (1999) *Do No Harm: How Aid can Support Peace – Or War*, Boulder, CO and London: Lynne Rienner Publishers, 1–66.

Anderson, M.B. (2003) *Collaborative Learning Projects and the Collaborative for Development Action, Criteria for Effectiveness*, at: http://www.cdainc.com/rpp/criteria_of_effectiveness.php.

Anderson, M.B. (2004) *Reflecting on Peace Practice Project CDA Collaborative Learning Projects and the Collaborative for Development Action*, at: http://www.cdainc.com/rpp/docs/ReflectingOnPeace PracticeHandbook.pdf.

Anderson, M.B. and Olson, L. (2003) *Confronting War: Critical Lessons for Peace Practitioners*, Cambridge, MA: The Collaborative for Development Action.

Arya, N. (2001) 'Preventing the adverse health effects of small arms', paper presented at the UN Conference on the Illicit Trade in Small Arms and Light Weapons in All Its Aspects, July, at: http://www.ippnw.org/SmallArmsAryaUN.html.

Arya, N. (2002a) 'Confronting the small arms pandemic: unrestricted access should be viewed as a public health disaster', *British Medical Journal*, 324: 990–1, also at: http://bmj.com/cgi/content/full/324/7344/990?eaf.

Arya, N. (2002b) 'Properly diagnose terrorism and work for a just response ', *Medicine and Global Survival*, 7, 2 at: http://www.ippnw.org/MGS/V7N2Aftermath.html#Arya.

Arya, N. (2003a) 'Ask the right questions!' *Ottawa Citizen*, 7 March, p. A17.

Arya, N. (2003b) 'Globalization: the path to neo-liberal nirvana or health and environmental hell medicine', *Conflict and Survival*, June 19, 2: 107–20.

Arya, N. (2003c) 'Healing our planet: physicians and global security', *Croatian Medical Journal*, 44, 2: 139–47, also at: http://www.pgs.ca/index.php/5/Healing.

Arya, N. (2003d) 'Human rights trumps security', *The Record*, May 16, A15.

Arya, N. (2003e) 'Winning the Peace: US offers little hope for winning Iraq peace' (letter), *Ottawa Citizen*, 4 May, A13.

Arya, N. (2004a) 'Peace through Health I: Development and use of a working model', *Medicine Conflict and Survival*, 20, 3: 242–57.

Arya, N. (2004b) 'Peace through Health II: A framework for medical student education', *Medicine Conflict and Survival*, 20, 3: 258–62.

Arya, N. (2005) 'Do no harm: towards a Hippocratic standard for international civilization', in *Re-Envisioning Sovereignty: The End of Westphalia*, United Nations University and Brooking Institute (ed.), 2006 (expected) at Australian National University Canberra: workshop April 2005, organized by Key School of Governance and Griffiths University and United Nations University, Tokyo.

Arya, N. (2006) 'The end of biomilitary realism? Time for rethinking biomedicine and international security', *Medicine, Conflict and Survival*, 22, 3: 220–229.

Arya, N. and Cukier, W. (2005) 'The international small arms situation: a public health approach', in P. F. Mahoney, W. C. Schwab, A. J. Brooks and J. Ryan (eds) *Ballistic Trauma: A Practical Guide*, London: Springer Verlag.

Arya, N. and Zurbrigg, S. (2003) 'Operation Infinite Injustice: the effect of sanctions and prospective war on the people of Iraq', *Canadian Journal of Public Health*, 94, 1: 9–12, also at: http://www.pgs.ca/pgs.php/Iraq/113/.

Ascherio, A., Chase, R., Cote, T., Dehaes, G., Hoskins, E., Laaouej, J., Passey, M., Qader, S.I., Shuqaide, S.F., Smith, M.C. et al. (1992) 'Effect of the Gulf War on infant and child mortality in Iraq', *New England Journal of Medicine*, 327, 13: 931–6, also at: http://content.nejm.org/cgi/content/abstract/327/13/931.

Ashford, M.W. and Gottstein, U. (2000) 'The impact on civilians of the bombing of Kosovo and Serbia', *Medicine, Conflict and Survival*, 16, 3: 267–80.

Baker, P. (2005) 'Bush estimates Iraqi death toll in war at 30,000', *Washington Post*, 13 December, A19.

Bilmes, L. and Stiglitz, J. (2006) The economic costs of the Iraq War: an appraisal three years after the beginning of the conflict, at: http://www2.gsb.columbia.edu/faculty/jstiglitz/Cost_of_War_in_Iraq.htm.

Böck-Buhmann, C. (2005) 'The role of health professionals in preventing and mediating conflict', *Medicine, Conflict and Survival*, 21, 4: 299–311.

Burnham, G., Lasta, R., Doocy, S. and Roberts, L. (2006) 'Mortality after the 2003 invasion of Iraq: a cross-sectional cluster sample survey', *The Lancet*, 368: 1421–8.

Bush, K. (1998) 'A measure of peace: Peace and conflict impact assessment (PCIA) of development projects in conflict zones', Working Paper No. 1. The Peacebuilding and Reconstruction Program Initiative and the Evaluation Unit, Ottawa, Canada: International Development Research Centre.

Bush, K. (2003) 'Hands-on Peace and Conflict Impact Assessment (PCIA)', *Walking the Path of Peace: Practicing the Culture of Peace and Peace and Conflict Impact Assessment*, Program P-CLGS (ed.), Manila, Philippines: Philippines-Canada Local Government Support Program: 71–109.

Butterfly Peace Garden Media Unit Website, at: http://www.thestupidschool.ca/bpg/background/introduction.html.

Cahill, K. (ed.) (1995) *Clearing the Fields: Solutions to the Global Landmines Crisis*, New York: Basic Books and the Council on Foreign Relations.

Canadian Medical Association Journal (2003) 'Editorial: the opportunity costs of war in Iraq', *Canadian Medical Association Journal*, 168, 9: 1011, at: http://www.cmaj.ca/cgi/content/full/168/9/1101.

Chapdelaine, A. et al. (1991) 'Firearm-related injuries in Canada: issues for prevention', *Canadian Medical Association Journal*, 145, 10: 1217–23.

Chase, R., Doney, A., Sivayogan, S., Ariyaratne, V., Sutkunanayagam, P., Swaminathan, A. (1999) 'Mental health initiatives as peace initiatives in Sri Lankan schoolchildren affected by armed conflict', Series on McMaster University's Health of Children in War Zones Project 1994–1996, *Medicine, Conflict and Survival*, 15, 4: 379–90.

Clark, J. (2002) 'War on Iraq could produce a humanitarian disaster, health professionals warn', *British Medical Journal*, 325, 1134, at: http://bmj.com/cgi/content/full/325/7373/1134.

Connolly, M.A. and Heymann, D. (2002) 'Deadly comrades: war and infectious diseases', *The Lancet*, 360: 23–4.

Cukier, W. (1998) 'Firearms/small arms finding common ground', *Canadian Foreign Policy*, 6: 73–87.

Diamond, J. (1997) *Guns, Germs and Steel: The Fates of Human Societies*, New York: W. W. Norton.

Elliot, G. (1972) *Twentieth Century Book of the Dead: Charles Scribner*, New York: Ballantine Books.

Forrow, L., Blair, B.G., Helfand, I. et al. (1998) 'Accidental nuclear war – a post-cold war assessment', *New England Journal of Medicine*, 338: 1326–31.

Galli, G. (2001) 'Humanitarian cease-fires in contemporary armed conflicts: potentially effective tools for peacebuilding', MA thesis, York: University of York.

Galtung, J. (1996) *Peace by Peaceful Means: Peace and Conflict, Development and Civilization*, London: PRIO/Sage.

Garfield, R.M. and Neugut, A.I. (1997) 'The human consequences of war', in B. S. Levy and V. W. Side (eds) *War and Public Health*, Oxford: Oxford University Press, 27–38.

Giacaman, R., Arya, N. and Summerfield, D. (2005) 'Establishing a mental health system: the Occupied Palestinian Territories', *International Psychiatry*, July: 16–18.

Gorbachev, M. (1987) *Perestroika: New Thinking for our Country and the World*, London: Collins, 154.

Gottstein, U. (1999) 'Peace through sanctions? Lessons from Cuba, former Yugoslavia and Iraq', *Medicine, Conflict and Survival*, 15: 271–85.

Graduate Institute of International Studies (GIIS) (2001) *Small Arms Survey 2002: Counting the Human Cost*, Geneva: Oxford University Press, 4.

Guerra de Macedo, C. (1994) 'Health, development and peacemaking: health as a bridge for peace', speech made at the international symposium on Health, Development, Conflict Resolution and Peacemaking, Copenhagen, Denmark, June.

Guha-Sapir, D. and van Panhuis, W.G. (2002) 'Armed conflict and public health: a report on knowledge and knowledge gaps', Centre for Research on the Epidemiology of Disasters CRED Université Catholique de Louvain, at: http://www.cred.be/docs/cred/publications/rocpressweb.pdf.

Healing Across the Divides Online. Available: http://www.healingdivides.org/.

Helfand, I., Forrow, L. and Tiwari, J. (2002) 'Nuclear terrorism' *British Medical Journal*, 324: 356–9.

Hendrickson, D. (1998) 'Humanitarian action in protracted crisis: an overview of the debates and dilemmas', *Disasters*, 22, 4: 283–7.

Hess, G. and Pfeiffer, M. (2006) 'Comparative analysis of WHO "Health as a Bridge for Peace" ', case studies website, at: http://www.who.int/hac/techguidance/hbp/comparative_analysis/en/index.html.

Hippocratic Oath Website (1999) at: http://members.tripod.com/nktiuro/hippocra.htm.

Holdstock, D. (2002) 'Morbidity and mortality among soldiers and civilians', in I. Taipale et al. (eds) *War or Health? A Reader*, London and New York: Zed Books.

Hoskins, E. et al. and International Study Team (2003) 'Our common responsibility: the impact of a new war on Iraqi children', at: http://www.reliefweb.int/rw/rwb.nsf/AllDocsByUNID/c5468f6f4d249a4885256cbf006da95f.

Hotez, P.J. (2001) 'Vaccines as instruments of foreign policy', *EMBO Reports*, 2: 862–8.

Human Rights Watch/Asia and Physicians for Human Rights (1991) *Landmines in Cambodia: The Coward's War*, New York: Human Rights Watch.

Hurst, Steven R. (2006) 'Iraq's health minister estimated at least 150,000 civilians have been killed in the war – 3 times previous accepted figures – 60 bodies a day at Baghdad morgue', Associated Press *Toronto Star* website, Nov. 10, 2006, 01:00 a.m.

International Action Network on Small Arms (IANSA) (2004) at: http://www.iansa.org/issues/documents/ippnw-report–2004.pdf http://www.iansa.org/ (accessed 4 January 2006)

ICBL International Campaign to Ban Landmines Online. Available: http://www.icbl.org/treaty (accessed 4 January 2006)

ICISS (2001) *The Responsibility to Protect*, Ottawa: International Development Research Centre, at: http://www.iciss.ca/.

International Committee of the Red Cross (ICRC) (1999) *Iraq: A Decade of Sanctions 1989–1999*, Geneva: ICRC, at: http://www.icrc.org/web/eng/siteeng0.nsf/iwpList322/4BBFCEC7FF4B7A3CC1256B66005E0FB6.

Iraq Body Count (2004) 'Civilian deaths in "noble" Iraq mission pass 10,000', London: Iraq Body Count, at: www.iraqbodycount.org.

Jabbour, S. (2005) 'Healing and peace making in the Middle East: challenges for doctors', *The Lancet*, 365: 1211.

Johnson, L. (1999) 'Life and Death in Iraq' *Seattle Post Intelligencer*.

Kater, M. (1983) *The Nazi Party*, Cambridge, MA: Harvard University Press.

Keen, S. (1986) *Faces of the Enemy: Reflections of the Hostile Imagination*, San Francisco, CA: Harper & Row.

Kellermann, A.L., Rivara, F.P. and Rushforth, N.B. (1993) 'Gun ownership as a risk factor for homicide in the home', *New England Journal of Medicine*, 329: 1084–91.

Kellermann, A.L., Rivara, F.P., Somes, G. et al. (1992) 'Suicide in the home in relation to gun ownership', *New England Journal of Medicine*, 327: 467–72.

Krug, E.G., Dahlberg, L.L., Mercy, J.A., Zwi, A.B. and Lozano, R. (2002) *World Report on Violence and Health*, Abstract, Geneva: WHO.

Large J. (1997) 'Considering conflict: concept paper for first Health as a Bridge for Peace consultative meeting', Les Pensières, Annecy, 30–31 October, World Health Organization, at: http://www.who.int/hac/techguidance/hbp/considering_conflict/en/print.html.

Leaning, J. (2000) 'Environment and health: 5. Impact of war', *Canadian Medical Association Journal*, 163: 1157–61.

Lee, P. (2002) Letter, at: http://www.cmaj.ca/cgi/content/full/168/9/1115-a.

Levy, B.S. and Sidel, V.W. (1997) 'The impact of military activities on civilian populations', in B. S. Levy and V. W. Side (eds) *War and Public Health*, Oxford: Oxford University Press.

Lifton, R.J. and Markusen, E. (1990) *The Genocidal Mentality: Nazi Holocaust and Nuclear Threat*, New York: Basic Books.

Macrae, J. (1998) 'The death of humanitarianism? Anatomy of the attack', *Disasters*, 21, 3: 309–17.

MacQueen, G. and Santa-Barbara, J. (2000) 'Peace building through health initiatives', *British Medical Journal*, 321: 293–6.

MacQueen, G., McCutcheon, R. and Santa-Barbara, J. (1997) 'The use of health initiatives as peace initiatives', *Peace & Change*, 22: 175–97.

MacQueen, G., Nagy, T., Santa-Barbara, J. and Raichle, C. (2004) 'War, water, and ethics: Iraq water treatment vulnerabilities', *Peace Magazine*, 20, 4: 16, at: http://www.peacemagazine.org/archive/v20n4p16.htm.

MacQueen, G., Santa-Barbara, J., Neufeld, V., Yusuf, S. and Horton, R. (2001) 'Health and peace: time for a new discipline', *The Lancet*, 357, 9267: 1460–61.

Manenti, A. (2001) 'Health as a potential contribution to peace: realities from the field. What has WHO learned in the 1990s?', Geneva: World Health Organization, Health and Conflict, Department of Emergency and Humanitarian Action.

Marks, J.A. (2005) 'The silence of the doctors', *The Nation*, 26 December, at: http://www.truthout.org/docs_2005/121405C.shtml.

Meddings, D. (1997) 'Weapons injuries during and after periods of conflict: retrospective analysis', *British Medical Journal*, 315: 1417–20.

Melf, K. (2004) 'Exploring medical peace education and a call for peace medicine', MA Thesis, University of Tromsoe.

Miles, S.H. (2004) 'Abu Ghraib: its legacy for military medicine', *The Lancet*, 364: 725–9.

Millennium Goals (2000) at: http://ddp-ext.worldbank.org/ext/GMIS/home.do?siteId=2 http://www.un.org/millenniumgoals/ http://www.undp.org/mdg/.

Montville, J. (1990) *Conflict and Peacemaking in Multiethnic Societies*, New York: Lexington.

Moodie, M. and Taylor, W.J. (2000) 'Contagion and Conflict, Health as a Global Security Challenge', a report of the Chemical and Biological Arms Control Institute and the CSIS International Security Program, January.

Murray, C. and Lopez, A. (eds) (1996) 'The global burden of disease: a comprehensive assessment of mortality and disability from diseases, injuries, and risk factors in 1990 and project to 2020', Cambridge, MA: Harvard School of Public Health.

Murray, C.J., King, G., Lopez, A.D., Tomijima, N. and Krug, E.G. (2002) 'Armed conflict as a public health problem', *British Medical Journal*, 324: 346–9.

National Priorities Project (2006) at: http://www.costofwar.com http://nationalpriorities.org/index.php?option=com_wrapper&Itemid=182.

Nuremberg Code (1949) *Trials of War Criminals Before the Nuremberg Military Tribunals Under Control Council Law* No. 10, Vol. 2, Nuremberg, October 1946–April 1949, Washington, DC: US Government Printing Office, 181–2, at: http://www.dreamscape.com/morgana/nurmberg.htm.

Orbinski, J. (1999) Acceptance speech on behalf of MSF for the 1999 Nobel Peace Prize, at: http://www.nobel.no/eng_lect_99m.html.

Orent, W. (2005) 'The evolutionary process may temper the avian flu', *The Record*, 27 October, A 11.

Ottawa Citizen (2003) 'War will provoke terrorism: Canada must support peaceful means to restrain Iraq and not take part in a military attack that could have dangerous consequences for the West, say Physicians for Global Survival', 24 January, A 17.

Paniagua, I., Crespin, E., Guardado A. and Mauricio, A. (2005) 'Wounds caused by firearms in El Salvador, 2003–2004: epidemiological issues', *Medicine, Conflict and Survival*, 21, 3: 191–98.

People's Health Charter (2000) at: http://phmovement.org/charter/pch-english.html.

Peters, M.A. (1996) 'A Health-to-Peace Handbook', *Journal of Humanitarian Assistance*, at: http://www.jha.ac/Ref/r005.htm or Hamilton: McMaster University, at: http://www.humanities.mcmaster.ca/peace-health/Resources/hlthpcbk.pdf.

Physicians for Global Survival (PGS) (2001) *Iraq Eyewitness*, fundraising letter, at: www.pgs.ca.

Physicians for Social Responsibility (PSR) (1962) 'The medical consequences of thermonuclear war', *New England Journal of Medicine*, 266: 1126–55.
Project Ploughshares (1996) *Armed Conflict Reports 1996–2000*, at: www.ploughshares.ca.
Roberts, L., Lafta, R., Garfield, R., Khudhairi, J. and Burnham, G. (2004) 'Mortality before and after the 2003 invasion of Iraq: cluster sample survey', *The Lancet*, 364, 9448: pp 1857–64.
Rodriguez-Garcia, R., Macinko, J., Solórzano, F.X. and Schlesser, M. (2001) *How Can Health Serve as a Bridge for Peace?*, Washington, DC: School of Public Health and Health Services, the George Washington University, at: http://www.certi.org/publications/policy/gwc–12-a-brief.htm.
Salvage, J. (2002) 'Collateral damage: the health and environmental costs of war on Iraq', at: http://www.ippnw.org/CollateralDamage.html.
Santa-Barbara, J. (1997) 'The psychological effects of war on children', in B. S. Levy and V. W. Sidel (eds) *War and Public Health*, Oxford: Oxford University Press, 168–85.
Santa-Barbara, J. (2004) 'Peace works–birth of an innovative group', *Croatian Medical Journal*, 45, 3, at: http://www.cmj.hr/2004/45/3/15185432.pdf.
Santa-Barbara, J. (2005a) 'Ethical pylons of Health as a Bridge to Peace', *Croatian Medical Journal*, 46, 1: 154–6. http://www.cmj.hr/2005/46/1/15726690.pdf.
Santa-Barbara, J. (2005b) at: http://www.humanities.mcmaster.ca/peace-health/Conf2005/Present/Joanna-PtH-Key%20Concepts.Ppt.
Santa-Barbara, J. and MacQueen, G. (2004) 'Peace through health: key concepts', *The Lancet*, 364: 384–5.
Seidelman, W.E. (1995), 'Whither Nuremberg? Medicine's Continuing Nazi Heritage', *Medicine, Conflict and Survival*, 2, 3, at: http://www.ippnw.org/MGS/V2N3Seidelman.html.
Shanks, L. and Schull, M.J. (2000) 'Rape in war: the humanitarian response', *Canadian Medical Association Journal*, 163, 9: 1152.
Sibbald, B. (2002) 'Attacks on US a crime, not act of war, conference concludes', *Canadian Medical Association Journal*, 166, 1, at: http://www.cmaj.ca/cgi/content/full/166/1/78.
Sidel, V.W. (1995) 'The international arms trade and its impact on health', *British Medical Journal*, 311: 1677–80, at: http://bmj.bmjjournals.com/cgi/content/full/311/7021/1677.
Sidel, V.W. and Levy, B.S. (eds) (1997) *War and Public Health*, Oxford: Oxford University Press.
Sidel, V.W., Geiger, H.J. and Lown, B. (1962) 'The medical consequences of thermonuclear war. II. The physician's role in the post-attack period', *New England Journal of Medicine*, 266: 1137–45.
Skinner, H., Abdeen, Z., Abdeen, H., Aber, P., Al-Masri, M., Attias, J., Avraham, K.B., Carmi, R., Chalin, C., El Nasser, Z., Hijazi, M., Jebara, R.O., Kanaan, M., Pratt, H., Raad, F., Roth, Y., Williams, A.P. and Noyek, A. (2005) 'Promoting Arab and Israeli cooperation: peace-building through health initiatives', *The Lancet*, 365: 1274–7.
Sloan, J.H. et al. (1988): 'Handgun regulations, crime, assaults, and homicides: a tale of two cities', *New England Journal of Medicine*, 319: 1256–62.
Stover, E., Cobey, J.C. and Fine, J. (1997) 'The public health effects of land mines: long-term consequences for civilians', in B. S. Levy and V. W. Sidel (eds) *War and Public Health*, Oxford: Oxford University Press, 137–46.
Stover, E., Keller, A.S., Cobey, J.C. and Sopheap, S. (1994) 'The medical and social consequences of land mines in Cambodia', *Journal of the American Medical Association*, 272: 331–6.
Summerfield, D. (1998) 'The social experience of war and some issues for the humanitarian field', in P.J. Bracken and C. Petty (eds) *Rethinking the Trauma of War*, London and New York: Free Association Press, 9–37.
Toronto Star (2003) 'Iraq body count ordered stopped', 10 December.
Toronto Star (2005) 'Coalition, not insurgents, killed most civilians: BBC', *Toronto Star*, 29 January.
UNICEF (1996) 'Children as zones of peace', at: http://www.unicef.org/sowc96/14zones.htm.
UNICEF (1999) *Situation Analysis of Children and Women in Iraq*. Baghdad: 1998, at the Campaign Against Sanctions in Iraq, at: http://www.casi.org.uk/info/unicef9804.html.
UNICEF (2005) *The State of the World's Children 2005* at: http://www.unicef.org/publications/index_24432.html.
United Nations (1948) *Universal Declaration of Human Rights*, at: http://www.un.org/Overview/rights.html.
United Nations (1959) *Declaration of the Rights of the Child*, General Assembly resolution 1386(XIV) of 20 November 1959, Geneva: Office of the United Nations High Commissioner for Human Rights, at: http://www.unhchr.ch/html/menu3/b/25.htm.

United Nations Development Programme (UNDP) (2005) Human Development Index, at: http://hdr.undp.org/ http://hdr.undp.org/statistics/data/indic/indic_12_1_1.html.

University of New South Wales (UNSW) (2004) *Health and Conflict Project Issues Paper 1 Health and Peace-Building Securing the Future*, December; see also: www.humanities.mcmaster.ca/peace-health/Conf2005/CaseStudies.htm.

Vass, A.J. (2001) 'Peace through health: this new movement needs evidence, not just ideology', *British Medical Journal*, 323: 1020, at: http://bmj.bmjjournals.com/cgi/content/full/323/7320/1020.

Vieira, O. (1998) Workshop on International Small Arms/Firearms Injury Surveillance and Research, Ryerson Polytechnic University, Toronto, 18 June.

Virchow, R. (1848) *Die medicinische Reform* 3, November 1848, at: http://www.uni-heidelberg.de/institute/fak5/igm/g47/bauervir.htm.

Wetmore, K. (2005) 'The Butterfly Peace Garden: A Programme Analysis', paper for PACS 301 course, University of Waterloo.

Woodside, D., Santa-Barbara, J. and Benner, D.G.I. (1999) 'Psychological trauma and social healing in Croatia', *Medicine, Conflict and Survival*, 15, 4: 355–67.

World Health Organization (1946) *Constitution of the World Health Organization*, Geneva: WHO.

World Health Organization (1978) *Declaration of Alma-Ata*, International Conference on Primary Health Care, Alma Ata, USSR, 6–12 September, at: http://www.euro.who.int/AboutWHO/Policy/20010827_1.

World Health Organization (1986) *Ottawa Charter For Health Promotion*, First International Conference for Health Promotion, 17–21 November, Ottawa, WHO/HPR/HEP/95.1, at: http://www.euro.who.int/AboutWHO/Policy/20010827_2.

World Health Organization (1997) *Report on the First WHO Consultative Meeting on Health as a Bridge for Peace*, Les Pensières, Annecy, 30–31 October.

World Health Organization (2001) *'Statistical Annexes', World Health Report 2001*, at: http://www-.who.int/whr2001/2001/main/en/pdf/annex2.en.pdf.

World Health Organization (2001) 'Global status of Polio eradication [information online], Geneva: World Health Organization, Division for Vaccines and other Biologicals, Expanded Programme on Immunization'.

World Health Organization (2005) at: http:/www.who.int/about/overview/en/.

Yusuf, S., Anand, S. and MacQueen, G. (1998) 'Can medicine prevent war?', *British Medical Journal*, 317: 1669–70, at: http://bmj.com/cgi/content/full/317/7174/1669.

Zwi, A. and Ugalde, A. (1989) 'Towards an epidemiology of political violence in the Third World', *Social Science and Medicine*, 28, 7: 633–42.

Part 5

Conclusion

25

Peace and conflict studies

Looking back, looking forward

Johan Galtung and Charles Webel

Looking back, say 50 years, the progress in peace and conflict studies is astounding, as evidenced by the chapters in this book. Perhaps one of the most important factors indicative of this progress, present in all chapters, is the use of the word 'peace' itself. Peace is used unashamedly, no apology needed, as a subject to be explored in all possible directions, no holds barred.

Run the time machine back 50 years, to the 1950s: in the West, 'peace' was often referred to derisively as a communist propaganda term, an invitation to lower one's guard against the 'Red Menace'. And in the Eastern part of the Occident, 'peace' was also a communist word, the strong card of international solidarity by 'peace-loving peoples and nations'. Today 'peace studies' benefits from increasing academic legitimacy, to some extent riding piggyback on its near cousin 'conflict studies', and often hyphenated with some less controversial term, like 'justice' or 'security studies'. Soon there will be unhyphenated peace all over the academic map. But many mainstream Anglo-American academics may still legitimize violence through 'security studies', emulated by some in other parts of the world.

More controversial is the old question, what does peace studies resemble? As can be seen very clearly from the chapters in this book, peace studies goes far beyond being some kind of left-wing version of international (actually inter-state) relations (IR), and well into a nascent human science of well-being, one in which handling conflict plays a major role.

Perhaps the most important affinity to explore is the resemblance between peace studies and health studies, both of individuals and peoples, a challenge lying well outside the field of social sciences. There are two important points here: first, health studies is highly interdisciplinary, as even the most cursory look at the curriculum of any medical or public health school will prove. In this handbook, the reader may enjoy some encounters with some more established academic disciplines (such as psychology, philosophy, and international relations), and some cases of interdisciplinarity. But, second, health studies is not only inter- or even trans-disciplinary. It is also inter- or trans-national. A medical doctor, ideally speaking, has no father/motherland. Not only can he practise medicine almost anywhere, but this profession has a value overriding even patriotism: health. The Hippocratic Oath demands of him to treat friend and foe alike.

We are moving in that direction also in the field of peace studies, meaning in the direction of promoting a value more important than national interests: peace. We are not there yet, nor is the task of inter/trans-disciplinarity carried as far as it merits. But conflict studies, or conflictology, which is as basic to peace studies as anatomy/physiology/pathology is to health studies, spans the whole spectrum from micro via meso and macro to mega conflict, meaning from individual psychology to global (not only inter-state and inter-nation, two aspects of IR) studies. Increasingly peace researchers feel at home at all these levels.

One reason for this is that the traditional, mainstream social sciences are closely related to the growth of the Western state system during the era of imperialism. Thus, world history usually parallels national, state and regional histories. The social sciences, especially political 'science', economics and sociology, are clearly dedicated to the three pillars of a modern state: State, Capital, and Civil Society, all endowed with a certain historicity, presumably absent from the colonized peoples for whom anthropology was invented as a Western master narrative description of their 'cultures'. This is not good enough. Contemporary economics is increasingly dedicated to the study (and advocacy) of only one particular economic system, capitalism ('capitalistics' would be a better word). The social sciences are badly in need of globalization.

But transcending state borders is only one of the challenges facing peace studies, peace researchers and peacemakers. There are other faultlines in the human constitution – including gender and generation; race, ethnicity and nationality; class (political, economic, military, cultural depending on the type of power involved); and ecology/environment.

Peace studies needs to create transcending paradigms for all of them, with no built-in assumption favouring one or the other side of a faultline. A major task of peace studies is to come to grips with *massive category killing*, one category of which is referred to as genocide. Killing of unborn and born women is one of the major forms of this kind of murder. Another is death by starvation and/or by preventable and/or curable diseases. Health studies is primarily focused on preventing, diagnosing and treating avoidable diseases, including pandemics; peace studies focuses on avoidable violence(s), including massive category killing. Both fields have to do much more work on positive health and positive peace, and not only as approaches to the prevention of disease and violence, but also as guideposts for higher levels of human self-realization.

Trans-disciplinary and trans-faultline peace studies may be around the corner. Unlike 'security studies', peace studies is not a ready target of upper-class, white, old male, patriotic and often Anglophonic countries exporting colonists and military bases to the lands of others, especially the Middle East. There is much to be insecure about. Peace studies and 'security through peace' would serve all peoples and nations, including the English-speaking ones, better than the global insecurity engendered by 'security and strategic studies'.

With globalization comes professionalism, also just around the corner, with the concomitant danger of self-righteous narrowness. Thus, the preservation of an independent, critical and emancipatory peace studies, able to analyze and critique the praxeology emerging from within its own ranks, is indispensable.

More challenges to peace studies and peace research will arise during the coming decades. Whoever pushes in any direction – like peace researchers who actively use their research to explore and bring about peace and who seek more ways of turning theory into practice – and vice versa – should not be surprised if counterforces appear. Action provokes reaction.

Other academic disciplines may react by trying to marginalize, eliminate, prevent and/or co-opt peace studies. They may also continue to claim that peace studies is superfluous, since the existing disciplines already allegedly cover what peace studies teaches: e.g. 'the problem of peace is basically a psychological problem', demanding courses in Peace Psychology, etc. This move is laudable if it results in even more students and teachers learning and making peace, and if it is combined with respect for a broader theoretical and practical perspective – a view of the forest, so to speak, and not just of a tree or two.

Strong reactions to peace studies, however, will not come only from academic disciplines whose turf needs defending, but from other professionals who also feel threatened. One of them is diplomats who have tried to hide behind the Track I/Track II formula: 'We do I, NGOs do II. Let us divide the turf.' Do they do I or rather –I? Inter-state diplomacy, dedicated to representation, information and negotiation, may in its present form be a dying institution, and not only because others may represent a state better than any embassy can, and often provide much better information. The problem goes deeper, into the traditional notion of peace as harmonized national interests, brought about by negotiating ratifiable documents. Where is nature's interest? The human interest? The local level interest? The corporate interest? The regional interest? The gender, generational, etc. interest? The global interest? The world is more complex today and more layered, thus demanding a multi-layered approach. The peace workers of the future can be useful all over the planet, but not if they should be tied to national interests that are the concern of very few.

Thus, it is far from obvious that a desirable place to turn theory of peace into practice is a foreign ministry, or even a peace ministry for that matter. We are moving away from the world as an inter-state system, and toward, not a world government, but the world as an inter-regional, inter-local authorities, inter-human, inter-gender/generation/race/class system – all in critical interfaces with the environment. To prepare for the world of yesterday, with a bit of fresh air blown into the traditional Westphalian, system of nation states with their own, often conflicting, security interests, is suboptimal. It is necessary to train the diplomats to do a better job for peace, and go ahead with all the other systems. They all badly need professionals, and should get them.

In conclusion: the research and theory needed to guide peace workers to produce more enduring and positive peace, not only more peace studies, have come to stay. Bridging the gap between peace movement moralism and foreign policy pragmatism is a major challenge facing everyone who seeks to achieve peace on Earth.

Index